BEN PIMLOTT has been Warden o⬛⬛⬛⬛⬛ ⬛⬛⬛⬛⬛ 1998. He was previously Professor ⬛⬛⬛⬛⬛⬛ tory at Birkbeck College. He is the author of *Labour and the Left in the 1930s*, *Hugh Dalton* (Whitbread Biography Prize), the best-selling *Harold Wilson*, and a collection of essays, *Frustrate Their Knavish Tricks*. A former Chairman of the Fabian Society, he is a frequent reviewer, political commentator and broadcaster, and has been a columnist for several newspapers. In 1996 he was elected Fellow of the British Academy. He has been described by the political analyst Andrew Marr as 'the best British political biographer now writing'.

PRAISE FOR *THE QUEEN*

'Pimlott has succeeded triumphantly in his unlikely project. He has written a book which can be enjoyed and admired by people who would never have imagined reading any previous royal biography.'

JOHN CAMPBELL, *Independent*

'This book is a strikingly impressive achievement. Professor Pimlott has shown what wit, scholarship and a wide-ranging historical imagination can do with a subject that must initially have seemed unpromising. There will not be a better royal biography for many years.'

PHILIP ZIEGLER, *Daily Telegraph*

'One of the many merits of Ben Pimlott's superbly judicious biography of Elizabeth II is that it understands [the] connection between monarchy and masses, and carefully evokes its political importance.'

ANDREW SULLIVAN, *New York Times Book Review*

'Excellent ... Mr Pimlott's biography of the Queen is first-class history: well-researched, well informed and gently ironic ... Junior members of the Royal Family should read it with care'. *Economist*

'While he is particularly strong on the political side, he never forgets that he is writing above all about a human being. Pimlott's book is the best all-round study of the Queen so far, showing understanding as well as amused irony'. JOHN GRIGG, *Sunday Telegraph*

'I found myself engrossed ... *The Queen* is really a fugitive political history of Britain and the Commonwealth during my lifetime, seen from the fascinating, if impotent, vantage-point of the throne and of the intelligent, philistine woman who is in every sense of the word constitutionally incapable of putting her foot down.'

JONATHAN RABAN, *Times Literary Supplement* Books of the Year

'Pimlott gives a masterly account of changing relations between the Royal Family and the media . . . Also exemplary is the account of the demanding role the Queen has played as Head of the Commonwealth . . . the author casts much light on both the defects and the strengths of our royal institutions.' PROFESSOR ANTHONY BRADLEY, *Scotsman*

'A marvellous narrative of post-war history with hilarious vignettes . . . Pimlott's book reveals the enormousness of the Queen's place in the political economy and society. He has written a superb biography.'

DENIS MACSHANE, *Fabian Review*

'Worlds apart from the tabloid candy floss that clutters the Royalty shelf in so many bookshops.'

IAN MCINTYRE, *The Times* Books of the Year

'A section in the middle of the book on the Queen as an individual is quite sparkling.' MALCOLM RUTHERFORD, *Financial Times*

'Ben Pimlott has carried out an extraordinarily difficult task with great skill. Never is he obsequious or snide . . . he has told a sad story with authority and insight. Within this biography lurks a requiem for a monarchy teetering on the brink of irrelevance.'

CHRISTOPHER BEAUMAN, *Ham and High*

'As we would expect from one of the best, if not the best political biographer in the country, his book is authoritative, comprehensive, lucid and readable . . . Professor Pimlott's biography of the Queen will certainly be the best study of the woman, the life and the reign, that we shall get in her lifetime, and possibly for a long time after that.'

KENNETH HARRIS, *Glasgow Herald*

'It is hard to see how the book could have been better written or presented.' MARTIN SEYMOUR-SMITH, *Scotland on Sunday*

'Excellent . . . The author is to be congratulated on a book about the monarchy that is scholarly, fair and entirely without vulgarity. It is a sad history of our times.' JULIAN CRITCHLEY, *Mail on Sunday*

THE QUEEN

Elizabeth II
and the Monarchy

Golden Jubilee Edition

BEN PIMLOTT

HarperCollinsPublishers

To my family

HarperCollins*Publishers*
77–85 Fulham Palace Road,
Hammersmith, London w6 8jb

www.**fire**and**water**.com

This paperback edition published 2002

1 3 5 7 9 8 6 4 2

First published in Great Britain by
HarperCollins*Publishers* 1996

A catalogue for this book
Is available from the British Library

ISBN 000 711436 2

Set in Postscript Linotype Minion and Photina by
Rowland Phototypesetting Ltd,
Bury St Edmunds, Suffolk

Printed and bound in Great Britain by
Clays Ltd, St Ives plc

LIST OF PLATES

Princess Elizabeth during a deck game on HMS *Vanguard*, April 1947 (*Popperfoto*)

Princess Elizabeth and Princess Margaret riding on the seashore in South Africa, 1947 (*The Royal Archives © 2001 Her Majesty Queen Elizabeth II*)

Princess Elizabeth and Prince Philip on their wedding day, November 1947 (*Hulton Archive*)

Princess Elizabeth arriving at Westminster Abbey with her father for her marriage to Prince Philip, November 1947 (*Hulton Archive*)

Prince Charles with Princess Elizabeth and Prince Philip, July 1949 (*Hulton Archive*)

Princess Elizabeth and the Queen at Hurst Park Races, January 1952 (*Hulton Archive*)

Princess Elizabeth with Mountbatten at a ball at the Savoy, 3rd July 1951 (*Hulton Archive*)

The Queen arriving at Clarence House after her father's death, 7th February 1952 (*Hulton Archive*)

The Queen as she drives to Westminster for the State Opening of Parliament, 1952 (*Hulton Archive*)

The Coronation of Queen Elizabeth II showing the Queen wearing her crown and preparing to receive homage, 2nd June 1953 (*Hulton Archive*)

The Queen Mother with Prince Charles at the Coronation, 2nd June 1953 (*Hulton Archive*)

Queen Elizabeth holding a model zebra with Princess Elizabeth, Peter Townsend and Princess Margaret in South Africa, 1947 (*Popperfoto*)

The Queen, and the Duke of Edinburgh with Sir Anthony and Lady Eden, 25th July 1955 (*Popperfoto*)

Daily Mirror front page 'Smack! Lord A. gets his face slapped,' 7th August 1957 (*By permission of the British Library/Mirror Syndication*)

Sir Michael Adeane (*Godfrey Argent for the Archives of the National Portrait Gallery/Camera Press London*)

The Queen with various members of the Government including Harold Macmillan, 16th February 1957 (*Hulton Archive*)

The Queen with Charles de Gaulle at Covent Garden, April 1960 (*Hulton Archive*)

The Queen with her corgis, 8th February 1968 (*Hulton Archive*)

The Queen on *Britannia*, 1972 (*Patrick Lichfield/Camera Press London*)

The Queen with Princess Anne, 1965 (*Camera Press London*)

The Investiture of the Prince of Wales, 1st July 1969 (*Hulton Archive*)

The Queen with Lord Porchester, 1966 (*Hulton Archive*)

The Queen at Aberfan, 29th October 1966 (*Hulton Archive*)

A student drinks from a bottle in front of the Queen at Stirling University, 12th October 1972 (© Scotsman Publications)

The Queen with Sir Martin Charteris on board *Britannia*, 31st October 1972 (*Patrick Lichfield/Camera Press London*)

The Queen on a Jubilee walkabout, 20th June 1977 (*Ian Berry/Magnum Photos*)

The Queen, Prince Philip and Prince Charles in Australia, 1970: 'as short as we dared' (*by permission of Sir Hardy Amies*)

The Queen with Harold Wilson, 24th March 1976 (*Hulton Archive*)

Prince Andrew returns from the Falklands, 1982 (*Bryn Colton/Camera Press London*)

The Queen with Margaret Thatcher and Hastings Banda, 3rd August 1979 (*Hulton Archive*)

Princess Elizabeth with President Truman, 4th November 1951 (*Hulton Archive*)

The Queen with Prince Philip and the Kennedys, 6th June 1961 (*Hulton Archive*)

The Queen with President Carter and Prince Philip, 10th May 1977 (*Hulton Archive*)

The Queen riding with President Reagan in Windsor Great Park, 1982 (*Tim Graham*)

The Queen and Prince Philip with the Clintons, 29th November 1995 (*Tim Graham*)

The Queen with a fireman at Windsor Castle, 21st November 1992 (*Hulton Archive*)

'HM The Queen' by Antony Williams 1995 (*Mall Galleries*)

Detail from a painting by Michael Noakes. Study for a group portrait commissioned by the Corporation of London 1972. (*Reproduced by kind permission of HRH The Prince of Wales*)

Princess Elizabeth seen through syringa, 8th July 1941 (*Hulton Archive*)

Princess Elizabeth and her mother at the Derby, 4th June 1948 (*Hulton Archive*)

Richard Nixon is filmed shaking Prince Charles's hand for the *Royal Family* film (*BBC © Crown*)

The Queen visits the Children's Palace, Canton, October 1986 (*Tim Graham*)

It's a Royal Knockout! June 1987 (*Photographers International Picture Library*)

The Queen and the Princess of Wales with bridesmaids, 1981 (*Patrick Lichfield/Camera Press London*)

The Princess of Wales in New York 1995 (*Tim Graham*)

Welcome the Queen (*British Pathe plc/National Portrait Gallery, London*)

Andy Warhol painting of the Queen (Queen Elizabeth II of the United Kingdom 1985 *by Andy Warhol © The Andy Warhol Foundation for the Visual Arts, Inc./ARS, NY and DACS, London 2002*)

Sticker artwork for single 'God Save The Queen', 1977 by Jamie Reid

The Queen as depicted by *Spitting Image*, 1985 (*Spitting Image Productions*)

Detail of *Trooping the Colour* by William Roberts (© *Tate London 2001*)

Queen Anne touching Dr Johnson, when a boy, to cure him of Scrofula or 'King's Evil' (*Private Collection/Bridgeman Art Library*)

The Princess of Wales meets a resident of the Lord Gage Centre, Newham, East London, September 1990 (*Tim Graham*)

'The Apotheosis of Princess Charlotte', oil painting by Henry Howard, 1818 (*National Trust Photographic Library*)

The sea of flowers and bouquets outside Kensington Palace after the death of Diana, Princess of Wales, September 1997 (*Justin G. Thomas/Camera Press*)

The Funeral of Diana, Princess of Wales, September 1997 (*Mark Stewart/ Camera Press*)

Mourners in Hyde Park during the funeral service of Diana, Princess of Wales, September 1997 (© *Chris Steele-Perkins/Magnum Photos*)

The Queen leaving HMY *Britannia* for the last time, 11 December 1997 (*Tim Graham*)

The Queen and Donald Dewar after the Scottish Parliament was officially opened in Edinburgh, 1 July 1999 (*Roger Donovan/PA Photos*)

The Queen joined Mrs Susan McCarron (front left), her son James and Liz McGinniss for tea in their home in the Castlemilk area of Glasgow, 7 July 1999 (*Dave Cheskin/PA Photos*)

The Queen gives Maundy Money to 150 Christian pensioners at Westminster Abbey, 12 April 2001 (*Camera Press*)

The Queen picks up a shot pheasant and rings its neck while out on a shoot on the Sandringham Estate, 18 November 2000 (*Alban Donohoe Picture Service*)

'The Queen and I' by Sue Townsend, March 1994 (*Donald Cooper/ Photostage*)

Camilla Parker-Bowles at Somerset House in London for a party hosted by the Press Complaints Commission, 7 February 2001 (*Tim Graham*)

The Queen and Pope John Paul II exchanging gifts in his private office in the Vatican City in Rome, 17 October 2000 (*Tim Graham*)

The Moon Against the Monarchy protest, 3 June 2000 (*Stefan Rousseau/ PA Photos*)

The State Opening of Parliament, 20 June 2001 (*Tim Graham*)

Prince William during his Raleigh International expedition in southern Chile, 11 December 2000 (*Tim Graham Picture Library*)

The Queen visits Kingsbury High School in Brent to launch the Royal web site, 6 July 1997 (*Tim Graham Picture Library*)

CARTOONS

The Flowers and the Princesses (*Reproduced by permission of* Punch. *Published on 28th April 1937*)

Birthday Greetings (*Reproduced by permission of* Punch. *Published 23rd April 1947*)

Vicky on the Altrincham affair (Mirror Syndication/*Centre for the Study of Cartoons, University of Kent. Published in the* Daily Mirror *14th August 1957*)

Jak 'Your Move!' (*Atlantic/Centre for the Study of Cartoons, University of Kent. Published in the* Evening Standard *5th March 1968*)

Steadman *'Up the Mall'* (*Ralph Steadman. Published in* Private Eye *4th July 1969*)

Rigby 'And Treble time . . .' (*News International Newspapers Ltd./Centre for the Study of Cartoons, University of Kent. Published in the* Sun, *3rd December 1971*)

Franklin 'Singing in the Reign' (*News International Newspapers Ltd./John Frost Historical Newspaper Service. Published in the* Sun *30th December 1976*)

Cummings 'I love red but not red carpets' (*Express Newspapers/Centre for the Study of Cartoons, University of Kent. Published in the* Daily Express *31st July 1981*)

Kal on the Commonwealth (*Kevin Kallaugher/Centre for the Study of Cartoons, University of Kent. Published in* Today *16th July 1986*)

Johnston 'Toe Sucking' (*News International Newspapers Ltd./John Frost Historical Newspaper Service. Published in the* Sun *20th August 1992*)

Franklin on the popularity of the Monarchy in Australia (*News International Newspapers Ltd./John Frost Historical Newspaper Service. Published in the* Sun *29th February 1992*)

Bell 'Orff with her ring!' (*Steve Bell. Published in the* Guardian *22nd December 1995*)

Bell 'The way ahead senior royals think tank' (*Steve Bell/Centre for the Study of Cartoons, University of Kent. Published in the* Guardian, *20 August 1996*)

Cummings 'I'm having a ghastly nightmare that the photographers stopped invading my privacy!' (*Mrs M. Cummings/Centre for the Study of Cartoons, University of Kent. Published in* The Times, *16th August 1997*)

Griffin 'The Queen of all our hearts' (*Express Newspapers/Centre for the Study of Cartoons, University of Kent.* Published in The Daily Express, *1st September 1997*)

Gerald Scarfe 'The Tidal Wave' (Centre for the Study of Cartoons, University of Kent. Published in the Sunday Times, *7 September 1997*)

Unny on the Queen (The Indian Express *(Bombay). Published in* The Indian Express, *12th October 1997*)

Trog on the death of Diana, Princess of Wales (*Wally Faukes/Centre for the Study of Cartoons, University of Kent. Published in the* Sunday Telegraph, *7th September 1997*)

Gerald Scarfe on the Australian referendum (*Centre for the Study of Cartoons, University of Kent. Published in the* Sunday Times, 7th November 1999)

Mac 'So Sophie. After that absolutely abysmal performance, you are the weakest link – goodbye' (*Atlantic/Centre for the Study of Cartoons, University of Kent. Published in the* Daily Mail, *9th April 2001*)

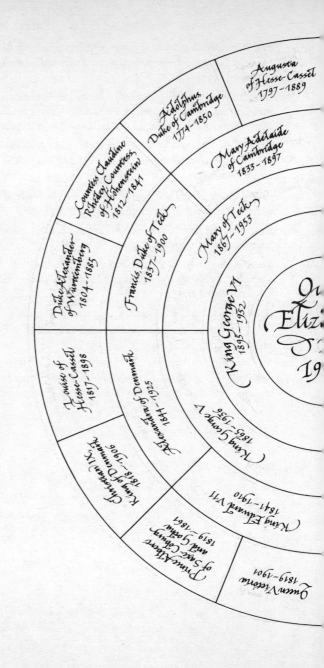

Augusta
of Hesse-Cassel
1797–1889

Adolphus,
Duke of Cambridge
1774–1850

Mary Adelaide
of Cambridge
1833–1897

Countess Claudine
Rhédey, Countess
of Hohenstein
1812–1841

Francis, Duke of Teck
1837–1900

Mary of Teck
1867–1953

Duke Alexander
of Württemberg
1804–1885

King George VI
1895–1952

Qu
Eliz
1
19

Louise of
Hesse-Cassel
1817–1898

Alexandra of Denmark
1844–1925

King George V
1865–1936

Christian IX,
King of Denmark
1818–1906

King Edward VII
1841–1910

Prince Albert
of Saxe-Coburg
and Gotha
1819–1861

Queen Victoria
1819–1901

Thomas George
Lyon Bowes
Lord Glamis
1801–1834

Charlotte
Grimstead
1797–1881

Claude, 13th Earl of
Strathmore and Kinghorne
1824–1904

Oswald Smith
1794–1863

Claude, 14th Earl of Strathmore & Kinghorne
1855–1944

Frances Dora Smith
1832–1922

Henrietta Mildred
Hodgson
1805–1891

Queen
Elizabeth
1
6

Lady Elizabeth Bowes-Lyon
1900–

Nina Cecilia Cavendish-Bentinck
1862–1938

Rev. Charles
Cavendish-Bentinck
1817–1865

Lord William
Cavendish-
Bentinck
1780–1826

Anne Wellesley
1788–1875

Caroline Louisa Burnaby
1832–1918

Edwin Burnaby
1799–1867

Anne Caroline
Salisbury
1806–1881

FOREWORD
TO THE GOLDEN JUBILEE EDITION

In my Preface to the paperback edition of *The Queen: A Biography of Elizabeth II*, published a year after the hardback, I excused myself for not adding new material by saying that 'an extra chapter would be part of another book'. I meant that any historical account is a snapshot, not just of its subject matter, but of the attitudes of the author when it is written. In this sense, *The Queen: Elizabeth II and the Monarchy* is another book. The first edition of *The Queen* was researched and written in the mid-nineties. It appeared in 1996, the year of the divorce of the Prince and Princess of Wales, and doubtless reflects that timing. This Golden Jubilee edition has been prepared several years later. It contains not one additional chapter, but five. The result is a book which has an altered shape from the original, while at the same time offering in the extra chapters a different snapshot.

Chapters 1 to 23 are little changed. There are a few corrections and stylistic tightenings, but I have not attempted to revise my interpretation. The new material is contained in Chapters 24 to 28. Here I have examined post-1996 events and sought to place them in the context of the Queen's life and reign as a whole. I have also looked more closely – partly in the light of 'Diana week' – at aspects of the Monarch's role that go beyond the purely constitutional or symbolic. If there is a new theme, it has to do with the ancient (but also apparently continuing) concept of 'royalty'. At the same time, I have tried to integrate the added chapters so that the reader who comes to the book afresh can take it as a single work, and move from old to new without too great a sense of the division. The revised title is intended to indicate the shift in the book's centre of gravity, and also to distinguish this edition from earlier ones.

I have included the original (hardback) Preface, and I would like to repeat my thanks to the people listed there, many of whom have been re-interviewed or who have given help with this edition in other ways. In particular, I would like to record my unique debt to the late Lord Charteris – a great royal and public servant with whom I spent many happy, instructive and sometimes hilarious hours in the cell-like interview rooms of the Palace of Westminster, and whose voice I often used to illuminate my text. In addition, I should like to thank the staff of the Buckingham Palace press office, and especially Geoff Crawford and Penny Russell-Smith, successively Press Secretaries to the Queen; together with Mary Francis, Peter Galloway, David Hill, Stephen Lamport, Robin Ludlow, Lady Penn, Frank Prochaska and a number of others who prefer not to be named. I should once again like to give my special thanks to Arabella Pike of HarperCollins, for her encouragement and ever incisive advice. I should also like to thank Aisha Rahman for her care and efficiency in guiding the Golden Jubilee edition through to publication. Caroline Wood has again provided invaluable help as picture researcher. At Goldsmiths, I am extremely grateful to Edna Pellett for typing an illegible (sometimes even to the author) manuscript with astonishing skill and without reproach. I would also like to thank Jef McAllister, London Bureau Chief of *Time Magazine*, and the staff at the Australian High Commission, for their kindness in providing access to newspaper and other files; and Dan and Nat Pimlott for their resourcefulness in sifting through them.

New Cross, London SE14
September 2001

PREFACE

'What a marvellous way of looking at the history of Britain', said Raphael Samuel, when I told him about this book. Others expressed surprise, wondering whether a study of the Head of State and Head of the Commonwealth could be a serious or worthwhile enterprise. Whether or not they are right, it has certainly been an extraordinary and fascinating adventure: partly because of the fresh perspective on familiar events it has given me, after years of writing about Labour politicians; partly because of the human drama of a life so exceptionally privileged, and so exceptionally constrained; and partly because of the obsession with royalty of the British public, of which I am a member. Perhaps the last has interested me most of all. To some extent, therefore, this is a book about the Queen in people's heads, as well as at Buckingham Palace. It is, of course, incomplete – no work could be more 'interim' than an account of a monarch who may still have decades to reign. However, because the story is still going on with critical chapters yet to come, it is also – more than most biographies – concerned with now.

It is an 'unofficial' study, and draws eclectically on a variety of sources. For the period up to 1952, the Royal Archives have been invaluable; documentation up to the mid or late 1960s has been provided by the Public Record Office and the BBC Written Archive Centre, alongside a number of private collections of papers, listed at the end of this book. For later years, interviews have been particularly helpful. In addition, there is a wealth of published material.

I have a great many individual debts. I am extremely grateful to Sir Robert Fellowes (Private Secretary to the Queen and Keeper of the Royal Archives, Charles Anson (Press Secretary to the Queen), Oliver Everett (Assistant Keeper of the Royal Archives) and Sheila de Bellaigue (Registrar of the Royal Archives) for assisting with my requests whenever it was possible to do so.

I would like to thank Anne Pimlott Baker, principal researcher for the book, for the care and resourcefulness of her inquiries, and for her skilful digests and research notes; Andrew Chadwick, for research into the archives of *The Times* and *News of the World*; Sarah Benton, for reading the whole text in draft and making many perceptive comments on it; Anne-Marie Rule for typing the manuscript with her usual combination of speed, precision and good-natured tolerance of unreasonable demands – the fifth time she has typed a book for me (am I the last author, incidentally, who still uses a pen and has his drafts typed on a pre-electric typewriter?); Terry Mayer and Jane Tinkler for their help in typing, and retyping, some of the chapters, and for many kindnesses; and my colleagues and students at Birkbeck, for their forebearance, interest and encouragement.

I am grateful to the many librarians and archivists, in the United Kingdom and elsewhere, who have helped me in person, on the telephone, or by correspondence. In addition to those already mentioned, I would especially like to thank Jacquie Kavanagh at the BBC Written Archive Centre at Caversham Park, Helen Langley at the Bodleian Library and the library staff of The Times Newspapers and the *Guardian*. I am also particularly grateful to Sir Hardy Amies, for generously making available to me his corespondence with the Queen and members of the Royal Family over a period of more than forty years; to Phillip Whitehead, for letting me see the unedited transcripts of interviews for his television documentary, *The Windsors*; and Vernon Bogdanor and Frank Prochaska for showing me the text of their excellent recent books, before publication. I am deeply indebted to the staff of the British Library at Bloomsbury, who continue to provide an outstanding service, despite trying conditions during the countdown to the move (regretted by so many) to St Pancras.

I am grateful to the following for permission to quote copyright material: Arrow Books (D. Morrah *To Be a King*); Collins (H. Nicolson *Diaries and Letters 1930–1939*); Duckworth (M. Crawford *The Little Princesses*); Hamish Hamilton (R. Crossman *The Backbench Diaries of Richard Crossman*; *The Diaries of a Cabinet Minister 1964–66*); Hutchinson (T. Benn *Out of the Wilderness: Diaries 1963–67*); Macmillan (J. Wheeler-Bennett *George VI: His Life and Reign*).

I would like to acknowledge the gracious permission of Her Majesty the Queen for allowing me the privilege of using the Royal Archives at Windsor Castle, and for granting me permission to quote from papers in the Archives. For the use of other unpublished papers and documents I am grateful to: Sir Hardy Amies (Amies papers); Lady Avon (Avon papers); Balliol College, Oxford (Nicolson papers); BBC Written Archive Centre (BBC Written Archives); British Library of Political and Economic Science (Dalton papers);

Christ Church, Oxford (Bradwell papers); Churchill College, Cambridge (Alexander papers; Chartwell papers; Swinton papers); Lady Margaret Colville (Colville papers); Dwight D. Eisenhower Library (Eisenhower papers); Mrs Caroline Erskine (Lascelles papers); House of Lords (Beaverbrook papers); John F. Kennedy Library (Kennedy papers); Lambeth Palace (Fisher papers); F. D. Roosevelt Library (Roosevelt papers); Harry S. Truman Library (Truman papers); University College, Oxford (Attlee papers); University of Southampton (Mountbatten papers).

I would like to thank the following people who have taken the time to talk to me about different aspects of this book: Lord Airlie, Lady Airlie, Ronald Allison, Sir Hardy Amies, Lord Armstrong of Ilminster, Sir Shane Blewitt, Lord Brabourne, Sir Alistair Burnet, Lord Buxton, Lord Callaghan, Lord Carnarvon, Lady Carnarvon, Lord Carrington, Lady Elizabeth Cavendish, Lord Charteris, Lord Cranborne, Jonathan Dimbleby, Lord Egremont, Sir Edward Ford, Princess George of Hanover, The Duchess of Grafton, John Grigg, Joe Haines, David Hicks, Lady Pamela Hicks, Anthony Holden, Angela Howard-Johnston, Lord Howe, Lord Hunt of Tamworth, Douglas Hurd, Sir Bernard Ingham, Michael Jones, Robin Janvrin, Lord Limerick, Lady Longford, Brian MacArthur, Lord McNally, HRH Princess Margaret, Sir John Miller, Sir Derek Mitchell, Lady Mountbatten, Michael Noakes, The Duke of Norfolk, Commander Michael Parker, Michael Peat, Rt Rev Simon Phipps, Sir Edward Pickering, Sir David Pitblado, Sir Charles Powell, Enoch Powell, Sir Sonny Ramphal, Sir John Riddell, Kenneth Rose, Lord Runcie, Sir Kenneth Scott, Michael Shea, Phillip Whitehead, Sir Clive Whitmore and Mrs Woodroffe. I also spoke to others who prefer not to be named. Where it has not been possible to give the source of a quotation in the text or notes, I have used the words 'Confidential interview'. None of these people, or anybody else apart from the author, is responsible for how the material has been interpreted.

HarperCollins has once again proved itself the Rolls Royce of British non-fiction publishing. I am particularly indebted to Stuart Proffitt, my publisher, for his persistent faith in the project and his shrewd author management, and to my incomparable editor, Arabella Pike, for whom my admiration has no bounds. I am also grateful to Caroline Wood for her inspired picture research, and to Anne O'Brien for vital last-minute help. Giles Gordon, my literary agent, has been a constant source of practical wisdom and advice.

Finally, I thank the people to whom the book is dedicated: my children, for keeping my spirits up; and my wife, Jean Seaton, for whom all my books are really written, whose thoughts about monarchy and royalty are now inextricably bound up with my own, and whose fertile historical imagination has been a daily quarry.

Bloomsbury, wc1
August 1996

1

APRIL 1926 was a busy month for every member of the Conservative Government, but for few ministers more than the Home Secretary, Sir William Joynson-Hicks. A long, bitter dispute in the coalfields was moving rapidly towards its climax – with drastic implications for the nation.

'We are going to be slaves no longer and our men will starve before they accept any reductions in wages,' the miners' leader, A. J. Cook, had declared in an angry speech that crystallized the mood in the collieries, while the men resolved: 'Not a penny off the pay, not a minute on the day'. On 14 April, the TUC leadership asked the Prime Minister to intervene. A week later the owners and men met, but failed to reach agreement. Thereafter, the chance of a compromise diminished, and the prospect grew closer of a terrifying industrial shutdown which – for the first time in British history – seemed likely to affect the majority of British manual workers. Alarm affected all levels of society. Even King George V – mindful of his right to be consulted, and his duty both to encourage and above all to warn – discreetly urged his ministers to show caution. Alas, royal counsels were in vain, and the General Strike began at midnight on 3rd May 1926, threatening not just economic paralysis and bankruptcy, but the constitution itself.

'Jix' Joynson-Hicks – best known to history for his zeal in ordering police raids on the decadent writings of D.H. Lawrence and Radclyffe Hall, and for the part he later played in defeating the 1927 Bill to revise the Prayer Book – was scarcely an outstanding or memorable holder of his post. This, however, was his most splendid hour. In swashbuckling alliance with Winston Churchill, Neville Chamberlain, Quintin Hogg and Leo Amery, the Home Secretary was a Cabinet hawk, in the thick of the fight, a scourge of the miners, opposed to an easy settlement.

If nothing else – it was said – he had nerve. It was Jix who, just after the Strike began, appealed for 50,000 volunteers for the special constables, in order to protect essential vehicles – and thereby raised the temperature of the dispute. For several critical weeks, Jix was at the heart of the nation's events, in constant touch with the Metropolitan Police, and sometimes with the Prime Minister as well.

Sleep was at a premium, snatched between night-time Downing Street parleys and daytime consultations with officials. A call in the early hours of 21 April to attend a royal birth, shortly before one of the most critical meetings in the entire dispute between the Prime Minister and the coal owners, was therefore not entirely a cause for celebration. But it was a duty not to be shirked, and Joynson-Hicks was equal to it. He hurried to the bedside of the twenty-five-year-old Duchess of York, wife of the King's second son, at 17 Bruton Street – the London home of the Duchess's parents, the Earl and Countess of Strathmore, who happened to be among the most prominent coal owners in the United Kingdom. The child was born at 2.40 a.m., and named Elizabeth Alexandra Mary, after the Duchess and two Queens.

Why the Home Secretary needed to attend the birth of the child of a minor member of the Royal Family was one of the mysteries of the British Monarchy. Later, when Princess Elizabeth herself became pregnant, an inquiry was launched at the instigation of the then Labour Home Secretary, Chuter Ede. Inspecting the archives, Home Office researchers rejected as myth a quaint belief, fondly held by the Royal Household and the public alike, that it had something to do with verification, James II and warming pans. After taking expert advice, Ede informed Sir Alan Lascelles, Private Secretary to George VI, that it was no more than 'the custom of past ages by which ministers thronged the private apartments of royalty daily, and particularly at moments of special significance such as births, marriages and deaths'.[1] In 1926, however, it was enough that it was customary – Jix was not the kind of man to question it. According to *The Times* the next day, Sir William 'was present in the house at the time of the birth' and conveyed the news by special messenger to the Lord Mayor.

It was a difficult delivery, despite the best attention. Not until 10 a.m. did the Duchess's doctors issue a guarded statement which revealed what had happened. 'Previous to the confinement a consultation took place,' it declared, '. . . and a certain line of treatment' – decorous code for a Caesarean section – 'was successfully adopted'.[2] The announcement had more than a purely medical significance. The risks such an operation then entailed, and would again entail in the event of subsequent pregnancies, made it unlikely that the Duchess would have a large family, and hence reduced the chances of a future male heir.

At the time, however, few regarded the Princess's proximity to the throne as important. Some later writers, looking back, argued that her succession was always likely.[3] But this was *post hoc*: in 1926 the Duke of York's elder brother was young and healthy, and was expected to marry and have issue. When Princess Elizabeth was born she was third in line for the throne after her uncle, the Prince of Wales, and her father, and under the 1701 Act of Settlement she took precedence over her father's young brothers – just as Queen Victoria had taken precedence over the Duke of Cumberland, younger brother of William IV, in 1837, even though her own father, the Duke of Kent, had predeceased him. Therefore, until either her uncle had a legitimate heir, or her father had a son, Elizabeth's eventual succession was possible, and she had a special standing as a result. But this chance initially seemed remote, and the Princess was much less afflicted during her earliest years by the isolating sense of an inescapable destiny than either her eldest uncle, or her own eldest son.

Despite the distance of the child from the throne, the newspapers took a keen interest in the birth. Perhaps they were responding to the deepening crisis with a bromide, or perhaps it was part of a patriotic reaction. Whatever the cause, far more attention was paid to Princess Elizabeth in 1926 than to George V's first two grandsons, George and Gerald Lascelles, sons of the Princess Royal, in 1923 and 1924, even though at the time of their births they had been similarly placed in the line of succession. Such, indeed, was the excitement that a crowd swiftly gathered in Bruton Street in the hope of seeing the Princess, to greet the messenger boys who arrived with telegrams and presents, and to cheer the Duchess's royal callers.

Among the first to arrive were the King and Queen. 'Such a relief and joy,' wrote Queen Mary in her diary, noting that the baby was 'a little darling with lovely complexion & pretty fair hair'. The Duke of York was beside himself. 'We always wanted a child to make our happiness complete,' he wrote to his mother. Kings, however, prefer male descendants. The Duke therefore added a little anxiously, 'I do hope that you & Papa are as delighted as we are, to have a granddaughter, or would you sooner have another grandson. I know Elizabeth wanted a daughter.'[4]

Then the nation was plunged into turmoil and uncertainty as, for six bewildering days, industries and services were halted, and workers took to the streets. The Duke of York attended debates daily at the House of Commons; at Buckingham Palace, sentries exchanged their red coats for khaki; and the royal entourage was cut to a minimum as an emergency measure, to allow the lords-in-waiting and most of the equerries to take up duties in Jix's army of special constables. Yet public interest in the royal baby was unabated. On 14 May, just after the ending of the Strike, Queen Mary's lady-in-waiting and friend, the Countess of Airlie, visited 17 Bruton Street to deliver the gift of a bottle of 'Jordan water' from the Holy Land, for use at the christening. She found such a throng in the street that the infant had to be taken out for her morning airing by a back entrance.

The christening took place at Buckingham Palace at the end of May, attended by ten 'children of the Chapel Royal' – small boys clad in crimson and gold, with neck jabots of old lace. The Princess wore a skirt several feet in length. She cried so much during the service that immediately after it her old-fashioned nurse surprised 'the modern young mothers present' (as Lady Airlie described some of the Duchess's friends), and much amused the Prince of Wales, by dosing her heavily from a bottle of dill water.[5] In spite of the puckering of the royal features, great interest was shown in the infant's physical appearance. One resourceful sketch-writer wrote of the Princess's 'pure cream complexion and blue eyes fringed with long, dark lashes'.[6]

The baby was no sooner baptized than an active debate began in the press about how she should, and would, be brought up. The issue of modernity versus tradition became a matter of particular concern, especially to women writers in the popular magazines, where prejudice and preference tended to merge with the little evidence that was available about what actually went on. There was also the question of whether royal child-rearing should be special – given the future responsibilities of a member of the Royal Family – or follow a pattern which any mother should treat as the ideal. Most commentators opted for the latter. 'Sensible' was a much favoured word: a sensible nursery regime involved strict, no-nonsense orderliness, with an emphasis on routine, and the avoidance of fads.

Above all – a point on which all agreed – there must be no excessive luxury. A distinction was made between the opulent symbols of royal status, which were considered both acceptable and desirable; and any kind of physical or especially dietary indulgence. Thus, the National Jewellers' Association was applauded for presenting the Princess with a silver porringer, with ivory handles carved in the form of thistles and a cover surmounted by an ivory and silver coronet. There were no objections when the chairman of the Association, Mr G. L. Joseph, declared after a little ceremony at Bruton Street his hope that the porringer would take its place 'upon the breakfast table of the first baby in the land, and may even be banged upon the table by her infant hands'.[7] It was also felt appropriate that royal baby clothes should be hand-made from the finest materials; and there was wide approval at the news that the Queen of England herself, together with Lady Strathmore and the Duchess of York, had personally stitched the Princess's layette, assisted by the inmates of charitable institutions where relevant skills were to be found. 'Many poor gentlewomen,' it was reported, 'have profited by the Duchess's order for fine lawn and muslin frocks, little bonnets and jackets, and all the delightful accessories of baby's toilet.' However, it was simultaneously claimed that, as 'a great believer in modern methods of bringing up infants,' the Duchess of York rejected the arguments of those who favoured long skirts for ordinary use.

Long skirts meant unnecessary waste. Yet if the Duchess was modern on the subject of skirts, she was old-fashioned on the matter of cloth. A battle raged in the 1920s between mothers and nurses who held to the tradition of clothing babies in cotton garments, and progressive advocates of warm, soft, cosy and absorptive wool.[8] The Duchess firmly rejected wool. After visiting a welfare centre where 'woolly babies' were the rule, she admitted that such apparel might be convenient and comfortable, but laughingly said that the infants 'looked rather like little gnomes, and that she preferred "frilly babies"'.[9] Yet she also rejected self-consciously showy clothes for children. Frilliness meant femininity, not unnecessary adornment. Cotton meant cleanliness and purity. The Duchess, suggested one account, had 'definite ideas about dressing a child, and they can be summed up in the single word Simplicity'.[10] When the Princess was a baby and toddler, she was dressed predominantly in white; when she grew older, she and her sister 'could not have been more simply dressed,' according to their governess.[11] Simplicity was linked to a sturdy, even spartan, approach: simple, sensible clothes as a feature of a simple, sensible upbringing. 'They don't wear hats at play, even on the coldest and windiest days,' wrote one commentator.[12] The Duchess's attitude seemed to rub off on her daughter who, in adolescence, 'never cared a fig' about what she wore.[13]

Such an approach seemed both patriotic and morally proper at a time when British was deemed best in the nursery, as everywhere else. At first, the Princess occupied a room at 17 Bruton Street which had been used by her mother before her marriage. Here, Lady Strathmore had made sure that 'in all the personal details that give character to a room,' the surroundings were 'typically English'.[14] After a few months, the nursery and its establishment of custodians moved to the Yorks' new residence at 145 Piccadilly, a tall, solid-looking building, later destroyed by a wartime bomb, close to Hyde Park Corner, and almost opposite St George's Hospital.

145 Piccadilly was a town house of the kind often maintained as a London base by aristocratic and other wealthy families who were happiest in the country. It was spacious (an estate agent's advertisement claimed that including servants' quarters, there were 25 bedrooms)[15] but unremarkable. When they were there, the standard of living of the King's second son and his wife was far from meagre. According to one account in 1936, staff kept at 145 Piccadilly included a steward, a housekeeper, the Duchess's personal maid, the Duke's valet, two footmen, three maids, a cook and two kitchen maids, a nurse, a nursery-maid, a boy and a night-watchman. A few years earlier, there had been an under-nurse as well.[16] Nevertheless, the Yorks' existence – cheek-by-jowl with the establishments of rich professionals, bankers and businessmen, as well as of landowners – was not unusual in aristocratic or plutocratic terms.

The photographer Lisa Sheridan first visited the Piccadilly house in the late 1920s (her mother happened to be a friend of the house-keeper). She later recalled a white terraced building, indistinguishable from those on either side of it. There was a semi-basement kitchen, 'like the giant's kitchen in a pantomime with its immense shiny copper pots and great fire-range'. The upstairs interior style reflected the taste of the Duchess more than of the Duke. Vast oil paintings, including a picture of horses, hung in heavy gilt frames in the dim, over-furnished entrance hall, alongside huge elephant tusks, mementoes of some-body's big game hunt. There was also a painted, life-size statue of a black boy.[17] An extensive garden at the back, shared with other houses, added an element of community. As the Princess grew older she was able to play on the lawns and paths with the children of the merely well-to-do, although a zoo-like atmosphere developed, as members of the public, tipped off by the press, acquired the habit of peering through the railings.[18]

Elizabeth lived in a suite of rooms at the top of the house, consisting of a day nursery, a night nursery and a bathroom linked by a landing, with wide windows looking down on the park. Here Mrs Sheridan remembered seeing the Princess, 'her pretty doll-like face . . . framed in soft silky curls'. Around her were the typical *accoutrements* of an inter-war upper-class infant's lair: a rocking horse, baby clothes hung up to dry, a nanny knitting in a rocking chair. The impression was of devotion and reassurance, but also of order, neatness and discipline; the Princess, at the crawling stage, was only allowed to play with one toy at a time.[19]

There was no question about who was in charge. The Yorks' gover-ness later aptly described the regime as 'a state within a state,' with the nanny, Clara Knight (known as 'Alla'), as ever-present benign dictator, 'a shoulder to weep on, a bosom to fall asleep on,' who 'would sit at evening in the rocker . . . mending or knitting and telling stories of "when Mummie was a little girl"'.[20] Alla was a former Strathmore retainer who had looked after the Duchess and her brother: Elizabeth Cavendish, a contemporary of the Princess, remembers her, from children's parties, as a 'formidable' figure.[21] Unmodern to a fault, she controlled the life of the Princess – health, dress and bath.

The tiny Princess, half-royal by birth, lived in her earliest years a half-royal existence. At first, much of it was spent with her parents, as they travelled restlessly around the great houses of people to whom they were related, like members of any great family. Soon, however, the requirements of royalty produced long parental absences, and the role of Alla and her assistants grew.

From babyhood, Princess Elizabeth was often in Scotland, either staying with her Strathmore (Bowes-Lyon) grandparents at Glamis Castle in Forfarshire, or with her royal ones at Balmoral Castle in Aberdeenshire. She spent much of her first summer in an ancient nursery wing at Glamis, or sleeping in the Castle garden 'to the rhythmic sound of tennis balls on hard courts where her elders played, and to the song of laden bees. And when she awoke it was to smile at her father and mother as they started off on some fishing expedition . . .' At the end of August, when Elizabeth was four months old, the Duke and Duchess of York left her in the care of the Countess of Strathmore while they went, like most of the young mothers and fathers, modern and unmodern, who were known to them, on 'a round of visits to friends'.[22]

This was the prelude to a much longer parting. Earlier in the year, the Duke of York had accepted an invitation to open the Commonwealth Parliament in the new Australian capital of Canberra. It was taken for granted both that his wife would accompany him and that their baby daughter would not. After Christmas, therefore, the Yorks took the Princess to the Strathmores' Hertfordshire home at St Paul's Walden Bury, and there they left her, for the duration of the royal tour. After they had sailed from Portsmouth early in January 1927, the Duchess wrote from on board the battle cruiser *Renown* to her mother-in-law that she had 'felt very much leaving on Thursday, and the baby was so sweet playing with the buttons on Bertie's uniform that it quite broke me up'.[23] Neither the King, nor the Queen, nor the Duke, however, would have seen anything unusual about such a trip. As Prince of Wales, George V had himself taken his wife on several foreign or imperial tours, without the encumbrance of their young children.

In any case, there was much to take the minds of the Duke and Duchess off their baby daughter. Prince Albert Frederick Arthur George, known as 'Bertie' to his family, had been made Duke of York in 1920, at the age of twenty-five. Yet he had not at that time sought a prominent royal role, and no exacting royal responsibilities had so far been asked of him. Shy and slow as a child, and the victim of a stammer since the age of seven or eight, he disliked and avoided occasions when he might be required to speak – so much so, that some had regarded him as not only reclusive, but intellectually backward. There had been some recent improvement. His marriage to Lady Elizabeth Bowes-Lyon in 1923 had increased his confidence. So too, during the months before the voyage, had a course of instruction from an Australian speech therapist. But his appearances before large audiences had been infrequent, and – except over events like weddings and births – the public had taken less interest in him and his wife than in other members of the Royal Family. 'The news-reels didn't bother them very much,' noted one commentator, a few years later, 'and the press left them pretty much alone.'[24] Australia, where the Duke was to represent his father before the people of an intensely loyal dominion, was his first major testing ground.

The tour was exacting, psychologically as well as physically, for it aroused huge public curiosity. The Yorks' itinerary involved going, via Panama, to Fiji and New Zealand before they reached Sydney. In Australia, a programme of visits took them to cities around the country, culminating in their arrival at Canberra for Bertie's painfully rehearsed, much feared speech at the opening ceremony. During the ominous build-up, the Duke and Duchess were fêted at each stop. The local press eagerly examined every available detail of the lives of the previously little-known couple, who seemed to embody the mother country, for which sentimental and nostalgic feelings remained strong. As the tour progressed, fascination increased, especially for the most humanizing detail of all: the distant and as yet inarticulate Princess. 'Wherever we go cheers are given for her as well,' Bertie wrote to his mother, '& the children write to us about her.'[25] The newspapers dubbed her 'Betty,' and she became the tour's unofficial mascot. The Duke and Duchess were soon besieged with questions about 'the World's Best Known Baby'. They also loaded with gifts for her, each locality or association vying with its rivals to produce the most loving, ingenious and appropriate present. The Brownies of Auckland delivered a large doll, the children of Fremantle gave a miniature bed, together with a box of miniature clothes, the National Council of Women sent a gold porringer, and the Melbourne Arts and Crafts Society proudly proffered an Australian Noah's Ark, complete with kangaroos, wallabies and other antipodean survivors of the Flood. In May 1927, it was estimated that three tons of toys had so far been presented for Betty, *in absentia*. The soldier who guarded them reputedly said there were more dolls in the collection than there were men in his regiment.

At home, however, Alla's one-toy-at-a-time regime did not alter. The Princess's first day without her parents was reported by the newspapers to be just like any other. Though it was the depth of winter, her nanny took her in a pram on a two-hour walk through Mayfair into Hyde Park, where she appeared perfectly content, fast asleep, and (suitably, for the granddaughter of a King-Emperor) clutching a golliwog under the covers. Supposedly, she 'seemed to miss her mother's regular morning visit to the nursery,' though how anyone could tell was not revealed.[26]

In February, the Alla establishment joined George V and Queen Mary at Buckingham Palace, and in April they followed the Court to Windsor, where the Princess spent her first birthday. The King and Queen enjoyed the idea of being *in loco parentis* (although it involved little contact with the child) and the Queen, particularly, took it very seriously. There was a daily ritual. Every afternoon, Alla would bring Princess Elizabeth down to her grandparents, 'and the appearance at the door of a very little person in a white gown and fringed sash would be greeted by the Queen's delighted cry of "Here comes the Bambino!"'[27] Photographs and written reports of the baby's progress were sent to her parents. 'She has 4 teeth now,' the King told them in March, 'which is quite good at eleven months, she is very happy and drives in a carriage every afternoon, which amuses her'.[28] The Strathmores were able to tell of other accomplishments. During the last two months of the Yorks' absence, the Princess stayed at St Paul's Walden Bury. Here, Alla patiently taught her to enunciate the word 'Mummy'. Since, however, there was nobody to whom the word could be accurately applied, she greeted everybody she came across, including family portraits, 'with the salutation "Mummy, Mummy!"'[29]

As one writer observed later in the Princess's childhood, 'the parents who came back to her from the other end of the earth were strangers'.[30] The Duke and Duchess returned in June after six months away, laden with toys, to greet a child they barely recognized, who was almost twice the age she had been when they departed. The reunion involved a poignant little ceremony in the Grand Hall at Buckingham Palace where the King and Queen and the Earl and Countess of Strathmore had assembled with the Household staff to provide a welcoming party. The Duchess, seeing the baby in its nurse's arms, rushed forward, exclaiming 'Oh you little darling', and kissed and hugged it repeatedly.[31]

Glad to be home, flushed with the unexpected triumph of their tour, and delighted to see their daughter, the Yorks were happy to relax for a while in London after such an arduous journey. However, they did not stay still for long. Within a few weeks, they had left the capital for the shooting season – the Duke to join the Duke and Duchess of Devonshire, the Duchess to visit her parents at Glamis. At first, Princess Elizabeth stayed in London, but after another short separation, she was dispatched to Scotland, where a mother-daughter relationship was re-established. 'Elizabeth is learning to walk – very dangerous!' wrote the Duchess of York at Glamis. In September 1927, the whole family joined the King and Queen at Balmoral. Then they returned south for the autumn months, in order to settle properly into their house in Piccadilly.

IN ALL ACCOUNTS of Princess Elizabeth as a child, legend and reality are inseparable. The observations of those with direct knowledge were fed, not just by what they saw, but also by popular beliefs and idealizations, colouring the way they treated her, and shaping the stories they passed on which, in turn, fed the myths. Two themes stand out in the early tales. According to the first, the Princess was an unusually bright and interesting child, as well as an exceptionally pleasing, generous, and sunny-natured one. According to the second, she was the essence of normality, and of a typically balanced yet fallible British girlhood. These contradictory versions – the ideal and the archetype – were held simultaneously and provided the frame on which every narrative of the Princess's childhood was built, including the anecdotes of those close to her. They also shaped the way the world came to see her as an adult and as a monarch.

The manufacture of a publicly known personality for the Princess began with her appearance. The world, peering into the royal perambulator, detected an ethereal quality. After a visit to the Bruton Street nursery, one early eulogizer wrote that the infant Elizabeth had 'the sweetest air of complete serenity about her. While we were talking, her nurse came in to fetch her, and the Duchess threw round her daughter's head . . . a filmy veil of gossamer, from which she looked down out of her nurse's arms smiling angelically at her mother, like a cherub out of a cloud'.[32]

Yet if the Princess's blond Botticelli curls, blue eyes and plump cheeks made it easy to cast her as an angel, it was important that she should also be seen as a mischievous one. After a Christmas party in 1927 for four hundred tenants on the Sandringham Estate, the press reported that the twenty-one-month-old apparition, wearing a white dress, silk socks and white shoes, suddenly materialized, standing upright on the table, 'chattering and bombarding the guests with crackers handed to her by her mother.'[33] There was also another version of the image of a small person bombarding big ones with harmless objects. At 145 Piccadilly, the Princess would allegedly get a small toy, such as a teddy bear or a ball, and drop it from the nursery landing down the stairwell onto visitors as they arrived at the house.[34] Other stories also emphasized that, for all the other-worldliness, the child was cheeringly imperfect. Ruth St Mawr, a friend of Lady Strathmore, told a story about taking tea at Glamis Castle when Princess Elizabeth, by then three, bounded in. 'You can't think how naughty I've been,' declared the child. 'Oh, *so* naughty, you don't know.' 'Well then tell me,' said Lady Strathmore, 'and I *shall* know.' 'No,' said Princess Elizabeth – and that was that.[35]

Normality required a pet-name and this, the press was delighted to discover, Princess Elizabeth herself provided early on. At two and a half, she was reported to be calling herself 'Tillabet'.[36] Later, this became 'Lisabet' or 'Lilliebeth,' before settling down as 'Lilibet,' the name her close family have continued to call her all her life. Normality also required a passion, and this, too, the Princess obligingly furnished in her lifelong love of horses and dogs, which could be dated to the autumn of 1928, when the Duke of York took Naseby Hall in Northamptonshire for the hunting season, and Elizabeth accompanied her parents there for much of the winter. According to one inter-war chronicler, it was at Naseby 'that Lisabet really fell in love with beautiful horses'. She enjoyed patting her father's animals, and her nurse had to watch her closely, because of her habit of running off to the stables at the slightest excuse at any time of day.[37] In addition, apparently, 'she especially loved the hounds with their nervous erect tails and their elemental eagerness to be off'.[38]

Horses and dogs had to be trained, and from a tender age, Princess Elizabeth was often portrayed in appropriate roles of command and authority in relation to them. But royal children required training too, and it was made clear, in every tale, that the Princess's mischief was never allowed to get out of hand. If Elizabeth had a sense of fun, it was also (commentators took care to point out) kept in check. 'Uncurbed without being spoilt' was how the *Sunday Dispatch* described the barely walking child in an article entitled 'The Roguish Princess'.[39] 'Roguish' was a favourite term in such accounts: it implied misbehaviour within acceptable and endearing limits. According to Alice Ring's royally sanctioned description of the Princess, published in 1930, on one occasion Elizabeth said 'My Goodness!' in the hearing of her mother. She was 'at once told that this was not pretty and mustn't be repeated'. However, if she heard an adult use the unseemly expression, 'up go her small arms in a gesture of mock amazement, and she presses her palms tightly over her mouth while her blue eyes are full of roguish laughter'.[40]

Uncurbed was never allowed to mean over-indulged. 'I don't think any child could be more sensibly bought up,' Queen Mary remarked. 'She leads such a simple life and she's always punished when she's naughty.'[41] Here was a useful moral tale, for the edification of millions. 'Once Lisbet had been naughty, for even princesses can be naughty, you know,' wrote Captain Eric Acland, author of a particularly cloying biography published when Elizabeth was twelve, 'and her mother, to punish her, refused to tell the usual bedtime story.'[42] According to another writer, if the Duchess of York was asked what her main duty was, 'she would reply, "Bringing up my children". She brings them up as she herself was brought up, with unremitting care and great practical intelligence.'[43] It was the accepted view. 'No child of Queen Elizabeth's will ever be spoilt,' the writer Stephen King-Hall summed up, at the time of George VI's Coronation.[44]

But how could any child receive so much attention, and be the object of so many admiring glances, yet not be spoilt, even allowing for parental firmness? Here was an even deeper paradox in the iconography, never satisfactorily resolved. The usual answer – and the one that dominated characterizations of the Princess until her adolescence – was that her innocence was protected, as if by wall and moat, from the corrupting effects of vulgar fame and even of excessive loyal adoration. Chocolates, china sets and children's hospital wards, even a territory in Antarctica, were named after her; the people of Newfoundland had her image on their postage stamps; songs were written in her honour, and sung by large assemblies of her contemporaries; while Madame Tussaud's displayed a wax model of her astride a pony. However, according to one chronicler in the early 1930s, 'of all this she is unconscious, it passes her completely by – and she remains just a little girl, like any other little girl . . . and passionately fond of her parents'.[45] There was also the idea of a fairy-tale insulation from the projected thoughts and fantasies of the outside world – a 'normal' childhood preserved, by an abnormal caesura, from public wonder. 'In those days we lived in an ivory tower' wrote Elizabeth's governess, many years later, 'removed from the real world'.[46]

Yet the very protection of the Princess, the notion of her as an innocent, unknowing, unsophisticated child who, but for her royal status, might be anybody's daughter, niece or little sister, helped to sustain the popular idea of her as a ray of sunshine in a troubled world, a talisman of health and happiness. This particular quality was often illustrated by tales of her special, even curative, relationship with the King, which juxtaposed youth and old age, gaiety and wisdom, the future and the past, in a heavily symbolic manner. From the time of the Yorks' Australian tour, when the Princess was fostered at Buckingham Palace, it had been observed that the ailing Monarch, whose health was becoming a matter of concern throughout the Empire, derived a special pleasure from the company of his granddaughter.

There were many accounts which brought this out. 'He was fond of his two grandsons, Princess Mary's sons,' the Countess of Airlie recalled, 'but Lilibet always came first in his affections. He used to play with her – a thing I never saw him do with his own children – and loved to have her with him'.[47] Others observed the same curious phenomenon: on one occasion, the Archbishop of Canterbury was startled to encounter the elderly Monarch acting the part of a horse, with the Princess as his groom, 'the King-Emperor shuffling on hands and knees along the floor, while the little Princess led him by the beard'.[48] When she was scarcely out of her pram, a visitor to Sandringham reported watching the King 'chortling with little jokes with her – she just struggling with a few words, "Grandpa" and "Granny"'.[49] The Princess's governess recalled seeing them together, near the end of the King's life, 'the bearded old man and the polite little girl holding on to one of his fingers'. Later, it was claimed that the King was 'almost as devoted a slave to her as her favourite uncle, the Prince of Wales'.[50]

Yet it was also stressed that she was taught to know her place. Deferential manners were an ingredient of the anecdotes, alongside the spontaneity. One guest noted that after a game of toy bricks on the floor with an equerry, she was fetched by her nurse, 'and made a perfectly sweet little curtsey to the King and Queen and then to the company as she departed'. This vital piece of royal etiquette had been perfected before her third birthday. When it was time to bid her grandfather goodnight, she would retreat backwards to the door, curtsey and say, 'I trust your Majesty will sleep well'.[51] Some accounts took the Princess's concern beyond mere politeness. For example, it was said that when the King was sick, she asked after him, and, on seeing her grandmother, 'flung herself into the Queen's arms and cried: "Lillybet to see Grandpar today?"'[52] There were also reports that when the royal landau passed down Piccadilly a shrill cry was heard from the balcony at No. 145: 'Here comes Grandpa!' – causing the crowd to roar with loyal delight.[53] There was much approval, too, for her name for the King: 'Grandpa England'.[54]

But the most celebrated aspect of the relationship concerned the Princess's prophylactic powers during the King's convalescence from a near-fatal illness in the winter of 1928–9. During this anxious time, the little girl 'acted as a useful emollient to jaded nerves,'[55] a kind of harp-playing David to the troubled Monarch's Saul.

In March 1929, the Empire learnt that the Princess, not yet three, was being encouraged to spend much of the morning with the recuperating King in his room at Craigweil House in Bognor, in order to raise his spirits. For an hour or so, she would sit with him by his chair at the window, making 'the most amusing and original comments on people and events'.[56] The King recovered, and his granddaughter was popularly believed to have played a part in bringing this about. Many years later, Princess Elizabeth told a courtier that the old Monarch's manner 'was very abrupt, some people thought he was being rude'.[57] The fact that he terrified his sons, and barked at his staff, gave the stories of the little girl's fearless enchantments an even sharper significance.

For her fourth birthday in 1930, the doting old man made Elizabeth the special gift of a pony. At this news public adoration, both of the giver and the recipient, literally overflowed. The same day, the Princess, in a yellow coat trimmed with fur, was seen walking across the square at Windsor Castle, with a band of the Scots Guards providing an accompaniment. Women waved their handkerchiefs and threw kisses. The Princess waved back, and 'her curly locks fluttered in the breeze'. The sight was too much for the crowd. People outside the Castle gate suddenly pressed forward, and swept the police officer on duty off his feet.[58]

THE DUCHESS OF YORK gave birth to a second child at Glamis Castle in August 1930. Although a Labour Government was now in office, traditional proprieties were once again observed – this time at even greater inconvenience to the new Home Secretary, J. R. Clynes, than to his predecessor. Summoned north for the expected event, Clynes was kept waiting for five days as a guest of the Countess of Airlie, at Cortachy Castle. He made no complaint, and seems to have enjoyed his part in the ritual. Later he described how, after the announcement, 'the countryside was made vivid with the red glow of a hundred bonfires, while sturdy kilted men with flaming torches ran like gnomes from place to place through the darkness'.[1]

The arrival of Princess Margaret Rose had several effects. One was to reinforce public awareness of her sister. The child was not a boy, the King's health remained uncertain, and the Prince of Wales showed no sign of taking a wife. A minor constitutional controversy, following the birth, helped to remind the public that Elizabeth's position was an increasingly interesting one. Although common sense indicated that, after the Prince of Wales and the Duke of York, she remained next in line, doubts were raised about whether this was really the case. Some experts argued that legally the two sisters enjoyed equal rights to the succession: there was nothing, in law, to say that they did not, and the precedence of an elder sister over a younger had never been tested. The King ordered a special investigation. The matter was soon settled, to the satisfaction of the Court, and as the Sovereign himself no doubt wished.[2]

Another effect was to give Elizabeth a companion, and the public an additional character on which to build an ever-evolving fantasy. The Yorks were now a neatly symmetrical family, the inter-war ideal. There were no more children to spoil the balance, or dilute the cast.

After the birth of Margaret Rose, 145 Piccadilly acquired a settled, tranquil, comforting air, and the image of it became a fixed point in the national and imperial psyche. When people imagined getting married and setting up a home, they thought of the Yorks. The modest, reserved, quietly proud father, the practical, child-centred mother, the well-mannered, well-groomed daughters; the ponies, dogs and open air; the servants dealing with the chores, tactfully out of sight; the lack of vanity, ambition, or doubt – all represented, for Middle England and its agents overseas, a distillation of British wholesomeness.

It did not matter that the Yorks were not 'the Royal Family' – that the Duke was not the King, or ever likely to be. Indeed, it helped that they were sufficiently removed from the ceremonial and servility of the Court to lead comprehensible lives, and for their daughters to have the kind of fancy-filled yet soundly based childhood that every boy and girl, and many adults, yearned for. At a time of poverty and uncertainty for millions, the York princesses in their J. M. Barrie-like London home and country castles stood for safety and permanence. The picture magazines showed them laughing, relaxed, perpetually hugging or stroking pets, always apart from their peers, doll-like mascots to adorn school and bedroom walls. Children often wrote to them, as if they were playmates, or sisters: little girls they already knew. Story books spun homely little tales around their lives, helping to incorporate them as imaginary friends in ordinary families.

The most dramatic attempt to appropriate them for ordinariness occurred in 1932, with the erection of a thatched cottage, two-thirds natural size, by 'the people of Wales,' as a present for Princess Elizabeth on her sixth birthday. This remarkable object made an implicit point, for no part of the United Kingdom had suffered more terrible unemployment than the mining valleys of the principality. Built exclusively by Welsh labour out of Welsh materials, it provided a stirring demonstration of the ingenuity of a workforce whose skills were tragically wasted. At the same time – loyally and movingly – its creators sought to connect the lives of the little Princess and her baby sister to those of thousands of children who inhabited real cottages. The point, however, could not be too political, and an abode, even an imitation one, intended for a princess had to be filled with greater luxuries than average families ever experienced.

Great efforts were made to ensure that it conformed to the specifications of a real home. Electric lights were installed, and the contents included a tiny radio, a little oak dresser and tiny china set, linen with the initial 'E', and a portrait of the Duchess of York over the dining-room mantelpiece. The house also contained little books, pots and pans, food cans, brooms, and a packet of Epsom salts, a radio licence and an insurance policy, all made to scale. The bathroom had a heated towel rail. In the kitchen, the reduced-size gas cooker, copper and refrigerator worked, and hot water came out of the tap in the sink.

It was scarcely a surprise present. Months of publicity preceded its completion. There was also a near-disastrous mishap. When the house was finished and in transit, the tarpaulin protecting it caught fire, and the thatched roof and many of the timbers were destroyed. Though some felt it lucky that the incendiary nature of the materials had been discovered before, and not after, the Princess was inside, the project was not abandoned. Instead, indefatigable craftsmen worked day and night to repair the damage and apply a fire-resistant coating, in time to display the renovated house at the Ideal Home Exhibition at Olympia.[3] Then it was reconstructed in Windsor Great Park for the birthday girl, and became a favourite plaything.

Whatever Elizabeth may have made of the house's message, she and her sister were soon using it for the purpose for which it was intended: to exercise and display their ordinariness. Elizabeth was 'a very neat child,' according to her governess, and the Welsh house provided an excellent opportunity to show it. The two girls spent happy hours cleaning, dusting and tidying their special home.[4] Thousands of people who had experienced a vicarious contact with royalty by inspecting the cottage when it was on public show, were later able to enjoy a series of photographs of the elfin princesses, filling the doorway of 'Y Bwthyn Bach' – the Little House – not just as children but as Peter Pan adults, miniaturized in a securely diminutive world, the perfect setting for the fantasy of 'royal simplicity'. The contrast between the oriental extravagance of the structure – fabulously costly in design, equipment, production and delivery – and the games that were to be played in it, highlighted the triumphant paradox.

It was also, of course, a *female* artefact, a point made by Lisa Sheridan, when the children proudly took her on a tour in 1936:

> In the delightful panelled living-room everything was in its proper place. Not a speck of dust anywhere! Brass and silver shone brilliantly. Everything which could be folded was neatly put away. The household brushes and the pots and pans all hung in their places. Surely this inspired toy provided an ideal domestic training for children in an enchanted world ... Everything in the elegantly furnished house had been reduced, as if by magic, to those enchanting proportions so endearing to the heart of a woman. How much more so to those young princesses whose status fitted so perfectly the surroundings?[5]

Y Bwthyn Bach gave Elizabeth a Welsh dimension. A Scottish one was provided shortly afterwards by the appointment, early in 1933, of a governess from north of the border, Marion Crawford. In a sense, of course, Elizabeth was already half-Scottish, and it was the Scottish networks of the Duchess of York that had led to the appointment. However Miss Crawford belonged to a different kind of Scotland from the one known to the Bowes-Lyons, or – for that matter – to the kilt-wearing Windsor dynasty. A twenty-two-year-old recent graduate of the Moray House Training College in Edinburgh, she came from a formidable stratum: the presbyterian lower middle class.

Miss Crawford stayed with the Yorks, later the Royal Family, teaching, guiding and providing companionship to both girls for fourteen years, until she married in 1947, shortly before the wedding of Princess Elizabeth. Three years later, she published a detailed account of her experiences in the royal service, against the express wishes of the Palace. 'She snaked,' is how a member of the Royal Family describes her behaviour today.[6] Perhaps it was the incongruity of a woman from such a background betraying, for financial gain, the trust that had been placed in her (as her employers came to see it) which accounted for the anger that was felt. She was not the last to snake, but she was the pioneer. Marion Crawford was soon known as 'Crawfie' to the princesses: 'doing a Crawfie' became an expression for selling family secrets, especially royal ones, acquired during a period of personal service. To the modern reader, however, Miss Crawford's *Little Princesses* is a singularly inoffensive work. Composed with the help of a ghost writer in a gushing Enid Blyton, or possibly Beverley Nichols, style, it does not destroy the Never-Never-Land mythology of 145 Piccadilly, but embraces it. Love, duty and sacrifice are the currency of daily life, and everybody always acts from the best of motives. Yet the book also has perceptiveness – and the ring of authenticity. Although effusively loyal in tone, it reveals a sharp and sometimes critical eye, and opinions which were not always official ones.

It shows a character with just enough of a rebellious edge to make the subsequent 'betrayal' explicable. Until she became notorious, Crawfie and her presence at the Yorks' hearth were regarded in the press (perhaps rightly) as evidence of the Bowes-Lyon belief in no-nonsense training for young girls. According to *The Times* on the occasion of Princess Elizabeth's eighteenth birthday, Miss Crawford 'upheld through the years of tutelage the standards of simple living and honest thinking that Scotland peculiarly respects'.[7] When the Duke of York became King, she was also felt to provide a politically useful bond between the kingdoms. The most important point about Crawfie, however, which escaped public attention at the time, was that she had aspirations, both for her charges and for herself.

She was no scholar, and seemed to share the Royal Family's indifference to academic and aesthetic values. Yet she did not share its lack of curiosity, and she had a strong, indignant sense of the Court as old-fashioned and remote. She deplored what she saw as the children's ignorance of the world, and her book – perhaps this was the most infuriating thing about it – describes her personal crusade to widen the little girls' horizons. There was a Jean Brodie, charismatic aspect to Miss Crawford, both in the power of her passionate yet selfishly demanding personality (sometimes she seemed to forget who was the princess) and in her evangelical determination to make contact with life outside. Although for part of the time she had Queen Mary as an ally, it was an uphill struggle. She did, however, take the children on educational trips, and conspired to satisfy their desire to travel on the London tube; and her greatest triumph was to persuade her employers, by then King and Queen, to allow a Girl Guide Company to be set up at Buckingham Palace. She was also a woman of her age: her other ambition was to get married, something which was incompatible with her employment and – if her own account is to be believed – one which her employers could never understand.

Crawfie was not a contented person. Indeed, the self-portrait unwittingly contained in her book suggests a rather lonely and restless one, an immigrant to England and an outsider to a strange tribe whose members, though friendly, persisted in their unusual and disturbing customs. She was a taker as much as a giver. But she was interesting, intelligent and forceful. Patricia (now Lady) Mountbatten – daughter of Louis and Edwina, and a second cousin of the princesses – remembers her from Guide meetings in the Buckingham Palace gardens as a tall, attractive, highly competent woman, 'with a good personality for bringing out somebody like Princess Elizabeth, who had a stiff upper lip ingrained from birth.'[8] There seems to have developed a mutual dependence, as she became, during critical years, the princesses' confidante and friend.

PRINCESS ELIZABETH's earliest years had been spent at 145 Piccadilly with her parents, at Glamis Castle and St. Paul's Walden Bury with one set of grandparents, or at Balmoral and Sandringham with the other. In 1931, the Yorks were granted Royal Lodge, in Windsor Great Park, by the King, and in the following year they took it over as their private country residence. Thereafter, the adapted remnant of George IV's *cottage orné* designed by John Nash, with its large, circular garden, screening of trees, and air of rustic simplicity, became one of Princess Elizabeth's most familiar homes. More than anywhere, Royal Lodge provided the setting for the Yorks' domestic idyll. Summers were spent there with a minimum of staff.

From the point of view of family life, it was an advantage (not mentioned in the newspaper profiles) that the Duke had little to do. He went on the occasional overseas visit, though never again, as Duke of York, on the scale of the 1927 Australian tour; he exchanged hospitality with relatives and friends; he gardened, he rode, and he shot. With time on his hands, he was often at home during the day and able to take luncheon with his family, and to play tag or hide-and-seek with his daughters in Hamilton Gardens. Until 1936 he and his wife seemed perfectly content with the undemanding routines of a minor member of the Royal Family, of whom little was required or expected. The Duchess had been a society beauty, fêted and wooed in her youth. After contracting a surprising if elevated marriage, however, she appeared to have no ambitions beyond the settled rhythms of an unremarkable aristocratic life, and the enjoyment of her children. Though her wit and charm made her friends wherever she went, and endeared her to other members of the Royal Family, she and her husband were not a fashionable couple, and they had little contact with the café society which held such a fascination for the Prince of Wales.

Crawfie, who disapproved of some of the grander and crustier aspects of the royal way of life, repeatedly stressed in her book that the York establishment concentrated on the children. 'It was a home-like and unpretentious household I found myself in,' she wrote. Life at 145 Piccadilly, at least as seen from the perspective of the governess, revolved around the nursery landing, or around the sleeping quarters of the Duke and Duchess. 'No matter how busy the day, how early the start that had to be made,' according to Crawfie, 'each morning began with high jinks in their parents' bedroom.' This was a daily ritual which continued up to the morning of Princess Elizabeth's marriage. The day ended with a bath and a bedtime ritual, also involving parental high jinks. 'Nothing was ever allowed to stand in the way of these family sessions.'[9]

Sandwiched between morning and evening high jinks came the Princess's education – or, as many observers have wryly observed – the lack of it. After breakfast with Alla in the nursery, Elizabeth would start lessons in a little boudoir off the main drawing-room, under the supervision of her governess. Later, she would make remarks (sometimes to put nervous, successful people at their ease) about her lack of proper schooling; and it is true that, even for a princess born out of direct line of succession to the throne, her curriculum was far from exacting.[10] According to a tactfully understated assessment in the 1950s, it was 'wide rather than deep' without any forcing, or subjection to a classical discipline.[11] It was, perhaps, a misfortune that there were no peers to offer competition, or examinations to provide an incentive. Most time was spent on English, French and history.[12] Elizabeth's dependence on a single instructor for a range of subjects was a limitation, especially as the instructor's own education went no further than a training college diploma. Other future Queens of England, also born out of the direct line, had been better served. Nevertheless, in the first half of the twentieth century a home-based education for upper class girls was normal rather than exceptional – the British equivalent of binding feet.

There were two rival versions of the Yorks' approach to the education of their daughters, and we may dismiss one of them, at least in its simple form. According to the first, semi-official, account the Duchess herself closely supervised her daughters' lessons, and personally devised a timetable which concentrated on relevant subjects, such as foreign languages, scripture, geography, imperial and constitutional history. This account was the one given to the press, especially after the Abdication. According to the second, the Duchess was quite properly concerned that Elizabeth and Margaret should not regard themselves as different from any other children of their background. 'She never aimed at bringing her daughters up to be more than nicely behaved young ladies,' reflected Randolph Churchill, after the war.[13] Sometimes the two versions were combined: the best training for a royal life, it was suggested, was a non-fussy, practical education.

Both, however, agreed on one point: the Duke and Duchess were determined, in the best traditions of the British Royal Family and aristocracy, that their children should not be intellectual. According to a newspaper report, when Elizabeth was ten, a regime which involved only seven and a half hours per week in the schoolroom had been designed with a purpose: to ensure that the elder Princess should avoid becoming a 'blue-stocking', with all the terrible consequences that that term of derision implied. With the avoidance of such a fate in mind, her studies had been planned 'in consultation with the leading educationalists in the country,' and after consideration by the Cabinet.[14]

If Crawfie is to be believed, the truth was actually more mundane. Whether or not the topic was ever seriously discussed in the Cabinet Room, it caused little anxiety at 145 Piccadilly. The attitude in the York household towards education seems, in general, to have been one of genial casualness, undisturbed in the early years by any premon-ition of what lay ahead. Crawfie stressed this last point: perhaps seeking a justification for the lack of pedagogic rigour. Nothing seemed less likely, she insisted, than that the two girls would ever have to play an important role in their adult lives, and consequently their parents' main concern was to give them 'a happy childhood, with lots of pleasant memories stored up against the days that might come and, later, happy marriages.'[15]

If the governess had little choice but to accept the relaxed view of her employers, the same was not true of the children's formidable royal grandmother. Queen Mary – the most serious member of the Royal Family – made purposeful forays into the Piccadilly schoolroom, and was perturbed by what she found. In an attempt to improve matters, she demanded to see a schedule of lessons, urged that Princess Elizabeth should read 'the best type of children's books,' and often chose them for her. She also thought up 'instructive amusements' for the children, like a visit to the Tower of London. 'It would have been impossible for anyone so devoted to the Monarchy as Queen Mary to lose sight of the future Queen in this favourite grandchild,' recalled the Countess of Airlie.[16] This, however, was after the Abdication. Until then, the impact of the Queen's concern was limited, partly because the Duke took as little active interest in his daughters' book-learning as the Duchess.

The Duke's relaxed attitude to female education did not mean, however, that he lacked a social conscience, or sense of royal responsi-bility. On the contrary: a willingness to keep his own daughters socially cocooned was combined with a strong, even progressive, interest in the plight of children from the urban slums. Before becoming King, as President of the Industrial Welfare (formerly Boys' Welfare) Associ-ation, he was involved in schemes to benefit working-class youth, and he lent his name to the pioneering Duke of York's Camp – a part paternalist, part egalitarian experiment much in the spirit of the East End universities' and public schools' settlements. Each year a hundred public schools and a hundred industrial concerns were invited to send two boys each to a summer holiday camp 'where all would be on equal terms'.[17] The aim, in the words of the organizer, Robert Hyde, was to 'tame young Bolshevists,'[18] by social mingling: each side of the divide would get to know the other and appreciate its qualities. The Duke made a practice of coming for a day or two and, appropriately clad in shorts and open-necked shirt, joining in the games and sing-songs. 'Class distinction was left outside the camp boundaries,' observed an admiring journalist.[19] At the last of the camps, at Aber-geldie near Balmoral in 1939, the princesses came daily to take part. One of the happiest and most natural of pre-war royal film clips shows the four of them, parents and daughters, sitting in a throng of laughing, chanting adolescents. It was the kind of educational activity – boisterous, slapstick, communitarian, classless – that appealed to the Duke and he was proud to show it off to his daughters.

This was as close as the princesses ever got, before the war, to any proper contact with ordinary children, middle or working class, of their own age. The question of whether a wider experience might be desirable was discussed, but discarded. For several years, there was whimsical newspaper speculation that Elizabeth might be sent to a girls' boarding school. When she was seven, the press reported a rumour that – in a daring break with royal precedent – the Princess was about to be enrolled at a preparatory establishment near London, and, furthermore, that 'one of our larger public schools' would be her eventual destination.[20] There was nothing in the story, though it is conceivable that the Duchess, who had spent two terms in her own adolescence at a day school in Chelsea, may have been behind it. A few weeks after the initial report, the *Sunday Express* announced under the headline 'Will Never Go to School: Too Embarrassing,' that the Duchess of York had asked that her elder daughter should go to school, so that she would be 'brought up like any normal girl'. But after discussion with the King, Queen and Prince of Wales, and consul-tation with Cabinet ministers – according to the paper – she had been forced to back down.[21]

Such an account is supported by the recollection of Lisa Sheridan, who remembered the Duchess telling her, just before the Abdication, that 'she regretted her own daughters would not be able to go to school,' and was concerned that they should grow up naturally and unspoilt.[22] This conversation, which took place during the brief reign of Edward VIII, coincided with fresh reports of a regal veto. The new King, it was stated, had decided against a school for Elizabeth, in accordance with the wishes of his father who had always been opposed. In addition to deference to a dead Monarch, three other arguments were reckoned to have weighed with the Princess's uncle: the jealousy the choice of any particular school would cause among schools not so favoured, 'the question of who would be her schoolmates' – that is, whether she could be protected from bad influences – and, even more spuriously, her need to study different subjects from those taken by most other girls.[23] However, neither George V nor his eldest son deserve exclusive blame for the denial to the Princess of the mixed benefits of 1930s boarding school normality. Indeed, their attitude may have been an excuse. Although it would have been difficult for the Duke and Duchess to defy the Head of State, there is no reason why, after his own accession, George VI and his wife could not have reversed the earlier decision, either for their ten-year-old daughter or their six-year-old one, if they had wished to do so.

But there was one aspect of the Princess's education that was not neglected: in view of the sporting pursuits of her parents, it would have been remarkable if it had been. Surrounded from earliest childhood by horses, and by servants who trained, fed and groomed, and relatives who owned, rode and talked about them, Elizabeth, like many aristocratic little girls, became a keen equestrian. Every account of her infancy suggests that an interest in horses and ponies was almost innate. George V, player of nursery equestrian games, was one influence: it may not be coincidence that Elizabeth's early interest in horses and ponies followed her grandfather's greatest racing success, when his filly Scuttle won the 1,000 Guineas in 1928. Her first reported riding 'lesson' took place in the private riding school in Buckingham Palace Mews in January 1930, when she was three and a half, under the supervision of the Crown Equerry, Colonel A. E. Erskine.[24] It was her parents, however, who became her first serious teachers. When she was five, the Duchess led her on Peggy, the Shetland pony given by the King, to a meet of the Pytchley Hounds at Boughton Cover. For a time the stud groom at the Royal Mews took charge of the children's riding. 'The Princess will undoubtedly be a keen horsewoman when she grows up,' it was accurately predicted when she was ten.[25]

In 1938, the royal riding instructor, Horace Smith, took over and began giving the two girls twice-weekly lessons at the Palace, accompanied by his own daughter. Training included mounting exercises, like touching their toes and leaning backwards until they were lying down on their ponies' backs, to improve their balance and confidence. Smith found Elizabeth, in particular, a good and eager pupil – a conscientious listener, and keen to improve her skills. He also noticed something else: she was as interested in the business of looking after horses as in riding them; and she would ply him with questions about their feeding and management. 'I think that in those days, when she was twelve years old, her chief interest in life lay in horses,' Smith later recalled. On one occasion she told him, a sentiment often later repeated, that 'had she not been who she was, she would like to be a lady living in the country with lots of horses and dogs'.[26]

Dogs mattered almost as much as horses: a point which also did not escape royal observers of the day. As ordinary children more often owned dogs than horses, the princesses' canine interest provided, in some ways, a stronger bond. It quickly became established that not only did Elizabeth and Margaret Rose like dogs, they had a special feeling, and even an empathy, for them. Articles and books about royal caninism became a genre. '. . . [F]ew people realise the marked similarity between the unaffected sincerity that so delightfully characterizes these royal but very human children, and the cheerful contentment of their dogs,' reflected an especially liquid work called *Our Princesses and their Dogs* in 1936. 'I doubt if I have ever encountered dogs who shared with their owners a quieter or serener companionship.'[27] Photographs of the children mercilessly mothering plump corgis – the family's favourite breed – filled the picture papers.

But it was the horse world that always took precedence. With Princess Elizabeth, horses were more than an interest: they became a passion, even an obsession. Rooms and corridors, first at 145 Piccadilly, then at Buckingham Palace, were filled with an expanding collection of toy and ornamental horses, of every material and size. Not just the indulgent old King but the governess as well were cajoled into the performance of equine role-play. A favourite game was to harness Crawfie with reins, as if she were pulling a grocery cart. Then she would be patted, given a nosebag, jerked to a standstill, or instructed to paw the ground. If the weather was cold enough for her nostrils to steam, so much the better. Sometimes, however, Elizabeth would weary of this ritual. She herself would become the horse, and make 'convincing little whinnying noises'. At other times, she and her sister would sit for hours at the window at 145 Piccadilly, watching for horses in the street.[28]

Were animals a substitute for other children? Her governess, in describing such pursuits, clearly implied that they were – indeed the idea of a 'poor little rich girl' who lived a well-ordered, comfortable, but isolated life is central to her account. The two images of simplicity and loneliness are juxtaposed. On the one hand, there is a stress on the gap between the luxury people imagined royalty to enjoy, and their disciplined real lives; on the other, Crawfie often describes the yearning of the girls to be just like other children, with the same kind of fun. In her version of the princesses' childhood, bedtimes were early, treats were few, seaside holidays rare, pantomimes visited only once a year. Other children seldom came to tea. For a time, Elizabeth made 'rather special friends' with the daughter of an eminent radiologist who happened to be a neighbour, but this unusual relationship ended when the child was sent away to school. It was, according to Crawfie, difficult for the children to gain other companions. The Duke of York was a private and unassuming man who, although he did not shun social life, did not seek it either. He and his wife rarely dined out or went to the cinema or theatre, and he was perfectly content to spend the evening at the family hearth, with his wife and daughters, indulging his hobby of needlework, pursued with such diligence that, during one burst of embroidering activity, he made a dozen chair covers in *petit point* for Royal Lodge. The impression is of cosiness, but also of domestic claustrophobia.

Perhaps such a picture of seclusion was exaggerated, and related as much to Miss Crawford's home-sickness for Scotland as to the actual feelings of her charges. Meetings with the offspring of suitable parents, mostly relatives and courtiers, did occur. Elizabeth seemed to mix with them happily and naturally. Yet there seems always to have been a gulf, unavoidably imposed by convention, which stood in the way of equality. Patricia Mountbatten remembers Elizabeth coming to tea as a little girl of five or six with curly blonde hair, at her parents' London home. She recalls a child like any other – except that she attracted special interest among the adults. There was a buzz of excitement among the nannies and governesses. 'She wasn't just another child of friends of my parents. She created a little flutter.'[29] An aristocratic contemporary remembers meeting Elizabeth for the first time at his birthday party when they were both three. He had received a pedal car as a present, and his father insisted that he should let her ride in it. 'She was a princess,' he says. 'You knew she was different.'[30]

As ELIZABETH grew, interest in her increased. Visitors inspected her closely and seldom failed to remark afterwards on her beauty and poise, and on a precocious maturity achieved (so it was said) without loss of childish innocence. At the same time, a constitutionally convenient contrast was drawn between her own character, and that of her younger sister. Crawfie was later blamed for inventing this distinction, but that is unfair. Long before the publication of her book, it had been firmly implanted in the public mind. The roguishness of Elizabeth faded, especially as her destiny became apparent, and weightier qualities took over. Early in the reign of George VI, one writer compared the artistic and musical leanings of Margaret with the 'serious turn of mind' of Elizabeth, who also had an aptitude for languages. In disposition, it was noted, the elder Princess was 'quiet, unassuming and friendly, yet she has inherited a dignity which properly becomes her position.'[31] In a book published in 1939, the journalist Beverley Baxter wrote of Margaret's talents as a mimic, and Elizabeth's tendency to frown on 'her sister's instinct to burlesque, while secretly enjoying it'.[32] Margaret was presented as impish and whimsical, Elizabeth as dutiful and responsible. 'Margaret's capacity for mischief, practical joking and mimicry,' maintained a typical account in 1940, produced an elder-sister sense in Elizabeth.[33]

On one point there was unanimity: individually and together, roguish and responsible, the princesses were a credit to their parents and the nation. 'A perfectly *delicious* pair,' wrote the diplomat Miles Lampson in his diary in 1934 after seeing the two girls at Birkhall, the Georgian house above the river Muick on the Balmoral Estate, lent by the King to the Duke and Duchess of York four years earlier. 'I have seldom seen such an enchanting child as Princess Elizabeth.'[34]

Their ageing royal grandfather felt the same. 'All the children looked so nice,' he wrote after the celebration of his Silver Jubilee in July 1935, 'but none prettier than Lilibet and Margaret.'[35]

The prettiness of the royal little girls – much more than the handsomeness of the Lascelles little boys – represented youth and renewal, and became one of the symbols of the Jubilee. It was a carnival time, but also a display of recovered national confidence, after the worst of the economic crisis. At the heart of the festivities was the King who – in his proud virtue, sound political judgement, unrelenting philistinism and limited intelligence – stood for so much in an Empire that stretched around the globe: country, deity, family and social order. The crowds were hard to contain.

The nine-year-old Princess Elizabeth was photographed in a carriage with the rheumy-eyed Monarch, grandfather to his peoples as well as to the child beside him. Not since the reign of Queen Victoria, and seldom even then, had a sovereign been so revered (and never, a sceptic might have remarked, on the basis of so modest an achievement). Yet the reverence pointed backwards: Elizabeth stood for the future beyond the present reign. Her portrait appeared on Jubilee stamps, and her personality and looks were compared with those of the erect, austere figure of the Queen. Her appearance, and character, were moulded in the press accounts to fit the requirements of the hour. 'Fair-skinned, blue-eyed, with regular features,' was an appropriate assessment, 'happy-natured but serious and quietly dignified.'[36]

Observing the enthusiasm of the massed well-wishers, the King was reported to be deeply moved. An uplifting year, however, had also worn him out. On Christmas Day he delivered his crackling wireless message to subjects all over the world, but with a noticeably weak voice. Over the next few days, he walked painfully in the estate at Sandringham, stopping every hundred yards to catch his breath. In the evenings, he had just enough energy left to play with his granddaughters.[37] Elizabeth had brought cheer to George V during his illness seven years earlier: once again, she appears in the stories told about him. Lord Dawson, the King's physician, later recounted how, as the end approached, the Archbishop of Canterbury, Cosmo Lang, asked the Princess if she would like to walk with him in the garden at Sandringham. 'Yes, very much,' she supposedly replied, 'but please do not tell me anything more about God. I know all about him already.'[38] F. J. Corbett, formerly Deputy Comptroller of Supply at Buckingham Palace, wrote that the last time he saw George V was on the private golf course at Sandringham, a few days after Christmas. 'Out of the mist came the King, mounted on his white pony, Jock,' he recalled. 'Walking by the head of the pony, as if leading it along, was the little figure of Princess Elizabeth. She was taking her grandfather back to the house.'[39]

On 17 January the princesses returned to Royal Lodge. The Duke of York had his own cause for anxiety in an age before antibiotics, for the Duchess was recovering from an attack of pneumonia. They had barely got home, however, when the Duke was summoned to his father's bedside. On 20 January, the King died, surrounded by the Queen and his children. Three days later his body was brought with great solemnity to London, and laid in state in the Palace of Westminster, where hundreds of thousands of mourners filed past. Four officers of the Brigade of Guards stood at the corners of the catafalque. On the last night, these were replaced by the dead King's four sons, including his successor and the Duke of York, each in uniform. Princess Elizabeth was taken by her mother to witness this extraordinary vigil, and to contemplate the coffin of her 'Grandpa England'. On 29 January, she attended the funeral at Windsor.

The accession of Princess Elizabeth's young, popular, forward-looking Uncle David as Edward VIII revived the monarchical excitement of the Jubilee. Such an event brings turmoil at Court, similar to the ferment at No. 10 Downing Street caused by the change of a Prime Minister. The hierarchy is turned upside down. Established officials fear for their jobs, or wonder whether the time has come to retire from them. The transition from the predictable George V to his febrile son was a particularly traumatic break, and it sent a tremor through the ranks of the old courtiers. Ancient customs were abandoned, rules and formalities were impatiently relaxed. The Queen was dispatched to live in Marlborough House, and unexpected faces appeared at the Palace.

The new reign also focused attention, with added intensity, on the Yorks. On the margins of the main performance, they continued to enjoy an adequate privacy. A few weeks into the new reign, Harold

Nicolson, official biographer of George V, spoke to the Duchess of York at the house of a mutual friend. He talked to her for some time, without recognizing her.[40] However, such anonymity could not last long, for the death of the old King, and the persistent bachelorhood of his replacement, brought the Duke of York a step closer to the throne. It also aroused a new kind of interest in his elder daughter. There was still no publicly acknowledgeable reason for expecting Elizabeth ever to become Queen. Yet her place in the line of succession had become much more than a statistic. It began to give rise to speculation, and romantic projection.

What if the King never married? In the run-up to the Coronation, such a possibility was tentatively aired. One commentator suggested that a female Sovereign would be rapturously welcomed, and argued that this in itself was a reason why meddlers into the King's private affairs should not seek to push him into matrimony. 'They do not realise how many of their fellow-subjects would, however respectfully, feel half sorry at such an event, however auspicious. It might deprive us of Elizabeth II.'[41] A similar thought may have occurred to Archbishop Lang, who had discussed (or refrained from discussing) theology with the Princess at Sandringham in January, and who stayed as a guest of the Yorks at Birkhall in the summer. At a time when the new King was becoming a serious worry, he was reassured by what he saw. 'The children – Lilliebet, Margaret Rose and Margaret Elphinstone – joined us,' he recorded. 'They sang some action-songs most charmingly. It was strange to think of the destiny which may be awaiting the little Elizabeth, at present second from the Throne. She and her lively little sister are certainly most entrancing children.'[42]

Yet, at first, life for 'the little ladies of 145 Piccadilly' did not alter. It may have been a symptom of her upward mobility that a marble portrait bust of Princess Elizabeth was commissioned in the spring of 1936. Over the next two years, Miss Crawford accompanied the child no fewer than eighteen times to the studio of the Hungarian sculptor Zsigmond Strobl in Pembroke Walk. Lajos Lederer, a Hungarian journalist employed to make conversation with her during these tedious sessions, recalled her as highly talkative, and extremely knowledgeable on the subject of thoroughbred horses.[43] Otherwise, the only direct effect on the princesses of the accession seemed to be that they saw less of their uncle, previously one of the Yorks' few frequent callers. The Duke and Duchess, though aware of gathering clouds, continued to ride, garden and embroider, much as before. Lisa Sheridan, visiting their London house before they left for Scotland, was led by a footman into the garden, where she found Princess Elizabeth and her mother feeding a family of ducklings which had wandered in through the railings from the adjoining park.[44]

There was no immediate mention of Wallis Simpson. When, eventually, the King's American companion was invited to tea at Royal Lodge, nothing was said about the significance of the visit. But Uncle David seemed to have lost interest in his nieces.[45] For some time, there had been 'King-tattle' – gossip which, as one loyalist claimed indignantly, 'rages without respect to decency and perhaps probability,' but which did not get into print.[46] The reason was not so much the laws of libel, as the fear of breaking a taboo. Editors and proprietors calculated that the opportunity was not worth the short-term boost in sales. 'No respectable paper would have thought it good circulation policy to print scandalous news about the Royal Family,' observed the anti-monarchist editor of the *New Statesman*, Kingsley Martin, afterwards. 'It would no doubt have sold for the moment, but it would have led to a storm of protest from readers.'[47] There was also a gap between the business side of running newspapers – whose circulation policy made use of incentives like free gifts and insurance policies to attract readers – and the editorial side, which held aloof. 'Editors were a traditional lot,' says Sir Edward Pickering, then on the *Mirror*, and later a leading editor and newspaper director. 'They didn't look on circulation in the way they do today. They felt themselves above all that.'[48] On this occasion they were also afraid of a backlash, in view of the popularity of a Monarch who, as Malcolm Muggeridge put it, 'was idolized as few men outside the Orient ever have been'.[49]

Yet the gossip was pervasive, the more virulent because of the gap between what those in the King's circle knew and the messages of the headlines and newsreels. 'Those who most strenuously maintained a decorous loyalty in public,' recalled Martin, 'were the most avaricious of scandal about the Monarchy in private.'[50] Princess Elizabeth may have been ignorant of what was going on, and the Duke and Duchess never spoke of it, but according to Crawfie, 'it was plain to everyone there was a sudden shadow over the house'.[51]

The whole Royal Family, together with the whole political and Church Establishment, and many ordinary people, were shocked and appalled by the prospect of an abdication, which seemed to strike at the heart of the constitution. But nowhere was it viewed with greater abhorrence than at 145 Piccadilly. According to his official biographer, the Duke of York viewed the possibility, and then the likelihood, of his own succession with 'unrelieved gloom'.[52] The accounts of witnesses suggest that this is a gross understatement: desperation and near-panic would be more accurate. To succeed to a throne you neither expected nor wanted, because of the chance of birth and the irresponsibility of a brother! Apart from the accidents of poverty and ill health, it is hard to think of a more terrible and unjust fate.

Alan ('Tommy') Lascelles, assistant private secretary to Edward VIII and later private secretary to George VI, wrote privately that he feared Bertie would be so upset by the news, he might break down.[53] There were lurid stories: that the Duke of York had refused to succeed, and that Queen Mary had agreed to act as Regent for Princess Elizabeth.[54] Rumours circulated in the American press that the Duke was epileptic (and that Princess Margaret was deaf and dumb).[55] There was also a whispering campaign, in which Wallis Simpson played a part, that he had 'a slow brain' which did not take on ideas quickly and that he was mentally unfit for the job.[56]

On 27th October, when Mrs Simpson obtained a decree nisi, the shadow darkened. The Duke braced himself for the catastrophe, as he saw it, that was about to befall his family and himself. 'If the worst happens & I have to take over,' he wrote, with courage, to a courtier on 25 November, 'you can be assured that I will do my best to clear up the inevitable mess, if the whole fabric does not crumble under the shock and strain of it all.'[57] Meanwhile, Crawfie and the children took refuge from the atmosphere of tension by attending swimming lessons at the Bath Club, with the Duke and Duchess sometimes turning up to watch.[58]

A week later, the press's self-imposed embargo on 'King-tattle' broke, and the headlines blazoned the name of Mrs Simpson. The Royal Archives contain a chronicle, written by Bertie, which shows the extent of his misery, bordering on hysteria, as he awaited what felt like an execution. In it, he describes a meeting with his mother on December 9th, when the Abdication had become inevitable, and how 'when I told her what had happened I broke down and sobbed like a child'. There are few more poignant testimonies in the annals of the modern Monarchy than George VI's account of the occasion he most feared, but could do nothing to prevent:

'I . . . was present at the fateful moment which made me D's successor to the Throne. Perfectly calm D signed 5 or 6 copies of the instrument of Abdication & then 5 copies of his message to Parliament, one for each Dominion Parliament. It was a dreadful moment & one never to be forgotten by those present . . . I went to R.L. [Royal Lodge] for a rest . . . But I could not rest alone & returned to the Fort at 5.45. Wigram was present at a terrible lawyer interview . . . I later went to London where I found a large crowd outside my house cheering madly. I was overwhelmed.'[59]

A kind of fatalism took over the Duke, now the King, as the Court which had surrounded – and sought to protect and restrain – his brother, enveloped him, guiding him through the ceremonies of the next few days. There was nothing he could do, except what he was told, and nothing for his family to do except offer sympathy. According to Crawfie's account, the princesses hugged their father before he left 145 Piccadilly, 'pale and haggard,' for the Privy Council in the uniform of an Admiral of the Fleet.[60] To Parliament and the Empire, and the man now called Duke of Windsor, the Abdication Crisis was over. But for King George VI and, though she did not yet appreciate it, his elder daughter, Heiress Presumptive to the Throne, it had just begun.

3

SIXTY YEARS LATER, it is still hard to assess the impact of the Abdication of Edward VIII. Arguably it had very little. In the short run, politics was barely affected; there was no last minute appeal by the resigning Monarch for public support, as some had feared there might be; no 'King's party' was put together to back him. Indeed, the smooth management of the transition was a cause for congratulation, and was taken to show the resilience of the Monarchy, and the adaptability of the constitution. Even social critics regarded it as evidence of English establishment solidarity. 'To engineer the abdication of one King and the enthronement of another in six days,' wrote Beatrice Webb, 'without a ripple of mutual abuse within the Royal Family or between it and the Government, or between the Government and the Opposition, or between the governing classes and the workers, was a splendid achievement, accepted by the Dominions and watched by the entire world of foreign states with amazed admiration.'[1] Nevertheless, it has always been treated as a turning point, and in an important sense it was one. It broke a spell.

In the past, public treatment of the private behaviour of members of the Royal Family had contained a double standard. Since the days of Victoria and Albert, the personal life of royalty had been regarded as, by definition, irreproachable; while at the same time occasionally giving cause for disapproval or hilarity – as in the case of Edward VII when Prince of Wales, and his elder son, the Duke of Clarence. Not since the early nineteenth century, however, had it been a serious constitutional issue. The Abdication made it one – giving to divorce, and to sexual misconduct and marital breakdown, a resonance in the context of royalty, which by the 1930s it was beginning to lose among the upper classes at large. At the same time the dismissal of a King provided a sharp reminder that British monarchs reigned on sufferance, and that the pomp and sycophancy counted for nothing if the rules were disobeyed. During the crisis, there was talk of the greater suitability for the throne of the Duke of Kent – as if the Monarchy was by appointment. It came to nothing, but the mooting of such a notion indicated what the great reigns of the past hundred years had tended to obscure – that Parliament had absolute rights, and that the domestic affections of the Royal Family were as much a part of the tacit contract between Crown and people as everything else.

In theory, the British Monarchy was already, and had long been, little more than a constitutional convenience. How could it be otherwise, with a Royal Family whose position had so frequently depended on parliamentary buttressing, or on a parliamentary decision to pass over a natural claimant in favour of a more appropriate minor branch? 'If there was a mystic right in any one,' as Walter Bagehot put it dryly in 1867, 'that right was plainly in James II.'[2] Yet, in practice, there had been accretions of sentiment and loyalty which had allowed the obscure origins of the reigning dynasty to be forgotten. As a result, a traditional right or legitimacy had replaced a 'divine' one, and a great sanctity had attached to laws of succession unbroken for more than two centuries. The Abdication cut through all this like a knife – taking the Monarchy back as far as 1688, when Parliament had deprived a King of his throne on the grounds of his unfitness for it.

On that occasion, the official explanation was that James II had run away – though in reality there were other reasons for wishing to dispose of a monarch who caused political and sectarian division. In 1936, the ostensible cause of the King's departure was his refusal to accept the advice of his ministers that he could not marry a divorced woman. Yet the Government's position was also regarded as a moral, and not just a technical or legalistic one. The King's relationship with Mrs Simpson was seen as symptomatic. The nation, as one commentator put it, took a dim view of tales of frivolity, luxury and 'an un-English set of *nonceurs*', associated with the new King and minded seeing its throne 'provide a music-hall turn for low foreign newspapers'.[3] Although the decision to force Edward VIII to choose between marriage and his crown was reluctant, it was accompanied by a hope and belief that his successor – well-married, and with a family life that commanded wide approval – would set a better example.

But the Monarchy would never be the same again. 'All the King's horses and all the King's men,' Jimmy Maxton, leader of the left-wing Independent Labour Party, reminded the House of Commons, 'could not put Humpty-Dumpty back again.'[4] Not only was the experience regarded, by all concerned, as chastening: there was also a feeling that, though the Monarchy would survive, it had been irrevocably scrambled. Even if George VI had possessed a more forceful character, the circumstances of his accession would have taken from the institution much of its former authority. As it was, the Monarchy could never again be (in the words of a contemporary writer) 'so socially aggressive, so pushy' as under George V;[5] nor could it be so brash as under Edward VIII, whose arrival 'hatless from the air,' in John Betjeman's words, had signalled a desire to innovate. After the Abdication, George VI felt a need to provide reassurance, and to behave with a maximum of caution, as if the vulgar lifting of skirts in the autumn of 1936 had never happened. Yet there could be no simple return to the old position of the Monarch as morally powerful arbitrator, a role played by George V as recently as 1931. Under George VI, royal interventions, even minor ones, diminished. The acceptance of a cypher-monarchy, almost devoid of political independence, began in 1936.

If the Abdication was seen as a success, this was partly because of an accurate assessment that the genetic dice had serendipitously provided a man who would perform the functions of his office in the dutifully subdued way required of him. Indeed, not only the disposition of the Duke of York but the familial virtues of both himself and his wife had been a key element in the equation. The point had been made by Edward VIII in his farewell broadcast, to soften the blow of his departure, when he declared that his brother 'has one matchless blessing, enjoyed by so many of you and not bestowed on me – a happy home with his wife and children.'[6] It was also stressed by Queen Mary, when she commended her daughter-in-law as well as her second son to the nation. 'I know,' she said with feeling and with meaning, 'that you have already taken her children to your hearts.'[7] Everybody appreciated that if the next in line had happened to be a footloose bachelor or wastrel, the outcome might have been very different. As it was, the Duke of York – despite, but perhaps also because of, his personal uncertainties – turned out to be well suited to the difficult task of doing very little conscientiously: a man, in the words of a contemporary eulogizer, 'ordinary enough, amazing enough, to find it natural and sufficient all his life to know only the sort of people a Symbol King ought to know,' and, moreover, one who 'needs no private life different from what it ought to be.'[8]

To restore a faith in the Royal Family's dedication to duty: that was George VI's single most important task. There was a sense of treading on eggshells, and banishing the past. As the Coronation approached, the regrettable reason for the King's accession was glossed over in the souvenir books, and delicately avoided in speeches. The monarchist historian Sir Charles Petrie observed a few years later that there was a tendency to forget all about it, 'and particularly has this been the case in what may be described as official circles'.[9] It was partly because the memory of the episode was acutely painful to the King and Queen, as well as to Queen Mary, but it was also because of the embarrassment Edward VIII's abdication caused to the dynasty, and the difficulty of incorporating an act of selfishness into the seamless royal image. Burying the trauma, however, did not dispose of it, and the physical survival of the Duke and Duchess of Windsor – unprotected by a Court, and often teetering on the brink of indiscretion or indecorum – provided a disquieting shadow, reminding the world of an alternative dynastic story.

By contrast, the existence of 'the little ladies of 145 Piccadilly' gave the new Royal Family a trump card. If, in the eyes of the public, the Duchess of Windsor was cast as a seductress, the little ladies offered cotton-clad purity, innocence and, in the case of Princess Elizabeth, hope. It greatly helped that her virtues, described by the press since babyhood, were already well-known. What if she had inherited her uncle's characteristics instead of her father's? Fortunately the stock of attributes provided by the sketch-writers did not admit of such a possibility. The ten-and-a-half-year-old Heiress Presumptive, it was confidently observed, possessed 'great charm and a natural unassuming dignity'. The world not only already knew, but already loved her, and hoped that one day she would 'rule the world's greatest Empire' as Queen.[10]

The discovery that she had become a likely future Monarch, instead of somebody close to the throne with an outside chance of becoming one, seems to have been absorbed by Princess Elizabeth gradually. Although her father's accession, and the elimination of doubt about the equal rights of royal daughters, placed her first in line, it was not yet certain that she would ever succeed. When Princess Alexandrina Victoria of Kent was told of her expectations at almost precisely the same age in March 1830, she was reported by her governess to have replied 'I will be good'. According to Lady Strathmore, when Princess Elizabeth received the news, she 'was ardently praying for a brother'.[11] It was still imaginable: the Queen was only thirty-six at the time of the Coronation in May 1937, and shortly before it a rumour spread that she was pregnant.[12] Increasingly, however, a view of the future with Princess Elizabeth as Monarch was widely accepted. There was even some speculation that Elizabeth might be given the title of Princess of Wales.[13] According to her sister, the change of status was something they knew about, but did not discuss. 'When our father became King,' recalls Princess Margaret, 'I said to her, "Does that mean you're going to be Queen?" She replied, "Yes, I suppose it does." She didn't mention it again.'[14]

There was also the matter of where they lived. According to Crawfie, Princess Elizabeth reacted with horror when she was told that they were moving to Buckingham Palace. 'What – you mean for ever?' According to Princess Margaret, the element of physical disruption was limited. 145 Piccadilly was only a stone's throw from Buckingham Palace, and they had often gone over to see their grandparents, and to play in the garden.[15] Perhaps the distrust was more in the mind of the governess, who likened setting up home in the Palace to 'camping in a museum'.[16] The living quarters were, in any case, soon domesticated after the long era of elderly kings and queens. Elizabeth's menagerie of toy horses acquired a new setting; and a room overlooking the Palace lawns, which had briefly been her nursery in 1927, was established as a schoolroom.

More important than the change of location was the ending of a way of life. In the months before the Coronation, public attention became unrelenting. Outside the railings at Buckingham Palace, a permanent crowd formed. Inside them, it was impossible to keep up the illusion of being an ordinary family. At 145 Piccadilly, there had been few visitors, most of whom were personal friends. At the Palace, the King had to see visitors or take part in functions for much of the day, and the Queen was busy every afternoon. Before, the little girls had been able to take walks in the park and play with the children of neighbours. At the Palace, royal headquarters of an Empire, there were no neighbours and different standards applied. A famous anecdote illustrated the change. Princess Elizabeth discovered that merely by walking in front of a sentry on ceremonial duty, she could make him present arms; and having made the discovery, she could not resist walking backwards and forwards to see it repeated.[17]

There was a sense of constraint, as well as of power. According to Lajos Lederer, the accession brought an immediate change to Princess Elizabeth's previously relaxed sittings for Strobl. A detective now accompanied her everywhere, a policeman was always outside, and she 'no longer referred to Mummy and Papa, but spoke of the King and Queen'.[18] The Queen seems to have been responsible for taking customary formalities seriously, and seeing that her children did so too. According to Dermot Morrah (a trusted royal chronicler), she insisted 'that even in the nursery some touches of majesty were not out of place, an argument that had the full approval of Queen Mary'.[19] One 'touch of majesty' involved the serving of nursery meals by two scarlet-liveried footmen. In addition, though nursery food was mainly 'plain English cooking,' the menu, for some reason, was in French.[20]

The biggest strain for the Royal Family, however, was the almost intolerable pressure placed upon the new King as he came to terms with his unsought and unwelcome role. 'It totally altered their lives,' according to Lady Mountbatten. 'To begin with, the King would come home very worried and upset.'[21] George VI's speech impediment, always a handicap, became a nightmare, and every public appearance a cause of suffering. Although British journalists tactfully avoided mentioning it, foreign ones were less reticent. To the American press, suspicious that the real reason for the Abdication was Mrs Simpson's American nationality, he remained 'the stuttering Duke of York'.[22] The Queen had always taken pleasure from public occasions, and continued to display a much-admired serenity: but the King at first seemed so gauche and unhappy that doubts were raised about whether he could get through his Coronation.[23]

HE MANAGED it none the less. In the early spring of 1937, British newspapers which had loyally kept silent about Mrs Simpson, now loyally built up George VI as a 'George V second edition'.[24] Yet there was a sense of him not just as the substitute but also as a reluctant Monarch. Kingsley Martin summed up the mood thus, apostrophizing the thoughts of a supposedly typical member of the public: 'We would still prefer to cheer Edward, but we know that we've got to cheer George. After all, it's Edward's fault that he's not on the throne, and George didn't ask to get there. He's only doing his duty, and it's up to us to show that we appreciate it.'[25] Martin noted a feeling of relief and sympathy, as much as of rejoicing, and of healing a personal wound.

The Coronation itself had a wider function than the consecration of a new King. It was also Britain putting its best face to the world – the more urgently so because of the international crisis which overshadowed the royal one. Many commentators, viewing the celebration with its hotch-potch of religion, nostalgia, mumbo-jumbo and military display, saw it simultaneously as a reminder to potential aggressors of British imperial might and a reaffirmation of British freedom. For such purposes, the Empire was unblinkingly described as if it were a democratic, almost a voluntary, association.[26]

Comparisons were proudly drawn between the symbols of liberty parading through the streets of London, and the choreographed vulgarities of European fascism. One fervent royalist saw George VI's Coronation as 'a pageant more splendid than any dictators can put on: beating Rome and Nuremberg hollow at their own bewildering best, and with no obverse side of compulsion or horror'.[27] The anthropologist Bronislaw Malinowski reckoned it a sound investment, as 'a ceremonial display of the greatness, power and wealth of Britain,' generating 'an increased feeling of security, of stability, and the permanence of the British Empire'.[28] Even the Left was impressed. Kingsley Martin agreed with the view that the British Establishment had upstaged Goebbels – and suggested that the propaganda purpose of the procession and festivities was to show that the Empire was still as strong and united as in 1914, and that Britain suffered from less class conflict than any other nation.[29]

Much depended on the central actor, who made little secret of his deep anxiety about the whole proceeding. Afterwards the King told the former Prime Minister, Ramsay MacDonald, that he had been so dazed by fear for much of the ceremony that he was unaware of what was happening.[30] However, the Westminster Abbey service went without a hitch, and the Monarch performed his part in it with appropriate gravitas. 'He carried himself well,' judged Chips Channon, who witnessed the ceremony as one of several thousand MPs, peers and other dignitaries in the congregation.[31]

A more privileged position among the spectators was given to the two princesses, who sat in the royal box with Queen Mary. For Elizabeth, particularly, the day was an important part of her education. Her governess prepared her for it by reading her Queen Victoria's account of her own Coronation, written exactly a century before, which began, 'I was awoke by the guns in the Park and could not get much sleep afterwards on account of the people, bands etc.' According to Crawfie, the elder princess took such a deep interest that she became 'one of the greatest living experts on Coronations'.[32] The girls rode to the Abbey in a glass coach. Chips Channon looked on as they 'whipped their robes on to their left arms as they had been shown, pushing up their frocks with the same movement and showing bare legs above socks'.[33] During the three-hour ceremony, Elizabeth watched intently as the Archbishop of Canterbury performed the complex rites, and her father, with the utmost difficulty, repeated the words 'All this – I promise to do'.[34]

For any child to view the Coronation at close quarters was a memorable experience: only a handful had the opportunity. For the Heiress Presumptive to see her own parents crowned, and to take part in the procession, must have been awesome. What did she think and feel? The Royal Library contains her own answer – an essay, both vivid and prosaic, written in pencil on lined paper just after the event, and carefully tied with pink ribbon. On the cover is inscribed, in neat red crayon, the words:

The Coronation
12th May; 1937
To Mummy and Papa
In Memory of Their Coronation
From Lilibet
By Herself
An Account of the Coronation

It describes how she was woken at five in the morning by the band of the Royal Marines outside her window (much as her great-great grandmother had been woken by the guns in the Park), and how, draped in an eiderdown and accompanied by her nurse-maid Bobo MacDonald, 'we crouched in the window looking onto a cold, misty morning'. After breakfast ('we did not eat very much as we were too excited') they got dressed and

> showed ourselves to the visitors and housemaids. Now I shall try and give you a description of our dresses. They were white silk with old cream lace and had little gold bows all the way down the middle. They had puffed sleeves with one little bow in the centre. Then there were the robes of purple velvet with gold on the edge.
>
> We went along to Mummy's bedroom and we found her putting on her dress. Papa was dressed in a white shirt, breeches and stockings, and over this he wore a crimson satin coat. Then a page came and said it was time to go down, so we kissed Mummy, and wished her good luck and went down. There we said Goodmorning to Aunt Alice, Aunt Marina and Aunt Mary with whom we were to drive to the Abbey. We were then told to get into the carriage . . . At first it was very jolty but we soon got used to it.

Princess Elizabeth describes the procession down the Mall, along Whitehall, to Westminster Abbey, and the walk up the aisle with her family, before she went up into the royal box with Queen Mary:

> Then the service began.
> I thought it all <u>very</u>, <u>very</u> wonderful and I expect the Abbey did, too. The arches and beams at the top were covered with a sort of haze of wonder as Papa was crowned, at least I thought so.

When Mummy was crowned and all the peeresses put on their coronets it looked wonderful to see arms and coronets hovering in the air and then the arms disappear as if by magic. Also the music was lovely and the band, the orchestra and the new organ all played beautifully.

What struck me as being rather odd was that Grannie did not remember much of her own Coronation. I should have thought that it would have stayed in her mind for ever.

At the end the service got rather boring as it was all prayers. Grannie and I were looking to see how many more pages to the end, and we turned one more and then I pointed to the word at the bottom of the page and it said "Finis". We both smiled at each other and turned back to the service.

. . . When we got back to our dressing-room we had some sandwiches, stuffed rolls, orangeade and lemonade. Then we left for our long drive.

On leaving the Abbey we went along the Embankment, North-umberland Avenue, through Trafalgar Square, St. James's St. Piccadilly, Regent St. Oxford St. with Selfridge's lovely figures, through Marble Arch, through Hyde Park, Hyde Park Corner, Constitution Hill, round the Memorial and into the courtyard.

Then we went up to the corridor to see the Coach coming in. Then Mummy and Papa came up and said "Goodmorning" and were congratulated. Then we all went on to the Balcony where <u>millions</u> of people were waiting below. After that we all went to be photographed in front of those awful lights.

When we sat down to tea it was nearly six o'clock! When I got into bed my legs ached terribly. As my head touched the pillow I was asleep and I did not wake up till nearly eight o'clock the next morning.[35]

PRINCESS ELIZABETH was eleven at the time of the Coronation, and it was an initiation for her, as well as for her parents. The day was not far off, as one writer put it in the royalty idiom of the time, when she would move out of childhood 'into a swifter current of life.'[36] Pretty and pubescent, she attracted nearly as much attention as the King and Queen during the two months of state drives, official tours and youth displays that followed. Although she continued to be dressed as a little girl, there was an increase in the number of grand

occasions in which she was involved. There was also a sudden seriousness about equipping her for future duties.

One new initiative was the establishment of a Girl Guide company
at the Palace, to which a Brownie pack was attached, with the specific
purpose of providing the two princesses with a training ground. Based
on a romantic myth of imperial kinship, the Scouts and Guides were
at their zenith, and several members of the Royal Family had honorific
titles within the movement. The Buckingham Palace Company met on
Wednesday afternoons and gathered together about twenty children of
friends and vetted acquaintances – some, like the royal princesses,
taught at home by governesses, others attending London day schools.
The Guides were grouped in three patrols. Princess Elizabeth was
second-in-command to Patricia Mountbatten, who was a few years
older, in the Kingfisher patrol. In winter they met in one of the vast
rooms in Buckingham Palace, in the summer in the gardens. There
were also trips to Windsor, involving the normal activities of Girl
Guides everywhere, though in an abnormal setting: tracking, bird
watching, trekking with a hand-cart, cooking sausages and 'dampers'
(flour balls on sticks) over a campfire. At the Palace, the long corridors
were used for signalling practice.

Princess Elizabeth received no special treatment, and mixed in well
with the other girls. According to Lady Mountbatten, she was 'a very
efficient and capable deputy,' already with an air of authority, and
popular in the Company, 'nice, easy to deal with, you'd want her
as your best friend'.[37] Another member of the Company, Elizabeth
Cavendish, confirms the impression of the Heiress Presumptive as a
highly competent Girl Guide, who took the various activities and
rituals seriously, and did well at them.[38] When a Scottish dancer came
to give them special instruction, Princess Elizabeth showed a particular
proficiency at dancing Highland reels.

The picture is of a conventional, unquestioning child, making the
most of what was presented to her. Yet if Princess Elizabeth was not
singled out, there was something different about her. 'She was very
aware that how she behaved in public was very important,' says Lady
Mountbatten. 'For instance, she couldn't burst into tears. If she hurt
her knee she knew she must try not to cry.'[39] The Company Captain
was a Miss Synge, held in awe by the girls, with Miss Crawford

ANOTHER CORONATION

THE FLOWERS AND THE PRINCESSES

Punch, 28th April 1937

assisting. Some of the Guides, Patricia Mountbatten and Camilla Wallop (later Lady Rupert Nevill), for instance, became lifelong friends.

It was not just cut knees. Incidents in the Kingfisher patrol were not, in general, leaked or reported. However, other events in Princess Elizabeth's life now were – as the press, less intrusive than later but no less curious, sought to cater for a huge public appetite for details about the royal children's lives. The princesses might not be able to cry over a minor mishap, but grazes and slight colds often got into the papers just the same. Even before their teens, public appearances had become performances. If the royal children were taken to the theatre, the newspapers automatically treated them as the main attraction – reporting every movement or gesture next day. Sometimes the theatre management, delighted by the privilege of entertaining royalty, would shower honours on them, and the spotlight would be turned in their direction. When the Heiress Presumptive attended the 1937 Christmas production of 'Where the Rainbow Ends' at the Holborn Empire, along with fifteen hundred other children, everybody was asked to stand and sing a specially composed children's verse of the National Anthem.[40] 'Normal' expeditions and natural behaviour were difficult.

The birthday of Princess Elizabeth, meanwhile, became a national event. Birthday presents were listed even in the serious newspapers, together with details of the guests and of how the anniversary was being celebrated. Stimulated by these public announcements, well-wishers would gather wherever the Princess happened to be, to cheer her and convey greetings, and she would be required to appear, and politely acknowledge them.[41] She also became the recipient of a flow of unsolicited mail, often from children in disaster areas, like Chinese orphans fleeing from the Japanese.

Some aspects of the princesses' lives did not greatly alter. The family continued to come together for weekends at Royal Lodge, where their existence remained much as it had been before. The press made much of the 'simplicity' of life at the Lodge, although actually the Royal Family enjoyed every luxury, opportunity for recreation, and service that anybody could wish for. Still, it was possible to enjoy a degree of informality. Here they could enjoy, if not simple living, then the kind of rustic domesticity which had been the greatest pleasure of the

Duke and Duchess of York before the upheaval, in the company of horses and dogs unconscious of rank, with grooms, stable boys and kennel hands to look after, handle and talk about them. Princess Elizabeth's ponies had names like Peggy and Comet; the dogs included corgis, labradors and a Tibetan lion dog, and had names like Dookie, Spark, Flash, Scruffy, Mimsey and Stiffy. The public took a keen interest in these animals. 'Dookie is unquestionably the "character" of the princesses' delightful canine family,' declared one authority in 1942.[42] On Sundays, the girls and their parents attended services at St George's Chapel or the Chapel Royal in the grounds of Royal Lodge; on Saturdays, and other days during holidays, the princesses went riding in the morning. Sometimes they walked in Windsor Forest, cycled in the royal gardens at Frogmore or swam in an outdoor pool at the Lodge. All that was lacking was the company of other children of whom they saw as little, or less, than at Buckingham Palace.[43]

Juvenile guests were rare. However, the King and Queen had to entertain official, and especially foreign, visitors who were invited to stay with increasing frequency as fears about the international crisis grew. According to Crawfie, Princess Elizabeth began to take an interest in politics at about this time, 'and knew quite a bit of what was going on in the world outside'.[44] She certainly had a unique vantage point compared with most other children of her age. In one month in 1938, four kings, a regent and a crown prince called on her parents, mainly on trips to London to rally support in defence of their countries. Visitors to Windsor early in the reign included the newly appointed American Ambassador, Joe Kennedy, and his wife Rose, who stayed for a weekend in April 1938. Rose Kennedy was moved by her brief contact with British royalty, especially its younger members. She recorded in her diary that she 'found it a great conversational convenience' that her own large brood included two children, Teddy and Jean, who were about the same ages as the princesses. During her stay, she watched out for the royal daughters, much as one might look out for rare and exotic birds when visiting their habitat, and she was not disappointed. While walking in the park surrounding the Castle, she and Joe 'ran into Princess Elizabeth hiding behind the shrubs. She had on a pink coat and was hatless and she smiled at us'. The Kennedys saw her again over luncheon, when

Elizabeth and Margaret appeared together, clad identically in rose dresses with checked blouses, red shoes with silver-coloured buckles, white socks and necklaces of coral and pearl. Elizabeth, not quite twelve, was placed next to the wicked old envoy, to his saturnine delight. After the meal, the princesses were required to accompany their parents and the ambassadorial couple as they walked 'very informally' over to Frogmore.[45]

Learning how to handle distinguished guests was one important part of an Heiress's education, and was soon extended. Shortly after the Kennedy visit, Princess Elizabeth was promoted from white socks to silk stockings, receiving a box from her mother as a birthday present.[46] She started to attend the huge, thousands-strong, garden parties held annually at Buckingham Palace. She also began occasionally to take a leading role at small-scale semi-public events, presenting rosettes at children's pony shows, and cups and shields to children at the Bath Club. When she was thirteen, she was allowed to accept the presidency of the Children's League of the Princess Elizabeth of York Hospital, which had been named after her.

There remained the question, both practical and philosophical, of what an Heiress Presumptive and future Queen should be educated to be like – a conundrum that had not faced the Court or Government since the 1830s, when Princess Victoria's education had been entrusted to the remarkable Baroness Lehzen. Marion Crawford had been employed to help the princesses become lady-like, not monarchical. After George VI's accession, there was a hesitant appreciation that being lady-like was not enough, but there remained a tension between the training felt suitable for a Head of State, and the needs of an idealized princess. The result was an incongruous mix. If the notion, as an authorized account claimed, that the Princess was subjected to 'a strenuous tutelage increasing in measure with the passing years',[47] was simply a pious invention, there was at least some expansion of the curriculum. Princess Elizabeth began to take twice weekly lessons in constitutional history at Eton College, close to Windsor Castle and Royal Lodge, given by the Vice-Provost, Henry (later Sir Henry) Marten. Later this tuition was supplemented by that of the Vicomtesse de Bellaigue, who taught both princesses French, French literature and European history.[48] Yet there was also a deep concern to avoid the taint of an 'intellectual' as opposed to 'practical' princess. It was therefore announced that she was taking cooking lessons in the Royal Lodge kitchens, that she sometimes baked cakes in her little Welsh cottage which were sent to children in hospitals or to unemployed areas, that she had learnt to sweep and scrub and to polish furniture, and that Queen Mary, 'a keen housewife,' had admired her efforts.[49]

Marten did his best. The theme of his tutelage combined the traditional and the modern, reminding the Princess of where she came from, but also of the changes wrought by modern conditions. Later, he recalled teaching her that the British Monarchy was exceeded in antiquity only by the papacy, that it went back more than a millennium to King Egbert, 'the first to unite all England,' and that the secret of its survival was its ability to adapt. He also taught her what he considered the two great events affecting the Monarchy in their own time, the 1931 Statute of Westminster and the advent of broadcasting. The Statute, he explained, had founded the modern British Commonwealth by making a common allegiance to the Crown the sole surviving link between Great Britain and the Dominions; while broadcasting enabled the Royal Family, by talking personally on the air, to sustain that link.[50] How much his pupil retained is hard to say, though he may have fired her interest in the past a little. When Princess Marie Louise apologized over dinner at Windsor during the Second World War for indulging in an old lady's reminiscences, the teenage Princess replied: 'But Cousin Louise, it's *history*, and therefore so thrilling.'[51] But perhaps she was just being polite.

Yet if the Princess began to build up an academic knowledge from her tutor, as well as an extraordinary acquaintanceship with some of the major players on the world stage, if she was known to millions of young people all over the world and occasionally seen by a few thousand of them – she nevertheless remained separate from all but a handful of carefully selected contemporaries, with few of whom she could ever be close. There is always a sense of the goldfish bowl, and the lack of any direct contact through the glass.

In some ways, she was very mature for her age. Physically, she developed early, with 'big bosoms just like her mother', as a member of a courtier family, who played kick-the-tin with her at Balmoral in the late 1930s, fondly recalls.[52] In other ways, silk stockings notwithstanding, she was held back in childhood. Marten remembered teaching 'a somewhat shy girl of thirteen who when asked a question would look for confidence and support to her beloved governess, Miss Crawford.'[53] Crawfie herself suggests a lonely, yet self-sufficient, child, and one with her own private world of perplexity. She recalled seeing her stand for hours at the window at Buckingham Palace, looking down the Mall towards Admiralty Arch, and that she would ask her questions 'about the world outside'.[54] The picture of a young princess who lacked nothing except social intercourse with people who did not think of her, first and always, as a princess, is confirmed by Elizabeth's own recollections. When she was having her portrait painted in the Yellow Drawing-Room by Pietro Annigoni shortly after her own Accession, she told the artist that she had spent hours as a child in the same huge, magnificent room, looking out of the windows. 'I loved watching the people and the cars there in the Mall,' she said. 'They all seemed so busy. I used to wonder what they were doing and where they were all going, and what they thought about outside the Palace.'[55]

WAR, AND THE threat of war, ups the value of Monarchy. As the danger from Hitler grew, and the rearmament programme gathered pace, the King and Queen became increasingly busy as hosts, ambassadors and patriotic symbols. Two days before the signing of the Munich agreement in the autumn of 1938, the twelve-year-old Princess Elizabeth travelled with her mother to Clydebank for the launch of the giant Cunard liner *Queen Elizabeth*, destined to be used both for civilian passengers and as a troop ship. Usually, however, the royal couple did their visiting and travelling unaccompanied by their children who, it was felt, were better off at home. In the case of the foreign trips which the King and Queen were now required to make, there was no sense that, quite apart from the advantages of keeping the family together, seeing other countries would be educational.

The most important royal visit of the decade took place in 1939. Following a brief and apparently successful trip to France in July 1938 to strengthen the Entente Cordiale, it was decided to send the royal couple to North America, to strengthen the special relationship. Before the journey, President Roosevelt invited 'either or both' the princesses, genially observing in his letter that 'I shall try to have one or two

Roosevelts of approximately the same age to play with them!' It was an exciting offer, but the King declined it, on the grounds that they were too young for the rigours of the Canadian part of the tour.[56]

By the time of embarkation in May 1939, Franco had taken Madrid, Hitler had marched into Prague, and a full-scale European conflict seemed imminent. Interest in the tour on both sides of the Atlantic was intense. Perhaps the wild excitement that greeted the King and Queen from the moment they landed in Canada on 17 May would have been even greater if their daughters had been with them. As it was, the visitors had to content themselves with the first-ever royal transatlantic telephone call, taken by the princesses at the Bowes-Lyon house at St. Paul's Walden Bury.[57] The King and Queen spoke through hand microphones; the children finished their end of the conversation by holding the Queen's corgi and making him bark by pinching him.[58]

After three weeks in Canada, the King and Queen were fêted in the United States by the President ('He is so easy to get to know,' wrote a grateful Monarch, '& never makes one feel shy'), before re-embarking from Canada on 15 June. Deeply moved by his reception, and relieved that it was over, the King 'nearly cried' – as he later confessed – at the end of his final speech before departing. It was, wrote his biographer, 'a climacture in the King's life,' while at the same time 'an undeniable wrench to leave homeland and family under such uncertain conditions'.[59]

Presumably it was also a wrench for his children, despite the telephone call. In the press, the six-week parting was widely discussed as an example of the high level of sacrifice the royal couple were prepared to make for the public good. Some interest was also taken in the feelings of their daughters, and the leave-taking at Portsmouth at the beginning of the trip became a moment of sentimental drama.

Keen attention was paid to the princesses as they were taken aboard their parents' ship before she sailed. Elizabeth at thirteen, it was observed, was nearly as tall as her mother. There was a change in the way she dressed – no longer in 'babyish, bonnet-shaped hats,' wearing instead a tilted cap, with the hem-line of her coat and dress lowered to below her knees.[60] The faces of both girls were scrutinized for signs of emotion. According to one witness, 'they looked somewhat forlorn when, at length, amid tremendous cheering, the hooting of sirens, and the God-speed of thousands of onlookers, the mighty liner, bearing their Majesties, slowly glided out of the harbour.'[61] According to another, when the princesses returned to the jetty, 'Margaret's face puckered up, Elizabeth looked tearful . . . ,' while the King and Queen could be seen gazing after them, 'until the two little figures merged into the blue of thronged quays'.[62]

During the tour, Elizabeth sent her mother photographs, and made a film of Margaret and the pets with a cine-camera. Various diversions of an educational sort were arranged by Queen Mary. One was a visit to the Bank of England to see the gold in the vaults. Naturally, the Governor, Montagu Norman, accompanied them. The old Queen was sincere in her didactic aims. However, in the prevailing mood such excursions almost inevitably became public events as well as private ones, despite strenuous efforts by Buckingham Palace to prevent, or at any rate contain, publicity. 'I think that the question of the press and press photographers in connection with the outings of T.R.H.s Princess Elizabeth and Princess Margaret will have to be seriously considered,' Sir Eric Miéville, the courtier responsible for press relations, wrote to the King's private secretary following a trip to London Zoo which was widely covered in the picture papers. 'What happens now is that by some extraordinary means, unknown to me, whenever they are due to visit an institution, news always leaks out ahead to certain members of the press . . . One has to remember that in these days such information given to the newspapers is worth money.'[63]

The homecoming of the King and Queen was almost as dramatic as the departure. The princesses prepared for it by spring-cleaning the 'Little House'.[64] The press did so by sending every available reporter to Southampton, where a destroyer, the *Kempenfelt*, had been ordered to carry the children to the liner *Empress of Britain* for a family reunion. 'Blue eyes sparkling, hair blowing,' the girls were piped on board the *Kempenfelt*.[65] Solemnly, they shook hands with each of the ship's officers, before sailing out to meet their parents in the Solent. After they had been brought together and returned to shore, the whole royal party proceeded by train to Waterloo, whence they rode in state to Buckingham Palace, the two princesses beside the King and Queen in the leading carriage.

4

'WE NEVER SEEMED to get really settled again after the Canada-America visit of 1939,' recalled Crawfie.[1] The trip marked the end of the tight family life that had survived the move out of 145 Piccadilly, and the start of intermittent separations and comings-together that lasted until 1945. The Royal Family had a good war – by the standards of almost every other royal house a stupendous one, emerging with its reputation enhanced, and much of the damage done by the Abdication repaired. Yet the psychology of the achievement was complicated. Much depended on the passivity of the Symbol King, and the serenity of his family life. Loyalty to the Monarchy waxed as the nation's fear grew, and acquired a character of hope and yearning – different from the sentimentalities and social conservatism of peacetime – which, as the end approached, turned to gratitude toward a King who had no way of affecting the outcome. Meanwhile, his children became representatives of what the fighting was about, their pre-war immaturity and innocence frozen in aspic. 'One felt,' in the words of a writer of the period, 'that these engaging little people would never grow up'.[2] The symbolism was heightened by a mystery. For security reasons, the whereabouts of the girls were kept secret, and the images of them that appeared in the press were set against an unknown, unidentifiable background, adding to a sense of them as magical princesses whose fate was linked to the national destiny.

The Royal Family was at Balmoral until just before the declaration of war on September 3rd. The King returned to London on August 23rd, his wife five days later. The children were despatched to Birkhall, the first of their mysterious locations, where they were cared for and guarded by a retinue headed by an equerry, and including a chauffeur, a police sergeant and several constables.[3] Lessons of a sort continued, Crawfie reading newspapers out loud, 'trying as far as possible to give them some idea of what was happening without too many horrible details.'[4] Marten posted history papers, and Princess Elizabeth sent him essays for correction. Girl Guide meetings took place in the village hall. So did 'war-work', which consisted of a large sewing party mainly made up of women from the royal estate. At Christmas they went to Sandringham, and then to Royal Lodge until May, with the Queen in residence for much of the time. Here there was more Girl Guiding, with the unusual ingredient of evacuees from the East End, bringing the girls into fleeting contact with urban working-class children.

'Thank you so very much for the books you and Mr Chamberlain sent me for my birthday,' Princess Elizabeth wrote to the Prime Minister's wife on 23 April 1940. 'It was so kind of you and I have always wanted to read them. I hope you are both well and that Mr Chamberlain is not too tired. Thanking you again so much.'[5] Mr Chamberlain was, however, shortly to be relieved of his responsibilities. On 8 May , following the debate on the Norway campaign, he was forced to resign. Two days later, Winston Churchill drove to Buckingham Palace to kiss hands as his successor. On 12 May, as Hitler invaded the Low Countries, the princesses were moved into the great fortress of Windsor Castle, where they were to live for most of the war. 'We went there for a weekend,' as Princess Margaret recalls, 'and we stayed for five years.'[6]

For a while, they slept in the dungeons. Princess Margaret remembers having to run to get to the shelter under Brunswick Tower. Yet she thought of it as a happy time.[7] Her sister felt much the same. She later told Harold Nicolson that she would like to make Windsor her home, rather than Buckingham Palace or Sandringham, since all the happiest memories of her childhood were associated with the Castle and the Park.[8] The girls lived in pampered seclusion, in conditions, as Morrah put it after the war, 'favourable to the quiet business of the schoolroom, though perhaps less for the enlargement of human contacts.'[9] There was a shifting band of soldiers, often Grenadier Guards, for company. With an informality hard to imagine in peacetime, they ate with their governesses and one or two officers in the State Dining Room, where a single light bulb hung from the ceiling in place of a chandelier.[10] At first, the King and Queen stayed at Windsor, commuting to Buckingham Palace. Later, after the worst of the bombing, they returned to London, visiting the Castle only at weekends.[11]

How should the royal children be used in wartime? Some of the best minds in the Ministry of Information addressed the problem with, as usual, contradictory results. On the one hand, it was decided to make much of the princesses' privations at a 'place in the country,' where they bore their loneliness stoically, for the national good. On the other, government propaganda used them as the centre-piece to a tableau of the perfect family hearth, confidently and comfortably immune to the threats of vulgar dictators. To project such an image, they would be shown, in pictures or prose, relaxing on sofas and rugs, surrounded by proud parents and placid pets. These two, separate, ways of imagining the King's daughters were sometimes combined. Later in the war, when victory was in sight, the second tended to predominate. Initially, when the need for sacrifice was greatest, the emphasis was on the first.

The presentation of the girls as victims of the family-rending impact of war provided the theme of Princess Elizabeth's first broadcast, delivered in October 1940 when she was fourteen-and-a-half, and directed at British children evacuated to North America, though actually intended to influence adult opinion in the United States, and the US Government, as well.

That the broadcast took place at all was a retreat by Buckingham Palace and a sign of how dire the emergency had become. Pre-war requests for Princess Elizabeth to speak on the air had been met by curt refusals. In 1938, the influential owner of the *New York Herald Tribune*, Helen Reid, was brusquely rebuffed when she asked if the Princess might make a five-minute broadcast to open National Children's Week in the United States. Mrs Reid had used the powerful argument that such a gesture would be in keeping with the British Government's policy of doing everything possible to bring America and Great Britain together. She had added, a little less tactfully, that it would also assuage American bitterness over the treatment of the Duke of Windsor at the time of his marriage.[12] Referring the matter to Buckingham Palace, the British ambassador wrote dismissively of such 'attempts to enlist the princesses for stunts'.[13] The Palace strongly agreed, and confirmed 'that there is, of course, no question of the princesses broadcasting, nor is it likely to be considered for many years to come'.[14] The autumn of 1940, however, was no time to be fastidious, where a chance of influencing American public opinion was concerned. When the Director-General of the BBC, Frederick Ogilvie, approached the King's private secretary, he immediately received a favourable answer.

The plan was to get Princess Elizabeth to introduce a series of 'Children in Wartime' programmes, intended to bring out the part children could play in the nation's defence. The Princess's brief statement would go out live in the short-wave service to the United States and Canada, and later be heard in recorded form all over the world. The unofficial aim of pulling adult heartstrings was made clear to the King and Queen. 'As Her Royal Highness's first broadcast, delivered at an historic moment,' Ogilvie explained to the Palace, 'it would reach the minds of the millions who heard it with a singular poignancy.'[15]

The broadcast went out on 13 October. The Princess read a carefully scripted text which linked her own recent life and that of her sister to the lives of displaced British children overseas. 'Thousands of you in this country have had to leave your homes and be separated from your father and mother,' she told her listeners, in a high-pitched, precise voice which *The Times* likened to that of her mother.[16] 'My sister Margaret Rose and I feel so much for you, as we know from experience what it means to be away from those we love most of all.' There was an expression of optimism ('We know, every one of us, that in the end all will be well.') A final exchange with the ten-year-old Princess Margaret was also in the prepared text: 'My sister is by my side, and we are both going to say good night to you. Come on, Margaret.' 'Good night,' said a smaller voice. 'Good night and good luck to you all.'[17]

Jock Colville, private secretary to the Prime Minister and later to Princess Elizabeth, wrote in his diary that he and Diana Sandys, Winston Churchill's daughter, who listened to the broadcast with him, 'were embarrassed by the sloppy sentiment she was made to express, but her voice was most impressive and, if the Monarchy survives, Queen Elizabeth II should be a most successful radio Queen'.[18] Sloppiness was what the occasion seemed to require: the broadcast was hailed on both sides of the Atlantic as a propaganda triumph, at a time when triumphs of any kind were sparse. It attracted particularly wide attention in the United States and made the front pages, with a picture in all the New York papers. 'Princess yesterday huge success here,' the local BBC representative cabled to Ogilvie. 'Some stations report telephone exchanges jammed with requests for repeat.'[19] Such was the quantity and enthusiasm of fan mail that the BBC turned the broadcast into a gramophone record for sale in America and throughout the Empire.

The guise of the princesses as typically lonely displaced children reinforced another part of the Ministry of Information's offensive: a projection of the King and Queen as typical Londoners carrying on regardless in spite of the Blitz. It helped to give the broadcast impact, indeed it might almost have been part of the plot, that Buckingham Palace had received a direct hit a few weeks earlier. Pictures of brave little girls in the country and their brave parents among the rubble mixed together in the public imagination. Mass Observation, the precursor of in-depth polling, recorded a mood of indignation and defiance, in which royalty played a part. 'If they hurt the King and Queen or the princesses we'd be so mad we'd blast every German out of existence,' declared a supposedly typical female clerk.[20]

Sometimes the children were shown on a pony cart with a corgi beside them, without adults, alone in a park. According to one early wartime account, walkers near their home would 'meet the two girls jogging along hatless, laughing, and talking merrily, taking it in turns to hold the reins, which they do gracefully with ribbons threaded in orthodox fashion over the first finger and under the thumb of the left hand'.[21] The impression was of free spirits, self-sufficient and unharmed in their own secret world. The contrast between this fairy land and bombed-out cities was stark. But there was also the other guise: children in the perfect family, whose domestic happiness was to be protected by the soldiers, sailors and airmen of the Empire as if it were their own. In this version, the children were never alone. Indeed, the presence of the King and Queen was a key ingredient.

It was important, as Simon Schama has observed, that a monarchy should appear as 'the family of families, at once dynastic and domestic, remote and accessible, magical and mundane'.[22] In a total war, the importance of the Windsors' as the 'family of families' increased because conditions on the home front, in addition to the foreign danger, were shaking non-royal family life to its foundations. The same had been true in the First World War. However, there had been a significant shift since 1914–18, partly because of the milder temperament of George VI, compared to his father, and the circumstances of his accession; and partly because his Royal Family, unlike the one he was born into, was conveniently young, nuclear and comprehensible. In the First War, George V had been portrayed as patriarchal, even god-like, a warrior monarch to whom duty was owed. In the Second World War, the whole 'family of families' was given prominence as a unit, with the King and Queen frequently shown in the company of their children, underscoring the domestic affections and virtues that the war was about.

Here it is particularly difficult to separate image from reality, because witnesses to royal domesticity were subject to the same media messages as everybody else, and the dutiful Windsors themselves, hounded by the pressures of what was expected of them, were on their best behaviour when being observed. In the context of such necessary and powerful myths, the royal actors had little choice but to play their allotted parts.

Would Edward VIII, had he lasted, have been selfish and truculent in wartime, or would he have risen to the occasion? It is an interesting speculation. As it was, the stammering King whom some had believed could not survive the ordeal of being crowned, seemed able to adapt in war, as in peace, to the requirements of his job. These consisted mainly of being photographed, taking part in public ceremonies, and personally bestowing honours – sometimes, because of the fighting, decorating several hundred servicemen in a single session. It also involved, and this was an especially vital role, making important visitors feel pleased to have had the opportunity of meeting him and his family. Surprisingly, this became something that George VI was particularly good at. The strange combination of his own social ineptitude, the Queen's ability to make whoever she addressed feel that they were the one person to whom she wished to speak, and their daughters' lack of affectation, provided a recipe for putting people at their ease.

Were they as genuinely pleased to see an endless flow of visitors as they seemed, or was it all act? Noël Coward asked himself this question after experiencing what he called 'an exhibition of unqualified "nice-ness" from all concerned' during a meeting with the Royal Family in 1942. He concluded that it did not matter. Putting oneself out was part of the job of royalty. 'I'll settle for anyone who does their job well, anyhow.'[23] Few others, however, came away feeling that it was just for show. For most who encountered the Family informally, the wonder of being in the presence of Monarchy in an Empire at war was combined with an uplifting sense of inclusion, as if they them-selves were family members. The result was a miasma of shared affec-tion, of which the grateful visitor felt both spectator and part. When Queen Alexandra of Yugoslavia (herself a refugee) met them in 1944, she immediately decided that 'this was the sort of home life I wanted, with children and dogs playing at my feet.'[24] General Sir Alan Brooke, Chief of the Imperial General Staff, who spent a shooting weekend with them in Norfolk in the same year, came away with a similar feeling – recording his impression of 'one of the very best examples of family life. A thoroughly close-knit and happy family all wrapped up in each other.'[25]

Nobody referred, in their descriptions of the King, to his intellectual capacities, his political judgement, or his knowledge of the war. Yet so far from being a handicap, George VI's limitations – and his aware-ness of them – were turned into a precious source of strength. One Gentleman Usher fondly described him as 'a plodder' – a man of simple ideas, with a strong sense of what he ought to do. Much was made of such decent ordinariness, which meant confronting what others had to face without complaint – and included such self-denials as not seeking to escape the Blitz, or trying to give his daughters a privileged immunity from danger by sending them with other rich children to Canada. It also meant frugality, and strict obedience to government rules – a topic which played a major part in the use of royalty for propaganda. Thus, in April 1940, the public was informed that at the celebration of Princess Elizabeth's fourteenth birthday, the Queen had decreed that the three-tier anniversary cake should be limited to plain sponge, as an economy.[26] There were many tales of economy with clothing coupons, and of how the Queen cut down and altered her own dresses for Elizabeth, adapting these in turn for Margaret, so that 'with the three of us, we manage in relays'.[27] This was not just for public consumption. When Eleanor Roosevelt visited Buckingham Palace late in 1942, she found an adherence to heat, water and food restrictions that was almost a fetish. Broken window panes in her bedroom had been replaced with wood, and her bath had a painted black line above which she was not supposed to run the water.[28]

Nevertheless, there remained a wide gulf between the life lived by the Royal Family, with their houses, parks and horses, and retinue of servants, and the conditions of their subjects. After a bomb struck the Palace, the Queen was supposed to have said: 'Now we can look the East End in the face'. The East End, however, was not able to retreat to Windsor to catch up on sleep, or to spend recuperative holidays in Norfolk and Scotland. Nor was the East End able to supplement its diet with pheasants and venison shot on the royal estates.

Indeed some aspects of royal life went on remarkably undisturbed. There was little interruption to the riding lessons given to the princesses by Horace Smith, which continued throughout the war. Training with Smith involved pony carts, which (as he later observed) had the particular advantage in wartime that journeys in them did not require petrol. With future troop-reviewing in mind, Smith also taught Princess Elizabeth to ride side-saddle. Occasions for demonstrating equestrian prowess did not cease, either. In 1943, Smith personally awarded Princess Elizabeth first prize in the Royal Windsor Horse Show for her driving of a 'utility vehicle,' harnessed to her own black Fell pony – a trophy she won again the following year, both times in the presence of the King and Queen.[29]

Watching was a developing interest, as well as riding or driving. In the spring of 1942, the Princess was taken by her parents to the Beckhampton stables on the Wiltshire Downs, where horses bred at the royal studs were trained, to see two royal horses, Big Game and Sun Chariot, which were highly fancied for the Derby and the Oaks. The jockey Sir Gordon Richards later recalled his meeting with the sixteen-year-old girl 'who took them all in', and was quizzed about them by her father as they worked, causing the royal trainer Fred Darling to remark loyally 'that Princess Elizabeth must have a natural eye for a horse'. Visits to see the mares and foals at the royal stud at

Hampton Court, and to see the royal horses in training at Newmarket followed.[30]

Other pursuits also involved opportunities not available to most compatriots. In October 1942, Princess Elizabeth made her contribution to the royal larder by shooting her first stag in the hills at Balmoral – using a rifle she had been taught to handle the previous year.[31] In the autumn of 1943, she hunted with the Garth Foxhounds, and later with the Duke of Beaufort's Hounds in Gloucestershire.[32] The decision to allow her to go hunting was taken, according to a report, 'in accord with the general policy of making her life as "normal" as possible' in the light of her position as Heiress Presumptive.[33]

There were also private entertainments. The King, despite his shyness, was a good dancer, and especially enjoyed dancing in the company of his children. He did not allow the war to curtail this particular pastime. A number of royal balls were held. Princess Elizabeth attended her first at Windsor in July 1941, when she was fifteen. A West End dance band played foxtrots, waltzes and rumbas to the Royal Family and their guests, who included Guards officers, until two in the morning, and Elizabeth danced several times with her father.[34] Later in the war, before the start of flying bombs in 1944, dances were held fortnightly in the Bow Room on the ground floor at Buckingham Palace. On one occasion the King, oblivious to cares of state, his stammer forgotten, led his family and other guests in a conga line through the corridors and state rooms.[35]

FOR MAXIMUM BENEFIT to the war effort, the privacy of the Royal Family needed to be less than complete. If life at Windsor and Buckingham Palace had been simply private, its exemplary virtues could scarcely have been known to loyal subjects. For this reason, as *The Times* observed just after the end of the war, 'many glimpses' of the Royal Family's home life had 'reached a wide public, through illustrated journals and the cinema'.[36] One avid supplier to the illustrated journals, and propagator of royal mythology, was the photographer Lisa Sheridan who, by her own testimony, never failed to come away from a professional visit to the Royal Family without feeling a better person. Her recollections of the princesses in wartime are interesting not only because her pictures of wagging puppy tails, happy children and proud parents became fixed in the Empire's imagination, but also because she provides a distillation of the 'family of families' miasma in its purest form.

In her memoirs, Mrs Sheridan described several wartime trips to see the princesses. Her account of the first, to Royal Lodge in early 1940, reflected the official line of the phoney war period, that the enemy had done little to change the traditional British way of life. The windows 'showed no signs of criss-cross sticky tape or nasty black-out'. The princesses were intent on their normal recreations. When she arrived, they were dressed for riding and carried crops; they changed into 'sensible' tweed skirts and pullovers, in order to be photographed in the garden, suitably equipped with rakes and barrows, digging for victory. The overriding impression, however, was of the Windsors as a household anyone would like to be part of. Apart from the King and Queen and a policeman at the gate, nobody else was visible. 'I never felt the presence of anyone at all other than the family,' she recalled. It was clear 'that home was to the Royal Family the source of life itself and that there was a determination on the part of the King and Queen to maintain a simple, united family life, whatever calls there might be to duty'. Later visits reinforced this picture of self-containment, though the background shifted from the unchanging domesticity of Royal Lodge to the warlike ramparts of the Castle. Here there were parables of life and death: the demise of a pet chameleon, for example ('Princess Elizabeth could not bring herself to speak of her tiny pet for quite a long time after his death') and, even more painfully, the death of a favourite corgi. The Queen, however, as always comforting and wise, told her elder daughter to keep things in proportion. It was, after all, the height of a world war.[37]

Sheridan's photographs, disseminated among dusty desert rats, weary Bevin boys, homesick land girls and traumatized evacuees, show a precious, sheltered intactness. In Sheridan's world, the princesses were happily free from the requirement to do anything except obligingly change their outfits, and display an exquisite politeness. Yet they were also shown to be greatly concerned about the worrying state of a world mercifully beyond their comprehension – a concern that helpfully linked the 'perfect hearth' portrayal of the photographic image to a view of the girls which provided the regular diet of Ministry of Information handouts: as dutiful models for every other daughter of the Empire too young to serve in the women's services.

A series of newspaper reports involving Princess Elizabeth, in particular, were designed, not so much to idealize the Heiress Presumptive, as to indicate royal approval for Government-sponsored schemes. Thus, the princesses did not only dig for victory, they knitted for it – the product of their labours being divided, with judicious impartiality, between the men of the army, navy and air force.[38] When they ran out of materials, there was a solution: in July 1941 it was announced that the two girls, aged fifteen and eleven, had personally arranged, and performed in, a concert in front of their parents and members of the armed services, from which between £70 and £80 had been raised, 'to buy wool for knitting for the Forces'. If a Ministry wished to exhort the population to greater efforts, or advertise an achievement, it turned to the Palace for help, and where appropriate, royal children were provided. On one occasion the princesses (to the envy of every school child) were shown over a Fortress bomber, and allowed to play with the controls. On another, orchestrated publicity was given to the Queen's decision to have both of them immunized against diphtheria. On yet another, the Heiress Presumptive was designated by the Ministry of Works as the donor of a prize open to Welsh schoolchildren 'for the best essay in English and Welsh on metal salvage.'[39] Meanwhile, there was a press story in 1941 about how the fifteen-year-old Princess (despite a Civil List income of £6,000 a year) was only allowed five shillings a week pocket money; and that more than half even of this small sum was generously donated to war-supporting good causes.[40] The same spring, royal dolls owned by the children were exhibited to raise money for the British War Relief Society,[41] and a special 'Princess Elizabeth's Day' was announced, for collecting for children's charities.

How could any teenager cope? One answer is that royalty lived its life in compartments: the public sectioned off from the private and, in the case of a young princess, often barely touching her personally at all. Another is that teenagers had not yet been invented – or at any rate, young people in their teens in the early 1940s had very different expectations from those either before or after the war. The Second World War was a time when adolescence was held in suspension. Children who went straight from school into war work or the armed services, enjoyed no intervening period of irresponsibility. In this, Princess Elizabeth was not unusual. The acceptance of a variety of honorific titles or the performance of symbolic acts was not necessarily more stressful than the tasks and ways of life of many contemporaries. Nevertheless, at a stage in life when it is hard enough to keep everyday private events in perspective, such a cacophony of public roles provided a strange accompaniment to growing up.

She was like other girls of her age, yet not like them. Winston Churchill was supposed to have remarked in an unflattering reference to Clement Attlee, that if you feed a grub on royal jelly, it becomes a queen. In the case of a human Heiress Presumptive, the equivalent of royal jelly is the world's perceptions: the drip feed of curtseys, deference, public recognition, combined with a knowledge of lack of choice, and of inevitability. The strongest instinct of many adolescents is to conform: it was an instinct with which Princess Elizabeth was well equipped. She seems to have dealt with the peculiarity of her position by becoming as unremarkable as possible in everything she could not change, while accepting absolutely what was expected of her. Her actual experience was unique: there was nobody with whom she could compare herself, no peer group to set a standard. Yet few young people could have been more conformist, more amenable, than George VI's elder daughter.

There remains the difficulty for the rest of humanity – grubs without a destiny – in understanding the mentality of somebody with such extraordinary expectations. A distinctive character, however, was beginning to emerge. Authentic portraits are rare – *vignettes* by passing visitors are generally coloured by excitement at meeting royalty, and tell more about the witness than the subject. But there are enough thoughtful descriptions to confirm the part-flattering, part-disconcerting impressions provided by Crawfie, of a reserved, strong-willed, narrow-visioned, slightly priggish child, without intellectual or aesthetic interests, taking what she is given as part of the natural order, but with greater mental capacities than any close member of the family cared to appreciate. When she was still thirteen, the Archbishop of Canterbury, Cosmo Lang, noted after 'a full talk with the little lady alone' before he conducted her confirmation service, that 'though naturally not very communicative, she showed real intelligence and understanding'.[42] More than two years later, Eleanor Roosevelt formed a view of her that was strikingly similar. The wife of one Head of State assessed the daughter of another as 'quite serious and a child with a great deal of character and personality ... She asked me a number of questions about life in the United States and they were serious questions.'[43]

The experience of her as an able, but above all single-minded, young person was shared by Horace Smith, who had more contact with her during the war than any of her other teachers apart from Crawfie, and who taught her in the subject that interested her most. The Princess was not, he considered, 'a person who takes up interests lightly, only to drop them just as easily a short time later. If and when her interest is aroused, she goes into whatever subject it is with thoroughness and application, nor does her interest wane with the passing of time or the claim of other new matters upon her attention.' In addition, he noted, she had 'a keen and retentive mind'.[44]

Such perceptions were combined, however, with a sense that she was young for her age, and remained in appearance and manner still a child until well into her teens. Perhaps there was an element of wishful thinking: the princesses' childhood was part of the *status quo ante bellum* which it was hoped to restore. Such a feeling may have been strongest of all in the King and Queen, who liked her to wear the clothes of a child after she had ceased to be one. Nevertheless an uncertainty about whether Princess Elizabeth was precocious or immature, or both, is a recurrent feature of the accounts. Chips Channon observed the princesses in procession at a service at St. Paul's in May 1943, 'dressed alike in blue, which made them seem like little girls'.[45] Peter Townsend, an RAF officer who joined the Royal Family as an equerry to the King nine months later, found that they were not too old to lead him in a 'hair-raising bicycle race,' and recalled Princess Elizabeth as 'charming and totally unsophisticated'.[46] Alexandra of Yugoslavia's recollection of meeting her British cousins at Windsor, describes a childish ritual involving the princesses and their dogs. When tea was brought in, they insisted on feeding (with the aid of a footman) their four corgis first.[47]

Preparation for her osmosis from child-princess, locked in a tower with her schoolbooks or playing in the park with her sister, to constitutionally responsible Heiress, was scratchy, like much else in wartime. For some time, the Crawfie and Marten regime had been supplemented with French lessons from the Vicomtesse de Bellaigue. According to one of the Queen's ladies-in-waiting, Lady Helen Graham, Elizabeth had been encouraged to attend closely to the news bulletins of the BBC.[48] 'Already the Princess has a first-rate knowledge of State and current affairs,' a courtier declared in 1943.[49]

Various accounts were given of the level of her knowledge, some of them doubtless exaggerated, in order to demonstrate her fitness for the tasks ahead. It was said that, in addition to French, she was fluent in German. When she was eighteen, *The Times* claimed she was highly musical and although 'like some others of her sex, she is no mathematician,' she was familiar with 'many classics' in English and French.[50] When a magazine editor wrote to the Palace to check a list, supplied by 'a friend near the Court,' of books and authors the Princess had allegedly read, a courtier replied firmly that the list could be published as correct. It consisted of 'many of Shakespeare's plays,' Chaucer's *Canterbury Tales*, Coleridge, Keats, Browning, Tennyson, Scott, Dickens, Austen, Trollope, Stevenson, Trevelyan's *History of England*, Conan Doyle, Buchan and Peter Cheyney.[51] To this remarkably large collection might be added the Brontës: at the end of the war, Lisa Sheridan found the Princess reading *Jane Eyre* and *Wuthering Heights*, and expressing a preference for historical novels and stories about the Highlands.[52] Was it true? If such accounts were even half accurate, the Princess would have been a strong candidate for a place at university, where she might have extended her intellectual range. Neither university nor even finishing school, however, was considered as a possibility. Instead, like a butcher or a joiner, she apprenticed for the job she would be undertaking for the rest of her life by doing it.

Her first practical experience of the grown-up world of royalty was to head a regiment. In January 1942, following the death of the Duke of Connaught, she was asked to take his place as honorary Colonel of the Grenadier Guards – a natural choice, some felt, in view of her contact with the Grenadiers at Windsor. The offer was accepted, and on her sixteenth birthday she carried out her first engagement as Colonel at Windsor Castle, inspecting the Grenadiers in the company of her father. Thirty reporters and ten photographers were granted press passes to cover the event.[53] Cecil Beaton marked it with one of his most famous pictures, which shows the Heiress Presumptive in uniform, fresh-faced and half-smiling, with her jacket unbuttoned and her hat at a coquettish angle. Afterwards, she was hostess to more than six hundred officers and men, entertained by the comedian Tommy Handley.[54] The Grenadier Guards were delighted by their acquisition, and those who dined with her in the officers' mess recall her as 'charming, and very sincere'.[55] Yet despite this dramatic début, Buckingham Palace kept up the fiction that the Princess was still a child, and American press requests for help with a story about her were met with the incomprehensible denial that she was entering public life.[56]

Adulthood could not be postponed for ever. Princess Elizabeth's coming-of-age, when she was entitled to succeed to the throne without need for a Regent, took place when she was eighteen, in April 1944. There was no débutante ball to celebrate the occasion. Instead, it was accompanied by the Princess's graduation from a nursery bedroom to a suite. Here she was pictured by Lisa Sheridan, as if she were part of the interior design. 'The upholstery is pale pink brocade patterned in cream,' it was revealed. 'The walls are cream, hung with peaceful pictures of pastoral scenes. The Princess's flowered frock harmonized admirably with her room.'[57] There were other changes, to mark her rise in status. She was assigned her own armorial bearings, and her own standard which flew in whatever residence she happened to be occupying. She also acquired a 'Household' of her own, including, in July 1944, a lady-in-waiting. Meanwhile, she had unwittingly stimulated a minor constitutional controversy which engaged the best legal brains for several months.

The 1937 Regency Act, which had been passed following George VI's accession, had provided for two forms of delegation of royal powers: to a Regent, in the event of a child under eighteen succeeding, or of the total incapacitation of a monarch; and to five Counsellors of State, composed of the Consort and the four next in line of succession, in the event of the Sovereign's illness or absence abroad. However, the provision disqualified anybody not 'a British subject of full age,' which effectively meant that Elizabeth could succeed her father as Monarch with full powers at eighteen, but not deputise for him as a Counsellor until she was twenty-one.[58]

Nobody noticed this anomaly until an eagle-eyed lawyer pointed it out to the King's private secretary, Sir Alexander Hardinge, in the autumn of 1942. Hardinge at first dismissed it. It was 'common sense,' he replied to the lawyer tartly, to regard the Princess as fully of age if she could succeed without a Regent.[59] The Lord Chancellor, Lord Simon, however, disagreed: due to bad drafting, the law and common sense did not coincide.[60] There the matter might have rested, had not the King himself indicated his desire to have his daughter as a Counsellor of State. The Lord Chancellor was once again consulted, and recommended to the Prime Minister that the law be changed in order to permit the Heiress Presumptive to become a Counsellor, bearing in mind 'the qualities of the young lady and the wish of her parents'.[61] As Allied troops invaded Sicily in July 1943, George VI spoke to Winston Churchill on the matter, and secured a promise that it should be brought up at War Cabinet, with a view to a quick Bill. 'He quite agrees this should be done,' wrote the King.[62] Cabinet assented, and in October, the Labour Home Secretary in the wartime Coalition, Herbert Morrison, introduced legislation, arguing that the responsibility would give the Heiress valuable experience.

The new Act received the Royal Assent in time for the eighteen-year-old Princess to become a Counsellor, along with her mother and three others, during her father's visit to Italy in July 1944. In his absence she performed her first constitutional functions, which included signifying the Royal Assent to Acts which had been passed by Parliament. Yet she was still not 'a British subject of full age', or legally old enough to vote in an election.

A further question also arose in connection with the Princess's eighteenth birthday: the possibility of a change of title. During 1943, letters and articles appeared in the press suggesting that, in view of her unchallenged position as Heiress, it would be appropriate to designate her 'Princess of Wales,' an idea first mooted in 1936. In August, Pwllheli Town Council petitioned the Prime Minister on the subject,[63] recommending the Princess's birthday as a suitable moment. At the end of the year, the *Carmarthen Journal* reported that no project in recent years had been more popular,[64] and early in 1944, the Welsh

Parliamentary Party, composed of Conservative, Liberal and Labour MPs, joined the campaign. It was pointed out, on all sides, that such a gesture would be greeted with enthusiasm in the Principality, with great benefits to Anglo-Welsh relations.

The Palace, however, demurred. While appreciating the sentiment behind such a proposal, it was unwilling to be swept along by a wave of populist fervour. The key issue, it decided, was the precedent for such a bestowal of title, and the lack of one. The title 'Prince of Wales' had only ever been given to the Heir Apparent. Princess Elizabeth was merely Heir or Heiress Presumptive. Could the Princess perhaps be promoted from Presumptive to Apparent? The Home Office was asked to investigate. 'I have looked into your question about HRH Princess Elizabeth', J. A. R. Pimlott, a Home Office official, wrote to Sir Eric Miéville. 'Where the heir to the throne is a woman her right of succession is defeasible at any time by the birth of a son to the reigning Sovereign. HRH Princess Elizabeth therefore remains Heir Presumptive till she in fact succeeds.' This had been true, he pointed out, of Victoria in 1837. Though Queen Adelaide, widow of William IV, had no child for seventeen years, it was thought constitutionally advisable in proclaiming the accession of Queen Victoria to guard against the possibility of a posthumous birth. The new Sovereign was therefore proclaimed Queen 'saving the rights of any issue of his Late Majesty King William IV which may be born of His Late Majesty's Consort'.[65]

This, however, was not the end of the matter. Though it dealt with the Presumptive-Apparent problem – by definition, no female could be Apparent – it did not dispose of the issue of whether there was any precedent for calling a female Heir, even though only Presumptive, by the Welsh title. Indeed, an inquiry seemed to show, on the basis of records kept by a sixteenth-century German ambassador, that Henry VIII had considered that whichever of his daughters was Heir to the throne should be known as Princess of Wales.[66] For a short time, there was consternation, and uncertainty. However, the evidence to support such a claim was shadowy, and when it was put to Sir Gerald Wollaston, Garter Principal King of Arms, he was dismissive. He also pointed out the danger of setting a new precedent, opening the doors to the alarming future possibility, if George VI had a son who then married, of there being two Princesses of Wales.[67]

The Palace view hardened. There remained, of course, the political complication of public opinion, which would be disappointed, especially in Wales, by a negative decision. But the King's new private secretary, Sir Alan Lascelles, regarded this as a minor factor. 'I have no doubt that the matter will be raised in Parliament before long, and of course the Commons have a right to do so,' he wrote to the King in January 1944, shortly before the Allied forces landed in Anzio. 'As long ago as 1376, they petitioned Edward III to make his grandson, Richard of Bordeaux, Prince of Wales.'[68] Not everybody, however, agreed that the views of parliamentarians should be as readily ignored in the twentieth century as in the fourteenth. One objector was Herbert Morrison, who suggested that to make the King's elder daughter Princess of Wales would deal neatly with any suggestion that the Government was anti-Welsh. It did not matter, Morrison reasonably suggested, if there was no precedent. Moreover, in the unlikely event of a male heir being born, the title could simply lapse.

The Home Secretary's minute on the subject of 28th January 1944 was sent to the Palace, but Lascelles, no mean politician on issues he regarded as important, deliberately withheld it from the King.[69] Probably it made no difference. A few days earlier, Jock Colville recorded in his diary that, while the Cabinet approved of the idea of making Elizabeth Princess of Wales, her father did not.[70] The royal will prevailed. At his weekly audience, Churchill promised the King that he would tell the Minister of Information to 'damp down all discussion of this question in the Press,' in order to avoid a row. In February, it was officially announced from Buckingham Palace that there would be no change in the Princess's title on her eighteenth birthday. 'This will check the spate of press comment and general chatter,' Lascelles recorded on 13 February. As a result, the principality was without a Prince or Princess until 1958. The oft-repeated explanation for this vacancy was 'the very real distinction between heirs apparent and presumptive'.[71]

To CONSOLE the Welsh, the King and Queen took Princess Elizabeth with them on a tour of mining and industrial areas in South Wales early in 1944. The crowds were welcoming and forgiving, and came from all classes and occupations. At Cardiff docks, according to one report, the Queen and Princess 'mingled with a crowd of coloured Merchant Navy seamen,' and stood beside 'an ebony giant from British Honduras'. People from the villages walked for several miles just to see the King's daughter, who smiled and bowed her head in acknowledgement of greetings.[72]

It was not just in Wales, however, that there was an upsurge of feeling in favour of Elizabeth. As the war entered its final phase, she found herself an emblematic heroine everywhere. All over the Empire, the health, beauty and emerging womanhood of the Princess were linked to the eagerly anticipated future, in which families would be brought together, sweethearts rejoined, babies born, bellies filled and freedom enjoyed. Encouraged by broadcasters and newsreels, young people took a special interest in her. On the Welsh tour, she caused particular excitement among children. In Valletta, on the island of Malta, a thousand school children assembled a few weeks before the Normandy landings to see and cheer a special film depicting scenes from her life.[73]

Requests for public appearances by the Princess now became frequent. For the time being the Palace was adamant: there could be no question of 'independent engagements,' though she might occasionally accompany her parents, as to South Wales.[74] Soon, however, this rule was relaxed. On 23 May 1944, Princess Elizabeth spoke publicly for the first time at the annual meeting of the Queen Elizabeth Hospital for Children in Hackney. In the autumn, she accepted an invitation to launch *HMS Vanguard*, the largest battleship ever built in the British Isles. The ceremony, in Clyde shipyards, was followed by a luncheon at which she read a short speech. The First Lord of the Admiralty, A. V. Alexander, wrote to Lascelles afterwards describing 'the clear and decisive way' in which she carried out both duties.[75]

There remained the question of whether she would enter one of the women's services, and if so, which. Early in 1945, it was decided that she would join the Auxiliary Territorial Service. It was not the obvious choice. In view of her family's naval traditions, the WRNS would have been more natural. The King and Queen were apparently reluctant: there is no reason to doubt Crawfie's account of an eager and determined young woman wearing down the resistance of her parents.[76] At the end of February she was registered as No. 230873 Second Subaltern Elizabeth Alexandra Mary Windsor. The rank was an honorary one, but the training in driving and vehicle-maintenance she underwent at No. 1 Mechanical Transport Training Centre at Aldershot, was genuine. She enjoyed this sole, brief experience of communal education. Several decades later, she told the Labour politician Barbara Castle that it was the only time in her life when she had been able seriously to test her own capabilities against those of others of her age.[77] After six weeks she qualified as a driver, and at the end of July, a few days before the final end to the war, she was promoted to Junior Commander.

'The Princess is to be treated in exactly the same way as any other officer learning at the driving training centre,' maintained the official report at the outset.[78] To back this up, the Queen requested that photographers should not be given any facilities.[79] This, however, did not deter the press, and during her short stay at the Centre she was photographed more intensively than at any time since the Coronation. As a result, she was scarcely just one of the girls. If it was not quite true, as a 1957 assessment put it, that 'the rule of seclusion was maintained and she did not mix with her fellows on the course,'[80] the extent of mucking in, on equal terms, was limited. She kept to the routine of the ATS mess, took her share of duties, and acquired the basics of driving, car mechanics and maintenance. But she returned to Windsor every night to sleep. She also became an unwitting mannequin for the uniform of the service – pictures of her with a spanner, at the wheel of a lorry, leaning on a bonnet, or peering purposefully and fetchingly under one, appeared in the newspapers and magazines of every Allied nation.

In such matters, it was always impossible to disentangle a private motive from the public effort. Since the enrolment of a royal princess could not be kept secret, her participation in the ATS inevitably became part of the morale-boosting display of the Monarchy. It was a similar story with other initiatives that started spontaneously. A particularly striking and, in its way, sad example of the way Royal Family behaviour spilled over from the personal to the public, so that domestic events were turned into courtly contrivance, was provided by a series of Christmas shows put on during the war by Windsor children, with the aid of adult mentors, and performed in front of parents and other members of the Castle community.

These began modestly in 1940 with a simple play, 'The Christmas Child,' in St. George's Hall, with Elizabeth playing one of the three kings, flanked by two boy evacuees. The occasion was enjoyed by everybody, and the princesses, who had been on stage since birth without knowing it, discovered an interest in, and even a talent for, amateur theatricals. The following Christmas, the stakes were raised slightly, and a pantomime, 'Cinderella,' was written for them by a local schoolmaster. Again it was a success, and once again there was a good deal of democratic sharing of tasks and banter in the preparations and rehearsals. The next year, they put on 'Sleeping Beauty,' and Lisa Sheridan described how Princess Elizabeth 'took the arms of the two "sailors" and sang "Mind Your Sisters"' and brought the house down.[81] The tradition continued, giving pleasure to both performers and audience, which always included the princesses' parents. Horace Smith, who attended the pantomimes of 1942–4, recalled seeing the elder princess 'full of confidence and vigour,' and reducing the King to hearty laughter.[82] The humour depended a lot on puns. 'There are three acres in one rood,' Widow Twankey, an office boy from the Castle, was required to say in the 1943 production of 'Aladdin'. 'We don't want anything improper,' replied Margaret. 'There's a large copper in the kitchen,' said the Widow. 'We'll soon get rid of him,' declared Elizabeth – and so on.[83]

Year by year, the performances became more polished, with increasingly elaborate costumes and sets. It was also established, as Court etiquette apparently required, that if the King and Queen were to attend, their daughters should have leading parts, regardless of the acting ability of the evacuees and village children who were also involved. Consequently, attention focused on the royal children and their skills, even more than would have been true in any case. Meanwhile audiences grew, bringing in large numbers of locally-based guardsmen and ATS girls. In 1943, there were three performances, including one specifically for soldiers. The show also became publicly known. Weeks before the 1943 pantomime, advance publicity produced a flood of inquiries, and more than a thousand would-be ticket holders sent in applications containing blank cheques. All were politely

Biker, 1931

From Queen Mary's album (captions in her handwriting): *above right* Princess
Elizabeth with her royal grandparents at Bognor, Spring 1929 and
opposite inspecting the guard: in the quadrangle at Windsor castle, May 1929.
Above left The Earl and Countess of Strathmore, 1931. *Below* 145 Piccadilly in the late
1930s (lefthand part of the central building)

Lilibet at Windsor *may*

Below With Alla and members of the Royal Family at a Balmoral charity fête, 1927

Above Second in line, with Edward VIII, Margaret Rose and the Duke of York at Balmoral, September 1936

Right Tube trip. The princesses and Crawfie, Tottenham Court Road, May 1939

Above Taming young Bolsheviks. King's Camp, Abergeldie, August 1939

Below 'I thought it all <u>very</u>, <u>very</u> wonderful.' Coronation of George VI, 12th May, 1937

Above Snapshot taken of
Princes Elizabeth and
Prince Philip of Greece
playing croquet in the
garden of the Captain's
House at Dartmouth
Naval College, July 1939

Right Pony and trap,
Windsor Great Park,
August 1940

Above ATS, April 1945

Below VE-Day

Above Princess Elizabeth preparing to hand Prince Philip her coat at the Brabourne-Mountbatten wedding, Romsey, 26th October 1946

Right Deck games with officers on board HMS *Vanguard*, 1947

Below With Margaret, East London, South Africa, 1947

refused.[84] However, those denied entry could still learn about the show second-hand, for reports appeared in the press. Particular interest was aroused by 'Aladdin' in 1943, in which the Heiress Presumptive, cast in the title role, and wearing utility shorts and top, performed a tap dance, and in one scene appeared as a charlady, in an apron of sackcloth. 'From the moment Princess Elizabeth popped out of a laundry basket,' enthused the *Sunday Graphic*, 'the King and Queen and the audience of 400 laughed and thoroughly enjoyed the show.'[85] After seeing the last of the three performances, Lascelles wrote in his diary that the principals and chorus alike would not have disgraced Drury Lane. 'P'cess Eliz. was a charming Aladdin', he noted, 'and P'cess M. a charming and competent Princess Roxana'.[86] Altogether the pantomime netted £200.

The final pantomime, at Christmas 1944, starred the Heiress Presumptive as a Victorian seaside belle. It also included a carefully choreographed 'ballet interlude,' arranged by the dancing mistress at Buckingham Palace.[87] By this time, however, it had been transformed into an ambitious, semi-professional extravaganza, widely discussed as an established rite, and, in effect, part of the public relations of royalty.

5

B EING ON STAGE was, of course, an inescapable part of a royal childhood. Indeed, the last of the Windsor shows was followed by a royal performance as theatrical as anything the princesses had yet experienced. In contrast to the run-up to the 1918 Armistice which was brought about by a sudden German collapse, the early months of 1945 provided a crescendo of victories and liberations. At home, faith in the cause, pride at survival, and the justice of the outcome, created a patriotic mood quite different from the nationalist frenzy of twenty-seven years before. As a result the celebrations marking the defeat first of Germany and then of Japan contained a communal spirit which expressed itself in the festival nature of the rejoicing, and also in an inclusive and grateful attitude to the Royal Family. On both VE and VJ-Days it was the crowds, as much as the Government, that placed the King, Queen and two princesses centre-stage.

Officially, Victory-in-Europe Day was 8 May. In practice, the cele-brations lasted at least three days, with attention directed at Bucking-ham Palace, and with the Royal Family in starring roles throughout. By mid-afternoon on VE-Day itself, the number of people gathered in the hot sunshine round the Queen Victoria Memorial in front of the Palace exceeded that at the Coronation. It was, according to *The Times*, 'a red, white and blue crowd,' with every other woman wearing a multi-coloured ribbon or rosette in her hair. Winston Churchill arrived in an open car and spoke briefly, before disappearing for lunch with the King and Queen. A lull followed. Then the call 'We want the King' rose from the crowd. Responding to it, the royal couple and the two princesses came out onto the balcony, the King in naval, and Princess Elizabeth in ATS uniform, to be met by prolonged cheer-ing and singing of 'For he's a jolly good fellow'. Only later did the Prime Minister appear with them, giving the 'V for Victory' sign. In the evening after Churchill had left, the Royal Family appeared for yet another encore, producing fresh waves of applause and community singing.[1]

That night, they were joined for dinner by a group of Guards officers who were friends of the princesses. After the meal, as the noise continued beyond the railings, Princess Margaret suggested that the younger members of the party should go outside, so that she and her sister could become, for an evening, part of the chorus. It was a frivolous idea which would have been dismissed as absurd on any other day. However, the exhilaration was such that the King and Queen agreed. Accompanied by a police sergeant, a small party left the Palace and went into the street.

They wandered among the chanting, cheering merry-makers. According to Lascelles, 'the Princesses, under escort, went out and walked unrecognized about St. James's Street and Piccadilly'.[2] One member of the group remembers a much more extensive itinerary – from Buckingham Palace to Parliament Square, then to Piccadilly, St. James's Street, Bennet Street, Berkeley Square, Park Lane, and into the Ritz and Dorchester Hotels, before crossing Green Park, and ending up, once again, outside the Palace. 'It was such a happy atmosphere,' he recalls. 'Such a tremendous feeling of being alive.'[3] Apart from Margaret, all were in uniform, making them barely distinguishable from thousands of others also moving almost aimlessly in the no-longer blacked-out city centre.

To be invisible in a crowd! For an instant, the fantasy of being ordinary and unknown became real. After five years of incarceration at Windsor, and a life sentence of the public spotlight, the nation's liberation gave them an exceptional moment of personal freedom. Many years later, Elizabeth recalled that they were terrified of being recognized, 'so I pulled my uniform cap well down over my eyes'. She remembered 'lines of people linking arms and walking down Whitehall, and all of us were swept along by tides of happiness and relief'.[4] One of the party snatched a Dutch sailor's cap as a joke, and the sailor kept chasing after them, not knowing and probably not caring who they had in their midst. In the atmosphere of carefree hysteria, they did the Lambeth Walk and the hokey-cokey. When they got back to the Palace, they stood close to the railings, and helped to orchestrate a new wave of 'We want the King' cries. Unlike most people, however, they were able to supply the King. One of them was sent inside, and shortly afterwards, the King and Queen reappeared on the balcony.[5]

Next day, the holiday continued with street parties and bonfires. During the afternoon, the princesses went with their parents on a tour of bombed-out districts in East London, including a council estate in Stepney, where two blocks of flats, and one hundred and thirty people, had been wiped out by a V2 rocket two months before. The King and Queen and their daughters appeared again on the Palace balcony in the evening, as a military band entertained the crowds from the forecourt.

Similar celebrations followed the Japanese surrender in August, with the important difference that, though the royal participants were the same, a Labour Government was in office, and a Labour Prime Minister now acknowledged the cheers and addressed the crowd. In place of the romantic Churchillian rhetoric, there was a clipped Attleean homily. 'We are right to rejoice at the victory of the people,' declared the new premier, from the balcony of the Ministry of Health, 'and it is right for a short time that we should relax. But I want to remind you that we have a great deal of work to do to win the peace as we won the war.' A speech read by the King, loyally described in the press as 'firm, resonant and strong,' was broadcast through loudspeakers. The Royal Family spent the rest of the day taking curtain calls on the balcony, waving to the multitude, and acknowledging the roars of approval.

That night, the princesses repeated the escapade of 8 May. This time, however, the attempt to behave like anonymous citizens – masked princesses at the ball – did not quite succeed. Perhaps the mood was less euphoric than on VE-Day; perhaps because Princess Elizabeth was not in uniform, she was easier to identify. At any rate, they were spotted. 'Big Crowds at the Palace,' headlined *The Times*. 'Royal Family on the Balcony. Princesses Join the Throng.' The paper revealed that the King's daughters had left the Palace shortly before eleven o'clock, and that they 'were here and there recognised and quickly surrounded by cheering men and women'. But police had told the crowds that 'the princesses wished to be treated as private individuals, and they were allowed to go on their way'.[6]

IN ITSELF, the coming of peace in August did not greatly affect the everyday lives of the Royal Family, who had been re-united at Buckingham Palace earlier in the year. There had already been various symptoms of the post VE-Day phoney peace. Early in August, Elizabeth was taken to Ascot. It was a doubly memorable day. Gordon Richards won five races, carrying the royal colours to victory in the Burghclere Stakes for the first time; and, during lunch at Windsor, the King received the news from President Truman that an atom bomb had been dropped on Hiroshima.[7] Despite such excursions, and weekend trips to Windsor, it took time to re-adjust to the cratered capital and bomb-damaged royal mansion. 'It was a nasty shock to live in a town again,' says Princess Margaret.[8] The King found himself as busy as at the height of the war: the exhortatory use made of the Monarchy, if anything, increased. Peacetime austerity had its own moralising. So did the newly elected Labour Government.

In 1940 the King had favoured Lord Halifax for the premiership. During the war, however, he had grown to like and depend on Churchill, who behaved towards him with extravagant courtesy, and he was distressed by the outcome of the general election in July 1945. Apart from his familiarity with the war leader, and his dislike of change *per se*, he was alarmed about the implications for his family, and his kind. 'Thank God for the Civil Service,' he is supposed to have remarked on hearing of the huge majority for a party committed to a programme of nationalization, redistribution and social reform. In private, he was unapologetically right-wing (his wife even more so), and was often moved to explosions of anger at the latest socialist outrage, especially if he felt he had not been consulted.

He need not have worried. Though he remained much more uneasy about the Attlee governments of 1945 and 1950 than his father had been about the MacDonald ones of 1924 and 1929, there was little in reality that the Labour Cabinet wished or dared to do to discomfort him. Indeed, the new Prime Minister went out of his way to provide reassurance. At Attlee's first audience, George VI expressed disquiet at the news that Hugh Dalton, the renegade son of George V's old tutor Canon Dalton, might be made Foreign Secretary. The Labour premier immediately bowed to the King's wishes, or at least allowed the Palace to think he was doing so. Ernest Bevin became Foreign Secretary, and Dalton was sent to the Treasury instead. Thereafter, Attlee treated the Sovereign with perfect correctness, and there turned out to be as little republicanism in the Labour Party after the Second World War as there had been before it. Soon, what some saw as the incongruity of a King-Emperor presiding over a social revolution – and over the granting of self-rule to the Indian sub-continent, jewel in the imperial crown – became accepted as natural and even valuable. Whereas, in the reign of George V, Buckingham Palace had stood at the pinnacle of a confident Establishment unshaken by the arrival of a Labour Government, in the late 1940s the Royal Family managed to avoid any outward appearance of discomfiture, as the Establishment took some knocks.

Indeed, George VI's passivity arguably became even more of an asset after the war than during it. On the one hand the Royal Family could be seen as a typically British piece of camouflage, disguising and making acceptable the Government's radicalism; on the other, its existence stood as a guarantee that pragmatic caution would prevail, and radicalism kept within bounds. Thus, when Labour took major industries into public ownership (but compensated owners generously) or made adjustments to the powers of the House of Lords (but only modest ones), both left and right thanked God for the Monarchy.

For Elizabeth, peace brought to an end her brief, token excursion into ATS 'normality'. It also produced an increase in the number of her solo engagements. She was nineteen, Honorary Colonel, occasional Counsellor of State, and a performer of royal duties: cast, it was increasingly clear, in the mould of her father and grandfather, though more self-assured than George VI, and cleverer than both of them. Was there ever a moment, in her early adulthood, when she questioned what she did, or wondered, in the prevailing atmosphere of equality, and fashion for the abandoning of pomp and circumstance, whether it was worth it? If she ever indulged in such a dissident speculation, she kept her thoughts to herself. There was no visible hint of rebellion, or suggestion that her own values and those of her parents and mentors ever clashed. She was now the almost certain future Queen, who, if she did succeed, would become the third monarch of the century who had not been born to such a fate but had had it thrust upon them. As the position became clearer with the passage of time, she accepted it, knowing that the possibility of an alternative did not exist.

She did as she was told in an enclosed world where loyal and experienced advice could be taken for granted. She became used to the ritual of the royal speech, consisting of a few platitudes crafted by courtiers skilled at the job. Her itineraries just after the war reflected the priorities of Buckingham Palace, and also of the Government. Thus, in the summer of 1945, she opened a new library of the Royal College of Nursing, presented prizes and certificates to students of the Royal Free Hospital School of Medicine for Women, inspected the Fifth Battalion and Training Battalion of the Grenadier Guards, and addressed (in her recently acquired capacity of Sea Ranger Commodore) three thousand Welsh Girl Guides. She also accompanied her parents on a visit to Ulster, travelling by air for the first time, in a flight from Northolt to Long Kesh.[9]

Some apparently promising requests, however, were refused. Lascelles turned down, on her behalf, an invitation to become the first woman ever to be awarded an honorary degree by Cambridge University – despite pressure from the Chancellor, Lord Baldwin.[10] Occasionally, the proposals of Labour politicians were considered excessive. In 1947, Lascelles rejected a request from Hugh Gaitskell, the Minister of Fuel and Power, for her to attend 'The Miner Comes to Town' exhibition at Marble Arch which had recently been opened by the Prime Minister, on the grounds that she was too busy.[11]

Generally, her visits expressed support for an officially approved, but non-controversial, good cause – though sometimes what the Palace saw as non-controversial turned out to be political dynamite. This was true of a tour of Northern Ireland without her parents in March 1946, for what was described as 'the most ambitious mission undertaken by the young Heir Presumptive'. The tour gave the Princess her first experience of being used, not as a symbol above domestic politics, but as a blatant political tool by one faction.

It was a mission to underline the Union, something which a visit from British royalty, personifying United Kingdom ties, achieved more eloquently than anything. The result was a welcome both vehement

and purposeful. This was a Protestant tour and the groups and institutions she met and addressed reflected it. Sometimes the message
remained implicit. At Dungannon High School 1,200 girls sang 'Come
back to Ulster, dear Princess' to the tune of 'Come back to Erin'. On
other occasions, it was crudely and disagreeably partisan. At Ennis-
killen, the Royal Ulster Constabulary put on a display that included
an illegal still, camouflaged with peat and foliage. The producers of
illicit 'poteen' were acted by local workers, heavily made up with
rouge, and wearing paddy-hats and green three-cornered scarves. An
almost hysterical atmosphere of loyalism lasted until the Princess's
departure from Belfast on 21 March, when a mob of schoolchildren
broke flag-bedecked stands and ran to the edge of the quay. As her
cruiser left the harbour, the whole crowd sang 'Will ye no' come back
again?' and 'Auld Lang Syne'.[12]

In Northern Ireland, enthusiasm was a symptom of sectarian anxiety. Elsewhere and on other occasions, the excitement the Heiress
caused is less easily explicable, especially so soon after the election of
a Government committed to dispossessing the better off. At the beginning of 1946, support for socialism was at its zenith: Gallup put
Labour twenty per cent ahead in the polls, as the Cabinet prepared
to introduce its most radical measures.[13] Yet, such popularity – and
apparent popular support for levelling down – was not accompanied
by any decline in pro-royal sentiment. In April, a gigantic crowd came
to watch the bands of the Royal Horse and Grenadier Guards playing
on the East Terrace of Windsor Castle, to mark Princess Elizabeth's
twentieth birthday. *The Times* estimated it at 40,000, a figure three
times as large as for any such event in the 1930s.[14] Perhaps the austerity
and restrictions, as great after the war as during it, sparked a reaction.
Such gatherings, and the carnival mood that infused them, may have
been a form of escape, a release from drabness. But there was also a
deep personal interest in the Princess: in her beauty, her clothes, her
shy smile, and, increasingly, her prospects.

When and whom would she marry? The assumption was that she
would do so soon; this, after all, had been the point of her education.
'That the Heiress to the Throne would stay unmarried', as Crawfie
archly but accurately put it, 'was unthinkable'.[15] The matter had been
discussed in the popular papers since the 1930s. The difficulty lay in

finding a suitable consort, at a time when suitability still entailed reasons of state. No heir to the throne had ever contracted a marriage for reasons that did not take dynastic considerations into account. However, conventions were changing. Although Edward VIII had been refused permission to marry the woman of his choice, the marriage of George VI had been a non-arranged, romantic and successful one. It was now accepted that a husband could not be forced upon the Princess. It was also accepted, however, that she could not be allowed unrestricted freedom, and that the range of possible suitors was limited to the diaspora of European royalty, few of whom were now in reigning families, and to the upper ranks of the British aristocracy. Though the Princess was well known, she did not know many people. Moreover, her small circle of friends, acquaintances and sufficiently distant relatives included hardly any young men who would be acceptable as a consort, or who would presume to such a role. That she was desirable, there was no question: but to pay court to the Heiress to the world's premier Monarchy required an exceptional degree of passion, confidence or gall.

Perhaps she sensed these difficulties, for in practice they never arose. There were minor flirtations, and stories of heirs to great titles who took liberties and were frozen out for ever. But there was never a phase of boyfriends, of falling in and out of love, of trial and error. From early in her adolescence she took a friendly and romantic interest in one man, and there is no evidence that she ever seriously considered anybody else. 'She fell in love with him,' says one former courtier.[16] According to another, it was a matter of coming contentedly to terms with what had to be. 'There really was no one else she could possibly marry but Prince Philip.'[17] Yet if Philip was, in a sense, hand-picked, it was not the Princess's parents, or the Court, who did the picking.

Prince Philip of Greece, nearly five years older than the Princess, had several commanding advantages: he was royal, on first acquaintance extremely personable and, though not British, he gave an excellent impression of being so. The British Royal Family had known him since he was a small child, when he had taken tea at Buckingham Palace with Queen Mary, who reported him 'a nice little boy with very blue eyes'.[18] He had been in the company of Princess Elizabeth at several pre-war family gatherings, including the wedding of the

Duke and Duchess of Kent in 1934, and the Coronation three years later. Even before the Coronation, Philip's name had been linked in the press with that of the Princess, as one of a tiny list of hypothetical bridegrooms.[19] The first significant encounter, however, took place on 22 July 1939, during the short interlude between the Canada-America trip and the outbreak of war, in the course of a Royal Family visit to the Royal Naval College, Dartmouth. According to Crawfie, the introduction took place in the nursery of the house of the Captain of the College. Philip, who had recently been admitted as a cadet, was taken in to see the princesses, who were playing with a clockwork train. Allegedly, the new friendship was sealed with ginger crackers and lemonade, and by a game of tennis.[20] As far as the adult, non-nursery world was concerned, however, the first important meeting took place at a tea party on board the royal yacht *Victoria and Albert*. This had been arranged – engineered might conceivably be a better word – by Lord Mountbatten, the King's cousin and Philip's uncle. 'Philip came back aboard *V & A* for tea and was a great success with the children,' Mountbatten wrote in his diary.[21] There are also filmic and photographic records of the day. One amateur snap shows the Greek cadet and the much smaller princess together alone, apart from the watching photographer, playing croquet in the Captain's garden. A still picture from a contemporary newsreal encapsulates the whole drama, as if it were a tableau: the child-like, solemn Princess Elizabeth, looking much younger than thirteen in a sea of adult faces, her parents and sister, Philip, laughing at some private joke, Mountbatten, also smiling, at his shoulder.

'It is hard to believe,' suggests Mountbatten's official biographer, discussing his subject's attitude towards the 1939 Dartmouth meeting, that 'no thought crossed his mind that an admirable husband for the future Queen Elizabeth might be readily available'.[22] In view of Mountbatten's character, his personal and dynastic ambition, his taste for intrigue, it is more than hard. We may take it for granted that one did. It is possible that such a thought had also occurred to the King and Queen. They were aware, after all, of the need to find a son-in-law before very long, and a foreign prince training for the British Navy was an obvious possibility. In Philip's case, however, there were some worrying features.

Indeed, the Prince's origins and early life raised the question of what 'royal' meant, if it was to be treated as a qualification. Should it be defined in terms of bloodlines, or did it relate to real-world wealth, reputation, and constitutional significance? By the first criterion, Philip was unquestionably royal, in one sense more so than Princess Elizabeth, for he had royalty on both sides of his family, instead of just one. He also happened to be related to the Princess several times over. His most important relationship was through his mother, Princess Alice of Battenberg, who was sister to Lord Mountbatten, mentor and cousin to George VI. But there were also other strands. He was even a fourth cousin once removed through collateral descendants of George III.[23] Moreover, he was not just descended from royalty, he had been born into a reigning Royal Family, the grandson and nephew of Greek kings.

On the other hand, by the second criterion, the current standing of his dynasty, Philip scored badly, or not at all. His birth took place at the Greek royal residence of Mon Repos on the Ionian island of Corfu in June 1921. This did not remain his home for long. Within eighteen months, following the passing of a death sentence by a Greek revolutionary court on his father, Prince Andrew, he and all his family became refugees. A few years later, Philip's mother recorded her thanks to George V for his personal intervention, 'realizing the deadly peril' her husband was in, to ensure that a warship got him 'out of the clutches of the military dictators and brought him and his family away from Greece' on the day after the trial.[24] The exile of Andrew, his wife, four daughters and baby son, turned out effectively to be permanent. Dispossessed, impoverished and in the case of Prince Andrew embittered, they settled in a house provided by Philip's aunt, Marie Bonaparte, at St. Cloud, on the outskirts of Paris.

It was to be a shambolic, meagre existence, built on fading dreams and painful memories. Philip's birthplace in Corfu had been lacking in amenities: in the early 1920s, there was no electricity, gas, running hot water or proper heating.[25] But it had been grand in style, and magnificent in location. By contrast, the villa in St. Cloud was humiliatingly unpretentious, 'a very simple country house,' according to one of Philip's sisters.[26] Cut off from the friendships and rivalries that mattered to him, Prince Andrew, the former commander of armies, immersed himself in the writing of a book appropriately called *Towards Disaster*, about the military endeavours, and their failure, for which he had stood trial. His wife, with five children to care for, suffered a nervous breakdown, and turned to religion. The couple separated in 1930, Andrew eventually moving to Monte Carlo, where he died in December 1944.

Against this troubled background, Philip began a cultural shift. Later, there was the question of whether 'Philip the Greek' was ever Greek at all; although born a Greek citizen, the son of a Greek prince, there were no 'ethnic' Greeks in his recent ancestry. In some ways this helped, but it also laid him open to a more damning charge. The description of him as a 'blond Viking', partly on the basis of his Danish ancestry, became a way of avoiding the fact, embarrassing in the 1940s, that his strongest family links were with Germany. All his four sisters married Germans and reverted to a German identity.

Until Philip was adult, he really belonged to no nation, except the freemasonry of Romanov, Habsburg and Saxe-Coburg-Gotha descendants, which conferred an entry ticket to the great houses and palaces of Europe. It was the benign interest of his mother's relatives, and perhaps a family appreciation that England was the most hopeful place for an uprooted royal to seek his fortune, that pushed him in a British direction. From early childhood, there were frequent English trips, especially to see Philip's Battenberg grandmother, the Marchioness of Milford Haven, herself the eldest grandchild of Queen Victoria and sister of the last Tsarina. Sophie ('Tiny'), youngest of Philip's sisters, recalls annual visits by the children to the Marchioness in the 1920s. She remembers sunbathing on the roof at Kensington Palace, where the old lady had an apartment, meetings with members of the British Royal Family, and most influential of all, being regaled with stories of their Europe-wide connections, which contrasted so dramatically with the life they lived in St. Cloud. These expeditions served as a reminder, and a tonic: if the children had any doubt about their social standing, the Marchioness removed them.

At about the time of his parents' separation, Philip left the American school in St. Cloud at which he had been a pupil, and was sent to Cheam, an English preparatory establishment in Surrey; and from there to Salem, in Baden, a school owned by one of his German brothers-in-law and run by the legendary Kurt Hahn. But for Hitler, the rest of his education might have been German. In 1934, however, Hahn moved to Scotland to escape the Nazis, setting up a new school, Gordonstoun. Philip became a pupil and, as a result, in the words of the Countess of Airlie, was 'brought up to all intents and purposes an Englishman,'[27] except that few Englishmen ever had to suffer the rigours and eccentricities of the Hahn–Gordonstoun form of educational progressiveness.

'I don't think anybody thinks I had a father,' Philip allegedly once complained. 'Most people think that Dickie's my father anyway.'[28] Philip had been much affected by the breakdown of his parents' marriage, and retained a great sympathy for Prince Andrew. 'He really loved his father,' says one close associate. 'He had a big image of him which persisted, and his death was a great shock to him.'[29] After 1930, however, he saw much more of his mother, Princess Alice, and was closer to her, despite all her difficulties – which were extreme. In addition to the psychological problems which developed during Philip's childhood, she was congenitally deaf. Later, she used to say that she could not communicate with her children until they were old enough to speak, when she became able to read their lips.[30] But the presentation of her as a demented recluse was false. Friends recall her, except when ill, as forceful, intelligent and amusing. Despite her marital and other difficulties, she was responsible for translating her husband's book from Greek into English. Conceivably, as one friend of Philip puts it, her eventual decision to found a Greek Orthodox monastic order, and become a nun in it, 'was a very clever solution to the problem of how she fitted into the world,' as an elderly royal widow without money, but with an interest in good causes.[31]

Nevertheless, Philip's early life, with an absent father and often psychologically absent mother, was by any standards disturbed and unstable. Much of it, especially when his mother had to go into a sanatorium, was spent migrating between schools and foster-homes provided by relatives. There was a confusion: uncertainty, neglect, and the feeling of being special mixed together. The only son, as well as the youngest child, Philip was a particular focus of family attention, especially to his four sisters who adored, petted and mothered him. However, within the space of a few months in 1931–2 all of them solved the problem of a disintegrating home by marrying German princes, scattering what was left of his family across Europe.

There were fixed points: Salem, for summer holidays, was one. When Philip was at school in Britain, his Uncle George, Marquess of Milford Haven and son of the dowager Marchioness, provided another, becoming his guardian in school vacations, and helping with fees. Although George was his main benefactor, Philip was also a frequent visitor at the house of his other uncle, Lord Mountbatten. 'He was around with us a lot from about 1934,' says Patricia.[32] Another refuge was Gordonstoun where Philip became a model pupil – athletic, outgoing, enterprising, effortlessly displaying precisely those attributes which it had been Hahn's vision to produce.

Yet the standard portrayal of Philip in his teens as a kind of *Boys' Own Paper* hero misses something out. There was a picaresque quality, the sense of the adventurer who lives by his wits, and for whom what one early writer called 'the lean upbringing of expatriate royalty,'[33] had provided as keen a training as any continental theory. Philip's cousin Alexandra, Queen of Yugoslavia (and a fellow expatriate), recalled him on holiday with her family in Venice, a year before the Dartmouth meeting, as a genial sponger, living in a style not uncommon among displaced princelings, and giving the impression of 'a huge hungry dog, perhaps a friendly collie who had never had a basket of his own'.[34]

The summer of 1938 was an especially waif-like moment. George Milford Haven had died the previous April, leaving Prince Philip, as Philip Ziegler puts it, 'stateless, nameless and not far from penniless'[35] and particularly in need of open-handed friends. Luckily, more substantial help was available. The death of one benefactor cleared the way for another, of incomparably greater influence. Observing Philip's predicament, George's younger brother Louis – 'Uncle Dickie' – stepped in, and took over what remained of the job of bringing his nephew up. It was a generous undertaking, but also, in view of the young man's obvious talents, a well judged one. Lord Mountbatten was a prominent naval officer and it had, in any case, already been planned that the best place for a *déraciné* young prince with a taste for travel, and no home base, was the British Navy. Hence, on 1 May 1939, Philip joined Dartmouth College as a Special Entry Cadet.

When Prince Philip and Princess Elizabeth met in July, he was an unknown young man barely two months into training. What did he make of his world-famous distant cousin, with her home in Buckingham Palace? Did he distinguish between the celebrity and the child-like person? It would be surprising if she did not have an impact, because of who she was: but it would also be surprising if, at this stage, Philip's interest was romantic. Handsome and confident eighteen-year-old young men are not often greatly attracted by thirteen-year-old little girls scarcely out of short socks. According to Queen Alexandra, the previous summer the Greek prince had shown himself a girl-crazy party-goer on the Venetian social scene. 'Blondes, brunettes and red head charmers,' she recalled, 'Philip gallantly and I think quite impartially squired them all.'[36] Hélène Cordet, a cabaret singer who had been a childhood friend (and who was later dubbed by the French press as 'the mystery blonde' and 'the one who will *not* be invited to the wedding') had a similar view of him.[37] Other accounts also show him as a happy-go-lucky enjoyer of female company, and player of the field. Yet Princess Elizabeth was pretty, royal, and obviously a catch. The thoughts that must have passed through his uncle's mind, may also have passed through his own. At the time, however, there were other pressing things to consider. War was imminent, with everything that such a prospect offered to a prize-winning naval cadet, with excellent connections.

If the British Royal Family had a good war, Philip in a more conventional sense, had a highly distinguished one. After a period of escorting contingents of troops from Australia to the Middle East, he was involved in several engagements in the Mediterranean. During the battle of Matapan against the Italian fleet, he controlled the searchlights of his ship, and was mentioned in dispatches. 'Thanks to his alertness and appreciation of the situation,' reported his Captain, 'we were able to sink in five minutes two eight-inch-gun Italian cruisers.'[38] Philip spent much of 1941 with the British Fleet in the East Mediterranean. In the spring, Greek resistance to the Germans crumbled, and on 23 April, King George of Greece and his Government were evacuated to Crete. The same day, Princess Elizabeth wrote to Winston Churchill thanking him for a bunch of roses he and his wife had sent her for her fifteenth birthday two days earlier. In her letter, she offered her sympathy, in view of the 'very worrying time' he had lately been having.[39] Perhaps she had Philip's recent dangers and exploits, and those of his royal house, partly in mind.

Such an officer was likely to be rapidly promoted in wartime, especially if he had ambition. In Philip's case, the energy and drive he had shown at Gordonstoun and Dartmouth, together with a view of his own long-term future which received ample encouragement from his Uncle Dickie, helped to push him forward. Mike Parker, a fellow officer who had also been a fellow cadet and later became his equerry, recalls thinking of the Prince as a dedicated professional and as a man heading for the very top: somebody who already 'had mapped out a course to which he was going to stick . . . a plan already in his mind that had probably been set before he left'.[40] In October 1942, Philip was made First Lieutenant and second-in-command of a destroyer, at twenty-one one of the youngest officers to hold such a post.

His adventures continued. The following July, while courtiers in Buckingham Palace exchanged learned memoranda about the date of Princess Elizabeth's coming-of-age and its constitutional significance, Prince Philip was aboard HMS *Wallace* off the coast of Sicily, helping to provide cover for the Allied attack and possibly bombarding one of his brothers-in-law, on the German side, in the process. In July 1944, his ship was sent to the Pacific, where he remained until after the dropping of atomic bombs on Hiroshima and Nagasaki, and until the final surrender of Japan.[41]

> Wherein I spake of most disastrous chances,
> Of moving accidents by flood and field,
> Of hair-breadth 'scapes, i' the imminent deadly breach . . .
> My story being done,
> She gave me for my pains a world of sighs.

It is hard to think of an experience of war further removed than that of the Heiress Presumptive, in her castellated schoolroom.

At first, Philip's busy war provided little scope for contact with the British Royal Family. Shore leaves were brief, makeshift and hectic. Parker felt that it was a bond between him and Prince Philip that both of them were 'orphans' (Parker was Australian), with a problem about where to stay.[42] In London, Philip was often put up by the Mountbattens, who had been bombed out of previous homes and were living in a house in Chester Street. Mountbatten's younger daughter Pamela recalls that she and a camp bed would move from room to room to provide space for her cousin, who would 'come and go and added glamour and sparkle to every occasion'.[43] His favours were distributed widely. Queen Alexandra, herself in London at the time, maintained that 'the fascination of Philip had spread like influenza, I knew, through a whole string of girls'.[44] But there was no special girlfriend. According to Parker, 'never once did I ever find him involved with any particular one. It was very much in a crowd formation'.[45] Other stories about Philip in wartime confirm the impression of a hedonistic, though also cashless, socialite whose uniform, looks, charm and connections opened every door – a character out of Evelyn Waugh or Olivia Manning, who popped up wherever in the world there were enough members of the pre-war upper class to hold a party.

Princess Elizabeth was sometimes in his thoughts. Alexandra met up with him in 1941 in Cape Town, where he was on leave from a troop ship. When she came across him writing a letter, he told her it was to 'Lilibet'. Alexandra assumed – such were the mental processes of displaced royalty – that he was fishing for invitations.[46] Perhaps she was right. It was not, however, until the end of 1943 that he was able to accept one of importance. This was to spend Christmas with the Royal Family at Windsor Castle, and to attend the annual Windsor family pantomime.[47] Philip accepted, with pleasure.

It was a private invitation. However, both the show, and the Prince's attendance at it, were reported in the press. In November, it was announced that a stage had been erected in a large hall in the 'country mansion' where the princesses were staying; that a cast of forty was rehearsing under the joint direction of Princess Elizabeth and a local schoolmaster, who had together written the script; and that twenty-five village school children would provide the chorus, accompanied by a Guards band.[48] A few days before Christmas, The Times reported that 'Prince Philip of Greece' had attended the third of three performances, sitting in the front row. Others in the audience included the King and Queen, various courtiers, royal relatives, and villagers.[49]

According to Lisa Sheridan, Prince Philip was more than just a passive spectator of the seventeen-year-old Elizabeth as she acted, joked, tap-danced and sang a few songs just in front of him. 'Both in the audience and in the wings he thoroughly entered into the fun, and was welcomed by the princesses as a delightful boy cousin.'[50] The pantomime was followed by Christmas festivities. On Boxing Day, there was a family meal at the Castle including retainers, Prince Philip and the young Marquess of Milford Haven. 'After dinner, and some charades,' Sir Alan Lascelles recorded in his diary, 'they rolled back the carpet in the crimson drawing-room, turned on the gramophone, and frisked and capered away till near 1 a.m.'[51]

Crawfie maintained it was a turning point: thereafter, Elizabeth took a growing interest in Philip's activities and whereabouts, and exchanged letters with him. The Heiress to the throne enjoyed the idea of being like other girls, she suggested, with a young man in the services to write to.[52]

IF ELIZABETH only began to think seriously about Philip in December 1943, she was way behind the drifting circuit of European royalty and its hangers on, which had been talking about the supposed relationship, almost as if a marriage was a *fait accompli*, for two or three years. Of course, Philip's eligibility as a bachelor prince, together with his semi-Britishness, was likely to make him the subject of conjecture in any case. However, before the end of 1943, the couple had little opportunity to get to know each other. What is curious, therefore, is the firmness of the predictions, and the confidence of the rumours, from quite early in the war.

One of the first to pick up and record the story of an intended marriage, in its definite form, was Chips Channon, befriender of Balkan princelings. He heard it at the beginning of 1941 during a visit to Athens, where the tale seemed to be current among the Greek Royal Family, whose interest had been sharpened by the presence of Prince Philip in their midst, on leave from his ship. After meeting Philip at a cocktail party, Channon noted in his diary, 'He is to be our Prince Consort, and that is why he is serving in our Navy.' The alliance between the British and Greek royal houses had supposedly been arranged by the finessing hand of Philip's uncle, Lord Mountbatten. Philip was handsome and charming, noted Channon, 'but I deplore such a marriage. He and Princess Elizabeth are too inter-related.'[53]

Such an item was, of course, no more than gossip, a symptom of the decadence and anxieties of the Greek court. Princess Elizabeth was fourteen at the time, and the notion of the British Government or Royal Family fixing a future marriage alliance with the Greek one is preposterous. According to Mountbatten a few years later, it was at about this time that Philip 'made up his mind and asked me to apply for [British] naturalisation for him'.[54] Perhaps it was news of this plan, combined with Philip's evident closeness to his British uncle, that inspired the tale. Nevertheless, the existence of such a lively and, as it turned out accurate, rumour nearly three years before a serious friendship is supposed to have started, puts the Prince's visit to witness the Princess performing into perspective. Had Mountbatten been involved behind the scenes? It is possible. 'He was a shrewd operator and intriguer, always going round corners, never straight at it,' says one former courtier from the 1940s, 'he was ruthless in his approach to the royals.'[55] Another suggests: 'Dickie seems to have planned it in his own mind, but it was not an arranged marriage.'[56] It would certainly have been in character for him to have followed up on the 1939 introduction. That, however, is a matter for speculation. What is clear is that in the course of 1944, despite the huge pressures on him, Lord Mountbatten took it upon himself to follow through his match-making initiative with operational resolve.

One effect of the Christmas 1943 get-together, and of its publication in the press, was to fuel the rumours. Prince Philip himself was reticent. Parker knew that Philip had begun to visit the Royal Family when he was in England, but he did not find out the significance of the visits until after the war.[57] Others had more sensitive antennae. In February 1944, Channon again got the story, this time from a source very close to the throne – his own parents-in-law, Lord and Lady Iveagh, who had just taken tea with the King and Queen. The Windsor party had evidently been a success. 'I do believe,' Channon reaffirmed, 'that a marriage may well be arranged one day between Princess Elizabeth and Prince Philip of Greece.'[58] Meanwhile, in Egypt, where the Greek royal family presided over the Government-in-exile, interest had deepened, and with good reason. Within months, or possibly a few weeks, of the Windsor meeting, Philip had declared his intentions to the Greek king. The diary of Sir Alan Lascelles contains a significant entry for 2 April 1944 in which he records that George VI had told him that Prince Philip of Greece had recently asked his uncle, George of Greece, whether he thought he could be considered as a suitor for the hand of Princess Elizabeth. The proposition had been rejected.[59] However, it was early days.

In August 1944, the British ambassador, Sir Miles Lampson, recorded meeting Prince Philip, once again on leave, at a ball in Alexandria, in the company of the Greek crown prince and princess. Lampson found him 'a most attractive youth'. In the course of the evening, the crown princess let slip 'that Philip would do very well for Princess Elizabeth!' an idea now of long-standing, and one on which the beleaguered Greek royal family was evidently pinning high hopes.

Philip's presence in Egypt, however, inspired more than a minor indiscretion from a relative. On 23 August, according to Lampson, Lord Mountbatten, now Supreme Allied Commander in South East Asia, arrived in Cairo by air and proceeded to unfold a most extraordinary cloak-and-dagger tale. The purpose of his mission, Mountbatten explained as they drove to the embassy from the aerodrome, was to arrange for Prince Philip, 'being a very promising officer in the British Navy,' to apply for British nationality. Gravely, Mountbatten explained that King George VI had become concerned about the depleted numbers of his close relatives, and believed that, if Philip became properly British, 'he should be an additional asset to the British Royal Family and a great help to them in carrying out their royal functions'. It was therefore his intention, he continued, to sound out Philip, and then the king of Greece, about his proposition. In the course of the same day, both were sounded, together with the crown prince, and all three agreed. Early that afternoon, a satisfied Mountbatten left by aeroplane for Karachi to resume his Command.[60]

What should we make of this very curious account? Mountbatten's explanation for his 'soundings' is obviously unconvincing – the one thing the British Monarchy did not need was functional help from a young foreign royal, let alone a Greek one, just because he happened to be on the market. The only way that Philip could be 'an additional asset' to the Windsors was by marrying into them, and this, as Lascelles's note the previous April shows, he by now wished to do. It seems much more likely that Mountbatten's mission was part of a considered plan, aimed at remoulding Philip for the requirements of the position both uncle and nephew wished him to hold. To make such an objective obtainable, Philip needed to be, not so much British, but non-Greek, in view of the unsavoury connections of his own dynasty. In short, the Egyptian whistle-stop visit was an opening move. Such an explanation is consistent with the behaviour of Lord Mountbatten over the next two or three years, as he bent ears and pulled strings in Buckingham Palace, Westminster and Whitehall, at every opportunity. So great, indeed, was Mountbatten's determination on his nephew's behalf, that at one point Prince Philip was moved to chide him gently for almost forcing him 'to do the wooing by proxy'.[61]

The wooing proceeded apace. There were meetings between Philip and Elizabeth at Buckingham Palace, and also at Coppins, the home of the Kents, as the ubiquitous Channon discovered when he inspected the visitors' book there in October 1944.[62] The problem from the start was not the Prince's courtship, but the British Government, concerned about its wartime Balkan diplomacy, and the hesitation of the Princess's parents. Despite Mountbatten's bold claim to Lampson in August that the British King was behind the naturalization initiative, nearly six months elapsed before Buckingham Palace made even tentative inquiries at the Home Office on Philip's behalf. 'The King asked me recently what steps would have to be taken to enable Prince Philip of Greece (Louis Mountbatten's nephew) to become a British subject,' Sir Alan Lascelles wrote to the relevant official in March 1945. The King, he explained, did not want the matter dealt with officially yet: he only wished to know 'how it could be most easily and expeditiously handled' at an appropriate time.[63] In August, Lascelles went to see the Permanent Secretary at the Home Office, at the King's behest, observing crustily, 'I suspect there may be a matrimonial nigger in the woodpile.'[64]

The question of Philip's naturalization, however, only became a matter for political discussion at the highest level in October 1945, by which time Greek politics, and the Greek royal family's embroilment, had become even more tangled. The Prime Minister, Foreign Secretary and Home Secretary now considered the proposal put to them by the Palace but, faced with the prospect of stirring a hornet's nest, postponed a decision. The danger, it was explained to the King, was that such a step would be interpreted in Greece as support for the Greek royalists. Alternatively, given the feverish nature of politics in the Balkan peninsula, it might be taken 'as a sign that the future prospects of the Greek Monarchy are admitted to be dark,' and that Greek royals were scurrying for safety abroad. In view of these competing risks, Attlee suggested that the question should be left until after elections and a plebiscite had been held in Greece the following year.[65]

When Prince Philip returned from the Far East early in 1946, the problem acquired a new urgency. Philip's undemanding peacetime job, as a member of staff of a naval training establishment in North Wales, provided ample opportunity for frequent visits to Buckingham Palace, where his charm worked, not only on Princess Elizabeth, but on Crawfie, who found him a breath of fresh air in the stuffy Court, 'a forthright and completely natural young man, given to say what he thought'. Above all, he could talk to Elizabeth as no outsider had ever dared to do before. Soon, she was taking more trouble over her appearance, and began to play the hit record 'People Will Say We're in Love,' from the musical *Oklahoma!* incessantly on the gramophone.[66] In May, in an atmosphere of continuing uncertainty, Philip went to Salem for the second marriage of his sister Tiny, whom he had not seen for nine years, and whose first husband had been killed in the war. He told her about his relationship with Princess Elizabeth. 'He was thinking about getting engaged,' Tiny recalls. 'Uncle Dickie was being helpful.'[67]

There was as yet no engagement, official or unofficial. The real reason for Philip's request for naturalization was coyly avoided in official memoranda – though the involvement of senior members of the Government indicated that it was known or suspected. Publicly, a pretence had to be kept up. If the Prince and Princess were present at the same party, they did not dance together, as a precaution.[68] However, there were clues which led to leaks. The addition of Philip's name to the guest list for Balmoral in 1946, when it had not been included on the advance list, aroused much below-stairs interest at the Palace.[69] A pattern developed which became the norm with royal betrothals: stories in the foreign press, picked up by British popular newspapers, followed by Palace denials whose cautious nature fuelled speculation. In September 1946, after a year of mounting gossip, Sir Alan Lascelles took the novel step of repudiating reports of an engagement, but without commenting on the future possibility of one. The story finally broke, not in words but − and it was another significant precedent − on celluloid: a newsreel shot of an exchange of tender glances at the wedding of Lord Mountbatten's daughter Patricia to Lord Brabourne, as Philip, an usher, helped Elizabeth, a bridesmaid, with her fur wrap.

A Greek plebiscite took place on 1 September 1946, restoring the Greek Monarchy: the restoration of George II, however, so far from reducing the political embarrassment of an alliance with the Greek dynasty, increased it, by highlighting King George's legacy of authoritarian rule.[70] In the meantime, the issue of Philip's national status, even his eligibility, as a foreigner, for a peacetime commission in the Royal Navy, remained unresolved. At first, he was told he could stay in the Navy;[71] then the Admiralty had second thoughts, and ruled that his retention depended on his naturalization.[72]

Matters ground to a virtual halt. The obstacle continued to be the attitude of the Government but also, it had become clear, the coolness of the Court. Faced with a Kafka-like civil service, a hesitant British King, and his dubious set of advisers, Uncle Dickie decided to harass the Palace.

It did the trick. The Palace's patience snapped. Following one particularly vigorous piece of Mountbatten lobbying, Lascelles informed the King somewhat testily that Dickie had telephoned him yet again on the subject of Prince Philip's naturalization, and that he had suggested that, as Prince Philip's uncle and guardian, there was no reason why he should not take up the matter himself, without reference to the Monarch.[73] Mountbatten took this as a *carte blanche*. Replying that 'nothing would suit him better,' he asked to see the King. Then he moved, striking hard and fast, making good use of his standing with the Labour Government. On 14 November, he saw the Home Secretary, and then the Prime Minister, and secured the agreement of both to the naturalization, and also that Philip would be known, in his new British persona, as 'HRH Prince Philip' – an extra bit of varnish to his nation-swapping nephew's image. Next day he wrote triumphantly to the Prince, sending him a form to fill, instructing him on what to put in it, and promising path-smoothing letters.[74]

The politics remained delicate. Backbench Labour MPs, many of whom took a keen interest both in foreign affairs and immigration policy, were liable to object not just that Philip was linked to an unpleasant dynasty but also that his naturalization, at a time when many aliens were clamouring for it, constituted favourable treatment. Mountbatten anticipated this danger by showering the press with detailed information designed to show that, in everything that mattered, Philip was already British.

In August, the Labour MP and journalist Tom Driberg, who was friendly with Mountbatten, took Philip on an educational trip round Parliament. Afterwards, he offered to help with newspaper articles. Mountbatten had replied with an urgent request that Driberg should not allow 'any form of pre-publicity to break, which I feel would be fatal' – while also sending the MP a biographical information pack for use later, which would show that his nephew 'really is more English than any other nationality.'[75] Now he asked Driberg to use this material, which recounted that Philip was the son of 'the late General Prince Andrew of Greece and of Denmark, GCVO,' that he had spent no more than three months in Greece since the age of one, and that he spoke no Greek. Mountbatten also asked Driberg to persuade his 'Left Wing friends' – that is, Labour MPs who might ask awkward questions – that Philip had 'nothing whatever to do with the political set-up in Greece, or any of our reactionaries.' Finally, he briefed the Press Association that 'the Prince's desire to be British dated back several years before the rumours about the engagement,' and somewhat disingenuously, had 'no possible connection with such rumours'.[76] To his great relief – as, no doubt, to that of Philip and Elizabeth – the press rose to the occasion. Most newspapers printed the Mountbatten memorandum almost verbatim, but without attribution, and as if it were news. *The Times* even obligingly suggested that, but for the war, Philip might have become a British subject on passing out from Dartmouth in 1939.[77]

Philip turned down the offer of 'HRH,' which was anomalous once he stopped being Greek, preferring to stick to his naval rank. There remained the question of his surname. On this, Dickie received his reward. Philip's Danish-derived dynastic name, Schleswig-Holstein-Sonderburg-Glücksburg, did little to assist the desired transformation. The ex-prince therefore turned to his mother's and uncle's family, adopting the appellation 'Mountbatten', itself the anglicized version of a foreign name changed during an earlier bout of xenophobia. Lord Mountbatten took the name change back to the King and Home Secretary, and fixed that too,[78] and on 18th March 1947 the change of nationality of Lieutenant Philip Mountbatten of 16 Chester Street appeared in the *London Gazette*.

There was a sequel to the saga of Philip's rushed naturalization. In November 1972 Lord Dilhorne, the former Lord Chancellor, replied to an inquiry from Lord Mountbatten with a remarkable piece of information. It was undeniably the case, he wrote, that under a 1705 Act of Parliament all descendants of the Electress Sophie of Hanover were British subjects. The point had, indeed, been tested in a 1956 case involving Prince Ernst August of Hanover, which concluded with a decision in the House of Lords that the Prince was a British subject by virtue of the same Act. Philip was, of course, a descendant of the Electress, through Queen Victoria. '. . . [S]o it appears,' wrote Dilhorne, 'that the naturalization of Prince Philip was quite unnecessary and of no effect for you cannot naturalize someone who is already a British subject . . .' The law was quite clear: the Queen's consort had had British nationality since the date of his birth.[79]

6

I F UNCLE DICKIE and his nephew believed that Buckingham Palace
was dragging its feet over procedures which, when complete, would
remove the major political objection to a marriage, they were probably
right. Buffeted by his daughter, the King made enquiries. A few days
before the Japanese surrender, Sir Alan Lascelles even wrote that
George VI was 'interesting himself keenly' in the question of Philip's
naturalization.[1] But the King did not press his advisers to speed things
along, and his advisers did not press ministers. It took the energetic
intervention of Lord Mountbatten to bring the matter to a conclusion.
Indeed, a profound ambivalence seems to have characterized the attitude of the entire Court, almost until the engagement was announced.

The Windsors were a harmonious family, and Elizabeth's views
were usually respected. It is interesting, therefore, that on something
so important there should have been a difference of opinion. The
explanation, common enough in royal romances through the centuries, seems to have been that the qualities that made the suitor
lovable to the Heiress, did not have the same effect on those who
guarded over the inheritance.

There were good grounds for approving of Prince Philip. In looks,
public manner, war record, even in his choice of the Royal Navy, he
fitted the part of 'crown consort' to perfection. The reasons for objecting to him were more complex. Some were obvious – in particular,
the fact that, as Crawfie unerringly put it, he was a 'prince without a
home or kingdom,' and hence, in seeking the hand of a British princess
who had both, was aiming too high.[2] But there were other factors. In
particular, ambivalence towards Philip reflected ambivalence towards
his uncle. Though Mountbatten was close to the King, he was also
known for his politicking and intrigue, and for his intimacy with the
Labour Government. There seems to have been a dislike of conceding

yet another round to Uncle Dickie's apparently ungovernable ambitions, and a fear that in doing so a fifth columnist might be introduced who would give Mountbatten the chance to exert a reforming influence on the style and traditions of Buckingham Palace.[3]

As far as the King and Queen themselves were concerned, there were personal reasons for not being rushed into a precipitate match. Lady Elizabeth Bowes-Lyon had been twenty-two when she accepted the proposal of the Duke of York in 1923. Her daughter was a mere seventeen at the time of Prince Philip's first formal request to be considered as a suitor. Queen Mary's belief, as related to Lady Airlie, that Elizabeth's parents simply considered her too young for marriage, may well be right. So too may Lady Airlie's own theory that the King was miserable about the prospect of letting her go, that his elder daughter 'was his constant companion in shooting, walking, riding – in fact in everything,' and he dreaded losing her.[4] Both views are also compatible with Wheeler-Bennett's suggestion that the King regarded Elizabeth as not only too young but too inexperienced, and found it hard to believe that she had fallen in love with the first young man she had ever met.[5]

In addition, there was the Prince himself – and here there was a contradiction that has continued to dog him all his life. Philip had a capacity to attract admiration and to cause irritation in equal measure. At the time, he was a man with enthusiastic supporters, but also with angry detractors. On the one hand, friends extolled his energy, directness, and ability to lead, attributes that brought him success at school and Dartmouth and in the Navy, and helped to win the hearts of many an English débutante and émigré countess. On the other, his forthright manner made some older people suspicious. What worked with naval ratings and princesses – abruptness, a democratic style, intolerance of humbug – grated at Court, and in the grander houses of the aristocracy. A courtier once told Harold Nicolson that both the King and the Queen 'felt he was rough, ill-tempered, uneducated and would probably not be faithful.'[6] According to a former adviser to the King: 'Some of the people who were guests at Balmoral thought him rather unpolished'.

There was also something else, alluded to in the last chapter: Philip's supposed (and actual) connections with the nation which, at the time of his first overtures, Britain was engaged in fighting. For all his acquired Englishness, there was something in Philip's character, in his tendency to put backs up, and in his mixture of rootlessness and dubious roots, that stirred in the previous generation of high aristocrats a mixture of snobbery and xenophobia. 'The kind of people who didn't like Prince Philip were the kind who didn't like Mountbatten,' suggests an ex-courtier. 'It was all bound up in the single word: "German".'[7]

In view of the Germanic links of the British Royal Family over the preceding two centuries, this was scarcely a rational prejudice, but it was undoubtedly there. The strongest evidence of its existence is provided by unpublished sections of the diary of Jock (later Sir John) Colville, who had been a private secretary to Neville Chamberlain and then to Winston Churchill, and became Princess Elizabeth's private secretary in the summer of 1947. During his first stay at Balmoral in the same year, Colville noted with fascination the prevailing atmosphere of bitterness towards the ex-Greek prince. 'Lords Salisbury, Eldon and Stanley think him no gentleman,' he recorded; 'and in a sense they are right. They also profess to see in him a Teutonic strain.'[8] 'People in the generation which had fought in the First World War were not very much in favour of what they called "the Hun",' says a former adviser to George VI.[9] An aristocrat linked to the Conservative Party used privately to refer to Philip as 'Charlie Kraut'.[10] One of the fiercest of Philip's opponents was the Queen's brother, David Bowes-Lyon, who did his best to influence his sister against the match.[11]

What exactly did being 'no gentleman' mean? There were several, generally unspoken elements. 'He wasn't part of the aristocracy', suggests a former courtier meaning that he did not share British aristocratic assumptions.[12] This point was linked to the unfortunate matter of his schooling. The problem was not its extent – if high scholastic attainment had been a requirement for joining the Windsor family, few twentieth-century consorts (let alone the royals they married) would have passed muster – but its location. It was a significant disadvantage that he was not a member of the freemasonry of old Etonians to which virtually everybody in the inner circle who was not actually a Royal Highness, almost by definition, belonged.[13]

Philip's unusual academy, regarded by the world at large as an interesting variation, contributed to the sense of him as an outsider – even possibly, like his uncle, as a kind of socialist. 'He had been at Gordonstoun,' points out a former royal aide. 'So he had very few friends. Eton engenders friendships. The more severe ethos at Gordonstoun leaves you without friends.' (Being 'without friends' should not, of course, be taken literally: what it meant was friends of an appropriate type. The same source acknowledges that, though Philip did have friends, they tended to be 'Falstaffian' ones.[14]) In addition, Gordonstoun's 'progressive' ethos could give rise to disturbing ideas. Thus, one member of the Royal Family apparently complained that the would-be consort 'had been to a crank school with theories of complete social equality where the boys were taught to mix with all and sundry.'[15]

There was no single, or over-riding, objection: just the raised eyebrow, the closing of ranks at which royalty and the landed classes were peculiarly adept. If there was a unifying theme, it was a kind of jealous, chauvinistic protectiveness – based on a belief that so precious an asset should not be lightly handed over, least of all to the penniless scion of a disreputable house who, in the nostrils of his critics, had about him the whiff of a fortune-hunter. Contemplating the presence of 'Philip of Greece' and his cousin the Marquess of Milford Haven at the Boxing Day party at Windsor Castle in 1943, Sir Alan Lascelles laconically observed: 'I prefer the latter'.[16] Whatever the full reason, a courtly and aristocratic distaste for the young suitor, and suspicion about his motives, hindered his full acceptance into courtly and aristocratic circles for years to come.

ONE PERSON had no doubts: Princess Elizabeth herself. 'She was a stunning girl', a close friend fondly remembers, 'longing to be a young wife without too many problems.'[17] In this ambition she was supported by most public opinion, apart from a sliver of the Labour Party on the pro-Communist left, which continued to associate Philip not with the Hun, but with the Greek right. In general, however, press and public took what they saw: a handsome, eligible naval officer, who happened to be a prince. So far from objecting, most early commentators found his combination of royal status, a British naval commission, and lack of celebrity, entirely appropriate for the back-seat but decorative role that would be required. Yet for the time being, Philip remained a shadowy figure.

Elizabeth, by contrast, was ever more visible in the popular magazines – with interest enhanced by speculation about the developing but unannounced romance. The American press, always ahead of the British, anticipated an engagement early in 1947 by turning her into a cover girl, a newsreel star, and – highest compliment – the ultimately desirable girl-next-door. In January 1947, the International Artists' Committee in New York voted her one of the most glamorous women in the world. In March, *Time* declared her 'the Woman of the Week', and praised her for her 'Pin-Up Charm'. Devoting four pages to her life story, it revealed her as a princess the magazine's readers could take to their hearts. She was practical, down-to-earth, human – the essence of suburban middle America. As well as being an excellent horsewoman she was, the article declared, a tireless dancer and an enthusiastic lover of swing music, night clubs, and 'having her own way'. She enjoyed reading best-sellers, knitting and gossipy teas with her sister and a few girlfriends in front of the fire at Buckingham Palace.[17]

According to Crawfie, she was an indifferent knitter.[18] However, the picture was not entirely false. Whatever she may have read in her teens, her adult tastes in literature and drama were, as a British observer put it delicately in the 1950s, 'those of the many rather than the few'.[19] In this respect, as in others, efforts to nip any blue-stocking tendency in the bud had succeeded.

It was also true that she enjoyed music, especially if it was not too demanding. She took a keen interest in the 'musicals' currently in vogue on the London stage. She liked the satirical entertainment *1066 and All That* so much that she obtained a copy of the song 'Going Home to Rome' from the management.[20] Jean Woodroffe (then Gibbs), who became her lady-in-waiting early in 1945, remembers that the two of them would while away the time on long car journeys to and from official engagements by singing popular songs.[21] After the war ended, weekly madrigal sessions were held at the Palace – either Margaret or a professional musician played the piano and both girls sang, together with some officers in the Palace guard.[22]

One madrigal singer was Lord Porchester (now the seventh Earl of

Carnarvon) who had known Princess Elizabeth when he was in the Royal Horse Guards at the end of the war, and had taken part in the Buckingham Palace VE-Night escapade. Porchester ('Porchey')* also shared the Princess's interest in riding, breeding and racing horses. During the war, they had seen each other at the Beckhampton stables on the Wiltshire Downs, where horses bred at the royal studs were trained. Porchester was the grandson of the fifth Earl of Carnarvon, who, as well as being the joint discoverer of the tomb of Tutenkhamun, had been the leading racehorse owner-breeder at the beginning of the century, and had set up the Highclere Stud at his Hampshire home. His father, the sixth Earl, had bred the 1930 Derby winner Blenheim. 'The King thought I was a suitable racing companion of her age group,' says Lord Carnarvon. 'There were not many people then who could accompany her to the races.' Since the 1940s, he says, 'We have developed our interest together, and it has got sharper.'[23] He was beside her at Newmarket in October 1945, and at almost every Derby since.

Before the war, horses had been Elizabeth's childhood fantasy. During it, her confidence as a rider had been built up with the help of Horace Smith. After 1945, the horse world became her chief relaxation and escape. She read widely on the subject, extending her knowledge of horse management, welfare and veterinary needs, and she developed a sixth sense as a trainer. 'She has an ability to get horses psychologically attuned to what she wants,' says Sir John Miller, for many years Crown Equerry and responsible for all the Queen's non-race horses, 'and then to persuade them to enjoy it.'[24] What started as a hobby later became a serious enterprise, and an area for her own independent professionalism. 'Prince Philip shrewdly kept out of it all,' says a former royal employee. 'Otherwise he would have dominated the discussion.'[25]

For Elizabeth, horse breeding was a family interest. The royal studs had been founded at Hampton Court in the sixteenth century, later moving to Windsor. In the late nineteenth century, the then Prince of Wales, later Edward VII, had re-confirmed the royal hobby by establishing the Sandringham stud. Royal interest seemed curiously,

* This is the Queen's own spelling. Others have 'Porchie'.

though perhaps not surprisingly, to mirror the royal fascination with dynastic genealogy. The result had been an exclusive attitude to bloodlines. 'Royal managers had avoided sending to some of the best stallions, often because they did not like the owner,' Carnarvon recalls. On one occasion, an otherwise ideal candidate for covering a royal mare was rejected by Captain Charles Moore, George VI's (and later his daughter's) Manager of the Royal Studs, on the grounds that it belonged to a bookmaker. In much the same way, the King – who took a mild interest in racing – had a patriotic approach to the sport. Not only did he prefer to send to British-based stallions, it upset him if French horses too often won British races.[26]

Lord Porchester, who had studied at Cirencester Agricultural College and had acquired a knowledge of the principles of 'hybrid vigour,' tried to advance royal practice by encouraging the family to be less fussy about equestrian social backgrounds. As Porchey and Elizabeth became more expert together, a quiet revolution came eventually to overtake royal breeding methods. After Elizabeth became Queen, her interest increased, and in 1962 she leased Polhampton Lodge Stud, near Overton in Hampshire, for breeding race horses – adding to the studs (Sandringham and Wolverton) at Sandringham. In 1970, Lord Porchester took over as the Queen's racing manager. Over the years their shared passion for horses became the basis for a close friendship. 'With Henry Porchester, racing and horses bring them continually together,' says a former royal adviser. 'Henry tells her a lot of gossip. She's very fond of him and he's devoted to her.'[27]

Princess Elizabeth's other recreations were also uncompromisingly those of royalty and the landed aristocracy. Like her grandfather, father and mother, she was relentless in her pursuit of the fauna on the Sandringham and Balmoral estates. She did not use a shotgun, but she became skilled with a rifle, and in stalking deer during Scottish holidays. One report described how, while staying on the Invernesshire estate of Lord Elphinstone, the Queen's brother-in-law, in October 1946, the twenty-year-old Princess followed a stag through the forest, 'aimed with steadiness and brought down the animal,' which turned out to be a twelve-pointer.[28] It was a sport for which she was well-equipped. After visiting Balmoral during the war, King Peter of

Yugoslavia, Alexandra's husband, expressed admiration at the quality of the rifle she lent him.[29] Later, Porchey gave her a .22 rifle as a present.

The pace quickened at the end of the war, in shooting as in everything else. Aubrey (now Lord) Buxton, a Norfolk neighbour who became a close friend of the royal couple – and who later helped to inspire Philip's interest in wildlife and conservation – described one extraordinary day's shooting at Balmoral, a fortnight after the Japanese surrender. A royal house party, headed by the Monarch, set itself the task of killing as wide a range of different birds and animals as possible. The King set out in search of ptarmigan, somebody else had to catch a salmon and a trout, and so on. After a hard day, the final bag in the game book was 1 pheasant, 12 partridges, 1 mountain hare, 1 brown hare, 3 rabbits, 1 woodcock, 1 snipe, 1 wild duck, 1 stag, 1 roe deer, 2 pigeons, 2 black game, 17 grouse, 2 capercailzie, 6 ptarmigan, 2 salmon, 1 trout, 1 heron and a sparrow hawk. Princess Elizabeth was the proud dispatcher of the stag.[30]

Margaret did not share Elizabeth's sporting enthusiasms – one of the factors which led to the growth of different and contrasting circles of friends. To some extent, despite the age gap, their circles overlapped. Weekend parties in the mid-1940s included the heirs to great titles, who were regarded as potential husbands for either of them. Names like Blandford, Dalkeith, Rutland, Euston, Westmorland tended to crop up. 'There was a good deal of speculation,' an ex-courtier remembers, 'about whether any of them would do.' When Philip became a fixture, the circles diverged. Margaret began to attract a smarter set: her friends thought of themselves as gaier, wilder, wittier, and regarded Elizabeth's as grand, conventional and dull.

As well as the gap in interests, the distinction reflected a difference in temperament. 'Princess Margaret loved being amused,' suggests one of her friends, 'in a way that her sister didn't.' It was also a product of the princesses' contrasting relationship with the King. Elizabeth, the introvert, had been brought up to be responsible; Margaret, the extrovert, to be pretty, entertaining and fun. 'George VI had a strong concern for Princess Elizabeth,' says the same source, 'but he had a more fatherly attitude towards her sister. I remember him leaning on a piano when she was singing light-hearted songs, with an adoring look, thinking it was frightfully funny.' While Margaret reached out to people, Elizabeth seemed never to give much away. A lady-in-waiting recalls her, in the mid–1940s, as 'very charming, but very quiet and shy – much more shy than later.'[31] Colville formed a similar impression. 'Princess Elizabeth has the sweetest of characters,' he recorded, shortly after joining her, 'but she is not easy to talk to, except when one sits next to her at dinner, and her worth, which I take to be very real, is not on the surface.'[32]

The impression of Princess Elizabeth is of a strangely poised young person used to going her own way, which tended to be the way of her class rather than of her age group, and making few concessions to fashion. Yet the sense of her as highly conventional – in contrast to her sister – depends partly on the vantage-point and the generation of the observer. Simon Phipps, friendly with Margaret when he was a theological student and young clergyman, and who later became Bishop of Lincoln, remembers the stiffness of royal protocol, including having to change twice in the evening (once for tea, and again for dinner), and turning at table when the Monarch turned. But he also recalls happy games of charades, including an anarchic one in which he was cast as a bishop, and the King as his chaplain.[33] When Lady Airlie, Queen Mary's friend and lady-in-waiting, visited Sandringham in January 1946, what shocked her was the extent of change since before the war. She found youth in control, with jig-saw puzzles set out on a baize-covered table in the entrance hall. 'The younger members of the party – the princesses, Lady Mary Cambridge, Mrs Gibbs and several young guardsmen congregated round them from morning to night,' she noted. 'The radio, worked by Princess Elizabeth, blared incessantly.' No orders or medals were worn at dinner, as they had been in the old days, and the girls related to their parents with – to Lady Airlie – startling informality. Modernity was also visible 'in the way both sisters teased, and were teased by, the young Guardsmen.'[34]

Teasing and teased Guards Officers were, however, only one aspect of their lives. The chasm that divided the King's daughters from the young men and women they were able to meet socially, widened early in 1947 when they accompanied their parents on a major tour of southern Africa which attracted world attention, and set the stage for Princess Elizabeth's *début* as a fully-fledged royal performer.

The end of the war had given a brief, almost paradoxical, boost to the imperial ideal. Partly, it was an effect of sheer survival – defending the Empire had been one of the causes for which the war had been fought. Britain's near-bankruptcy had made the vision of a shared, transoceanic loyalty all the more necessary to national self-esteem: a necessity which the granting of self-government to India seemed, if anything, to increase. At the same time, the British Government was aware that the bonds that tied together the Commonwealth were in need of repair. Nowhere was this more apparent than in the case of Pretoria, capital of a Union still bitterly divided between English-speakers and Afrikaners.

Officially, the tour – which involved a total of four months' travel – was supposed to be a chance for the King and Queen to rest after the ordeal of war. In practice, the schedule prepared for the Royal Family was strenuous, and the objectives highly political. Wheeler-Bennett later called it a 'great imperial mission'[35]. That was one way of describing it. From the South African point of view, the visit was (in the words of another historian) 'essentially a mission to save Smuts and the Crown of South Africa'.[36] English-speakers were enthusiastic about it, Afrikaners on the other hand, were cynical – seeing George VI (according to the High Commissioner, in a telegram to the Palace) 'as the symbol of the "Empire-bond" which they had pledged themselves to break.' General Smuts was accused of having arranged the trip in order to rally the English section round him for the coming general election.[37] But there was also something else, which in one sense made nationalist Boers right to be suspicious: the royal trip had an 'imperial' aspect that went beyond the attempt to improve relations with the Union. South Africa was important in a new 'multi-cultural' definition of the Commonwealth – in the light of Indian independence – because it was the only 'white' dominion that was in reality predominantly black. The royal visit was to be a way of showing Windsor and Westminster interest in what one (pro-British) Natal paper described as 'the complex problems of race relationships – problems which are certain to assume an increasing importance in the years ahead,' in the many countries which owed allegiance to the Crown.[38]

These factors, however, were not the ones that got the most publicity. In the eyes of the world, the tour also had a personal and dynastic interest: Princess Elizabeth and Prince Philip would be apart for four months. Since the invitation was accepted by the King on behalf of the whole Royal Family in the first half of 1946, the trip could hardly be seen as an attempt to break up the friendship. Yet the visit took place as speculation was at its height; and the irony did not escape the gossip-writers that the first major tour on which the King and Queen proposed to take their elder daughter was also one on which she had reason to be reluctant to accompany them.

Why was there no engagement announcement before they set out? A belief that all was not going smoothly added to the press excitement. One former courtier suggests that – whatever the original intention – the King and Queen saw the visit as an opportunity for reflection. 'Undoubtedly there was hesitation on the part of her parents,' he says. 'They weren't saying "You must or mustn't marry Prince Philip," but rather, "Do you think you should marry him?" It wasn't forced. The King and Queen basically said: "Come with us to South Africa and then decide".'[39]

With Philip's naturalization due to be gazetted in a few weeks, however, any pretence that the relationship did not exist was abandoned. A couple of nights before the departure of the Royal Family, Elizabeth accompanied both her parents to dinner with the Mountbattens, including the about-to-be Philip Mountbatten, at 16 Chester Street – serenaded by Noël Coward. 'The royal engagement was clearly in the air that night,' recalled John Dean, Mountbatten's butler and later valet to Philip.[40] It was a farewell meal in two senses. While the King prepared to inspect one of his domains, Uncle Dickie was about to negotiate the transfer of power, as George VI's Viceroy of India, in another.

MUCH OF THE journey to Cape Town, aboard the battleship HMS *Vanguard*, was uncomfortably rough, confining the Royal Family to their cabins. When she returned to South Africa as Queen several decades later, Elizabeth recounted how sea-sick they had been. However, as they travelled south they left Europe's worst winter weather of the century behind them. 'Our party seems to be enjoying themselves, especially the princesses,' Lascelles wrote to his wife, describing 'crossing the line' festivities, and a treasure hunt involving the King's daughters and the midshipmen. 'Peter T[ownsend],' he added, referring to an equerry who was a member of the party, 'tries hard and is doing well.'[41]

For the two young women, the experience was breathtaking – not least because it was the first time either of them had been abroad. In the 1930s, they had been considered too young to accompany their parents on foreign visits, and during the war it had been too danger-ous, or impracticable, to do so. Thus, Princess Elizabeth had reached the age of twenty before setting foot outside the United Kingdom. The impact of the voyage and then of the journey around a very different kind of country was therefore all the greater. South Africa – with its varieties of terrain, race, wealth and culture – was a powerful reminder to Elizabeth of the Commonwealth duties that lay ahead. Both girls were struck by the open spaces: Princess Margaret recalls her sense of the vastness of the country and the contrasts with austerity Britain. 'There was an amazing opulence, and a great deal to eat,' she says. She remembers the change from a country still restricted by food rationing, and her delight at the endless series of meals with their abundance of delicacies, including an enticing array of complicated Dutch pastries. Huge fir cones seemed to symbolize the outsize scale of everything they encountered. The South Africans lent them horses, and they rode on the beaches, wearing double felt hats.[42]

The royal party arrived in Cape Town on 17 February to a tumultu-ous welcome that banished fears of republican hostility. There was a glittering state banquet the same night. Next day, Lascelles wrote home that while he had never attended a more dreary and miserable dinner in thirty years of attending public functions, the Royal Family seemed to enjoy it, especially the princesses. 'Princess E[lizabeth] is delightfully enthusiastic and interested,' he noted; 'she has her grandmother's passion for punctuality, and, to my delight, goes bounding furiously up the stairs to bolt her parents, when they are more than usually late.'[43] The plan was to bring the British Monarchy into direct contact with every part of the Union – in the words of the tour's official souvenir – from the seaboard of the Cape and Natal 'to areas where African tribes live in peace and security under conditions which still suggest the Africa of history.'[44]

The royal party slept in a special 'White Train' for a total of thirty-five nights, travelling to the Orange Free State, Basutoland, Natal and the Transvaal, and then to Northern Rhodesia and Bechuanaland. South Africa was a society rigidly divided on racial grounds: but it did not yet have strict apartheid laws, and the royal party met people from different communities, even attending a 'Coloured Ball'. The King's daughter attracted particular attention. Africans shouted from the crowds 'Stay with us!' and 'Leave the Princess behind!'[45] The presence of British royalty also aroused keen interest in the small, enclosed white South African world, dominating popular entertainment. At a huge civic ball held in Cape Town the night following their arrival, five thousand guests danced to a fox-trot composed in honour of Elizabeth, called 'Princess'. The tune accompanied a song which became the catch of the season. 'Princess, in our opinion,' went its loyal refrain, 'You'll find in our Dominion/Greetings that surely take your breath,/For you have a corner in every heart,/Princess Elizabeth'.[46] Elsewhere, there were other musical tributes. At Eshowe, Zulu warriors pounded out the 'Ngoma Umkosi,' the Royal Dance before the King. One verse was omitted at the last minute: 'We hear, O King, your eldest daughter, Princess Elizabeth, is about to give her heart in marriage, and we would like to hear from you who is the man, and when this will be.'[47] On 1st April, close to the end of the tour, the not unwelcome or unhelpful news came through of the death of King George of Greece. Lascelles reported home that while there would be a week's court mourning in London, no notice at all would be taken 'by anybody out here because we haven't any becoming mourning with us – a typical Royal Family compromise!'[48]

At East London, the second city of Cape Province, Elizabeth had to open a graving dock – it was a windy day, and she had to struggle to keep her hat on, her dress down, and her speech from blowing away.[49] For much of the trip, however, the princesses' most demanding duty was to walk behind their parents at ceremonies or sit beside them at displays. It was a long time to be away, on holiday yet constantly on show – and out of touch with ice-bound Britain, where Philip, at his naval base, lectured his students in his naval greatcoat and by candlelight, because of the fuel crisis. According to below-stairs gossip, spread by Bobo MacDonald, who had graduated from children's nursemaid to become the Princess's maid and dresser, 'Elizabeth was very eager for mail throughout the tour, and so was Philip.'[50] She also wrote to other friends. Lord Porchester, for instance, received letters from her wherever she went. She wrote vividly, about the tour and meeting Smuts, but also about home. In one letter she asked about her horse, Maple Leaf.[51]

The passivity, however, did not last until the end of the tour. The Royal Family's departure date was fixed for 24 April. Princess Elizabeth's twenty-first birthday fell three days earlier – a happy coincidence of timing which enabled the South African government to make it the climax of the visit. It could scarcely have been celebrated on a more elaborate, and extravagant, scale. As a token of the importance Smuts attached to the royal tour, 21 April was declared a public holiday throughout the Union. In addition, the royal birthday was marked by a ceremony, attended by the entire Cabinet, at which the Princess reviewed a large contingent of soldiers, sailors, women's services, cadets and veterans; by a speech given by the Princess to a 'youth rally of all races'; by a reception at City Hall in Cape Town; and by yet another ball in the Princess's honour at which General Smuts presented her with a twenty-one-stone gemstone necklace and a gold key to the city.

The Royal Family made its own most dramatic contribution to the day's events in the form of a broadcast to the Empire and Commonwealth by Princess Elizabeth, which became the most celebrated of her life. The author was not the Princess, but Sir Alan Lascelles, a straight-backed, hard-bitten courtier, not given to emotionalism – though with a sense of occasion and (as his memoranda and diaries reveal) a lucid, if somewhat old-fashioned, literary style. The speech was both a culmination to the tour, and a prologue for the Princess.

When Princess Elizabeth was consulted in the White Train near Bloemfontein during the preparation of a draft, according to one account, she told her father's private secretary, 'It has made me cry'. The effect on many listeners and cinema-goers was much the same as they heard or later watched the solemn young woman making her commitment, like a confirmation or a marriage vow. That her message came from a problematic dominion added to the impact of words which already sounded archaic, and a few years later might have seemed kitsch, yet which seemed strangely to capture the moment.

BIRTHDAY GREETINGS
APRIL 21st

Punch, 23rd April 1947

The effect was the more surprising because Lascelles had made no concessions to populism, and had not attempted to write the kind of speech a young woman might have delivered, if the thoughts had been her own.

'Although there is none of my father's subjects, from the oldest to the youngest, whom I do not wish to greet,' the Princess read from her script, 'I am thinking especially today of all the young men and women who were born about the same time as myself and have grown up like me in the terrible and glorious years of the Second World War. Will you, the youth of the British family of nations, let me speak on my birthday as your representative?' She quoted Rupert Brooke. She spoke of the British Empire which had saved the world, and 'has now to save itself,' and of making the Commonwealth more full, prosperous and happy. Thus far, her speech belonged alongside other truistic utterances forgettably spoken by royalty when required to address the public. It was the next part that took listeners by surprise. Unexpectedly, she changed tack, launching into what amounted to a personal manifesto, that combined two themes of Sir Henry Marten in his tutorials – the Commonwealth, and the importance of broadcasting:

> There is a motto which has been borne by many of my ancestors – a noble motto, "I serve". Those words were an inspiration to many bygone heirs to the throne when they made their knightly dedication as they came to manhood. I cannot do quite as they did, but through the inventions of science I can do what was not possible for any of them. I can make my solemn act of dedication with a whole Empire listening. I should like to make that dedication now. It is very simple.
>
> I declare before you all that my whole life, whether it be long or short, shall be devoted to your service and the service of our great Imperial family to which we all belong, but I shall not have the strength to carry out this resolution alone unless you join in with me, as I now invite you to do. I know that your support will be unfailingly given. God help me to make good my vow and God bless all of you who are willing to share in it.[52]

What was it in this nun-like promise – about a crumbling Empire that in a few years would cease to exist – that captured the imagination of those who heard it? It was partly the youth of the speaker, the cadences of the delivery, and the confidence of the performance; partly the knowledge that a royal betrothal was imminent; partly the earnestness of the sentiment in an earnest decade.

In fact, though the Princess may not have known it, the message was highly political – directed at several distinct audiences. One of its aims was to help Smuts and the cause of English-speakers in South Africa. It was designed to help Uncle Dickie, as Viceroy, in his task of seeking to retain Indian friendship within a Commonwealth that would no longer be able to differentiate between self-governing white dominions, and imperially ruled black colonies. At the same time, the speech was for domestic consumption in Britain – it offered a population that was exasperated by restrictions, and worn out after the added hardships of a terrible winter, the bromide of Commonwealth and imperial ideals. Finally, it was a royal speech, written by a courtier for a royal anniversary: it reaffirmed the British Monarchy as the one reliable link in an association of nations and territories whose ties had become tenuous, because of war, British economic weakness, and nascent nationalism.

But it was the Princess herself, and the feeling she conveyed as an individual, which, as it was said, brought 'a lump into millions of throats'.[53] For a moment, the Empire seemed as one. In South Africa, the English-speakers could not have felt prouder, and even the Afrikaners acknowledged the effect. 'I feel . . . a bit exhausted by the tremendous success of the whole thing,' Lascelles wrote to his wife, as he packed his bags in Cape Town, 'and for Princess Elizabeth's speech, on which I had lavished much care.'[54] A few days later, as the *Vanguard* sailed for home, the King's private secretary was able to reflect a little more on his handiwork. The tour, he concluded, had amply achieved its most important objective, as far as the Court was concerned, of demonstrating the value to South Africa of the British Monarchy. The biggest revelation had been the blossoming of the King's elder daughter:

> From the inside, the most satisfactory feature of the whole business is the remarkable development of P'cess E. She has got all P'cess Marg's solid and endearing qualities plus a perfectly

natural power of enjoying herself . . . Not a great sense of humour, but a healthy sense of fun. Moreover, when necessary, she can take on the old bores with much of her mother's skill, and never spares herself in that exhausting part of royal duty. For a child of her years, she has got an astonishing solicitude for other people's comfort; such unselfishness is not a normal characteristic of that family.

In addition, he noted with approval, the Princess had become extremely business-like: she had developed the 'admirable technique,' if they were running late, 'of going up behind her mother and prodding her in the Achilles tendon with the point of her umbrella when time is being wasted in unnecessary conversation'. When circumstances required, she also 'tells her father off . . .' Both princesses must have found moments in the tour very dull, Lascelles concluded. But, on the whole, both had been 'as good as gold'.[55]

Lascelles's optimism about the impact of the tour turned out to be misplaced. Indeed, if the aim had been to save both Smuts and the Crown in South Africa, it was a double failure. The following year, Smuts was ousted by Malan and the isolationists, and a new government adopted a programme of racial laws that weakened still further the Commonwealth links of the Union, and led eventually to South Africa's withdrawal from the association thirteen years later. Yet it would be wrong to dismiss the trip as politically negligible. In a way it was a marker: remembered, with nostalgia and also hope, for the affirmation it had provided of more elevated values than those later imposed. The memory was still there when, nearly half a century later, Nelson Mandela's democratic republic re-applied for Commonwealth membership. There was also a directly personal effect. Elizabeth's first tour, which was also one of her longest, profoundly affected her outlook, helping to establish a Commonwealth interest and loyalty that became a consistent theme of her reign.

AT HOME, every paper carried a birthday profile of the Heiress Presumptive, in each case seeking to meet a public desire for as happy and as rosy a picture of the Princess as the meagre details available about her short life permitted. Descriptions highlighted the qualities an idealized princess ought to have, alongside those she actually did.

Since it was an egalitarian, democratic era, much ingenuity was exercised in presenting her as a people's princess.

The Prime Minister set the tone. The simple dignity and wise understanding of the King's elder daughter, he declared, had endeared her to all classes.[56] The sentiment was echoed, universally. The *News Chronicle* helpfully noted that, unlike a male heir, who would have been created Prince of Wales and a member of the House of Lords, she was technically a commoner, and had appropriately simple tastes in personal adornment.[57] *The Times* saw the point as more than technical. Elizabeth belonged to a Monarchy that had become 'social and unpretentious,' it declared, acting as 'the mirror in which the people may see their own ideals of life'. From this firm base, the Princess would provide the rising generation with a model that was progressive in the widest sense, 'standing for the aspirations of the men and women of her own age, for everything that is forward-looking, for all the effort that seeks to build afresh.'[58]

Such a 'representative' view of royalty, of course, begged a few questions: did being 'representative' mean representing the interests and ideals of ordinary young people in a symbolic sense, or actually being like them? Dermot Morrah, always ready with a loyal argument, claimed that the Princess was as representative in the second sense as in the first – and that her representative status came from the happy chance of her intellectual and cultural limitations. Like her father and grandfather, he pointed out, she was 'normal' – that is, average – in capacity, taste and training. The result was an Heiress Presumptive with normal, average values. That she was 'simple, warm-hearted, hard-working, painstaking, cultivated, humorous and above all friendly' helped to make her 'a typical daughter of the Britain of her time'.[59]

Like the trumpeted 'simplicity' of the Princess's pre-war upbringing, however, the reality was somewhat different. Most of the 'normality' of her early adulthood was a product of the ambition of observers to present her as somebody with whom genuinely simple and normal people could identify. The only hard, publicly available evidence was that she was untypical – in particular that she was rich and about to become richer, with a Civil List income rising from £6,000 per annum to £15,000 on her majority, a sum over which she would have full control. She was also untypically, even uniquely, famous: one newspaper suggested that the twenty-one-year-old Princess was 'unquestionably the most publicized young woman in the world,' easily out-distancing Shirley Temple, her nearest rival.[60]

Privately, the Princess felt no particular need to pretend to be what she was not. Indeed, her reluctance to step outside her own class in her social relations caused her royal grandmother, who continued to watch her progress carefully, some disquiet. At the beginning of July, Jock Colville recorded a conversation with Queen Mary in the garden at Marlborough House, in the course of which the elderly lady, nearing eighty, 'said many wise things' about her grand-daughter, 'including the necessity of travel, of mixing with all the classes (H.R.H. is inclined to associate with young Guards officers to the exclusion of more representative strata of the community) and of learning to know young members of the Labour Party.'[61]

Yet there was also, perhaps, a quality that did not entirely belong to the categories of cliché or necessary myth. Unremarkable in capacity, abnormal in experience, wealth and friends, the Princess nevertheless possessed an attribute which radio listeners and filmgoers believed they could hear and see for themselves. This could best be described as 'wholesomeness' and stood in unremarked contrast to the decadence associated with the former Heir Apparent to George V. The Princess's involvement in the Guides and ATS, her outdoor interests and pursuits, and her supposedly happy upbringing, had already been the stuff of wartime propaganda. After 1945, a belief in the Princess's decency, straightforwardness, honesty, rather than in any visible talent, did much to elevate the idea of Monarchy during anxious years when – against ideological trends, or pre-war expectations – its psychic power seemed to soar. When Lord Templewood, who as Sir Samuel Hoare had been a Cabinet minister at the time of the Abdication, wrote of the 'growing influence of the Crown,' and of its 'moral power,' which was now 'so firmly established that we can look forward with undoubted confidence to the reign of Queen Elizabeth the Second,'[62] he expressed a common feeling, for which the Cape Town broadcast had provided confirmation, that the institution would remain in clean hands.

The future of the Monarchy, however, was also linked to the question of who the Princess would marry. By now, an engagement to Prince Philip was assumed. During the South African tour, the BBC – planning ahead – began to consider a talk on the Princess 'by someone who had known her since childhood' to follow a betrothal announcement, and a similar one on the Prince.[63] But no announcement was made, either on Princess Elizabeth's birthday, or on the Royal Family's return. To damp down speculation, the couple tried to be seen less together – thereby sparking rumours that the relationship had been broken off.[64]

One royal adviser recorded that, during a meeting with the Princess's grandmother, Princess Elizabeth's coming engagement had been discussed and that Queen Mary evidently had grave doubts about it.[65] Perhaps there was a last minute rearguard action by opponents of the match. If so, it swiftly collapsed. Prince Philip's small sports car began to reappear at the side entrance to Buckingham Palace,[66] and on July 8th, the Palace declared its hand. 'It had long been rumoured,' noted Colville.[67] A few weeks after the official announcement, the Princess's private secretary wrote of the lobbying that had taken place against the Prince by his critics. Whether they had been unable to block the engagement, he wrote, 'because, as they think, the Queen's usually good judgement has failed her, or because Princess Elizabeth was so much in love as to overcome her parents' antipathy to the match, I do not know'.[68]

7

U NCLE DICKIE had prepared the ground well. The press reaction
to the betrothal, at a time when the Princess's popularity had
never been greater, was one of unqualified enthusiasm. Newspapers
vied with each other to point out, not only that 'this was clearly a
marriage of choice not arrangement,' but also that it was an extremely
suitable match, made all the more so by Philip's British bearing and
attachments.[1] 'An effort had obviously been made,' as Colville drily
observed, 'to build him up as the nephew of Lord Louis Mountbatten
rather than a Greek Prince.'[2] The effort came primarily from Dickie,
and it worked. Glücksburg antecedents took a backseat. Profiles
focused on Philip's British relatives, education and service record,
which made a neat package. As one account put it, the Prince was
'thoroughly English by upbringing, has that intense love of England
and the British way of life, that deep devotion to the ideals of peace
and liberty for which Britain stands, that are characteristic of so many
naval men'.[3] Others tactfully suggested that, although technically a
member of the Greek Orthodox Church into which he had been born,
Princess Elizabeth's fiancé had 'regarded himself' as a member of the
Church of England since entering Dartmouth;[4] that he did not look
Greek; and that his royal rank was a bonus – even though the naturalization had set aside any significance it ever had. Meanwhile, in Athens,
the continuing Greek royal family – which had leaked the news of
the engagement the day before its official release – had no doubt
about its own reaction. Philip had hit the jackpot.[5]

Philip himself acquired a valet and a detective, who accompanied
him wherever he went. He also received a degree of public attention
which he had never been subjected to before, and which he would
now have to put up with for the rest of his life. His face, shown on
all the newsreels, became recognizable everywhere. So did his car –

suddenly everybody in Britain seemed to know that he drove a black, green-upholstered sports car with the registration HDK 99, and they looked out for it. For the time being, however, he continued to live on a lieutenant's pay. According to his valet, his wardrobe was 'scantier than that of many a bank clerk,' and often didn't include a clean shirt.[6] His naval wardrobe wasn't much better. Appraising the King's future son-in-law at a royal garden party a few days after the announcement, Lady Airlie noted, not entirely disapprovingly, that his uniform was shabby, with 'the usual after-the-war look'.[7] For a short time, the image of the Prince as a genteelly poor, male Cinderella became a newspaper staple. Crawfie – who had been won over by the Prince from the beginning – took secret delight in the raffish style he introduced into the Palace, and in the pursed lips of servants and courtiers when he arrived hatless, with flannel trousers, and in an open-necked shirt with rolled-up sleeves.[8]

In August, after the King and Privy Council, including the Prime Minister, Archbishop of Canterbury and Leader of the Opposition, had formally approved the match (as they were required to do under the 1772 Royal Marriages Act), Lieutenant Mountbatten joined the Royal Family at Balmoral. Here the Court was able to assess, soberly, the new recruit. According to one below-stairs tale, Philip annoyed the King when they were in Scotland by bobbing a mock curtsey at him while wearing a kilt.[9] Whether or not the story is true, it fits in with a picture of the Prince's uneasy first summer in possession of the prize, regarded with caution by the King's aristocratic friends, and potentially as dynamite by his courtiers. Jock Colville – in mellow mood, after his own first Balmoral working holiday – recorded his impressions of the royal life north of the border. He was struck by the contrasts with austerity London, even as experienced in Buckingham Palace. 'There was luxury, sunshine and gaiety,' he wrote, with 'picnics on the moors every day; pleasant siestas in a garden ablaze with roses, stocks and antirrhinums; songs and games; and a most agreeable company with which to disport oneself.' The company included Lord and Lady Eldon, the Salisburys, the Duke of Kent, David Bowes-Lyon, and Lady Violet Bonham Carter's son Mark – several of them avowed disapprovers of the Prince.

Colville and Philip overlapped for a week, long enough for the

Princess's private secretary to form a provisionally favourable opinion, though also a cautious one. He liked the young naval officer, appreciated his difficulty in fitting into 'the very English atmosphere that surrounds the Royal Family,' especially when people like the Eldons and the Salisburys were around, and felt that he was intelligent and progressive, especially on the Commonwealth. But he was puzzled by the Philip–Elizabeth relationship. He recorded that the Princess was certainly in love with her fiancé. But he wondered about the apparently 'dutiful' appearance of the Prince.[10] Perhaps Philip did not show his deeper feelings, perhaps Colville's attitude was tinged with a little jealousy: he, after all, was the person who saw more of the Heiress than almost anybody – including, probably, her fiancé. Other impressions varied. One royal adviser remembers games of 'murder' at Balmoral, and bumping into the couple in the dark. 'Somehow', he recalls, 'they always seemed to find each other when the lights went out.'[11] Another, however, confirms Colville's impression of a mysterious imbalance. 'She was in love with him, you know', he says. 'Whether he was with her, I couldn't say'.[12]

The marriage was fixed for November 20th. In the meantime, Princess Elizabeth took over from the Duke of Gloucester the function of the King's ceremonial understudy. In October, she accompanied her father at the State Opening of Parliament for the first time, riding to the ceremony in the glass coach, with a lady-in-waiting. Royal Wedding fever – which was to reach epidemic proportions a few weeks later – had already gripped the capital: people began to line the procession route from Buckingham Palace to Westminster in the early hours of the morning, in the hope of catching a glimpse of the Princess as she passed.

However, the idea that the marriage of the Heiress Presumptive should be treated as a major national and imperial event was a novel one – in Eric Hobsbawm's terminology, an invented tradition. Walter Bagehot had written a famous passage in *The English Constitution*, in which he declared that the women of Britain cared more about the marriage of a Prince of Wales than a ministry. Yet nineteenth and early twentieth century royal weddings had been comparatively modest occasions, and the marriages of the children of recent monarchs were essentially family events. Although the wedding of George VI as Duke of York had taken place in the Abbey, this was a departure from earlier practice. Edward VII, as Prince of Wales, had married in St. George's Chapel, Windsor and George V, as Duke of York, had married in the Chapel Royal at St. James's Palace. The wedding of Victoria, which took place after she had become Queen, was also at St. James's Palace.

The choice of Westminster Abbey as the venue – made in consultation with the Prime Minister and Cabinet – was a decision to turn the day into a popular celebration of a kind, and on a scale, that had not taken place since before the war. It was to be a jamboree fit for a people's princess, which would show that the Labour Government knew how to give everybody a good time, even in the depths of economic adversity. There were also – as at the time of George VI's Coronation – diplomatic points to be made. In place of the restrained show of imperial might of 1937, the wedding of a decade later would be a peace-loving Empire parade, reminding people – as the South African tour had also sought to do – of the continuing strength of Commonwealth and imperial ties in the wake of Indian independence. Finally, Princess Elizabeth's wedding to an undivorced, unforeign, relative provided both Monarchy and public with the Heir-to-the-Throne marriage of which they had been deprived in the 1930s, and which – it was fervently hoped – would blot out the memory of an unsuitable match with a suitable one, while perpetuating the new Windsor line.

Yet the arguments did not wash with everybody. Hugh Dalton, the Labour Chancellor of the Exchequer, described 1947 – in a phrase echoed by Elizabeth in a different context many years later – as his own, and the nation's, 'annus horrendus'. Not only was it an exceptionally uncomfortable year because of the protracted freeze-up in the first part of it. It was also economically a catastrophic one, with a fuel crisis which stopped factories, put millions out of work, and helped to precipitate a financial collapse that stalled the Government's reform programme. In August – a few days after the Abbey announcement – the large North American dollar loan which had helped to pay for early post-war reconstruction ran out, and the free exchange of dollars and sterling was abruptly ended. In a restructuring of the Government in September, Sir Stafford Cripps, the President of the Board of Trade, was given the powerful new post of Minister of Economic Affairs, in order to strengthen the export drive. An Emergency Budget was scheduled for November, and Dalton was expected to announce the most restrictive package of measures since Labour came to office.

Against such a background there was some feeling, especially on the left, that a major state occasion was out of keeping with the rigour of the times. The Communist MP, William Gallagher, attacked the marriage both on the grounds of Philip's ancestry ('I am quite certain that he has not forsaken the family politics,' he told the Commons), at a time of Greek repression, and because of the 'lavish expenditure' involved.[13] A group of Labour MPs added their own voice, sending a letter to the Chief Whip in protest at the likely cost.[14] On October 28th, Dalton responded to the attacks by declaring that only the decorations in Whitehall and outside the Palace would be funded by the taxpayer – everything else would be financed by the King's Civil List.[15] On the eve of the Wedding, Chips Channon reckoned that Labour had got the worst of both worlds, laying itself open to criticism for spending too much, while actually appearing mean. Somebody in the Government he noted, 'apparently advised simplicity, misjudging the English people's love of pageantry and a show'.[16]

There was certainly fierce pressure on the Palace not only to limit expenditure but, above all – at a time of foreign-exchange shortage – to buy British. Indeed, such were the jitters of the Government on the subject, that it became the cause for behind-the-scenes friction. In October, Lascelles responded with extreme testiness to a request for information from the Prime Minister, who was facing a hostile question, about a suggestion that 'Lyons silk' was being used for the bride's dress. 'The *wedding dress* contains silk from Chinese silk worms but woven in Scotland and Kent', replied the courtier. 'The *wedding train* contains silk produced by Kentish silk worms and woven in London. The *going-away dress* contains 4 or 5 yards of Lyons silk which was not specially imported but was part of the stock held by the dress maker (Hartnell) under permit.' (Norman Hartnell had his own say. Faced with the accusation that, in troubled times, the silk might be ideologically suspect, he made a firm answer: 'Our worms are Chinese worms', he coldly informed his accusers, '– from Nationalist China, of course !'[17]) As for the suggestion that the Palace was insufficiently careful on such matters, Lascelles tartly reminded the Prime Minister that, only recently, the Privy Purse had found it necessary to tick off the Board of Trade for recommending an Austrian ornament-maker for the wedding dress's trimmings, a recommendation which had threatened the Palace 'with an appreciable amount of embarrassing publicity'.[18]

A bigger problem, however, than the cost of the Wedding was the cost of the Princess. The marriage of an Heir to the Throne automatically involved a review of the Heir's Civil List – and the month in which this was taking place could scarcely have been less propitious. Buckingham Palace asked for a total of £50,000 per annum for the couple – a net increase of £35,000. The Government – conscious of left-wing backbenchers whose working-class constituents had been told to tighten their belts – replied that this was politically impossible. It did not ease discussions on such a delicate matter that the Chancellor, responsible both for the Budget and for finding the cash for the King's daughter, happened to be the son of a former tutor to George V, and – for complex domestic reasons – was heartily disliked by the Royal Family, which regarded him as a turncoat. Dalton, anti-royal since his youth, was not particularly good at concealing the wry pleasure he derived from the twist of fate that had made him royal paymaster.

The Cabinet had a single objective: to avoid a parliamentary row at a difficult time on what they regarded as a minor matter. On October 22nd, less than a month before the Wedding, Attlee and Dalton saw Lascelles and Sir Ulick Alexander, Keeper of the Privy Purse, in order, as Dalton recorded, to discuss 'a new Civil List Bill and much more money for Princess Elizabeth and Prince Philip'.[19] It was a sticky meeting. In reply to the courtiers' request on behalf of the royal couple, the premier and Chancellor threatened a full-scale Select Committee, which might open a pandora's box, and bring every item of royal expenditure under review. In particular, Attlee pointed out, 'it might even be impossible to prevent questions being asked as to the extent of any private fortunes belonging to the King and to other members of the Royal Family'.[20] Dalton added that if the annuities were too high, 'It would raise discord, and many awkward questions, and would impair the popularity of the Royal Family.'[21] Why, asked the Chancellor, should the King not solve the problem himself, by increasing the Princess's present allowance out of the Household Balances which were in credit, and were likely to continue so? When Alexander insisted that the surplus was only temporary, Dalton drew attention to £200,000 which had been lent by the King, out of these balances, to the Government – and which might be used to pay for Elizabeth and Philip. At this point Lascelles suggested that Dalton should have a personal audience with the King, to discuss the matter[22] – and laid the ground for such a meeting by proposing to the Prime Minister a compromise. Parliament, he suggested, should make provision for the Princess – thereby avoiding the setting of a dangerous precedent by not doing so – but on the understanding that, while the difficult times lasted, the money would not be spent.[23]

Dalton's audience took place on October 27th. It appeared to go well. Lascelles wrote afterwards that the Chancellor was 'greatly pleased by his talk with HM,'[24] and Dalton told the Prime Minister that he found the King 'in a very happy mood'. The meeting seemed to resolve one of the royal difficulties – how to preserve the principle of provision by Parliament, without a Select Committee – by agreeing a formula that established a Select Committee in name, but not in reality. A royal message would announce that no burden should be placed on public funds while economic difficulties lasted. Then the Chancellor would propose the setting up of a Select Committee that would merely note that it was normal for provision to be made for an Heir on marriage, but that this would be delayed for the time being.

The affair, 'so delicate from so many different points of view,' Dalton wrote to Attlee, 'has moved forward with an unexpected smoothness.'[25] But had it? One thing it had not disposed of was the problem of how much the Princess and Prince would get, and how they would be paid. 'The essential point,' Dalton reminded the King, 'was to prevent the development of an embarrassing debate.' That, however, was more the Government's problem than George VI's. The royal concern, the King told the Chancellor, was 'that he could not go on indefinitely making the additional provision from his own resources . . .'[26] The gap between these two positions remained a wide one, and in the fortnight before the Budget it became the cause of a heated argument, which turned on the status of the royal wartime loan. The Government saw this as a fund of public money to be tapped; the Palace, on the other hand, regarded it as the product of royal frugality, and an essential part of the King's accounts. It did not help Government-Palace relations that at the end of October it was decided, for technical constitutional reasons, that a proper Select Committee would be necessary after all.[27]

On November 7th, Dalton returned to the attack, sending the Palace a detailed proposal: the King should surrender the £200,000 saved during the War, and out of this sum a £10,000 annuity should be paid to Elizabeth (over and above the £15,000 Civil List income she was already getting), and £5,000 to Philip, making a joint total of £30,000, part of which should be taxable. If he imagined that this would do the trick, he was mistaken. The Palace was incensed at an amount which it considered derisory, and a poor return on its £200,000 wartime saving. Lascelles recorded the next day that the King considered the offer to be unacceptable.[28] The prospect of a negotiated peace having thus faded, both sides now dug trenches. As Dalton approached the day on which he would have to give the most difficult Budget speech of his career, his attitude became even less tractable, and more infuriating to the Court. On November 10th, he returned to the Palace for another discussion with Lascelles and Alexander, and explained that his earlier offer had just been a bargaining position. The admission confirmed everything the Palace believed about him already. 'He began by saying that he was not at all surprised that the King had rejected the offer,' noted an exasperated Lascelles, who added that this was particularly remarkable in view of the fact that he had been told that Dalton had Cabinet backing.[29]

There, for the next few days, the matter rested. In his Budget speech on November 12th, Dalton – as expected – announced a series of tax increases and other deflationary measures. Next day, in Cabinet, his sole recorded contribution to the morning's discussion concerned the forthcoming marriage of HRH Princess Elizabeth for which, he said, Parliament should be asked to make further financial provisions.[30] A Draft Message from the King, in which His Majesty expressed willingness to 'place at the disposal of the faithful Commons a sum derived from savings on the Civil List made during the war years' was passed without a dissentient voice. Even the left seemed happy. The Minister of Health, Aneurin Bevin – who might have been expected to make a critical or at least quizzical comment – merely remarked that so long as Britain had one, 'we ought never to lower the standards of the Monarchy', and that he hoped the Select Committee would do its work quickly, and settle the whole matter while the Wedding was fresh in people's minds. No figures were mentioned. 'That is quite satisfactory', Lascelles wrote to the King cautiously, 'as far as it goes.'[31]

The same night, however, an unexpected development altered the picture in a fundamental way. Released from Budget concerns, Dalton might now have turned his attention fully to the Civil List problem. Instead, the discovery that he was the inadvertent source of a Budget leak, which appeared in an evening paper while he was still giving his speech, forced him to offer his resignation as Chancellor of the Exchequer. It was accepted. His friends were shocked, while the Opposition congratulated itself on an unexpected scalp.

Buckingham Palace could be forgiven if it secretly rejoiced as well. At any rate, it is unlikely that the King remonstrated with Attlee about the departure. Indeed, he now had a double reason for gratitude towards his Prime Minister on the subject of Mr Dalton. In 1945, Attlee had obliged by not appointing the renegade Etonian as Foreign Secretary; two and a half years later, he obliged once again by accepting Dalton's resignation as Chancellor, at a moment of maximum convenience to the Palace.

In the negotiations, Dalton had appeared both resistant and devious, even – most maddeningly of all – gleeful. His successor, Sir Stafford Cripps, was none of these things. Despite his reputation for austerity (perhaps partly because of it), he was not only straightforward in his dealing with the Palace on the Civil List issue, he was also accommodating. As a result, a much more generous provision than Dalton had ever envisaged went through without a hitch.[32] In December, the new Chancellor recommended to his colleagues a total provision of £50,000 – including a £25,000 increase for Elizabeth, with £10,000 for Philip – £20,000 more than Dalton's offer. He also suggested that the King should make available only £100,000 of accumulated savings, for a period of four years.[33] He was, however, taking a risk. The provision required Parliamentary approval which, in view of the need for a Select Committee, could not be taken for granted. Moreover, if they did not accept it, serious damage would be done to the prestige of the Monarchy, as well as to relations between Palace and Parliament.

The Committee began hearing evidence on December 3rd. A key witness was the King's private secretary, who impressed MPs with a dire warning that the Civil List 'may have to face a crisis of insolvency,' if it did not receive adequate provision. Should this happen, three major economies would become necessary: the abolition of horse-drawn carriages, the disbandment of the Gentleman at Arms and Yeoman of the Guard, and the closing of Windsor Castle as a royal residence. 'I don't think any member of this Committee,' he declared – repeating Bevan's remark in Cabinet – 'will disagree with me when I say that, so long as we have a Monarchy, the Monarchy's work has got to be done well'.[34]

It was a close-run thing. Under only slightly different circumstances – with a less persuasive Chancellor, or one who commanded less authority among MPs – the decision might have gone the other way. As it was, five out of the twelve Labour MPs on the Committee, including the Chairman of the Parliamentary Party, were in favour of substantially lower annuities for the royal couple, backing figures of £35,000 for Elizabeth and £5,000 for Philip. In the final vote, Labour MPs, split evenly, and the higher figures proposed by the Chancellor required Tory and Liberal support to carry them.[35]

THE DEBATE over annuities for the Heiress and her husband had many echoes over the next half century, as inflation bit into the Civil List, while rising asset values simultaneously added to royal wealth. The question of what Parliament should provide, and what it was fair to ask the Monarch to pay out of private or accumulated resources, remained one of the central issues surrounding the institution.

In 1947, however, few matters were of smaller interest to the public. Despite the Government's misgivings, 'Royal Wedding Week' in mid-November provided the national carnival of the decade: a spectacular display of conspicuous consumption, for royalty and subjects alike, which revealed – to those who cared to note it – the public longing for a relaxation of controls after eight years of tight regulation. If there was popular criticism or resentment, little of it ever became public. Mass Observation discovered discontent, here and there, about the extravagance. People questioned about the 300 clothing coupons and £1,200 spent on the wedding dress split evenly on whether it was reasonable or not. The journalist Jill Craigie described the decision to design a calf-length trousseau for the Princess as 'a major victory for the vested interests of the fashion houses.'[36] However, opinion polls showed a mellowing of opinion as the day approached, with a rise between July and November from 40 to 60 per cent of people actively approving of the arrangements.[37]

During the autumn, pre-nuptial excitement focused fetishistically on the physical details of the preparations, including the wedding presents which arrived by the crate-load from all over the world. A souvenir book was published listing all 2,428 of them, and the gifts themselves were put on show, tickets a shilling each, at St James's Palace. 'After the scarcity, the make-do of the war years,' wrote Crawfie, who beat Princess Elizabeth to the altar by getting married, more modestly, in September, 'this sudden lavishness was unnerving.'[38] Presents ranged from a gold tiara from the Emperor of Ethiopia to a large number of nylon stockings, home-knitted jumpers and hand-made tea cosies.[39] There were political gifts, like a 175-piece porcelain dinner service from Chiang Kai-Shek and his wife; well-chosen ones, like a chestnut filly (Astrakhan) from the Aga Khan; and puzzling ones, like the item given by the Mahatma Gandhi, which the catalogue described as a 'fringed lacework cloth made out of yarn spun by the donor on his own spinning wheel.'[40] Queen Mary thought it was the Indian leader's famous loincloth, and took a dim view. 'Such an indelicate gift,' she told Lady Airlie.[41] Not included in the exhibition were hundreds of tons of tinned food from British communities abroad, which were distributed to needy widows and pensioners, with a message from the bride.[42]

All exhibited gifts were carefully and democratically itemised in the catalogue, regardless of splendour. The *pot pourri* of the exhibition, appropriate for the times, was reflected in a preview party for donors, attended by rich and poor, 'peers and factory workers, statesmen and schoolgirls, old age pensioners and housewives, visitors from the provinces, the Continent and the United States.'[43] Such social mixing, however, was not to everybody's taste; nor were many of the gifts. Chips Channon, caught in the crush, noted with admiration a wreath of diamond roses given by the Nizam of Hyderabad, but 'was struck by how ghastly some of the presents were, though the crowd made it difficult to see.'[44] He owed his own invitation to gift No. 797, listed as a 'silver cigarette case, sunray pattern set with a cabochon sapphire in a gold thumb piece.'[45]

The Princess herself spent much of her time before the Wedding thanking the more important corporate donors in person. For such occasions, she had a set speech, which was like a cutdown version of her Cape Town broadcast and a wedding rehearsal combined. 'As long as we live', she recited in her thank-you to the City of London, 'it will be the constant purpose of Lieutenant Mountbatten and myself to serve a people who are so dear to me and to show ourselves deserving of their esteem'.[46]

Of almost as great interest as 'the presents' was 'the cake' – a topic of special fascination because younger members of the population, reared on sugar rationing, found it difficult even to imagine a culinary creation of such opulence. The problem of having the wedding cake made was solved by a neat and characteristic royal exploitation of professional snobbery, vanity and loyalty. Royal-connected cake manufacturers were graciously permitted to present an example of their work, in return for an invitation to the viewing party in the mirror-lined State dining-room, in the presence of the King and Queen, who wandered around, asking polite questions about the ingredients. The winners had the satisfaction of knowing that their cakes had been consumed by royal guests.[47] There were twelve cakes in all, the biggest of which stood four feet high, and took four months to make.[48]

Finally, there was 'The Dress'. Of all the totemic artefacts associated with the royal wedding none drove the press and public to greater frenzy than this garment – partly, again, because of the shortages, which had made fine materials hard or impossible even for well-off people to obtain. Accounts of the wedding dress were caressing: according to Norman Hartnell's own description, it was made of 'clinging ivory silk', trailed with jasmine, smilax, seringa and rose-like blossoms, and included a large number of small pearls. Others were even more lyrical. James Laver, fashion expert at the Victoria and Albert, spoke of Hartnell's creation of Botticelli curves, and of the raised pearls arranged as York roses, entwined with ears of corn. By the device of reversed embroidery, the design had 'alternated star flowers and orange blossom, now tulle on satin, and now satin on tulle, the whole encrusted with pearls and crystals.'[49] A mythology surrounded the production. Hartnell himself liked to recount that his manager, returning from America after a component-hunting expedition, had replied to the question at the customs about whether he had anything to declare, 'Yes, ten thousand pearls, for the wedding dress of Princess Elizabeth.'[50] Like the presents, the dress was put on display, and at times the queue of people waiting to see it stretched the length of the Mall.

After the build-up, the Wedding became, in the words of an American monarchophile, 'a movie premiere, an election, a World Series and Guy Fawkes Night all rolled into one'.[51] It was also, at its core, a gathering of the remnants of European royalty – a vast, rivalrous, beleaguered, mutually suspicious and mutually loyal, and frequently impoverished, extended family. In this respect, the Wedding was different from a Coronation, which was a state more than a personal event. Because of the background of the groom, special attention was directed at the least significant members of this inter-related, uniformed, bemedalled and be-jewelled *galère*, who included the flotsam of two world wars and many revolutions – and for whom Lieutenant Mountbatten was both an object of envy, and a morale-boosting proof that they still had a place in the world.

Since 1918 – if not before – the British Royal Family had been the premier dynasty; and now, with fewer surviving monarchies than ever, its pre-eminence was even more apparent. 'You are the big potato,' Smuts was overheard saying to the King's mother at the wedding-eve party; 'all the other queens are small potatoes.'[52] Nobody doubted it or that this was an occasion for big potatoes to show cousinly solicitude to small ones, whatever their circumstances. Lady Airlie cast her mind back to 1939 or even 1914. Old friends were reunited, she wrote, old jealousies swept away.[53] 'It was a tremendous meeting place,' recalls Princess Margaret. 'People who had been starving in little garrets all over Europe, suddenly reappeared.'[54] Queen Alexandra of Yugoslavia likened the atmosphere to that of a boarding school, in which all the royal families belonged to the same house: the Wedding reminded her of a reunion of school friends, all 'shedding their grown-up facade, and romping together in an abandon of gossip, leg-pulling and long-remembered family jokes'. Many of the visiting royals – especially the mendicant ones, who had their travel expenses discreetly paid by the Windsors – crowded round a communal table in the dining room at Claridges, where they were put up, adding to the illusion of an unruly and cacophonous academy.[55]

However, simple accounts of happy high jinks, and of bygones being bygones, did not give the whole picture. Delicate decisions had to be made. Though Philip's mother was invited, his three surviving, German-married sisters were not. Nor was the Duke of Windsor, who spent the day morosely in New York in his Waldorf Towers suite. A few who came might have done better to have stayed away. 'When I am back behind the Iron Curtain,' Queen Helen of Romania remarked during her brief stay, 'I shall wonder whether this is all a dream.'[56] Her words acquired a special poignancy because the Government in Bucharest used the opportunity afforded by King Michael's absence to declare a republic.

On the eve of the main event there was a dinner for foreign royalty, and a grand party at the Palace, attended by crowned heads, presidents and premiers. Much was made of the down-at-heel condition of royal adornments, of tiaras taken out of storage and dusted down: as though the ostentation was easier to justify if it was seen as a fancy dress parade, rather than the display of real luxury. Crown jewels were worn as if they were paste, almost apologetically – leading some of the kings and queens who still had thrones to feel superior. 'Queen Juliana of the Netherlands was frightfully scathing about everybody's jewellery,' recalls Pamela Hicks, a bridesmaid. '"It's so dirty," she kept saying.'[57] Lady Airlie wrote that 'anyone fortunate enough to have a new dress drew all eyes'. However, all the famous diamonds were visible, 'even though most of them had not been cleaned since 1939'.[58]

ONE TICKLISH question, which exercised the finest and most anti-quarian minds at Buckingham Palace almost until the Wedding itself, was what Philip Mountbatten should be called and how he should be styled. Since he was no longer Greek, his royal title was meaningless, and anyway he had abandoned it; yet it was taken for granted that the Heiress's consort could not remain a commoner. The problem was finding a suitable English title, and an appropriate rank. In choosing one, future children – including the future Heir or Heiress – had to be taken into account. Would they be named after their father or their mother? Consulted on this point, the Lord Chancellor, Lord Jowett, replied that the 1917 Proclamation which changed the Royal Family's name to Windsor, did not include under the general rubric George V's married female descendants. Elizabeth, and her issue, were excluded, and would take their names from her husband.[59]

At the end of July, Dermot Morrah – who had covered the tour of South Africa for *The Times* and felt a passionate concern about the minutiae of royal etiquette – sent a memorandum to his editor, who passed it on to the Palace, listing some twenty alternative labels for Lieutenant Mountbatten, with comments on each. He gave 'Edinburgh' a high ranking. Though it had the drawback of lacking antiquity, 'having been first conferred only in 1726,' the adoption of it, he suggested, would be seen as a compliment to Scotland. Lascelles added his own notes, and passed on the list to the King.[60] In view of Philip's naval background, either the Earl or Duke of Greenwich was considered a possibility.[61] Finally, Baron Greenwich, Earl of Merioneth, Duke of Edinburgh was agreed. However, the question of a 'Royal' Dukedom – whether Philip should be called 'His Royal Highness', following his marriage – still had to be sorted out. The King became greatly exercised on this issue. 'Can you find out how Prince Henry of Battenberg who was Serene Highness was created Royal Highness by Q. Victoria on his marriage to Princess Beatrice?', the King pencilled to Lascelles in August. 'This will give me a Precedent in this case.' In September, after consultations with the Home Secretary, it was decided to bestow the 'HRH' title which Philip had turned down before the engagement, but which his marriage to the Princess would justify. The King's attention now turned to the complex question of his future son-in-law's coat-of-arms. Rough sketches were commissioned, and the Monarch spent many productive hours poring over them, noting down his comments.[62]

At the end of September, Philip's transmogrification into an Englishman was completed with his formal reception into the Anglican Church by the Archbishop of Canterbury in the chapel at Lambeth

Palace – at roughly the same time as his mother, Princess Alice, was making arrangements for the founding of her own Greek Orthodox order of working nuns. There was one more detail: in November, the King bestowed the Garter on both the Princess and Philip – though too late for the wedding service sheets, which described him as 'Philip Mountbatten, RN'. Popularly, however, he had always been known as 'Prince Philip' – a title to which his wife, as Queen, finally gave regal sanction ten years later.

Courtiers continued to weigh him up. In late October, Philip accompanied Elizabeth on her last pre-marriage engagement, to launch the Cunard liner the *Caronia* from the Clydebank shipyard of John Brown and Co. On the way back, the royal train was delayed in a siding, and Jock Colville walked down the line with his employer's fiancé, climbing with him into the signal box. 'I watched P. narrowly,' he recorded. 'He is a strong believer in the hail-fellow-well-met as opposed to the semi-divine interpretation of Monarchy.' However, during a conversation with some of the railwaymen, there was one 'appalling gaffe'. When the signalman said jokingly that he was waiting for promotion until somebody died, noted Colville, 'Philip replied, "Like me!" No doubt he meant in the Navy, but another interpretation was obvious.' Colville wrote that he expected the future consort to be popular with the crowd, but that he could also be vulgar, and that his manner towards Princess Elizabeth at times was quite off-hand.[63] However, even the Princess's acidic private secretary was not immune from the rising tide of sentiment towards the young couple, and the sense of a storybook romance. Close contact with both of them also caused him to revise his opinions. 'As the day drew nearer', Colville acknowledged immediately after the Wedding, 'I began to think, as I now sincerely do, that the Princess and Philip really are in love.'

He also wrote that Elizabeth 'bore the pre-wedding strain with great good nature and cheerfulness'.[64] Sometimes, it must have been hard. To the worries of any young bride were added an uncertainty about what to expect as the first married Heiress to the Throne of modern times, and the almost suffocating attentions of the world. Crawfie, seeing her former pupil's nervousness, tried to help – by offering some advice. This took the form of a homily on the condition of matrimony, which reveals much about British attitudes (or at any rate Scottish lower-middle-class ones) in the 1940s. It was unwise, the governess explained, even in a royal union, to be too jealous or possessive a wife. 'When you marry, you must not expect the honeymoon to last for ever,' she told the young woman she had helped to bring up. 'Sooner or later you will meet the stresses and strains of everyday life. You must not expect your husband to be constantly at your side or always to receive from him the extravagant affection of the first few months. A man has his own men friends, hobbies and interests in which you cannot and will not want to share.'

Princess Elizabeth started her wedding day much as she had begun the morning of her father's Coronation ten years before – looking out of the window of Buckingham Palace in her dressing-gown.[65] Despite the cold November weather, crowds had gathered in the Mall the night before, in preparation for an all-night vigil. 'There was a tremendous crowd reaction', says Pamela Hicks. 'Suddenly to see the state coach was marvellous, with Princess Elizabeth with her wonderful complexion and Prince Philip so devastatingly handsome – they were a dream couple.'[66] The theme was popular monarchy. The day's events, including the service, were broadcast to forty-two countries. The address by the Archbishop of York, Cyril Garbett, stressed the universality of the occasion. Never, he said, had a wedding been followed with such interest by so many people, yet the ceremony was 'in all essentials exactly the same as it would have been for any cottager who might be married this afternoon in some small country church in a remote village in the Dales'.[67] One of the essentials – despite a few protests from 'extreme advocates for sexual equality' – was the promise by the Heiress Presumptive 'to love, cherish and obey' her husband.[68] Non-essentials included the attendants, the list of whom made no concessions to social equality. All were either royal or aristocratic. Philip's cousin, the Marquess of Milford Haven, was best man.

The congregation of two thousand included, as Wheeler-Bennett put it, 'one of the largest gatherings of royalty, regnant and exiled, of the century'.[69] There were so many kings and queens and their offspring, together with foreign heads of state, that other categories were squeezed – British MPs, for instance, had to ballot for places, much to their irritation. Many of the guests were unknown to either the bride or the groom. Others were known to the entire Abbey. When the Leader of the Opposition, Winston Churchill, arrived a little late, 'everyone stood up', as Channon observed, 'all the Kings and Queens'.[70] There were also eccentrics. Lady Munnings, wife of Sir Alfred, President of the Royal Academy, sat through the whole service with her Pekinese dog, Black Knight, concealed in her muff.[71] To be invited was bliss: to be left off the list, when you thought you should be on it, was torture. 'Miserable royal wedding day', wrote Lord Reith, former Director-General of the BBC, in his diary. 'Didn't get up till 10.30. Completely out of phase with everything and everybody through not being asked to the Abbey.'[72]

The lucky ones felt the kind of excitement people feel when they attend events everybody else wishes they were at: they found beauty and wonder everywhere, in the building, the words, the music, the congregation, the Royal Family, the royal couple and especially the bride. There were many accounts from people eager to display their privileged access, and inside knowledge. Faces were studied for expressions, clothes critically examined for the minutest detail. Mrs Fisher, wife of the Archbishop of Canterbury, thought the Princess looked 'very calm, absolutely lovely' coming up the aisle. The effect of her outfit, she wrote, 'was a diaphanous one with her lovely train of silk tulle and her veil'.[73] Channon 'thought Princess Elizabeth looked well, shy and attractive, and Prince Philip as if he was thoroughly enjoying himself'.[74] Others were impressed by the theatricality of the event. 'The King looked unbelievably beautiful', Sir Michael Duff wrote to Cecil Beaton, 'like an early French King and HRH the Bride a dream.'[75]

After the signing of the register in the Chapel of St Edward the Confessor, the couple returned, the Prince bowing to the King and Queen, the Princess dropping a low curtsey, her train billowing out behind her. Then they returned together in the Glass Coach to Buckingham Palace, for an 'austerity' wedding breakfast for 150 guests. At the end of it, the King made no speech. He simply raised his glass to 'the bride'.[76] The going-away involved an additional ritual. As Philip in naval uniform and the Princess in a coat of 'love-in-a-mist blue'[77] left the Palace forecourt for Waterloo Station, they were chased by bridesmaids and relations, including the King and Queen, pelting them with rose petals. Queen Alexandra recalled that the Monarch and his wife were hand in hand,[78] Crawfie that the Queen lifted her skirts to join the farewell party by the railings, as the couple disappeared into the crowds that lined the route.[79] According to *The Times*, 'Roll upon roll of cheers followed the carriage', on its journey.[80]

Press coverage was even greater than for the Coronation – the start of an inflation in the news value of the Monarchy which eventually took its toll. In 1947, it helped to inflame a public interest in the display of royalty which had lain dormant since before the war. Radio was the dominant medium – used by the BBC to create images in the minds of listeners that were reverential, awe-inspiring and atmospheric. 'Into London's gathering dusk this afternoon', the six o'clock newsreader intoned, 'Princess Elizabeth and the Duke of Edinburgh – man and wife – drove away in an open landau from Buckingham Palace for their honeymoon ... It's been a day which London will long remember.' The written script was broken up, with strokes between words and phrases, to indicate pauses for solemn effect.[81] Afterwards, radio and its world-wide audience became part of wedding lore, with tales of huddles of avid listeners in unlikely places – for example, it was reported that the skipper of the New Zealand ship *Pamir* hove to in the middle of the South Atlantic so that all his crew could listen properly to the broadcast.[82] Mass Observation noted that in a typical provincial office, the radio was switched on all day. 'We couldn't get into the room', reported an informant, 'and just joined the crowd clustered outside.'[83]

As well as listening to the radio, a small number of people in Britain were able to watch some of the day's events on an apparatus described by the press as 'television's magic crystal' which had recently resumed broadcasting. A TV camera placed over the Palace forecourt was able to follow Princess Elizabeth's coach as it came out of the gates, and another took over outside the Abbey. The service itself was filmed, and shown on television the same evening, while the film and other press and broadcasting materials were flown for distribution next day in the United States. So great was the international interest that the Wedding film was even screened in Allied-occupied Berlin. The 4,000 seat cinema in which it was shown in the still devastated city was fully booked, seven days a week.

For British children, the most potent symbol of the Wedding was probably 'the cake'. Many schools celebrated with feasts of ices and buns, often (so it was reported) 'without recourse to special supplementary permits from the Ministry of Food', and in spite of a request from the Ministry of Education to head teachers to be as modest as possible in their spending. Universities treated it as an unofficial rag. Oxford had 'its gayest celebration since the war,' with community singing and fireworks in the streets, and undergraduates dancing eightsome reels.[84]

What was it really about? People were as puzzled then as they are now. Apart from the chance to escape austerity, if only for a day, there was what a woman in Leatherhead described to a Mass Observer as 'a delighted sort of family feeling. I always get it when watching any sort of royal do.'[85] The Archbishop of York had alluded to such a feeling in his marriage service address, and John Masefield, the Poet Laureate, displayed it in a mawkish but revealing *Prayer for the Royal Marriage*. 'To those dear lands, still calling Britain "Home",' he versi-fied, 'The Crown is still the link with Britain's past, The consecrated thing that must outlast / Folly and hate and other human foam.' A less embarrassing version of the same sentiment was provided by the historian G. M. Trevelyan who wrote in the official souvenir of a King above politics, and a symbol of national unity, yet one 'who appeals below the surface of politics to the simple, dutiful, human instincts which he and his own family circle represent,' and 'who holds the Commonwealth together by the common bond of his royal authority'.

In short, the Wedding was to be regarded – in the Establishment, but also in the Labour Government version – as a reminder of the direct link that supposedly existed between royal familial virtue and the constitutional and political functions of the Monarchy; and the public rejoicing as a celebration of a democratic system which worked. The whole occasion could be seen as a kind of victory parade for liberty, for a constitution, 'still the most sea-worthy of all political craft,' which had 'weathered the storms of two world wars', and for a family which provided a vital human ingredient. Trevelyan's argu-ment was pragmatic, yet also romantic. 'In Great Britain the Crown is the least criticised of our domestic institutions', he claimed; 'throughout the Dominions and Colonies it is the point on which the eyes of loyalty are turned from across every ocean. Affection for a

King's person and family adds warmth and drama to every man's rational awareness of his country's political unity and historic tradition. It is a kind of popular poetry in these prosaic times.'[86]

What Trevelyan did not say – something which provided an important element in the Empire-wide celebration of an essentially personal event – was that 'family' had come in the dozen years since George V's death to encroach still further on the other aspects of Monarchy. As the author of an internal Cabinet Office paper on the functions of the Prime Minister put it in June 1947, not only was it absolute doctrine that the King did nothing political except on ministerial advice, 'the tendency has been to regard more and more matters as having political significance'.[87] The Second World War, the election of a highly political Labour Government, and the personality of George VI, had all contributed to this tendency, which had rendered the areas of royal activity that were controversial, or open to normal criticism, nugatory, and narrowed the range of public interest in royal figures and royal lives, without removing its intensity.

Thus, the reduction of the Royal Family to picture book iconography did not diminish public enthusiasm: indeed, by removing all remaining partisan elements, it enhanced it. Appreciation of the virtues of the British system turned into an appreciation of personages from whom all hint of blame had been removed for anything that went wrong – yet who could be thanked for the things that had gone right. The biggest of these was survival. In the late 1940s, apart from the United States, British democracy had no major-state rival, and this was a point, not just for patriotic pride, but also for sober contemplation on the constitutional reasons why it should be so. The point was contemporary and urgent: amongst other things, the Wedding – the 'splash of colour' as Churchill called it – was a propaganda blast against totalitarianism at the start of the Cold War. 'To every foreigner present,' Wheeler-Bennett was able to write a few years later, the ceremonies, processions and public enthusiasm were 'an object lesson, doubly expressive in the existing distressed state of Europe, of the stability of Britain's political institutions, and of the unity of the nation in its respect for tradition and its loyalty to the throne'.[88]

8

Any hope that, by leaving London for a supposedly private honey-moon in the country, Elizabeth and Philip could escape national attention or at any rate pretend it did not exist, was quickly dis-appointed. The public hunger, raised to such a level, could not simply be switched off at the moment when it became convenient to do so. The couple were due to spend the first part of their honeymoon at Uncle Dickie's house Broadlands, near Romsey in the New Forest. When they got off the train at Winchester, the Princess was observed to have a corgi with her – symbol of the domesticity she longed for. But the crowds would not allow it. Having learnt of the whereabouts of the Princess and the Duke, sightseers lay in wait. On the first Sunday after the Wedding, in a foretaste of what was to come, a mass of them surged into Romsey Abbey, where the couple were due to attend Matins. Some – unable to get seats in the church – carried ladders, chairs, and even a sideboard into the churchyard to stand on, in order to get a better look. After the service, less voracious royal enthusiasts queued (it was an age of queuing) outside the Abbey, in order to take their turn at sitting in the seats that royalty had sat in.[1]

After a week under siege at Broadlands the royal couple at last evaded their pursuers by travelling north to Birkhall.[2] They returned to the Palace in time for the King's fifty-second birthday on December 14th. 'The Edinburghs are back from Scotland,' Colville wrote the following day. 'She was looking very happy, and, as a result of three weeks of matrimony, suddenly a woman instead of a girl. He also seemed happy, but a shade querulous, which is, I think, in his charac-ter.'[3] One reason for querulousness was that, among all the pre-wedding preparations, one aspect of their future had been neglected: where they planned to live. Following their engagement they had chosen Sunninghill Park, near Ascot, as their future country home.

In August, however, Sunninghill was gutted by fire. Chips Channon recorded that he had been asked if he would let or lend his house to the couple for several months while they found somewhere else, but had turned down the request on the grounds that it would mean too much upheaval.[4] Instead, they obtained a lease on Windlesham Moor, near Sunningdale in Surrey. This was not immediately available, and in any case was only for weekend use. Their London residence was to be Clarence House in Stable Yard, at the south angle of St James's Palace. This imposing four-storey mansion had been built for William IV when Duke of Clarence in 1824. Its most recent occupant had been the Duke of Connaught, who had died in 1942, since when it had been unoccupied. In addition to the neglect of an elderly royal duke, there had been serious damage from bombing. Renovations took more than eighteen months, and the couple were unable to move in until July 1949.

In the meantime, they lived in Buckingham Palace. Crawfie believed that this was a mistake, that the Princess needed to get away from her parents.[5] Philip – beginning to experience the brutal consequences to his own life of such a marriage – may have felt the same. However, as the popular papers eagerly pointed out, the Palace was convenient for the office: Philip had been given a desk job working for the Director of Operations at the Admiralty, and was able to walk there every morning along the Mall, despite the stares of passers-by.

It was an odd period for both of them: Elizabeth at first living a life which on the surface had altered remarkably little since before her engagement, Philip undergoing the profound change of outlook, circumstance and expectation that accompanied his choice of mate. Both worked, though neither of them very strenuously. They took a keen interest in the Clarence House renovations, often visiting the initially gloomy building. Sometimes they joined in – Elizabeth amusing herself by mixing the paints for the walls of the Adam-style dining-room, which was hung with Hanoverian portraits, and by furnishing the house with wedding presents. When eventually they moved in, the Princess and her husband had separate but communicating bedrooms, with the dressing-tables only a few feet from the joint door, so that they could talk through it when they were getting ready for dinner. According to the Duke's valet, John Dean, when Bobo

MacDonald was helping Elizabeth and he was helping Philip, the couple 'would joke happily through the left-open door.'[6]

Getting settled into suitable accommodation took some time to sort out. Money was quicker – though by no means automatic. The Select Committee report on the Civil List was delivered promptly on December 11th, and discussed on the floor of the House six days later. The debate – as the *Manchester Guardian* put it – was of 'peculiar interest'.[7] Against the background of the Wedding on the one hand, and the split vote in the Committee on the other, it provided the first opportunity since the Abdication for a proper public exploration of the role and function of the Monarchy. It was also an exercise in temperature taking: for the vote was a free one, and the House, with its large Labour majority, was as far tilted away from automatic monarchism as at any time since 1918.

Conservatives and Liberals supported the report proposals. The difficulty was on the Government side. Sir Stafford Cripps, moving the acceptance of the report, spoke of the importance of the functions the Princess and Duke had to perform, and of the proof of that importance provided by 'the intense interest and enthusiasm displayed by all sections of the population at the time of their marriage'. For the Conservatives, Anthony Eden reminded the House that the British ambassador in Washington spent £20,000 a year just on entertaining. Labour left-wingers responded with arguments that were to become staple fare on such occasions. There was talk of the excessive cost of the 'servants and hangers-on of the Court,' and of 'spivs and drones and butterflies' around the royal couple. A Scottish MP compared the Duke's £10,000 ('in addition to a cushy job at the Admiralty') with the forty shillings a week paid to men blinded in the war. Others suggested that the 'Scandinavian type' of monarchy was cheaper and better.

In addition, there was a 'moderate' opposition to the Cripps-Lascelles package – not republicanism, but a belief that (in the words of Maurice Webb, a Select Committee member) the country both wished to retain the Monarchy 'and desired it to be simple, austere and democratic'. From the Palace's point of view, such an argument was much more dangerous than that of the Monarchy denigrators, because it struck a genuine chord among the loyal but luxury-denied public; and because it sought, in reasonable tones, to reassert parliamentary control of royal expenditure. The decisive group, however, was the powerful body of Labour MPs who both believed in the Monarchy as a useful device, and felt – with Nye Bevan – that if it was to be done at all, it had to be done in style: in the words of Arthur Greenwood in the debate, 'with proper dignity'.

It was to this group that the Prime Minister appealed when he spoke in support of a 'ceremonial' monarchy – whose value, he implied, derived both from its ability to meet a need for public theatre, and from the exemplary behaviour of the principal actors. In what amounted to a Labour theory of Monarchy, Attlee spoke of the need for 'simple lives and approachable people' at the heart of a democracy, and of royal ceremonials as an alternative to the sinister rituals of totalitarianism. The financial details before the House, he suggested, were intended to make such ceremonials and necessary symbolism possible, by giving 'these young people the facilities for doing the kind of work the general public wanted them to do, of visiting and getting into contact with people in the United Kingdom' and outside, especially in the Dominions.

Attlee's advocacy worked, but it failed to supply the all-party support for the Select Committee recommendations which the Palace would have liked. Although no more than thirty-three MPs voted for a left-wing amendment to give no increase in the Civil List at all, an amendment proposed by Webb to limit the couple's total to £40,000 was defeated only by 291 to 165 – indicating a large dissentient vote among Labour backbenchers, and a significant rate of abstention among ministers. A mere 122 Labour MPs opposed Webb's amendment, while 106, including eleven ministers, were unaccounted for. In short, if Labour had voted on its own, the Webb reduction to the List payments would have been carried. As it was, the Princess and Duke got their increases in spite of, not because of, the votes of the governing party.[8]

'There was much criticism of the sums proposed but none of the Monarchy as such,' noted Colville who, with other courtiers, keenly watched the proceedings from the Distinguished Strangers' Gallery. 'There was, however, a large school on the Labour backbenches which said the country wanted a "Scandinavian monarchy" with less pageantry and pomp rather than a "ceremonial monarchy". Cripps spoke admirably and was most effective in debate and Eden was also telling.'[9] Chips Channon blamed the Palace for the tactical error, as he saw it, of failing to invite enough ordinary MPs to the Wedding, which had resulted in a lengthy and embarrassing debate. He concluded that 'the Royal Family had, I think, a deserved jolt.'[10]

THE FIRST DUTY and ambition of an Heir to the Throne was swiftly accomplished: early in the New Year, Princess Elizabeth became pregnant. The announcement was not made until the summer. In the meantime, the publicity created by the Wedding, combined with the Princess's new status, helped to increase her list of engagements.

With the marriage, as Ziegler has written, 'the monarchy gained a new and incomparably brighter focus of attention. The King was in no sense forgotten . . . but in a curious way he was written off. Elizabeth was the future.'[11] The young Princess who signed no documents, made no decisions and uttered few words in public that were her own, continued to have a hypnotic effect wherever she went. As time passed, however, there was a shift in the tone and quality of the adulation. By chance, the marriage had coincided, not just with a crisis, but with the nadir of the nation's peacetime fortunes. Thereafter, both the economy and living conditions began to improve. It was as if the Wedding had been a good omen; and the Princess – a healthy, composed, pretty, wifely symbol of post-war youth and possibility, with her exquisitely designed couture that made imaginative use of clothing coupons, and her picture-book war-hero husband – stood for a new alternative to drabness.

It was an enjoyable life, and less demanding than the frequency of her newsreel appearances made it appear. Yet it was also – as Colville perceived – a remarkably aimless one, devoid of any content apart from pleasing and being seen. The Princess's private secretary, an ambitious and high-flying diplomat on secondment, had had a more exciting life than this, and he determined to inject some element of purpose, or at least of understanding, into the repetitive royal round. Once the Wedding was out of the way, he set himself the task of extending his employer's political education.

He found the Princess easier to instruct than her husband. After going through some paperwork with both of them, he noted that Philip became impatient if his interest was not immediately aroused; and that Elizabeth concentrated better on details.[12] In order to advance the Princess's knowledge, though possibly also to increase his own, he hit on the idea of getting her included in the distribution of Foreign Office telegrams. The less technical ones, he wrote to Lascelles, 'would give HRH an idea of world affairs which she cannot possibly get from the newspapers.'[13] The Foreign Office consented, as did the King, and the first box of telegrams arrived on January 16th. In addition, rather like Crawfie and Queen Mary before the war, Colville decided to take the Princess on educational trips. Shortly after the arrival of the first FO box, they sat and watched a Foreign Affairs debate in the House of Commons. As the Princess entered, 'all eyes there turned in her direction,' according to the press.[14] The Princess sat demurely, while the Duke, who accompanied them, made lively comments.

Compensating for the deficiencies of a royal education was an uphill struggle. Though she appeared to read the telegrams, Colville was disappointed to find Princess Elizabeth at first uninterested in politics. However, his attempt to widen her experience continued. In February, he took her to a juvenile court for a day, in the not very optimistic hope of persuading her to improve her knowledge of the social services.[15] In this, he achieved more success than he perhaps realized. At any rate, the Princess picked up enough to assist her in one of the most necessary of royal skills, that of talking brightly to distinguished guests about areas that concerned them. When Eleanor Roosevelt stayed at Windsor Castle the same spring during a visit to England for the unveiling of a statue of her husband, she was greatly flattered that the King's daughter sought her out with a question about homes for young women offenders. She found the Heiress 'very serious-minded' and she was impressed 'that this young Princess was so interested in social problems and how they were being handled'.[16]

There were also other horizon-expanding excursions in addition to the formal round. In May 1948, Tom Driberg complained to Lord Mountbatten that the Princess and Duke had made the wrong kind of visit to the Commons at the wrong time. Before the war, he pointed out, members of the Royal Family had dined informally in private rooms at the House with MPs of the then ruling party. He suggested taking the Princess to the House at Question Time. 'To get the ethos, the feel, of Parliament', he wrote, 'she really ought to watch Bevan, Gaitskell, Harold Wilson, Morrison etc. parrying the everyday cuts, often pretty effectively and wittily.'[17] If this particular suggestion reached Clarence House, it was ignored. However, Driberg's belief that the Princess had no contact with leading Labour figures was not quite correct. In fact, a meeting with a couple of the Labour politicians on his list had occurred only the month before.

This took the form of a small dinner party held by the Prime Minister and his wife for the royal couple, to which a few of the younger members of the Government, including the President of the Board of Trade, Harold Wilson, and the Minister of Fuel and Power, Hugh Gaitskell, and their wives were invited. The gathering was indeed a strange one. The politicians could not decide whether it was appropriate to admit to the kind of feelings their constituents would have had at such an intimate meeting with royalty, or to put on a show of jacobin disdain. While they waited to greet the royal guests in the drawing room at No 10, they made nervous schoolboy jokes. 'We had been talking about capital punishment,' Gaitskell recorded. 'Harold reminded us that it was still a capital offence to rape a Royal Princess!' When the Princess and Duke arrived, the ministers and their wives were faced with the problem which often seems to beset prominent socialists in the presence of royalty: whether it was sillier to bow and curtsey, or not to. Dora Gaitskell could hardly bring herself to curtsey, but Mrs Attlee, entering into the spirit of things, 'suddenly swung round and curtsied low to the Duke.'

After dinner, each minister was summoned to the sofa, to spend a quarter of an hour in conversation with the twenty-two-year-old guest of honour, who must have found the experience as taxing as they did. Gaitskell formed the same opinion as Colville. 'She had a very pretty voice and quite an easy manner but is not, I think, very interested in politics or affairs generally', he concluded. She tried hard, but evidently found it more difficult to think of things to say about the fuel economy than about homes for bad girls. Gamely, she remarked that her grandmother's house was the coldest she knew. Why? inquired the minister. The Princess replied that 'it was because of her national duty'.[18]

Colville's ambitions to extend his employer's range (and also to extend his own) did not cease. In February, he proposed that the Princess and the Duke should visit Paris to help strengthen ties with an ally that was beginning to recover its economy and self-confidence after the war. The proposal was accepted by the Foreign Secretary and the King, but at first it encountered difficulties with the royal couple. Elizabeth was enthusiastic about the prospect of a trip that would take her to a city and country she had never visited, and which would be a good deal more exciting than speaking to women's organizations in the provinces, or sitting on sofas with middle-aged politicians. Philip, on the other hand, who had spent most of his childhood in or around Paris, was less thrilled. He also resented the way Colville did things that affected him without getting his opinion first. There was a row, but eventually he agreed.

The notional purpose of the visit was the opening of the Exhibition of Eight Centuries of British Life at the Musée Galliera in Paris, in a ceremony to take place in the presence of President Auriol on May 14th. The real aim, however, was to give the Anglophile section of the French public a chance to show its sympathies, after a decade of confusion. It was the first official visit by British royalty since the King and Queen had been sent on a similar mission of bridge-building in 1939. The precedent was not entirely propitious: though British royalty had been welcomed on that occasion, the visit had failed in its purpose of helping to create an unbreakable bond between the two peoples. Since 1940, French attitudes towards Britain had contained a complex mixture of emotions, including those of comradeship and suspicion in equal measure.

So it was a gamble – but it worked. The French government did everything in its power to build up the diplomatic importance of the visit, and the French public – mystified and fascinated by the royal wedding – seemed delighted at the opportunity to see and cheer a newly married Princess. The royal party was escorted to Versailles and given lunch at the Grand Trianon, where the tablecloths and napkins had been embroidered with 'E's and 'P's in their honour. A triumphal progress down the Seine was followed by a dinner and reception at the British embassy, where the Princess glistened with the Nizam of Hyderabad's jewels; and there were visits, through thick crowds, to Fontainebleau, Barbizon, Vaux-le-Vicomte. It was, said the papers, the Norman Conquest in reverse: Elizabeth had conquered Paris. It helped that the Vicomtesse de Bellaigue had done her work well, and that the Princess spoke almost faultless French. Even the Communist press abandoned its normal silence on such occasions, and paid the Princess the indirect compliment of complaining that the police arrangements for her security made it impossible for ordinary Parisians to get a close enough look.[19]

The British Foreign Office privately expressed its satisfaction. 'The latent enthusiasm of the French people for the pomp and pageantry of monarchy was clearly revealed,' the British ambassador, Sir Oliver Harvey, wrote to Ernest Bevin. 'It was an unusual experience to see the townsfolk of Paris cheer an English Princess from the Place de la Bastille.' Yet the visit caused offence to some. General de Gaulle – opposed both to the current French government and to the Fourth Republic Constitution – was left off the Embassy invitation list, for fear of offending the President, and they had to do make do with the General's brother, who was President of the Municipal Council of Paris, instead.[20] At home, some Scottish church organizations criticized the couple for visiting a racecourse and a Paris nightclub on a Sunday, and hence setting a most regrettable example to the Empire's youth, 'who look to their Royal Highnesses for guidance and inspiration'.[21] The Princess used the trip as an opportunity to stock up with goods not available in Britain. When she got the HM Customs bill, she startled her private secretary by asking him crossly why he had made a full declaration.[22]

The appeal of the Princess to the French lay partly in her international celebrity following the Wedding; partly in her appearance, especially what Colville, a keen connoisseur, described as her 'beautiful blue eyes and superb natural complexion';[23] and partly in a feeling that she stood for those who had grown up in the war, and could look hopefully ahead. In Britain too, the vision of the Princess as the ambassador, not just of her country, but of her generation, seemed to justify hopes for a freer, more fulfilling future for the war's young inheritors. Invitations to speak to, and on behalf of, younger people proliferated. At the end of May, she attended a parade of youth organizations in Coventry; later she delighted dons and undergraduates in Oxford with a speech in the Sheldonian in which she declared that the universities were 'a powerful fortress against the tide of sloth, ignorance and materialism.'[24]

Meanwhile, the idea of the Princess as standing for the future was enhanced on June 4th, Derby Day, by the announcement of her pregnancy. The Princess broke precedent by appearing the same afternoon, 'smiling and unabashed,' at the Epsom Downs racecourse.[25] No child *in utero* arouses more interest than a royal one in the direct line. As Crawfie later pointed out, the only truly private period in the existence of a member of the Royal Family is between conception and the moment when the coming event is publicly known.[26] For Prince Charles, that period was now over. The world's most famous foetus became the hapless recipient of baby clothes from all over the world, together with matinée coats, bootees and pictures of storks.

PRECEDENT was about to be broken in another way: the custom that had got 'Jix' Joynson-Hicks out of bed in the middle of the night in 1926 was discontinued. Royal propaganda presented the decision as an independent initiative by the King and Queen, and further evidence of their modernity. In fact, it only came about after a fight, and the forces of reaction nearly won the day.

Lascelles later claimed to have been the instigator of change. 'I had long thought that the practice of summoning the Home Secretary to attend, like a sort of supernumerary midwife, at the birth of a royal baby was out-of-date and ridiculous', he wrote in 1969, after his retirement. 'The Home Office made exhaustive researches and assured me that it had no constitutional significance whatever, and was merely a survival of the practice of ministers and courtiers, who would flock to the sick-bed, whenever any member of the Royal Family was ill.'[27] The Home Office assurance was indeed categorical. 'The custom is only a custom,' Chuter Ede, the Home Secretary, wrote in June. 'It has no statutory authority behind it and there is no legal requirement for its continuance.'[28]

It was an opportunity to do away with a time-wasting and embarrassing distraction. The matter was one for the King, but the King demurred. According to Lascelles's later account, when he put the proposition to him in the autumn of 1948, George VI agreed at once, 'but the Queen thought differently, seeing in this innovation a threat to the dignity of the Throne. So I was told to hold my hand.'[29] However, Lascelles's memory of what happened was not exact. Contemporary records suggest that a period of indecision preceded the royal negative. Correspondence in the Royal Archives includes a letter from Lascelles himself to the Home Secretary, written at the end of July, putting off an answer. In it he explained that the King had been particularly busy lately, 'but hopes to give his full consideration to the question of your attendance at Princess Elizabeth's accouchement when he gets to Balmoral next week.' It was another month before the period of full consideration was complete, and the verdict communicated. 'It is His Majesty's wish', wrote Lascelles on August 21st, 'that you, as Home Secretary, should be in attendance when Princess Elizabeth's baby is born.'[30] There the matter rested until November when, a few weeks before the birth, the King changed his mind. The clinching factor was not a sudden progressive impulse, or a newly acquired desire to dispense with a meaningless ritual – but a shocked discovery of the constitutional implications of hanging on to it.

What turned the tables was a visit to the Palace, on other business, by the Canadian High Commissioner. In the course of the conversation with the King's private secretary, the envoy happened to speak of the Princess's condition. Since the Dominion governments had as much stake in the birth of a future heir as the British one, he remarked, he supposed that when the baby arrived, he and the representatives of the other Dominions would be asked to attend, along with the British Home Secretary. It was a eureka moment. The point had never occurred to Lascelles, to the Home Office, to the Dominion Governments or – apparently – to anybody at all in 1926, at the time of the Princess's birth. However, constitutionally it was indisputable – and, at a time of Commonwealth transition, politically it was unavoidable.

When Lascelles spoke to the King later that day, he was able, quite casually, to mention that 'as he had no doubt realized, if the old ritual was observed, there would be no less than seven Ministers sitting in the passage.'[31] The perpetuation of a custom popularly believed to involve the Home Secretary attending 'as a sort of super-inspector to guarantee that the Royal baby is not a suppositious child!' could scarcely be seen as an act of homage[32] – least of all, if there were seven super-inspectors. According to Lascelles, the King was horrified at such a prospect, and his resistance immediately crumbled.[33] On November 5th, Buckingham Palace announced the ending of 'an archaic custom'.[34]

Perhaps a more personal factor also affected the Monarch's judgement. The King had been unwell for some time, and in the autumn of 1948 his health took a sharp turn for the worse. On October 30th, a medical examination showed that he was seriously ill. Thirteen days later, his doctors firmly diagnosed early arteriosclerosis – with such a severe danger of gangrene to his right leg that they considered amputating it.

How much did the Princess know? The full significance of the diagnosis may have been kept from her, as it was from the King. However, the physical discomfort of her father, and the acute anxiety of her mother, must have communicated themselves to her during the last few days before her first confinement.[35]

The burdens of being a monarch were not easily shed. Despite his illness, and the concern for his survival, the King was required to perform a constitutional function which the courtiers regarded as urgent. 'As things stand at present,' Lascelles wrote to the King on November 9th, while the doctors were considering their provisional diagnosis, 'Princess Elizabeth's son would be "Earl of Merioneth", her daughter "Lady X Mountbatten".' To ensure that the child would be known, instead, as HRH Prince X or Princess Y, Letters Patent had to be prepared '*before* the baby is born,' Lascelles stressed, 'so that the official announcements may refer to him, or her, as a Prince or Princess.'[36] The King did as he was advised, and Letters Patent were rushed through and issued the same day. The move had an incidental consequence: it finally resolved, for the benefit of constitutional purists, an issue first raised after the birth of Princess Margaret, when it had been argued that the two princesses might have equal claims to the succession. By placing Princess Elizabeth in the same position as if she were the King's son and heir, any theoretical doubt on this point was finally eliminated.[37]

With Clarence House not ready and Windlesham Moor unsuitable, arrangements were made for the Princess's confinement to take place at Buckingham Palace, just below her second floor bedroom, looking out towards the Mall. The American press reported 'medical reasons' for expecting the baby to be a girl[38] and a Ceylonese astrologer sent a horoscope – which Lascelles passed to the King for his amusement – promising a boy.[39] The astrologer was right. The Princess went into labour early in the evening of November 14th, and – attended by four doctors – gave birth to a baby boy shortly after 9 o'clock. Her husband, who played a game of squash during her contractions, was summoned from the Palace court immediately after the delivery to hear the news.[40] According to the official statement, the Duke 'went into the Princess's room to see her' and then 'went to see his son, who had been taken to the nursery.'[41] Meanwhile, the crowd outside the Palace, far greater than the little gathering in Bruton Street twenty-three years before, became so large that the police had to cordon off the road. Despite appeals for quiet, the cheering continued until after midnight. 'The bells rang, and a man going down the street outside our flat called "It's a boy,"' recorded Hugh Dalton. Pondering the future for such a child, and the future of the British Monarchy, he added: 'If this boy ever comes to the throne . . . it will be a very different country and Commonwealth he'll rule over'.[42]

Few others looked so far ahead. Most newspaper commentary combined anodyne leading articles about the value and virtues of royalty with sentimental descriptions of the baby's appearance. Crawfie thought he looked like George V,[43] John Dean described him as 'a tiny red-faced bundle, either hairless or so fair as to appear so'.[44] A few days after the birth, Cecil Beaton was called to the Palace to take the first official pictures of mother and baby. 'Prince Charles, as he is to be named, is an obedient sitter,' he noted. 'He interrupted a long, contented sleep to do my bidding and open his blue eyes to stare long and wonderingly into the camera lens, the beginning of a lifetime in the glare of publicity.'[45] As a royal gesture, the Princess instructed that food parcels made up from gifts received at the Palace should be distributed to mothers of all children born on November 14th.[46]

The baby Prince was placed in a gilt crib, with lace frills around it, and the entire Palace staff was invited to visit the nursery to take a peek. A royal pram was brought out of storage, along with a royal rattle once used by the Princess.[47] According to Crawfie, in order 'to give him as good a foundation as possible,' for the first few months the Princess breastfed him.[48] Before the Prince had reached the age of two months, however, there was an unfortunate hiatus. In January, it was announced from the Palace that Princess Elizabeth had contracted measles. There were no complications. Nevertheless, it was feared that the baby might catch the infection. It was therefore decided that mother and baby should be separated, until the disease had run its course.[49]

IF THE PERIOD following the Wedding was a happy one for the Princess, the immediate aftermath of her first confinement was tense and anxious, as the full gravity of her father's illness – with its terrible implications, not just for him, but for her as well – was brought home to her. Two days after the birth, the King yielded to the advice of his doctors that a long-projected tour of Australia and New Zealand, similar to the one he and the Queen had undertaken as Duke and Duchess of York in 1927, should be postponed. The decision was a bitter disappointment, but he had no choice – he had been told that such a journey might delay his recovery, and even endanger his leg.[50]

The moment was a turning point. From this time on, the Heiress Presumptive and her young, healthy family became the present, as well as the future – her energy and composure linked in the public mind to the visible fatigue of the ailing King. Though still in his early fifties, the King looked and behaved like a man much older, and had become increasingly difficult for his family and advisers to handle. He remained a loving and deeply devoted father, who enjoyed nothing so much as a private family occasion. In matters of state, he was punctilious, honest, and stoical to a fault. But his ability to deal with complicated matters, never great, diminished still further under the impact of his illness. Although, ultimately always willing to take advice, he became increasingly obstinate.

There was also an intensifying of some long-established traits: and in particular his bad temper. 'He had his explosions,' says one of his former advisers. 'He would explode if he read something in the paper that the Prime Minister hadn't told him about. We used to call them his "gnashes". When they occurred Princess Margaret was very good at defusing them.'[51] One friend of the princesses, who used to stay at

Sandringham and Balmoral, recalls the King's 'prep-school sense of humour,' and rollicking enjoyment of practical jokes. He also remembers his 'Hanoverian bark' if something annoyed him. The subject of his displeasure was often politics. However, everyday incidents could also provoke an outburst. Once, when they were shooting at Sandringham, a man walked past and the King said, 'He didn't take his bloody hat off.'[52] According to another ex-courtier, the Monarch 'used to lose his temper with anyone around.'[53]

Some people wondered whether he had a touch of the *petit mal*. Others put it down to the frustration caused by his own intellectual limitations, and the need to cover up. Alec Vidler, a canon at Windsor who often dined with the Royal Family, found him 'really very simple,' and also 'difficult to get on with because he talked in an excitable manner'.[54] Another aide, meeting the King for the first time in 1947, was taken aback by his irascibility and apparent inferiority complex. It was as if, he recorded, the Monarch's displays of wrath and emphatic manner were devices to hide his ignorance and weakness.[55]

In March 1949, the King underwent major spinal surgery to restore circulation to his leg, carried out in a surgical theatre constructed at Buckingham Palace. He was well enough by June to be driven in an open carriage to watch the Ceremony of Trooping the Colour, while his elder daughter rode confidently at the head of the parade. Pictures of him, however, show a drawn, tired old man. He was now a semi-invalid, and the rest of his life was to be a series of alarms, remissions and new alarms, with alternating episodes of relief and anxiety, against the background of an unspoken foreboding. His wife and two daughters admired, adored, and felt protective towards him – as they always had. But as his health deteriorated and his ability to cope diminished, his dogmatism grew, and so did the pressure on those around him. It was heightened by a desperate resistance to the truth. 'The Queen never allowed you to contemplate the fact of the King's illness,' recalls a former aide.[56]

The result was a collective self-deceit at Court, which made a realistic look into the future impossible to discuss. The King's ill-health also had the effect of increasing his elder daughter's sense of independent responsibility, as she assumed more and more of his functions. Outwardly, the Princess showed no sign of strain. Indeed, she and the Duke – with a male heir promptly provided, and efficiently nurtured by a retinue of helpers – embarked on a brief episode of social gaiety. As pre-war Society began to re-emerge from hibernation, the royal couple were to be seen at the houses and events frequented by others of their kind, or in the company of show business personalities, for whom both princesses had a particular penchant. Ordinary citizens bought photos of their favourite film stars. The King's daughters invited them to dinner, or to stay. When Princess Elizabeth celebrated her twenty-third birthday in April 1949 at the Café de Paris, a fashionable restaurant in Coventry Street, following a visit to *The School for Scandal* at the New Theatre, the royal party was joined by Laurence Olivier and Vivien Leigh, the leading actor and actress of the show. Together, the royal and theatrical party 'tangoed and sambaed, waltzed and quick-stepped' the night away, before going on to a nightclub for more of the same.[57]

For a time, both princesses took up with Danny Kaye, then at the height of his fame. John Dean recalled seeing the American comedian 'capering round Princess Elizabeth' on the lawn at Windlesham Moor.[58] At grand social occasions, the Princess and the Duke were inevitably the main attraction, and they learned to play their parts. In June 1949, Chips Channon recorded his impression of the couple at a ball at Windsor Castle, mainly attended by the clever, artistic, smart members of the emerging 'Princess Margaret set'. Elizabeth was wearing a very high tiara and the Garter, and Philip, also with the Garter, was in his naval uniform. 'They looked like characters out of a fairy tale', wrote Channon, 'and quite eclipsed Princess Margaret, who was simply dressed.'[59] This was one kind of fancy dress. There was also another. At a ball given by the American ambassador in July – in a curiously snobbish piece of royal whimsy – the Duke appeared as a waiter, wearing a white apron, and his wife as a maid.[60]

That summer they moved into Clarence House, away from the direct surveillance of the King and Queen. For a few months, they were able to lead the semblance of a normal family life – husband, wife and infant son, a single, separate unit under the same roof. The arrangement, however, was soon upset by the resumption of Philip's active naval career. In October 1949 – following a period at the Royal Naval Staff College at Greenwich – he was appointed First Lieutenant and second-in-command of HMS *Chequers*, leader of the First

Destroyer Flotilla of the Mediterranean Fleet, based in Malta. During the next two years, the Princess's existence became, in one respect, the most 'normal' of her entire life. Crawfie wrote later that when Elizabeth was in Malta with her husband, she 'saw and experienced for the first time the life of an ordinary girl.'[61] Mike Parker, who had become a private secretary to the Princess and the Duke jointly, agrees. 'This was a fabulous period,' he says, 'when it was thought a good idea for her to become a naval officer's wife. It seemed it was the King's wish that she should do so.'[62] The negative side of such normality, however, was that she saw her husband only on those occasions that his location and leaves made possible.

Philip flew out to Malta on October 16th. The Princess was due to join him a few weeks later. Meanwhile, her emblematic role as young mother continued to develop. It was an age of exhortation, and the Princess's demeanour and speaking style equipped her well for the task of delivering homilies to others – especially women – whose experience seemed to relate to her own. A couple of days after her husband left, she returned to the theme of 'materialism' – already denounced in her Oxford University speech – when she addressed a Mothers' Union rally of young wives at Central Hall, Westminster. 'Materialism' in 1949 meant wasteful and unnecessary consumption – and therefore was subject to Government as well as moral disapproval. At the same time, she was required to lend her own moral authority – as a royal newly-wed and home-maker – to the Mothers' Union condemnation of divorce.

In her speech, she spoke scathingly of the 'current age of growing self-indulgence, of hardening materialism, of falling moral standards'. She also praised her audience's emphasis on the sanctity of marriage.[63] The young wives applauded warmly when she declared that broken homes caused havoc among children, and that 'we can have no doubt that divorce and separation are responsible for some of the darkest evils in our society today'. Children, she said, learnt by example, and would not be expected to do what parents were too lazy to do themselves. 'I believe there is a great fear in our generation of being labelled priggish', she added – indicating that the fear should not prevent responsible people from doing or saying what they believed to be right.[64]

The speech plunged her into unexpected controversy. Advocates of changing the divorce laws reacted strongly. The Mothers' Union, they claimed, was notorious for its conservatism on the subject, and they complained that royal sanction should not have been given for a standpoint that was increasingly contested. 'The harm to children can be greater in a home where both parents are at loggerheads than if divorce ensues', protested the chairman of the Marriage Law Reform Committee. Of course, the Princess had not written the words she had spoken, but – having allowed her personal image and reputation to be used in order to bolster a contentious point of view – she could not entirely escape responsibility for the sentiment. However, according to one member of the Royal Household, writing a few years later, there was no reason for the Princess to distance herself from her script. 'King George and Queen Elizabeth were completely satisfied that their daughter had been right, for their views on marriage and family life were the same.'[65]

Princess Elizabeth flew to Malta to join her husband on November 20th, accompanied by a party that included a lady-in-waiting, Lady Alice Egerton, Mike Parker, her maid Bobo, and Philip's valet John Dean.[66] Prince Charles was left in the charge of nursery staff, much as Princess Elizabeth herself had been left in 1927, when her own parents, as Duke and Duchess of York, had embarked on their antipodean tour.

According to Dean, the Princess's life in Malta was not markedly different from that of anybody else similarly placed. However, normality and ordinariness were only relative. Most service wives did not have a retinue of devoted helpers. There was also something else that singled her out: the presence and hospitality of Uncle Dickie. It added greatly to the convenience and comfort of the Princess that the ever-solicitous Lord Mountbatten happened to be based at Malta in his current role in command of the 1st Cruiser Squadron of the Mediterranean Fleet, and that he was more than happy to make his house, Villa Guardamangia, available to the royal couple.

The Princess's party stayed till the end of December, when *Chequers* was sent with six other warships to patrol the Red Sea, following disorders in Eritrea. Dean recalled later that Princess Elizabeth had been very excited about her first Malta trip, 'although she was probably a little sad at leaving Prince Charles behind'.[67] She did not, however, display any obvious consternation or – as some mothers might, after five weeks' separation – find it necessary to rush back to him as soon as she returned to England. Instead, she spent four days at Clarence House attending to engagements and dealing (according to the press) with 'a backlog of correspondence,' before attending Hurst Park races, where she saw Monaveen, a horse she owned jointly with her mother, win at 10–1. Only then was she reunited with her son, who had been staying with her parents at Sandringham.

Yet the Princess could be forgiven for enjoying the novelty of her visits to Malta – a haven of comparative privacy, and freedom from official duties. 'They were so relaxed and free, coming and going as they pleased . . .' recalled Dean. 'I think it was their happiest time.'[68] Philip was delighted to have returned to the life he knew and loved, and which depended on his abilities, not on his marriage. What for him, however, was a restoration of the *status quo ante* was a revelation for her. Though she lived in greater luxury than others, she did many of the same things as them, and in a similar way. Parker recalls that she would go down to the ship at the bottom of the road which led from the villa and 'generally mucked in with the other wives'. There was a lot of social visiting, having tea and dining with other couples. 'She spent only ten per cent of the time being a Princess,' he says. The ten per cent was mainly accounted for by Uncle Dickie who 'tried to get her into the admirals' strata'.[69]

There were some necessary courtesy calls. She was required to visit Archbishop Bonzi, and admire the views from his hilltop residence. Otherwise, to a degree that was barely imaginable in Britain, she was left alone. When Philip was busy, she drove her own Daimler, either solo or with a female companion, around the island. When he was free, she accompanied him on swimming expeditions with the Mountbattens, who would take a launch to the creeks and bays around Malta and Gozo, and they would sometimes sleep on board. She would watch her husband at some sporting event, or dine and dance with him at the local hotel – protected by the management and unharassed by the press. If she missed Charles, helping with a party given by Lady Mountbatten for a hundred children on board ship may have provided some consolation.[70]

In April, Princess Elizabeth's second pregnancy was announced. She spent her twenty-fourth birthday on Malta, watching her husband and uncle playing polo. Then she returned to England. The baby was due to be born in August, this time at Clarence House. As her time approached, thousands of people gathered outside, many of them hoping for a glimpse of the heavily pregnant Princess.[71] Bobo Mac-Donald responded to the tension by whipping herself up into a frenzy of work.[72] On August 15th, her mistress gave birth to a baby girl. Afterwards, Prince Charles, aged twenty-one months, was held up to the window to wave back at the onlookers.

The Princess took some time fully to recover. She had been expected to resume her public duties in October, but – on doctor's orders – had to postpone or cancel all engagements for another month. There were further cancellations in November because of a 'severe cold'. Later the same month – shortly after Charles's second birthday – she flew to Malta to spend Christmas with her husband, while the children were taken to Sandringham to stay with their grandparents. Meanwhile, Philip had been promoted to Lieutenant-Commander, and at the beginning of September 1950 he was given command of the frigate HMS *Magpie*. The *Magpie* had been ordered to provide an escort for the Commander-in-Chief's despatch vessel, HMS *Surprise*, for a visit to Philip's relatives King Paul and Queen Frederika of Greece, in Athens. Princess Elizabeth accompanied her husband on the trip – and together they were warmly welcomed in the Greek capital.

Not everybody shared the devotion of a Bobo MacDonald. In January, the whole Royal Family's education was dramatically advanced by the unexpected treachery – as they saw it – of Crawfie, now Mrs Buthlay, who had decided to cash in on her royal experiences. A letter from Princess Margaret to her former governess in March 1949 indicated concern at the Palace at the preparation of a revelatory book.[73] There may have been an element of misunderstanding. After the book was written, the Queen was approached for permission, and even saw proofs.[74] However, there was no doubt about the royal displeasure when the book was serialized, against the Royal Family's express wishes, in the American *Ladies' Home Journal*.

In March – spurred by the excitement caused in the United States – *Woman's Own* ran it in Britain, advertising extracts as 'The Loving,

Human, Authentic Story of The Little Princesses'. The Palace tried to throw doubt on the accuracy of the account at every opportunity. 'The Princess is not a bad sailor' insisted the Comptroller of the Household in reply to a well-wisher who, on reading that the Heiress suffered from sea-sickness, had helpfully donated a patent remedy, 'and to show how facts can be distorted, the voyage to the Channel Islands – on which occasion Miss Crawford reports that Her Royal Highness was prostrate – was in fact so calm that it was impossible to tell one was at sea, except for the subdued hum of the engines'.[75] Undeterred, Mrs Buthlay wrote a stream of additional books and articles over the next few years, drawing on the same store of knowledge, though ever thinner and more repetitive as the store ran out.

Eventually, to the great satisfaction of Buckingham Palace, she overreached herself by writing in imaginative detail about a royal event as if she had witnessed it, before it had taken place, and then finding herself unable to prevent publication of the article after the event had been cancelled. Her literary career ended forthwith. Mrs Buthlay died in 1986, unmourned at Buckingham Palace. According to a royal aide who went to the Palace a few years after the rumpus, 'the only thing I was told was that letters signed Bongo or Biffo should not be put in the bin because they were probably from cousins. Letters from Marion Crawford should be handled with a very long pair of forceps.'[76] Her name is still taboo: mention Crawfie to older royalty, and they stiffen. Yet there remains a little tragedy about the lack of a reconciliation. For the princesses, and especially Princess Elizabeth, were closer to Crawfie than almost anybody during their most formative years, and the bonds of understanding and affection had been strong.

Today it is difficult to appreciate an age of innocence in which Crawfie's recollections caused such a sense of outrage. As A. N. Wilson puts it in his introduction to the 1993 reprint of Marion Crawford's *The Little Princesses*, 'though few books were written so mawkishly, few can have been written with such obvious love'.[77] Kenneth Rose suggests that the Royal Family was angry because 'their privacy had been purloined and sold for gain'.[78] Yet there had been earlier accounts of the princesses' childhood, almost as mawkish, and also for gain. Perhaps it was the disobedience that caused most fury, rather than either the content or the motive.

The Little Princesses marked a watershed. For the former governess had stumbled on a discovery that was to blight the Royal Family for the rest of the century: the market in intimate details of royal lives was a rising one. The financial value of revelations was already known, and had been remarked upon within the Palace before the war. What had changed, and would henceforth grow with increasing rapidity, was the voracity of the public appetite, and the profits-led crumbling of inhibitions about feeding it.

There was an irony: Crawfie's writings caused a *frisson* because of the tightness with which royal privacy had been guarded, and the refusal to treat even the most modest press request for personal information as legitimate. The instrument of this policy was the King's press secretary, Commander Richard Colville – an unbending ex-naval officer with no knowledge of the press, which he treated with a combination of distrust and lordly contempt. There was also a grundyish aspect: former colleagues fondly recall his countenance when, confronted by the latest newspaper *lèse-majesté*, the corners of his mouth would turn down in horror.[79] Journalists called him 'the Abominable No Man', fellow courtiers dubbed him 'Sunshine'. At the time of Crawfie's offence, he had been in post for three years. The affair seemed to have a traumatic effect on him. So far from encouraging him to liberalize, it produced secrecy, greater *hauteur*, and greater prudery.

Commander Colville stayed at the Palace until 1968, a source of continuing aggravation to those on the press side who had to deal with him. His legacy – a belief that any titbit of above or below-stairs royal gossip was inherently interesting, because of the irritation its publication would cause to the Palace – still has its baleful effect. The Commander, however, was not alone in his attitude to the media. While George VI lived, his views received active support from Sir Alan Lascelles, who to some extent shared – even helped to inspire – the view that the Palace owed the press nothing, and that it would be better if the newspapers confined themselves to publishing official handouts.

Though author of the Princess's Cape Town BBC speech, Lascelles regarded the technology of radio with a special wariness. Over-exposure, he believed, through such a direct medium as broadcasting, was one of the biggest potential dangers to the Royal Family – and a temptation to be resisted strongly.

At the height of the Crawfie furore, it was proposed that Princess Elizabeth should accept an invitation to broadcast to the Youth of the Empire on Empire Day. She herself was keen. Lascelles's reaction, however, was unhesitatingly negative. 'The world, as a whole,' the courtier wrote in an internal Palace minute, 'is pretty surfeited with broadcasts, and the last thing we want is for the world to feel that way about royal broadcasts.' Christmas broadcasts, together with the occasional VE-Day or Silver Wedding, were quite enough. He therefore strongly advised against the Princess undertaking 'an "out of the blue" broadcast this summer – or indeed at any time'.[80] No Empire Day broadcast took place; and Princess Elizabeth remained – Crawfie outpourings apart – tantalizingly visible yet inaccessible, until many years after her accession as Queen.

9

PHILIP RETURNED FROM MALTA in the summer of 1951 and bowed to the inevitable: that it was impossible to combine an active naval career with the role of active partner to the Heiress Presumptive – especially one who, because of the King's illness, was expected to take on an increasing share of royal duties. It was a major sacrifice. He was barely thirty and, but for his marriage, his prospects of promotion to a high rank within the Navy of his adopted country were reckoned to be good. But he could not simultaneously accompany his wife, and command ships; his wife could not adapt her royal functions to suit his career; and he could not repeatedly take sabbaticals. When he left Malta, it was announced that he would not take up any further active naval appointments until after the return of the King and Queen from a Commonwealth tour now scheduled for the autumn. In fact, the break was a permanent one.

The result was a painful period of transition, which expressed itself in bursts of undirected energy and dismissive intolerance. According to his manservant, 'he loved the sea and adored the Navy, and some of my gayest times with him were when he was serving'. After his return from the sea, he was 'inclined to be moody and impatient', and it was some time before he settled down to public engagements.[1] One of the butts of his impatience was the royal establishment, which he regarded as stuffy and old-fashioned. 'Prince Philip was very hostile to Buckingham Palace – he didn't like it, and he wanted his own show', recalls a former courtier. 'The gap between the Palace and Clarence House was very big.'[2]

It was some compensation that, by 1951, the much smaller households of the Princess and Duke at Clarence House did constitute a quite distinct show – and one that worked with a degree of efficiency and harmony that would have been impossible if they had stayed longer in the same building as the King and the Queen. It may have helped that at the beginning of 1950 the suavely intelligent Jock Colville returned to the Foreign Office. In some ways, Colville had been a progressive influence, with an ambition to make the Heiress and her husband more socially aware. On one occasion he even made the suggestion to the Duke that he should work as a coal miner for a month – a proposal which was rejected on the grounds that 'it would be playing to the gallery'.[3] Colville's frequently possessive devotion to the Princess, however, had not made him the easiest of advisers for her husband to work with, and the atmosphere at Clarence House was more relaxed without him. His place was taken by Major Martin (later Lord) Charteris, a professional soldier who had spent much of the war in the Middle East, eventually running Military Intelligence in Palestine. Charteris worked for Elizabeth at Clarence House and then at Buckingham Palace for the next twenty-seven years. With the exception of her later Deputy Master of the Household, Lord Plunket, he came to know her as well as any courtier. His particular blend of wisdom, dry humour, friendliness, conservatism and selfless loyalty fitted her needs well.

Those who worked at Clarence House in the short period of its occupancy by the royal couple recall a happy, close-knit group of helpers, over which the influence of the busy and contented Princess, enjoying her duties and her pleasures, shone benignly. 'Martin and I both loved to bask in her light', says Mike Parker. 'She was very good at making you feel part of her team and family.'[4] The mornings would be filled with letters and other business, the afternoons with visits. She and her husband would often lunch with the staff in the dining-room, in conditions that were less formal and much more intimate than anything possible at the Palace.[5]

'When we were planning daytime journeys, she was very good at making suggestions', Parker recalls. 'She showed an early maturity in discussing things and making decisions.'[6] Her responsibilities were widening. As yet, however, she had little knowledge of the conduct of Government business. Jock Colville had made his own contribution, by persuading the Foreign Secretary to let her see Foreign Office telegrams. In the summer of 1950, Charteris took a leaf out of Colville's book, and raised with the Cabinet Secretary, Sir Norman Brook, the possibility of letting her see Cabinet papers as well. Brook consulted the Prime Minister, suggesting that the Princess should see minutes as well as memoranda, apart from any Confidential Annexes, as 'a temporary experiment forming part of the general plan for giving Her Royal Highness a wider experience of public affairs'.[7] Attlee spoke to the King. Then he scribbled a note to Brook: 'I think it should be permanent', and it became so.[8]

The Princess's experience of public affairs extended in other, more traditional ways over the next eighteen months. In 1951 – year of the Festival of Britain – the Royal Family was in exceptional demand for ceremonial duties, and Elizabeth had to deputize for her father, because of his illness, on many occasions. In June, she hosted a dinner for her uncle, King Haakon of Norway. This time her father was too ill to attend the King's Birthday Parade of the Brigade of Guards, with the ceremony of Trooping the Colour, on Horse Guards Parade. It was a vivid *début*. The tiny, compact figure, riding side-saddle in the scarlet tunic of Colonel of the Grenadiers – 'a woman alone', as *The Times* put it, at the centre of an all-male military event – was a telling reminder of her significance, not just as under-study, but as successor to the sick Monarch.[9]

In the summer, the medical suspicion that George VI had cancer became stronger. In September, exploratory surgery confirmed it, and the King underwent the removal of his left lung. Once the severity of the illness was established, a variety of arrangements had to be made. To ensure that the constitutional functions of the Monarchy should continue without interruption, Lascelles took the necessary steps to have the Queen, the two princesses, the Duke of Gloucester and the Princess Royal designated Counsellors of State. Princess Elizabeth wrote to her father's private secretary agreeing that this was the best thing to do, 'for it will relieve the King of so much of the ordinary routine things'.[10]

One routine thing was the general election. Before the operation, the King had asked the Prime Minister to make a decision about a poll before the start of his Commonwealth tour, planned for January. After it, Lascelles wrote to Attlee explaining that when this request had been made, the King had had no inkling that the trip would have to be put off.[11] The decision was now taken to hold an election on

October 15th. On October 4th, Princess Elizabeth presided over the Privy Council preceding the Dissolution. Meanwhile she had been making her own preparations. 'In view of the unfortunate turn in the King's health,' she wrote to her young dress designer Hardy Amies on September 24th, and 'in the strictest confidence . . . I have strong reason to believe that he will be unable to undertake the tour of Australia and New Zealand. I would very much like you to prepare some sketches for me to see . . . as a precaution against any sudden decision for us to go in the King's place.'[12] On October 9th, the King's already postponed South Sea tour was cancelled.

It was to be a busy winter – the busiest, indeed, of the Princess's life so far. Despite anxiety about the King, she and her husband decided to go ahead with a long-projected tour of Canada. This particular venture had first been mooted three years earlier. Elizabeth had been keen, but – as over the French trip – Philip had initially been opposed, saying that he wanted to settle down and start a family.[13] Their family was now well started and they had, at Clarence House, a settled home. With the other obstacle – Philip's naval duties – also removed, the trip was scheduled for October 1951. Meanwhile, the proposed tour had expanded in ambition. The visit had at first been envisaged as a purely Commonwealth undertaking. However, in July, Lord Halifax – a former ambassador in Washington – had suggested that it would be impolite for the royal couple not to include in their itinerary a brief detour south of the border. So what Lascelles called a 'pop-over' holiday visit to the United States was tacked on, as an extra.[14] The royal party flew out to Newfoundland on October 7th, for a tour that was overshadowed by fears for the King's health. To guard against the possibility of his death, Charteris kept papers about the holding of an Accession Council under his bed throughout the trip.[15]

They had a mixed reception. A few days after their arrival, the Canadian Governor-General wrote soothingly to the King that the *Quebecois* had been impressed by the Princess's French, and that the crowds in Ottawa were bigger than those during the state visits of either President Truman or President Auriol of France.[16] However the press – unaware of the seriousness of the King's illness and looking for an angle – quickly decided that the Princess looked distracted, and even bored. 'At the end of some of the long trying days,' declared one Canadian broadcaster, 'you'd hear people worrying about how tired the Princess is.'[17] The royal party had an uncomfortable feeling of the trip having got off to a poor start. 'There was a lot of comment about Princess Elizabeth not smiling,' according to Lord Charteris. It was to become a common complaint. 'My face is aching with smiling,' he recalled her saying in exasperation.[18] Yet there was no lack of interest. Such was the crush of photographers wanting to get a picture of her face, smiling or blank, that splinters of glass from exploding flash bulbs were found on her coat.[19]

As in South Africa in 1947, much of the tour was spent cooped up in a special train. The mood in the royal car varied. To relieve the monotony as they travelled into every province of the dominion, Philip developed a line in practical jokes. On one occasion he left a booby-trapped tin of nuts for his wife to open, on another he chased her down the corridor wearing a set of joke false teeth.[20] At other times, tempers frayed. One member of the party remembers the Duke loudly denouncing the Heiress Presumptive as a 'bloody fool' in the breakfast room.[21] Meanwhile, as they chugged across the vast open spaces, from the industrial lowlands of St Lawrence to the west coast, the nation's enthusiasm – dormant at first – grew into an extraordinary excitement, focusing on the Governor-General's train. People travelled colossal distances to gather at each stop. There were vivid incidents. Dean particularly remembered the arrival of the royal train at a small settlement deep in the Rockies, late at night in falling snow. As the couple dismounted, they were greeted by the town band and the entire population singing 'The Loveliest Night of the Year'.[22]

The high point was the hastily-added pop-over. On October 31st, they flew to Washington, where – to ensure a fitting welcome – President Truman had ordered that all Federal employees should be given time off.[23] What guaranteed the success of the visit was partly the Canadian preamble, which gave the American press time to get used to the idea; partly the brevity of the trip, which gave no time for boredom; and partly that Truman decided to make it the climactic celebration of his own presidency. 'He fell in love with her', according to Charteris.[24] The British ambassador, Sir Oliver Franks, wrote to the King that when the President appeared with Princess Elizabeth in public he conveyed 'the impression of a very proud uncle presenting his favourite niece to his friends'.[25] As Federal workers lined the streets to cheer, the President behaved as if the Princess and her husband had been responsible for some magnificent achievement. 'We have many distinguished visitors here in this city,' he declared in a speech in the Rose Garden, 'but never before have we had such a wonderful couple, that so completely captured the hearts of all of us.'[26] The Washington papers wrote of 'little Lilibet' – recently made familiar to the American public through the pages of the *Ladies' Home Journal* – who had 'suddenly matured into the lovely young mother who one day is to be the ruling Queen of England'.[27] At a big British embassy reception, the Princess and the Duke had to shake the hands of 1,500 guests.

There were matters of protocol. One, which caused a flurry of diplomatic telegrams, was the question of where the Princess should return the President's hospitality. As the pop-over took place during a tour of Canada, she came to the United States not as future Queen of England but as future Queen of Canada, and consequently was required to entertain President Truman at the Canadian, not the British, embassy.[28]

Afterwards, there was the question of thank-you letters. When the royal couple had returned to Canada, Philip wrote to Mrs Truman – as one consort to another – thanking her for her kindness, and describing his 'rather blurred memory of our rush round Washington'. It was the job of the Princess to write to the President. She did so after talking to her father on the telephone. 'He sounded much better,' she wrote, hopefully.[29] Across the Atlantic, the King was shown glowing extracts from the *Washington Evening Star*, and read the famous remark of Harry Truman: 'When I was little boy, I read about a fairy princess, and there she is.'[30]

IN MID-NOVEMBER, the Princess and Duke returned to England, and to a new political landscape. A few years earlier, Labour had seemed so firmly entrenched that many people believed it would retain office for a generation. The 1950 election, however, had cut its majority to a handful. In the general election of October 1951, a tired Labour Government – depleted by retirements and resignations – faced a re-invigorated Conservative Party campaigning for a bigger confla-gration of controls. The result was tight. Labour polled more votes, but the Tories obtained a small working majority. At seventy-seven, Winston Churchill was called to the Palace and asked by the convalesc-ing King to form the first purely Conservative Government since Baldwin left office in 1929. The Monarch was not sorry. Although Attlee had treated him with civility and respect, the King and Queen made little secret – in private – of their High Tory opinions.[31] During the war the King had come to depend personally on Churchill, whose exaggerated shows of deference he found reassuring and flattering, and he welcomed the return of a Prime Minister who took an almost child-like pleasure in the pageantry and show of Monarchy.

Elizabeth and Philip did not have long, however, to adjust to the change. Following the cancellation of the tour of the King and Queen, arrangements had been put in train for the Princess and her husband to undertake it instead – including, in their itinerary, a few days in East Africa *en route*. There were two reasons for such an excursion. The Kenyan colonial government, which had given the Princess and Duke a farm, Sagana Lodge, as a wedding present, had been keenly asking for a royal visit. Furthermore, such a pause in the journey gave an excuse for not stopping in Egypt, currently in the throes of a political crisis. 'Going to Kenya is a good way of skipping the Mediter-ranean,' the King pencilled in a tremulous note to his private secre-tary.[32] The intention was to make the Kenya leg of the journey largely a holiday, before they went on from Mombasa, aboard HMS *Gothic*, to Ceylon.

The Kenyan settler community was delighted at the news. The *East African Standard* spoke for the colony when it welcomed the visit of two young people whose charm, devotion to duty and 'personal example of homemaking family life' had endeared them to the Commonwealth: it hoped that they would enjoy what Kenya had to offer in terms of fishing, riding, shooting and travelling on safari. As with the South African tour, the fiction was preserved that the royal visit – intended to provide symbolic reassurance to the white settlers in increasingly uncertain times – was purely recreational.[33] The couple's example of homemaking did not include bringing their children with them. Though they expected to be away for six months, longer even than the Yorks' 1927 trip, the question did not arise. 'It was absolutely taken for granted that they would be left behind,' says an ex-courtier. 'It was simply what one did in those days.'[34]

As soon as he knew they were coming, the Governor of Kenya, Sir Philip Mitchell, made an imaginative suggestion. '. . . [P]lease try to get them here so that their visit includes the period of three days on either side of the full moon,' he wrote to the Colonial Office on October 13th. 'In that case I would reserve Treetops for them for a night, that is the hotel in the branches of a giant fig tree overlooking a salt lick about ten miles from their Lodge in the Aberdares . . . I am sure that H.R.H. would enjoy it enormously; it really is something not to be missed and it does require, for its full enjoyment, as much moonlight as possible.' The moonlight was for viewing the big game that came to the water-hole under the tree.[35]

In his Christmas broadcast, the King expressed his pleasure that 'our daughter, Princess Elizabeth' and her husband would be taking his and the Queen's place on the tour. It was the first and last time that he ever referred to his heir on such an occasion by name.[36] After recording the programme – piece by piece, as his strength allowed – the King spent Christmas with his family in Norfolk. 'I am progressing well since my operation, I am glad to say', he wrote to General Eisenhower from Sandringham on January 7th.[37] On January 30th, he returned to London for a visit to the American musical *South Pacific* in Drury Lane. The following day he accompanied his elder daughter and his son-in-law to London airport and said good-bye to them on the tarmac as they boarded their plane for Nairobi.

The royal couple were greeted on arrival next morning by Sir Philip Mitchell, in plumed hat, and whisked off for a series of engagements. Then the royal party set out for Sagana Lodge in Nyeri, a hundred miles north of the capital, where they spent a couple of days elephant-watching, fishing and filming – before driving to Treetops. The hotel, as Mitchell had indicated, was an outpost only for the sturdiest of tourists. Getting to it was regarded as hazardous, because of wild animals at the foot of the tree. There may also have been another hazard, because it was in the heart of Mau Mau territory – during the rebellion which erupted shortly afterwards, it was burnt down. At the time, however, the Princess and the Duke were able to spend a safe and peaceful evening watching Kenya's most imposing fauna from the hotel's observation balcony.

On February 4th, Lascelles wrote to Mitchell from England thanking him, on behalf of the King and Queen, for helping to make the visit a success.[38] Next day, in Downing Street, the Cabinet discussed a Labour motion complaining about a planned royal visit to South Africa, in the course of which the King was due to stay in Dr Malan's official residence as his guest. Ministers agreed that the matter was one for the Union Government to decide, and that it would be 'constitutionally inappropriate' to offer advice.[39] In Sandringham, the King went out shooting, and returned for dinner with his wife and younger daughter. 'There were jolly jokes,' Princess Margaret recalls, 'and he went to bed early because he was convalescing. Then he wasn't there any more.'[40] That night, he died in his sleep.

When did Elizabeth succeed? 'She became Queen,' wrote Harold Nicolson, 'while perched in a tree in Africa watching the rhinoceros come down to the pool to drink.'[41] This became the legend, and it was not far from the truth. When the King's fatal heart attack occurred in the early hours of the morning, the Princess was either asleep or eating breakfast (watching, not rhinoceros, but baboons) or taking pictures of the sunrise. Mike Parker, a member of the royal party, believes he was with her at the precise moment when her reign began. He had invited her to climb up to a look-out point at the top of the tree to watch the dawn coming up over the jungle. While they looked at the iridescent light that preceded the sunrise, they saw an eagle hovering just above their heads. For a moment, he was frightened that it would dive onto them. 'I never thought about it until later', he recalled, 'but that was roughly the time when the King died.'[42]

Although for several months his death had been a medical inevitability, the news of it came as a surprise both to the public and to the Royal Family. 'He died as he was getting better,' says Princess Margaret.[43] Remarkably, the ground had not been prepared and the arrangements for telling key people had rapidly to be improvised. The Queen had been the first to know, after the King's valet had discovered his body, at 7.30 a.m. An hour or more elapsed before Edward Ford, the assistant private secretary, was sent by Sir Alan Lascelles to tell the Prime Minister and the King's mother. Ford drove to Downing

Street, and was shown up to Churchill's bedroom. The premier was propped up in bed writing, surrounded by paperwork and a candle for his cigar. 'I've got bad news,' Ford recalls saying, '– the King died this morning.' Churchill seemed shaken. 'Bad news?' he exclaimed. 'The worst!' He flung aside the papers. 'How unimportant these matters seem. Get me Anthony Eden.' Then, according to Ford, 'he got onto the phone and said, in an absurd attempt at security, "Anthony, can we scramble?" But they couldn't scramble. He went on in a kind of code, "Our big chief has gone – we must have a Cabinet."'[44] The Prime Minister's distress was more than momentary. Jock Colville – who, with the change of Government, had been brought back into No 10 as Churchill's joint private secretary – found him in tears. When he tried to cheer the premier by saying how well he would get on with the new Queen, 'all he could say was that he did not know her and that she was only a child'.[45]

Getting hold of the Prime Minister was a great deal easier than finding the new Monarch, who had returned from Treetops to Sagana Lodge. It was more than four hours before the Queen knew that she had succeeded. 'Because of where we were,' says Pamela Hicks, who was in the party as a lady-in-waiting, 'we were almost the last people in the world to know.' Another lady-in-waiting – aboard the *Gothic* at Mombasa in anticipation of the royal party – only learnt of the King's death when she asked why people were taking down the decorations.[46] Eventually the story was picked up from the radio by Martin Charteris, a few miles away at the Outspan Hotel. He telephoned Sagana Lodge and spoke to Parker. There was no way to check officially. It was confirmed, however, when Mike Parker switched on his own radio, and heard the announcement on the overseas wavelength of the BBC.[47] Parker told Philip who – at about 2.45 p.m., 11.45 a.m. London time – told his wife.[48] 'He took her up to the garden,' according to Parker, 'and they walked slowly up and down the lawn while he talked and talked and talked to her.'[49]

THE DEATH of a British monarch changes little in practical terms. It does not shift a Prime Minister, alter the party of Government, reverse its policies, or influence the economy. Yet – in a way that is hard to define – it affects the mood. This is because the British public relates to its kings and queens, who it regards with a variety of emotions, but always with interest. It even imagines that the relationship works both ways: the question in A. A. Milne's rhyme about changing the guard at Buckingham Palace – 'Do you think the King knows about me?' – is an adult fancy, as well as a childhood one. Hence such an event is often experienced with genuine grief, as a family loss. But there is also a wider, social relationship, which makes a change of reign more than a nominal transition. It is not just for convenience that the culture, mores, architecture, style of dress of a period have often been identified by the name of the monarch – 'Victorian', 'Edwardian' and so on. A link is made between the supposed character of the titular ruler, and some facet of the age. Even in the mid-twentieth century, after the abandonment of this kind of epochal labelling, monarchs still give a flavour to the attitudes and outlook of the episode over which they formally preside.

Politically, there was little to bind the reign of George VI together. Spanning a turbulent fifteen and a half years from the Depression and the rise of fascism, through a world war, to post-war austerity, the building of the welfare state, Indian independence, the Cold War, and the beginnings of consumer affluence, it had no single theme. Yet its very instability gave the King's nervous courage and mule-like conservatism an historical role. Indeed, his lack of imagination was seen by many as an advantage, placing him below statesmen and closer to the bewildered common man. In private, prime ministers found him almost intolerably slow, yet they respected his honesty and decency, and his desire to do his best, and they felt protective towards him. There was also relief, and gratitude, that he should have provided the most domestically admirable 'Royal Family' since the days of Prince Albert.

The press became filled with images of black drapery, coffins, tombs and catafalques. Even the *New Statesman* – whose editor, Kingsley Martin, was a rare critic of Monarchy – became convulsed by an argument about whether the front page should have a black band around it. However, the mourning was not just a media indulgence. Affection for George VI was felt everywhere. A few days after the death, Richard Crossman, a left-wing MP and iconoclast, recorded his impression of a 'hard-boiled' attitude in Parliament, but 'directly you got outside, you certainly realised that the newspapers were not sentimentalizing when they described the nation's feeling of personal loss'.[50] The feeling was intensified by the King's relatively young age, and by sympathy for his widow; and by a mixture of concern and excited, expectant curiosity towards his elder daughter, who had been so closely watched since childhood, who had recently become an almost mythic being, but about whom very little was yet known. It was around this small and mysterious person that the national senti-ment rapidly became – in the unironic phrase of the Annual Register for 1952 – 'a religion of royalism'.[51]

A variety of procedures automatically followed the King's death, even before Elizabeth – now the Queen – knew of it. An emergency Cabinet met at 11 a.m., and decided to hold an Accession Council the same afternoon. There was a discussion of the wording of the Proclamation, which had important long-term effects. It was also decided to extend the Council's composition. 'Representatives of other members of the Commonwealth' were now to join the 'Lords Spiritual and Temporal, members of the Privy Council, and other Principal Gentlemen of Quality, with the Lord Mayor, Aldermen and Citizens of London'.[52] At the Council later in the day, the Lord President, Lord Woolton, read the draft declaration proclaiming the new Monarch as Queen Elizabeth the Second – the first to have been proclaimed *in absentia* since the accession of George I.

Proclamations echoed around the world, as never before – and never again, for the phenomenon of one individual as hereditary Head of State in so many different colonies and self-governing states is unlikely to be repeated. There was a plethora of invented traditions. In Australia, for example, the proclamation of George VI in 1936 had been read by a secretary in the Prime Minister's department to a handful of people assembled in the King's Hall at Parliament House. His daughter's proclamation was read by the Governor-General from the steps of Parliament House, and similar ceremonies were conducted before large crowds in state capitals around the country.[53] In some places, the implications of what was proclaimed caused local diffi-culties. A particular complaint was made in Scotland, where the National Committee of the Scottish Covenant Association pointed out that, north of the border, she was Elizabeth I. There was a fierce legal argument. On February 20th the Edinburgh Court of Sessions resolved the matter by announcing that, as far as official documents and declarations were concerned, she would be styled 'the Second'. The result was a grievance against the British Monarchy that was not forgotten.

In Kenya, it was difficult for 'the lady we must now call the Queen' – as Charteris began to refer to her – to come to terms, simultaneously, with the loss of a father and becoming Head of State for the rest of her life. It was also hard for her husband. After they got the news, the royal party rapidly prepared for the return journey to London. 'I have this picture in my mind,' according to Lord Charteris, 'of going into the Lodge on 6th February 1952 and the Queen sitting at her desk, pencil in hand, and Prince Philip lying back on a sofa and holding open *The Times* over his face. And I felt then that something had changed, and it had.' He recalls her 'sitting erect, no tears, colour up a little, fully accepting her destiny'. He asked what she wanted to be called as Queen. 'My own name, Elizabeth, of course,' she said.[54] When Pamela Hicks expressed her sympathy, the Queen's reaction was 'I'm so sorry, we've got to go back. I've ruined everybody's trip'.[55] Parker felt that 'her feelings were deep, deep inside her'.[56]

They left Sagana – the Queen still wearing blue jeans – before five. 'When all the luggage had been packed,' a servant wrote in Swahili a few days later, 'Their Royal Highnesses came to us and said, "Goodbye, and thank you, we shall meet again". They got into their car and went away.'[57] Charteris asked the press not to take any pictures. 'As the motor cars left the Lodge, the world's press lined the road', he recalled. 'Yet not a single photograph was taken.'[58] At seven o'clock, the royal party flew from Nanyuki to Entebbe, where they had to wait for two hours in the airport lounge, because of a thunderstorm. Then they began the twenty-four-hour flight home – monitored stage by stage by the world's news agencies as the plane made refuelling stops. There was little talk on the journey. Dean recalled that once or twice the Queen left her seat, and when she returned she looked as if she had been crying.[59] 'She was looking out of the window on her own,' says Lord Charteris. 'At one point she called me over. She said: "What's going to happen when we get home?" I realized that she didn't know.'[60]

The first thing to happen was a solemn greeting on the tarmac from the Prime Minister, the Leader of the Opposition, and other prominent political figures. At Clarence House, she was met by Queen Mary, veteran of five reigns, who curtseyed and kissed her grand-daughter's hand. It was Churchill, however, who set the scene for what he called a new Elizabethan Age. 'Famous have been the reigns of our Queens,' he declaimed in a broadcast that night. 'Some of the greatest periods in our history have unfolded under their sceptre.' He also spoke of the Monarchy, 'the magic link which unites our loosely bound, but strongly interwoven Commonwealth.'[61]

The Queen's first public presentation took place at a full meeting of the Accession Council at St James's Palace on February 8th. It was attended by an assortment of Privy Councillors – 'people one didn't remember were still alive,' Dalton noted, 'and some looking quite perky and self-important.' The Queen, he thought, looked 'very small – high pitched, rather reedy voice. She does her part well, facing hundreds of old men in black clothes with long faces. She will take up this task "which has come to me so early in life".'[62] The contrast with her stumbling father on such occasions was stark. Harold Mac-millan noted 'her firm yet charming voice' as she said her lines.[63] Harold Wilson found the Council 'the most moving ceremonial I can recall'.

Deep emotions stirred. There were uncomfortable features. It was one of the ironies – or hypocrisies – of the hereditary system that death and renewal were combined: grief at the loss of one monarch was supposed to be accompanied by joy at the arrival of another. Churchill spoke of the thrill in once more invoking the prayer and the anthem 'God Save the Queen'.[64] Yet the thrill at placing a young woman on a pedestal normally reserved for men was a complex one. If there was something grotesque – a distortion of past glories – about the protracted rituals and obeisances associated with the public mourning, there was also a peculiarity about the prostration of old gentlemen before a twenty-five-year-old Queen who had no choice but to accept the part she was asked to play.

Some spoke or wrote about her with barely concealed sexuality. Cecil Beaton described her, after a brief encounter at the theatre in July, as if she were Garbo. 'The purity of her expression,' he wrote, 'the unspoilt childishness of the smile, the pristine quality of her pink and white complexion, are all part of an appearance that is individual and gives the effect of a total entity.'[65] Lord Kilmuir, the Lord Chancellor, found 'something breathtaking' in her swift changes of costume and role. He recalled how moved he felt watching her out of the window at the Palace, as she knelt on the grass in a yellow shirt and jodhpurs, calling a dog to come to her – and knowing that, within a quarter of an hour, she would have changed and become a sovereign receiving her subjects.[66] Churchill himself soon became besotted. 'All the film people in the world,' the premier rhapsodized to Lord Moran, 'if they had scoured the globe, could not have found anyone so suited to the part.'[67]

It did not take long for the popular newspapers, mixing the lugubrious and the prurient, to see the opportunities. For if the Queen at her Accession had been, in the press imagery, 'a girl in unrelieved black whom [the King's] death had brought back from Kenya's tropic sunshine to the searching chill of Norfolk in mid-winter,'[68] she was also a pretty face to brighten the front page. Some of the finest pre-Coronation pictures show her in mourning. There was an erotic splendour to the line of queens and princesses, Elizabeth II at their head, that attended the lying in state in Westminster Hall, 'like Moslem women,' as Crossman put it, 'clothed in dead black, swathed and double swathed with veils so thick that they couldn't read the Order of Service through them'.[69]

THE QUESTION of how the Queen should be described in the Proclamation – discussed in Cabinet within hours of the King's death – was of more than ritual significance. The words chosen, and amended, helped to determine the relationship of the Queen to her realms – and those that would cease to be realms – for many years to come. There was agreement that account needed to be taken of changes. Ministers felt that the traditional formula 'was not wholly in accord with present constitutional conditions in the Commonwealth.' The old wording contained anomalous references to 'Ireland' – no longer a member state – and to the 'British Dominions' which some of the countries so described might not like. It was therefore decided to drop 'Imperial Crown,' and include a reference to the Sovereign's position as 'Head of the Commonwealth'.[70]

The problem reflected the growing diversity of the dominions since the Second World War; and it helped to determine the future nature of their relationship with the United Kingdom. Much was to flow from the designation of the Queen as 'Head of the Commonwealth' – a title formally acquired by George VI less than a year earlier, through the Royal Titles Bill, which had recognized the 'divisibility' of the Crown. Divisibility (the product of diversity) was officially adopted as a principle at the first Commonwealth Prime Ministers' Conference of the reign in December 1952, when it was agreed that each state should think up a title to express its own relationship with the Crown.

Apart from the United Kingdom, six self-governing nations – Canada, Australia, New Zealand, South Africa, Pakistan and Ceylon – retained the British Monarch as head of state. Three of them felt that 'Defender of the Faith' was inappropriate. In all of them 'Queen of the British Dominions beyond the Seas' was replaced by 'Queen of her other Realms and Territories'. Finally, the words 'Great Britain, Ireland' in the full title were replaced by 'the United Kingdom of Great Britain and Northern Ireland'. The changes accelerated a movement away from the notion of the British Monarch as sovereign over 'dominions' and towards a personally-based link, in which the Monarch enjoyed a separate identity in each country.[71]

Advocates of 'divisibility' maintained that it was unavoidable and desirable. Not only were the dominions growing apart constitutionally in any case, a sober recognition of political and cultural realities would have the effect of promoting rather than diminishing Commonwealth unity.[72] Others argued both that the idea of a 'personal union' was absurd, and that the idea of a 'Head of the Commonwealth,' who would have any area of discretion distinct from the advice given to her by the ministers of her governments, and primarily the British Government, was a dangerous heresy.

The sharpest proponent of this view was Enoch Powell, a young Conservative MP who had spent much of the war in India, and who – from the start of the new reign – established himself as a lynx-eyed guardian of parliamentary rights *vis-à-vis* the Crown. Three weeks after the Accession, he wrote to the Prime Minister complaining about the attendance of the Duke of Edinburgh in the peers' gallery of the

House of Commons during a debate – something, he pointed out, a royal consort had not done since 1846 – in the course of which the Duke seemed to make his opinions of what was being discussed unconstitutionally obvious.[73] The Government Chief Whip backed the complaint, remarking that the consort had not been 'exactly poker-faced,' and the Duke was privately ticked off.[74] Powell returned to the topic of royal interference on many occasions, as the Queen's titular 'divisibility' – which many people in 1952 saw as just an exercise in linguistic tidying – grew in significance as the Commonwealth evolved.

As well as Commonwealth titles, there was also another problem of nomenclature – which touched the Sovereign herself, and more particularly her husband, personally. This was the question of what the Royal Family, and its descendants, should be called.

Was the Queen a Windsor? Would Charles III remain one, or become the first King in the House of Mountbatten? The point had been considered in 1947 by the then Lord Chancellor, who had been in no doubt that, according to the law as it then stood, any children of the marriage would bear Philip's name. Although most British Queens regnant had failed to produce issue that survived to adulthood, and so there were few cases to go on, this seemed to accord with past practice. There was the recent example of Edward VII, who reigned as a member of the House of Saxe-Coburg-Gotha, not of the House of Hanover. Yet there was also a different kind of precedent. As George V showed during the First World War, the name of the House could be changed if the Sovereign, or the Government, so wished it. George VI's death left the question unresolved.

The issue came rapidly to a head in the first months of the new reign – and in the process seriously ruffled Prince Philip, causing considerable bad feeling between him and the Government. According to Jock Colville – who acted as a kind of go-between, passing messages from premier to royals, although his first loyalty was now on the other side – the Duke argued that his children should not be Mount-battens but Edinburghs of the House of Edinburgh.[75] If this had been the main proposal, it might perhaps have been acceptable. However, Edinburgh was a bestowed royal title, not a family name, and in any case, it seems only to have been put forward as an afterthought. The obvious name for the Royal Family to acquire in the next generation, following the Prince Albert–Edward VII precedent, was Mountbatten and this seems to have been the main suggestion. What ensured the retention of 'Windsor' – with its neutral, Home Counties ring – was an alliance between older royalty, the Royal Household, Winston Churchill, and the Conservative Cabinet. All deplored the prospect of linking the British dynasty to the Duke's uncle, a politically engaged and often controversial figure who, though related to royalty, had none of the passive attributes considered desirable in a constitutional monarchy.

It was the new Sovereign's grandmother who sounded the alarm. Twelve days after the death of her son, a grieving but angry Queen Mary summoned the Prime Minister's private secretary in order to deliver a protest. Prince Ernst August of Hanover had told her, she announced, that at a recent house party at Broadlands attended by royalty, Lord Mountbatten had been heard to boast 'that the House of Mountbatten now reigned'.[76] Colville passed on this remarkable piece of intelligence to the Prime Minister, who did not take long to decide how to react. Churchill had long regarded the Duke's Uncle Dickie as a dangerous and subversive rival, who had sacrificed India; he was determined to put the old Queen's mind at rest. Cabinet was immediately informed, and put in no doubt about the Prime Minister's opinion.

Churchill's ministers, as outraged as Queen Mary, would have none of it. 'The Cabinet's attention was drawn to reports that some change might be made in the Family name of the Queen's Children and their descendants,' record the Cabinet minutes for the same day. 'The Cabinet was strongly of the opinion that the Family name of Windsor should be retained; and they invited the Prime Minister to take a suitable opportunity of making their views known to Her Majesty.'[77]

Perhaps the Broadlands indiscretion meant nothing. However, the rumours, leading to suspicion and uncertainty, could not have come at a worse time – so soon after the Accession, when Palace nervousness was at its greatest, and the Queen was feeling her way. Raised later and more tactfully, the matter might have been settled in a spirit of amity. As it was, the Queen found herself caught in the crossfire. According to a sympathizer of the Duke, Churchill steam-rollered her into the decision, pleading the national interest, and she was not strong or mature enough to resist. 'But it really did upset Philip. If she had realized how hurt he was going to be, a way round would have been found from the beginning.'[78]

Philip did not give up without a fight. 'I am the only man in the country not allowed to give his name to his children', he complained to friends. However, he had little support and, indeed, could scarcely campaign publicly. Even his Battenberg grandmother thought it a storm in a teacup. 'What is it he wants them to be called?' the Dowager Marchioness of Milford Haven went round saying. 'Mountbatten? Montgomery?'[79] Colville – whose message-bearing had sparked the whole rumpus – felt that although Philip had precedent on his side, he had not shown wisdom or tact, and he had placed the Queen in a dilemma, caught between pressure from her husband, and an ardent Windsor faction composed of her mother and grandmother.[80] The effect of Philip's advocacy had been to irritate ministers, and raise fears as to his future behaviour.[81]

On February 20th, Churchill reported to the Cabinet that the Queen had bent to its will, as, indeed, she was required to do. 'The Prime Minister said that it was The Queen's Pleasure that She and her descendants should continue to bear the Family name of Windsor,' the Cabinet minutes record.[82] The Royal Household was much relieved. The Queen gave her formal approval to a proclamation to this effect on April 4th. When she did so, Sir Alan Lascelles – whom she had inherited as private secretary – stood over her, in his phrase, like 'one of the Barons of Runnymede'. Even so, Queen Mary continued to rumble with indignation. 'What the devil does that damned fool Edinburgh think that the family name has got to do with him,' she muttered a few days later.[83] On April 10th, it was reported officially that the Queen had taken the unprecedented step of declaring in Council that she wished her family and descendants to 'bear the name of Windsor' – thus ensuring that she herself was not the last of the House and preventing the launching of a new one.[84]

It remained a sore point on both sides, adding to the friction that already existed between Philip and some members of the Court. Meanwhile Lascelles – who had derived much satisfaction from Churchill's firmness – proved a valuable ally to the Prime Minister in a bitter exchange that took place a few days after Queen Mary's 'House of Mountbatten' protest. For some time there had been concern, both political and medical, about Churchill's failing health and mental powers. The difficulty lay in conveying this concern to the Prime Minister himself. The new reign opened up an interesting constitutional possibility. It was the right of the Monarch to be consulted, to encourage and to warn the Prime Minister – and moreover she had the opportunity to do so regularly, and in complete privacy. Might not the Queen be the appropriate person to raise the delicate matter of Churchill's retirement in an audience?

After Churchill's doctor had made this suggestion to Jock Colville and Lord Salisbury on February 22nd, it was put to Lascelles, who rejected it. 'If she said her part, he would say charmingly: "It's very good of you Ma'am, to think of it –" and then he would politely brush it aside,' said the Queen's private secretary, for whom the Prime Minister had just proved such a staunch ally in the Mountbatten dispute. 'The King might have done it,' he added, 'but he is gone.'[85]

Churchill stayed, and so did the Windsor name. In June, the Prime Minister observed to an aide that although he wished the Duke of Edinburgh no ill, he neither liked nor trusted him and only hoped that he would not do the country any harm.[86] Meanwhile the Duke contracted jaundice, and for three uncomfortable weeks lay prostrate, depressed and irritable, contemplating the red silk walls and heavy furniture of his new bedroom at Buckingham Palace.[87]

PHILIP was not the only person to find the change in his wife's status difficult. It created problems for the whole Royal Family. The biggest arose from the need to move into Buckingham Palace. It was the second time in her life that the ending of a reign had made such a step necessary, though on this occasion, after less than three years' absence, the Palace held no surprises. In 1936, however, going to the Palace had mainly been a matter of changing homes. Now it meant assuming command of a large, inward-looking, and in many ways ramshackle organization, set in its ways, and ruled in practice by the iron will of Sir Alan Lascelles. It also meant ejecting the sitting tenants. 'It was difficult for Princess Margaret and Queen Elizabeth to move out and for the Queen and Prince Philip to move in,' says a former Lady of the Bedchamber. 'Neither side wanted to do it.' The Queen

Mother (or Queen Elizabeth, as she is always referred to by insiders) was especially unhappy about leaving. Margaret tried to comfort her, but found her prickly. 'Like many people who have to face such a terrible wrench,' says a close relative, 'Queen Elizabeth got very cross.'[88] At first, she was overwhelmed by grief. 'It is difficult to grasp the fact that he has left us,' she wrote to General Eisenhower in March; 'he was so much better, & so full of ideas & plans for the future. One cannot imagine life without him, but one must carry on as he would wish.'[89] In September, she wrote to Edith Sitwell that there were still days 'when one felt engulfed by great black clouds of unhappiness and misery'.[90] In the spring of 1953, she was still at the Palace. Cecil Beaton came to photograph her, and found her marginalized, and under pressure from the staff to move out.[91] She and her younger daughter were due to go to Clarence House, but the move took time to prepare, and for the time being she remained an uncomfortable presence in the establishment that had been her home for a decade and a half, and where she had been used to being obeyed.

Meanwhile, the new occupants took over the first and second floor apartments on the north side of the central quadrangle, with the nursery above them on the top floor.[92] Nursery routine for the two children, now aged three and eighteen months, changed little, though the Queen ended the traditional rule that royal children (when they become old enough for it to be relevant) should bow and curtsey on entering the presence of the Sovereign.[93] The relaxation did not, however, extend to Queen Elizabeth or Princess Margaret, who formally curtseyed to their daughter and sister when they met her in company.[94]

The Queen and the Duke brought several members of their staff with them, including Martin Charteris, who became assistant private secretary at the Palace, alongside Edward Ford, and Mike Parker, who continued to work for Philip. The Duke meanwhile made his presence felt among the established Palace courtiers, who did not always relish it. He and Parker embarked on a private study of the whole organization, and its methods. In the course of their investigations, they explored the labyrinthine spaces below ground level. 'We were fascinated by the wine cellar, which went on for miles and miles,' Parker recalls, 'and there were one or two very ancient wines indeed, plus some very old menus from the early Victorian period, which were utterly fascinating.'[95] Yet as long as Lascelles's sometimes baleful influence remained, attempts to put the Palace on a more business-like footing had little impact.

According to John Dean, one of the migrants from Clarence House to the Palace, 'the whole tempo of life changed,' and both the Queen and the Duke became much busier.[96] The question of whether the Queen was under too much pressure became a matter of comment in the press, where the idea of a mother of small children – even if she did not have to look after them – working at all, was regarded with ambivalence. Lady Airlie saw the Queen in Edinburgh in the summer of 1952. Busybodying as ever, she expressed concern that the courtiers 'will not kill the poor little girl' by burdening her with too many engagements.[97] Meanwhile, the National Federation of Women's Institutes passed a resolution urging that the nation 'should endeavour not to overwork our beloved young Queen, remembering that she has her duties also as wife and mother'.[98] The medical establishment backed this up. The *Lancet* even suggested that until her children were older, she should be allowed to withdraw from public view. It was important, it argued, that she should put her family life first, and protect her 'health and vitality'. For the next few years, her advisers would do well 'to resist all calls for her official presence except on really great occasions'.[99]

The Queen showed no inclination to take such advice. As the shock of her father's death eased, so the duties of the Monarchy, and above all the preparations for the Coronation, absorbed the greater part of her attention. 'My father died much too young and so it was all very sudden,' she said forty years later, adding that 'it was a matter of making the best job you can . . . and accepting the fact that it's your fate.'[100] Over the next eighteen months, she allowed fate to take its course.

After the Proclamation, the most pressing royal matter for the Government to decide was the date of the Service. 'The King's death really has swamped politics,' wrote Crossman, a few days after the Accession.[101] In fact, the timing of the Coronation, first discussed in Cabinet on February 11th, was a highly political matter. From the Government's point of view, there was the desirability of having the patriotic celebration as close to the next general election as possible, in the hope of stirring pro-Conservative sentiment; there was the question of the ill-fated Australia–New Zealand tour, now postponed twice, which might be arranged to take place before the Queen was crowned if the Coronation happened later rather than sooner; finally, there was the unresolved issue of the Prime Minister's longevity in office. Churchill indicated his preference for a distant date in the early summer of 1953 – even though Australia and New Zealand quickly made clear that they wanted a visit after, not before, the ceremony.[102] His retirement plans were not directly mentioned as a reason. However, there was a keen awareness that the Prime Minister found playing Melbourne to the Queen's Victoria a perfect excuse for procrastination.

Churchill had 'set his mind on seeing the Queen crowned before he gave up office,' his doctor recorded[103] – which meant that, since he seemed set to stay in office as long as he could, he was in no hurry to see her crowned. Eventually the date was fixed for June 2nd 1953 – providing a sixteen month gap between the Accession and the Coronation that allowed time for the combined forces of officialdom and commercialism to build up an extraordinary momentum. Changes in the economy also contributed to the gathering excitement: unlike the prelude to the royal wedding which had coincided with an emergency, the run-up to June 1953 was a time of relaxing controls, rising prosperity and rising expectations – and of a brittle optimism that nurtured the 'new Elizabethan' myth, as though the appearance of a young woman on the throne had opened a chapter in the nation's history.

There were preliminary rituals, watched with obsessive interest, which had the novel aspect of a fashion parade. In November, the Queen opened Parliament for the first time. The occasion had been preceded by a tricky protocol debate about what to do with the Duke. The Lord Chancellor considered precedents, and concluded that the best thing – following the practice of Prince Albert, and requiring no new legislation – was to give him a chair of state on the left of the Throne. The Queen agreed.[104]

The Queen's Speech from the Throne was preceded by a formal declaration that she was a 'faithful Protestant' and would ensure the Protestant succession. Then she began with words written for her by the Prime Minister: 'My thoughts turn first to my beloved father . . .'[105]

Members of both Houses contrasted her firm delivery, through seven minutes of reading, with the painful enunciations of the late King at such events.[106] Cecil Beaton, watching from the public gallery, assessed her performance as though she were the star of a costume drama, which in a sense she was. 'The Queen wore gold and stolid white,' he observed. 'The long red velvet train, miniver-edged, splendid against the gold and scarlet setting, her stance, with the rigid little head and the well-curled hair around Queen Victoria's Crown, was marvellously erect.' Not only her clothes, but also her face, were subject to the minutest examination. The Duke of Wellington was particularly struck by 'her lovely teeth, hair and eyes, and that amazing quality of skin. Then add the wonderful voice and romance, and you have a deeply moving effect.'[107] Beaton judged that 'her eyes are not those of a busy harassed person. She regards people with a recognition of compassion – and a slight suggestion of a smile lightens the other-wise cumbrous mouth.'[108]

Nobody, of course, ever wrote of a male Monarch like this. How-ever, it was not just the beauty of the Queen which her observers found spell-binding. It was the combination – as they saw it – of beauty, innocence and earnestness. Subjects were fascinated by the idea that, like a caged bird, she too was a subject – the prisoner of her circumstances, and willing slave to her people. 'Dedication' was a word much used by her speech writers. 'At my Coronation next June, I shall dedicate myself anew to your service,' she said in her first Christmas broadcast, which contained yet another echo of her Cape Town speech. She went on to ask her listeners to pray that she might faithfully serve God 'and you all the days of my life'.[109] Yet if the impact of such clichéd phrases came from the disturbing sense that she meant them, there was also the feeling that she was not a natural or spontaneous communicator like her mother. This was the other side of earnestness: the need to work to create an effect. She was hard to talk to, and some found her stiff. Though there was a grace and dignity about her, noted Harold Nicolson in February, 'it was a well trained young woman manufacturing grace and dignity'. Sometimes he observed, 'her face lost all vivacity and lapsed into a bored, even a sulky, mask.'[110] She was nervous of cameras, perhaps afraid that they would catch her when the mask dropped. She refused to allow her Christmas broadcast to be televised,[111] and made it clear to the BBC that she would be embarrassed if the television cameras were trained on her face for too long when she was taking the salute at her Birthday Parade.[112]

While the media profile of Elizabeth underwent a swift evolution, perceptions of Philip also changed. In some ways he was harder to deal with. A monarch, even a female one, invited comparison with a gallery of predecessors. In the case of a male consort, only Prince Albert was available as a model, and Philip was sufficiently different in outlook and character to preclude attempts to construct a parallel. Nevertheless, there was a move away from the simple portrayal of the princely mannequin in naval uniform that had accompanied the Wedding. A style started to emerge. Philip began to be presented as a man's man, an appropriate accessory for a woman of high authority who, in her critically important 'wife and mother' persona, epitomized traditional femininity. Philip's job, it became apparent, was to talk bluff common sense, and keep the Queen domestically in order. His interests fitted this image, for they were regarded as suitably masculine ones. So was his layman's curiosity about, and support for, industry: although no intellectual, he was – like Albert – interested in science and technology, and he acquired a reputation for visiting advanced installations, and speaking plainly about them. His remarks, which did not always please those who had invited him, had the particular quality of appealing over the heads of the Establishment to ordinary people. He was on the side of modernity. Thus he would admit his own lack of knowledge of a particular field, and then berate unidentified authorities for their failure to take steps to ensure that more people were not expert in it. He was refreshingly impatient of protocol, and shared the man-in-the-street's ambivalence – sometimes irreverence – towards ritual. If the Queen was acknowledged to be shy, he was seen to have the common touch. 'He goes about the country mixing on the friendliest terms with all sorts of people, high and low,' it was claimed. 'He is a born leader of men and a strong right hand to the Queen.' For the time being, the adulation bestowed upon his wife included him as well. Only later did his desire for independence, and for a role, make him vulnerable.

The emergence of one consort was accompanied by the passing of another. In March 1953, Queen Mary died and the Court went back into mourning. A male consort is never as acceptable, or as assimilable, as a female one: the old Queen, widow, mother or grandmother of four Sovereigns, had not only become the incarnation of royal traditions and virtue, she had stood, in the public imagination, for a particular kind of Victorian rectitude. Yet she had been more liberal in her outlook than many of her relatives, and she had taken a more active and progressive interest in the education of Elizabeth and Margaret than either her son or her daughter-in-law. Churchill described her in Parliament as 'practical in all things'.[113] Apart from her successful campaign to defend her husband's chosen family name against usurpers, one of her last concerns had been to widen the social horizons of her grandchildren in tune with the changing times. Her coffin replaced that of her son in Westminster Hall. Soon, however, Queen Mary's lying-in-state and funeral were overshadowed by the preparations for the Coronation, as the royalty religion – dressed in the patriotic colours of the Union Jack – became a festive mania.

'THE CORONATION was like a phoenix-time,' says Princess Margaret. 'Everything was being raised from the ashes. There was this gorgeous-looking, lovely young lady, and nothing to stop anything getting better and better.'[1] The moment was right: just as the slow post-war recovery was turning into a rapid advance. Yet it was also a time of real or masked fears – of communism, imperial decline, foreign competition. Despite the death of Stalin early in the year, there was no thawing of the Cold War. Although Britain retained a large and scattered colonial Empire, its value to the mother country was questionable, and its future uncertain. There was also a bewildering contrast between the new prosperity British people could see and feel at home, and the nation's shrinking share of world markets, especially compared to the defeated powers of the Second World War. 1953 was thus a good year in which to celebrate survival and revival, using history as an excuse for hope. As the historian David Cannadine puts it, the Coronation could be seen as 'stressing stability in an age of change, and celebrating the continuity of Britain as a great power'.[2]

At the heart of the celebration was the most visible – and some felt most appropriate – contrast of all, between youth and innocence, and age and experience. The juxtaposition of the angelic Sovereign and the cherubic premier delighted the public. It also seemed to delight the incorrigibly – and, as he got older – increasingly sentimental Winston Churchill, who took a very personal pleasure in his weekly audience with a young Queen who knew so little, and had so much to learn. In the past, meetings between Prime Minister and Monarch had been respectful occasions. Now they took on an almost jaunty air. The premier would arrive wearing a frock coat and top hat, with a gleam in his eye, and disappear happily into secret conclave. In the spring and summer of 1952, Jock Colville noticed that the length of these meetings increased. 'What do you talk about?' he asked the Prime Minister curiously. 'Oh, mostly racing,' was the genial reply.³ According to Edward (now Sir Edward) Ford, who had become the Queen's assistant private secretary, there were also other favourite topics: polo, for example, which Churchill had played as a young subaltern in India.

'He acted upon her lightest word,' says Ford. On one occasion, the Prime Minister's weekly audience took place on the day after the Queen had attended a royal film performance of *Beau Brummell* – a film apparently picked on the principle that royalty would enjoy watching dramas about its own kind. During their conversation, she remarked that she did not enjoy it. 'Churchill came out of the audience muttering,' Ford recalls. 'He said, "The Queen has had an awful evening. This must not recur".' Before the next day was over, the Home Secretary had been instructed to arrange for the choice of films for the annual royal film performance to be scrutinized, and Lord Radcliffe had been appointed chairman of the resulting selection committee.⁴ In September, the Prime Minister joined the royal party at Balmoral, at his own self-invitation – a venerable guest in an otherwise youthful party. The Queen treated him with courtesy, and grave respect, and in the spring she offered him the supreme honour in her personal gift. Nothing could have pleased him more. 'I'll tell you a secret,' he confided in Lord Moran on April 24th. 'You mustn't tell anyone. She wants me to accept the Garter.'⁵ 'I took it because it was the Queen's wish,' he wrote to Pamela Lytton, an old friend. 'I think she is splendid.'⁶

There were ample grounds for honouring Churchill in any case, but the timing seemed appropriate for such an heraldic elevation, as for its traditions of courtly dedication. It added to a sense of the great statesman as secular high priest of the coming ceremony, uniquely placed to identify with a ritual that evoked past glories and looked forward to new ones. Churchill's profound and personalized belief in the Monarchy chimed with the moment. So did his use of language – with its echoes of Shakespeare, the Book of Common Prayer, Macaulay. The institution, he believed, had never been stronger. The Crown, as he said in his tribute to Queen Mary, 'so soon to be set with all solemnity on the head of her granddaughter,' was now 'far more broadly and securely based on the people's love and the nation's will than in the sedate days of her youth, when rank and privilege ruled society'.[7]

Yet if the Monarch was unquestioned and uncriticized in 1953, unlike in the late nineteenth century when it had been the subject of a lively debate, the love and will were buttressed in ways that could not be sustained indefinitely. Love for Elizabeth, as for her father, was partly a product of the need for a personal focus, above nation, in a fragile yet still functioning Empire. It was monitored by an Empire-minded press which linked respect for the Crown with patriotism. The decline in the imperial role of the Monarchy, however, had already diminished its grandeur; the disappearance of Empire would inevitably weaken its hold on the popular imagination. At the same time, the assumption that the Victoria-George V-George VI-Elizabeth tradition of publicly dutiful and domestically impeccable monarchs and heirs could continue without any repetition of the 1936 lesion, and without any temptation for the newspapers to abandon their habitual docility, was a dangerous one.

For the time being an alliance of proprietors and readers, and the complicity of editors and journalists, ensured that the media would regard anything that was potentially embarrassing to the Royal Family as untouchable. Such restraint required little effort of will. The war had developed habits of self-censorship, which newspaper owners – eager for British Establishment respectability – encouraged. At the same time, a Fleet Street consensus believed that 'disloyal' stories and comment were dynamite: any short-term gain in circulation would be wiped out by a longer-term loss of reputation. The message from the public appeared clear. People wanted warm, comfortable and reassuring coverage of the Royal Family, and would not buy newspapers that offered anything else.

It was a climate that gave Buckingham Palace, and especially the dour figure of Commander Colville ('ashen-faced and like the wicked uncle in a pantomime,' as Cecil Beaton described him in mid-1953, '... who deals so sternly with all of us who are in any way connected with the Press'[8]) an extraordinary negative power. For if editors had no reason to print anything derogatory, the Commander felt little need to supply the press with information or facilities that did not directly support the impression Buckingham Palace wished to convey. Taking public enthusiasm and saccharine press coverage as a royal right – and, indeed, deriving satisfaction from it – the Court felt no obligation to give anything in return, or to feed the loyal appetite for innocuous details which, in Coronation Year, became a compulsive hunger.

Even the BBC, a propaganda mouthpiece for the Monarchy during the war, and still ultra-sycophantic in all its coverage, was treated by the Palace press office in the run-up to the Coronation with a disdain that suggests not so much a constitutional democracy preparing to celebrate its historic liberties, as an authoritarian regime in which all channels to and from the Head of State were strictly guarded. Rules were tight, and transgressors sharply rebuked. Thus the BBC Northern Regional Controller received a severe reprimand for unwisely stating in the *Radio Times* that he was sure the Corporation's handling of the death of George VI had met with the approval of the Royal Family. The point – the Palace made coldly clear – was not that the Queen, or anybody else, disapproved of the coverage. It was that, on such matters, royalty must never be held to have an opinion. The Director-General, Sir William Haley, did not dissent. Instead he ordered the editor of the *Radio Times* never again to publish articles about the Royal Family's views on broadcasting. 'There ought to be an absolutely rigid policy,' he instructed, 'that so far as the BBC is concerned they can be guaranteed complete privacy.'⁹

The 'privacy' injunction applied with equal force to television, the medium whose rapidly emerging importance was to be greatly strengthened by the Coronation. The routine became established: the BBC would float a mild-sounding proposition, and the Palace would slap it down; or the Palace would protest at some Corporation misdemeanour, and an unfortunate official would have his ears boxed. As the pressure built up, so did the slappings, protests, and ear-boxing. In May 1952, B. E. Nicolls, Director of Home Broadcasting, wrote tentatively to the Queen's press secretary asking permission to film the arrival of the Queen at Balmoral for Television News. The reply was a firm refusal. 'Since Her Majesty and her family are going to Balmoral privately for a short holiday,' wrote Commander Colville, 'I do not think it at all appropriate to suggest filming the arrival scenes.'[10] Colville had already proposed that, in view of the BBC's record of intolerable intrusions, royal appearances in newsreels should be rationed. In May and June he followed up with a series of edicts. In future, he told the BBC, if it wished to film the Queen live, it should seek his permission first. It was also announced that nobody would be allowed to film any of the royal residences, internally or externally, before the end of the year.[11]

The regulations, however, did not just restrict coverage of the reigning Monarch. They also extended to her dead predecessors. In August 1952, Nicolls approached the Palace press officer about a proposed BBC documentary, in which the producer wanted to include a scene showing the first night of the new Gaiety Theatre in 1906, which had been attended by Edward VII and Queen Alexandra. The actors, he explained, would not speak, or do anything other than enter their box and sit down. What – he asked trepidatiously – were the rules about impersonating past royalty? The answer came back: both the Lord Chamberlain's Office and the British Board of Film Censors forbade the representation, on stage or screen, of any British sovereign, under any circumstances, more recent than Queen Victoria.[12] That, however, was not the limit of the prohibition. Just after the Coronation, an internal BBC paper reminded staff that, even with Queen Victoria, the Lord Chamberlain's ruling 'lays down that impersonations should be in a serious historical vein'.[13] In such a context, it is scarcely surprising that a biographical documentary about Elizabeth II, entitled 'The Young Queen', and intended both for home use and export, should have been heavily censored, or that an interview with Mrs Buthlay should have been clinically excised from it.[14]

ONE JUSTIFICATION for such sensitivity over the historical record was the argument that to rake up the past, or to offer the Royal Family as a vehicle for entertainment, would be insulting to the Queen and detrimental to the dignity of her office. The underpinning of this case, however, was the belief that the Royal Family was what it presented itself to be: a family beyond reproach, in which relationships were conventional ones, and social rules were unquestioningly observed. Such an assumption was not doubted. But the very reticence of the press – against a background of exceptional adulation – added to the thrill caused by the remotest hint of a transgression. The erecting of taboos does not abolish prurience – far from it. While nobody in the early 1950s expected to hear anything bad about the Royal Family, press and public together looked out, with the keenest interest, for any unusual variation.

The person most watched was Princess Margaret, who had been cast since infancy as the 'mischievous' daughter. The stereotyping did not change. Throughout her teens, and into adulthood, there was, as one observer put it in the 1960s, 'a pantomime-simple idea that while the Queen must be portrayed as an icon of seriousness, opposite qualities must be found in her sister'.[15] The first years after the war had seemed to justify the idea of royal symmetry. While the Heiress Presumptive had acted out her prescribed role – with a well-timed marriage, the swift provision of heirs, the carrying out of royal duties – Margaret had apparently played to hers. 'Between the ages of fourteen and eighteen', says one of her friends, 'she made her own independent stand. She emerged from the shadows, and impressed herself on the public mind.'[16] In party-going and irreverence, as in her challenging good looks and playful smile, she had stood for youthful rebellion against the greyness of the age. The gossip columnists linked her to a circle that included the Earl of Dalkeith, his sister Lady Caroline Montagu-Douglas-Scott, Judy Montagu, and the daughter of the American ambassador, Sharman Douglas. These were sharp, fashionable people, and Margaret became a trend-setter – her hair-styles, dresses and haunts subjected to close examination. Her habit of smoking through a long cigarette-holder became the trade-mark, in the popular papers, for a particular kind of devil-may-care, West End decadence.

The mischievous sister, adored and spoilt by her father, had grown up into the excitable, sparkling, cheeky and slightly naughty one, who made wicked jokes, and charlestoned till 4 a.m. But she was also turning out to be the erotically interesting one, an aspect which the best endeavours of Commander Colville could not prevent the public from observing. If Elizabeth had an icy allure, it was Margaret who had, as Cecil Beaton noted in 1953, 'a sex twinkle of understanding in her regard'.[17] While Elizabeth behaved in public as if the cameras did not exist, Margaret teased them with a look. It was a style in some ways reminiscent of the Duke of Windsor as Prince of Wales: an intimate, colluding charisma, made the more intriguing by a hint of restlessness. Where Elizabeth's rural interests did not conflict with the rhythms of traditional royal life, Princess Margaret seemed a princess on a leash, eager to enjoy the company of a café society that the older courtiers believed should be out of bounds. People often said that she would have been a good actress – meaning, not just that she had theatrical talent, but also that, as a member of the Royal Family, she was not quite reliable. Queen Mary's adjective to describe her granddaughter was *espiègle* – not bad, but adventurous.[18] It was not a coincidence that the suggestion to embark on the VE-Day escapade had come from her, not her sister. She was also the still-unmarried daughter, and thus – especially after her sister's wedding – the subject of continuous gossip.

The gaiety of the fun-loving princess collapsed in 1952. 'After the King's death, there was an awful sense of being in a black hole,' she recalls. 'I remember feeling tunnel-visioned, and didn't really notice things.'[19] The Queen, centre of the Empire's attention, had no choice but to throw herself into public engagements, which provided their own balm. Margaret did not have the same consolation. Effectively abandoned by the sister with whom she had always been close, and left to cope with a turbulent mother, she became reclusive and withdrawn. There had always been a darker, less self-confident side to her personality, and an awareness of the isolating effects of her status. Now, grieving and lonely, she sought comfort in religion. 'She did not wish to see any of her usual circle of friends,' recalled a former member of the royal staff, 'but frequently left the Palace early in the morning with her lady-in-waiting to visit unheralded and privately a church'.[20] She also turned to one of her father's assistants, Peter Townsend.

Townsend had been appointed to the royal service as a much-decorated Battle of Britain pilot during the war. His job, as an equerry to the King, was that of an aide-de-camp and general factotum. He was expected to make sure that visitors came on time and, when they did arrive, were well looked after, to remove problems in any itinerary, and to anticipate and deal with any little difficulty that might crop up in the daily routine of his employer. It was not an intellectually demanding occupation, but it required a degree of psychological subtlety: it was necessary to be available, agreeable and inconspicuous at the same time. Townsend did it well.

One of the requirements was to be liked. 'To survive in that very close-knit *galère*,' says a former insider, 'you've got to be liked or off-loaded.'[21] Not everybody liked Peter Townsend. One of Princess Margaret's friends felt that he was narcissistic, and – when troubles arose – that he was as much in love with the royal life as with the King's daughter.[22] However, this was an exceptional view. Townsend fitted in with the King's family, almost as a substitute son and brother. He became particularly skilled at handling the royal 'gnashes'. Courtiers got on well with him. 'He was very attractive,' says one; 'a little bit fey, with rather rigid views, but delightful company.' When the Air Ministry asked to have him back, the King and Queen resisted. 'They said "Dear Peter, we can't lose him,"' recalls the same source.[23] That Townsend was much older, married, and had small children, may have contributed to their naïvety.

According to friends, it was in the close proximity of the White Train in South Africa in 1947, while Elizabeth's thoughts were in North Wales, that the equerry approaching middle-age began to develop a friendship with the seventeen-year-old princess that was more than fraternal. The death of Margaret's father, and the break-up of Townsend's marriage helped to bring them closer together. It was not until a year after the Accession that they first discussed their feelings with one another – although by this time the relationship had become obvious to others. Margaret told her sister – her most natural confidante – and a meeting was arranged between the two couples. If Townsend had hoped for encouragement, he did not get it. The Queen was sympathetic, but non-committal. She did not indicate disapproval. Nor, apparently, did she offer to do her best to help. Instead, she asked that 'under the circumstances' – and the most pressing circumstance was the forthcoming Coronation – they should wait a year.[24]

Townsend had grounds for expecting sympathy at this meeting because the Queen, too, had fallen for a handsome but impecunious war hero whose ambition to marry into the Royal Family had encountered resistance in Buckingham Palace and elsewhere. Townsend's difficulties, however, were of a different magnitude. To begin with, he was not a prince. Unlike Philip, he was not already a member of the extended network of European royalty, with its set of secret shared assumptions. As a middle-class courtier, he had – by encouraging, or not resisting, the affections of the King's daughter – breached the code which required all those who worked on terms of intimacy with the Royal Family to behave like Palace eunuchs. 'If you probe underneath it all', reflects a former courtier, 'you are their servants, and servants ought not to marry their masters.'[25] Townsend's suit crossed a boundary of caste. It also, incidentally, shattered the Peter Pan idyll that had surrounded the Royal Family since 145 Piccadilly, and which had allowed courtiers and governesses to mix with royalty on terms of superficial equality, pretending that inconvenient passions did not exist.

But the much bigger stumbling block was Townsend's marital status. That he required a divorce to marry Princess Margaret, albeit as the innocent party, revived the still recent memory of 1936. Margaret was third in line. If she could marry a divorced man, why had Edward VIII been forbidden to marry Mrs Simpson? Should he not still be King? 'You must be mad or bad,' Lascelles, who had been Edward VIII's assistant private secretary at the time of the Abdication, told Townsend – contemplating the hornet's nest.[26] There had been some changes in the intervening seventeen years. The old rule, which had allowed divorced officers in the armed services to kill the King's enemies, but had not permitted them to kill his pheasants in royal shooting parties, had been relaxed during the Second World War.[27] Yet divorced people were still not asked to royal garden parties, or to attend other functions at which royalty was present. Meanwhile, the Church of England, with the ardent approval of the Primate, refused to re-marry people who had been through the divorce courts. Liberal pressure to change the divorce law, so far from easing the path to royal acceptance of divorce, encouraged the Church hierarchy to react with even greater indignation against any behaviour that seemed likely to open the flood-gates. If Townsend had had an Uncle Dickie, the outlook might have seemed better. As it was, the obstacles were mountainous.

For the time being, the problem was contained and, indeed, had not publicly arisen. Sir Alan Lascelles advised the Queen of her right to refuse permission for the marriage of her sister, until Princess

Margaret's twenty-fifth birthday, under the 1772 Royal Marriages Act, and of the right of veto of the British and Dominion Parliaments thereafter. He also told her that, on such a matter, her ability to consent depended on the advice of her Prime Minister. Churchill was consulted: he replied – no doubt with the months after the Accession of Edward VIII in mind – that the granting of permission for such a match would be disastrous in the same year as the Coronation. Rumours began to appear in the American and Continental press. As yet, the British papers ignored them.[28]

IN MANY WAYS, the Coronation of Elizabeth II in 1953 was the most magnificent and affecting royal ceremonial of the century – despite, or because of, the decline in the importance of the Monarch. George VI's crowning had been a nervous event, the 1947 royal wedding a splendid dress rehearsal. By contrast, the 1953 Coronation combined the personal drama of the Wedding with the solemnity of a great state and religious occasion. Only the 1935 Silver Jubilee was comparable.[29] Even that, however, had lacked the magic ingredient of the vernal Queen, her adult years ahead of her, and – in the public imagination – able to offer a new future for the nation.

Great ceremonies are seldom explicit about their purposes, even if those who organize them know what they are, or seek to impose them. Rituals are taken from the record of what happened before, amended to fit what is currently felt to be suitable and acceptable. If the mood of 1953 combined a sense of the restoration of the *status quo ante bellum* and an anxious optimism, there were also other elements. Some saw the official celebrations as directly political. At a time when Britain was holding aloof from European discussions, ardent European Federalists viewed the whole occasion as 'a gigantic British festival of isolation, a thunderous nation-wide re-assertion of British sovereignty, separateness and exclusiveness'.[30]

In retrospect, the 1953 event seems to have acquired a character that was more universalist than nationalistic – so far from causing hostility on the continent of Europe, it aroused admiring interest. Nevertheless, Government ministers undoubtedly saw it as a tradition-alist sequel to the Festival of Britain – a celebration of Britishness, British achievements, an independent British destiny. If it was not anti-European, it was partly envisaged as a demonstration of a 'Commonwealth unity' that was needed to fill the vacuum created by the collapse of European power. There was a paradox here: for the very circumstances of the Coronation had changed the nature of that unity. On the one hand, the pulling-apart of member states had been accelerated by the Accession Proclamation, and by a series of Acts during the 'uncrowned' part of the Queen's reign. These had ended the idea of a Commonwealth 'united by a common allegiance to the Crown' (in the words of the 1917 Balfour Declaration), making Elizabeth II the Queen, separately, of each of her realms.[31] On the other hand, international pressures had made the idea (or fantasy) of the Commonwealth as a power bloc comparable to the United States appear a necessary goal, and the only available way to give substance to the polite fiction that Britain remained a great power. The Accession had coincided with what one historian has described as 'the short-lived imbalance between Britain and the super powers'.[32] The Coronation provided an opportunity to display a new kind of imperial greatness, by reaffirming the Monarchy as a cord tying together the Empire and Commonwealth into a group of diplomatically, economically and even militarily associated nations.

'Without the Crown there can obviously be no Britain and no Commonwealth,' asserted a 'Coronation Supplement' of the *Westminster Bank Review* in an extreme version of this approach. 'Without Britain and the Commonwealth, there can be no tolerable future.'[33] Such contemplations, however, did not touch or fully explain the feelings of those who covered their houses in red-white-and-blue and turned out to cheer. For most ordinary celebrants, the reasons – though complex – were largely instinctive. One element was what a quizzical Canadian psychologist called 'a regal feeling' – widely held in Britain and the old dominions – which, he suggested, had been acquired like a mother tongue, through birth or residence.[34] There was also a romantic concept of the 'British Empire,' for which, supposedly, two World Wars had been fought, and which meant more to many people than 'the Commonwealth'. Despite the invention of the Commonwealth republic, to cater for Indian sub-continent independence, the Commonwealth remained closer to what it had been in the days of the Queen's grandfather than to the multi-cultural associ-

ation it later became; and many people who applauded Commonwealth troops half-imagined that they were welcoming the soldiers
of a still-unitary British Crown. The Coronation might have been
'celebrating the continuity of Britain as a great power'. But it was also
the last great imperial display, a magnificent funeral tribute to a world
order that was ending.

As a social and national phenomenon, the Coronation was not a
single event, but a rolling programme that began with the Accession
and did not subside until months after the ceremony itself. The most
rabid period began in the spring of 1953. Shops decked themselves in
the colours of the union jack, and filled their shelves with orbs,
sceptres, maces, coaches and crowns. Town councils discussed street
parties, and school children – revved up for a mid-summer Christmas
– were whipped into a frenzy of iconographic pasting, painting and
modelling. A craze for periscopes, designed to help small people see
over tall ones in front of them in the crowd, spread among people
who had no prospect of being in London on Coronation Day.[35]

One thing, however, that made the 1953 Coronation different from
its predecessors was that most people did not have to be in London,
with or without a periscope, to see it. For the first time, televisions
were widely enough available for the majority of those who wanted
to do so, to watch the day's events live, on the screen. Indeed, if the
Coronation was a burial service for the Empire, whose passing took
away one of the main roles of the Monarchy, it was also a baptism
for a new kind of mass participation in national events, which changed
for ever the way in which royalty would be perceived.

It nearly did not happen. At the outset, a distinction was drawn
between the procession, which would be televised as it had been in
1947, and the Coronation service, seen as a sacred and even as a
privileged occasion. The press stoked up public interest and the television industry, eager to expand, campaigned to allow cameras into
the Abbey. Resistance, however, was strong – especially in Buckingham
Palace.

In March 1952, it was suggested to the Prime Minister that Philip
'who is insupportable when idle,' should be given a responsible job.[36]
The Coronation provided him with one. The arrangements – astonishingly, for such a major logistical operation – were not entrusted to

somebody with a proven organizational talent, on the basis of their competence, but to the 'Earl Marshal', an hereditary office held by the Duke of Norfolk. However, a Coronation Joint Executive was set up to help him, and Prince Philip was made Chairman. In July, this body, composed of prominent people involved in the ceremony or the procession, discussed the proposal that the service should be seen live on television, and rejected it.

The main reason (indeed almost certainly the overriding one) was the reluctance of the Queen herself. 'The Committee was almost unanimous in considering that television of the actual ceremony should not be allowed,' Jock Colville informed Churchill, in a Downing Street memo. 'Whereas film of the ceremony can be cut appropriately, live television would not only add considerably to the strain on the Queen (who does not herself want TV) but would mean that any mistakes, unintentional incidents or undignified behaviour by spectators would be seen by millions of people.' The news soon leaked. 'The chief opponent of television seems to have been the Queen herself,' Edward Pickering, editor of the *Daily Express*, wrote to Lord Beaverbrook in October. 'It was because of her known antipathy that the matter was never fully examined.'[37] The Queen's hesitancy was backed up by an alliance of the Prime Minister, the Archbishop of Canterbury and the Abbey clergy, who believed that a large casual audience watching the religious service 'over the coffee cups' would detract from its dignity. Fears were also expressed that television in the Abbey might 'steal the crowds' and stop people from coming to watch the procession.[38] The Cabinet, however, regarded the impact on the Queen as paramount. Influenced, according to the minutes, 'by the importance of avoiding unnecessary strain for Her Majesty and upholding the sanctity of the ceremony,' it endorsed the Executive's position. However, that was not the final word. There was an avalanche of letters to the press, and protests from MPs. In October, ministers reconsidered their verdict. After a lengthy discussion, they decided 'in the light of serious public disappointment' to reverse it.[39]

According to one account, a key influence was the BBC journalist, Richard Dimbleby, who came down firmly in favour of television, rather than radio, as the best vehicle for his commentary.[40] When state papers for 1953 were made available thirty years later, Jock (by now Sir John) Colville gave his own account, from memory, of what had happened, in order – as he saw it – to put the record straight, and to counteract the obvious inference to be drawn from newly released Cabinet documents. In particular, he maintained that it had been the Queen herself who had instigated the eventual decision by the Cabinet to allow the cameras in after all. Following the initial decision by the Joint Executive, backed by the Cabinet, to keep them out, he claimed, the Monarch told the Prime Minister in an audience that 'all her subjects should have an opportunity of seeing it'.[41] If this recollection is correct, it constituted a regal about-face: for both Colville's own contemporary note and the Cabinet minutes make indisputably clear her initial opposition to live television. In any event – despite such a change of heart – the Queen remained deeply suspicious of the medium. The same autumn, she declined to have her Christmas broadcast televised, opting for the BBC to show a still photograph of herself at the microphone instead.[42]

There was still the question of what parts, and how much, of the Coronation service should be shown on the screen. Great anxiety was expressed about close-up shots of the Queen's face, and about the danger of some gaffe or error reaching a mass audience. Attitudes softened, however, when it was explained that 'live' did not mean unedited, that close-ups could be excluded, and that any shot could be previewed – and, if necessary, censored – before transmission.[43] At the end of October, the Cabinet Secretary presented the Prime Minister with the arguments for and against allowing an 'inclusive' approach. On the plus side, he suggested, public opinion was in favour, not out of idle curiosity, but from a natural desire to participate. It should also be born in mind that 'television is here to stay'. On the minus side, providing unlimited access would make it difficult to resist future requests to televise royal marriages, funerals and other ceremonies where the cameras might be considered even less appropriate.[44] Eventually, an inclusive formula was adopted – though wrangling continued about the siting of the cameras both in the Abbey and at the Palace. The whole day was given over to coverage of the Coronation – procession, service, and crowning.

The result was a media revolution that transformed the industry and turned Britain into a nation of couch potatoes. Licence holders doubled from 1½ to 3 million in anticipation of Coronation Day; in addition, a large number of people who rented sets just for June 2nd, decided to retain them. A breakthrough in international broadcasting also occurred. A European link-up extended coverage to much of France, West Germany and Holland. American TV networks were allowed to telerecord the BBC's coverage inside the Abbey, and fly it across the Atlantic.[45] The outcome, as one awe-struck commentator put it, was that for the first time ever, 'a whole nation, and indeed a considerable part of the population of the world,' saw a crown being put on the head of a Queen.[46]

In Britain, an estimated twenty-seven million people watched the Coronation live for at least half the day. The sense of everybody seeing the same event, itself a novelty, added to the community spirit – especially as owners and hirers of sets invited others into their homes. It also changed the iconography. From now on, the expectation that royal events would be televised became automatic; popular images of royalty were animated ones, and television became the means by which the public would perceive the Royal Family and – with ever more fascinated intimacy – relate to it.

A POWERFUL, non-televised image of Commonwealth unity, and of the monarchical cord, was provided at a dinner in Westminster Hall on May 17th, six days before the Coronation. The Queen and the Duke sat beside Commonwealth Prime Ministers at a high table placed on the steps where Charles I had stood trial and – in the presence of representatives of fifty-two legislatures – listened to the British premier describing what had become, in Coronation year, the dominant theory of Monarchy. In his speech, Churchill stressed first the importance of continuity – he reminded the Queen that he had 'served your Majesty's great-great-grandmother, great-grandfather, grandfather, father, and now yourself'. He spoke, not just of the personal virtues of the Monarch whose Coronation they were celebrating, and of her recent forbears, but also of the 'burden' she would willingly bear. Finally, he drew attention to the unifying role of the Crown which helped to make it 'the central link in all our modern changing life, the one which above all others claims our allegiance to death'.[47] The trinity of continuity, duty and unity accorded to the institution and the occupant a far more active role than Attlee had offered as a justification for increasing the Civil List in his 'ceremonial' account six years before.

The Queen – star of the show, with a complicated part – meanwhile learnt her lines. The Minister of Works, David Eccles, told Richard Crossman that she enormously enjoyed the Coronation rehearsals.[48] There was some relaxation of the rules about who was allowed into the Abbey. This time, the war was judged sufficiently distant to allow Philip's German-married sisters to attend the ceremony – though they were strictly rationed to two children each. But other German relatives were firmly put off.[49] The most ticklish issue concerned the Duke of Windsor. When the Queen discussed with the Archbishop of Canterbury the possibility of the former King taking part, both agreed that, even if he wanted to come, he should not be invited. 'The Queen would be less willing than any one to have him there,' recorded Dr Fisher, after their conversation.[50]

The invasion of the capital began on May 23rd – on that day alone, a million people came to London to see the decorations along the procession route. Four days later, traffic problems became so bad that the police had to forbid all but priority and public service vehicles from entering an area within a two-mile radius of Westminster. In the last few days, the press virtually gave up on non-Coronation news, filling their columns almost entirely with royal-related features and information. The build-up continued with a huge garden party on May 29th which reminded one observer of a Hollywood epic in an interval between shooting: including an enormous cast of extras composed of bishops, sultans, sheikhs, generals, African tribesmen, and a vast array of beautifully dressed women 'in their silks and taffetas and gros-grain'.[51] This was followed by a dinner and ball given by the Household Brigade at Hampton Court – by which time the temperature of the crowds had reached boiling point. 'Never has there been such excitement,' wrote Jock Colville, 'never has a Monarch received such adulation.' Thousands cheered the Queen's departure from the Palace, and waited on the pavement to cheer her as she drove past.[52] Hospitality for Commonwealth leaders reached its climax on the eve of the Coronation, with a prime ministers' lunch at Buckingham Palace. Cecil Beaton, at the Palace on other business, stumbled in as they were lining up for the official photograph, and observed the Queen 'quite obviously elated at being the delightful, gay and attractive cynosure of it all'.[53] Others found her cool, the encapsulation of Britishness. 'You must be feeling nervous, Ma'am,' a lady-in-waiting said to her the same day. 'Of course I am, but I really do think Aureole will win,' she is supposed to have replied, referring to a horse she owned that was running in the Derby.[54]

The Coronation took place on Tuesday, June 2nd, and on the Sunday people who had not obtained seats in the stands along the procession route began to bed down in the streets in order to secure a standing place. By dusk on the Monday, half a million people were already lining the route, in pouring rain and driving wind. The timely news that a couple of climbers from a Commonwealth expedition had got to the top of the highest mountain in the world reached the waterlogged encampments in the early hours of the morning. 'All This – And Everest Too!' hyperbolized the *Daily Express*, above an 'exclusive' drawing of the Queen's robes, and a picture of huddled-but-happy spectators, 'Crowds singing in the rain'. Yet there was solemnity as well as rejoicing. Comparisons were made with Armistice, VE- and VJ-Days. The 'extraordinary stillness and tranquillity' of the campers on the route was noted. Many people went to church to pray, meditate or take communion.[55]

There had, indeed, been a religious build up to the Coronation, as well as a secular one. From the Church of England's point of view, it was an important moment. The service offered a rare example of an ecclesiastical event – other than a wedding or a funeral – that aroused intense public interest. Conscious of shrinking attendance and the rivalry of other denominations, the Anglican Church was glad of a chance to assert its pre-eminence, while drawing attention to its historic link with the Monarch as its Supreme Governor. Partly for these reasons, the Archbishop of Canterbury took his own role in the proceedings with great seriousness, becoming – during the months in which anybody remotely connected with the drama acquired a celebrity status – one of the Coronation's most familiar actors. He also made a close, conservative, study of the Coronation liturgy, which he explained in a series of sermons in the weeks preceding the main event.

Dr. Fisher's exposition is of interest, both because of the care with which it was prepared and the standing of its author, and because of the emphasis it placed on the character and duties of the Sovereign. Like Churchill, though with greater emphasis and meaning, Fisher saw the life of a Monarch as a 'burden,' which – though not chosen – was willingly assumed. He also saw it as involving a spiritual dimension. In this respect, his interpretation was even further at odds with the workaday, ceremonial version of Attlee.

Fisher did not speak of divine right, but of the Queen as 'God-called' to perform duties which were much more than merely symbolic. He argued that the diminution of the temporal power of the Monarchy, so far from reducing the institution's importance, had enhanced it – giving the Sovereign 'the possibility of a spiritual power far more exalted and far more searching in its demands: the power to lead, to inspire, to unite, by the Sovereign's personal character, personal convictions, personal example'. Such a power might be inoperable, he suggested, in the wrong hands. Fortunately, however, the Queen had been well equipped, through upbringing and Christian faith, to exercise it, and, by doing so, to uphold 'the pillars of a true society', whose goals included 'domestic fidelity' and 'united homes'.

There was also another aspect, however – and here the Archbishop got to the crux. The Coronation was not just about the power of leadership. It was also about sacrifice. By bringing the Queen 'into the presence of the living God' at the Anointing, the service defined her special relationship with the Deity – a relationship based on self-denial. The physical weight of the Crown, meanwhile, would symbolize the burden of the demands that would be made upon her, 'to her life's end'. Sacrificing herself and bearing this burden on behalf of country and Commonwealth, she would be 'giving herself and being herself at all times'.[56]

In practical terms, of course, such an account was as unreal as it was terrifying: no modern Monarch, victim of inheritance, could be expected to become a semi-priest and campaigner for family values, even if the constitution had allowed it. Possibly the Primate, in his zeal, over-reached himself. 'Doubtless there was something about a young and beautiful Queen which moved him emotionally,' observes his biographer, '. . . thus encouraging him to use to the full all the opportunities, pastoral and otherwise, which the Coronation provided for an Archbishop.'[57] Nevertheless, his interpretation had some basis in the strange hotchpotch of ancient rites and recent accretions contained in the service, which had, at its medieval core, both the ritual of anointing, and a primitive idea of a sacrifice.

Nobody seemed quite sure how the service had begun, though all authorities pointed to origins that were Anglo-Saxon or older. As the anthropologist S. B. F. Price points out, royal rituals and insignia had been used 'to define the nature of the King and hence of the state itself' since classical times.[58] In his major study of kingship, A. M. Hocart suggests that coronations in all cultures contained rituals – such as communion, unction, special clothing, investing with regalia and processing – that pointed to a common, primitive origin.[59] The English ritual was authoritatively traced to the Coronation of King Edgar in 973 which, according to the medieval historian Professor B. Wilkinson, already expressed a mixture of elements ('Christian anointing combined with Teutonic acclamation and with Roman crowning'), which survived into the twentieth century. The most dramatic survival, made much of by the Archbishop, was anointing, originally with oil that had miraculous powers, and then as a symbolic act.[60] 'Not all the water in the rough rude sea,' Shakespeare wrote in *Richard II*, 'can wash the balm from an anointed king'. The idea retained its power – and the modern ritual, including the disappearance of the Monarch under the canopy accompanied by the Church's highest priest – was later believed to have affected the Queen deeply.[61]

The service, however, was more than a mystic initiation, or an opportunity for archiepiscopal projection. Some traditionalists saw it as a 'medieval pageantry in patriotism, transfused with religion'.[62] But it was also possible to view it, with all its additions, subtractions and permutations, as (in Professor Wilkinson's words) 'a synoptic view of the whole development of modern democracy,' which provided 'a covenant to preserve the great Anglo-Saxon political tradition, and a pledge to maintain the historic process by which this was translated into the procedures of the modern state'.[63] The essence of it was a legitimation, not of spiritual, but of temporal power – and, in the modern era, of the institutions of a liberal society. Constitutionally, the most important part was the Oath, which required the Queen to swear 'to govern ... according to their respective laws and customs' the people of her different realms, to uphold Law and Justice, and to maintain in the United Kingdom 'the Protestant Reformed Religion,' together with the Church of England settlement. There was some criticism that the Archbishop, who cared so deeply for the theology, made no adjustment to meet the sensibilities of Ceylon and Pakistan, 'realms' which retained the Queen as Head of State, yet contained an overwhelming majority of non-Christians. A young journalist called John Grigg (later Lord Altrincham, before reverting to his original name) suggested that one constructive reform would be to swap eminent Canadians, Australians, Pakistanis and other Commonwealth leaders for many of the disproportionately large number of British aristocrats in the congregation.[64] Such suggestions for change, either to the service or the participants, however, met with a wall of opposition from the Earl Marshal and the Archbishop of Canterbury, while the Queen had no suggestions to make.[65]

The Day itself was remarkable mainly for the size of the crowds, and the enjoyment they seemed to derive from the procession, despite weather that was unseasonably cold and wet. The Queen's own mood seemed to range from apprehension before the crowning to carefree animation after it. *The Times* opened the day echoing the theme of the Archbishop: that the Queen was willingly sacrificing herself to the Almighty and to the nation. 'Having made service her career,' it proclaimed, 'she has the reward of the selfless in the pure joy of duty amply, generously, done.' The Queen's duty on her Coronation Day was to be the almost silent actress, acting herself as she was supposed to be, in a pageant that commanded the thoughts and emotions of almost everybody in Britain and the dominions, and many people elsewhere in the world as well. A continual roar, through the drizzle, accompanied her gold coach down the Mall, and in an extended circular route to Westminster Abbey. What were they cheering? A twenty-seven-year-old woman who had had no chance in her life to do anything except make polite conversation and launch ships? The Monarchy? The nation, the Commonwealth, the system of Government – or themselves?

At the Abbey, the Queen 'grave-faced' – according to a token 'ordinary' member of the public admitted to the service – moved 'slowly to an unheard rhythm . . . Her face was pale, her youth and tenderness intensified by the cherishing – I can only use that word – of her supporters'.[66] Some felt she showed the strain.[67] Others cast her in various ways, according to their lights. Princess Alice, Countess of Athlone, saw her as 'a young and beautiful Queen and sovereign who looked like a débutante . . .'[68] Cecil Beaton described her as if she were a wedding cake at a magical feast:

> The cheeks are sugar-pink: her hair tightly curled around the Victorian diadem of precious stones straight on her brow. Her pink hands are folded meekly on the elaborate grandeur of her encrusted skirt; she is still a young girl with a demeanour of simplicity and humility. Perhaps her mother has taught her never to use a superfluous gesture. As she walks she allows her heavy skirt to swing backwards and forwards in a beautiful rhythmic effect. This girlish figure has enormous dignity; she belongs in this scene of almost Byzantine magnificence.[69]

The service began with the Archbishop's declaration to the bishops in the sanctuary. 'Sirs, I here present unto you Queen Elizabeth, your undoubted Queen.' Then came the Oath, and Holy Communion, including the antiphon 'Zadok the priest and Nathan the prophet anointed Solomon king,' sung by the choir to music written by Handel for the Coronation of George III. After this, the Queen shed all her robes and adornments and put on a white dress for the hidden act of anointing. As she sat on the Coronation Chair, Knights of the Garter put a canopy over her head, and – out of view of the cameras or congregation – the Archbishop of Canterbury made a sign of the cross on her hands, chest and head, intoning the extraordinary words:

> Be thy Head anointed with holy Oil: as kings, priests, and prophets were anointed. And as Solomon was anointed King by Zadok the priest and Nathan the prophet, so be thou anointed, blessed and consecrated Queen over the Peoples, whom the Lord thy God hath given thee to rule and govern . . .

People were moved by the divestment, by the sense of exposure, and by the simplicity of the anointing dress – as though the sacrifice were a physical one, and the rite performed under the Canopy an act of violation. 'I thought how young she looked and how vulnerable, how resolved and how steadfast,' commented one witness. 'Her young, rounded arms were uncovered, in contrast to the formality of her magnificently embroidered dress and long-trained crimson Robe of State.'[70]

The ceremony then moved to the crowning, when the Archbishop held the crown for a few moments above the Queen's head. The expression on her face, Beaton noted, was 'one of intense expectancy' until the Archbishop thrust the crown down, with speed and force.[71] This was the signal for the self-crowning of the peeresses, which had so impressed Princess Elizabeth in 1937, a movement of robes and jewels which was compared to the corps de ballet in *Lac des Cygnes*.[72] Homages from the Archbishop, Duke of Edinburgh and the nobility followed. Finally, there was the acclamation 'God Save Queen Elizabeth. Long live Queen Elizabeth, May the Queen live for Ever!' – a form of words derived from the earliest Anglo-Saxon and Frankish practice.[73] The crowned Queen then returned to the coach, which carried her, with Sceptre and Orb, through the capital, accompanied by 13,000 troops, twenty-nine bands and twenty-seven carriages along the seven-mile route – a 'great deep thunder' of acclamation heralding and pursuing her.[74]

Beaton, photographing the Queen in the Picture Gallery at the Palace afterwards, found her 'cool, smiling, sovereign of the situation,' though looking tired, after wearing the heavy crown for three hours. Her husband was in the background, making wry jokes, and 'definitely adopting a rather ragging attitude towards the proceedings'.[75] That evening, the Queen broadcast a speech, relayed through loudspeakers to the damp yet still exhilarated crowds in the Mall. In it, she repeated Cape Town, yet again – giving her pledge 'to your service, as so many are pledged to mine'.[76]

11

'FOR THE FIRST FEW YEARS of her reign,' wrote Sir Charles Petrie in 1961, 'she was the subject of adulation unparalleled since the days of Louis XIV.'[1] It was obvious, or should have been, that such a mood could not possibly last; moreover, that the unreal reverence must eventually exact a price. In retrospect, it was a time when the institution had an opportunity to re-examine its purpose. Since anything it did was virtually beyond criticism, Buckingham Palace might have been able to carry through unexpected, even imaginative, reforms without causing offence, and without being pushed. However, popularity is not normally seen as a reason for self-appraisal – it is more likely to encourage a belief that the existing formula is a successful one. In any case, the twentieth-century British Monarchy was not in the habit of taking initiatives. Hence in the mid 1950s, on the back of the fragile post-war recovery, and cosseted by governments that were happy to bask in the reflected glory, the Monarchy wasted its most bountiful years – taking what it was given in mindless admiration as its due.

The Coronation was followed by an irrational expectancy: as if so great a drama required a consummation. This feeling was combined with a desire to extract some kind of meaning from an event that was so inexplicable, and of which the popular mood had been the most remarkable part. The Queen wrote to the Archbishop of Canterbury, thanking him for his help in sustaining her through 'the strain of that long day,'[2] while Fisher recorded in his diary that the only mistake she had made was 'that she forgot to curtsey when she got to the North pillar'.[3] Meanwhile, she relaxed at the Derby, watching Aureole come second. 'Congratulations on winning the Derby,' she said to Norman Bertie, trainer of the horse that beat Aureole to the post as she handed him the trophy. 'May I congratulate you, Your Majesty, on winning the world,' Bertie is supposed to have replied.[4] The Archbishop took longer to come down. 'You will, I expect, find it as difficult as I do to give your minds to anything else,' he admitted in his Sunday sermon. 'Every train of thought or conversation comes back to it. The wonder of it, the unforgettable bearing of the Queen, the overwhelming sense of dedication to God, of worship of God, consecration by God and communion with God, embracing everyone in the Abbey . . .' There was, however, a shift of emphasis. Before the service, the stress had been on duty, burden, sacrifice. Now, viewing the day's events in exhilarated retrospect, he described it as, above all, a 'tremendous family event'.[5]

Others agreed. But whose family? The Royal Family itself could once again be portrayed, as in the 1930s, as an ideal young family – the kind of brisk and open-shirted nuclear unit that breakfasted on corn flakes and believed in outdoor fun and restrained procreation. The periodical *Twentieth Century* put it well. 'The quick commonsense of the Queen, and the shrewd modernity of the Duke of Edinburgh' not only made them excellent parents. Such royal virtues helped the Crown to give the state 'the sense of family,' while 'our loyalty to each other is stimulated by the person of our young Queen'.[6] Thus, the Coronation had shown that familial virtues were infectious and, in the liturgical language of the Archbishop, 'we found ourselves sharing her dedication and receiving in her consecration a portion of her spirit and a place beside her in the blessing of Almighty God'.[7]

A secular version of this argument was provided by two sociologists, Edward Shils and Michael Young, who described the celebration in an article at the end of the year, as 'an act of national communion' – citing Durkheim's theory that a society needed from time to time to reaffirm the collective ideas which characterized it. Television and radio, they suggested, had helped to reinforce the sense of universal participation, and of the British people as 'one great national family' through its identification with the Monarchy. So too had the moral unity created by the Second World War, and by a Labour Government which had shown concern for the poor without alienating the middle-classes. As a result, Britain had entered the Coronation period with an exceptional degree of moral consensus.

Where, however, Shils and Young particularly agreed with the Archbishop – as well as with Churchill, and with *Twentieth Century* – was in their sense of the importance to this equation of the Royal Family's moral example, and especially its family virtues. 'Devotion to the Royal Family thus means in a very direct way devotion to one's own family, because the values embodied are the same,' they concluded. Against such a background, the Coronation could be seen as an extension of the idea of the whole of society as one large family, and of the Commonwealth as a 'family of nations,' and of the Crown as a moral cord binding the consensus together.[8]

Shils and Young were challenged by a fellow sociologist, Norman Birnbaum, who accused them of describing a moral unity that did not exist, and of romanticizing feelings for the Queen and her family which were little different from the cult of adulation built round certain film stars.[9] In the 1980s, Tom Nairn joined the attack, accusing Shils and Young of 'the Sociology of Grovelling'. However, Nairn acknowledged that such royal occasions were of greater significance than the mere 'tinsel' dismissed by Birnbaum.[10] Read today, Shils and Young's essay has the flavour of a period piece, but one which accurately perceived, without solving the mystery, that the Coronation was more than mere flummery: and that it helped to define, not just royalty, but the British identity for the next generation.

EXCITEMENT related to the Coronation lasted many weeks. The first few days were filled with banquets and displays, as medals, jewels and tiaras glittered round London. The nation's obsession with tinsel did not cease. Attempts at serious culture seemed out of place. On 8th June, Benjamin Britten's opera *Gloriana*, written for the occasion, was performed before the Queen at Covent Garden. The Earl of Harewood had put the idea to Britten, after reading *Elizabeth and Essex* by Lytton Strachey. The original intention was for a 'national' opera – a British equivalent to *Aida* for the Italians. Harewood's personal access to the Palace enabled him to overcome resistance to anything so innovatory, and it was arranged that extracts should be tested out on the Queen and Duke in advance. The result was a rare example of an important artistic creation that was a product of royal encouragement. However, it received a mixed reception at the première – which Harewood attributed to the general mood of hysteria produced by the event for which the opera had been written. It was clear, he recalled, that what the critics wanted was 'some sort of simple-minded glorification . . . not the passionate, tender drama inside the public pageantry that Ben had contrived.'[11]

Coronation kitsch remained the dominant motif as the round of festivities continued. There was a fetishising of anything, or anybody, royal. The personality of the post-Coronation week was not Benjamin Britten but Queen Salote of Tonga, whose large and genial presence in the Coronation procession had been taken as a reassuring symbol of imperial multi-culturalism, and whose royal progress round the dinners and canapé trays that followed was keenly observed, as an alternative, earth-motherly, image of Queenship. It was a climate that incubated any kind of royalty news or rumours – making it impossible to keep a royal secret, especially one that had become servants' hall gossip at Buckingham Palace and Clarence House.

The trigger for press dementia over Princess Margaret and Peter Townsend was provided, appropriately, at the Coronation service itself. Just as speculation about Elizabeth and Philip had been sparked by intimate gestures at the Brabourne–Mountbatten wedding, so a friendly movement by the Queen's sister, as she 'brushed with a tender hand' the lapels of the Group Captain in an ante room to the Abbey, fired gossip about their romance.[12] The New York press ran the story next morning. Eleven days later (such was the extent, and limit, of Commander Colville's power), the British Sunday *People* revealed to its readers that foreign newspapers had been openly asserting that Princess Margaret 'is in love with a divorced man and that she wishes to marry him'.[13]

'It was Tommy Lascelles and also Winston, or rather Clemmie, who objected,' says a former courtier.[14] Lascelles had spoken to the Prime Minister the day before the story broke. According to Churchill's doctor and Boswell, Lord Moran, the premier's first reaction was to say that 'the course of true love must always be allowed to run smooth'. However, the Prime Minister was checked by his wife, who told him that if he adopted this line, 'he would be making the same mistake that he had made at the Abdication,' when he had done himself political damage by backing Edward VIII.[15] The Lascelles–Clemmie view rapidly became that of the Court and Cabinet. Princess Margaret blamed Lascelles. Later, she was quoted as saying, 'I shall curse him to the grave.'[16]

At the end of June, Margaret accompanied her mother on a visit to Rhodesia. In their absence, Peter Townsend – technically still in the RAF, although currently employed by Queen Elizabeth as Master of her Household – was suddenly posted to a sinecure job as air attaché in the British Embassy in Brussels. It was a humiliating, as well as a brutal, move. 'Queen "exiles" RAF ace linked to Princess Meg,' declared the American press.[17] It was the Government, doubtless in collusion with Sir Alan Lascelles, that did the exiling. However, the Queen might have tried to stop it. There is no evidence that she made such an attempt.

The moment was stressful, coming so soon after the Coronation, whose celebration had not yet ceased. Noël Coward played before the Monarch and her husband at Hurlingham on 18th July, the day after Townsend had taken up his Belgian posting, and the day before Margaret got back from Africa. 'The Queen, poor dear, scowled through most of the performance,' he noted. 'One can only assume that the "advisers" in Buckingham Palace and the Lord Chamberlain's office are a poor lot.'[18] In the popular press, Townsend became a folk hero, Margaret – once again – the princess in a tower. The *Daily Mirror* ran a poll, which produced more than 70,000 responses, of which 67,907 thought the couple should be allowed to marry, 2,235 that they should not.[19] 'It is all so incredibly vulgar,' wrote Coward, expressing the Mayfair view, 'and to me, it is inconceivable that nothing could be done to stop these tasteless illiterate minds from smearing our Royal Family with their sanctimonious rubbish.'[20] The newly established Press Council did its best, censuring the *Mirror*. Not for the last time, it was ignored. Lord Beaverbrook's *Evening Standard* defended the *Mirror*. 'Princess Margaret is not a private person,' it argued. 'She is the potential Regent of Great Britain. And that being so, her marriage is of the utmost importance and consequence not only to herself but to all the people.'[21] *The Times* regretted that 'these royal and remarkable weeks' following the Coronation had been 'saddened for the Queen by public gossip,' yet it took the same line on press freedom as the *Standard*.[22]

At this stage, however, public discussion of the Margaret–Townsend question was in one sense a debate about nothing. In 1936, the options facing the King had been to renounce or abdicate. In 1953, no immediate engagement was envisaged, and it was not a constitutional offence to be in love. The key date in the diaries of the Group Captain and the Princess was 21 August 1955, when she was released from the authority of her sister (that is, of the Prime Minister) under the Royal Marriages Act. In the meantime, Townsend relieved the boredom of his Belgian banishment by reading poetry and the Bible, and taking up amateur horse-racing. He wrote to Princess Margaret daily. 'Our own world was a vacuum which had to be endured day in, day out,' he recalled, 'and during the yearning hours of the night.' The press called him 'the loneliest man in Brussels'. It was a year before he was allowed back to England to see Princess Margaret, and incidentally to see his children.[23]

The Queen, under pressure from statesmen and Palace advisers, did not help. 'She was very fond of Peter in the old days,' says a former courtier. 'If she had been on her own, she wouldn't have minded about Princess Margaret's desire to marry him.'[24]

If Sir Winston Churchill bothered much about the problems of the Queen's sister, he did not do so for long. On 23 June, a few days after the Townsend relationship became public, he suffered a severe stroke. At first he seemed likely to die. Then he made a spectacular recovery. When he was well enough, the Queen sent him a letter from Scotland, telling him about her visit to Edinburgh. The Scottish capital, she wrote, had been 'thrilled by all the pageantry'. The Prime Minister replied carefully and at length, describing what had happened, and expressing his hope to remain in office until the autumn when the Foreign Secretary, Anthony Eden – who was also ill – would be able to succeed him.[25] As his strength returned, however, Churchill's plans for retirement became more vague. By the beginning of August he had recovered sufficiently to see the Queen. During his audience, he told her that he intended to make his decision a month later, by which time – he explained – he would be able to see clearly whether he would be well enough to face the Commons, and to make a speech at the Conservative Party Conference in October.[26]

His colleagues despaired. Churchill was now seventy-eight, and both his physical energy and his mental agility had been declining for some

The Wedding.

Left Bride and groom, 20th November 1947

Below The Dress. Princess Elizabeth arrives at Westminster Abbey with the King and bridesmaids

Above Prince Charles with his parents, July 1949

Opposite top The Queen and Princess Elizabeth talking to a jockey at Hurst Park Races, January 1952

Opposite below Dancing with Dickie. Charity ball at the Savoy, July 1951

Left Accession.

Arriving by car at Clarence House from the airport, 7th February 1952

Below Driving to Westminster for the first State Opening of Parliament of the reign, 4th November 1952

Opposite 'As Solomon was annointed King by Zadok the priest and Nathan the prophet.' The Coronation of Elizabeth II, 2nd June 1953

Left Royal box at the Coronation

Centre Equerry. Peter Townsend with royal ladies during the 1947 tour of South Africa

Below New premier. With the Edens and Philip at a military parade, 25th July 1955

aily
irror

WED AUG 7 1957

FORWARD WITH THE PEOPLE
No. 16,687 +

SMACK!
LORD A. GETS HIS FACE SLAPPED

By HARRY LONGMUIR

LORD ALTRINCHAM, critic of the Queen and her advisers, was slapped in the face last night as he came out of Television House, London, after appearing on ITV.

The incident occurred as the thirty-three-year-old Peer was walking towards a car.

Two policemen seized a man and held him against the walls of Television House.

Cheeks Flushed

Lord Altrincham's cheeks were flushed as he watched the man being escorted away.

Later, Philip Kinghorn Burbidge, 64, of Elmhurst, Holly-park, Crouch Hill, was charged at Bow-street Police Station with insulting behaviour outside Television House whereby a breach of the peace might have been caused.

Burbidge, a member of the League of Empire Loyalists, was allowed bail and will appear at Bow-street Magistrates' Court today.

After the street incident, Lord Altrincham got into a car with Ludovic Kennedy of Independent TV News.

As Lord Altrincham and Mr. Kennedy drove away a 6ft., red-bearded figure approached. It was Mr. Austin Brooks, 33, deputy chairman of the League of Empire Loyalists.

Mr. Brooks said: "I wish it had been me.—His Lordship is just about my age."

'She's the Boss'

Before driving away Lord Altrincham told me: "The article I published (in the National and English Review, which he edits) was the climax to years of personal criticism I have made about the Queen's advisers.

"I have written and spoken personally to most of them. Some have ignored me. Others have said: 'What can we do? We are only lackeys.'

"I have found that the majority of the Queen's advisers would have been out-dated in the Court of Charles II. And that criticism includes some young men.

"I tried every way possible to make my feelings known to them.

"Now I consider it is a question for the Queen and public opinion. She is the boss. She has the power to fire them."

WHAT LORD ALTRINCHAM SAID ON TV—See Page 16

Kinghorn Burbidge, 64, is led away by police after last night's scene.

Lord Altrincham (right) has an argument with a man outside Television House after his broadcast last night.

Lèse majesté, August 1957

Above Tweedy. Sir Michael Adeane, the Queen's private secretary 1953–72

Top right Airport departure. With Harold Macmillan and other members of the Government, February 1957

Above Dogs. Returning to Liverpool Street from Sandringham, 8th February, 1968

Left Fantasy of flowers. With President de Gaulle at the Royal Opera House, Covent Garden, April 1960

time before his stroke. His unfitness for office was manifest to all who worked closely with him. Yet no mechanism existed for getting rid of a Prime Minister for whom there was so much regard and affection, and who refused to budge.

Was this a good moment for the Head of State to use the privileged secrecy of the audience to consult with the Prime Minister about the future of her Government, encourage him to step down – as Lord Moran had suggested the year before – and warn him of the harm he might do if he put off his departure for too long? If she had done so, nobody could have challenged the constitutionality of such advice, which fell within the scope of her prerogative, and few would have disputed her wisdom. Yet it was difficult for a woman in her mid-twenties, who knew little about politics, to say such a thing to a great statesman thrice her age, who behaved as if he were her twinkly-eyed uncle. No tactful words seem to have been uttered, and the opportunity for a change that would have benefited the nation, the Monarchy and Churchill's own reputation was lost. Later in August, the Queen invited him to join her at the St. Leger. The trip was a tonic. The crowds greeted the convalescing premier with welcoming cheers, and his spirits rose. 'I don't think they want me to go,' he declared. 'I am really very popular.'[27] The month had soon passed. There was no retirement in October, and the year ended with his determination to stay in office stronger than ever.

Not everybody who served the Queen stayed in his post. After the Coronation, Sir Alan Lascelles, adviser to four monarchs, retired as private secretary, and was replaced by Michael Adeane. Though the choice of successor was obvious and expected, it scarcely indicated a progressive royal impulse. Lascelles had been a wily, cultivated, didactic, austere and hidebound counsellor. Adeane was cast in the same mould. An hereditary courtier, assistant private secretary to George VI from 1937, and then to his daughter, he maintained the traditions of personal self-effacement, meticulous administration and a reluctance to allow anything to happen that had not been done before, of his predecessor. He had devotion, humour, and a fitting humility. 'Because you happen to be in Whitehall terms the equivalent of a Permanent Under-Secretary,' he once said, 'it is no use thinking you are a mandarin. You must also be a nanny. One moment you may be writing to the Prime Minister. The next you are carrying a small boy's mac.'[28] As a nanny to the institution he served, however, he belonged to the old school. Like Lascelles, he was against the vulgarities of the modern world. He remained in his post for nineteen years – personifying 'the Court' as well as the ramrod values of the caste to which he belonged.

In November, the Queen and Duke of Edinburgh embarked on a new Commonwealth tour – in effect, a resumption of the trip abandoned in Kenya at the time of George VI's death. The scale and scope, however, had increased. Originally the tour had been planned for an ailing King, then for an Heiress Presumptive. Now it was for a Monarch at the height of her glory, the 'world's sweetheart,' as the American financier Bernard Baruch called her,[29] and the Queen of a world-wide Empire. The tour lasted five and a half months, and involved visits to Bermuda, Jamaica, Fiji, Tonga, the Coco Islands, Aden, Uganda, Malta and Gibraltar. The major part of the trip was to be in New Zealand and Australia, where she and her husband would spend three months, with an additional ten days in Ceylon. Such a marathon of travel, speeches, national anthems, handshakes, troop inspections, Parliament openings, performances, banquets, bouquets and gifts, had never before been undertaken by a British Head of State – or perhaps by anybody.

The tour made the South African and North American trips pale into insignificance. It was also unrepeatable. Not only was it the last occasion for an extended royal tour of a still-surviving Empire and of dominions that fervently believed in their Britishness, it was also the last time the crowds could be so large. This was the apogee of the Windsor Monarchy's world repute: thereafter, public adoration declined, or became a different kind of feeling, while television made it unnecessary for people to line the roadside or assemble in a main square in order to have the experience of seeing the Queen. Preparations were thorough. One requirement was a huge wardrobe: months in advance, Norman Hartnell discussed with the Queen the designs and fabrics needed for such a wide range of climates.[30]

The night before they left, as a private *finale* to the Coronation festivities, the Queen and Duke stayed till 3 a.m. at a party given by Queen Elizabeth at Clarence House, entertained by Peter Ustinov.

Noël Coward, a Queen Mother favourite, was among the guests. Later, with an actor-playwright's trained eye, Coward watched the televised departure of the Hartnell-clad Monarch and her husband from London airport. 'The Queen looked so young and vulnerable and valiant,' he wrote, 'and Prince Philip so handsome and cheerful. A truly romantic couple, star quality *in excelsis*.'[31]

The absence of the Sovereign momentarily quietened interest in royalty at home; it also produced a lull in speculation about a possible change of Prime Minister. There was no precedent for the appointment of a new premier – even when the choice was clear – when the Monarch was out of the country. Counsellors of State, appointed to deputize for constitutional functions, had no power to exercise royal discretion. They could not dissolve Parliament, or as Edward Ford pointed out in a letter to No. 10 during the tour, make 'any other decisions on which the Sovereign has the right to question'.[32] British politics was placed on ice. '. . . [N]ow I must carry on until the Queen returns in May,' Churchill reflected cheerfully to his doctor.[33]

The royal party arrived at Bermuda on 24 November, proceeding via the Panama Canal to Fiji, and thence to the island of Tonga. Much of the tour was spent on board HMS *Gothic*, which provided long, relaxed interludes between the tumultuous visits. 'The Queen could be very funny about some of the stops,' says Pamela Hicks. 'On Fiji, the local greeting involved three grunts and solemnly clapping hands while seated on the ground – when the Fijians did it, it was quite dignified. I remember the Queen sitting on the floor of the day saloon on the *Gothic*, and doing three impressive grunts. A crew member came in, and got a shock.'[34] On Tonga they were serenaded with nose flutes and photographed with a giant turtle allegedly hatched in the days of Captain Cook.

The main part of the tour began in Auckland, New Zealand, where months of Coronation and post-Coronation news from the other side of the world had whipped-up Queen-mania into a national delirium. The Sovereign of New Zealand was welcomed like a deliverer. 'Nobody *wanted* the King dead,' Ziegler observes, 'but there were many who looked forward to a new reign as heralding a brighter and more successful future.'[35] The social historian Ruth Brandon suggests that the fervour had a special intensity in New Zealand because of post-war anxiety both about economic ties with Britain and about relations with the rest of the Commonwealth. The result was a popular identification with the Monarchy that invaded many aspects of national culture. Thus, children's books linked a definition of the community New Zealand was seeking to be, with an idealized, and localized, account of British royalty – projecting a national self-image on to members of the Royal Family. In a near-contemporaneous 'royal' edition of the New Zealand *School Journal*, the Windsors were shown as modern, egalitarian, progressive and committed to social justice. Privilege, it was implied, was merely a convention forced on them by the class-conscious British. Pictures in the journal suggested that what they really liked doing, when not shouldering royal responsibilities, was being just like New Zealanders.[36]

The same kind of projection can be seen elsewhere. The popular literature of other dominions and colonies also shows the Royal Family, and especially the Queen, shifting identity wherever they happened to be, with stories and paintings that remoulded them for local conditions. At each royal stopping point, books, magazines and hoardings expressed the collective desire to reaffirm links with Britain and the Commonwealth after a difficult period – and did so by claiming the Monarchy as a domestic possession. In Fiji, posters showed the Queen with a widened jaw and thickened lips; in Australia, magazine graphics depicted her wearing a casual, airy dress and giving a broad antipodean grin. In this cultural equivalent of the doctrine of 'diversity,' it helped that Philip was the chameleon, non-British, possessor of Commonwealth qualities; and that the Queen seemed to avoid holding, let alone expressing, controversial opinions of any description.

New Zealand's wild enthusiasm was the apéritif. In Australia, where the royal party stayed for two months, interest was so great that an estimated three quarters of the entire population turned out to see the Queen in person.[37] The tour had been built up by the arch-royalist Prime Minister, Robert Menzies, into what one historian has described as 'the most elaborate and most publicized sequence of official events' the country had ever known.[38] As in New Zealand, there was a political and economic context, with evocations of the past linked to concern about the future. The visit followed a strengthening of scientific, military and diplomatic links with the United Kingdom. These had reached a proud and triumphant climax with the exploding of a British atomic bomb on Australian soil in October 1953, an event widely applauded as a tribute to Anglo-Australian co-operation, and – against a background of Cold War anxieties – as a demonstration that the Commonwealth of Australia had at last 'caught up in the stream of great world events'. The Queen's visit was regarded as an opportunity to consolidate such advances, by linking up with the modernization Britain still represented, and encouraging closer ties with the fast-recovering West. Thus, so far from being an antiquarian relic, the Australian Monarchy stood for progress, and a world view. Great significance was attached to the presentation to Philip – seen as a forward-looking man of action – of a box of mulga wood, containing samples of South Australian uranium.

There was also an element of historical continuity, important for a recently established nation. The trip was a chance to welcome Betty, heroine *in absentia* of the 1927 trip, when her father, as Duke of York, had opened the Federal Parliament in Canberra, and who now did so herself. Once again, the visit was unimpeded by royal children. However, as in 1927, children played a significant part in the tour. Great efforts were made to ensure that schoolchildren and new immigrants, who together constituted the dominion's future identity, should see and meet the Queen.[39] As in North America, the tour gathered pace, the crowds growing in size and the applause rising to a pinnacle of rapture. With the mounting excitement came displays of sentiment and loyalty. At receptions, old soldiers would come up to the Queen's assistants moist-eyed, and say, 'Now I know what I fought for'.

In the sprawling towns, the Queen sometimes had to give half a dozen short speeches in a day, and then drive for a couple of hours at snail's pace, past a crowd spread thinly for miles along the route. 'She was very meticulous in the motorcades that the car should go slowly enough for people to get a proper view,' says Pamela Hicks, a member of the party. 'She used to say, "What's the point in coming unless they can see me?"'[40] The smiling problem, which had arisen in Canada, was a perennial concern. At home, it had been noticed on ceremonial occasions, when she had to greet large numbers of important people, each of whom expected the same attention. In Australia, a similar difficulty arose after protracted exposure to the crowds. Sometimes, she would overhear a comment about it as the car crawled past. 'It's awful,' she told a helper, 'I've got the kind of face that if I'm not smiling, I look cross. But I'm not cross. If you try to smile for two hours continuously it gives you a nervous tic. But the moment I stop smiling, somebody will see me and say "Doesn't she look cross?"'

The Duke had no difficulty in smiling. He had some difficulty, however, in keeping awake. To relieve the tedium of interminable motorcades, he devised a game. As the royal car passed a pub, its occupants would surge out unsteadily to take a look, some grabbing lamp posts for support. Philip would single out the lamp post clutchers and wave at them personally – inviting them to wave back, release their grip, and fall over.

The royal party travelled great distances by train, adopting the Canadian routine of halting at remote places, often at odd hours of the night, to greet a few dozen people waiting at a railway siding. It was hot and uncomfortable, and when they went to functions in the towns, there was often a lack of privacy. One lady-in-waiting felt that the constrained conditions of the journey bothered the Queen, and that the shock of always being stared at was still with her. 'We would arrive, after travelling all day or all night, and be shown the cloak-room,' she recalls. 'A film star would take it in her stride if she had to make up in front of other people. But for the Queen it was disconcerting – she'd never had to use a public cloakroom. There'd be this drawback that the cloakroom attendant would be there, whose great moment it would be, thinking this was something to tell her grandchildren – but for the wretched Queen who was tired out, it was awful to be gawped at when she was trying to do her hair and get her hat straight. I remember saying, "I'll get rid of them," and the Queen replied, "Can you? You're so brave. Do you think they'll mind?"' In front of members of the public – cloakroom attendants, well-wishers, dignitaries – she always exercised a tight self-control. But sometimes, in private, after an endless repetition of receptions and dinners, the mask would come off completely. 'Goodness they're boring,' she once said to her husband and aides. 'All these mayors and councillors are so boring, boring, boring. Why are they so boring?'[41]

The royal party returned to England in mid-May, and was met on board ship by the British Prime Minister. Churchill was entranced by the Queen's casual attire, particularly her khaki trousers. 'Philip came in and said, "Come and meet your mother". She laughed,' the premier reported happily. '"How can I, like this?" She is so completely natural.'[42] It was not everybody's description. Some found her stiff, and hard to talk to. But all agreed that privately she was herself. She did not pretend. They also agreed that her straightforward style, smiling or unsmiling, had made the tour a triumphant success, 'an exercise in bonding,'[43] which had shown the reality of Commonwealth loyalties, and strengthened ties with the dominions.

The Palace gave its own assessment. 'The structure and framework of Monarchy could easily stand as an archaic and meaningless survival,' said the Queen, in characteristically stilted courtier-prose, at the Guildhall, shortly after her return. 'We have received visible and audible proof that it is living in the hearts of the people.'[44] Certainly it is hard to watch the old newsreels of the delighted couple amongst the huge, cheering, Commonwealth crowds, and not be struck – moved even – by the mutuality of the feeling.

Yet to what long-term end? What did it really mean to describe such a dazzling, contentless royal progress as a 'success'? From the British Government's point of view, it was fair to imagine that a Commonwealth royal trip that increased interest in and affection for the Queen, also strengthened emotional and hence diplomatic ties with the mother country. There was also the point – at the start of a debate that was to dominate foreign policy for the rest of the century – that a tightening of Commonwealth and imperial links was one way to counter the argument of those who wanted to take part in a European trade agreement. Yet the Queen's post-Coronation tour cannot just be seen as a British diplomatic mission – if, indeed, it was that at all, for the visit of the Monarch of one country to other countries which also regarded her as their Monarch stood outside the normal sphere of international diplomacy, and Head of State visits. In the old dominions, the communion that existed between Sovereign and subjects was personal, with a unique psychology, and the Queen was sometimes regarded with a simpler, deeper loyalty than at home. It was, however, inevitable that the psychology could not be sustained. Just as the over-heated emotions of the Coronation were followed in Britain by a sense of anti-climax and non-fulfilment, so the intense emotions aroused in the Commonwealth by the tour gave way to disappointment. It was as if a distant parent had made a longed-for call, and then simply gone away again. The great wave of popular feeling was remembered, often with nostalgia. But it also became a high-water mark against which the relative failures of later royal tours, in a changing world, were judged.

There were other effects. The global excitement had implications for the future behaviour of the press. The Coronation and then the Commonwealth tour unleashed a new type of interest in Royal Family personalities – just as rapid changes in the mass media were making it harder for governments or press authorities in one country, through censorship or restraint, to seal themselves off from news that was uncensored in others. Television was spreading, radio broadcasting was increasing in sophistication, news agencies were becoming more closely interlocked. In the 1930s, Edward VIII had been able to conduct his relationship with Mrs Simpson without British publicity, until a crisis point was reached. In the 1950s, a combination of improved technology, changed press economics, and world-wide news demand, was making it virtually impossible, despite the stone-walling efforts of Commander Colville, to preserve a royal news-exclusion zone. For a while, the conservatism of editors and proprietors held out against the rising tide of royalty demand, and the rising possibility of feeding it. It was not long, however, before the Royal Family found that it could not hope simultaneously to be famous, and indifferent to the requirements of the modern press.

The change was gradual. In one small way, however, the tour accelerated the cross-border advance of the electronic media. While the Coronation had the incidental effect of expanding the television industry, the Commonwealth visit facilitated global access to broadcast news. Big surges of demand stretch technological ingenuity. A breakthrough occurred because of the BBC's attitude to the Queen's Christmas broadcast, normally heard by many millions, which it regarded as an almost sacred event. At Christmas 1953, the Queen was in New Zealand – as far away from the British listening public as it was possible to be. Here was a challenge, and also a risk – for existing radio communications between New Zealand and the western hemisphere were unreliable. There was an opportunity for 'a spectacular triumph for Commonwealth Communications' – according to a BBC memo – 'opening a new chapter in the tradition of royal Christmas broadcasts'; but also the danger of a fiasco, and of besmirching the reputation of the Australasian broadcasting authorities, with potentially serious consequences for Commonwealth relations.[45] The BBC decided to go for it, while seeking to minimize the risk. To guard against the possibility of a radio blackout, a pre-recording of the speech was made on the *Gothic* at Fiji, and flown to Sydney for transmission to London – though still with some danger that it would not get through. On Christmas Day, the millions turning on their wireless sets in Britain were not disappointed: the Queen's words could be heard clearly from twelve thousand miles away, live. The pre-recording was not needed, and the BBC could claim its spectacular technological triumph.

THE QUEEN'S return in May 1954 did not immediately signal the retirement of the Prime Minister. On the contrary: recovered in health and will, Churchill now determined to carry on until after the London Conference on European security and integration in the autumn, if not – as some feared – indefinitely. The frustration of Anthony Eden, eager to step into the premier's shoes, was intense. When the Conference was over, the Queen sent the Foreign Secretary a solicitous letter from Balmoral congratulating him on its success. 'No-one has worked harder,' she wrote, adding, '. . . perhaps we can hope for a more peaceful time and not so many crises.' She also expressed friendly concern about his health which, though improved, had succumbed to a new infection. She was sorry, she noted, to learn that Eden had 'caught the germs which we read that M. Mendes-France had got – I must say it seems a poor way of expressing gratitude!'[46] The same month, she took the unusual step of awarding Eden the Order of the Garter, apparently in anticipation of his succession to the premiership.

It was not until the spring of 1955 that Churchill was finally persuaded to go. The Queen was not the instrument of this decision: indeed, Churchill even tried to get her to collude in yet another postponement. On 27 March, he told her that he was thinking of putting his resignation off. 'He asked if she minded,' recorded Jock Colville, 'and she said no!'[47] Adeane later wrote to Churchill that she fully understood why 'there still seemed to be some uncertainty' on the point. However, the moment came, and there was no going back. On 31 March, Churchill told the Queen's private secretary to inform the Sovereign of his intention to resign five days later. Now, at last, Buckingham Palace blocked off the escape route. Though Adeane wrote that the Queen would miss the Prime Minister's weekly audience which, he said, she had found both instructive and entertaining, he also wrote firmly that Her Majesty 'recognized your wisdom in taking the decision which you had,' a formula which may have been designed to discourage any last minute recantation.[48]

The Queen felt genuine sadness: Churchill had first kissed hands as her father's Prime Minister when she was fourteen. To mark the departure, he gave a farewell dinner at No. 10, with the Queen and Duke as his guests. It was an occasion for sentimental memories, and rolling prose. Raising his glass for the loyal toast, the Prime Minister said that it was the same that he had drunk, as a cavalry subaltern, to her great-great-grandmother. He spoke of 'the sacred causes, and wise and kindly way of life, of which Your Majesty is the young, gleaming champion'.[49] Then, young and gleaming, the Queen appeared outside with the deeply bowing statesman, for the benefit of the photographers. She wrote warmly to him afterwards. 'I had a lovely letter from her,' he remarked. 'It took me a whole morning to reply.'[50]

The retirement of Churchill confronted the Queen with the first important exercise of the royal prerogative of her reign. The decision about whom to appoint as premier was not a difficult one. More than almost any other mid-term succession of the century, it was regarded as automatic. Nevertheless, the constitutional position was plain: the Sovereign retained the right to ask whoever she wished to try to form an administration, limited only by the requirement that the person called should be able to command the confidence of the House of Commons. At a time when the Conservative Party did not elect its leader, this right was more than token. On past occasions when such a transfer had occurred, the Monarch had taken a close interest in the choosing. This time, however, the choice was treated for some time before Churchill's eventual resignation by everybody, including Buckingham Palace, as a foregone conclusion.

'No rival candidate existed,' as one writer has put it, expressing the accepted view, 'so there was no discussion or controversy of any kind.'[51] Yet the appointment of Sir Anthony Eden had not always seemed so inevitable. Churchill himself had had doubts, though possibly self-serving ones, about the Foreign Secretary's fitness for the job. Others had wondered whether, through all Churchill's waverings, Conservative support for Eden would sustain itself. When the issue of the succession was discussed at Court before the Coronation, Sir Alan Lascelles (still the Queen's private secretary) seemed far from certain. He told Eden's private secretary at the Foreign Office, Sir Evelyn Shukburgh, at the beginning of 1953 that 'if Winston were to die tomorrow' then Eden would definitely be called. However, if present trends continued, he thought that by the end of the year the succession would be in doubt. 'There might be at least 50 per cent opinion in the Party and in the City by that time in favour of Butler.'[52] The remark turned out to be prescient. When Churchill was taken ill in June, Eden was also out of action. If the Prime Minister had died or had felt compelled to resign, Butler, as acting premier, might well have succeeded. Eden's own poor health – which was to precipitate his retirement less than two years later – remained a cause for concern, and might have been considered a reason to hesitate before appointing him. Moreover, though Eden was the expected and welcomed choice among Conservative MPs, he was not leader of the party at the time of his appointment: that position was only acquired after he became Prime Minister, when the title was proclaimed at an *ex post facto* coronation, attended by MPs, peers, candidates and party activists. His position as 'deputy prime minister' gave him no special precedence.

The Queen had an absolute right to make soundings, before asking somebody to form a government. But did she make any, and who did she sound? If consultations took place, they were narrow in range, and extremely discreet; and a mystery continues to surround the process by which the inexperienced young monarch came – 'unadvised,' as Elizabeth Longford puts it[53] – to call Eden. Lord Avon's

biographers are silent about such an important moment in their subject's career. Avon himself was also reticent. In his memoirs, he wrote
only of his 'long era as crown prince,' as though the designation of
such a status by Churchill, years before, bestowed a right.[54]

Like everybody else, Churchill – despite earlier doubts – seems to
have accepted the appointment of Eden as his successor as a *fait
accompli*. According to Butler's later account, on 30th March – the
day after the resignation letter to Adeane – Churchill told Butler and
Eden together, in private, 'I am going and Anthony will succeed me'.
Presumably he discussed the matter with the Queen. He did not,
however, advise her. In his final audience on 4th April, he carefully
stuck to what he considered to be the proprieties. 'She asked me
whether I would recommend a successor,' he recorded when he got
back to No. 10, 'and I said I preferred to leave it to her.' However, it
was clear that she had made up her mind, or had had it made up for
her. 'She said the case was not a difficult one,' Churchill added, 'and
that she would summon Sir Anthony Eden.'[55] Later, Jock Colville
recalled that Churchill spoke to him about his reticence – and that
he described it as an important constitutional point. 'The theory that
an outgoing Prime Minister can just say, "Oh, by the way, I think
the person you ought to send for is so-and-so" is rubbish,' Churchill
told him. 'Once the Prime Minister resigns he can't advise.'[56] However
it was easy to be a constitutional stickler in the confident knowledge
of what the Queen would do in any case.

No doubt there were discussions of a very private kind, which
pointed in a single direction. Yet it is possible to see with hindsight
that the Queen's *modus operandi* (or lack of one) had a greater importance than was apparent at the time. Non-events set precedents, as
much as dramas. The smoothness of the first prime ministerial changeover of the reign, and the absence of even a token assertion of royal
independence, helped to establish the expectation that, at any future
moment of transition, the Palace would not seek an active role.

IN CHOOSING a successor to Sir Winston Churchill, it is unlikely that
the Queen, or her advisers, gave any thought to the bearing such a
decision would have on the matrimonial plans of Princess Margaret.
The two matters were, however, indirectly linked, because the appoint-

ment of Sir Anthony Eden meant that, for the first time ever, the Monarch had a Prime Minister who was himself divorced. That this should have been possible was a sign that attitudes had changed. The effect, however, was to neutralize – or at any rate limit the involvement of – No. 10 Downing Street in the debate about Peter Townsend. On this issue, Eden was a constrained politician: to have come down firmly on one side would have seemed hypocritical, while to have backed the other might have looked like special pleading. Hence the matter was pushed back to Buckingham Palace, just as it reached its climax.

Margaret's birthday, 21st August, was the date watched by the press. However, though reaching the age of twenty-five removed one obstacle, it did not make a marriage possible. The approval of the United Kingdom and dominion parliaments was still required if Princess Margaret wished to continue to avail herself of the official rights and privileges of her 'royal' status. It was this hurdle that was to prove insurmountable.

'Nothing could have been worse handled than Princess Margaret's romance with Group Captain Peter Townsend,' concluded Sir Charles Petrie a few years later.[57] Noël Coward called it 'a silly, mismanaged lash-up'.[58] On this, matrimonial conservatives and liberals agreed. In contrast to the swift dispatch of the matter of Mrs Simpson by Baldwin in 1936, the Townsend affair was allowed to cause a maximum of embarrassment to all those involved.

Townsend blamed his former colleagues at the Palace, especially Commander Colville. '. . . [N]ot once during the whole affair,' Townsend complained, 'right up to the bitter end, did he contact me or attempt to evolve a joint front with me towards the press.'[59] Yet the problem was not just that the Queen's press secretary refused to regard the private life of his employer's sister as a matter of legitimate public interest, and therefore believed there was nothing to discuss. It was also that, in a sense, he was right. Unless and until an engagement was requested, no constitutional issue arose. The 'crisis' was really a crisis of fevered media anticipation, fuelled by the ending of Townsend's exile, and a colossal public fascination with the Princess, who, as one of her biographers has shrewdly written, had two, intriguingly contradictory, sides to her character. On the one hand there was the tragic lover, waiting for her crusader to return, but on the other, 'a wilful, attractive young woman who remained the greatest catch in Britain and wanted to live for the minute, experiencing as much and as quickly as possible'.[60] Fifty names had been linked to Princess Margaret romantically, according to one paper – but none had usurped that of the Group Captain.

The press campaign built up in stages. Other, sniping stories had already begun to prick the post-Coronation euphoria, sorely trying Commander Colville's patience. Some came from the Beaverbrook press, which had long had a slightly maverick view of royalty, but other papers were also involved. In October 1954, the *Daily Express* took Buckingham Palace to task for failing to supply an appropriate royal message of sympathy for the victims of floods in Canada.[61] In November, the *Daily Mirror* complained that some members of the Royal Family were underemployed. What was there for them to do in Britain, it asked. 'Twiddle their thumbs? Visit one another? Do the dreary social rounds?' The attack was read in the Palace. Next day, the Duke of Edinburgh riposted during a visit to a factory, 'Of course, Ladies and Gentlemen, you know what I am doing – I am twiddling my thumbs'. The *Mirror* was overjoyed. 'For the first time in the present century,' it boasted, 'a member of the Royal Family publicly replied yesterday to a newspaper comment on the activities of the Royal Household.'[62] A new era had begun.

A bigger strain on the Commander, however – and perhaps also on the Duke – was the serialization of a book by John Dean, for several years valet to Philip, describing his experiences. This early example of 'doing a Crawfie' (though Dean had much less to reveal) was the subject of a sharp complaint by Colville to the Press Council. 'You will, I am sure, readily agree that the Queen is entitled to expect that her family will attain the privacy at home which all other families are entitled to enjoy,' declared the royal press secretary at the end of January 1955.[63] It was a sentiment he and his successors would repeatedly express, with decreasing impact, as market pressures grew.

The dispute left the popular newspapers in a war-like mood, and a bruised Commander on the defensive. 'Are events now creeping closer?' asked the London evening *Star* on 25th January, speculating that a visit by Princess Margaret to the Caribbean was the prelude to an announcement. But what kind of announcement? Would she marry and be damned, giving up her royal rights? And what kind of step-mother would she make to the 'two lusty schoolboys' who were Townsend's children by his first marriage?[64] The press examined such questions, and came up with conflicting answers. In April, the Arch-bishop of Canterbury, visiting Cape Town, rashly complained that rumours of an impending engagement were a stunt put up by London newspapers, and then fuelled the same rumours by denying that he had said anything of the sort.[65]

There was the question of the attitude of the Queen. Was she for or against a marriage? 'She was absolutely determined,' says a close friend of the Princess, 'that nobody should influence Princess Margaret over her decision, and that she should be free to make up her own mind.'[66] There was no pressure to renounce, but no encouragement to marry either. Meanwhile, the press failed to find any hint of a division between the two sisters. At the end of April, they were seen cheerfully racing each other along the Royal Mile at Ascot. Wearing coloured head scarves, and followed by a riding master in a top hat, they rode neck-and-neck at full gallop, until Princess Margaret broke away up the straight and won by three lengths. 'They were laughing as they pulled up after the race,' said a workman on the course, 'and then trotted out the way they had come.'[67]

'Come on Margaret!' demanded the *Daily Mirror* two days before her birthday, as three hundred journalists and photographers con-verged on Balmoral, where she was staying. 'Please make up your mind!'[68] Townsend, in London, was in touch with Princess Margaret on the phone. Elizabeth Cavendish acted as go-between, putting through calls to Princess Margaret and then handing over to Towns-end, who stood beside her. 'I felt he had no realization of what life for her would be like had she married him,' she recalls.[69] In Scotland, the press laid siege. When Princess Margaret left for a long-awaited meeting with Townsend, the Queen made a point of being out in the estate, according to a guest at the Castle, 'so she wouldn't have to say anything to her sister about it'.[70]

For weeks there was a torrent of pictures, exhortations and specu-lation, frequently fed by the more adventurous foreign press. On 18th October, the matter was discussed in Cabinet, and the Prime Minister had an extended audience. Next day, Margaret dined with the Arch-bishop of Canterbury. Later, Fisher angrily rejected allegations that he had put pressure on her[71] – though it is scarcely likely that the purpose of a meeting *à deux* between a Primate and a Princess at such a time was to make small-talk, and the Archbishop was not reticent about his firmly held opinions on the subject of divorce and re-marriage. The terms for a Bill of Renunciation were set by Cabinet on 20th October – to be presented to Parliament, if required. On 21st October, the Queen – in the company of the Prime Minister, Leader of the Opposition, members of the Cabinet and of the Royal Family – unveiled a statue of her father in Carlton Gardens. It was an unusual moment, mingling the public and the acutely personal, and her speech received particular attention. The Queen spoke of duty, sacrifice, faith and accepting the cards you were dealt. 'Like his father,' she said of her own father, 'he expected to support the throne rather than fill it.' Princess Margaret had the same expectation. Even more pointedly, as it seemed, the Monarch described how George VI had not only 'enjoyed the blessings of a happy family life,' but had 'shirked no task however difficult,' and 'never faltered in his duty to his peoples'.[72]

On 23rd October, the *Sunday Pictorial* published a New York maga-zine's agony aunt competition, which offered $100 for the best letter offering a solution to the 'Princess Meg' problem. Another British paper logged all the entrances and exits to Clarence House, where Margaret lived with her mother, since Townsend's return from exile.[73] The Press Council castigated newspapers which had 'offended against good taste'. The Princess Meg problem, however, was by now on everybody's lips, with opinion divided, and anybody who could come up with an answer that satisfied the requirements of Church, state and human charity, deserved the prize.

It was *The Times* that articulated the Establishment position on royal deviatons. In a long leading article on 26th October, Sir William Haley – who had moved from the BBC to become editor – castigated fellow members of his profession for the 'odious whipping-up' of public emotion for 'motives of gain'. Sir William then proceeded to define the issue as he saw it. At the nub was the concept of the family. His exposition provides a remarkable snapshot of royalty doctrine at the time. The matter, suggested Haley, was neither ecclesiastical nor constitutional. It had to do with an idea of royalty as an element in the lives of all the Queen's subjects throughout the Commonwealth. It was that idea that made Princess Margaret's marital intentions – if such they were – of public concern; for it was vital that the model family which the Royal Family constituted, and in which all Commonwealth subjects organically participated as members of the Queen's 'many-sided society or family' – should not be tarnished. Hence, the view of Britain's most authoritative newspaper was unequivocal. *The Times* regarded the issue of the proposed Margaret–Townsend marriage as fundamental to the institution of Monarchy itself.

The problem, Haley continued, was the symbolic role of the Queen, who stood for every side of the society which made up her world-wide subjects. She was the universal representative of that society, and it was in her that people saw their better selves ideally reflected. Since part of the popular ideal was family life, it followed that the Queen's family – including her sister – played a part in this process of reflection. Here was the difficulty facing the Queen, the Princess, the nation and the entire Commonwealth:

> If the marriage which is now being discussed comes to pass, it
> is inevitable that this reflection becomes distorted. The Princess
> will be entering into a union which vast numbers of her sister's
> people, all sincerely anxious for her lifelong happiness, cannot
> in conscience regard as a marriage.

This then was what all the highly personalized adulation, the intense interest in members of the Royal Family as individuals – which reached such a remarkable zenith with the Coronation and Commonwealth tour in the previous two years – had come to. No matter that the first twentieth-century King had consorted with mistresses; that there were many Christians who did regard the marriage of a divorced person as legitimate; and that a high proportion of the Queen's subjects, in Ceylon, Africa and elsewhere, were non-Christian. For the whole society of the Commonwealth, the Royal Family existed as 'the symbol and guarantee of the unity of the British peoples'. 'If one of the Family's members became a cause of division,' wrote Haley, 'the salt has lost its savour. There is no escape from the logic of this situation.' The logic, he concluded sadly, was that if the Princess went ahead with the match, the price should be, not just the loss of her constitutional rights but a full withdrawal from royal public functions into private life.[74]

It is a mark of how much has changed in British society, and the Commonwealth, in the last forty years that such an argument today should seem, not merely monstrous, but almost incomprehensible. Yet at the time it was not dismissed as the ravings of an eccentric bigot. On the contrary, it was believed to reflect the views of, amongst others, the Archbishop of Canterbury and the Queen's private secretary; and it was widely quoted and discussed. It was also decisive. It was after reading it that Townsend and Princess Margaret privately agreed that they could not go ahead with a marriage.[75] On 31st October, a communiqué – drafted by Townsend – was issued in Princess Margaret's name, in which she conceded the essence of Haley's argument. She was aware, she declared, of the option of a civil ceremony; but, 'mindful of the Church's teachings that Christian marriage is indissoluble, and conscious of my duty to the Commonwealth,' she had resolved to put these considerations before others. Afterwards, both Margaret and Townsend blamed Palace officials for misleading them – and giving the impression, when the matter was first raised in 1953, that if they waited, the marriage would be acceptable.[76] Townsend returned to Brussels. In 1958, he married a much younger Belgian woman instead.

Following the announcement, the *Church Times* printed a smiling portrait of the Princess with the horrible caption 'Life begins anew'.[77] Yet there was also popular sympathy. Harold Nicolson saw Margaret's decision as an act of self-sacrifice, and wrote that 'the country will admire and love her for it'.[78] 'With half the world religiously exulting,' as Noël Coward put it, 'and the other half pouring out a spate of treacly sentimentality,'[79] few drew attention to the issue of double standards. The *Manchester Guardian*, however, crisply reminded its readers of the irony that Eden, the innocent party to a divorce, could appoint archbishops; while a princess who had only a remote chance of succeeding to a largely ceremonial throne was denied by ecclesiastical prescription the right to marry an innocent party to a divorce.[80]

According to the loyalist *Daily Mail*, the Monarchy emerged 'calm, serene and unshaken' by the episode,[81] but that was a moot point. With extraordinary care, the Queen had managed to remain outside the argument – neither alienating her sister, nor seeking to force her hand. 'She was distressed by the situation,' says a former courtier, 'but it seemed impossible to combine her sister's romance with constitutional necessities. She accepted that nothing could be done to sanction the marriage without the approval of Parliament, the Cabinet, and the Commonwealth. But the key to it was that Princess Margaret was not prepared to give up her royal status. If she'd been willing to take herself out of the line of succession and the Civil List, they couldn't have prevented it.'[82]

Yet, if it is difficult to see how the Queen could have intervened to allow her sister both to become Mrs Townsend and remain fully royal, it would have been neither improper nor unconstitutional for her to have let it be known that, unadvised, she would have accepted the marriage. Instead, she gave no whisper of a hint, one way or the other. Her private opinion remains a matter for speculation. 'She was clear as Queen about what she hoped would happen,' suggests a friend of Margaret's who spent time with the Princess during this episode, 'though as a sister she wanted her to feel free.'[83]

THE PROBLEM over Peter Townsend was the first of importance that required the Queen to exercise her independent judgement. Her handling of it signalled a future pattern. On delicate matters, she would let events unfold, not take sides, and – if a decision was unavoidable – make scrupulously certain that any blame for a mistake would be taken by 'advisers', if not in Downing Street, then at the Palace. As yet, she was feeling her way: it would in any case have been hard as a young Monarch to ignore the older men around her. However, avoiding partisanship, and shrinking from controversy, also came naturally.

Indeed, despite her comparative youth and inexperience, she very rapidly settled into a mode of Queenship with which she would be comfortable, and which she would see no reason to change. This was partly because of the circumstances of the Accession. She was not – like a politician – eager for power, nor – like a middle-aged or elderly Heir – restlessly in search of a role. Becoming Queen was something that happened without her wishing for it. Hence she was content to take guidance.

In this she was her father's daughter. Though she had more preparation for the throne than George VI, and was in some ways better equipped, he remained her model. She spoke of him often – consciously trying to behave as he might have done, or as if she was still deputizing for him. Despite the politician-talk of renewal and a dawning age, the most striking personal feature of the succession was a sense of continuity from one reign to the next. Yet Elizabeth was not unhappy to be Queen. Though her apprenticeship had been brief compared with most predecessors, she was fully adult when she succeeded, and – as an active performer of ceremonial duties during her father's illness – she had had time to acquire confidence and poise. She enjoyed the theatre, the ritual, the attention, and the admiration, as well as the sense of achievement that came from doing the limited tasks that were required of her to the best of her ability.

'Theatre', however, is only partly right as a word to describe what happened when the curtain went up, and she did her visible job as Monarch. Elizabeth did not have two personalities, one for public display and the other for family and friends. Being looked at and remarked on had been part of her expectation of the world for almost as long as she could remember: her Accession emphasized, but did not fundamentally alter, this consequence of her position in the direct line. As Monarch, she was always on call, seldom not on show, ever conscious of being observed and of having to set an example.

In such conditions, to be 'natural' was to be regal. Yet there were different sides to her character, and different styles. Those who knew her privately were aware of a precious ability to enjoy her pleasures, and to display a biting humour, spiced with mimicry. This side was hidden from the public, which saw only the fixed smile or, when the mask dropped, a solemn and even sad-seeming countenance, and which never heard her utter a casual remark.

People who were presented to her found her initially shy, difficult to talk to, and platitudinous in conversation, with an anxious desire to avoid getting too deeply into any topic. She was nervous, as one close friend puts it, about meeting 'people of a higher academic field,' and became embarrassed if she was drawn into a discussion she felt was beyond her.[84] To talk of her as lonely was in a way absurd: nobody was more constantly surrounded by people, or had a more devoted circle of helpers. Yet there was always a sense of being in an ethnic minority of one: a Sovereign not a subject, universally known, automatically of interest, requiring respect. It did not prevent her relating to people, but it gave her friendships and attachments a lopsided quality.

'If you're the centre of such adulation you never have entirely normal relationships,' says an ex-lady-in-waiting from the early years. 'Even your best friends like Porchey, or oldest courtiers like Martin Charteris, treat you with special courtesy.' There was a vicious circle: nobody could treat her just like anybody else because to have done so would have been presumptuous and rude. This had been true when she was Heiress. The same former aide, who knew her as a child, remembers being told by Queen Mary that when she entered the royal service she must train herself to stop saying 'Lilibet' and to say 'Ma'am' instead. 'She was a very friendly person,' another member of her pre-Accession circle recalls from this period, 'but she was capable of giving you a very old-fashioned kind of look – nothing snobbish or pompous about it – that said she was a princess, and was going to be Queen.' The gap widened when she became Monarch. 'Anybody could unbalance her if they were too familiar,' says a close friend. The problem continues. 'Whenever she meets ordinary people,' according to a present-day helper, 'they are always in a terrifically over-excited state so she can't really talk to them in a normal way.'

Later, the Queen's ability to cope with different kinds of people improved. She had an excellent memory for facts and faces, and – despite the lack of training which continued to make her shy away from any kind of conceptual discussion – those who met her were made aware of a sharp, perceptive intelligence. As her experience grew, people were often surprised – partly, perhaps, in the manner of Dr Johnson and women preachers, but also with real admiration – by her grasp of public affairs. In the early days, however, conversation could be arduous, on both sides.

With people she knew well, there was never the same difficulty. 'She speaks very freely among her friends,' says a duchess who has known her for half a century. 'In a private situation,' says another member of her close circle, 'if people come up, she has always been able to show much more spontaneity.' There was a difference between the face she showed to the public – 'the public' was everybody, even Prime Ministers, she met formally – and the one she permitted her inner retainers, a few very old friends, and her family, to see. She could change faces almost as quickly as dresses. One moment she would be performing a public duty, the next she would be entertaining her ladies-in-waiting with a savage, acted-out account of the people she had met. 'She's very observant,' says a female aide for several decades. 'She'll remember exactly what a lady councillor or mayoress was wearing: "a ghastly green dress, and the strap fell off".'

There was also an iron control, born of early conditioning. She lacked her father's explosive vehemence. 'The Queen doesn't get furious,' says a present-day adviser. 'Unless you tread on one of her corgis' tails. Then that's pretty bad news.' 'She might say "I am absolutely furious" but not directly to anybody's face,' says a former courtier who has known her since she was a young woman. Her anger was kept inside, or only revealed to intimates. Some witnessed occasional outbursts, though always minor ones. 'She has a stamping temper,' says a close friend, 'throwing a book on the floor, that kind of thing.' Her animals – especially her dogs – loom large in most accounts of lapses of this kind. 'She might ring up and say something like, "Oh, the stupid vet didn't completely get the thorn out of the dog's foot",' says the same source. She could also be irritated by untidiness – for example, an ornament not where it should be. 'Disorder would upset the Queen terribly,' says a friend. 'But if you told her the Japanese had invaded Cornwall, she'd just say: "I must let the Lord Lieutenant know".'

Animal mishaps could seriously disturb her. Once, after a pack of her mother's corgis had inexplicably chased and savaged to death one of her own members of the breed, she wrote a friend with whom she seldom normally corresponded a six-page letter, 'full of doggy language,' about 'not blaming the dogs,' which revealed the extent of her distress. But she seldom let anybody see her emotions towards people. 'We are not bad at concealing what we are feeling,' as one member of the Royal Family puts it. She was almost never seen to cry. 'She has learned how to control her feelings and how much she can divulge,' says one of her ladies, ' – she has acquired introversion.' She could seem withdrawn. 'She is not a demonstrative person,' says another helper. 'She's very English in this respect. She'd only been married for a few years when she had this enormous burden thrust upon her, this incredible job for life. It must have been a great strain, while also being a wife and mother. It's probably true to say she was a bit uptight.' Gradually, she began to relax and soften. 'After the first five or six years, she was possibly a little less aware of what she might be doing, and found her own equilibrium.'

As a young Queen, especially before television destroyed the possibility even of moments of anonymity, it was possible to make occasional forays with friends into the outside world, and pretend to be a normal person. There were even daring ventures to the cinema, comparable to the VE-Day sally: the trick was to arrive unannounced and unexpected, and go in just as the lights dimmed. Once, she and Prince Philip went with a couple of friends and sat in the sixth row of the stalls: when the lights went up for the interval, a delegation of Russian miners in the row behind could scarcely believe their eyes. But people were good about not crowding round. 'The rule was that if you don't tell anybody, you can get away with it,' says a companion. Balmoral – for the long summer break – became the territory on which relaxation was most possible, and a kind of normality took over. It remains the Queen's favourite refuge. 'She behaves quite differently when she is there,' says a friend, ' – rushing around in tatty clothes, laughing, joking, joining in, singing dirty songs.' But there was still the mask that guarded what everybody refers to as a 'very private person,' shutting people out and reminding them of her inner, inescapable awareness: 'I am different, I am the Queen.'

Part of the equilibrium she acquired in the opening years of the reign was based on the discovery that – unlike her father, who hated any kind of performance – she could gain satisfaction from the expert way in which she carried out her public functions. Where George VI had been terrified and Edward VIII nonchalant, Elizabeth II performed the often strange practices inflicted on her by courtiers and churchmen with every appearance of taking them seriously – an appearance given piquancy by her youth and freshness. Bit by bit, she acquired her own measured, unvarying style – devoid of brilliance or special effects, but also of mistakes. 'She believed implicitly in the ceremonial,' says a friend. It was as if the concentrated care and attention to detail which, in her childhood and adolescence, she had devoted to equestrian matters – horses, stables, bridles and pony carts – were now directed at the baubles and rituals of the human world. Instead of horses and bridles, she acquired an encyclopedic knowledge of the history, leading people, uniforms and traditions of the regiments with which she was associated, and – as a landowner as well as a Monarch – of the names, families, and problems of every tenant farmer on her estates.

The equilibrium was also maintained by the reassurance of a fixed timetable, and the traditional cycle of the royal year. 'The Queen is a person who accepts what has to be done with so little question,' says one ex-courtier from the 1940s and 1950s. 'She says "I'm seeing the Prime Minister tonight," and she does it. She knows what she's going to do and absolutely accepts it.' Other aides contrast her punctiliousness with the behaviour of more easy-going relatives. 'A facet of the Queen's character was that she was very efficient and accessible as an administrator – unlike her uncle and her son,' says one. When a red box went up to her on a Friday night, it would be down, with documents signed and comments made, by Monday morning. She no longer read books, if she ever had. But she became a conscientious student of briefing papers – despite her lack of constitutional power (and usual lack of desire) to do much about what they contained. The speed with which she returned to her boxes after the birth of her younger children was part of Palace lore. Civil servants and courtiers regarded this aspect of her character with relief: Adeane was apt to remark on how much of an advantage it was to have a Sovereign who earned the respect of Whitehall.

The other side of a love of routine, however, was conservatism. 'Sometimes,' recalls a past courtier, 'it was difficult to persuade her to do something outside the normal run of things.' Others put it more emphatically: she hated the unexpected. A respect for tradition was at the heart of an hereditary Monarchy – it would be difficult to imagine one without it. Yet there was a constant danger of clinging to habits present-day citizens could no longer relate to. It was not one the Monarch – even at the beginning of her reign – was ever inclined to address. Unlike her husband, whose bursts of modernizing energy made him unpopular at Court but had an occasional impact, the Queen was seldom to be found pushing on the side of royal or monarchical reform.

Part of the reason was innate, part of it was the power over her of staff who, by their choice of occupation and acquired habits of mind, tended to be deeply cautious. A major part was her mother. It was not easy for Queen Elizabeth, only fifty-one at the time of the Accession, to come to terms with the loss, not just of a husband, but also of regality and the blandishments that went with it, and to assume the role of dowager. After a couple of years of semi-withdrawal, however, she adjusted. Recovered in strength and energy, and holding a candle for the man she continued to speak of as 'the King', she exercised an influence that often seemed pervasive. She maintained an important place in the lives of both daughters, as of the nation. 'The Queen's picture of her role was derived from her father, and very much reinforced by her mother,' says an ex-courtier. 'Queen Elizabeth seemed to favour the Monarchy as it was pre-war, and was not embracing the idea of changing things.' The Queen was in daily contact with her mother, on the telephone or – if either of them was abroad – by letter, detailing everything she was doing, and often discussing the issues of the moment. She indulged her, helped to finance her – and was sometimes overawed by her. In the early, unsure days, she allowed herself to be led by her in the way she behaved as Monarch. As a result, as one former aide puts it, 'there was a tendency to stick with the way things had always been done.'

There was humour in the way the two women related. 'Oh, Mummy, grow up,' the Queen was apt to say about her mother's no-tomorrow spending habits. There was also companionship, and an example. Queen Elizabeth provided a link – psychological as well as social – to the network of Scottish and English nobility that was half her daughter's heritage. They shared, too, an equestrian passion. 'Queen Elizabeth is the Queen's talking person on racing,' says a friend. There remained tensions: the indomitable will of the extrovert, socialite, aristocratic Queen Mother seemed at times almost to eclipse her royal children. 'Queen Elizabeth has always been much flashier,' says a lady-in-waiting. 'The Queen has always refused to imitate her Hollywood film star style.' Nevertheless the strong, ambitious, worldly, charismatic personality of the older woman remained for many years one of the rocks upon which her daughter's difficult life rested.

A few others were also close to the Queen. There were childhood friends and relatives – like the Brabournes, with whom the Queen and Prince Philip often stayed, and vice versa, especially in the early days, and Lord Rupert Nevill, who became private secretary to Prince Philip, and his wife Micky. Non-relatives with whom the Queen exchanged visits mainly belonged to the landed, aristocratic, and horse-and-dog worlds. The most important friend in this category was Lord Porchester, the Queen's other equestrian 'talking person,' who became the dominant figure in this part of her life, while her husband, who took no interest in racing, followed other pursuits. The Queen often stayed with Porchester and his American wife at Milford, and then, after Porchester succeeded his father as Earl of Carnarvon, at Highclere castle – finding in their shared enthusiasm a refuge from the royal rounds. Porchester was regarded as the Queen's closest non-family friend. 'He talks a lot to her in a secret way,' says a former aide. 'There's real love there, I think, on both sides. I expect they talk intimately – but I also expect she keeps her own counsel.'[85]

The Queen developed good, loyal friendships with ladies-in-waiting and Ladies of the Bedchamber – part-practical, part-ceremonial assistants recruited almost invariably from an aristocratic background or married into one, who answered letters from ordinary subjects, accompanied the Monarch on trips, fed her gossip, and sometimes stayed loyally in her employment for decades. In general, however, the Queen related better to men than women. Among male courtiers, pride of place – for day-to-day advice but also for encouragement and emotional support – was taken by the charming and magnificently tasteful Lord Plunket, a former Guards officer who had succeeded to his father's barony in his teens, served as an equerry to George VI from 1948, and was made Deputy Master of the Household in the year after the Coronation. Only three years older than the young Queen, he combined the roles of older brother and Jeeves-like personal factotum.

'Handsome and debonair,' as Kenneth Rose observes, Plunket was 'one of those bachelors of easy manners' always in demand at Court, partly because he lived out, in his manners and obsessions, the royal fantasy. He had a passion for the details of royal entertaining. He was a chooser of exquisite little gifts for distinguished visitors, and an arranger of flowers at state banquets – specializing in great pyramids of white flowers alongside treasure troves of silver: sometimes his creation would be a palace, sometimes a country house[86]. His relationship with the Queen, intimate and fond, contained a kind of camp normality which people admired, envied, and were amused by. 'He was in a position to say things to the Queen which others couldn't,' says one ex-courtier. He used to scold her about her clothes. 'You can't possible wear shoes like that,' he would say. 'Well I can't see what's wrong with them,' she might reply – and then meekly or petulantly, 'If you say so, I mustn't say any more.' His impact extended beyond the Queen to those around her. 'Patrick Plunket made everybody feel comfortable,' says a Lady of the Bedchamber. 'He had a happy way with people.'[87]

Plunket's influence was complemented (and offset) by Bobo Mac-Donald – nursemaid since 145 Piccadilly, and dedicated dresser and helper to the Queen thereafter. Bobo was a woman of formidable authority, something of which those who sought access to her mistress were sometimes made cruelly aware. Nobody was closer, or more loyal. 'Total devotion to the Queen oozed from Miss MacDonald,' recalls one who grappled with her power.[88] The Queen told her everything of a day-to-day kind that was on her mind, and they would gossip together about below-stairs affairs – the latest mishap of the pantry boy, and so forth. But Bobo had a public, as well as a private and comradely, importance. In the sartorial sphere – apart from the occasional forays of Lord Plunket – she reigned unchallenged. It helped Bobo that the Queen's own interest in clothes was, at best, half-hearted. Where her daughters-in-law later applied thought and large sums of money to how they looked, the Queen tended to regard the topic as an occupational chore. Her concerns were practical: she wanted to wear dresses that were comfortable and not too expensive, and which would not cause offence.

The last was important. Norman Hartnell later recalled that when he was making the Coronation dress, the Palace had to worry about more than just the national origins of silkworms: the design itself had to avoid showing favours to one realm over another. His initial sketch included a tudor rose, a thistle, a shamrock and a daffodil: the Queen instructed him to weave in the emblems of the Dominions as well.[89] Related problems – sometimes involving local customs and taboos – frequently cropped up over the years that followed. At home, the Queen's first concern was to be suitably clad for ceremonial occasions. 'She used to be fanatical about getting into training for Trooping the Colour,' an ex-courtier recalls. 'Two months beforehand she would start losing weight because she had to fit into the uniform.' Uniforms (other people's, as well as her own) often seemed to excite her more than dresses. Like her father, she was a stickler for the correct detail of military apparel.

As far as her non-ceremonial, non-military clothes were concerned, her main interest was in making sure that they did not get in the way of whatever she had to do. She did not employ any particular designer exclusively. Though Hartnell made her Wedding and Coronation dresses, he was not permitted a monopoly of commissions. In a canny distribution of favours that stimulated price as well as artistic competition, the Queen varied her patronage, and made frequent use of the up-and-coming Hardy Amies, who was able to offer a range of day as well as formal wear. Amies – recommended by a lady-in-waiting, Lady Margaret Colville (married to Jock Colville) – obtained his first royal commission just before the 1951 Canadian tour. He rapidly discovered the importance of paying court to Miss MacDonald, as much as to her employer. Bobo would arrange the time of the fitting, receive the designer when he arrived, and seat him in the waiting room. She did not decide how the Queen would dress, but – like Plunket – she had an effective power of veto, and helped to determine which great couturier would be given a particular job. She also set a demarcation line, to the despair of the Hartnells and the Amieses, as she frequently made clear: 'frocks' might be their sphere, but hats and handbags were hers.

Unfortunately, Bobo's taste in hats and handbags was regarded by the dress designers as execrable. The Queen took even less interest in hats than in dresses, except that she hated having to wear them. 'Hats make me look like a sheep,' she once said to friends. 'Why should I want to look like a sheep?' (She preferred crowns and tiaras – part of her official uniform – to hats. 'Oh, the Queen's marvellous,' Bobo once remarked. 'She's the only person who can go downstairs putting on a tiara without looking in the glass. She's so used to it, she can do it by feel'.) But it was the handbag problem that made the couturiers almost suicidal. In vain, they tried to stop the Monarch carrying large, ungainly, box-like objects in garish colours, whose purchase had been arranged at the Palace. 'Bobo was the origin of the Queen's ugly handbags,' says one of them, bitterly.[90] Eventually a solution of a kind was found – a conspiracy theorist might suspect a deliberate plot. The result of the couturiers' desperation, and Miss MacDonald's obduracy, was a steady flow of Christmas gifts of accessories, especially handbags, thoughtfully chosen by the Queen's dress designers.

Dresses – especially dresses for foreign tours – conveyed messages, and had to strike a balance between dignity, fashion, and the avoidance of opportunities for photographers to take unflattering or embarrassing shots. The balance was hard to maintain, especially in the 1960s, as the Queen approached her fortieth birthday and hemlines rose mercilessly. 'As a designer,' Amies recalled in his memoirs, contemplating his royal commissions, 'I was not happy with the mini-skirts era.'[91] Cloth had to be thick enough not be transparent with the light behind it, yet flexible enough not to crush on car seats – a problem made slightly easier because, as one dress-maker approvingly remarks, squirming is the main cause of crushed materials, and the Queen was a 'non-squirmer'.

The Queen's other preoccupation, of which her couturiers were made acutely aware, was cash, even though the huge commercial value of a royal warrant did not incline them to overcharge. A high proportion of a large number of handwritten letters from the Queen to Amies over the years concerned, sometimes quite tartly, the cost of his designs. 'Thank you for the enormous bill,' she wrote in characteristic style on one occasion, 'which will take a little time to pay.'[92] 'With the Queen,' reflects Sir Hardy Amies, 'you've got to be dead simple.'[93]

Vanity was not one of the Queen's vices, as her dress designers discovered: she did not wear clothes to make herself alluring, or even elegant. It was the fate of a Monarch, however, to be examined minutely by large numbers of people, and this made it impossible to ignore the visual impression she created. It was also a regal fate to be painted formally more often than almost anybody else in the world. As a result, there was another category of people – portrait painters

– who had a close contact with the Queen, involving hours spent with her *à deux*, through repeated sittings.

Where dressmakers focused on the body of the Monarch – her small (five foot four inch) stature, tight waist when young, prominent breasts, narrow shoulders – painters looked at the face, which was generally in animation. They noted the darting eyes and bright smile, a look that would suddenly cloud over, and then re-emerge from the clouds. 'She has no intermediate expression,' says Michael Noakes, who painted one of the best pictures of her. 'She's either looking – ping! – wonderful with a great smile, or dour in repose.'[94] Pietro Annigoni, painter of two famous portraits, made a similar observation. 'As she posed her facial expression was mercurial,' he recalled, 'smiling, thoughtful, determined, uncertain, relaxed, taut, in rapid succession.'[95] There were familiar patterns of behaviour, observed by artists and dress-makers alike. She would be courteous, co-operative and patient, accepting the business of being painted (or dressed) as a professional obligation like everything else. She was also – and it is interesting that several painters have observed it – a chatterbox.

Portrait-painting generally took place in the Yellow Drawing-Room at Buckingham Palace – on the balcony floor on the extreme left of the front of the building, with windows on two sides. When a session was due, the Queen would arrive slightly late for the appointment, place herself before the artist with a glass of water in front of her, and talk non-stop. Sometimes, her conversation took the form of a running commentary. During one of her sittings for Annigoni, she described the aftermath of a minor crash she had just seen through the glass, involving a car and taxi. 'In the meantime,' she recounted, 'the clock ticks up and the poor thing in the taxi will have to pay.' Another painter remembers her looking out as darkness fell, with the curtain undrawn and the light on, and imagining the conversation between a couple she could see beyond the Palace railings, peering up at the window. 'An American has stopped,' she said in an American accent, 'he has seen us, he has seen us, he has said to his wife, "Gee mam, it can't be!"'

The soliloquy flowed from topic to topic – the royal children, minor misfortunes, famous people. When Annigoni first painted her in 1954, somebody asked him if she talked during sittings. 'Well, yes,' he replied, '– perhaps too much.' The remark got back, and the next four sessions took place in stony silence. However, when he painted her again sixteen years later, she was as loquacious as before. 'At every sitting,' he recalled, 'the Queen chatted to me in the most natural way and her disarming frankness never failed to surprise and fascinate me, even at those times when, for the purpose of the portrait, it would have been better if she had kept silent.' Towards the end, the painter 'longed for silence, but the Queen wanted to talk and in the end I gave myself up to conversation.'[96] One dress-designer's fitter held a similar view to Annigoni's, and used to remark that he wished the Queen's rapid fire of comments would stop, so that he could get on with his work.[97]

12

At the beginning of 1956, the Queen and Duke of Edinburgh spent three weeks in Nigeria, largest of the African colonies. Norman Hartnell designed a canopy to be transported with them, to act as a saluting platform and sunshield, as they toured the country attending religious and tribal ceremonies. The itinerary included a visit to a leper settlement – a royal gesture regarded as a propaganda coup against the continued and irrational fears attached to any physical contact with the disease, much as the Princess of Wales's hospital and hospice-visiting was felt to help the cause of leprosy and AIDS sufferers several decades later. Nigeria had only a small expatriate British population. Yet it responded with all the enthusiasm of a white dominion. Tribal leaders competed in the splendour of their displays. The visit culminated in Lagos, with a dance of ten thousand masked warriors, and a million-strong crowd chanting 'Our Queen'.[1]

In April, the Queen was herself host to the new Soviet leaders Marshal Bulganin and Nikita Khrushchev. The Government saw the visit as a breakthrough, marking a thaw in the Cold War; and the Monarch, incongruously, was presented as one of the attractions. 'Eden told us that we would find the Queen to be a simple, but very bright and very pleasant woman,' wrote Khrushchev in his published memoirs, believed to be genuine. The Soviet General Secretary agreed with this assessment, and likened the British Sovereign to 'the sort of young woman you'd be likely to meet walking along Gorky Street on a balmy summer afternoon'. He found her 'completely unpretentious,' and lacking in the haughtiness he had expected to encounter in a Queen.[2] Unfortunately, any gain derived from the royal hospitality was swiftly obliterated by the embarrassing case of Commander Crabbe whose body, in a frogman's suit, was fished up from the harbour where the warship that had brought the Russian leaders was docked; and by crises that arose in East Europe and the Middle East later the same year.

On July 26th, Egypt nationalized the Suez Canal, precipitating three months of diplomatic turmoil. Faced with the refusal of the Egyptian leader, Colonel Nasser, to meet their demands, the British, French and Israeli governments agreed secretly – and illegally – that Israel should attack Egypt, thereby providing the pretext for a forcible Franco-British occupation of the Canal Zone. Israel launched its attack on October 29th, and Britain and France followed with their independent assaults.

During this rapid series of events, the Queen found herself the hapless witness as her Prime Minister exhausted the possibilities, as he saw them, and moved towards a military operation. She had no direct role. There was even a story, which seemed to underline the peripheral nature of the Monarchy, about her signing an emergency Order in Council calling out the Army Reserve 'on the rump of her racehorse in the Goodwood paddock,' with a scratch group of Privy Councillors around her.'[3] The story was not far from the mark. In fact, on 2nd August, Sir Michael Adeane presented her with a hastily-prepared Proclamation, not in the paddock, but in her private room in the Duke of Richmond's box – her approval was required before it could be read out in the House of Commons the same afternoon. The actual signing of the document took place at a special Privy Council at Arundel Castle, where she was staying as a guest of the Duke of Norfolk.[4]

The anecdote can be taken as an example of royal frivolity; or, alternatively, as a demonstration that the Suez crisis was something the Monarch could not escape. Indeed, if Lady Eden came to believe that the Suez Canal flowed through her drawing room, the Queen must have felt pretty damp as well. For Buckingham Palace was in the uniquely frustrating position of knowing everything, yet being able to do nothing. 'The Queen received all the Foreign Office telegrams and papers,' according to one former adviser, 'and so in some ways was better informed in advance of the operation than many members of the Cabinet.'[5] 'She knew the inside story,' says another. 'Nothing was kept from her. She knew about the secret deals beforehand.'[6] It was an extraordinary vantage point – not just for the Monarch, but for her courtiers, who included two assistant private secretaries, Edward Ford and Martin Charteris, with experience of the Middle East.

Not only was the Queen told more than many ministers, some of whom were notoriously kept in the dark; she (and her staff) may even have been better informed on some matters than No. 10, for the Queen was the recipient of messages from Commonwealth governments that were not directed at the Prime Minister, especially as tensions within the Commonwealth increased. In September, Robert Menzies – who backed Eden but wanted to patch up divisions on the issue within the Commonwealth – visited the Queen at Balmoral. 'I called in to give Her Majesty a little background of my talks with Colonel Nasser regarding the future of the Suez Canal,' the Australian premier explained to a member of the Royal Household.[7]

There is the interesting question of how much the Queen told her Commonwealth Prime Ministers, including those who were opposed to Britain's aggressive stance. Did she swap information about talks with Nasser, or other up-to-date details provided by the Commonwealth leaders, for a run-down on her own talks with Eden? Or was conversation in one direction, with the Queen keeping silent, for fear of giving anything away? Finally, did she – was she expected to – pass on to her British ministers any news or opinions thus acquired? It was an anomaly of her position that she had to choose between leaking secrets or deceiving prime ministers and high commissioners who looked to her as Head of State or Head of the Commonwealth by withholding information that was relevant to their interests.[8] In addition to the Australian Prime Minister, who clearly saw the Queen as a potential route to Eden, there were also other lobbyists. One was Lord Mountbatten who passionately opposed the attack, both on diplomatic and military grounds. 'Dickie was talking to her,' according to a former royal adviser. 'He wanted her to know what he thought about it – he was saying something like, "I think they are being absolutely lunatic". He was typically devious. He didn't mean it as a message to be conveyed directly to Eden, but he hoped she would pass it on to him as her own thoughts.'[9]

'The impression we got was of consternation in the embassies in the Middle East,' says an ex-courtier, 'and of general concern in the

Foreign Office – ninety per cent of which was strongly against it.'[10] The Palace itself was divided. Adeane was personally pro-Eden, and professionally concerned that the Queen should maintain the constitutional proprieties. Ford and Charteris were both vehemently opposed. What view did the Queen take? 'I think the Queen believed Eden was mad,' according to one former Palace aide, who recalled that when the Prime Minister came for his weekly audience, the premier 'ranged up and down and wouldn't sit still. He was edgy, jumpy'.[11] Another has similar memories. 'There was not a comfortable atmosphere at meals together,' he remembers, 'not the same benign atmosphere as with Churchill.'[12] She certainly felt the pressure. 'I'm having the most awful time,' a friend remembers her saying at a private dinner party at the height of the crisis. 'My lady-in-waiting thinks one thing, one private secretary thinks another, another thinks something else.'[13]

Many years later, when a journalist suggested in the draft of a book that the Queen had protested strongly against the Suez operation, Lord Avon angrily denied it, and pressed to have the reference removed.[14] Former courtiers however, remember a less than neutral royal position. 'She may have said to Eden,' ventures one, 'something like: "Are you sure you are being wise?"'[15]

BRITISH and French troops moved against Egypt on 29th October. For the next few days of fighting, the Queen received daily bulletins from No. 10 Downing Street, including details of casualties.[16] On 6th November, international pressure and the threat of financial collapse forced the London and Paris governments to order a cease-fire. Shortly afterwards, an emotionally and physically exhausted Eden left for Jamaica to recuperate.

The Queen spent Christmas at Sandringham with her children – without Philip, who had left London two weeks before the Suez action on a protracted world tour. Friends visited for the New Year. In January, Sir Anthony and Lady Eden came to stay, with a specific purpose. In the course of an audience on 8th January Eden told her of his decision to resign, on medical advice.[17]

This was a statement of intent, not the act itself. Buckingham Palace was felt to be the appropriate place for handing in, and accepting, the seals of office. Eden therefore returned to London. On January 9th he went through the informal and formal steps involved in a prime ministerial departure. The same afternoon he told three key figures – the Chancellor, Harold Macmillan, the Lord Privy Seal and Leader of the House, R. A. Butler, and the Lord President, Lord Salisbury of his intention. He attended a full Cabinet, and then went to see the Queen, who had returned from Norfolk in order to receive him, and told her again what he had already told her at Sandringham. She responded by offering him an earldom, either immediately or whenever he wished.

The resignation occurred against a background of deep national crisis and uncertainty, following the Suez *débâcle*, with the Conservative Party and the Government bitterly divided. For Eden, it had been an astonishing change of fortune. Nineteen months earlier, his appointment had been unquestioned – his authority confirmed by a general election at which the Tories had increased their majority. Now his departure was greeted with relief, not least in Buckingham Palace. There had been no easy rapport. 'He didn't give you the feeling he trusted you with sensitive information,' says one former courtier. Members of the Household had been alarmed by the symptoms following the Prime Minister's return from the West Indies: a high colour, which 'made it look as if he had a temperature all the time,' and – in Norfolk – a visible nervousness.[18] Jock Colville, who had been a guest at Sandringham a few days before the Edens arrived, recorded that nobody in the royal party seemed to suspect that the Prime Minister's resignation was imminent; however, it was his impression that everybody, including the Queen, thought it was to be desired.[19]

The vacancy placed the Queen in a dilemma which she had not faced in 1955: this time, there was no undisputed dauphin. The choice lay between Rab Butler and Harold Macmillan. Butler was the favourite. In the press, only the *Evening Standard* correctly predicted the outcome. However, the Lord Privy Seal had many detractors in his party, and a peculiar flair, as Anthony Sampson later observed, 'for not rising to the occasion.'[20] Hence the contest seemed open – except that, in the conditions then prevailing, no contest was involved. Instead, there was a recognized arbiter, whose method of arbitration was unspecified, beyond the requirement that she should find a candidate acceptable to the House of Commons.

Such a difficult decision had not been required of a Monarch since 1923, following the resignation of Andrew Bonar Law, when George V had examined the rival merits of Stanley Baldwin and Lord Curzon, and had surprised many people by choosing the former. In the whole of George VI's reign, there had been only two mid-term changes of premier, neither involving any serious uncertainty, although there might have been some in 1940 if Halifax had not declared his reluctance to serve. Since 1923, the need to take political guidance had increased – yet no mechanism existed for assessing who should appropriately provide it.

'We took the view that it was for the Conservative Party to select its leader,' says one former courtier, 'and that the Queen should not do anything until she was sure what the Party had decided.'[21] What constituted the Conservative Party for these purposes, however, was a metaphysical point. The Party was not, and did not consider itself to be, internally democratic. Tory doctrine held that on some matters it was right to defer to rank and authority. The choice of a Prime Minister was one of them. Conservative MPs fully accepted that the Monarch had an area of discretion at such a time, and they were prepared to defend it.

Yet if the Queen was to exercise a judgement, there remained the question of criteria. Should her decision be a verdict on Suez, still the dominating issue of the time? Should she appoint a stop-gap, whilst the political temperature cooled? Finally (a point of interest to the Labour Party), should the royal prerogative be used for the appointment of somebody whose main merit, in the eyes of colleagues, was an ability to help the Conservatives to recapture votes in time for the next election?

After Eden's departure for the Palace, events moved fast. At the end of the Cabinet meeting, two senior ministers, Lord Salisbury and the Lord Chancellor, Lord Kilmuir – both non-contenders – invited their colleagues to stay behind for a process of consultation which was, to say the least, cursory. Later, Butler made the reasonable complaint that 'Cabinet ministers were "corralled" to give an immediate judgement'.[22] Each minister, apart from the two expected candidates, was interviewed in the Lord President's room in the Privy Council office, which could be reached without leaving the building. One by one, they were asked versions of Lord Salisbury's subsequently famous question: 'Is it Wab, or Hawold?' After this interrogation, the two peers widened their survey to include former ministers and the chairman of the back-bench 1922 Committee. Kilmuir later claimed that the verdict was never in doubt. An 'overwhelming majority' of Cabinet Ministers supported Macmillan, who was also the choice of back-benchers.

On the morning of 10th January, the Queen summoned Lord Salisbury and Sir Winston Churchill to the Palace, in order to take their advice. According to Macmillan, Lord Salisbury acted as spokesman, and 'did not give his views' – merely presenting 'the general view inside the party'.[23] Churchill – who arrived in a car with a union jack rug covering his knees – backed him up. As the old statesman emerged from his audience, he was heard to remark, 'I said Macmillan. Is that right?'[24] Macmillan was called to the Palace at noon the same day, and at 2 p.m. he was premier. The process was not only quick. It was smooth. There was no time for unseemly wrangling – or for second thoughts, either about the decision, or the method of making it. One moment Butler had seemed the likely successor, the next his rival was kissing hands.

The more important of the two opinions offered to the Queen was that of Lord Salisbury, who spoke for the Government and the Conservative Party. (An interesting situation would have arisen if Churchill had pressed for Butler, though it was obviously unlikely that he would advise against the outcome of the sounding-out.) Once the advice had been sought, the Queen had no option but to take it. However, she did have a choice about accepting the method of consultation in the first place, and it was this that gave rise to criticism.

A legend later grew that Eden had held aloof from the choice of his successor, much as Churchill had done in 1955, and left the matter entirely to the Queen and his former colleagues. 'There is no evidence that Eden was asked for his advice,' Anthony Sampson wrote in his biography of Macmillan a decade later.[25] Lord Avon himself encouraged this view. Others have disagreed. Another Macmillan biographer, the former Tory MP Nigel Fisher, claimed 'that the Queen did consult Eden'.[26] According to Avon's official biographer, Eden's personal preference was for Butler, whom he expected to be chosen, 'but he was careful not to make any recommendation at all' to the Queen.[27] However, a memorandum in the Avon papers, dictated by Eden on 12th January as a record of his final audience and sent to Sir Michael Adeane, shows that while he did not advise, he did state a preference. 'Her Majesty spoke of the future and of the difficult choice that lay before her,' Eden recorded. 'I agreed that it was certainly difficult. The Queen made no formal request for my advice but enabled me to signify that my own debt to Mr Butler while I have been Prime Minister was very real and that I thought he had discharged his difficult task during three weeks while I was away in Jamaica very well.'[28] Constitutionally, if a Prime Minister 'advises' the Monarch, the advice has to be taken. Eden was not asked for, and did not give, such binding advice.[29] But he very unequivocally recommended Butler to the Queen as the best person to succeed him.

He did so, however, in the context of other proposals which, when followed, meant that such a recommendation could not be put into immediate effect. Eden's own private account shows that the Prime Minister spoke to Adeane about the succession in advance of his resignation, suggesting that a senior minister who was not a candidate should be asked to take soundings in Cabinet. The minister he suggested was Lord Salisbury. He did not indicate any procedure.[30] This accords with the version given by Kilmuir – joint Cabinet interrogator with Salisbury – that the initiative for the 'Wab or Hawold' consultation came from Salisbury after talking with Eden.[31] It is also consistent with the account given by Dermot Morrah, whose writings on royalty had a semi-authorized status, in a book published a year later, which again suggests the involvement of both Eden and Adeane in the choice. According to Morrah, 'it was reasonable to suppose' that the Queen discussed the succession with Eden in earlier audiences; and that in the weeks before the resignation, 'a considerable number of men and women who might be able to illuminate one or another facet of the problem unburdened themselves in the discreet room in the North Wing of Buckingham Palace where Sir Michael Adeane collects all possible opinions that may help the Queen to make a decision'. Since the writer fulsomely acknowledged Adeane's help, we may guess that the source for this information was the Queen's private secretary himself, perhaps seeking to justify the Palace's role, following criticisms.[32]

Thus the sequence of consultation seems to have begun with Eden, who suggested to Adeane that Lord Salisbury should act as the sounder-out. The Queen's private secretary himself discussed the matter with Salisbury, who in turn brought in Kilmuir. There remained the question of how they were to proceed. Should they restrict their enquiries to ministers? To what extent should back-benchers be involved? In their discussion, the Lord Chancellor cast his own possibly decisive weight against too much democracy. Having, as he wrote, 'considered the constitutional position very carefully,' he declared himself opposed to putting the matter to a meeting of Conservative MPs – on the loyal, if curious, grounds that to do so would jeopardize the Queen's prerogative.[33] His fear was that such a meeting – tantamount to a Labour-style leadership election – would take the choice out of the Queen's hands where, he believed, it should remain for use in emergencies. He seems to have imagined that an informal procedure would put the prerogative on ice, permitting the Conservative hierarchy to do the choosing this time, while preserving for the Monarch the right to take an independent initiative on some future occasion. In fact, what put the Queen's prerogative most in jeopardy, was precisely the method that was adopted. An active use of the royal prerogative might have shown that it was in working order. Handing it over to the Tory old guard set its own precedent, signalling that it had become a doubtful instrument.

Ironically, criticisms occurred because of the Queen's desire to keep out of the political arena, rather than to enter it. 'Nothing in her temperament would have induced her to exercise her own judgement,' as the journalist Malcolm Muggeridge observed, 'even assuming – which is unlikely – that she herself had any particular preference or opinion.'[34] In 1923 George V had conducted soundings through his private secretary, Lord Stamfordham (who happened to be Adeane's grandfather) and made an unexpected choice – though not a disputed one. A generation later, George V's granddaughter had effectively allowed her private secretary to delegate her prerogative power – making herself vulnerable to the charge not of exercising an arbitrary judgement but of allowing the Monarchy to become the pawn of a Conservative faction.

There were no immediate repercussions. Talk of a censure motion against the Government came to nothing. However, the controversy produced a small but significant statement of principle from the Labour Party – which had not so far had to face the problem of finding a new leader while in office, and which now made it clear that, if such a problem arose, the Parliamentary Party would insist on a vote before accepting a new Prime Minister. 'We believe that it is important that parties themselves should decide on their leaders,' declared James Griffiths, the Labour deputy leader, in a television interview – stating a view that the Conservatives would later accept, 'and that the Crown should not be put in the embarrassing position of having to make a choice between rival claimants for the premiership of the same party. This is bringing the Crown into internecine party warfare, which is very bad for the constitution.'[35] For the time being, however, the constitutional position in the event of a Tory changeover remained muddier then ever – adding to nervousness and contention when six years later the prospect of another succession arose.

THE QUEEN, meanwhile, had taken a key educational decision on behalf of her son. Following Philip's departure in October, Prince Charles was admitted to Hill House, a small pre-preparatory establishment in Knightsbridge – becoming the first Heir to the Throne to attend school. The decision to send him was regarded as enlightened, especially as Hill House was unconventional and cosmopolitan, with a large intake of foreign pupils. At home Charles and Anne were in the charge of Mabel Anderson, a young Scottish nanny who looked after the two children for most of the day, apart from a pre-bedtime 'romping' session with the Queen, comparable with the high jinks of her youth.[36] Mabel Anderson, previously assistant nursemaid, had taken over from their former keeper, Helen Lightbody ('a bitch, who was rough on Anne and spoilt Charles,' according to one former member of the Household)[37]. By this time Anderson had become a mainstay, solving the problem of royal childcare.

From Hill House, Charles proceeded to Cheam, his father's prep school. Boarding school was regarded as a progressive choice – encouraging a greater degree of mingling with children from non-royal and non-aristocratic homes. It soon became clear, however, that he hated it. The Queen seems to have had few qualms. '. . . Charles is just beginning to dread the return to school next week,' she wrote to Eden from Sandringham in January 1958, '– so much worse for the second term!'[38]

One reason for choosing boarding school was the nature of the Queen's life. Her duties frequently took her away from her children, not just during the day, but also when she travelled, and she showed little inclination to have them accompany her. In view of her absences, the issue has been raised of whether she was a 'good mother'.[39] The question defies an answer – partly because criteria vary, from one generation and one social group to another; but also because the jury is still out on the long-term effects. In style, her method of upbringing was not unusual among aristocratic families of an old-fashioned sort. For those who could afford it, dependence on a surrogate mother was as common then as it is now: to be Head of State and a fully engaged parent are not obviously compatible occupations, and there are many women today who find it necessary to delegate responsibility for their children because of employment that is less demanding than being a Monarch.

She was not demonstrative. 'The Queen was a very tight mother,' says a courtier. 'She's not very tactile,' according to one friend. 'A child wants a mother to be emotional, hugged, kissed – and that's not what the Queen's good at,' says another, 'she's tough, totally unsentimental.' Yet some felt that, so far from being too tough with her children, she was not tough enough – that, because she was Queen, she did not assert herself. 'She has always been reluctant to stop her children doing anything,' says a former courtier. 'The burden would fall on the Duke.' If the Queen stood back, Philip overcompensated. 'He misinterpreted Charles on many occasions,' says a relative. 'His attitude was based on himself. Here was this child – he would have to make his way in the world. People spoiled him. He needed to counteract the spoiling.' According to a friend of Philip, however, 'He was nicer to them than many people I know are with their children.' Yet it was hard to imagine a father and son more unalike. 'Prince Charles was a very sensitive little boy, very kind, very sweet,' says a friend of the Queen. 'He was always giving one little presents – it was very touching.'

Those who knew the Royal Family when the children were growing up dispute that there was anything unusual about them – except, of course, in the obvious ways in which they were completely different from anybody else. 'At Balmoral they were a very normal, ordinary, country-loving couple with two small children,' one friend recalls from the earlier years. The picture is of picnics, fishing on the loch, pony rides, 'anything privileged children did in England, and always with their parents'. If there was some nervousness at first, the Queen became more relaxed as the size of her family increased. 'She was a less natural mother with Charles and Anne,' suggests a helper, 'whereas she was much more the besotted parent with Andrew and Edward'.[40]

One of the things privileged children did in the 1950s (and for aristocratic boys and girls it was virtually *de rigueur*) was ride horses. In the case of the children of Elizabeth II, an equestrian education was backed by a serious maternal passion. The Queen's own interest in the riding, breeding, training and racing of horses had been greatly reinforced by the weight of family tradition, and by the impact of inheritance.

So long-standing was the connection of the British Monarchy with the Turf – including the ancient, inbred bloodlines of the royal studs – that it seemed inseparable from the dynasty and the institution. In the reign of Henry VIII, there had been royal studs at Hampton Court, Tutbury and Malmesbury; Elizabeth I went racing at Salisbury just before the Spanish Armada, Charles II founded Newmarket Turf Plate which was 'to be run over the New Round Course on the second Thursday in October forever,' and in 1667 rode the winner in the same race himself; Queen Anne founded the Ascot Races; as Prince of Wales, George IV bred two of the great horses of the British Turf, Herod and then Eclipse (so named because it was foaled on the day of a solar eclipse in 1764). Edward VII, also as Prince of Wales, founded a new stud at Sandringham – and it was here that George V bred Friar Marins, the sire of Feola, one of the outstanding brood-mares of the time. On the day that Scuttle won the Derby in 1928, the King wrote that he was 'very proud to win my first classic and that I bred her at Sandringham!'[41]

As we have seen, George V's grand-daughter acquired an interest in horses early on. The essence of the traditional royal obsession, however, was ownership. The direct involvement of Elizabeth began in the late 1940s when she received the filly Astrakhan as a wedding present from the Aga Khan. The Princess acquired her own racing colours of 'scarlet, purple hooped sleeves and black cap' when she and her mother jointly bought the steeple-chaser Monaveen. There were early successes: in October 1949, Astrakhan finished second in a race for two-year-olds at Ascot, and a few days later Monaveen won at Fontwell. Astrakhan won again at Hurst Park in the spring of 1950, and the Duke of Norfolk telegraphed the Princess in Malta with the news. From then on, the Queen's first interest was in flat-racing. However, Philip's *Chequers* posting limited her opportunities to indulge it, and it was not until after she became Queen that she was able to develop it further.

At first, a sudden increase in her duties pushed it to the margins. It was the sense that horses were part of the extended, complicated business of being a Monarch-landowner-farmer with a matrix of inherited responsibilities, of which the royal studs were one, that brought it back. Included in her inheritance were some trusty mares, including the nineteen-year-old Feola and her three daughters, and a two-year-old colt called Aureole, the first foal of Angela, a bay mare that had been the 'best staying filly' of the year in 1948. With such a legacy, the Queen found herself guardian of a stock of horses that seemed an important part of her new proprietorship. Very quickly she made clear that she regarded it as a sacred trust.

Her keenness on the Turf was further encouraged by the ever-improving form of the fast but temperamental Aureole – 'tricky from the start and very difficult to catch in a paddock'. His second place in the 1953 Derby became a staging-post on the way to a series of triumphs. In 1954, he won the felicitously named King George VI and Queen Elizabeth Stakes at Ascot. After this victory, the Queen, 'delighted and thrilled' by the race, greeted the horse in the unsaddling enclosure with a display of public affection which she seldom showed towards human beings. At the end of the season the Coronation Derby near-miss had made the Queen easily the top British owner in terms of winning stake money. 'Cecil Boyd-Rochford, leading trainer, from

Elizabeth R, leading winner-owner 1954,' read the inscription of a lacquered cigarette box she gave the man most responsible for her success that Christmas. By the time of Aureole's retirement the following year, he had won seven of his fourteen races, and been placed second or third in five of the rest. When he was eventually put down in 1973, after many lucrative years at stud, it was like a state event: the body was buried in the paddock where he died, and a copper beech marked the grave.

In 1957, the Queen's reign on the Turf reached its peak. At the end of a year in which Lester Piggott rode Carozza – leased by the Queen from the National Stud and trained by Noel Murless – to victory in the Oaks, the Jockey Club handicapper rated three of her fillies the best three-year-olds of the year, and she became leading owner for the second time. The following year, she won the 2,000 Guineas with Pall Mall, ridden by Doug Smith. The high performance of the 1950s, however, could not be maintained: it was followed in the early 1960s by a period of embarrassing decline. The Queen's breeder, Captain Moore – another inheritance – was widely blamed. Critics saw him as fuddy-duddy, with an antiquated attachment to in-breeding, and pointed to the irony that the Queen's biggest successes of the 1950s, Aureole and Dontille, were among the least in-bred. Whatever the reason, no more horses of the calibre of Aureole (bred before the Queen came to the throne) came from the royal stud before Boyd-Rochford's retirement in 1968. After several bad seasons, the octogenarian Moore was replaced in 1962 by his deputy, Brigadier A. D. R. Wingfield. Rival doctrines now gained ground – strongly encouraged by the Queen's racing confidant, Lord Porchester. In the same year, at Porchester's suggestion, the Queen decided to lease Polhampton Stud near Kingsclere on the Hampshire Downs, a few miles from the Carnarvon stud at Highclere. The impact of proximity was psychological as well as practical, and 'hybrid vigour' gained ground.

'The Queen's enthusiasm for racing has been tested time and again by her lack of luck,' writes Alastair Burnet, in his official history of the Derby.[42] That is not quite fair: though she has never won the Derby or in the last four decades come close to doing so, her horses have won all the other classics. However, winning or losing never really seems to have been the point as far as the Monarch has been concerned – which may be one reason why she hasn't won more often. The Queen's horse world, central to her life, has been as much aesthetic and sensuous as competitive. It has also become a reassuring part of the royal ritual. From the beginning, she enjoyed having a field of knowledge in which she could be expert – as well as the open air, the sights and smells, the physicality of horses, the shared language of fellow enthusiasts, and the ceremonies of the race track. 'She has a certain earthiness,' says a close horse-world friend. 'She is very interested in stable management – and happiest with the minutiae of the feed, the quality of wood chipping and so forth.'[43] Her approach has been like that of a distinguished and obsessive art collector. She is also, of course, the owner of many great paintings: but she takes a far deeper interest in her horses, and knows much more about them. 'If she sees a horse out of her window, she knows instinctively if it has got three shoes or four,' says Sir John Miller, former Keeper of the Royal Mews.[44] Others stress her understanding of pedigree, of 'conformations' (including the body and muscles of a horse) and her ability to 'read a race,' by describing precisely what happened during it.[45]

In addition, she is seen as an intuitive equine psychologist. One old retainer contrasts her with her eldest son, a keen but impatient horseman. 'Prince Charles expects a horse to do what he wants,' he says. 'That is something she would never think of doing. Instead, she works out the horse's own intentions, gets the animal attuned to what she wants, then persuades it to enjoy it.'[46] The skill was developed, sometimes painfully, over a long period, for duty as well as pleasure. Not many modern Heads of State are required to ride a horse as part of their functions: until the last few years, the Queen was the exception. A high point of the ceremonial year was Trooping the Colour in June, always an occasion for careful preparation. For weeks beforehand, as well as careful weight-watching to ensure that the right uniform would fit, the Queen would ride four times a week to adapt her muscles for the lengthy event.[47]

THE PROBLEM of Prince Philip's lack of a constitutionally defined role increased in the late 1950s, as the Queen settled into her new duties. When she travelled abroad, he generally accompanied her as the most important member of the supporting cast. In the autumn of 1956, stimulated by a desire for a more rugged kind of adventure than the Court rounds allowed, he embarked on an ambitious world tour of his own. Like the Queen, he did not find it hard to spend long periods away from his children. On this occasion – and it was a point that gave rise to controversy – he planned to spend several months away from his wife as well.

Since they moved in after the Accession, Philip had found the atmosphere at Buckingham Palace a stultifying one. 'When he first arrived on the scene, the courtiers were a bunch of old starched shirts,' comments a friend. 'It was assumed that everything would go on in the old way.'[48] The Queen was more comfortable with the 'old way', having grown up with it, than her husband. In the early months, in which she was still somewhat in awe of people like Sir Alan Lascelles, he fought them. Philip was in awe of nobody: his arrival, an ex-courtier gratefully recalls, was like a 'breath of fresh air.'[49] He had a vision of popular monarchy that derived partly from a personal history of coming from an unpopular one, partly from the social radicalism of Uncle Dickie, and partly from his contact, whilst in the Royal Navy, with other ranks. 'He was always asking "What am I doing here? Why am I here?" says a close friend. He believed, with a healthy and uncomplicated passion, in the need to bring the stuffy Palace closer to the lives of ordinary people.

The Household had regarded Philip warily from before his marriage, and nothing happened after the Accession to alter that view. The central problem was simple: the Prince had opinions, generally of a radical nature, about the organization of the Monarchy, which brought him up against the Court, and about many aspects of British life, which brought him up against the elected politicians – and he wished to follow them through. The requirement of being a caged royal butterfly, however, was that he should not do so – and, to ensure that he kept within bounds, the starched shirts took care to keep official papers from him. There were frequent clashes. He could be intolerant, abrasive, argumentative. 'He always began a sentence with the word "No!" pointing his finger,' says one ex-courtier.

It was intensely frustrating: marrying a future Queen gave him prominence, and the certainty that anything he said would be noted;

but the rules stated that he should bridle his tongue. In fact, he did not always do so. Instead, he developed a recognizable style, which involved a bluff, short-tempered intolerance of pompous people and public humbug, so that the press never knew quite whether to deplore his incivility or applaud his down-to-earth verities. Few doubted his ability and drive. 'If he had worked for somebody like Rupert Murdoch,' says a friend and admirer, 'he would have been a high flyer, because of his searching mind and restless energy. On the other hand, he might have caused too much offence.'[50]

He had an impact, generally on the side of innovation. It was at his initiative, for example, that regular luncheon parties were introduced, taking in a range of people who would not otherwise have been invited to the Palace. It was also his idea to take the annual Maunday Services, traditionally only held at Westminster Abbey, out to all the major cathedrals in the provinces; and it was he who led the way in relaxing some of the stiffer aspects of Palace protocol. He also interpreted the outside world to the Queen, who – sometimes to the intense irritation of courtiers – relied on him for help with speeches and broadcasts that fell within her sphere. But he was never allowed, and he gave up trying, to have anything equivalent to the part in the working of the Monarchy that Prince Albert had enjoyed in the reign of Victoria.

In his public life, Philip combined the application of creative energy to a number of often influential schemes, with fierce prejudices, which he did not take much care to conceal. Journalists were a lifelong bugbear. There were famous occasions when he went too far – giving the press an excuse to hit back. Diplomatic *faux* and gaffes became his trade mark: 'dontopedalogy', the science of putting your put in your mouth, was what he himself labelled it. He had a particular habit, the cause of much angst to politicians and officials, of making an unfortunate remark, and leaving aides to explain to his nonplussed listeners that he was, of course, only joking.

Though many of the stories were embellished, and others were apocryphal, they had the cumulative effect of shaping how he was regarded, and what was expected from him. 'It's a pleasant change to be in a country that isn't ruled by its people,' he was supposed once to have said to the General Stroesser, the dictator of Paraguay.[51] There was the occasion when he visited the ape enclosure at Gibraltar, and spotted some reporters watching him. 'Which ones are the monkeys?' he was supposed to have asked.[52] Another time, he allegedly asked a Brazilian admiral whether he had won the impressive row of medals on his chest on the artificial lake at Brasilia. ('Yes, Sir,' the sailor reputedly replied, 'not by marriage'.)[53] Such tales reflected an essential truth: that Prince Philip's multifarious interests and hobbies – farmer, manager, lecturer on philosophy, industry and the environment, educationalist, patron of charities, pilot, Sunday painter, polo player, driver four-in-hand – never made up for the loss of a professional career, and the lack of a defined role or major responsibility.

He did not like sycophancy. When the journalist Basil Boothroyd wrote a gushing biography of him and sent him the manuscript, he responded with a reference to Proverbs 28,23: 'He that rebuketh a man, afterwards shall find more favour than he that flattereth with the tongue.'[54] However, though he freely rebuked others, he did not brook opposition. His frustration spilled over into his private life, or perhaps from it: gruffness with the world and with his family may have been of a piece.

He was a martinet not just with his children, but with the Queen. Lord Mountbatten used fondly to recount an anecdote that encapsulated one aspect of the marriage, as it appeared to those who knew the couple closely. Once when Philip – who had a notorious record for minor motoring accidents – was driving his wife and uncle to Cowdray Park, accompanied as usual by police cars and outriders, the Queen, worried about the speed at which they were travelling, started to tense herself and draw in breath at critical moments. Eventually her husband turned to her and said, 'If you do that once more I shall put you out of the car.' She stopped. When they got to their destination, Dickie asked her, 'Why didn't you protest? You were quite right, he was going much too fast.' She looked puzzled. 'But you heard what he said,' she replied.

A friend explains how their relationship worked: 'Nothing makes a woman less happy than being able to get away with everything.' 'Prince Philip is tough, which is why she loved him,' says an ex-courtier. Sometimes, he could be brutal. 'He was always liable to say things like "Don't talk such rubbish! You're completely wrong!" –

Those sorts of explosions,' says one of the Queen's closest friends. 'She would clam up and wouldn't fight back. It was very much like that in the first ten or fifteen years of their married life.' Some people would take him on, but most would just give up. 'He used to make everybody slightly uncomfortable. The Queen would try and jolly things back again.' Later, she learnt to resist. 'There were occasional cross words,' says a former aide, who knew them from the 1960s, 'and they were not inhibited by having the courtiers around.' 'I'm not going to come out of my cabin until he is in a better temper,' another recalls her saying, during an incident on *Britannia*. 'I'm going to sit here on my bed until he's better.'[55]

In the end, they achieved a kind of harmony. In the 1950s, however, it was difficult for a man with such a forceful, enterprising personality to accept the constraints and humiliations of his position. In particular, his defeat on the Mountbatten name issue continued to grate: few people appreciated how bitterly, as a displaced person, he felt about it. Three years after the Coronation, therefore, Buckingham Palace was a place from which he needed to take a rest.

The trip lasted from mid-October 1956 to mid-February 1957, and took in New Zealand, Ceylon and the Gambia, with brief visits to Antarctica, the Galapagos and the Falklands. To the surprise of some, Philip did not curtail his tour at the outbreak of hostilities in the Middle East – even though he had to miss out a planned stop in Singapore, because of anti-British riots. It was the duration of the trip, however, and an incident that occurred towards the end of it, that gave rise to a flurry of rumours about a supposed rift in the royal marriage.

The catalyst was the abrupt resignation from the Duke's service of Mike Parker, his old naval friend and now his equerry, which followed news of Parker's separation from his wife. Parker's brisk departure from the royal yacht at Gibraltar, was accompanied by a wave of newspaper comment that echoed the Townsend affair of two years before, and inspired the American press to add a new ingredient. It was the *Baltimore Sun* which furnished the story. The British capital, the *Sun*'s London correspondent proudly revealed, was awash with a rumour that the Duke of Edinburgh was involved with an unnamed woman, whom he was meeting regularly in the apartment of a court photographer.

Other American papers ran with it. 'Report Queen, Duke in Rift Over Party Girl,' they declared. 'Not since the first rumours of a romance between the former King Edward VIII and the then Mrs Simpson have Americans gobbled up the London dispatches so avidly,' reported Alistair Cooke.[56] The story was soon elaborated. It was pointed out that two royal children was not very many; that Philip's apparently last-minute decision to spend ten days in Gibraltar instead of returning to England, was not entirely consistent with the idea of a homesick husband rushing home to see his wife; and that, even when they were both in the United Kingdom, the Queen and her consort were frequently apart, and seemed content that this should be so. The basis for the tale seemed to be the well-established fact of Philip's membership of the mildly louche Thursday Club, an eating and drinking society that included a number of celebrities, and met for what were called 'rip-roaring stag parties' which allegedly were 'not always stag'.[57] 'People wondered', says one former royal aide, 'whether this was an appropriate milieu.' Another, however, who was taken to a Thursday lunch recalls nothing more daring than the telling of tasteless jokes.

What really gave momentum to the rumour of a royal rift was the decision to deny it. According to Parker, Prince Philip was 'very hurt, terribly hurt, very angry' about the press story.[58] Perhaps that was why Commander Colville decided to issue the unwise statement: 'It is quite untrue that there is any rift between the Queen and the Duke.'[59]

'Rift Far-Fetched, Royal Aides Say,' declared the American press, or – more mischievously – 'London Hushes Royal Rift'. In Britain, however, the impact was different. British papers had found, as usual, that getting any information out of the Abominable No Man was like trying to squeeze blood out of a stone. Now, without any explanation, the Commander had suddenly come up with a fulsome response – albeit a negatively fulsome one – for the American press, while continuing to regard British journalists with his usual cold contempt. The moral seemed clear: sticking to the rules got you nowhere. 'Was it assumed that Britain and the Commonwealth were made up of good chaps who would play the game and not mention this tittle-tattle to each other?' asked the *Mirror*.[60]

The effect was to provide British papers with the excuse they needed to give the 'rift' – now the non-rift – a full airing. Though *The Times*, *Telegraph*, *Mail* and *Sketch* remained decorously silent, the *Manchester Guardian*, *Express*, *Herald* and *Mirror* all splashed Colville's denial.[61] The reporting of 'the news that was no news at all'[62] was not, however, the limit of Fleet Street's revenge. The press also retaliated by finding other grounds for attacking the Duke. There might have been no marital rift: that Philip seemed content to be away from home, however, was undeniable. Why had he failed to fly back from Gibraltar, at the earliest opportunity, to see his children? The Royal Family, the *Sunday Pictorial* reminded its readers, 'is loved and envied throughout the world because it *is* a family ... How can you expect youngsters to understand that Daddy is so near yet cannot come home?'[63]

The fracas was not forgotten. Royal stories, once lodged in the cuttings, never are. Reports of the Duke of Edinburgh's friendships with women surfaced from time to time, given plausibility by the Duke's restless character and visible enjoyment of female company.[64] They did not prevent the royal marriage from developing into a strong and supportive one. Few people ever saw them as a close couple, and they did not lead conventionally joint lives. They had separate dining rooms, sitting rooms, bathrooms (' Bobo would come and sit at the end of the Queen's bath and talk to her,' says a friend, 'so it wouldn't have done for her and Prince Philip to have their rooms together.') But friends and advisers had the sense of a relationship which, though there had been difficult periods, worked for both of them; and that they enjoyed being together as much as they often enjoyed travelling and living apart. 'They have enormous regard and respect for each other,' says a former helper of the Queen, 'although his head may occasionally have been turned by a pretty face'.[65]

It was the new Prime Minister who helped to give the 'rift' affair a tidy ending. On 22nd February, the day after Prince Philip's return, Macmillan told Cabinet that he had proposed to the Queen that her husband should be given 'the style and dignity of a Prince of the United Kingdom,' and that she had agreed. In future, the Duke would be known officially, as he was already known familiarly, as 'the Prince

Philip, Duke of Edinburgh,' in recognition of the affection in which the people held him, and of his services to the nation and the Commonwealth, 'culminating in the tour which had just concluded.'[66]

AFTER APPOINTING Macmillan as Prime Minister on 10th January, the Queen returned to Sandringham to complete her holiday. She composed a long and sympathetic letter to Sir Anthony Eden, thanking him for his life of public service, and commiserating over his plight. 'There is no doubt that you took the only possible course after the doctors had given you their verdict,' she wrote, adding, almost tenderly, 'but one can only guess at what it must have cost you to do it.'[67] Eden, greatly moved, wrote back that he had 'looked forward to my weekly audiences knowing that I should receive from Your Majesty a wise and impartial reaction to events, which was quite simply the voice of our land.'[68] Over the next few years, a friendly correspondence developed between the Queen and the broken statesman, in which she treated him with consideration and gentle humour. However, she soon found Macmillan – as pleased as he was surprised to find himself Prime Minister – a more relaxing mentor.

Indeed, the gesture over 'Prince of the United Kingdom' was a symptom of Macmillan's feline understanding of the kinds of things that pleased her. Unlike her husband, the Queen seldom indicated directly what she wanted to happen. 'She has excellent passive judgement,' says a former courtier.[69] She expected others to make suggestions, and then she would react with caution, reserving her most positive responses for ideas that fitted her own needs precisely – as in this case, by giving Philip reassurance in the one area in which he lacked confidence, which was his name.

In some ways, it was a return to the Churchill era of deferential gallantry, except that Macmillan was not yet in his dotage. Where Eden had, in practice, tended to regard the Monarchy as a distraction,[70] Macmillan made the Queen his ally, and also part of his own emotional system – turning his formal subservience to a woman young enough to be his daughter into a kind of chivalrous fantasy. Those who worked closely with the new premier recall that, in female company, he often showed a curious inadequacy – patronizing women or telling them jokes in an awkward effort, as he saw it, to come down to their level. With the captive Queen, however, he had her attention without seeking it. He could also act out the idea, which both seemed to find pleasing, that he was not at her level but below it.

'The Prime Minister is above all the Queen's First Minister,' he wrote later. 'His supreme loyalty is to her.'[71] Throughout his premiership, he behaved towards her as if this constitutional fiction was a fact, treating her opinions as if they mattered to him, and that, indeed, he was just her humble adviser. In his memoirs, he argued that although the effective power of the Monarch had been reduced, 'in many ways the royal influence has grown,' both because of 'the example that the Head of the Royal Family gives to her people,' and the wisdom of the advice she gave to the Prime Minister. Great appointments under the Crown, he insisted, 'must never be a matter for formal approval'. It was true that, with appointments as in policy matters, the Queen had to yield to the advice of her ministers. But she had the absolute right, he observed, 'to know, to criticize, to advise – or, as a great authority has put it, "to advise, to encourage, and to warn"'[72] – a misquotation of Bagehot which is significant, for the Victorian constitutionalist did not accord to the Monarch the right to advise, but only the much weaker 'to be consulted'.[73]

From the beginning, Macmillan took extravagant pleasure in the intimacy of his meetings with the Queen, almost as if they were trysts. 'One of the most agreeable aspects of my job is the weekly audience,' he recorded in his diary, just a month after taking office. 'The Queen is not only very charming, but incredibly well informed.'[74] This became a theme. He was impressed by her knowledge, her intelligence and her insight; he was frequently 'astonished' by her grasp of detail in messages and telegrams. His memoirs are sprinkled with the lengthy and obsequious memoranda he was in the habit of sending her, and with her own friendly and informal replies. He recalled that he particularly enjoyed discussing Church politics and personalities with her, and regaling her with impressions of important meetings. According to aides, he adopted the practice of reading papers to her at such length that on one occasion his private secretary had to restrain him.[75] Nevertheless, she seemed to be happy in his company.

Obviously not all of Macmillan's flamboyant style can be taken at face value. 'He had assumed the mantle of an aristocrat,' says one ex-courtier, recalling the old entertainer coming out of audiences, 'burbling something or other'.[76] The appropriate analogy is not with Melbourne, but with Disraeli: Macmillan's indisputably genuine admiration for his Sovereign was combined with the knowledge that nothing but good could come from it. Like Disraeli, he saw the political value and convenience of identifying popular conservatism with a popular myth of Monarchy that was both inclusive, yet had a flavour of *noblesse oblige* snobbism.

Of all post-war Prime Ministers, Macmillan was the one who paid most attention to the Monarchy's residual rights. 'As soon as he came to power,' according to his official biographer, 'Macmillan determined to do what he could to strengthen the Queen's prerogative.'[77] This was in theory. What it seemed to mean in practice, however, was appropriating the royal aura for his own brand of 'One Nation' conservatism, at a time when class hierarchy was still in place, yet many of the old certainties were breaking down. Though the Coronation remained vivid in the nation's memory, Suez had made manifest Britain's loss of world power, and the 'Elizabethan Age' had become, not a period of widening horizons, but of imperial disintegration. It had also demonstrated that Commonwealth unity was more an emotional than a political idea: in contrast to the Second World War, when the dominions rallied round, Suez had produced the spectacle of a majority of Commonwealth nations voting against Britain in the United Nations. Indeed, Suez was almost immediately seen as a turning point: the moment when even the Conservative Government was forced to acknowledge that the days of Empire were over.[78] In 1959, Iain Macleod was appointed Colonial Secretary to perform the task of winding it up – something which, despite Indian sub-continent independence, would have been unthinkable at the time of the Accession. Macmillan's passionate monarchism, therefore, was part of an elaborate subterfuge – what Tom Nairn has called 'the Glamour of Backwardness'[79] – which disguised the retreat that was taking place, from its perpetrators as well as from the public. The inflexible traditionalism of Buckingham Palace – the presentation parties, the Season, Royal Ascot and the rest – offered a form of reassurance that nothing had changed when, undoubtedly, it had.

It was a climate that invited a serious analysis of the nation's institutions, starting at the top, yet one which produced a rigid fear of what such an assessment might uncover. A wider social critique, affecting literature and the arts, and spreading to politics, had already begun, eventually bearing fruit in the liberalized climate of the 1960s. Some would even call for a reform of Parliament, and the Civil Service. But the Monarchy remained out of bounds.

In private, the upper classes were condescending about royalty, but not on a platform, or in print. Serious criticisms were seldom voiced. The right found the subject embarrassing, like sex. The left regarded it as irrelevant. There were marginal objectors – Irish Republicans, for instance, and British Communists. The Royal Family occasionally offended opponents of field sports, or Protestant sects with a firm view on Sunday observance. Such 'conscientious' opposition tended to confirm the identification of anti-monarchism with extremism and eccentricity. Thus, an article by the journalist Malcolm Muggeridge in the *New Statesman* in September 1955 in which the author declared that there were probably many people who 'feel that another photograph of the Royal Family will be more than they can bear,' was placed in such a category.[80] '. . . [T]he Queen Mother,' he went on, 'Nanny Lightbody, Group Captain Townsend, the whole show is utterly out of hand.' But few people, apart from readers of the *New Statesman*, took any notice.

A different reaction, on the other hand, greeted a special issue of a small circulation journal called *National and English Review,* published in August 1957, which took as its theme 'the future of the Monarchy,' and which attempted, for the first time on such an ambitious scale since the nineteenth century, a serious and uninhibited examination of the institution, by a range of authors expressing a variety of points of view.[81] The article which provoked the sharpest response was by the journal's editor, Lord Altrincham (later John Grigg, the historian and biographer), whose elegant and incisive argument today seems both constitutionally innocuous and entirely consistent with the monarchism it professed.

Scandals are usually explicable in terms of the atmosphere of the time, rather than the substance. Usually there is an explosive cocktail. In the case of the *National Review*, a fissile combination was provided by Altrincham himself, a young, well-connected, and far from eccen-

tric hereditary peer who had stood as a Conservative candidate; by a
rawness on imperial and hence other 'patriotic' issues following Suez;
and by a few biting phrases which expressed what others had begun
to think, but did not dare utter. Altrincham's interest in the topic came
partly from a family connection – his father, who became Governor of
Kenya, had toured the world with the Prince of Wales in 1919. His
views reflected those of a rising generation of democratically-minded
younger Tories who had become unhappy about the aristocratic links
of their party and the Establishment.

There was a warning, which Altrincham and his colleagues failed
to notice. The year was one of post-Suez, fence-mending royal visits
– to Portugal in February, France in April, Denmark in May, and
later to Canada and the United States. Because of the pressing purpose
of these trips, they aroused an unusual degree of political comment,
especially in Commonwealth countries such as India, which had
strongly opposed the Suez attack. In March, a piece appeared in a
Congress Party journal, *Economic Review*, taking violent exception to
a speech made by the Queen in Portugal. In the article, the nationalist
author lambasted the Head of the Commonwealth as 'Queen of all
Britons, now of fading glory, fast descending from the zenith of power
to its nadir, cursed as they are by millions and millions of world
humanity, whom British imperialists have crushed, oppressed and
butchered . . .' and so on.[82] The Queen was not Indian head of state,
and the article was more anti-imperial than anti-monarchist. Nevertheless, it was immediately treated as a personal attack. *The Times*
called it 'vituperative and hysterical,' the acting High Commissioner
made a complaint, and – astonishingly – the Indian Prime Minister,
Nehru, made a public apology.[83]

The immediate aftermath of Suez was a time when reassessment
was urgently needed: hence it was also one of hyper-sensitivity and
even paranoia. Altrincham, however, did not anticipate that the
National Review special issue would arouse unusual interest, and kept
the print-run to its customary level of 4,500.[84] Contributors were
mainly Conservatives. They included Humphry Berkeley, who wrote
about royal finances and argued that the Royal Family gave value for
money; the indefatigable Morrah, who described the role of the
Queen's private secretary; and B. A. Young, a journalist who provided

a trenchant analysis of recent royal public engagements, and concluded that the Queen did not have enough to do. Thirty-odd public appearances in ninety days, Young wrote, was 'hardly a back-breaking programme for a company whose principle *raison d'être* is the making of public appearances'. He also pointed out that 'culture' accounted for only three out of thirty-four engagements listed for the May–July 1957 season and concluded that – as judged by the performances they attended – the Royal Family had deplorably bad taste.[85]

Young's article made a serious point about patronage of the arts. However, its tone had an edge of flippancy. What distinguished the Altrincham article was the breadth of its assault, the care of its construction and – breaking the ultimate taboo – its focus, like that of the unfortunate Delhi *Economic Review*, on the Monarch herself. Hitherto, the acceptable limit of any criticism of the Royal Family was to attack peripheral members, like Prince Philip, or the Court for giving bad advice, while absolving the Queen. Altrincham caused consternation by going right to the heart of the matter, arguing that the guardian of Britain's constitutional monarchy was the Monarch; that there was a sphere of responsibility that was distinctly her own, outside the control of ministers; and that her advisers were, in the end, no more than that – personal appointees whose demeanour ought to reflect her own style and wishes, not the other way round.

Having thus identified his target, the author suggested that the British Monarchy had become complacent and hidebound. It could not regard the fervour aroused by the Coronation four years earlier as permanent or inevitable – least of all in the non-white parts of the Commonwealth. Monarchy, he maintained, required its leading figures to use their imagination by performing the 'seemingly impossible task of being at once ordinary and extraordinary'. Unlike the Whig magnates, who had exalted the institution of the Monarchy while ignoring or despising its occupants, many influential people in contemporary Britain combined a high regard for the Royal Family as individuals with 'a fundamental scepticism as to the viability of the institution'. The danger, he argued, was that the high personal regard might not last. When the Queen had 'lost the bloom of youth,' she would need to assert herself as a distinctive personality who was prepared 'to say things which people can remember, and do things on her own initiative which will make people sit up and take notice'. It was a cause for concern that, as yet, she had failed to do so.

There was also social class. Here Altrincham compared the Queen unfavourably with her grandfather, whom he saw as the ideal constitutional monarch, and shaper of the modern institution. In contrast to the 'classless stamp' of George V, Elizabeth II and her sister still bore 'the debutante stamp,' largely because of their conventional aristocratic education. Picking up Churchill's 'New Elizabethan Age' fantasy, he cruelly inverted it:

> "Crawfie," Sir Henry Marten, the London season, the race-course, the grouse-moor, canasta, and the occasional royal tour – all this would not have been good enough for Elizabeth I! It says much for the Queen that she has not been incapacitated for her job by this woefully inadequate training. She has dignity, a sense of duty, and (so far as one can judge) goodness of heart – all precious assets. But will she have the wisdom to give her children an education very different from her own? Will she, above all, see to it that Prince Charles is equipped with all the knowledge he can absorb without injury to his health, and that he mixes during his formative years with children who will one day be bus drivers, doctors, engineers, etc. – not merely with future land-owners or stockbrokers? These are crucial questions.

But they were not the only ones. There was also the matter of how the present-day Monarchy conducted itself, after several years of the 'New Elizabethan Age' in which the Queen had had opportunities to make changes, yet had failed to take them. Altrincham had a particular scorn for snobbish *accoutrements* of royalty like debutante presentation parties at which, in a kind of apostolic laying on of hands, socially selected young women were initiated as members of the upper class. Such customs were a symptom of the Court's 'social lopsidedness' which, he complained, favoured people of 'the "tweedy" sort' – that is, members of the landed aristocracy, or their relatives, with country house-party assumptions – who were almost exclusively British.

Altrincham's proposal for a 'truly classless and Commonwealth Court' was startling enough. What, however, aroused the excitement of the press and the ire of starched shirts throughout the Establishment was Lord Altrincham's comment on the style and content of royal speeches. This was specific, personal, and – it was widely admitted in private – very close to the mark:

> She will not . . . achieve good results with her present style of speaking, which is frankly "a pain in the neck". Like her mother, she appears to be unable to string even a few sentences together without a written text . . . But even if the Queen feels compelled to read all her speeches, great and small, she must at least improve her method of reading them. With practice, even a prepared speech can be given an air of spontaneity.
>
> The subject-matter must also be endowed with a more authentic quality. George V, for instance, did not write his own speeches, yet they were always in character; they seemed to be a natural emanation from and expression of the man. Not so the present Queen's. The personality conveyed by the utterances which are put into her mouth is that of a priggish schoolgirl, captain of the hockey team, a prefect, and a recent candidate for Confirmation. It is not thus that she will be enabled to come into her own as an independent and distinctive character.[86]

August 1957 was a quiet month for news, and the popular and middle-range newspapers seized on this unusual invective with joy. 'Peer Attacks the Queen' declared the *Daily Express*. The *Mail* added a judgmental adjective: 'Peer's Strange Attack on the Queen'. The Sunday *People* – few of whose readers had ever heard of the *National Review* – devoted several pages to a discussion of the miscreant article, including the reactions of fellow members of the House of Lords, who variously recommended that the young editor should be horse-whipped, hanged, drawn and quartered, or shot.

It was not so much the cheekiness of the attack as the shock of the new: a wicked tweaking of the skirt around the piano leg. Some greeted the article with relief, as an antidote to gush. *Reynold's News* congratulated Altrincham on 'saying out loud what many people are thinking,' and Francis Williams wrote in the *New Statesman* that the author had broken the unassailable Fleet Street law 'that the Queen is not only devoted, hardworking and young – but also a royal paragon of wit, wisdom and grace'.[87] Those who breach unassailable laws, however, have to suffer the consequences, and most conventional journalists gave Altrincham a taste of his own medicine. The *Mail's*

Henry Fairlie denounced him for 'daring to pit his infinitely tiny and temporary mind against the accumulated experience of centuries,' the *Sunday Times* declared that only a coward or a cad would attack somebody who could not answer back, while the normally liberal *Observer* turned 'priggish schoolgirl' around and accused him of 'schoolboyish gaucherie'. 'What a cowardly bully you are!' one woman wrote to him, in a letter he published in the next issue of the *Review*, 'I can well imagine what a beastly specimen you were at your preparatory school – the sort who hit boys smaller and weaker than yourself, no doubt.'[88]

The Archbishop of Canterbury, crowner of the Monarch, denouncer of divorce, identified Altrincham with irreligion, blasphemy and even, implicitly, indecency, by remarking that a young girl at her confirmation had nicer thoughts than he had had in all his years since his.[89] More reflectively, the *Spectator* – owned and edited by Altrincham's friend and political associate Ian Gilmour –- accused him of 'monarcho-mysticism,' of exaggerating the influence of the Monarchy, and seeking, unrealistically, to elevate the Queen to the position of 'a life-force'. Nevertheless, it joined the attack on presentation parties, and acknowledged that the Monarchy leant too heavily on the upper class.[90]

The BBC put the story in the same category as the Philip infidelity rumour by blacking it altogether. However, commercial television and the cinema newsreels gave it full coverage, providing the author with a chance to state his case, which he did with a mild reasonableness that aroused his opponents to greater fury. It was a bad doctrine, he told Robin Day, then of ITN, that the Queen should be immune from criticism: if the Court was wrong on something which was not subject to ministerial responsibility, there was no choice but to criticize the boss, 'because only the "boss" can get rid of the bad servants'.[91]

Such was the public fascination with the phenomenon of the 'Etonian peer' – as the popular press referred to him – that cameras followed him everywhere. When he emerged from Television House in the company of Ludovic Kennedy on 6th August, the newsreel film-makers were waiting for him. So was a Mr B. K. Burbidge, who stepping forward from the crowd, slapped him hard across the face, and shouted 'Take that from the League of Empire Loyalists!' Photographs of the incident appeared in most papers next day, and it was prominently covered by the newsreels. Fining Mr Burbidge twenty shillings for his assault, the Chief Metropolitan Magistrate expressed sympathy for the defendant's motives. 'Ninety-five per cent of the population of this country,' he observed, 'were disgusted and offended by what was written.'[92]

THERE WERE different aspects to the disgust, or – to put it another way – the Altrincham article touched a variety of raw nerves. One concerned accent. It was a time when speech-related distinctions were a touchy subject, splitting the bourgeoisie. The upper middle class regarded it as impolite to talk about them, while lower-class writers singled them out aggressively as a symptom of Britain's moral torpor. By apparently referring to the Queen's diction (a careful reading showed that it did not, but that was how 'priggish schoolgirl' was interpreted), the article drew attention to what everybody knew, but ardent royalists preferred not to think about, that the Queen's version of received pronunciation – what Nairn has since called 'the ultra-distilled by-product of drawing-room, shoot and London club'[93] – placed her in a social group that half the population instinctively voted against at every election.

Such an unnerving reminder was part of what people meant when they described Altrincham's essay as caddish, cowardly and in bad taste. As important, however, was its supposed attack on the British Empire, at a moment, less than a year after Suez, when bewilderment over imperial decline was at its height. The idea that criticizing the Head of State was tantamount to an attack on the imperial and Commonwealth ideal had been behind the sharp British reaction to the criticism of the Queen in the Delhi *Economic Review* in the spring. The notion that it was unpatriotic, and a comfort to Britain's rivals, lay behind the violence of Mr Burbidge, a member of the nostalgic and racist League of Empire Loyalists. 'Due to the scurrilous attack by Lord Altrincham I felt it was up to a decent Briton to show resentment,' Burbidge explained to the sympathetic Chief Metropolitan Magistrate. 'What I feared most was the overseas repercussions and publication in American newspapers. I thought our fortunes were at a low ebb and such things only made them more deplorable.' The

Daily Mirror, 14th August, 1957

Archbishop of Canterbury, in the United States for the World Council of Churches, took much the same view. The peer's article, he declared, had caused much misunderstanding in America, and was especially regrettable in view of the Queen's forthcoming visit.

Privately, though Fisher wrote that he considered Altrincham's use of language 'impudent and disrespectful seeing that he was a private citizen talking about his sovereign,' he did not suggest that the arguments themselves should not have been expressed.[94] At Buckingham Palace itself, opinion – perhaps surprisingly – was similarly mixed. There was a defensiveness about the practicalities ('Did one really want to break the kind of relationship the Queen had with people like the Lord Chamberlain,' says one member of the Household of the period, 'even though they came from a small section of society?')[95] However, some of the younger courtiers relished the opportunity for a debate. 'This is the best thing that has happened in my time,' Martin Charteris told Altrincham, early in the furore.[96] It was also widely reported that Prince Philip – who had fought his own battles against tweediness – agreed with many of the Altrincham arguments.[97]

In one respect, however, Mr Burbidge and the Primate were quite right. It was impossible to contain the incubus within the British Isles, or to prevent it from crossing the Atlantic, and affecting the Queen's reception in the United States. On 12th October, the Monarch began her trip to North America by flying to Ottawa, before travelling south to take part in the State of Virginia's 350th anniversary celebrations. The underlying aim was to resuscitate Anglophilia after the embarrassment of Suez. 'I do hope our visit will be of value between the two countries,' the Queen wrote to Sir Anthony Eden before her departure; '– there does seem to be a much closer feeling between the U.S. and ourselves, especially since the Russian satellite has come to shake everyone about their views on Russian scientific progress!'[98] In the United States, she expressed her surprise to President Eisenhower at the press hysteria over evidence of the Soviet lead in the space race.[99] She was also apprehensive about the media coverage ('. . . [T]he television is the worst of all,' she wrote to Eden '– but I suppose when one gets used to it, it is not so terrible as at first sight').[100] In fact, she need not have worried: the Americans were also keen to restore friendship, and her visit achieved the remarkable feat of pushing Russia off the front pages. There was intense interest when the royal couple visited football games and supermarkets, meeting ordinary citizens – an early form of walkabout which provoked journalists to ask, 'If this can happen in America, why not in Britain?' At Williamsburg, the Queen's advisers caused a happy *frisson* by inserting into her speech a passage about being delighted that Virginia had counties named after every British monarch from Elizabeth I to George III – 'even George III'.[101]

The Queen was full of delight at the impact she felt she was having – a young and energetic hereditary Monarch contrasted by some commentators with the slowed-down American elected one. It was the first chance in her reign to compare the two roles. She felt that the Americans she met, and especially the President, displayed a surprising lack of self-confidence. When she got back, she told a friend that she had found herself having to offer – as if on Britain's behalf – a shoulder to lean on, and that she had been taken aback by the American need to be liked. She was struck by the enormous weight of the President's responsibilities, which would have been a strain for anybody, but particularly for Eisenhower, whose health had recently been poor. It seemed to her a dreadful life, and she was both flattered and a little shocked by the eagerness of the garrulous old man – a figure from her wartime adolescence, now in the middle of his second term – to unburden himself to her.[102]

However, the visit also had a side-show – provided by the still-simmering Altrincham debate. At the height of the tour, the New York *Saturday Evening Post* – intrigued by the British debate – gave its own stir to the pot, publishing an article by Malcolm Muggeridge in which the writer developed some thoughts about the Royal Family which he had first expounded in the *New Statesman* two years previously.[103] Muggeridge's essay was more an ascetic assault on the consumerist age than on the Queen, which was one reason why, in the original *New Statesman* version, it had been ignored. It was judged by the editor of the *Post* to be of particular interest to the more sophisticated American public during a British royal visit because, unlike the Altrincham essay, it attacked the Monarchy as such, implying that it had outlived its usefulness.

Muggeridge focused in particular on the implications of the existing Monarchy for social class. He presented the Head of State as the pinnacle of an hierarchical system. 'The impulses out of which snobbishness is born descend from the Queen,' he wrote, 'at the apex of the social pyramid, right down to the base.' Thus, the 'effulgence of royalty' shone on social distinctions, giving them validity. 'If it is considered,' he concluded, ' – as I consider – that such a social set-up is obsolete and disadvantageous in the contemporary world, then the Monarchy is to that extent undesirable.' He was also direct in his personal barbs. 'Duchesses,' American readers were told, 'find the Queen dowdy, frumpish and banal.'[104]

Muggeridge was editor of *Punch*. He was also a well-known BBC broadcaster – which put the Corporation into a quandary. On the one hand, the BBC was proud of its special relationship with royalty, and was prepared to put up with any amount of humiliation at the hands of Commander Colville in order to maintain it. It was conscious that its own television coverage of royal events, especially the Coronation, had contributed to the cult of monarchy; but it was also aware of a two-way process – the cult had boosted interest in television. On the other hand, the introduction of commercial TV in September 1955, and the rapid success of the new station in capturing audiences, had caused a division of opinion on the Board of Management about the old Reithian principle of obeisance to the Palace in return for a most-favoured-network status. By taking a high moral tone over Altrincham, the BBC had lost out to ITV. In the case of Muggeridge, it risked losing, not just short-term ratings over a topical issue, but a broadcasting star who brought in viewers precisely because of his iconoclastic style.

A debate raged within the Corporation, with deep implications for the future of royal broadcasting. At first, the Board took a tough line. Muggeridge's immediate appearances were cancelled, and a plan to discuss the issue on *Panorama* was dropped on the grounds that it was already receiving a great deal of publicity[105] – an odd inversion of normal news values. When extracts from the *Post* article appeared in Britain, a planned appearance by Lord Altrincham on *Any Questions* was dropped as well, for good measure. Meanwhile, the Director of Current Affairs, Harman Grisewood, wrote to the BBC Director-General that Muggeridge had been over-used, because of a 'journalistic urge' to go for a showy personality, and that there was a worrying tendency within the Corporation to be too topical. Once, he acknowledged, the BBC had not been topical enough. Now, some departments were making topicality the only test. As far as Muggeridge was concerned, there had been more support for taking him off the air than for any other recent action. The only supporter Grisewood actually cited, however, was Harold Nicolson – who privately volunteered his own services as a commentator on Monarchy, instead.[106]

Gradually, the hard line was relaxed. Both Altrincham and Muggeridge were allowed back on to *Any Questions*, on the strict understanding that no discussion of Monarchy would be permitted.[107] Just before Christmas, the Governors decided – too late – to allow Muggeridge to be re-engaged. By now, however, Granada had enticed him away, and he told the BBC that in view of their behaviour, he did not want to work for them.[108]

Grisewood continued to try to lay down guidelines. His impression of outside opinion, he wrote in a further memo, was that while discussion of the monarchical system might sometimes be proper, it was 'not proper or fair to broadcast a discussion, pro or con, about the conduct of the reigning Monarch.'[109] Pandora's boxes, however, once opened, are difficult to shut; and in any case there was little evidence to back up Grisewood's assertion about outside opinion. A survey for the *Daily Mail* showed that although a majority (fifty-two per cent) of people disagreed with Lord Altrincham's criticisms in general terms, on particular points he had public support. Fifty-five per cent wanted the Court circle widened, against only twenty-one per cent who were happy with the status quo; and there was little suggestion that examining the conduct of the reigning Monarch was itself illegitimate.[110]

There was the question of whether the BBC should agree to be the self-censoring voice of the Establishment, excluding debates the Establishment did not like; whether liberty in Britain extended to the right to discuss all aspects of the constitution, including the individuals responsible for them; and whether (as Altrincham put it in a follow-up article) all institutions 'should be part of the community and subject to normal democratic investigation and control'.[111] Finally, there was the question, in the words of the *New Statesman*, of whether the British Monarchy could continue to flourish 'if the royal family is wrapped in tinsel and protected against rational and constructive criticism by a host of self-appointed champions – archbishops, metropolitan magistrates, mayoresses and sycophantic press proprietors'.[112]

Politicians did not seek to answer these questions, or to acknowledge their importance. The Labour leadership strove to keep out of dangerous waters. When the royal couple returned from North America, Macmillan dealt publicly with the issue by denying that there was one. 'In all its long history,' he told the Queen at a dinner of the Royal Society of St George, 'the Crown has never stood so high.' The Society's President, the Duke of Devonshire, backed him up. The success of the Queen's tour, declared the Duke, had given the lie 'to those miserable men who try to cast aspersions on her Majesty'. However, what the Duke of Devonshire called 'the bleatings, or shall I say bleepings, of a publicity-seeking sniffle group,' had one immediate victory. In November 1957, the Lord Chamberlain announced that, after the following year, presentation parties would be abolished and replaced by more garden parties, so that larger numbers of people could be invited to Buckingham Palace.[113]

This was not the only consequence of the Altrincham–Muggeridge storm, whose reverberations continued to be felt for many years to come. It was a moment of cultural shift, occurring – as Christopher Booker later put it – just as 'the old social "myths" which had seemed to hold British society together in a great organic whole' were about to lose their force.[114]

It was the trigger, as Roy Strong has argued, which enabled the image of royalty, frozen for so long, to advance.[115] There was no sudden break in press treatment of royal subjects – the Commander

Colville era had more than a decade to run. However, the tone of discussion slowly became more quizzical. In all talk of royalty, there was now a caveat. Meanwhile, Buckingham Palace came to realize the truth of what Lord Altrincham had said: that it could not take the adulation of the past for granted. In the next phase of the Queen's reign, the Palace began cautiously to consider the seemingly impossible task Altrincham set the Monarchy – how to be ordinary and extraordinary at the same time.

13

I⟨T WAS A NICE IRONY⟩ that the medium which brought the Altrincham–Muggeridge rumpus into the nation's living rooms was also
the one that had over-heated public feeling at the time of the Coronation, and kept it simmering ever since. Yet, in a way, it was not so
ironic: part of the interest taken in what Altrincham called 'the rumpus' was merely royalty prurience in a different form. People were
shocked by the renegade peer; but they were thrilled to be shocked,
and watched more television as a result. It was a bigger irony that the
BBC should have let commercial television make the running during
the affair – precisely because of its own anxiety about ratings, in the
new, complicated battle for the expanding TV audience.

One reason for BBC *hauteur* was that the Corporation was in danger
of losing out whatever it did. If it refused to talk about criticisms of
the Monarchy, and banned broadcasters the Palace did not like, then
the Independent Television Authority would steal its viewers; but if
it failed to refuse, and courted royal disfavour, the Palace might decide,
huffily, to become more even-handed in its favours, and commercial
TV would steal its viewers in any case. Faced with this dilemma, the
BBC preferred to lose viewers the first way, rather than the second:
in the end, it cared more about Establishment approval than about
ratings. Nevertheless, it was worried. In the summer of 1957 it was
particularly nervous because the Queen had just agreed to allow her
Christmas Day broadcast to be televised – and the ITA was hammering
on the door of the Palace, demanding a piece of the action.

The Queen had resisted television on Christmas Day ever since the
Accession. The excuse given was that most of the Commonwealth did
not have TV, while the only other two countries that did, Australia
and Canada, would need a pre-recording, which meant a loss of
spontaneity. The real reason was a mixture of traditionalism and the

Queen's reluctance to allow the strain, and paraphernalia, of television – if it was to be live in the UK – to interrupt her family celebration.[1] However, the refusal obviously could not go on indefinitely. As the majority of people acquired TV sets, ratings for the radio Christmas Day broadcast had dipped embarrassingly. At last, therefore, the Palace decided to accept the inevitable. Discussions began at the beginning of 1957,[2] and in March, Adeane signalled the Queen's agreement – subject to the condition that the programme should not be a televised broadcast as such, but a televised radio broadcast, with the Monarch shown in front of a microphone reading a script.[3] There would be no use of a teleprompter. The reason, staff were informed, was that Her Majesty was 'very averse from artificiality'.[4]

The BBC was delighted once again to be the chosen instrument of royal communication. It had controlled the sound broadcast – over which it still had a monopoly – for a quarter of a century, and was immensely proud of the way in which the Sovereign's annual utterance to the Commonwealth had come to be regarded as a part of the traditions of Monarchy itself. It saw the decision as an honour, and a challenge. Yet there were reasons for disquiet. First, though the BBC was given responsibility for all the arrangements, the existence of independent television, and the intolerable possibility that people might switch over to see if there was anything better on the other side, meant that commercial TV would have to be allowed to show the broadcast simultaneously. Second, the decision to televise the Christmas Day speech indicated a change of heart at the Palace which opened up a range of exciting but also anxiety-making possibilities. Indeed, once the Queen had lost her shyness over the Christmas broadcast, there seemed to be no stopping her. In October 1957 – perhaps in response to the 'rumpus' – Commander Colville told the BBC that 'the Queen herself would not mind if her speech from the throne was televised to her subjects,' and he suggested that a formal request should be made.[5]

The Christmas broadcast with its BBC tradition was one thing. Where, however, an occasion had never been televised before, it was much harder to ward off Independent Television Authority competition. Thus, the unreported background to the banning of Malcolm Muggeridge from BBC programmes and to the high moral tone adopted by Harman Grisewood, was acute concern at the BBC about an approach from the ITA and the Programme Companies to the Corporation suggesting a rota system for the handling of broadcasts involving the Queen on occasions when television camera access was limited. Jacob flatly refused, and turned to Sir Michael Adeane for support. At the end of October – a few days after imposing a judicious ban on Muggeridge – the Director-General spoke urgently to the Queen's private secretary, warning him plaintively that the Palace might in future 'be faced with an awkward choice'.[6] Adeane replied that this was a matter for the Government. The BBC therefore lobbied the Home Secretary, R. A. Butler, arguing strenuously that for such occasions as the Christmas broadcast, coronations, royal weddings and the State Opening of Parliament, 'experienced people in whom the Queen has confidence should conduct the proceedings,' and that such people were not to be found in the commercial companies. A general ruling was needed, because at any moment an event might happen which would bring forward the ITA's claim, with the risk of 'an unseemly wrangle breaking out in public'.[7]

For the time being the BBC retained its pre-eminence. However, November and December 1957 were tense months at Broadcasting House. A few weeks before the first-ever televised Christmas speech, a Corporation official was unwise enough to say in a public handout that the BBC had been charged with the broadcast 'on behalf of the BBC and the ITA' – a Palace-inspired formula, designed to take account of the fact that both channels were showing it.[8] There was an explosion in the Director-General's office. 'There is no question of bringing the ITA into this,' thundered Sir Ian Jacob. 'This is a Corporation broadcast . . . The fact is, as previously stated, that the arrangements for the Queen to be televised while she makes her Christmas broadcast have been made by the BBC.'[9]

As Christmas Day approached, there was concern about making the Queen seem 'natural' – harder with TV than radio. Part of the problem was that the words were supposed to be the Queen's own, but had been written for her. 'The final draft was, in fact, Prince Philip's,' recorded a BBC official. 'I think the very fact that the Queen had nothing to do with the script made our job a tough one, since it is the most difficult thing in the world to give a personal message that is in fact not personal.'[10] But it worked. Perhaps recent debates had something to do with it. Harold Nicolson wrote privately that the Queen came across 'with a vigour unknown in pre-Altrincham days'.[11] The novelty of seeing the Queen performing the annual electronic ritual, instead of just hearing her, united the nation on Christmas afternoon. According to Audience Research, the 3 p.m. broadcast was seen by sixteen and a half million people. It also produced the largest number of press cuttings for any single television broadcast since the Coronation.[12] There was great satisfaction at Broadcasting House – and little inclination to get on the wrong side of Commander Colville by giving air time for criticisms of Buckingham Palace. The importance of retaining the good will of the Palace could not be stressed enough, noted an internal memo a year later, after the number of royal outside broadcasts had increased for the third year running. 'Any clash with the Palace,' it warned, ' is likely to jeopardize our future requests.'[13]

There were also other reasons why critical discussion of the Monarchy rapidly closed down again after 1957. One was the lack of an incentive to take it any further. The Royal Family was not unpopular – far from it – and so there was no political advantage to be gained from pointing out its failings. In the Conservative Party, which had always identified itself particularly strongly with the Monarchy, the episode was regarded with distaste – as Altrincham discovered to his cost when, six years later, he renounced his peerage and tried to find a Tory seat.[14] On the Labour side, though there was sympathy for the Altrincham critique, there was little support for the Muggeridge argument that the Monarchy was the fount of social snobbery. Labour right-wingers were afraid of the electoral repercussions of any attack; left-wingers thought it let capitalism off the hook. The wealth and privilege of the Royal Family were seen as the symptoms, rather than the cause, of class distinction and social inequality, while its surviving political influence was considered unimportant; at the same time, there was a rueful acknowledgement that working-class people enjoyed royal occasions. There was also, of course, the Empire. However, when socialists became aroused by imperial or colonial questions, they made the Americans and Tories their targets, not the Queen. Thus serious MPs across the spectrum – like serious journalists, historians and novelists – tended to view the subject as infantile politics, and to regard the institution itself as both unavoidable and, for most practical purposes, irrelevant.

Nevertheless, the rapid changes both in British society and in Britain's position in relation to its present and former colonies made some re-evaluation of the place of the Monarchy inevitable. Indeed, though there was nothing that could be called a 'debate', there was an emerging difference of emphasis between those (like Altrincham) who took a loyal but down-to-earth view of monarchical functions, and others who wished to retain a reverential, semi-religious approach. The most significant theorist of the second kind was Dermot Morrah, who had been accorded by a grateful Palace the splendid and ancient, if empty, title of 'Arundel Herald Extraordinary', and whose study *The Queen at Work*, published in 1958, provided the best available justification for what Altrincham (as John Grigg) later called the 'British Shintoism' of the 1950s. Morrah's ideas are of interest because they both influenced and reflected Court thinking, while showing (from a working journalist's point of view) an appreciation of the perspective of the press; and also because they elaborated the 'family on the throne,' placing it in the forefront of the institution's roles.

Morrah's book raised to a principle the very passivity which Altrincham had criticized: Altrincham had asked that the Queen should actively set an example and offer moral leadership. Morrah, by contrast, maintained that the importance of the Monarch should lie 'not at all in what she does, but entirely in what she is'.[15] Downplaying the Monarchy's discretionary functions, he argued in effect that what mattered was the iconography of royalty, based on its actual private behaviour; and that the Queen's 'being' – as opposed to public doing – involved her exemplary family.

The idea of the Monarchy as the provider of the Commonwealth's ultimate family had existed in a variety of forms since the Commonwealth first came into being. It had been expressed by the first Lord Altrincham, father of the editor of the *National Review*, in a book published during the war, in which the author argued that the Crown had provided part of an axis around which the Commonwealth had developed, and that the 'moral unity' of the British Empire had begun with 'a strong sense of family,' to which common interests and ideals were added.[16] Morrah's theory took this idea a stage further, stressing both the passive symbolism, and the private behaviour, of the Monarch herself.

This was a different version of the 'family on the throne' from Bagehot's. The Victorian pragmatist had been careful to distinguish between an idealized family, and a family whose behaviour was ideal. 'We have come to believe that the domestic virtues are as likely to be found on thrones as they are eminent when there,' he wrote in *The English Constitution*. But he had then gone on to point out that Queen Victoria – who was the basis for such a belief – was the exception, and likely to remain so, because the temptations available to royalty made them less likely to be privately good than other people, rather than more.[17]

Morrah ignored this warning. Where Bagehot had counted Victoria's private standards as a bonus, without basing his case for Monarchy on them, Morrah not only extolled the virtues of Elizabeth and her kin, but made them the linchpin of his thesis. The Monarchy in the late 1950s, he maintained, was not so much a system of government as a way of life, an aspect of being 'British' which was still the uniting quality of the peoples of the Commonwealth. The Queen was the 'universal representative' of the Commonwealth, whose position drew its strength from the magical roots of kingship, and met a universal human need. She was the expression of an idea. But – because she was flesh-and-blood rather than an abstraction – she was able, as she travelled around the countries that recognized her Sovereignty or Headship, to translate the idea into real human relationships that were essentially familial ones. 'Wherever she goes,' he reflected, in a passage that made her sound more divine than human, 'that spot is momentarily the centre of the Commonwealth, and the soldiers on parade, the artisan at his bench, the nurse by the bedside and the patient under her care are enabled to feel themselves exalted by the recognition of their place in a world-wide family and a vast design.'

This physical (as well as charismatic) approach to the 'family' concept required a corporeal family to sustain it that was more than just a grandiloquent metaphor. If the Queen was to be 'the embodiment of ordinary English life,' which enabled her to encapsulate Britishness in her relationships with the 'world-wide family' of the Commonwealth, then the public had to be able to see her enjoying a normal home. Hence, in Morrah's view – and here was an interesting logical step – the apparently intrusive interest of ordinary people in the Queen's world was not only justified; it was desirable and necessary. Manifestations of that interest might sometimes be trivial or crude. However,

> they proceed from the healthy fact that the people have before their eyes a picture not of an ideal woman but of an ideal group, so that families in mansion or cottage may be strengthened in their inward relationships by the feeling – it scarcely amounts to a thought – that the little social unit they are maintaining is one that also lives and develops in its most admirable form in Windsor Castle or Buckingham Palace.[18]

Thus the Monarchy – 'necessarily popular,' 'always changing and always the same,' and 'always up-to-date' – had nothing to fear from having a little light shed on it. If the Queen was at the apex of the Commonwealth family in a personal sense, and people related to her in a familial way, then it followed that they should want to see for themselves her everyday family life in action.

Morrah's ideas – a mixture of the mundane and the metaphysical – were developed by others, and became part of the understanding of Monarchy in the early post-imperial phase: the retreat from the notion of a remote 'Emperor' into that of a bourgeois *mater familias*. In 1959, for example, Dorothy Laird – author of a descriptive account of monarchical functions – picked up the Morrah doctrine and followed it to its logical conclusion. Not only were family virtues a visible feature of the existing institution, they were central to its working. Indeed, she wrote:

> so much has a happy family life become identified with the British Royal Family that it is doubtful whether a sovereign could sustain his sovereignty were this shattered . . . We think, 'There is Queen Elizabeth II: she has everything in the world, but look, she chooses to spend her leisure much as we would, with her husband, her children, her dogs, in her own home, in the country'. We are reinforced in our belief that the greatest and basic happiness lies in such a simple and sound way of life.[19]

Unlike Morrah, Laird saw a danger in such a psychology, as well as a benefit. The trouble with it, she shrewdly pointed out, was its unrealistic pursuit of perfection. Others saw the parallel risk of public enthusiasm getting out of hand. In 1962, Anthony Sampson likened popular interest in royalty to a balloon that had broken from its moorings. Some courtiers he reported, had 'an uneasy feeling that the balloon might eventually hit something and explode'.[20] Nobody, however, now questioned the idea, central to Morrah's thesis, that the private mores and family life of royalty – as distinct from the public virtues of the old, Bagehotian, symbolic family – were vital to the cameo.

'FAMILY LIFE' is not static. It requires events to mark its changing seasons. Early in 1959, the Queen became pregnant. The announcement was delayed until after a six-week royal tour of Canada, in June and July, in the course of which the Queen and President Eisenhower opened the St. Lawrence Seaway. The Queen and Duke also spent a day in Chicago. They saw the Eisenhowers again in August, when the President and his wife came to Europe and visited Balmoral, joining a house party largely composed, as usual, of members of the landed aristocracy – the Earl of Westmorland, the Porchesters, the Salisburys, as well as the royal Gloucesters. The Americans did not seem to mind. Ike, who had known Elizabeth since the war, and wrote to her and her husband as 'old friends,'[21] mixed convivially in this tribal company. One topic of conversation was food. The President expressed his appreciation of some home-made drop scones served at tea, and the British Monarch promised to send him the recipe. There was also shooting. When the Eisenhowers left Balmoral for Chequers, they took with them some royal grouse for consumption at the Prime Minister's dinner table, during the next leg of their itinerary.

The announcement that the Queen would have another child took the world by surprise. '. . . [M]y wife and I are delighted about the coming "event",' wrote Eisenhower in his thank-you letter, 'as is everyone in your Kingdom.'[22] British delight was coupled, however, with speculative curiosity. Charles was eleven, Anne nearly ten. Was it an example of royal carelessness? It became a talking-point. 'What a sentimental hold the monarchy has over the middle classes!' Harold

Nicolson noted. 'All the solicitors, actors and publishers at the Garrick were beaming, as if they had acquired some personal gift.'[23] Royal engagements for the autumn were cancelled, giving Macmillan – so it was argued – a wider choice of election dates. He chose well. The poll was held on 8th October. In a remarkable recovery of fortune since the Suez fiasco, the Government increased its majority to a hundred. It was the third Tory victory in a row, and the easy identity of Monarchy, Conservative Party, and traditional social hierarchy continued undisturbed.

The prospect of a new addition reawakened the dormant, but not forgotten, issue of the family name. This time, a helpful cleric took the Duke's side. In December, the Bishop of Carlisle declared that he did not like to think of any child 'born in wedlock' being deprived of the right and privilege of every other legitimate child. Since, he reminded his congregation, the Windsor dynasty unquestionably 'set a noble example of family life,' he hoped that the Queen would secure her future child's birthright.[24] His hope was fulfilled.

It was the Queen who brought up the issue which had so rankled with her husband, and sought to remedy the damage done in 1952. Macmillan was in South Africa. At the end of January, Butler – as acting premier – sent him a telegram in Johannesburg saying that at his first audience the Queen had raised the 1952 decision, and that she had 'absolutely set her heart' on a change.[25] Lord Mountbatten, ever interested in such matters, may possibly have had something to do with it. According to Lord Beaverbrook, the Queen, while wishing to retain 'Windsor' in the name, 'sympathizes with her husband's feelings and more particularly with the overtures of his uncle'.[26] At the beginning of the reign it had been Uncle Dickie's 'overtures' that had bothered Churchill. Macmillan, however, bore none of the fierce prejudices of his predecessor-but-one against the Mountbatten clan, and wanted – once again – to please the Queen. A double-barrelled name for future generations was therefore proposed.

Macmillan recorded at the time that the Lord Chancellor came up with a formula according to which 'the name of the House, Family and Dynasty [is] to be Windsor – the name of any "de-royalized" grandson, etc., of the Queen and Prince Philip to be "Mountbatten-Windsor".'[27] The matter was soberly discussed in Cabinet, with

Butler presiding. According to the Lord Chancellor, the Queen had no desire to alter the name of 'the Royal House and Family of Windsor,' but she indicated that 'those members of the Royal Family who would have to use a surname,' because they were no longer entitled to be called Prince or Princess, should use the new one.[28] Some ministers expressed misgivings, but eventually agreed that the Queen's wishes on this occasion, unlike eight years earlier, should be respected. Afterwards Butler conveyed the news to the heavily pregnant Monarch, who asked him to tell the Prime Minister that 'it took a great load off her mind'.[29]

While the Queen awaited her confinement, she amused herself by writing to the President of the United States. 'Seeing a picture of you in today's newspaper standing in front of a barbecue grilling quail,' she wrote, one Head of State to another, 'reminded me that I had never sent you the recipe of the drop scones which I promised you at Balmoral. I now hasten to do so, and I do hope you will find them successful.' She enclosed a list of ingredients (4 teacups flour, 4 tablespoons caster sugar, 2 teacups milk etc.). These quantities were for sixteen people. However, when there were fewer, 'I generally put in less flour and milk, and use the other ingredients as stated'. Golden syrup or treacle, she explained helpfully, were a good alternative to sugar. 'I think the mixture needs a great deal of beating while making,' she concluded, 'and shouldn't stand about too long before cooking.'[30] 'I hope we may soon use it,' Eisenhower replied politely. 'You will understand my rather woeful ignorance of culinary practices when I tell you that I did not recognize the term "caster" as a type of sugar. But when I called the British Embassy for help, the problem was promptly solved for me.'[31]

A fortnight later two thousand people – a perceptible shrinkage since the birth of Anne – gathered outside the Palace railings to see the announcement of the birth of a boy, the first child born in a 'family on the throne' since Princess Beatrice in 1857. It was called Andrew, happily combining the name of Scotland's patron saint and of the baby's paternal grandfather. 'Our rejoicing is personal,' said the Archbishop of Canterbury. An anonymous leader in The Times, which may well have been written by the Arundel Herald Extraordinary, expressed the hope that the Queen might enjoy many happy hours among her children, disturbed as little as possible by public curiosity, 'which cannot be rebuked because it expresses spontaneous sympathy'.[32] It was widely agreed that the family of the universal representative was now more representative than ever, with members at every stage of life.

The Archbishop had another reason for personal rejoicing. The birth was shortly preceded by the announcement of the engagement of Princess Margaret to Antony Armstrong-Jones, a photographer employed by the Royal Family for official portraits. 'I hope she will not take to religion in a big way and become a frustrated maiden princess,' Noël Coward wrote at the time of the Townsend break-up. 'I also hope that they had the sense to hop into bed a couple of times at least, but this I doubt.'[33] The sense that the Princess had been hard done by over Townsend helped to remove any possible objection to the proposed match. A few years earlier, the idea of a young man living by his abilities, who was neither aristocratic nor royal, marrying the reigning Monarch's sister, would have caused consternation. Now it was greeted with guilty relief, not least by ministers who – in a benign and conciliatory mood – ruled that in future it would only be necessary to tell Cabinet in advance of the proposed marriage of 'a person close in succession to the Throne,' to whom the Royal Marriage Act applied, and that 'Ministerial advice would not have to be sought'.[34]

Royalty seemed to have a penchant for society photographers. Armstrong-Jones was by no means the first of his profession to gain social access to the Windsor circle: Cecil Beaton, a favourite since the war, and Henry Nahun (Baron), a friend of Prince Philip, and fellow member of the Thursday Club, had preceded him. Part of the explanation may have lain in a shared interest in the visual image. Few kinds of pictures were more powerful, or more sought after, than those of royalty, as royalty was itself aware: and the shots taken by a Beaton, Baron or Armstrong-Jones, like those of Lisa Sheridan in the 1930s and 1940s, defined the Royal Family and the Monarchy for the whole world. It was also true that society photographers fell into the tiny category of non-upper-crust people who, for professional reasons, mingled easily and eagerly in titled circles. Unlike Philip, Armstrong-Jones was not just technically a commoner, but actually one, with no folk memory of a royal identity; unlike Townsend, he had no knowledge of the royal way of life. Even so, the social leap took place within a restricted sphere. Armstrong-Jones might not be aristocratic: but he had been to Eton and his mother's second husband was an earl.

Some expressed doubts. The journalist Jocelyn Stevens, a school friend of Armstrong-Jones, recalled trying to warn him off.[35] There were bad omens, which suggested a marriage on the rebound. The couple became engaged in the month of Peter Townsend's second marriage. Princess Margaret is herself reported to have said that she decided to marry on the day, in October, when she learnt of Townsend's intentions.[36] Most people, however, saw the engagement as a hopeful one, and approved of the intelligent and tactful fiancé. In contrast to Philip at an equivalent stage, he was liked by other members of the Royal Family. Indeed – and it was a sign of the more democratic times – there were many who counted his commoner status an advantage, while his professional and creative skills were an answer to criticisms that the Court was out of touch, or had little contact with the arts.

The wedding took place in Westminster Abbey in May – the first such event since the marriage of Elizabeth and Philip and the Coronation. The atmosphere was incomparably different. The 1947 wedding had celebrated the end of the war, the Coronation, the end of austerity and the survival of the Empire. Princess Margaret's wedding, by contrast, took place against a background of unprecedented affluence, at a time when the Empire was rapidly ceasing to exist.

The Archbishop of Canterbury married them. Unlike the day of the Coronation, the sun shone. 'The morning was brilliant,' observed Coward, who attended the service, 'and the crowds lining the streets looked like endless, vivid herbaceous borders.'[37] The carnival atmosphere, the huge throng, the cries of 'We Want Margaret!' were part of a newly established tradition, which helped to ensure that all future royal weddings would be big national events – fixing in the public mind, ever more firmly, the idea of nuptials and matrimony as a centre point of the royal fable.

* * *

'ALL BUT a few cynics,' wrote Bagehot, 'like to see a pretty novel touching for a moment the dry scenes of the grave world.'[38] Margaret, with her beauty, romance and broken heart provided the ingredients of a pretty novel. However, not only did Bagehot's idea of a family on the throne as a convenient simplification for the ignorant masses, differ from Morrah's universal, Commonwealth family, with its semi-mystical overtones. Bagehot's 'grave world' was not the same as the one contemplated by guardians of the Constitution nearly a century later. Bagehot wrote of nation, rather than of Empire, which did not exist in its twentieth-century form, and which he did not mention in the context of the Monarchy. By contrast, Morrah was post-imperial and nostalgic. The idea, first of the Monarchy as a binding cord and then as a psychic force, helping to maintain Commonwealth unity, had been produced by the fear that the Empire and Commonwealth might fall apart. It is thus scarcely surprising to find the theory in its most florid form just as the Empire entered the phase of terminal disintegration; and that it should have been propagated at a time when the value of the Commonwealth itself was being brought into question.

At the beginning of the reign, it had been possible to imagine the Empire going on much as before, minus the Indian sub-continent, and with the Commonwealth itself as an association of nations held together by close ties of politics, economics and sentiment. By 1960, however, two developments had put this hopeful vision under strain. One was the accelerated process of colonial divestment, not anticipated in 1952, and the creation of new states which became, according to the Nehru formula, Commonwealth republics. The other was the alternative magnetic force and alarming rivalry of the Common Market, established by the Treaty of Rome in 1957.

Britain did not take part in the new, ambitious trading group – partly because of the ideology, and the shackles, of the Common-wealth. However, the rapid expansion of European economies soon changed the minds of many people, including that of the Prime Minis-ter. A debate developed that was to cause more dissension, and split-ting of parties, than any other since the Second World War. Initially, most leaders were hesitant or hostile. It took much to overcome the Commonwealth-mindedness of many politicians, and of public opinion. At first, however, the biggest obstacle to British participation in the Common Market was not domestic opposition, but President de Gaulle, architect of the newly established French Fifth Republic, who was suspicious that Britain's Commonwealth and American links would make her a half-hearted member.

Early in 1960, the French President was invited to London for a state visit, in the hope of winning him over. The three-day trip took place in April, with a maximum of splendour. Not only the Queen, but Prince Philip and other members of the Royal Family were paraded for the ceremonial welcome, involving a procession to Buckingham Palace with an escort of household cavalry and landaus. Later, there was a State Dinner at the Palace which Macmillan believed (and hoped) 'gave considerable pleasure to the French'.[39] On the third day there was a Gala Performance at Covent Garden, with a 'fantasy of flowers' – 25,000 pink carnations in a design by Cecil Beaton, who was rewarded with the *Legion d'Honneur* – decorating the Royal Opera House, in a re-creation of the gala night of 1903 in honour of President Loubet.[40] President de Gaulle acknowledged the ovation he received from the audience with a wave of both arms, and returned to the Elysée apparently impressed. In his memoirs, he wrote warmly of his reception in London, noting with pride and satisfaction how, as he and the Queen drove side by side in her open carriage, 'the Sovereign went out of her way to encourage with gestures and smiles the enthusiasm of the crowd massed along the route'. He was delighted by the fireworks display that followed the banquet, and by the number of people who assembled to cheer the two Heads of State as they appeared on the balcony to watch it. He noted, with gratification, that the entire Royal Family attended a dinner he gave at the French Embassy.

He also formed a favourable impression of the British Monarch. He came to realize, he wrote, 'that she was well-informed about everything, that her judgements, on people and events, were as clear cut as they were thoughtful, that no one was more preoccupied by the cares and problems of our storm-tossed age'. She even, with appropriate humility, asked him what he thought her role ought to be. The French President treated the remark as more than a pleasantry. 'In that station to which God has called you, be who you are, Madam,' he told her; 'that is to say the person in relation to whom, by virtue of the principle of legitimacy, everything in your kingdom is ordered, in whom your people perceive its own nationhood, and by whose presence and dignity the national unity is upheld.'[41] He was not, however, persuaded that Britain was ready to join the Common Market.

Nothing increased the desire of pro-Marketeers, and especially the Prime Minister, to join the European club more than the awareness that, if an application were made, Britain might be refused entry. For several months after the President's inconclusive visit, the British Government strove to make its intended bid more acceptable. Part of that effort was directed at the Commonwealth.

'The wind of change is blowing through the Continent,' Macmillan had told the Joint Assembly of the Union Parliament in Cape Town on 3rd February, 'and whether we like it or not, this growth of national consciousness is a political fact.'[42] The Commonwealth, in Asia as well as Africa, was changing by the month. Ghana and Malaya gained independence in 1957, Nigeria did so in 1960, and other colonies were following in their path. South Africa, opposed to the trend, responded by tightening its apartheid laws: the following year it left the Commonwealth and became a republic.

Two problems thus faced Commonwealth Prime Ministers when they met in London in May, in the wake of the de Gaulle visit: Britain's European bid, and the discordant note provided by South Africa. Neither was solved. However, new Commonwealth countries seemed more anxious, not less, to strengthen ties with the United Kingdom, and one outcome was a set of formal invitations to the Queen, which she was encouraged to accept, to visit the Indian sub-continent.[43]

The Queen and Duke embarked on a five-week tour of the region at the beginning of 1961. It included Nepal as well as India and Pakistan, with stops in Cyprus and Iran *en route*, and Italy on the way back. The visit to Iran was at the instigation of Lord Mountbatten, who had recently visited Tehran, and who passed on a personal invitation from the Shah.[44] As India and Pakistan were now both republics, the British Government arranged the itinerary.[45] The Queen was invited to India as Queen of the United Kingdom, not as Head of the Commonwealth – on the grounds that the latter would have implied the continued existence of her authority over the country. Only a dozen years after the trauma of Indian partition, there were fears about how the cousin and nephew of the last Viceroy might be received. They were unnecessary. Half a million people welcomed the Queen in the streets of Delhi. However, the difficulties of being a 'universal representative,' in terms of shared values throughout a heterogeneous Commonwealth – as well as the impossibility of keeping world-wide media coverage within the old, reverential, tram-lines – were underlined during a tiger hunt which had been organized for the royal couple by the Maharajah of Jaipur in the Sawai Madhopur game reserve.

It was the kind of event, with echoes of Sagana Lodge and Treetops, that the Queen and Duke enjoyed. The British Sovereign – dressed in linen slacks and bush jacket, with a head-scarf and sunglasses, and suitably equipped with cameras – did not carry a rifle. However, it was no mere sight-seeing trip. On the second day, the Royal Treasurer, Rear-Admiral Bonham Carter, shot a tiger; while the Duke – photographed by his wife from a separate *machan* ten yards away – shot a tigress. The Duke's beast measured an impressive 8 feet 9 inches from head to tail. Together with its fellow victim, it was skinned and cured, ready to be taken home as a trophy at the end of the visit. The Sawai Madhopur shoot was followed by other big game expeditions, producing a bag that included a crocodile and a Nepal rhinoceros – whose killing reportedly orphaned a baby calf.

The shooting trips were intended as relaxation, a gesture by one princely family to another. Unfortunately, the Duke's well-aimed bullets ricocheted around the world, blanketing other aspects of the visit. Out of range of non-Indian public opinion the organizers – and their guests – had made a misjudgement. In Britain, there was conservationist and animal welfarist uproar. Calls were made for the Queen to use her personal authority to exclude from future tours such 'elements of unnecessary barbarism,' as the normally ultra-polite *Church Times* put it, and ministers were blamed for not advising against 'something which must revolt the feelings of millions of subjects'. The royal couple's sporting activities did not, however, have such an effect on people in the countries they visited. In India, millions of Commonwealth citizens were unperturbed. The leader of the anti-violence Ahimsak Party went on a week-long fast. But the main press

reaction was one of irritation at the Anglo-Saxon sentimentality of
the critics.

Here was a test case of Morrah's idea of the 'universal representative'
as the centre of the Commonwealth wherever she went. Should she
stay British in India, or adopt Indian practices? Though few Indians
attacked her for the tiger hunt, some expressed disappointment that
she failed to reciprocate President Prasad's gesture of joining her in
a church service, by taking part in a Hindu temple service; and for
failing to give the traditional 'Namaste' salutation of bringing the
palms together in front of the chest. To have shown politeness in this
way, pointed out one resident of Bombay, would have satisfied an
Indian hope 'that the Queen would amply reflect the changing nuances
of the Commonwealth'.[46]

A bigger difficulty than tiger hunts faced the Government over a
proposed royal visit to Ghana, which had recently become a republic,
while remaining in the Commonwealth. The visit had been planned
for 1960, but postponed until November 1961 because of the Queen's
pregnancy. 'I am going to have a baby,' she told Martin Charteris just
before setting out for Canada in June 1959, 'which I have been trying
to do for some time, and that means I won't be able to go to Ghana
as arranged. I want you to go and explain the situation to Nkrumah
and tell him to keep his mouth shut.' Lord Charteris recalls that he
flew to Accra, where he was taken to see the Prime Minister to whom
he passed the confidential message. Nkrumah sat silently for several
minutes. Charteris went through his message again. There was another
silence. Charteris asked whether he had understood. At last the
premier spoke. 'I put all my happiness into this tour,' he said. 'Had
you told me my mother had just died you could not have given me
a greater shock.'[47]

By 1961, the position in Ghana had altered. Kwame Nkrumah had
been the first black African to lead his country to independence.
He was also one of the first to move towards single-party rule and
dictatorship. This unexpected development, swiftly copied elsewhere,
set a new kind of Commonwealth dilemma. How should Britain, and
the Head of the Commonwealth, behave towards the leader of a
member state who denied civil liberties to its citizens, sacked British
officers in the army, and made anti-British speeches? Some MPs called

for the Queen's postponed trip to be cancelled. While the Left and Centre protested about the arbitrary behaviour of the Ghanaian government, the Right worried about protecting the Queen from an African mob. It was a test case. Would the Commonwealth tolerate civil rights abuses in member states, regarding the issue as an internal matter?

Macmillan, however, saw it as a test case in another sense. Was Nkrumah's defiance of Western opinion to become the trigger for the break-up of the 'new' Commonwealth – with implications for the Western alliance? His immediate fear was that the cancellation of the Queen's visit might give Nkrumah, now President of the Ghanaian republic, the excuse to leave the Commonwealth altogether, and align with the Soviet Union instead. He advised the Queen accordingly.

The situation was fluid. Just before the Queen's planned departure, Nkrumah arrested fifty members of the opposition. The atmosphere in Ghana was reported to be dangerously anti-British – and likely to become more so if President Kennedy, who had succeeded Eisenhower in the White House at the beginning of the year, announced the withdrawal of US financial support for the Volta Dam project before or during the visit. Macmillan was now in a quandary. To cancel would look weak, with possibly serious effects. But to go ahead would lay himself open to the accusation of using the Queen as a diplomatic pawn, and of being indifferent to her safety. It was another complication, and one which was to arise again in the future, that the Queen was not just United Kingdom property. On such a matter, the British Prime Minister had to explain his advice in appropriate messages to his Commonwealth counterparts, especially in those countries of which the Queen was Head of State.

This was Macmillan in a different guise: outwardly calm, but inwardly a bundle of nerves. On 3rd November, six days before the Queen was due to depart, he again advised her to go ahead, promising that there was 'no foreseen risk' of violence. This advice, however, was almost immediately put into question by a bomb explosion in Accra. To assuage his critics, he sent the Commonwealth Secretary, Duncan Sandys, to Ghana personally to inspect the Queen's intended route. But domestic opposition had become so fierce that Macmillan was afraid that a Commons vote might either force him to change his advice to the Queen, or resign.

Here was an interesting constitutional scenario, not in the text-books. What if the Prime Minister, confronting the House on the issue, offered his resignation on the grounds of parliamentary pressure? Speculating feverishly – with, as he put it, 'a sort of mock seriousness' – Macmillan calculated that in such circumstances the Queen might refuse the offer, and go to Ghana anyway, flouting Parliament but quite properly taking the advice of the man who was still her Prime Minister. The fantasy of Queen and Prime Minister *versus* Parliament was not put to the test. Much to Macmillan's relief, his opponents passed over the opportunity to corner him, and there was no division. The trip took place without incident, though Adeane sent the Prime Minister twice-daily telegrams to reassure him.

At the heart of this strange little diplomatic whirlpool was the Queen herself – passive as always, yet impatient with the politics, and especially (as Macmillan recorded) 'of the attitude towards her to treat her as a *woman*, and a film star or mascot . . .' She was eager to work for the Commonwealth, in which she believed. 'If she were pressed too hard,' he wrote, in a curious passage which seems to reveal how much the to-ing and fro-ing had irritated her, 'and if Government and people here are determined to restrict her activities (including taking reasonably acceptable risks) I think she might be tempted to throw in her hand. She does not enjoy "society". She likes her horses. But she loves her duty and means to be a Queen and not a puppet.'

Macmillan described the week of the visit as 'one of the most trying of my life'.[48] The diary of Harold Evans, his press secretary, suggests that he wasn't exaggerating. 'To and from the Grocers Hall in the car he talked almost solely about the Queen,' Evans noted on 18th November. ' "What a splendid girl she is." She had been indignant at the audience just before we left at the idea of having the trip cancelled. The House of Commons, she thought, should not show lack of moral fibre in this way. She took very seriously her Commonwealth responsi-bilities, said the P.M., and rightly so for the responsibilities of the UK Monarchy had so shrunk that if you left it at that you might as well have had a film star.'[49] Evans evidently leaked something of the kind to the press, for a few weeks later journalists reported that she had told Cabinet, 'with some vehemence, that she did not know how she could carry on if they did not allow her to go'.[50]

In Accra the Queen's prepared speech was about the Common-wealth 'family'. A 'wide degree of disagreement and intelligent dis-cussion' was possible, she said, given the recognition 'that the views of other members of the family . . . are . . . genuinely and sincerely held.'[51] Such a speech could still be made, in such a set-up, without a sense of its absurdity. A photograph was taken of her at a state ball in the arms of the Ghanaian President, a picture which – not unhelp-fully – caused outrage in South Africa, now out of the Commonwealth, where the nationalist *Die Oosterlig* complained of 'the honoured head of the once mighty British Empire dancing with black natives of pagan Africa.'[52] The Ghanaian press hailed her as 'the greatest socialist monarch in the world'.[53]

On November 23rd, the Queen made a brief state visit to Liberia, before sailing to Sierra Leone, arriving on the 25th. She gave her own vivid account of the Ghanaian and Liberian trips in a letter to Lord Porchester, written on *Britannia* on November 24th, as the royal party left Monrovia – revealing a keen interest in African politics, a clear understanding of the motivations of political leaders, and a longing, in this strange setting, for English autumnal sights and smells. She wrote wistfully of horse auctions, of the opening of the shooting season, the end of ploughing, leaves falling off trees, and news of her mother's racing triumphs. She also described how the Ghana trip had seemed a success, but had also been a strain. Much of it had been spent in the company of Nkrumah – an experience which gave her a disturbing insight into the tortuous workings of the Ghanaian leader's mind. She was surprised by how muddled his views on the world seemed to be, and how naïve and vainglorious were his ambitions for himself and his country. She was struck, too, by his short-term perspective: she observed that he refused to look beyond his own lifetime.

After this, Monrovia had offered light relief. Everything in the Lib-erian capital had felt like a carbon copy of the United States, except that it was organized with cheerful inefficiency. She was amused that Mrs Tubman, wife of the veteran President, had a female ADC dressed in uniform. There were jokes in the British royal party, she reported to Porchey, that her own ladies-in-waiting should follow suit.[54]

Macmillan believed the visit had been a political triumph, vindicating his decision not to cancel it. Later, he claimed that it was directly responsible for Kennedy's decision in December to support the Volta Dam project – which was partly a result of the American President's 'chivalrous recognition' of the Queen's courage. Whether that was true or not, it was a rare example of the physical involvement of the Queen in an international political tangle; and it had provided a glimpse of a cool Monarch, and a Prime Minister in a flap. It was also a rare example of an instruction to the Monarch which, in the opinion of some, put her physically at risk. 'She must sign her own death-warrant if the two Houses unanimously send it up to her,' Bagehot had laconically observed.[55] Macmillan wrote of the 'terrible responsibility' of giving advice to travel, which, constitutionally, she was obliged to take.[56] In fact, the responsibility was made less terrible by her evident willingness to go, and impatience over impediments. Indeed, she had been obeying another Bagehotian injunction: for the decision to send her was effectively a joint one, and the clearest example of her exercise of 'the right to be consulted, the right to encourage, the right to warn,' of her reign so far. Significantly, it was on a matter of Commonwealth importance.

'THE MONARCHY in Britain is established and safe,' observed a *New Statesman* critic at the time of the Margaret wedding; 'indeed, the age of mass-communication has brought it a degree of popularity which would have seemed inconceivable even to the Victoria of the Jubilee. But for this reason, it cannot afford to make mistakes.'[57] The wedding had been an uncomplicated affair – a happy echo of the Coronation, but without the same earnestness, a festival more than a sacrament, which seemed to show that the public-royal relationship was in good repair. However, the pageantry was losing much of its former meaning. Despite the world-wide audience, the elaborate ceremonials had become harder to justify, except in terms of an ill-defined – and, in the case of a royal wedding, largely non-existent – national tradition.

In the past, the processions had been 'imperial'. Empire and Commonwealth, however, were not the same. Indeed, as Professor

Mansergh has put it, the two notions 'represented incompatible and antithetical concepts'[58] – as the contrasting politics and ideas of old dominions and new Commonwealth republics had begun to show. The Margaret wedding coincided with the Commonwealth conference – yet it scarcely represented the Royal Family's relationship with the Commonwealth as it had become. A yawning gap was opening up between the Commonwealth as it was still supposed to be, and the reality – something that the Prime Minister's 'trying week' over the Queen's visit to Ghana made apparent. Macmillan had been concerned to keep Ghana as part of an association seen as the successor to the British Empire. The myth of such an association remained powerful. It was still possible to believe, as the cultural critic Martin Green had recently claimed in *A Mirror for Anglo-Saxons*, that the combined resources of Britain and the Commonwealth – old and new – provided 'a potentiality far greater than Russia's or the USA's'.[59]

What was the role of the Queen to be, as far as countries like Ghana were concerned? In 1958 Morrah had tried to cope with the problem of African self-assertion in relation to the Monarchy by proposing the Queen as the bearer of a post-colonial 'white man's burden,' who could remind semi-savage peoples of British political values. Differentiating between the dominions and the new republics, he argued that whereas in the former, the Queen stood 'as a symbol and pattern of a way of life' first developed in Britain and taken overseas, in the latter, especially in Africa, she was a reminder of the British heritage. To the African continent, he maintained, the British Empire

brought contact with an admittedly higher civilization than any that was native to the soil. Advancement in civilization was therefore synonymous with the adoption of an increasing measure of the British way of life, including generally the Christian religion which is the source of its ideals. That is to say, the African communities . . . have aspired to take the colour of British civilization even while working to release themselves from British political control. Their tendency is to become, so to speak, agnatic members of the family of which the Queen is head, and they can without difficulty receive her as the symbol of their internal cohesion . . . To each independent nation, and indeed to each dependent colony, she can be and is a symbol of unity, of the ideas common to all of the British allegiance concerning justice, tolerance, liberty, the love of peace, the fundamental decencies of family life.[60]

It was an almost risible idea – or would have been, but for Morrah's habit, in what he wrote, of replicating attitudes current in the Palace – and it showed how convoluted the theory had become in the face of the changing reality. Thus the problem in the 1960s was how to reconcile the 'unity' myth, which had been expressed at the time of the Accession, when the same writer had spoken of the Crown as 'the mysterious link, indeed I may say the magic link' uniting the 'strongly interwoven' Commonwealth – with the reality of growing diversity.[61]

Not everybody was as backward-looking as Morrah. Although the whole decolonization process was beset with wishful thinking, some people were certainly more prescient: including writers who, themselves, had a Commonwealth perspective. For example, Percy Black, a sharp Canadian critic of the Monarchy, had caused irritation at the time of the Coronation by suggesting that the Queen needed the Commonwealth more than the other way round.[62] Others had since developed the point. In 1956, Professor F. Underhill, also Canadian by birth, observed that while it was almost useless to protest against the sentiment currently surrounding the Monarchy, he could not help feeling that if all the dominions suddenly became republics, the Commonwealth would go on just as before. What held it together, he suggested, was the presence of common interests and ideals. If these disappeared, or were replaced by conflict, 'the symbolism of the Monarchy would soon turn out to be a very weak bond of union'. The danger facing the British Monarchy was that its loyal supporters would try 'to puff it up to a much greater importance than it can possibly maintain,' and that 'old' Commonwealth loyalty to the Crown would alienate new members – creating, not unity, but the opposite.[63] A similar point was made in the same year by the Commonwealth and constitutional expert C. J. Hughes, who accurately predicted that the republic-within-the-Commonwealth idea, pioneered by India, would be adopted by most non-European new member states. 'Monarchy, at any rate, is no longer an essential part of the Commonwealth,' he wrote, in an article published a year before the Altrincham critique.

'The Commonwealth no longer stands or falls with the Monarchy'.[64]

Thus Morrah – and Buckingham Palace, if Morrah accurately reflected its views – had little excuse. Yet the proposition that 'the Monarchy needed the Commonwealth more than the other way round' could be stated more generously: the Monarchy with its imperial memory, keenly sought a Commonwealth role, partly to justify itself, but also because it had taken its supra-national role seriously, and – in a way that was never quite understood by politicians – it continued to relate to distant communities which showed their loyalty in ways that did not necessarily come to the attention of Whitehall.

Here was a point on which Altrincham and the Palace were at one. Where Muggeridge regarded the whole monarchical enterprise with puritanical scorn, Altrincham passionately believed that the Monarchy had a part to play in the Commonwealth which, so far from becoming less important, ought to be extended. '. . . I am more concerned with the Queen's new and revolutionary function as Head of the Common-wealth', he wrote early in 1958, 'than with her traditional function as a national sovereign'.[65] Unlike Morrah, however, he wished to abandon the notion of the Queen as a symbol of 'Britishness'. In a speech to the Commonwealth Correspondents' Association in January of the same year, he proposed that 'British Commonwealth' – a term still commonly used, though formally dropped as long ago as 1949 – was a misnomer. He also suggested that what had been a largely non-British association should be defined not by reference to a single nation, but by common ideals such as the extirpation of racialism, a belief in liberal democracy, the pursuit of peace, and the redistribution of wealth from richer to poorer nations. At the end of George V's reign, Sir Charles Petrie had foreseen that the Monarch would become ever more mobile, travelling from one part of the Empire and Common-wealth to another, in an effort to hold it together.[66] Altrincham went a daring step further. He suggested that the Queen should cease to be a resident of the United Kingdom and a mere tourist abroad, and should show her dedication to the world community by varying her country of residence. Her children would benefit from the experience of living abroad, and growing up as 'true Commonwealth citizens'.[67]

It might even be beneficial, he suggested on another occasion, if they contracted inter-racial marriages.[68]

The Queen did not adopt his suggestions – although later, starting with Prince Charles at Geelong, her children received part of their education in Commonwealth countries. When the question of the Queen residing for two months of the year in the 'old' Commonwealth countries in rotation was raised in the press a few years later, the Palace protested her Britishness. 'As you know Her Majesty never shirks a duty,' Adeane wrote to No. 10. '. . . All the same everyone, except a nomad, needs a Home, and the Queen is no exception.'[69] Yet she did not take the Commonwealth for granted. On the contrary, more even than her father and grandfather, she increasingly saw it as her special sphere. As Macmillan observed, the Commonwealth offered opportunities for a monarchical role, carved out for herself, that the United Kingdom could not provide. 'I suppose that, between us, my husband and I have seen more of the Commonwealth than almost any people alive,' she said when opening the new Commonwealth Institute building in Holland Park in 1962.[70] Familiarity with Commonwealth political leaders who (although sometimes for sinister reasons) often lasted longer than British ones, also helped to encourage her developing and committed interest, and to give the Palace a Commonwealth perspective that was separate from that of the British governments which advised it.

14

'PUBLIC CRITICISM of the person of the Queen is unheard,' wrote Patrick O'Donnell in the *Observer* just before the tenth anniversary of the Accession, 'and in private it is usually a signal of a consciously daring arrogance. Virtually no one in public life comes out and declares himself a republican and it is doubtful that any political career would at present survive such a declaration.'[1] Yet if criticism – which briefly appeared in the late 1950s – slid from view in the next decade, there was a significant change in the tone of the praise.

The Queen fulfilled her role impeccably, avoided spontaneous gestures or remarks (in contrast to her sometimes pilloried husband), gave away little of what she actually thought and offered no hostages to fortune. She remained popular, admired, fêted wherever she went. Nearly half the population watched or listened to the Christmas Day broadcast in 1961, even though – to the despair of the BBC – it had ceased to be delivered live.[2] Nevertheless, excitement about the Monarchy, and about the Monarch, had quietened. There was no longer the glamour, the 'star quality *in excelsis*', which had been associated with the British Empire's Indian summer, and the Queen's youth. Instead, there seemed to be a settled quality about the not quite middle-aged Sovereign and her family – Philip with his outdoor and conservationist interests, Charles at Cheam and then at Gordonstoun, Anne and her ponies, the grandmotherly Queen Elizabeth, the fashionable Snowdons, the unfashionable Gloucesters and Kents leading respectable, mainly rural, lives. The approach of the press had become less awe-struck, and the content focused more on everyday gossip.

With Charles away at school, and impossible to protect from photographers around the clock, the opportunities for illicit pictures increased. The Palace tried to treat intrusions as a distracting nuisance – wasps at a summer picnic – but the relationship was becoming more complicated. The Royal Family was not, in fact, averse to being in the newspapers, provided the publicity was favourable; and even the misanthropic Commander Colville had an uneasy awareness of royalty's dependence on the papers it found most irritating. On one occasion, Prince Philip – whose spats with the popular press had become legendary – was goaded into calling the *Daily Express* a 'bloody awful newspaper'.[3] But it was papers like the *Express* which conveyed the image and idea of the Monarchy to a world-wide audience, and generated the enormous crowds that greeted the Queen in every city from Chicago to Bombay. Thus the attitude of the Palace contained an ambivalence – classically expressed in a letter from Colville to newspaper editors after the Queen and Prince Philip had refused to allow facilities for the press on sports day at Cheam, shortly after Charles entered the school in 1957. Charles's parents, explained the royal press secretary, were 'most anxious to strike a reasonable balance between the very natural desire of people to know how the Duke of Cornwall is growing up, on the one hand, and their own wish that he should be treated as nearly as possible as an ordinary boy'.[4] Such a balance, however, had become impossible – as Jonathan Dimbleby's account of the Prince's early life reveals.

The serious papers meanwhile paid less and less attention to royalty. In the liberal and leftish press, a post-Altrincham inverted snobbery on the subject was reflected in a condescending tone. The *Guardian* called the Queen dull, with insufficient interest in intellectual, cultural or social affairs.[5] Others affected a protective loyalism, condemning what one writer called the 'monstrous and gushing sentimentality'[6] of their downmarket rivals. The excuse or explanation given by editors for the paucity and brevity of their royal reports, was that the Monarchy offered little hard news: the very aspect which enabled it to escape criticism. Indeed, at the end of the Queen's first decade on the Throne, it could be claimed that, on none of the important matters facing the nation, had she ever publicly expressed, or even hinted at, an opinion. The Sovereign's adherence to the requirement of strict political neutrality became the more remarkable in the 1960s, when it was put to its sorest test over an issue that struck at the heart of the Monarchy's identity. The debate over the Common Market, and Britain's relations with it, became a matter of intimate concern to the

Crown after the political decision was made in July 1961 to seek entry. Although the Government denied it, few doubted that a successful bid to join the European Six would be a turning point for the Commonwealth, not only ending preferential trading arrangements, but destroying the idea of a Brito-centric, mutually supportive, world-wide bloc. The implications divided both Right and Left. Right-wing anti-marketeers were concerned about the 'old' Commonwealth, left-wing ones about the new.

Part of the preparatory diplomacy involved the United States, whose 'special relationship' with Britain was one of the reasons for de Gaulle's suspicion. Macmillan was keen to carry American support, as a prelude to calming French fears. In June 1961, President Kennedy visited Britain to talk to the Prime Minister, and dined at Buckingham Palace with the woman who, as a little girl, had once been required to make polite conversation with his father. The contact with the Kennedys was strengthened in March 1962, when the Queen invited Jackie, who was on a private visit to London, to lunch at the Palace.[7] In May 1962, Macmillan paid a return visit – prompting the Queen to write a friendly Head-of-State letter to the White House. 'I have seen my Prime Minister who has just returned from his visit to the United States and Canada,' she began, 'and he has told me how much he enjoyed being there, and particularly how much he valued this chance to talk personally with you at this present difficult stage in the affairs of the West.' The letter went on in similar vein, pointing, perhaps too obviously, to Macmillan's guiding hand. Nevertheless, its characteristic Windsor style – a blend of the hostess, the headmistress, the woman of affairs and the well-brought-up schoolgirl who knew how to write polite letters to order – suggest a royal participation in the drafting:

> It is a great comfort to me to know that you and he are so close, and that you have confidence in each other's judgement and advice; I am sure that these meetings and this personal trust and understanding are of the greatest importance to both our peoples. I was also glad to hear from Mr Macmillan that my Ambassador and his wife are getting on so well, and that you are finding them useful. David [Ormsby-Gore] is, as you know, very highly thought of here, and so it is excellent news that he

and Cissie are making their mark in Washington.   It was a great pleasure to meet Mrs Kennedy again when she came here to lunch in March at the end of her strenuous tour. I hope her Pakistan horse will be a success – please tell her that mine became very excited by jumping with the children's ponies in the holidays, so I hope hers will be calmer! During the C.E.N.T.O. meeting last month, I had the chance of a very enjoyable and interesting talk with Mr Rusk when the Foreign Ministers dined with us. My husband who is now in Canada is going to have the pleasure of visiting the World Fair in Seattle in June, and then a week later will be in New York for a dinner engagement. I envy him the chance of being in the United States again – we have had two such happy visits there.
Your sincere Friend
Elizabeth R.[8]

Macmillan's biggest headache, however, was not the United States but the Commonwealth countries themselves. At the September 1962 Commonwealth Conference – after heads of government had expressed their anger and concern privately to the Queen – Macmillan tried publicly to persuade them that entry would 'not be incompatible with the Commonwealth; the two associations being complementary'. Most were sceptical. So, perhaps, was the association's Head. Before the Conference, the Queen expressed herself 'worried about Commonwealth feeling' to Macmillan in his weekly audience.[9]

The constitutional position, in view of her divided status, was complex. What if Britain decided to go in, and the Commonwealth governments advised the Queen that they wanted it to stay out? What happened to the concept of the 'Crown' which provided the framework for government and law in those countries of which the Queen was Head of State? Technically, no problem arose. Unlike the Monarch, the 'Crown' was an abstraction, which could be everywhere simultaneously, and also in incompatible situations. It could even, as one writer pointed out, be both at war and not at war – as happened in 1939 when there was a short gap between the ending of British and Canadian ultimatums against Germany. Indeed, in view of the wide variety of uses to which the concept was put throughout the territories in which it was employed, it made more sense to talk of the Crown wearing the Monarch, rather than the other way round.[10]

Such contradictions, though entertaining to lawyers, were bewildering to the Commonwealth public. It was a unified concept of the 'Crown,' and of citizens as equal 'subjects' throughout its dominions, that seemed to give point to its symbolism. The Common Market proposal involved the acceptance by one Commonwealth state, Britain, of an external authority beyond the Crown, and an authority, moreover, which would be accorded increasing power. In addition, there were questions of national identity and loyalty – especially if Europe, including Britain, developed a common foreign policy. Thus, while joining Europe could reasonably be presented as in Britain's self-interest, it took a Houdini to argue that there was much benefit for the Commonwealth, and that it would not tear apart Britain's traditional relationships with countries of which the Queen was Head of State, or took an interest in, as Head of the Commonwealth.

Macmillan attempted to be Houdini. He told the Queen that such anxieties were 'a combination of Little Englandism and Jingoism,' and that he was asking his Conservative colleagues 'to turn their minds from the old Imperialism which no longer has its old power, to a new concept of Britain's ability to influence the world'.[11] Yet he was forced to apologize to the Queen for the embarrassment the quarrel in the Commonwealth had caused her, and to admit, in a letter on 21st September 1962, that the Common Market problem and its Commonwealth impact had 'raised difficulties which I would have wished during my Premiership to have spared Your Majesty'.[12]

In January 1963, the problem was postponed for the time being when President de Gaulle gave a firm 'Non' to the British application. However, the spell had been broken. Notice had been served to the Commonwealth of Britain's ambitions, and member states looked for an alternative destiny, forging non-British links and alliances, as the Queen began to discover for herself. A two-month royal tour of Australasia and the Pacific was planned to start at the end of January. 'It will be interesting to see their progress since 1954,' the Queen wrote to Eden, now the Earl of Avon, thanking him for the gift of a copy of his memoirs.[13] The trip replicated the triumphant tour that had followed the Coronation – except that it turned out to be less triumphant. Crowds were warm and respectful, but notably smaller. In both Australia and New Zealand, the affection was qualified by a circumspect attitude towards Britain, because of the European bid.

On the British side, there were no illusions. There was also an appreciation that one requirement, if the Common Market countries were to be convinced of the United Kingdom's European-ness, was to treat the Commonwealth roughly. When the Queen returned, she made a Government-crafted speech at the Guildhall, in which she referred to the divergent economic interests of Britain and the antipodean dominions, and called for 'hard realism' on both sides.[14]

In the meantime, the political climate had been changing at home. The Common Market bid had been partly an attempt to get the Tories out of a trough. Opinion polls showed a commanding Labour lead, and there had been unexpected by-election losses. Many blamed the Prime Minister himself for the Government's difficulties, and there was increasing talk of his retirement. In June 1962, Macmillan spoke gloomily to the Queen about giving up his administration. 'Does Uncle Harold seriously contemplate the fall of the Government,' wondered his press secretary, 'or his own fall?'[15] The answer turned out to be neither. On 13th July, the premier took the nation, and his party, by surprise when he summarily dismissed a third of the Cabinet – a purge which kept the Monarch busy for much of the day, offering a shoulder for unexpectedly sacked ministers and a hand to unexpectedly appointed ones, who were invited to enter Buckingham Palace by a different door.

The aim was to sharpen the image of the Government, and protect himself. However, the anger and bewilderment caused by the 'Night of the Long Knives' did him more harm than good, and the pressure for a change at the top quickly returned. The Prime Minister was looking and sounding older; the Conservatives, many commentators agreed, had been in power too long; Labour was winning by-elections, and at the beginning of 1963, following the death of Hugh Gaitskell, it acquired an energetic, media-conscious new Leader in Harold Wilson. Finally, the accident-prone Tory administration was hit by a major scandal, following the resignation in June of the War Minister, John Profumo, who admitted lying to the House of Commons about his relationship with a model, Christine Keeler.

The resulting epidemic of allegations and rumours – symptomatic of a wider malaise – seemed for a time to engulf the Government. At one point the Prime Minister privately expressed a fear that 'the tide of gossip might even lap around the Royal Family'. It lapped – and then receded. There was a tangential association between Stephen Ward, the Society osteopath and portrait painter who was Christine Keeler's procurer, and Prince Philip. Old newspaper cuttings were dug up, and the popular press ventured one or two ambiguous head-lines. The rumour-mongers were no respecters of rank. However, royalty was never seriously affected. The main sufferers were the Conservative hierarchy and the Prime Minister. Macmillan was made to seem inept, and out of touch with the world's harsh realities. Privately, he wrote to the Queen, apologizing in emotional terms, 'for the undoubted injury done by the terrible behaviour of one of Your Majesty's Secretaries of State.' He admitted that he himself had 'no idea of the strange underworld' in which Profumo and others had been entrapped, and hinted that behind the accusations that followed the minister's resignation lay 'something in the nature of a plot to destroy the established system'. The Queen sent a consoling reply, in which she remarked on how hard it was for people with high standards to suspect others of lacking them.[16]

'It *is* a moral issue,' wrote Sir William Haley,[17] who believed the same about Princess Margaret's proposed marriage to Group Captain Townsend. For many people in journalism and the arts, however, it was also an opportunity to change the rules of engagement. A 'satire boom' which had helped to sound the alarm over Profumo, widened the range of social criticism. The ground shifted, from accusations of orgiastic parties and the like, to indictments of upper class hypocrisy and corruption of a more general kind. In a sense, Macmillan was right about an anarchistic plot: but the plot was as much against the Sir William Haleys and other starched shirts of the Establishment as against the Tory Government.

The Monarchy was not immune from the assault. How could it be? The satirists' weapon was laughter, its enemy was pomposity – and there was much about the Court, and those who took obsequious delight in its performances, that was both pompous and funny. In March 1963, before the Profumo scandal broke, Ned Sherrin's path-breaking programme *That Was The Week That Was* signalled the changing mood at the BBC with a sketch entitled 'The Queen's Departure,' which lampooned Richard Dimbleby's commentary when the Queen set out for Australia a few weeks earlier. In the sketch, the royal barge sank while the band of the Royal Marines played the National Anthem. 'Perhaps the lip readers among you can make out what Prince Philip, Duke of Edinburgh, is saying to the captain of the barge as she sinks,' ran the offending commentary. 'It looks to me like "Oh dear, I think we are sinking". And now the Queen, smiling radiantly, is swimming for her life. Her Majesty is wearing a silk ensemble in canary yellow.' The attack was levelled at the inane sycophancy of BBC coverage of royal events, rather than the Monarchy. Though the sketch was shown on television, it ran into difficulty elsewhere. After the management of a revue at the Duchess Theatre dropped it in anticipation of a Lord Chamberlain ban – simply because it mentioned royalty[18] – it became a *cause célèbre*, and part of an ultimately successful campaign against theatre censorship. In Australia, where the Lord Chamberlain's writ did not run, an actress imitated the Queen in a Brisbane revue called 'Roll Yer Socks Up'. 'Why shouldn't the Queen be part of a stage joke in this day and age?' asked the director, in reply to protests.[19]

It had become hard to find an answer, especially as Princess Margaret and Lord Snowdon's show business and design world friends were precisely the kind of people who, in permissive, trend-setting London, were engaged in demolishing the ramparts the Lord Chamberlain defended. In the Labour Party, nose-thumbing at the trappings of royalty became one way for middle-class MPs, and activists, to demonstrate their egalitarian disdain for the aristocratic and capitalist embrace. Addressing Oxford undergraduates in May, a young MP called Anthony Wedgwood Benn suggested some 'mood-changing measures' for an incoming government – 'like no dinner jackets for Labour ministers at Buckingham Palace, mini-cars for official business and postage stamps without the Queen's head on them'. The last suggestion, he recorded, got the biggest cheer.[20]

On the far left, the fragments of the early 1960s anti-nuclear campaign coalesced round new targets. At the beginning of July 1963, King Paul and Queen Frederika of Greece came to Britain for a state visit which was intended to strengthen the relationship of the two NATO countries. The invitation was unwise. The Greek Government had been under attack because of its civil rights record, and Queen Frederika became a particular target because of her history of right-wing involvements that went back to the pre-war Hitler Youth. There was also the complicating embarrassment of Prince Philip's close relationship to the Greek royal family.

The visit, hosted by the Queen, was accompanied by demonstrations and arrests. When the two royal couples attended the performance of a play at the Aldwych Theatre, jeers and catcalls greeted the arrival of both, indiscriminately. The Government expressed outrage. 'The Queen of England was booed tonight and I am furious,' declared the Home Secretary, Henry Brooke. 'I never thought such a thing would happen in Britain. I don't know when it last happened in this country that a reigning monarch was given such treatment.'[21] Harold Wilson, the new Labour leader, turned down an invitation to the state banquet at Buckingham Palace, in order to show his party's disapproval of the visit.

Brooke was making a political point, against the Left. But he was right that such a demonstration would never have occurred ten years before. What had happened in the meantime? If part of the explanation was that society had lost some of its rigidities, another part was that the Monarchy had ceased to be revered in the same way. The two factors were perhaps connected. A journalist observed that the nation had grown 'bored with the splendidly dull, utterly safe and inoffensive middling image of the monarchy'.[22] One symptom was a decline in the practice of playing the national anthem at public gatherings. The reason was not so much that the management of cinemas and theatres found it inconvenient. It was more that it had turned into a farce. Where before there had been the solemn ritual of the audience standing in patriotic silence during a playing of the first verse of 'God Save the Queen', there was now an unseemly scramble for the exit, until the first bar sounded – at which point convention still required everybody to freeze, grandmother's-footsteps fashion, wherever they stood.

There was also the beginning of an alarming slippage in the ratings of the Queen's Christmas broadcast – which had previously been almost obligatory listening or watching in many households. There were complaints about its blandness, and even about the Queen's delivery. 'We can never rely on the Queen doing a much better performance than this Christmas,' noted a BBC official glumly, after criticisms of the 1962 programme. 'The text is however all important, and needs to be less stilted and more human if the Queen is to continue to command full attention as the years roll by.'[23] The Palace blamed the box. 'Television has ruined the whole thing,' Adeane complained, when the Prime Minister's press secretary raised it. 'The Queen is gay and relaxed beforehand, but in front of the cameras she freezes and there is nothing to be done about it.'[24] In August, in a desperate bid to inject some more life into the broadcast, the Prime Minister was persuaded to use his weekly audience to request a change in the method and content. 'He failed,' Kenneth Adam, Director of Television, recorded bleakly, after the audience had taken place.[25] In 1964, the BBC – which had fought so hard for a televised broadcast – informed the Palace that, in the interests of spontaneity, it would gladly give up television altogether and return to sound only, provided it were live.[26]

It did not add to the Monarchy's lustre, either, that it had for so long been associated with one government, and one Prime Minister. Since attacks on the Conservatives were frequently linked to criticism of a social and political 'Establishment,' of which the Monarchy was seen as part, it was difficult to avoid being linked in the public mind. In the autumn of 1963, the Queen had reason to hope for a respite from such difficulties. In September – just before she accompanied Princess Anne to her new school, Benenden – the Palace announced that she was pregnant with her fourth child. A respite, however, was not granted. Unhappiness over the Government's performance did not lessen during the summer, and calls for a change at the top became more and more insistent. Early in October, the Prime Minister at last yielded to the combined pressures of politics, ill health and sheer exhaustion – precipitating a chain of events which brought the Monarchy more directly into controversy than ever before in the reign.

HAROLD MACMILLAN not only wrote about the Queen in more unctuous terms than any other Prime Minister. He also declared, with greatest frequency, his over-riding concern to preserve the royal prerogative. It is odd, therefore, that he should have been the premier who, by the manner of his departure, did most to undermine it. However, he was not solely to blame. The Queen's Palace advisers, and the Queen herself, shared responsibility for the most confused and unsatisfactory transfer of office of the post-war period. Macmillan's motives were complex, and devious. The Queen's were, as ever, simple. She wished to avoid constitutional impropriety, and believed that this was to be achieved by taking the line of least resistance. As a result she allowed herself to be turned, disastrously for what remained of royal discretionary power, into a political pawn. Indeed, the whole sorry tale of the selection of Macmillan's successor shows how easily, if the Monarch forgoes her or his role as arbiter, it can be exploited by unscrupulous politicians, with agendas of their own.

Like most Prime Ministerial resignations, Macmillan's was both long-awaited and precipitate. In August 1963, Sir Michael Adeane refused an invitation to a shooting party in Scotland that would also include the Prime Minister, on the grounds that to join it might give rise to speculation that would embarrass the Queen.[27] Speculation grew in any case. In the early autumn Macmillan decided provisionally to resign – if indeed such a 'decision' can be said to have been made if it is merely provisional. He dithered about the date, expressing his despondency about the prospects if he carried on, but remaining open to persuasion to do so. On 20th September, he told the Queen in his audience that he intended, in three weeks' time, to announce that his resignation would take place early in the New Year. The Queen expressed appropriate consternation. It was clear to Macmillan, however, that her main reason for concern was a fear of repeating the difficulty she had found herself in six years earlier. They discussed at length the possibilities. 'She feels the great importance of maintaining the prerogative intact,' noted Macmillan. 'After all if she asked someone to form a government and he failed, what harm was done! Of course, it would be much better for everything to go smoothly, as in my case.'[28]

It was a curious conversation, which Macmillan later took as an invitation to handle the business of 'maintaining the prerogative intact' himself. For the moment, however, he carried on. On 25th September, he wrote to Sir Michael Adeane, confirming what he had said to the

Queen. Five days later, he told Lord Swinton the same over lunch at Chequers, saying that he thought Lord Hailsham the best available successor.[29] But he did not make any statement to Cabinet, and he soon began to have second thoughts. On 6th October, he observed – as premiers sometimes do at such a juncture – 'a growing wave of emotion in my favour,' and on the 7th he seems to have determined to stay on and fight the general election.[30] That night he was taken ill. Next day, in serious pain, he was admitted to King Edward VII's Hospital for Officers for an immediate prostate operation.

On October 9th – sick, and with surgery pending – he wrote to the Queen telling her that his immediate resignation was necessary. He also summoned Lord Home, the Foreign Secretary, to his bedside, and gave him a written message which he asked to be read to the Conservative Party Conference, then assembling at Blackpool. This declared that, despite his wish and previous intention to remain in office until the election, his incapacitation had made this impossible. He also used the opportunity provided by the Foreign Secretary's visit to press that Home might allow his own name to be considered for the leadership. Failing that, he suggested the Lord President, Lord Hailsham – almost anybody, in fact, apart from the obvious, most popular choice. Indeed, one thing soon became apparent – the Prime Minister's driving, abiding intent, despite illness, weakness, fear and pain, that the one person who should not succeed him was the deputy premier, R. A. Butler.

With Macmillan still technically in office, the next three days were taken up by the operation – and by the impact of the message dispatched, in Lord Home's pocket, to Blackpool. Perhaps if he had not sent the letter, or if the Foreign Secretary had not read it, Macmillan might once again have had second thoughts about resigning, after he had recovered his strength. Home did not wait to discover. Obeying the Prime Minister's instructions, he read out the letter to the 4,000 delegates, and unleashed a whirlwind.

If the Queen had been worried about the implications for the prerogative, she had reason. The choice was now certain to be a complex one. In 1955 there had been one candidate for the succession, in 1957 two. In 1963, there were at least five. In addition to Butler, who was once again regarded as the front-runner, Lord Hailsham

quickly announced his candidature, declaring his willingness to relinquish his peerage under the newly enacted Peerages Act (incidentally
demonstrating how little store, even in the Conservative Party, was
now set by an hereditary title). The names of Reginald Maudling, the
Chancellor of the Exchequer, Iain Macleod, Leader of the House, and
Edward Heath, the Lord Privy Seal, were also mentioned. In addition
there was the distant possibility, raised by a few, of Lord Home.

Here was a new situation facing the Monarch, for which the stage
had been unwittingly set in 1957. After Eden's departure, the relative
simplicity of the choice between Butler and Macmillan, the alacrity
of the sounding-out, and the belief still held in the Conservative
Party that the Queen should be the arbiter, had stood in the way of
campaigning for particular candidates. Yet the very smoothness of the
operation had given rise to suspicion and controversy. This time, the
party and the Sovereign had the worst of both worlds. Because of
what had happened in 1957, it was assumed that the Queen would
conduct a wide-ranging consultation, involving different levels of the
party. Forewarned, MPs began to lobby for their favoured nominees,
yet no agreed mechanism, formal or informal, existed for carrying
such a process out.

As the Tory Party Conference ended chaotically, the Prime Minister,
'in a still half-drugged coma,' considered the precedents for advising
the Monarch himself.[31] Gladstone had not been consulted by Queen
Victoria in 1894, he reflected, and Bonar Law had indicated that he
was too ill to advise George V in 1923. Macmillan was also ill, which
might have excused him – though not as ill as Bonar Law. Why did
he not follow Bonar Law's example? The answer, he later insisted,
was that 'it was intimated to us quite clearly from the Palace that the
Queen would ask for advice . . . It therefore became necessary for me
to do what I would have preferred to avoid – become involved in the
situation as it was after my colleagues had returned from the Blackpool
Conference.'[32]

The 'intimations' are puzzling, to say the least. There had been no
such intimations in 1955, when they had not been needed, and in 1957
the Queen had accepted Eden's suggestion that not he, but a senior
colleague, should carry out consultations. When the succession had
been discussed at No. 10 two years before Macmillan's resignation,

Timothy Bligh, the Prime Minister's principal private secretary, had remarked that 'if Uncle Harold fell down the stairs tomorrow . . . the understanding is that the Queen would consult the Lord Chancellor and the Chancellor of the Exchequer'.[33] The Chancellor of the Exchequer was himself a candidate. However, there was no obvious reason why the principle of consulting Cabinet ministers directly, other than the outgoing premier, should be abandoned; and the idea of 'intimating' on such a matter to an elderly man hours after major surgery was, to put it mildly, bizarre. Macmillan, however, was still Prime Minister. When Salisbury and Kilmuir conducted their 'Wab or Hawold' interviews on 9th January 1957, Eden had ceased to be so. The explanation for the Palace 'intimations' seems partly to lie in this difference of status: as long as Macmillan remained premier, he was technically the person the Monarch was required to turn to, on any major topic.

Once re-involved by the Palace, Macmillan – though 'still woozy from the anaesthetic,' according to Alistair Horne, his biographer[34] – moved with impressive speed. On 14th October, the Foreign Secretary's campaign was effectively launched by an inspired story in *The Times*. The same day, the Prime Minister had revived enough to see the Chief Whip, Sir Martin Redmayne, and the Lord Chancellor, Lord Dilhorne. What the Prime Minister discovered, according to his own later account, was that the Hailsham (about to be Hogg) bandwagon had met resistance; and that a 'draft Home' movement, designed to keep out Butler who was still the favourite to succeed, was gaining strength. That night the sick premier – whose wooziness was fast fading as the plot thickened – recorded that 'the party in the country wants Hogg; the Parliamentary Party wants Maudling or Butler; the Cabinet wants Butler,' and that the position seemed settled.

It was at this point that Macmillan wrote a 'minute of instruction' for a consultation procedure, to be read by Butler as Deputy Prime Minister to Cabinet next day. In it, he instructed (it is important to note that, on such a matter, his colleagues accepted the premier's right to 'instruct') that Lord Dilhorne should sound out the opinions of the Cabinet; Redmayne, all other MPs and ministers, Lord St Aldwyn (Chief Whip in the Lords), the Tory peers, and Lord Poole (joint Party Chairman) opinion in the extra-parliamentary party. 'It was now clear,' maintains Horne, 'that, sick as he was, Macmillan was still going to hold all the strings in his hand until the very last minute, controlling events from his bed in King Edward VII's.'[35]

So here was a novelty within a novelty. Where Churchill had declined to advise the Queen at all, and Eden had advised her about an adviser, Macmillan – on the basis of 'intimations' from the Palace – took it upon himself to be rule-maker, appointer of sounders-out, and final judge of the outcome, a role made possible by the authority over his colleagues and access to the Queen which his continued status as Prime Minister gave him.

On 15th October, Macmillan saw the contenders one by one. Other ministerial interviews followed over the next two days. These allegedly revealed that the largest group of MPs, though not an overall majority, supported Home, but that the constituency parties backed Hailsham against Butler 60–40, with Home a non-runner. In addition, Macmillan was presented with the surprising, and to some implausible, information that ten Cabinet ministers supported Home as their first choice, against nine for Butler, Maudling and Hailsham put together. Some ministers later complained that the soundings were by junior whips, and involved loaded questions.[36] Nevertheless, Macmillan treated the Cabinet statistic presented to him by Lord Dilhorne as decisive, and immediately dictated a memorandum for presentation to the Queen, 'should she ask for my advice'.[37]

This was, of course, tendentious: everybody by now knew that she would ask for it, which had been the reason for the exercise. By 9.30 pm the same night, 17th October, Macmillan's likely advice had been leaked to the press. There followed hurried meetings, including one in Enoch Powell's house, attended by a number of ministers including Maudling and Macleod, to which the Chief Whip was also invited in the almost pathetic hope that he would be impressed by the evidence of dissent, and communicate it both to the Prime Minister and to the Queen.[38]

That night, Buckingham Palace – which had done everything possible to avoid involvement in the fray – became, through its attempt at disengagement, the focus of intense speculation. 'Backbench MPs like Tony Lambton and Charles Mott-Radclyffe were ringing up to express their view that Home or Rab would be disastrous choices,' recalls Sir Edward Ford. 'Meanwhile Michael Adeane was hearing from Macleod and Powell that they wouldn't serve under Home. Our response was "You're the party, choose your undoubted leader and we will inform the Queen".'[39]

The 'Revolt of the Night' had some effect, but in the wrong place. It alerted Macmillan to the need to ward off possible objections to his intended recommendation. As the morning papers splashed the name of Home, the Prime Minister – his wooziness now a thing of the past – tacked on an addendum to his note for the Queen, but without changing the substance of his advice. Then, at last, he sent his formal letter of resignation to the Palace – raising the curtain for the royal part of the drama. The choreography of the next two hours, which had been carefully worked out in advance with Sir Michael Adeane, was constitutionally significant – for on it turned the precise status of anything Macmillan would say to, or give, the Queen in his final audience. On the evening of Tuesday, 15th October, Sir Michael Adeane had spent an hour with Lord Swinton telling him exactly what had been pre-arranged. 'He outlined the proposed drill,' Swinton recorded at the time, 'that when Harold was ready to advise H.M. on his successor, the Queen would visit him in hospital and accept his resignation and receive his advice'. Adeane added that he thought it very important that he himself should not see the Prime Minister, as it would look as if the Palace was intervening.[40] Adeane warned Swinton 'to check and approve all the drill'[41] – three days in advance of putting it into operation. The 'drill' was for Macmillan's letter to leave the hospital at 9.30 a.m., and for the Palace to announce the resignation at 10.30 a.m. In fact, there was a hitch, and Bligh – the Prime Minister's messenger – set out half an hour late. Nevertheless, the Palace announcement was made at 10.30 a.m. as scheduled.[42]

As soon as Macmillan ceased to be Prime Minister, Buckingham Palace wasted no time. Three-quarters of an hour after the announcement, the Queen arrived at the hospital for a half-hour farewell meeting that was to be the most remarkable audience in modern monarchical history – the more extraordinary because, constitutionally, there was no need for it to take place at all.

According to Randolph Churchill's account shortly afterwards, Bligh returned to Macmillan in the hospital after delivering the resignation letter 'with the news that the Queen wished to consult him' and was proposing to come over at 11.15 a.m.[43] The 'news' was scarcely a surprise: it was the meeting the Cabinet, Conservative Party, and nation eagerly awaited. Yet the audience itself occupied a curious constitutional no-man's land – it was not, emphatically, the same as the final audiences given by the Queen to Churchill and Eden, at each of which the outgoing premier had declined to offer 'advice' about a successor. In Macmillan's case, there was a difference between the moment when the audience was arranged – during his premiership, when his advice was binding and his recommendations unlikely to be disobeyed – and when it took place, when he had lost all constitutional authority. At the same time, with no new Prime Minister in office, the aura of the six-year relationship between Sovereign and now ex-premier remained.

The physical conditions of the audience – the enfeebled former Prime Minister before the Monarch, both regnant and pregnant – matched the peculiarity of the constitutional ones. 'Never before in the history of the office of Prime Minister,' as Lord Hailsham wrote later, with forgivable acidity, 'had advice as to his possible successor been tendered to his sovereign from a bed of sickness, based on hearsay evidence prepared for him by others which he apparently had no possible means of verifying.'[44] According to Macmillan's diary entry for 18th October, the Queen came into the hospital board-room, where he had been installed, with a bottle beside him, 'with a firm step, and those brightly shining eyes which are her chief beauty. She seemed deeply moved; so was I'.[45] His doctor, Sir John Richardson, claimed to see tears in the royal eyes[46] – if so, it was unusual. To the patient, she expressed regret at his departure, and then, on cue, asked his opinion about what to do next.

Macmillan gave two accounts of the conversation that followed. The second, in an interview given to his biographer many years later, suggested an almost spur-of-the moment exchange, as though the issue of the succession was an after-thought:

> [The Queen] then said: 'Have you any advice to give me?' And I said, 'Ma'am, do you wish me to give you any advice?' And she said 'Yes I do' . . . So then I said 'Well, since you ask for it,

Ma'am, I have, with the help of Mr Bligh, prepared it all, and here it is.' And I just handed over my manuscript . . . then I read it to her, I think.[47]

However, a less casual, and almost certainly more accurate, version is contained in the diary record included in Macmillan's memoirs, which suggests that the exchange was more formal, as well as premeditated. According to this, the ex-premier began by asking if he could read the memorandum on the grounds that he was not strong enough to speak without a text, mentioning that he had up-dated it to take account of 'the so-called "revolt"' of the night before. At this point,

> She expressed her gratitude, and said that she did not need and did not intend to seek any other advice but mine. I then read the memorandum. She agreed that Lord Home was the most likely choice to get general support, as well as really the best and strongest character. But what of the revolt? I said that I thought speed was important and hoped she would send for Lord Home immediately – as soon as she got back to the Palace. He could then begin to work. She agreed.

Knowing that his recommendation of Home would be contentious, Macmillan advised the Queen, 'both verbally, and in the second part of the memorandum,' not to make Home Prime Minister at his first audience, but 'to use the older formula and entrust him with the task of forming an administration' so that he could consult his colleagues before giving an answer.[48] He then asked that the memorandum he had read should be kept in the Royal Archives as a full justification for any action the Queen might take on his advice. The Queen thanked him, they talked a little more, and then she left.

'When they came back from the hospital,' Lord Charteris recalls, 'the Queen wanted to send for Alec.' It is interesting that she should have felt such an inclination, without any doubts: for the man she had just spoken to had no more constitutional authority than any other MP, a point of which she was firmly reminded in the car on the way back to the Palace by Adeane, who stressed that as the advice was 'non-constitutional' she did not have to take it.[49] Politically, it would have been difficult to hold back – having permitted and encouraged the sounding-out process, and with the world waiting – but she would have been within her rights, even more so than in 1957 when advised by Salisbury and Churchill, to have done so, if she had wished.

There is no sign, however, that she did so wish. On the contrary, she seems to have been perfectly happy with the choice. As one former courtier puts it, Macmillan's recommendation, though incomprehensible to the public and many Tories, was 'pushing at an open door' as far as the Queen was concerned – a point which may have crossed the ex-premier's mind as he raked around for a stop-Butler candidate. She seems to have found Butler too remote and complex for her taste. 'Rab wasn't her cup of tea,' suggests an aide. 'When she got the advice to call Alec she thought "Thank God". She loved Alec – he was an old friend. They talked about dogs and shooting together. They were both Scottish landowners, the same sort of people, like old school friends.' Thus, while she knew that she was 'constitutionally justified in sending for Rab,' she felt no temptation whatsoever to do so.[50]

'The Queen was a victim of a violation of the Constitution,' argues Enoch Powell, a rebel in the night. 'It is unthinkable that a Prime Minister should say "Here is my resignation" and then "Here is my advice".'[51] It was, however, of critical importance that, like Salisbury in 1957, he was offering advice which he could claim was the 'official' opinion of his party. 'He was determined to put himself in a position so that, if his opinion was asked, he would be able to give advice of a realistic and acceptable character,' wrote Randolph Churchill, 'so as to ensure that the Queen did not have to "shop around" for a successor or for advisers on the succession. If he were to do a Bonar Law and refuse, when asked, to give advice, the Queen would be put in the intolerable position of seeming to interfere in the internal affairs of one party.'[52] However, Macmillan did not prepare for the *possibility* that he would be asked his opinion: he knew he would be, and may have known for some time.

By, in effect, advising her, while still Prime Minister, to consider his advice, he made it harder for her to refuse, if she had been inclined to do so, or to seek an alternative channel. 'As Prime Minister, Macmillan presumed to advise the Sovereign and then he resigned having declared his intention,' Powell maintains. 'He had it both ways. It was difficult for her, in the circumstances, to say "You are not my Prime Minister and I don't want your advice".'[53] Nevertheless, though difficult, it was not impossible. Indeed – given the confusion in the Conservative Party – it was precisely an occasion when the royal prerogative might have been taken out of mothballs, and used in a decisive manner, without inviting complaint from a party which traditionally defended its use.

One thing should have been apparent: Macmillan was not disinterested, and his behaviour can only be understood in terms of his paramount concern to prevent Butler from succeeding him. He enjoined the Queen to act with 'speed,' because of his fear that a stop-Home movement might gather momentum – and demonstrate that Home was, in fact, less acceptable to the party than Butler. The Queen took the point. The problem of finding a new Prime Minister was not yet over. One journalist who spoke to Sir Michael Adeane just after the hospital audience, remembers the Queen's private secretary saying that it was the duty of the Sovereign to find a premier who could command a Commons majority – she had no obligation to seek, or find, the best Prime Minister.[54] The question remained, however, whether even the minimum requirement had been fulfilled. 'We knew it was not just a straightforward situation,' says Charteris. 'The Queen couldn't just send for Alec and everyone would shout "Hurrah". Though the Queen and Adeane had made up their minds, in effect, by asking Alec, they were also saying "Oh well, we'll find out, and if he succeeds there will be no more to say".'[55]

Just before 1 p.m., the Palace announced that the Earl of Home had been received in audience, and had been asked to form a government. Home himself recalled that, at his audience, he 'explained to the Queen that I must ask leave to go away and see if I could form an administration'.[56] It was a request for which there was no precedent since the Duke of Wellington and Lord Aberdeen had accepted invitations to form governments in the nineteenth century, but had not promised that they would be able to do so.[57] Home wrote that he considered it critical, at the least, to secure the support of Butler, Maudling and Hailsham. The key figure, however, was Butler. 'We all understood that Alec could not form a government unless Rab agreed to serve,' says Charteris, 'and, if not, the Queen would have had to call for Rab.'[58]

Lord Home, with the authority, not of Macmillan's dubious selection procedure, but of the Sovereign, behind him, immediately began to interview ministers to see if he could rally the support he needed. It was soon clear that the Queen, bounced by Macmillan into asking Home, had effectively bounced most of the Cabinet into accepting him. An attempt by Hailsham to get agreement between himself, Maudling and Butler to refuse to serve failed, because Butler refused to be galvanized. In vain, Hailsham told Home that all four leading contenders – himself, Home, Butler and Maudling – were needed in any administration, and that if they were not included, the Queen might have to send for the Leader of the Opposition.[59] By next morning, only Macleod and Powell, among Cabinet ministers, were still holding out, and Home felt able to go to Buckingham Palace to kiss hands as Prime Minister. Thus the outcome was as the tired and recently anaesthetized – but absolutely single-minded – ex-premier wished. That night Harold Wilson told a meeting in Manchester that the message had gone out to the world that the Government party in Britain selected the country's leader through the machinery of an aristocratic cabal.

Many on the Tory side agreed. The most astringent analysis of the way Lord Home had 'emerged' was written by a Conservative, Iain Macleod, in January 1964 in the *Spectator*. This identified a 'magic circle' of old Etonians whom it accused of fixing the succession, and declared that, 'at all times, from the first day of premiership to the last, Macmillan was determined that Butler should not succeed him'. Amongst defeated candidates and their most ardent supporters, bitterness against the 'magic circle' – and a feeling that there had been trickery – was intense. But there was little direct criticism of the Queen. This was for several reasons. The convention of political discussion, particularly firm on the Conservative side, that the Sovereign was above reproach, meant that any attempt to blame the Palace would almost certainly have been self-defeating. As important was the feeling in the pro-Butler camp that Macmillan was the main villain, and that once his advice had been given it was hard to refuse. There was also a recognition that the Queen was not, in any sense, the instigator.

Should she be blamed retrospectively? The choice of selection method and the decision to abide by its result were political acts, and political acts have to be judged both by intentions and results. The effect of the 1963 major confusion, on top of the 1957 minor one, was to end forever the Monarch's discretionary power over the mid-term appointment of a Prime Minister, except in the most exceptional of hypothetical circumstances. This was the opposite of the intention of the Queen – who, indeed, allowed herself to be duped by Macmillan, a still-engaged politician with personal concerns of his own. Enoch Powell later accused Macmillan of 'having deprived the Queen of her principal prerogative ... deliberately (and, in retrospect, conclusively).'[60] He might also, however, have accused the Queen of co-operating in her own deprivation. For this – and for the appointment of a premier who, though he fulfilled the requirements of the moment, was felt by most people within and outside the Conservative Party to have been a less satisfactory choice than Butler – the Queen and her Palace advisers were partly culpable. Her decision to opt for passivity, and in effect to collude with Macmillan's scheme for blocking the deputy premier, must be counted the biggest political misjudgement of her reign.[61]

LORD HOME – Sir Alec Douglas-Home, as he became – was the closest to the Queen in background, interests and temperament of her Prime Ministers. All Home's predecessors had been aristocrats or closely linked to the aristocracy – Churchill was the grandson of a duke, Macmillan the son-in-law of one, Eden the son of a baronet. However, the renouncing Earl was the one with whom she felt most comfortable. The age gap was beginning to close – Home was nine years younger than Macmillan. More important, he was the first the Queen could talk to with a set of shared values and assumptions. There was a feeling of kinship between Douglas-Homes and Bowes-Lyons that went back generations. When the Homes stayed at Balmoral, they did so as personal friends.

Because of her pregnancy, the Queen was little seen in public during the early months of the new premiership. The baby was born on 10th March 1964 in the Belgian suite at Buckingham Palace, and christened Edward Antony Richard Louis. Capitals throughout the Commonwealth greeted the news with twenty-one-gun salutes, and the new Archbishop of Canterbury, Dr Ramsay, welcomed the birth in terms archbishops habitually employ on such occasions, by reference to the nation's model hearth. It meant much, he said, that at a time when not all homes were as lucky, 'there was around the throne a Christian family united, happy and setting to all an example of what the words "home and family" most truly meant'.[62] The Queen did not resume public engagements until late May. It was a distracting, and worrying, summer, apart from the new baby. There were growing indications that Prince Charles – now fifteen and at Gordonstoun – was lonely and unhappy there. In July, Charles's difficulties were compounded by illness when he contracted pneumonia, following a fishing trip, and had to spend ten days at the Walson-Frazer Nursing Home at Aberdeen.[63]

The same spring the Queen became indirectly and improbably embroiled in the, as yet, secret affair of Sir Anthony Blunt, Surveyor of the Royal Pictures, and 'fourth man' in the espionage ring which involved three former Foreign Office officials, Guy Burgess, Donald Maclean and Kim Philby. Blunt had been appointed in 1945, in succession to Sir Kenneth Clark, to look after the art collections at Buckingham Palace, Windsor Castle and Hampton Court. An outstanding and resourceful art historian, and the author of many distinguished works, he had done much to build up the Courtauld Institute of which he was simultaneously Director. As Surveyor, he was responsible for the immense and highly valued *Catalogue* of Old Master drawings in the Royal Collection, and for the first exhibition of the new Queen's Gallery, in one of the conservatories in the Palace gardens, which took place in July 1962. The Queen herself took only a sporadic interest in the Royal Collection, and since Blunt seldom attended royal parties or functions, he was rarely in her company.[64] Nevertheless, his appointment was a royal one, and his link with the Queen sufficiently close for her private secretary to be informed of his treasonable activity, when it was confirmed.

How much did the Queen know? Blunt made his confession to an MI5 interrogator on 23rd April 1964, admitting that he had been recruited to work for Soviet intelligence while still at Cambridge, that he had recruited others, and that, while working for British secret intelligence during the war, he had passed on a large quantity of information to the Russians.[65] Before the meeting, it had apparently been agreed with Sir Michael Adeane, not only that Blunt should be offered legal immunity to avoid alerting the KGB, but also, for the same reason, that he should keep his job in the royal service. After it, a memorandum was sent to Adeane describing what had been revealed. Blunt stayed in his post. Though his link with the Philby network was widely rumoured, the story did not break publicly until 1979, when Mrs Thatcher, as Prime Minister, was forced to reveal it in the House of Commons.

By then, Blunt had retired from royal employment, and so could not be dismissed. He was, however, hastily stripped of his knighthood – a dishonouring which encouraged the obvious question of whether, if the Queen knew at the time about the confession, she was right to accept the arrangement, and to continue to employ a known traitor; or, if she did not know, why she was not told. The mystery deepened when Lord Home claimed that, as Prime Minister, he had himself not been informed of the confession or immunity – raising the additional question of why, if the Queen knew, she did not raise such an extraordinary development with him in an audience.

What the Queen knew or did not know has never been resolved. Some have assumed that her private secretary would not have been involved without telling her.[66] According to one ex-courtier, when Sir Burke Trend, as Cabinet Secretary, made enquiries on the subject in the early 1970s, the Queen 'gave the impression that she already knew,' though by this time Blunt had retired in any case. A senior official recalls being told that, when she was briefed by Mrs Thatcher in 1979, the Queen commented: 'It doesn't surprise me one bit,' which could be taken as an indication either that she knew – or that she did not, but had her suspicions. According to a former courtier who believes that she did know, 'Michael Adeane was given a clear indication that Blunt should be left in the Household, but without access to documents. The Queen was just taking advice.'[67] Whatever the state of the Queen's awareness, however, Adeane was certainly kept informed of the position; and for the next eight years, until both retired in 1972, the extraordinary situation existed in which the Queen's principal Palace adviser worked as a colleague of the Queen's principal adviser on her collections, in the full knowledge of the latter's criminal treachery.

On 5th October 1964, the Queen marked her full return to public life after the birth of Prince Edward with a nine-day visit to Canada, accompanied by her husband, for the centennial of the 1864 meetings which resulted in the formation of the Dominion. The trip was partly in response to a demand that had been voiced in the press for shorter, 'ad hoc' Commonwealth visits, which would enable the Queen to visit particular countries for special occasions, without taking on a marathon tour of a region or hemisphere.[68] The plan was to visit Charlottetown and Quebec City. After the visit had been fixed, however, an upsurge of French separatism in Quebec raised the question of whether it was wise to go ahead with it – especially after activists threatened to disrupt the tour with methods recently used in the American civil rights movement, like lying down in front of the royal car. Death threats against the Queen, only months after the assassination of President Kennedy, added to the concern. Lester Pearson, the Canadian premier, dismissed reports that there would be disturbances,[69] but anxieties continued to be expressed in Britain – creating a constitutional ambiguity which the Queen's divided status inevitably gave rise to.

There was some similarity to the scare and uncertainty that preceded the Ghana visit. As in 1961, the Queen herself was keen to go. 'She is personally unmoved by this sort of thing,' Adeane wrote in April, when cancellation was mooted.[70] In the case of Ghana, however, the Queen had travelled to a Commonwealth republic as Head of the Commonwealth, on the advice of her ministers in Britain, who were politically accountable for the decision to send her. This time, it was proposed that she should travel to and in a dominion of which she was Head of State, on the advice of her Prime Minister in Canada, and in theory the British Government had no say in the matter.

Here was an interesting hypothesis. What if the Queen's British ministers, judging the outlook less favourably than their Canadian equivalents, advised her in the interests of the United Kingdom to stay at home? The British Government considered this question. The constitutional position was quite clear, the Cabinet Secretary advised the Prime Minister a few days before the Queen's intended departure. 'The Queen would be going as Queen of Canada and could only look for advice to the Prime Minister of Canada.'[71] The only matter on which she needed to consult the British Government, suggested *The*

Times, was the convenience of the date. Even when in Britain, it suggested, 'the Queen remains Queen of Canada as well as of her other realms. She is guided exclusively by their governments in her relations with them.'[72]

Unlike Anglo-Ghanaian relations, Anglo-Canadian relations were close enough for the matter to be amicably resolved, in a way that allowed the trip to take place without the British Government either appearing unconcerned about the Queen's safety or seeking to pull constitutional rank. On 22nd September, Sir Alec Douglas-Home told Cabinet that Pearson had agreed to a formula whereby the British Government would announce that it was in touch with the Canadians on the safety issue, and that it was satisfied that all precautions were being taken.[73] However, the interests of the two states were not identical, and – quite apart from the Queen's physical safety – it was not necessarily in Britain's diplomatic interest, in terms of international prestige, for its own Head of State to make a locally unpopular visit. Thus, the period of uncertainty over the Canada trip highlighted a 'divisibility' problem that was bound to arise again as the Commonwealth became more diverse.[74]

As it turned out, the 1964 Canadian tour was one of the most difficult the Queen had ever undertaken. Anticipating trouble which they had earlier predicted would not take place, the Canadian authorities over-reacted. When the Queen arrived in Quebec City, the police charged a peaceful crowd, beating up and arresting people indiscriminately. As a result, interest in the tour focused on the controversy over the security measures, and the nationalists seemed vindicated. 'The royal visit has won virtually no popular acclaim,' reported Hella Pick, in the *Guardian*, 'and unless the Queen's car was sound-proof as well as bullet-proof, her ears must still be reverberating to the unaccustomed sound of booing.'[75] The public reaction in Quebec, and the lack of it elsewhere, led Pearson – who had initiated the visits in the first place – to warn the Queen that the Monarchy's days in the dominion were numbered.[76]

There was another aspect to divisibility, apart from different opinions about the safety of the Queen when she was abroad. If the Queen was required to perform duties in two of her realms simultaneously, which took precedence? The question arose over the Canadian trip, because of the possibility that the British Prime Minister might wish to ask for a dissolution – which required the Sovereign's physical presence – during the period in which the visit was due to take place. Early in the year, it was agreed that to ask the Canadians to cancel the tour because of such an eventuality would create a very awkward situation constitutionally, and would also give, as Sir Michael Adeane put it, 'a certain colour to the Quebec extremists' worst accusations of Colonialism'.[77] In the event, Douglas-Home asked for Parliament to be dissolved in late September, with polling day on 15th October, which allowed the Canadians to squeeze in their royal visit during the British election campaign.

The timing of the election, however, and the question of how Parliament should be dissolved, raised a constitutional issue of a different kind. In the normal way, as Parliament was in recess, it would be necessary for it to be recalled in order to be prorogued – That is, brought to an end ceremonially prior to dissolution. However, as it was close to the end of its full five-year term, and there was no matter that needed urgently to be put before it, the Prime Minister decided that the most sensible procedure would be for the Queen merely to dissolve by Proclamation – even though this had not been done since 1922.[78]

The Palace was informed accordingly. But was Douglas-Home at liberty so to decide? It did not occur to him or his advisers that there was any difficulty about doing so until the Queen raised an objection following a Privy Council meeting on September 2nd. Buttonholing the Clerk to the Council, Godfrey Agnew, she told him, in no uncertain terms, that 'she was not altogether happy with this idea since it represented a break with tradition and tradition is all important'. Though she accepted the point that because Parliament was time-expired, it was not worth recalling it, 'she considered that it should be made clear at the time of the announcement from No. 10 that there was no intention of setting a precedent for the future'.[79] The Prime Minister won her round, though the Clerk continued to protest, on the Monarch's behalf, that 'Her Majesty said She regarded tradition to be of value and importance and would not like to see, in the future, this occasion being used as a reason for abandoning the normal procedure.'[80]

At issue was the vexed issue of the royal prerogative, and its preservation. The Queen was quite prepared to travel from Balmoral, where she was in residence, to Buckingham Palace, for the Privy Council at which she would make the Proclamation (once it was agreed), on the grounds, put to her by the Prime Minister, that for 'so important an exercise of the Prerogative power' London was the appropriate place.[81] But she insisted on Douglas-Home travelling to Balmoral in order to make the formal request for a dissolution. Her sharp-eyed private secretary, moreover, was insistent that the request should be couched in the language of entreaty, not demand or recommendation. Spotting an errant word in the draft press notice, Adeane swiftly informed No. 10 that 'From the Queen's point of view the important point on these occasions is that the Prime Minister asks for a dissolution rather than that he advises one because this makes clear the royal prerogative in such matters'.[82] On September 13th, when all was in place, Douglas-Home wrote to Harold Wilson, as Leader of the Opposition, telling him that he would be going to Balmoral next day to ask the Queen to proclaim an early Dissolution, without prior Prorogation. 'If she complies with this request,' he wrote in the Alice-in-Wonderland language deemed suitable, 'Dissolution will take place on Friday, September 25th.'[83]

There remained one issue, before the royal party set out for Canada, that was not raised with the Monarch. What if she was assassinated while she was there? It was the duty of civil servants, when planning such an expedition, to consider every contingency. A couple of days after the Dissolution, Derek Mitchell, the Prime Minister's private secretary, discussed this grim hypothesis with Sir Burke Trend and the Government Chief Whip. Together, they clinically considered the implications for British politics at a moment of uncertainty and hiatus. After due deliberation, they concluded that – as Counsellors of State would be in existence, and the Election could go ahead under Statute – the Constitution would be able to cope.[84]

'THE ARRIVAL OF WILSON was taken calmly,' recalls an ex-courtier. 'There was no feeling of a problem, though when he came to the Palace with his family it was a bit of a culture shock.'[1] Whether or not the election result was to the Court's liking, there had been plenty of time for it to compose itself. The Government had been behind in the polls since 1962, and for most of the time since Wilson became Labour Leader the gap between the parties had been wide. However, during the summer of 1964, opponents of change were given reason for hope. With the margin narrowed almost to vanishing point, the campaign was a tense one, and there was talk of a 'hung' Parliament – the first for thirty-five years. What should the Queen do then? No. 10 prepared a position paper, just in case. This concluded that even if Labour was the biggest party, but without an overall majority, the Queen would not have to accept Sir Alec Douglas-Home's resignation, or ask Harold Wilson to form a government. It was open to her to ask the Prime Minister to stay until defeated in the House, or to press him to try to form a Coalition, or to send for somebody, not a majority party leader, in the hope of forming a compromise government, pending the calling of another general election.[2]

However, the paper did not have to be put to the test; and on 16th October, the zestful and ebullient Mr Wilson, accompanied by his wife, two sons, father and political secretary – all in a state of culture shock as big as the Court's – arrived to see the Queen. It was the first time Labour had taken power from the Tories since 1945, and also the first time, after a dozen years on the throne, that the Queen had been required to appoint a new Prime Minister because of an election. The transaction was a straightforward one. 'She simply asked me if I could form an Administration,' Wilson later recounted. Unlike Lord Home in 1963, he was not in doubt, even though his majority was small. He replied in the affirmative, 'and I was made Prime Minister on the spot'.[3] The Queen's husband, who was on tour, telegraphed his congratulations. In his message, he referred to Mr Wilson's bungalow in the Scillies. 'Delighted to see that resident of the Duchy of Cornwall is new tenant at Downing Street.' 'Do I have to present my humble duty etc.?' the new Prime Minister asked an official. 'No,' was the answer, only to the Sovereign. So he cabled back: 'Thanks to the generous attitude of the Duchy, my residence within the Duchy of Cornwall is a freehold as against the tied cottage status of my tenure at Downing Street.'[4]

For the Queen, the switch from a fourteenth Earl to the fourteenth Mr Wilson (as Home had dubbed him) was a startling one. Unlike any of her previous Prime Ministers, the new premier came from something approaching an ordinary background. The gulf between them, therefore, was enormous. A shared experience of the doctrines of Lord Baden-Powell gave them a little to talk about. 'At Balmoral,' a Wilson aide recalls, 'Harold liked the boy scoutish things, like collecting wood for the barbecue, and rubbing two sticks together.'[5] However, the differences between the 20th Huddersfield Scout Troop and the 1st Buckingham Palace Guide Company were as great as the similarities.

Otherwise, the Monarch and her first minister had little in common. Yet, in some ways, this helped. The Queen was intrigued by Wilson – socially, politically and intellectually from a different planet. Wilson, for his part, was delighted by the Queen. It was partly what she stood for, as the ultimate symbol of his own success, linked to his identification with the man-in-the-street, along the lines, as one of his officials puts it, of 'who would have thought of a chap like me ending up in a place like this.'[6] He enjoyed the pageantry. 'I have a great respect for tradition,' he told a reporter. 'I like the real ceremonies of the Monarchy ... the Opening of Parliament, the Coronation. All that.'[7] In addition, he had a strong attachment to the romance, and political idea, of the Commonwealth, partly derived from a boyhood trip to Australia.

But it was also personal. Wilson enjoyed the company of strong, business-like, and intelligent women, and he was unhindered by, because he was oblivious to, the nuances of upper-class etiquette and courtly behaviour. He neither patronized the Queen, nor treated her as if he were a knight errant. He behaved towards her – unexpectedly – as an equal, and talked to her as if she were a member of his Cabinet. This, of course, she was not, which helped: she was one of the few people, outside his own entourage, he was able to deal with on a regular basis without treating them as rivals, or calculating their motives. He was fond of saying that a Prime Minister had to do his homework or she was likely to catch him out. He valued her as a sounding-board. 'He thought her advice often quite wise,' says his former press secretary, Joe Haines.[8]

The Queen meanwhile was flattered by his eagerness to take her into his confidence, without condescension. 'She appreciated that he was very communicative,' says a former courtier, '- that he appeared to want to inform her about what he intended to do.'[9] Audiences, as a result, grew longer – a point observed with interest below stairs. '. . . [W]e all knew that a great respect had grown up between the Queen and Sir Harold Wilson,' a royal servant later recalled. 'The old guard who made up some of the Household were very suspicious.'[10]

In addition, there was a political dimension. Every vote-hungry premier wants to be liked by a popular monarch, and none more so than a left-wing one, with a wafer-thin majority, seeking to provide the electorate with reassurance. If Wilson's pleasure in the Queen's company and her apparent pleasure in his were sincere, they were pleasures he was happy to let the public know about. The press, briefed by No. 10, was soon commenting on the 'extraordinary relationship' that now existed between Downing Street and the Palace, and on the audiences which involved detailed briefings, for example over the position in Vietnam.[11] But it was also genuine. 'The Russians are in an interesting "cleft stick" position in Vietnam as their influence in Hanoi is negligible unless they can get the Chinese to do it,' the Queen wrote knowledgeably to Lord Avon in August 1966, thanking him for a copy of his new book, *Towards Peace in Indo-China*. She added, indicating her source, 'and I believe Harold Wilson discovered some interesting hard facts about this when he was in Moscow.'[12]

The attitude of other Labour ministers towards the Head of State varied. Barbara Castle, one of the most left-wing members of the Cabinet, enjoyed royal occasions, and found her easy to talk to, woman to woman. Richard Crossman, the new Housing Minister, on the other hand, regarded the rituals with distaste – though also, as the author of an introduction to *The English Constitution* – with professional fascination. Both elements were combined in his account of the 'kissing of hands' ceremony, at which new ministers were sworn in as Privy Councillors. He described how he and his colleagues were first coached in the drill of kneeling, holding the Bible, taking the royal hand, and walking backwards, and were then ushered into a great drawing-room at the Palace. 'At the other end there was this little woman with a beautiful waist,' he recorded, 'and she had to stand with her hand on the table for forty minutes while we went through this rigmarole. We were uneasy, she was uneasy. Then at the end informality broke out and she said, "You all moved backwards very nicely," and we laughed. We were Privy Councillors: we had kissed hands.'

Crossman found it 'two-dimensional, so thin, so like a coloured illustration in *The Sphere*, not a piece of real life.'[13] Wedgwood Benn meanwhile, advocate of no dinner-jackets at Buckingham Palace, was filled with democratic outrage. To show his disapproval of the whole proceedings, he chatted to a fellow minister during the rehearsal, which he considered 'terribly degrading as we were told that we had to kneel on a footstool before the Queen and assent to the Privy Council oath which had a real Mau-Mau quality.' In the actual ceremony, he made his feelings felt by doing 'the most miniature bow ever seen.' He left the Palace 'boiling with indignation' at 'an attempt to impose tribal magic and personal loyalty on people whose real duty was only to their electors'.[14] Later, to differentiate himself from servile colleagues, he turned down an invitation to a sherry party at the Palace.[15]

The new Prime Minister's eagerness to explain his actions to the Queen, and her willingness to listen, made it easier for them to work together over an issue of major importance to the Commonwealth which arose as soon as Labour came to office. The 'winds of change' which Macmillan had identified in 1959 had brought independence to most of the remaining British colonies and territories in Africa, on the basis of black majority rule. The significant exception was Southern Rhodesia. Here, the Labour Government inherited a developing crisis, produced by the clash between the British (and world) insistence that full autonomy must be accompanied by democracy, and the intransigence of a white settler government in Salisbury, headed by Ian Smith, which wanted to maintain white minority rule. The issue affected the Queen directly, in a way that many colonial matters did not, because of the fierce passions it aroused in the new Commonwealth republics, especially in Africa, and also – conversely – because of the old-fashioned, 'imperial' loyalty many British settlers felt towards both the idea and the incarnation of the Crown. Consequently, during the discussions that took place between London and Salisbury, much attention was paid on both sides to the 'royal' factor – each trying to exploit it to its own advantage.

The involvement of the Queen is interesting because it showed the Monarchy's continued psychological power, and also the confusion that could arise from any attempt to harness it for a political purpose. For more than forty years, the Crown had provided a vital link between the Rhodesian governments and the United Kingdom, in a way that was different from its role elsewhere. Since 1923 the government of Southern Rhodesia had been in the hands of European settlers for most domestic purposes, while remaining legally subject to ministers in London. After the break-up of the federation of Rhodesia and Nyasaland in 1963, the Rhodesian white community – used to conducting its own affairs without interference, while continuing to regard itself as 'British' – sought independence within the Commonwealth on its own terms. As a result, Salisbury and London came into increasing conflict over the provision for eventual black majority rule.

Sir Alec Douglas-Home's Government had firmly resisted Smith's demands. The new Labour Government, strongly committed to racial equality, was expected to be even firmer. In fact, there was little change. Wilson simply maintained the stance of his predecessor. He stood out against those in the Commonwealth, and his own party, who threatened military action. But, like Douglas-Home, he made clear that independence would not be granted without guarantees; that a 'unilateral' declaration of independence would be regarded as illegal and unconstitutional; and that such a step would be met with economic sanctions. What altered was the nature of Rhodesian hopes. The Salisbury regime had friends on the Tory back-benches; it had none on the Labour side. Consequently, Ian Smith became more truculent, and prepared for a breakaway. In his effort to prevent this happening, and – after it had taken place – to bring the rebellion to an end, Harold Wilson enlisted the direct, political help of the Queen who, from the start, he saw as a potentially vital ally. He took exceptional care to keep her informed and up-to-date about his latest actions. His particular aim was to disabuse white Rhodesians of the notion that the Queen could be regarded as separate from her ministers in London, and that it was possible to deal with her on an independent basis. He therefore secured her co-operation, early on, in an announcement that there would be no question of her accepting the role of Head of State of a rebel regime.[16] He also persuaded her to send messages to Rhodesia which indicated a personal support for the policy of her Government in London that went beyond what was constitutionally required. Ironically, however, such statements in themselves proved that a separation existed. At the same time, the Monarch laid herself open to the criticism, both from Ian Smith sympathizers, and from constitutional purists, that she was improperly partisan.

The most dramatic use of the Queen to back up Wilson's diplomacy occurred in October 1965, by which time UDI seemed almost inevitable. In a last minute bid to change Smith's mind, the British Prime Minister himself flew to Salisbury – carrying with him a royal message, in which the Queen entreated the Rhodesian premier to find a solution to the problem.[17] On his arrival in the Rhodesian capital, Wilson brandished the Queen's hand-written letter – jointly drafted by his own private secretary, Derek Mitchell, and by Sir Michael Adeane[18] – like a magic wand. The object of the letter was to remind Rhodesia of their allegiance to the Crown. However, Smith was able to turn the bland words of hope and encouragement in the message to his own advantage, using them as evidence of the Queen's sympathy for the Rhodesian government in its predicament. Instead of seeking to play the message down, he read it out loud to the guests at the banquet held for the British Prime Minister, as if it were a personal triumph – describing it as 'a wonderful message from this gracious lady,' which was 'the sort of thing that we live for in Rhodesia – our association with the Queen, with Britain and with the Commonwealth.' It also gave Smith an opportunity to appear to be in friendly and direct communication with the Monarch, which was the opposite of the plan. 'We have embarked upon discussion with Mr Wilson in a spirit of utmost sincerity, frankness and goodwill,' he wrote to the Queen in reply, concluding: 'The Rhodesian people have a special affection for Your Majesty and for Her Majesty the Queen Mother.'[19]

Invoking the Queen's name did not end there. During the last few days before UDI, Smith stepped up his declarations of loyalty, as part of the Rhodesian government's campaign to reassure the white population that independence would mean the maintenance of traditional values, rather than a break with them. 'The Crown in the person of the Sovereign, is dear to all the people of Rhodesia,' announced a letter sent to the Head of State on 9th November, signed by the whole Cabinet. '. . . [W]hatever happens there will still be found among all Rhodesians that same loyalty and devotion to the Crown which have guided and sustained us since our country was founded.'[20] The Queen was advised not to respond directly, on the grounds that Rhodesians had no constitutional rights of access to the Palace.[21] Instead, a reply was routed through the Commonwealth Secretary, saying that she acknowledged with gratitude the assurances of loyalty expressed, and was 'confident that all her Rhodesian people on whose behalf the message speaks will demonstrate their loyalty by continuing to act in a constitutional manner.'[22]

Both sides claimed the Monarch; each dismissed the other's claim as spurious. While the Salisbury government strove to distinguish between the Sovereign, to whom it was devoted, and her first minister in Britain, whom it deplored, Wilson attempted to detach the Queen's 'subjects' in a Crown colony from an administration whose threatened rebellion, he sought to make clear, had the Monarch's strong disapproval. This curious dance continued right up to, and beyond, a 'Proclamation of Independence' on 11th November by the Rhodesian Cabinet, which mimicked the American Declaration of Independence with the significant difference that it retained the Monarchy. Instead of breaking with the past by setting up a republic with an elective presidency, the proclamation provided for the Queen to be Head of State (something which Wilson had specifically stated she would not be), and ended with the words 'God save the Queen'. Wilson reacted by publishing the recent correspondence between the Queen and the Rhodesian Cabinet. 'Her Majesty had sent a beautifully formal reply,' observed Barbara Castle, '. . . Harold has certainly got her superbly organised.'[23]

If anything, the 'battle for the Queen' hotted up after UDI, with both the Salisbury government (which had practical power) and the London Government (which had control of the Monarch's actions and declarations) claiming the legitimacy derived from her name. It was more metaphysical than real. At Cabinet on 8th October, a month before UDI, Wilson stated his position: in the event of illegal independence, members of the Salisbury government would be regarded as traitors, 'and the Queen will take over the government'. But what did this mean? Ministers were puzzled. In such a context, 'the Queen' normally meant 'ministers of the Crown'. However, in the case of Rhodesia – since Wilson had ruled out the use of force – the only available ministers were the 'traitors' in Smith's cabinet.

Crossman asked the pertinent question. Would 'the Queen' act through the Governor in Salisbury, Sir Humphrey Gibbs, or the British Prime Minister? The answer was both, and neither. Gibbs stayed in Rhodesia, symbolizing the Queen. The Queen made him a KCVO, an honour in her personal gift, which heightened the symbolism. He took orders from the British Government. But he had virtually no influence over events. Although he 'sacked' Smith and his ministers, they remained in control. Hence 'taking over the government' meant only that the British Government did not relinquish what little authority the name of the Queen could bestow.

Following UDI, Wilson considered playing the royal card in a more direct way. He rejected a suggestion that the Queen should make a broadcast. He also rejected a scheme, put forward by Sir Humphrey Gibbs, that British planes should bombard Rhodesian cities with leaflets containing a personalized royal message.[24] On the other hand, he briefly envisaged sending Lord Mountbatten – ex-Viceroy, friend of Labour and a cousin of the Monarch – as a 'direct emissary of the Queen' on a special mission to the Governor. On 16th November, he raised the idea with the Queen at his audience. Though she expressed concern about Mountbatten's personal safety, she reacted positively. Lord Mountbatten was even more positive, and indeed seemed to relish the idea of such a dramatic and high-profile role. Developing the idea, he proposed taking Sir Solly Zuckerman, the government's chief scientific adviser, and his own son-in-law, Lord Brabourne, with him. He also suggested that he should fly out in an RAF Comet, specially painted to identify it as part of the Queen's Flight.

The stumbling block turned out to be the Court, which had serious constitutional worries about the wisdom of the Monarch – represented by a royal 'emissary' who could easily become a loose cannon – getting too closely embroiled in the politics and policies of the British Government. Confronted with the scheme, the two leading Palace officials, Sir Michael Adeane and the Lord Chamberlain, Lord Cobbold, formed a joint front, insisting (according to a No. 10 memorandum) that 'the proposal should be treated with the utmost caution and that the Queen's personal position would need to be fully protected'. In short, the 'direct emissary' could only be sent on the specific instructions of the Government. If the Prime Minister wanted to pursue the idea, they made clear, the Queen 'would want very definite advice on the terms, in writing and preferably publishable'. Only on such conditions would they give their own advice to her to agree.[25] However, if the mission from the Queen was publicly acknowledged to be 'on advice' from the Prime Minister, that would have negated most of its point, which was to demonstrate, once again, which side the Queen was on. Despite vigorous lobbying by Lord Mountbatten, both with Wilson and the Queen,[26] the idea was dropped.

Yet royal authority continued to count for something in Rhodesia. The condemnation of the Smith regime as 'traitorous' turned out to be hollow – nobody was prosecuted for treason, and the British Government quickly absolved Rhodesian civil servants and members of the armed services from any duty to disobey orders. Nevertheless, Gibbs's beleaguered survival in Rhodesia was a nagging reminder of Smith's illegitimacy in the eyes of the world – making it harder to regard independence as a closed chapter. The idea of an ostracized Governor holding a torch for democracy was an affecting one. 'It was a moving experience to dine at Government House – black ties, ADCs etc.,' recalled one British visitor, a Conservative, a few years later '- and to drink the toast to the Queen with a sense of its significance which does not always impinge at banquets in Britain.'[27] One bit of evidence of its significance was Smith's tolerance of the Governor's presence. Instead of ejecting Gibbs and installing a replacement, the Rhodesian Prime Minister went to extraordinary lengths to maintain the fiction that Rhodesia, though independent, was a Monarchy. Two weeks after UDI, he offered the Queen 'advice' that Clifford Dupont, one of his ministers, should be made Governor-General, 'praying that Your Majesty may be pleased to appoint him to that office'.[28] Gibbs was instructed by his controllers in London to reply that the Queen was unable 'to entertain purported advice of this kind'.[29]

Why the charade? The battle for the Queen was much less important than the battle to cut off or maintain oil supplies, which Rhodesia won hands down. Yet Smith was conscious of the need to move carefully, in the face of his own, ultra-conservative constituency. Most important of all, in his calculations, were the Rhodesian armed forces, who had seen themselves as 'soldiers of the Queen,' and for whom the idea of loyalty to the Crown had a continued meaning. The Chief of Staff of the Rhodesian Armed Services, Major-General Anderson, had found the break impossible to bear, and had been dismissed for opposing independence. 'I have taken an oath to the Queen,' he declared, 'and to me that means one is an upholder of constitutional government.'[30] Others lived uneasily with a divided loyalty. For a time after UDI, an extraordinary situation existed in which Rhodesian service chiefs reported both to Smith, as Prime Minister, and to Gibbs, representing the Queen, while – according to the account of Ken Flower, former head of the Rhodesian Secret Service – the intelligence services of London and Salisbury kept in close contact with each other.

Flower paints a vivid picture of the complicated life of the illegally independent, yet studiously 'loyal' country, as it tried to carry on with rituals and ceremonials – necessary for a sense of the British civilization it believed itself to represent – as if the distant Monarch was still a part of them. Thus, at the first 'Opening of Parliament' following UDI, the new Commander of the Army, Major-General Paterill, was invited by the Smith government to officiate in place of Sir Humphrey Gibbs. In the strange constitutional limbo in which Salisbury politics now operated, Paterill felt he should consult Gibbs first. The Governor advised him to accept, but to make a point of not appearing to enjoy himself. The result, according to Flower, was a most remarkable

" Your move ! "

Ian Smith and Harold Wilson, as depicted in the Evening Standard, 5th March, 1968

performance. Afterwards, the official photographs 'depicted an unhappy general standing amongst bewildered politicians – bewildered because they had taken UDI in the name of the Queen, had then excluded the Queen's representative from taking part in the ceremony and now found themselves in the company of an unhappy general who, on the instructions of the Queen's representative, deemed that there would be no royal salute . . . and no Queen's Colours on parade.'

As the Smith regime became more established, the need for such elaborations declined. One concrete effort of the Salisbury government's desire to retain an appearance of Monarchy-sanctioned legitimacy, was the hesitancy Smith showed over the carrying out of death sentences – appeals from which, under pre-UDI law, required a Privy Council hearing. After two and a half years, however, it decided to go ahead with them, in defiance of the Queen's exercise (on British ministerial advice) of the prerogative of mercy. A republic was declared in March 1970. Yet even then royalist sentiment remained strong in the armed services, and some leading commanders objected on the grounds that UDI had been proclaimed 'in the name of the Queen, Christianity and civilization. The Union Jack was to continue to fly and the National Anthem to be played.' Though the Oath of Allegiance might not mean much to the politicians, they protested, it meant a great deal to servicemen.[31]

In retrospect, the Rhodesian dispute was full of contradictions. One of the biggest was that the Rhodesian white community identified itself with the code of an Empire that had ceased to exist, and with a Monarch who was the Head of a Commonwealth and constitutionally the property of a British Government, with different values. Refusing either to shed their 'Britishness' or to believe that the bipartisan policies of the Westminster Parliament embodied it, some Rhodesians became *plus royalistes que la reine*, half-believing that the Queen (and, for some reason, her mother) would see their point of view, were it not for the pressure from a cynical left-wing Government.

Wilson's attempt to counter this misapprehension, by detaching the Queen as a person from the constitutional being, was a questionable tactic – if anything confirming the half-belief that the Monarch could be considered independently. When was she expressing a genuinely personal opinion, and when was she the mouthpiece of prepared texts? In a speech at the Lord Mayor's banquet in November 1965, Wilson insisted that any instruction issued 'by Her Majesty's ministers in the name of the Queen could not and would not in any circumstances be issued without the specific authority and approval of Her Majesty herself'.[32] He repeated this assurance in communications with Sir Humphrey Gibbs,[33] and the state papers reveal much coming and going between No. 10 and the Palace on the topic. However, few doubted that the Queen's 'personal' letters and actions were as much a product of plotting in Whitehall as Smith's 'personal' replies were of plotting in Salisbury.

'Personal' communications also put the Monarch in an invidious position, as the Queen's Palace advisers were nervously aware. It could be argued that the Monarch should not express a more than formal interest in a matter of policy under any conditions; and that, as Grigg has argued, she committed a 'constitutional error' by writing to Smith on a political issue, blurring 'the vital distinction between the sovereign as an individual and *the Crown*' which was really a code-word for the Government.[34] If the Queen made a practice of expressing opinions that were her own, her constitutional authority, which depended on her neutrality, would be undermined. On the other hand, not to have countered white Rhodesian illusions about her private sympathies, might have caused embarrassment in the Commonwealth.

With and without the Queen, the Rhodesians continued their rebellion until 1980, outlasting Wilson, whose attempts to end it 'in weeks rather than months' manifestly failed. The Queen – along with the exhortations of politicians, and UN sanctions – was part of that failure. Nevertheless, she remained relevant to the dispute. Smith waited more than four years before cutting a link that was central to the white Rhodesian identity. Even after 1970, the idea of 'restoring the Queen' – a personalized, as well as a symbolic notion – was always regarded as the first step in any possible settlement.

IN THE FIRST half of 1965, the Queen and Duke embarked on a series of state visits, the first to non-Commonwealth countries since 1961. Such trips were less common in the Queen's early years on the throne than they later became, partly because of the established principle that a state visit to any one country only took place once in a reign,[35] a somewhat arbitrary rule, which failed to take into account that some reigns were longer than others.

In February, the royal couple travelled to Ethiopia and the Sudan, and in May to Germany. The North African tour followed the death, in January, of Sir Winston Churchill, at the age of ninety. He had been ailing for some time, and Buckingham Palace had prepared for the event long in advance. When Churchill was taken ill in 1958, it had occurred to the Queen, according to Lord Moran, 'that he was very old and very frail and might die,'[36] and plans, code-named 'Operation Hope Not', had been initiated by Sir Michael Adeane for a full state funeral.[37] Hope Not was now activated, with due magnificence and solemnity, and the British congratulated themselves on their unique ability to give a great statesman a good send-off. During the lying-in-state, the Queen, accompanied by her husband, sister and brother-in-law, visited Westminster Hall quietly to pay their respects to the most justly honoured British leader of the century. The royal group stood before the catafalque for five minutes, little noticed by the column of mourners who continued to file past.[38]

It was a season of evocations. The Ethiopian tour – hosted by Haile Selassie, who had much to thank Churchill for – was conducted with opulent splendour. In March memories of a different sort were revived by the announcement that the Duke of Windsor, now seventy-one, would visit a London clinic for an operation to secure the detached retina of his left eye to the eyeball. The question arose of whether the Queen should abandon her family's tradition of pretending that the Duke and Duchess did not exist, or maintain it. She decided on a minimal gesture. On 15th March, she called at the hospital and talked to her pyjama-clad and bandaged uncle, and to her aunt, for twenty-five minutes – to the intense, lugubrious interest of the world's media.[39]

In May there was a national as opposed to personal gesture of reconciliation. The month of the twentieth anniversary of the ending of the Second World War in Europe was marked by a royal visit which was intended to show the amity that now existed in Anglo-German relations. The decision to embark on such a trip, taken a year earlier under the Conservatives, had been a long time in gestation. The possibility had been mooted since a brief visit to the United Kingdom by President Heuss in 1958, but successive British premiers had ducked it. When the Germans raised the possibility of a visit by the Queen in 1961, the London Government refused, partly because it was felt, in the words of an official, that 'more time was needed for British public opinion to develop towards closer Anglo-German relations'.[40] The following year, Macmillan raised the matter with the Foreign Office, noting gloomily, 'I suppose it will have to be faced sooner or later.'[41] But the Cabinet put it off again, this time on the convoluted grounds that it would be improper to use the Queen as an 'inducement' in the Common Market negotiations – which amounted, as a senior Foreign Office official tartly pointed out, to saying that the Queen could not visit another country if it might do any conceivable good to Britain.[42]

In April 1964, after the negotiations had failed, the Foreign Secretary, R. A. Butler, returned to the idea, and approached the Palace, suggesting that the Queen should make a state visit to Germany in May of the following year. He got a curiously frosty response. Sir Michael Adeane replied that the Queen and her husband would be willing to make the trip, but only if it was made clear that they had been told to do so. The reason was not anti-German feeling at Court. It was, rather, that the Royal Family had its own worries about public opinion. When there had been rumours about an impending royal visit in the past, there had been a tendency, according to Adeane, 'to represent the Queen and the Duke of Edinburgh as pressing strongly to go to Germany because of their private ties and relationships'. This, the Queen's private secretary insisted, was 'all wrong and is untrue'. The Germans had made the running. The Queen herself had always made clear that 'she would only consider such a visit on the advice and at the request of the British Government. This is still her position.'[43] The Government advised and requested, and the next month it was announced that Elizabeth II would become the first British Sovereign to visit Germany since George V attended the wedding of Princess Victoria of Prussia in 1913.

The visit, inherited by Labour – which was beginning to consider the possibility of a renewed Common Market bid – turned out to be a remarkably successful one. British public opinion remained quizzical. The Germans, however, responded with curiosity and an almost embarrassing degree of delight, especially in Berlin. The *Guardian* noted a 'jubilant, rejoicing crowd'. As the Queen processed to John F. Kennedy Square, faces peered from every window, and people lined the streets, tight-packed and several deep, waving and shouting. There was even interest across the Berlin Wall. When the Queen and the Duke, accompanied by Willy Brandt and the Chancellor, Dr Erhart, drove up to the Brandenburg Gate, a crowd of several hundred East Germans could be seen on the other side, apparently hoping to catch a glimpse of the Queen if she stood on the viewing platform.[44]

It was a new, and not quite comfortable, experience to be cheered so fervently in a city that had recently applauded very different leaders and causes. Twenty years was not such a long time, and members of the British party, some with painful memories, had mixed feelings. Nicholas Henderson, who accompanied the royal party as private secretary to Michael Stewart, the Foreign Secretary, observed that the noise got louder every time an attempt was made to get silence so that the Queen could speak.[45] Stewart himself recalled that there was an edge to the enthusiasm of the Berlin crowd, especially in the rhythmic chanting of 'Elizabeth – Elizabeth,' that the Queen found disturbing. 'I think she thought this was a bit too much of a good thing,' he noted, '- too reminiscent of ritual Nazi shouting'.[46] Others, however, saw the excitement in a different light. Professor Carlo Schmid, Vice-President of the Bundestag, suggested that it reflected Germany's sense of the end of its status as a moral outlaw. In Britain, he maintained, the Queen was seen as capable of doing no wrong – and therefore the sight of her extending her hand to Germans would encourage her subjects to follow suit.[47] The Queen and Duke were in Germany for ten days, travelling for much of the time (as so often on her tours) by special train. The trip ended in Hamburg, with a banquet on board *Britannia* for the Federal President, President Lübke, and the Chancellor. 'Our visit to Germany was of absorbing interest,' the Queen wrote to Lord Avon when she got back.[48]

In addition to giving pleasure and satisfaction to foreigners, great royal dinners – on the royal yacht, or in a royal residence – had an undoubted power to please Labour politicians. In July, the Queen hosted a visit by President Frei of Chile. She gave a state banquet at Buckingham Palace, attended by Government ministers – including the Minister for Overseas Development, Barbara Castle, who unashamedly enjoyed herself. The setting, Mrs Castle wrote in her diary, was 'pure Ruritania,' with gold plate, knee-breeched footmen serving courses in an organized phalanx, minstrels in the gallery, roses everywhere, and the dining-room dominated by a huge canopied throne. Afterwards, Mrs Castle was summoned by a lady-in-waiting to talk to the Queen, who was sitting on a sofa with Mary Wilson. The Minister gave 'my usual half-bow because I won't curtsey' (half-bows seemed to be the Labour style). They discussed her own recent visit to Africa, until the Queen was called away to talk on the telephone to Prince Charles, who was taking his O Levels next day. When the Monarch got back, the conversation turned to everyday family matters.

> The Queen was very relaxed. I liked her enormously. She chatted on about Charles and said he was nervous, but she thought he'd get on all right. Weren't these exams awful? Turning to Margaret,

she said, 'You and I would never have got into university'. I said I was sure they would: it wasn't as formidable as it seemed. I told her how beautiful her dress was . . . and she thanked me with obvious pleasure. Margaret then pointed to the Order which was perched on the Queen's right breast and chipped, 'That's rather prominent, darling. Well it does rather stick out.' The Queen laughed and said, 'It's all right for the men; they can wear it in the lapel, and I have to pin it on somewhere.' Then Margaret murmured, 'I suppose we ought to permeate,' so we all moved into the outer drawing-room . . . [49]

Prince Charles performed adequately at his O Levels – but not much more. He failed two, including mathematics. Unlike some of his royal forebears – George V and George VI, for example, both of whom had been considered slow – he was above average. He was energetic, with wide interests. He played the cello, took the lead in the Gordonstoun school play, *Macbeth*, in November 1965, and in December won a Silver Award in his father's 'Duke of Edinburgh's Award Scheme' after getting through an obstacle race of character-building tests. But he was scarcely a brilliant student academically, and the view was taken that his aptitudes were physical and practical rather than cerebral. On this basis – and as a gesture to a favoured dominion – he was despatched for six months at the beginning of 1966 to Timbertop, the outback section of Geelong Church of England Grammar School near Melbourne.

Charles was seventeen when he went to Timbertop – still with a year and a half at school. But what then? Was it appropriate to set a new precedent by sending him to read for a degree at University, and if so, which? Just before Christmas, as solemn a gathering assembled as had ever met to discuss the future of one not very gifted boy. A dinner was held at Buckingham Palace on 22nd December to consider his fate, attended by the Prime Minister, the Archbishop of Canterbury, the Dean of Windsor, the Chairman of the Committee of University Vice-Chancellors and Lord Mountbatten. Notably absent was the Prince himself. It was the kind of occasion that Harold Wilson relished. Next day, the premier told Crossman that the discussion 'had gone on for a couple of hours because it was so interesting'.[50] Wilson recommended a provincial university, which was the right level, given the evidence so far of Charles's academic potential; such a destination would also have helped to meet the point made by Lord Altrincham, eight years before, about the need for the Heir to get to know contemporaries from ordinary backgrounds. However, his parents, who knew nothing of higher education, recoiled. Instead, Uncle Dickie's advocacy of 'Trinity, Dartmouth and the Royal Navy' prevailed. Nevertheless, it was agreed that at Cambridge, Charles – unlike previous royal students, who had lived sheltered lives without exams – should occupy rooms in college, and be treated like any other undergraduate.[51]

AT THE GATHERING of Heads of State that took place in London at the time of Churchill's funeral, the Queen mentioned to President de Gaulle that she would like to see some of the French studs: two years later she did so. In May 1967, she made the first of two private trips to Normandy. Porchester – helping with her racing interests more than ever, as Moore and Boyd-Rochford approached retirement – was the instigator. Since the Accession, she had been sending one or two mares to French stallions every year. The aim of going to France was to enable her to see for herself the way in which they were bred, as well as to meet French owners and breeders. The small royal party included Sir Michael Adeane, and Porchey's wife Jeanie, who acted as lady-in-waiting. They spent several days touring, with massive security – armoured cars and tanks watched them closely from the woods, roads were blocked off, and the motor convoy travelled at high speed. Although there was supposed to be no publicity, peasants in the villages knew they were coming. Some doffed their caps and shouted 'Vive la Duchesse!' ('Well I *am* Duke of Normandy,' said the Queen).[52] The tour ended with a visit to Baron Guy de Rothschild's Haras de Meautry, near Deauville. Later there were similar royal missions on private equine business to the United States.

Two years later, the Queen made Porchester her Racing Manager, with the job of representing her at race meetings and advising on bloodstock and mating questions – making official what had been the position *de facto* for some time. At the end of her lease of the Polhampton Stud, she bought it outright, and thereafter royal yearlings went to Polhampton after they were weaned and until they went into training. In 1970 Michael Oswald took over the running of the Royal Stud, based at Sandringham.

The two appointments turned out to be fruitful: after the trough of the sixties, royal racing and breeding fortunes sharply improved. In 1970, the Queen – in what proved a triumphantly successful demonstration of the benefits of 'hybrid vigour' – sent her broodmare Highlight to be covered by Queen's Hussar, owned by Porchester's father, which stood at the Highclere stud. The product of this match, Highclere, became the outstanding mare of the decade. Ridden by Joe Mercer, she won the 1,000 Guineas in 1974, giving the Queen her first English classic victory for eighteen years. The Queen also watched Highclere win her next race, the Prix de Diane at Chantilly (the French Oaks), after which – 'radiant with excitement' and surrounded by a huge crowd that was more interested in a British Monarch than in her victorious racehorse – she came down to lead in the winner. As she did so, the press of onlookers became so alarming that Porchester, Oswald and Charteris had to link arms to keep them from crushing her. Highclere was named after the Carnarvon stud and home: her first foal, three years later, was called after the Porchesters' home, Milford.

In 1974, the Queen won £140,000 in stake money, mainly because of Highclere. In 1977, her filly Dunfermline won the Oaks and St Leger, trained by Major Dick Hern. Not every year was as good. A mixed performance in the 1980s led to the forced retirement in 1989 of Hern, while recovering from a paralysing hunting accident, and to his replacement as trainer by William Hastings-Bass (later the Earl of Huntingdon). Ironically, Hern's career ended with a run of successes. His departure caused a furore in the racing world. Many people felt that it was unnecessary, and had been tactlessly handled. 'Criticism of the royal decision was unprecedented,' according to one racing authority. 'The bland statement in typical Palace fashion was seen to be callous.'[53] There was the question of where to lay the blame. Some pointed a finger at Lord Carnarvon. Others maintained that the Queen decided – on this delicate matter within her own expert sphere – unadvised. Whatever the reality, it was accepted in the racing world that on equestrian affairs she was no constitutional monarch, and, moreover, that she had firm views which she would vigorously express to any interested or knowledgeable visitor, and on which she was prepared to act.

Horses remained her refuge. Sir John Miller, formerly Keeper of the Royal Mews at Buckingham Palace, recalls that he found that the best time to ring the Monarch was early on a Tuesday evening. 'She was quite exhausted by talking to the Prime Minister,' he says, 'and it was a relaxation to talk about horses.'[54] Following her purchase of the Hodcott House stables from the Weinstock family in 1982, she frequently visited the downs to watch her string at work. She continued to have mixed luck: Highclere's daughter, the celebrated Height of Fashion, proved to be outstanding at stud, but only after the Queen had sold her to Hamdan Al-Maktoum. However, the Queen won her first Group One Race in the United States in 1989 with Unknown Quantity, and the following year won in Germany with Starlet.[55] She rode whenever she could – at Windsor, Sandringham or Balmoral. As throughout her life, news of thoroughbreds, pedigrees, races, racing personalities, auctions, provided a balm. In later years, when the media offensive against Royal Family became intolerably oppressive, she would quietly retreat into the comforting columns of *Sporting Life*.

THE QUEEN did not have a seamlessly easy time with all her Labour ministers. One more problematic than most was the young MP for Bristol South East who took a markedly different view of the Monarchy from that of the Minister for Overseas Development. Barbara Castle was a Bevanite, on the left of the Labour Party, with a family background of north country socialism, and a political record as a scourge of the Labour leadership, as well as of Tory governments, on such issues as British colonialism. Her critique was of social privilege and injustice, with little interest in constitutional matters. Wedgwood Benn came from a different heritage. The son of a former Liberal MP who became a Labour Secretary of State for India, Benn inherited a radical suspicion of authority and a scorn for tradition. With youth, vigour, wit, generosity, persistence, populist passion and a serviceable streak of paranoia on his side, he was already a phenomenon. A proselytizer of technocratic socialism, he was the enemy of class distinctions and – having fought a successful battle to change the law regarding the automatic inheritance of an hereditary peerage, so making it possible for him to renounce his own – inherited titles. It was against such a background that the newly-appointed minister launched a one-man crusade against an institution he regarded as an affront to democracy.

Though close to Harold Wilson in Opposition, Benn was not sufficiently senior in the Labour Party to receive the immediate reward of a Cabinet post. Instead, he entered the Government in 1964 in the unexalted office of Postmaster-General. It was not one he intended to hold for long. It did, however, provide an opportunity to demonstrate his Cromwellian fervour on an issue of daily relevance to the whole population, which he had identified as symbolically important before the election – namely the design, pictorial themes, and iconography of postage stamps. During his first few months as a comparatively inconspicuous member of the administration, Benn focused with remarkable single-mindedness on what he called 'stamp policy,' and on his radical ambition to remove the portrait of the Queen.

Since 1843, Britain had maintained its unique right not to include a national name in the design of its stamps, but to use the Monarch's head as its symbol instead. Now Benn questioned the value of this privilege – ostensibly on grounds of good design, but actually for reasons of democratic (or, as traditionalists darkly believed, republican) principle. At the time, the controversy received little attention in the press, or indeed from other politicians. Perhaps it should have got more: for it provides an unusual twentieth-century example of a minister of the Crown identifying the Crown itself as the enemy. It also showed, as Benn was forced ruefully to admit, that the Monarch was no mean fighter. From the Postmaster-General's point of view, however, it was always an uphill struggle. The Queen had on her side the powerful weapons of a Stamp Advisory Committee, chaired by the former Surveyor of her Pictures, Sir Kenneth Clark; the old-fashioned loyalties of civil servants in the Post Office; and a weekly audience with the Prime Minister.

Lacking big guns, Benn applied to his stamp war a vulpine ingenuity. He began by trying to remove the Queen's head by stealth – proposing that a large stamp, with a tiny head, should be issued. The death of Sir Winston Churchill in January 1965 enabled him to extend this tactic: he suggested, as a particularly cunning manoeuvre, a special

Churchill stamp, with the heads of the former premier and the Queen side by side. Finally, he enlisted the help of the stamp designer, David Gentleman, who bitterly complained, from an artist's point of view, that having to include the Monarch's head on every stamp cramped his style.

At first, there was some encouragement. Benn learnt that Lord Snowdon, with an interest in design, and Princess Margaret, both took a relaxed view of the matter. But there were reverses as well. From his officials, Benn faced a wall of hostility to change. Meanwhile, his double-headed Churchill stamp was shot out of the water by the Queen's personal fiat that she 'did not wish to appear with the faces of other people, however famous, who were dead'. Facing an impasse – but as determined as ever to behead his stamps – the Postmaster-General asked the Prime Minister if he could speak to the Queen directly, to sort the matter out. An audience took place on 10th March, in the state apartment at Buckingham Palace. The young minister went in, clutching a black box. He bowed, shook hands, accepted an invitation to sit down, and launched into a carefully prepared speech about the importance of stamp design. Then he got to the point. Up till now, he said, it had been understood at the Post Office that 'by the Queen's personal command,' stamp designs without the Monarch's head could not even be considered. He did not know whether the understanding accurately reflected the Queen's own views, 'but it seemed to me the straightforward thing to do was to come along and ask whether this was the result of a personal command of this kind.'

The Queen's reaction was not quite what he expected. He had been prepared for a polite but firm argument. Instead she seemed embarrassed, 'and indicated that she had no personal feelings about it at all'. Emboldened, the Postmaster-General knelt on the floor, opened his box, and spread Gentleman's headless designs on the carpet. After a forty-minute audience scheduled to last fifteen, Benn left believing himself triumphant. He was convinced – like many others with a complaint against the Palace – that the real villains were those who whispered poison in the Monarch's ear. He was also, like practically everybody else after their first proper meeting with the Queen, in a mood of elation:

So I went back to the House of Commons feeling absolutely on top of the world. The fact is the Palace is determined not to get into any controversy in which they might be seen to be responsible for holding back popular clamour for change. The real enemies of course are those forces of reaction – the Tory Party, the Civil Service, the palace flunkeys and courtiers – who use the Queen as a way of freezing out new ideas . . . I am convinced that if you went to the Queen to get her consent to abolish the honours list altogether she would nod and say she'd never been keen on it herself and felt sure the time had come to put an end to it. Of course when you do that you have to be terribly charming and nice and I tried as hard as I could to do a little Disraeli on her with all the charm I could muster.

However, it was not quite clear who had charmed whom. Still walking on air, Benn told the Prime Minister about his audience. Wilson, who was beginning to get to know the Queen, listened with grave interest. All he said was, 'Did she get down on the floor with you?'

It soon became clear that – Disraeli or not – the Postmaster-General's problems were not over. The Queen may have nodded disarmingly, but the civil servants in the Post Office who regarded the matter as one in which she had a legitimate interest, simply ignored their Minister's instructions. Soon Benn was having to cede ground.

In July, he began to doubt the wisdom of taking the Queen's image off stamps commemorating the Battle of Britain. 'In view of the bad press I'm getting and the delicate political situation,' he ruminated, 'I could foresee that if these stamps were published – since the Queen is more or less constitutionally obliged to accept my advice – I would be violently attacked in the Tory press, and this would be presented as the final straw: "Benn knocks Queen off stamps".' Prudently, he contacted Sir Michael Adeane, who seemed to confirm that, after all, the Queen had rejected the 'headless' stamps. Here was a problem. Face-to-face, she had appeared to accept headlessness. Now, the discreet message reached him, via one of the forces of reaction, that she was, in fact, dismayed by it. Benn felt obliged to capitulate. A few weeks later, instead of 'Benn knocks Queen off stamps,' the *Sun* splashed, 'Queen rejects stamps that left her out.'

Was the Queen constitutionally obliged to accept his advice or not?

Above left With Princess Anne, 1965

Above right Liege man of life and limb, Caernarvon Castle, 1st July 1969

Right With Lord Porchester at the Newbury Races, 1966

Previous page The Queen on *Britannia*, 1972

Left The Queen at Aberfan with children from bereaved families, 29th October 1966

Below Stirling University, October 1972

Top With Sir Martin
Charteris on *Britannia*,
1972

Above Silver Jubilee walkabout, St Pauls, London,
20th June 1977

Right From the album of
Sir Hardy Amies,
Australia Tour, 1970

As short as we dared

Above Wilson farewell, March 1976

Right Andrew back from the Falklands, June 1982

Below Emollient. With Mrs Thatcher and Hastings Banda of Malawi at Lusaka, August 1979

Presidential guests.
With Truman at the Canadian
embassy in Washington, 1951; the
Kennedys at Buckingham Palace,
1961; Carter at Buckingham
Palace, 1977; Reagan in Windsor
Great Park, 1982; the Clintons at
Buckingham Palace, 1995

Horribilis. Windsor fire, November 1992

Portrait by Antony Williams, 1995.

The answer seemed to be, only if the Prime Minister backed him. Wilson, however, had bigger fish to fry than headless stamps, and was keen not to displease the Monarch, whose help he needed over Rhodesia. Hence the forces of reaction were able to press home their advantage. In October, Benn received a letter from Wilson's principal private secretary, Derek Mitchell, telling him that in some circumstances the Queen could reject the advice of her ministers – and also forbidding him from commissioning headless stamps, or showing headless designs that already existed to the press, without permission.

The chastened Postmaster-General detected the handiwork of Sir Michael Adeane, in cahoots with the official staff at No. 10. 'Whether or not the Queen cares personally about it, Adeane and all the flunkeys at Buckingham Palace certainly do,' he brooded. 'Their whole position depends upon maintaining this type of claptrap.' Benn, however, was not a quitter. Instead of giving up, he decided on a last, defiant Machiavellian ploy. The Queen had indicated one thing, the Palace another, and No. 10 had rapped his knuckles, apparently put up to it by the Palace. He would go back to the starting-point, and write directly to the Queen, in the hope of getting a reply which asked him to drop headless stamps once and for all – thereby obtaining constitutional ammunition against the Palace, which would be shown to be interfering in a political matter. Alternatively, faced with such a letter from the Postmaster-General, the Palace might be shamed into accepting his arguments. Having conceived the plan, he drafted his epistle with the utmost care, so that – he recorded – 'it looks absolutely obsequious but contains a threat of cancelling the stamp policy'.

However, it was never sent. His private secretary, alarmed at the danger of an escalation, persuaded him that even to hint to the Queen that her principal adviser had lied, or to suggest that she herself had changed her mind, was over the top. Benn also learnt that Sir John Wilson, Keeper of the Queen's Philatelic Collection, had told an increasingly pro-Monarch and anti-Benn Stamp Advisory Committee that the Queen would never accept stamps without her head on them. 'The plain fact is that I shan't get the Queen's head off the stamps,' Benn wrote just before Christmas, facing up to cruel reality at last, 'and it's probably rather foolish of me to go on knocking my head against a brick wall'. Bitterly, he blamed Wilson, arch-betrayer of socialist values. '. . . [I]t is clear that Harold's intentions are that we should be more royal than the Tory Party and he finds the Queen a very useful tool,' he recorded. '. . . I doubt whether he is so foolish as to be taken in by smiles from the Queen and the flunkeys at Buckingham Palace and for that I am grateful. But I am sure that in the long run his attitude simply strengthens the reactionary elements in our society and cannot help those who want to make change.'

Benn did not get the Queen's head off the stamps, but he did eventually succeed in shrinking it. Following the general election in March 1966, which Labour won with an increased majority, he obtained clearance to display an album of David Gentleman designs to the press. He also got agreement that – though the head would be included – it would only appear as a very small black or gold silhouette. Honour was now satisfied on both sides, and diplomatic relations were restored. In June, Adeane wrote the Postmaster-General a genial letter, saying that Her Majesty hoped that 'the wide public interest in British stamp design which you have aroused in this country . . . will continue to have fruitful results'.

The following month, Benn was promoted into the Cabinet, and left the Post Office. The controversy ended: his successor, Edward Short, took no interest in the design of stamps. But the two rival generals in the stamp war had not forgotten their dispute. When Benn went to Buckingham Palace to be sworn in for his new post as Minister of Technology, he went down on one knee, held up his hand, and picked up the Queen's hand to kiss it in the approved manner. Afterwards, she shook hands with him and said, 'I'm sure you'll miss your stamps'. He replied, 'Yes indeed I shall. But I shall never forget your kindness and encouragement in helping me to tackle them.' He then bowed, and went out backwards.[56]

RICHARD CROSSMAN, successively Minister of Housing, Lord President, and Social Services Secretary in the 1964–70 Governments, presented yet another view of Monarchy. Crossman was a Wykehamist rebel – an Establishment-reared opponent of his contemporaries, with a sophisticated understanding, both social and intellectual, of the system he attacked. He was not impressed by the Monarchy, nor did he feel indignant about it: he regarded it with the sort of studied contempt that, as a schoolboy, he had felt towards the prefects, or as an aesthete at Oxford towards the bloods. It was a stupid institution, in his eyes, staffed by stick-in-the-mud people who wasted his and everybody else's time. Where lower-middle-class and sentimental Harold Wilson loved the ceremonial aspects of Monarchy, Crossman was impatient with them.

At any rate, this was the theory. Like Benn, he often recorded in his diary his irritation and disdain for things monarchical. Yet the frequency with which he did so suggests that they affected him much more than he was prepared to admit. A few years later Eric Heffer, hard left and proletarian, described to a comrade how, when he went to the Palace to be sworn in as a Minister of State, 'he had been pleased to go but felt that, by being pleased, he was somehow betraying the working class movement.' Crossman did not have the same conflict, or self-knowledge. Nevertheless, his attitude was not free from ambivalence, as his diary – in its most honest moments – admits.

He began by adopting a mode of dismissive and (his own term) 'self-conscious' contempt, both for the person and the institution. 'In our ten minutes she talked, as I am told she always does, about her corgis,' he recorded after an early meeting, in the company of the beasts, camouflaged against the carpet, in November 1964. 'She remarked how often people fell over her dogs.' A few months later, he grew fidgety over the reading by the Lord President of Orders in Council, describing it as the 'most idiotic flummery' which made him feel morally superior to his colleagues because he despised it. When he himself became Lord President, he extended his complaint, objecting that a busy minister should have to fly to Scotland for a Privy Council meeting, just because the Head of State, with time on her hands, happened to be there.[57] Like other ministers – Castle with her half bow, for instance – Crossman liked to underline his lack of deference with little gestures of autonomy – in his case, by arriving five minutes late for Council meetings, in order to keep the Queen waiting.[58] Constitutionally, he argued that Privy Council meetings were in any case unnecessary, and the whole procedure should be replaced by a time-saving royal signature.

However, Crossman's attitude to the Queen herself – as opposed to the institution – softened after he got into 'one of my furious intellectual rows' over dinner with Lord Porchester in the summer of 1964, in which he explained pedagogically to his host 'the Bagehot theory of monarchy as part of the dignified element in the consti-tution,' dilating 'on the snobbery of the people who love the Monarch and the dreary role both of the Monarch and the Court'. This was more than purely intellectual, and Porchester retorted that the Queen was one of his greatest personal friends, and that he was a tremendous admirer. 'Well maybe,' Crossman barked back, 'but she finds me boring and I find her boring and I think it is a great relief that I don't have to see her.'

Even Crossman realized that he had gone imprudently far, in such company. When the Queen said to him, a few days later, 'Ah, Lord Porchester was telling me about you,'[59] he assumed that it was a pointed remark. According to Lord Carnarvon (as Porchester has since become), it wasn't – he had not reported the conversation.[60] Yet Crossman – who liked it when people stood up to him – was impressed. 'It was very clever of her to mention it straight away and let it be known that Lord Porchester had passed on my remarks,' he noted, ' – and I found it was perfectly simple and straightforward to get on with her.' Instead of freezing relations, it felt like a secret bond, and they had an easy conversation.[61] Thereafter, his comments became increasingly favourable. He found her shy, but – on closer acquaint-ance, when he was Lord President – warm and natural. 'She has a lovely laugh,' he wrote in September 1966. 'She laughs with her whole face . . .' By the end of 1967, he was recording, with pride, in spite of himself, a 'cosy chat' with her. He also noticed – what she herself was impatiently aware of – the gap that sometimes existed between the message given out by her facial expression, and what she was actually feeling. He agreed with a Privy Council official that her sour look could be deceptive. 'When she is deeply moved and tries to control it she looks like an angry thunder-cloud,' he noted. 'So, very often when she's been deeply touched by the plaudits of the crowd she merely looks terribly bad-tempered.'[62] 'Cosy chats' became the Labour solution to the problem of how to deal with the Monarch, and how she would deal with Labour politicians. George Brown, for example, called the Queen 'my dear,' without intending or causing offence.

Meanwhile, cosiness was beginning to define the relationship of the Monarch to the public, in an era without an Empire and in which the idea of the Queen as the pinnacle of a social pyramid, kept alive during the long period of *noblesse oblige* Toryism, ceased to be relevant. Society was becoming less hierarchical: the introduction of comprehensive schools, the expansion of higher education, laws against racial discrimination all expressed an aspiration for social equality, if they did not establish the fact. Even the hereditary principle itself was challenged, when in the 1968 Queen's Speech the Government announced its intention to reform the House of Lords. While members of the Royal Family were sent off to the independence celebrations of the last remaining colonies, which almost immediately became republics, the Monarchy at home seemed reduced in scale.

The Queen's own habits and seasonal rites changed little: a dozen or so Investitures, the Maundy Thursday ceremony, Queen's Scout Parade, Cup Final, Birthday Parade, Derby, Ascot, Holyrood House, Garter Service, Thistle Service, garden parties, Goodwood, Braemar, Opening of Parliament, British Legion Ceremony, Remembrance Day, Diplomatic Corps party, Christmas Broadcast, together with Sandringham, Balmoral and Windsor, and royal tours and visits.[63] But their significance, beyond the traditions of the institution itself, and the pleasures of its occupant, seemed to diminish. There were still crowds, but they were smaller. Occasionally cheers were mixed with boos, as demonstrators turned out to protest, not against the Queen, but against some Government policy or other to which they happened to object. In the late 1960s, university campuses became places to avoid. When the Queen visited the University of East Anglia in May 1968, for example, students protested against the extravagance of redecorating a lavatory for the royal visit. An open-air seminar was held to coincide with the Queen's arrival. Afterwards, over tea, she complained about one protester who 'kept bellowing in my ear'.[64] As always, she carried out the formal part of her inspections with unflinching aplomb. But her reception, in such an environment, was a far cry from the wild, helpless enthusiasm that had greeted her wherever she went a few years earlier.

The Queen was not unpopular. But the double negative was becoming appropriate: she was ceasing to be a person, or a topic, about whom most people became excited. Surveys revealed an attitude of bland, broadly favourable, acceptance. A Mass Observation Poll of 3,000 people conducted nation-wide in 1964, and published a couple of years later, painted a picture, both comfortable and domestic, of the Queen as somebody people believed they could relate to, but about whom they had no very strong emotions, one way or another. According to its findings, the Monarch was widely regarded as kindly, motherly, natural, charming, unhypocritical and unselfish; though a sizable minority also considered her obstinate, cold and with insufficiently wide interests. Support was strongest among Anglican churchgoers, women, the middle-classes, the middle-aged and the elderly; and weakest among working-class men.[65]

Much the same picture was provided by another survey in a single city, Glasgow, with a strong radical and anti-English tradition. Here, research found remarkably little evidence of hostility to royalty – but little sense that it mattered, either. Bagehot's notion of the Monarchy as a disguise, which 'enables our real rulers to change without needless people knowing it,'[66] did not apply in Glasgow, where eighty-six per cent saw the Queen as a figurehead, signing laws and doing as she was directed. Although seventy per cent saw her as voting Conservative and only four per cent Labour, sixty-six per cent (in a Labour voting city) said she did her job well, against three per cent who felt she did it badly. There was no antagonism, and almost no republicanism. But the popularity was passive. The social scientists who carried out the survey likened her image to the picture on a chocolate box. 'The photograph gives pleasure to some, while others hardly think about it.'[67]

It was a photograph that was developing lines – and a recognizable character. 'She exacts her due,' wrote a critical, yet respectful, profile writer in the *New Statesman*. 'She speaks her mind. She tolerates no familiarity . . . No successful businesswoman in mid-career can outdo her in settled habit and fixed opinion.'[68] The sense of her as dutiful, kindly, yet unbending – simultaneously remote and sincere – was impressed on the public, with harrowing impact, after the most horrific disaster of the decade.

On 21st October 1966, a pit-heap collapsed in the mining village of Aberfan in South Wales, engulfing a school, killing a hundred and forty-six people, mainly children, from families in the same community. The Prime Minister immediately visited the scene. So did Lord Snowdon and the Duke of Edinburgh. The Queen held back. It was the moment for a spontaneous gesture: she did not make one. The reason given was that she did not want to interrupt the work of rescue and rehabilitation. Nevertheless, there was a feeling that her presence was needed, and an opportunity missed. 'She is negative,' reflects a former courtier. 'She never says things like "For Christ's sake, let's go to Aberfan". She regrets that now – she would say it was a mistake, that she should have gone at once.'[69]

Six days after the accident, she went, and spent two-and-a-half hours with the villagers and rescue workers. Reports suggest a simple, moving and appropriate tour of the devastated area. The police were told to make no effort to isolate her, and she was surrounded wherever she went by silent groups of villagers, dressed in black. 'As a mother, I'm trying to understand what your feelings must be,' she said to bereaved parents. 'I'm sorry I can give you nothing at present except sympathy.' A little girl presented her with a bunch of flowers with a card marked 'From the remaining children of Aberfan'.

With her husband, she clambered in mud over broken planks, corrugated iron and shattered desks, to the top of the heap of slag covering the school. 'There were tears in her eyes as she talked to us,' one woman was quoted as saying. 'She really feels this very deep. After all she is the mother of four children. We had four too and now we have only two.' The Queen placed a wreath at the cemetery where eighty-one children had been buried, and she and the Duke walked to the house of Councillor Jim Williams, who lost seven relatives in the disaster. Mrs Williams gave them tea. 'She was very upset,' said Mrs Williams afterwards. 'She was the most charming person I have ever met in my entire life. Really down to earth.'[70]

16

THE QUEEN AT ABERFAN was a throwback: reconjuring her parents in the rubble of the East End in the blitz, or her uncle, the Prince of Wales, in the mining valleys saying that something must be done. It was an image of communion, above politics, showing royalty not as ordinary or familiar but as available and in touch with the people at times of trouble. She performed this ancient function with dignity, though it did not come easily to her. Other roles were fading: it was becoming increasingly hard for the Monarchy to maintain traditions which had a future, as well as a past.

This was particularly true in the sphere which had involved the institution in its biggest upheaval of the century. On the subject of personal morality, and especially the sanctity of marriage, the Royal Family was in danger of becoming beached – defending a code in which privately it had ceased to believe, but which it was tied to by public expectations and its own heritage. A key issue, both for the nation and for royalty, was divorce. Reform of the divorce laws became an important part of the 'permissive' revolution of the 1960s. A liberal campaign which had gathered pace in the late 1950s came to fruition in the Matrimonial Causes Act of 1967, and in the Divorce Reform Act two years later. Thereafter, the number of divorces rapidly increased. In 1960, 25,672 were made absolute, a lower figure than in 1950. Ten years later, the number had more than doubled to 62,010.[1] Even before the changes in the law, divorce had lost much of its stigma. Yet at Court, the word continued to cause a tremor – because of Church doctrine, because of 'family on the throne' mythology, and, most of all, because of the legacy of the Royal Family's traumatic encounters with non-royal divorcees.

Aristocratic divorces had become common. Royal ones were unknown. This continued to be so until 1967, when the Earl of Hare-

372

wood, son of the late Princess Royal and first cousin to the Queen, was sued for divorce on the grounds of his adultery with Patricia Tuckwell, with whom he lived and who, three years earlier, had borne his child. The action threatened to open old wounds. The issue was not the Countess's right to a divorce, of which there was no doubt, but the Earl's right to re-marry. Though Harewood was not in the immediate line of succession, he was sufficiently close for his re-marriage to require the permission of the Queen, under the 1772 Royal Marriages Act – 'the most totally outdated piece of legislation . . . still on the books', as he later put it, a description with which Princess Margaret would undoubtedly have agreed.[2]

The British Monarchy lived by precedent, tempered by the need to adjust to changing attitudes. Where its own private behaviour was concerned, however, adjustment was more difficult. It seemed hypocritical to apply one standard in one decade, and then, because the fashion had changed, to permit a different one in the next. The Church, moreover, faced the same problem. If marriage had been wrong for Edward VIII in 1936 and for Princess Margaret in 1955, when, in each case, what was proposed was a union with a divorcee, how could re-marriage now be sanctioned for a Royal Family member who was himself divorced? It helped that Lord Harewood was a highly respected patron of music. It did not help that the Countess was the wronged party. The situation was embarrassing, as Harewood acknowledged. 'I doubt if it is possible to exaggerate the horror with which I initially looked upon the idea of divorce', he recalled, 'which was less prevalent in England in those days and seemed to me at first . . . the refuge of despair.'[3]

The Queen fervently wished not to be involved, and yet unavoidably she was. At the time of her sister's marriage to Antony Armstrong-Jones, the Cabinet had specifically – and generously, as it thought – removed any ambiguity in the interpretation of the 1772 Act by absolving the Monarch from the duty to seek advice before giving permission under its terms. The only requirement was that she should inform her ministers of what she intended to do. On this occasion, however, the first on which it had seriously arisen, the Queen wished to give permission, but she also did not wish to be exclusively associated with giving it. She appealed to the Prime Minister. With the help of his friend and solicitor Lord Goodman, who also happened to be a friend of Harewood, he devised a solution.

'Harold brought it up in Cabinet and told us that the Queen expressly wants to be advised by us,' recorded Crossman, after presiding, as Lord President, at the relevant meeting of the Privy Council. 'It was my duty . . . formally to give her the Cabinet's advice which of course she was duty bound to take.'[4] According to the Goodman-Wilson formula, 'the Cabinet has advised the Queen to give her consent and Her Majesty has signified her intention to do so.' By 1967, it would have been inconceivable for Cabinet to have given different advice. The point of the baroque if ingenious arrangement whereby her cousin asked the Sovereign's permission to marry, she asked the Cabinet for guidance knowing what its answer would be, and Cabinet obliged by giving her binding advice, was to avoid compromising the traditional royal position on divorce. In retrospect, however, it might have been better to have faced the matter squarely. By passing the buck, the Queen left the Monarchy's attitude murky. As it was, divorce became one of the forces of the modern world which crept up on the Royal Family – until it had to be accepted because there was no other choice.

The conventions which had hitherto made royal personages seem different from most people were being eroded in other ways as well. One involved the rules forbidding the portrayal of royalty on the stage. Here a matter of traditional deference, which bothered few people in itself, got mixed up with a fierce struggle against theatre censorship in general. The two became intertwined because of the ancient, and anomalous, 'Lord Chamberlain system' of licensing plays, which incongruously linked the role of watchdog over public taste with the exercise of the royal prerogative. 'Abolish it, root and branch,' wrote Bernard Shaw of the system in 1899. However, it survived, and had become by the 1960s – when as many as 800 applications for theatre licences were submitted each year – a symbol, in the world of British theatre, of philistine illiberalism.[5]

The Lord Chamberlain's prudery and his protectiveness towards the Royal Family were regarded by critics as part of the same package. Indeed, they were justified in similar terms. The ban on the theatrical representation of any recent Head of State was not defended on the grounds that it was an insult to the Crown, or an attack on the dignity of the state. Supporters of the rule put forward the characteristically British argument that it was in bad taste: the public, traditionalists maintained, regarded the frivolous portrayal of the Queen and her close relatives as improper, and would be outraged. By the mid–1960s, however, frivolity had become hard to check. Actors and producers took little – indeed virtually no – interest in contemporary royalty as such. What did concern them was theatre freedom, and making fun of one of the most ridiculous aspects of the Lord Chamberlain's grundyism became a way of cocking a snook at the Establishment. By inviting a prohibition, Queen-acting highlighted the absurdity of censorship in general.

For the libertarians, there were victories and reverses, and reverses which became moral victories. Sometimes, performances became better known by not being shown than they would have been if they had gone ahead. Thus, there was a flurry of protest in December 1965, when a production of Marlowe's *Doctor Faustus*, in which the Queen was portrayed as one of the Deadly Sins – Sloth – by an actor in a mask, was cancelled by the management of the Chase Theatre in Glasgow, after the American producer refused to cut the scene. Eventually the system became impossible to operate, as radical playwrights challenged it with plays that were unlicensable because of their sexual explicitness and use of banned words, and managers got round it by putting on unlicensed plays in theatre clubs. Its abolition in 1968 – welcomed by successive Lord Chamberlains – marked an important retreat by the Court from what remained of its role as an arbiter of public mores.

The matter did not just affect the professional stage. One significant row involving a representation of the Queen was political rather than thespian, and reflected the new restlessness of the far Left. Once again the attack was not on the Monarchy as such, but on the system of which the Monarchy was part, using Monarch-mimicking as a way of gaining attention. Early in 1967, the radical 'Committee of 100' concocted a plan to impersonate the Queen at an anti-Vietnam War rally in Trafalgar Square. The idea was for a protester to wear a crown or tiara and sit on a throne, and present a medal to an Australian soldier surrounded by corpses. The fifty-seven-year-old woman, Mrs

Kathleen Farr, detailed for the role, insisted that she 'meant no disrespect to the Queen'. Nevertheless, she received a warning from Scotland Yard that the impersonation might be regarded as offensive. The dispute sparked a furious exchange in the press. While some people objected on grounds of common decency, others pointed out that nobody objected when actors pretended to be President Johnson or President de Gaulle. Why, they asked – and the question did not go away – should a British Head of State be treated in a special way? The demonstration went ahead, but only after the organizers had made the tactical concession of using the name 'Queen Kathleen' for the impersonation, and of denying that it was an impersonation at all, in order to avoid criminal prosecution.[6]

The incident was a symptom of the increasingly irreverent times, as the satirical and underground press embraced notoriety and wove the Royal Family into its fantasies in a way that was inconceivable at the time of the Altrincham–Muggeridge critique. The erosion continued, aided by television – simultaneously royalty's most dedicated and powerful celebrant – which, abreast of the new climate, pressed as hard as the other media against the old restraints. While 'Mrs Wilson's Diary' in *Private Eye* incorporated the Queen as a staple character into its Pooterish world, Ned Sherrin's *TW3* again stretched the limits of acceptability, this time with a pop song about the Queen, which led Mrs Mary Whitehouse, the 'Clean Up TV' campaigner, to protest to the BBC Governors on the grounds of the song's 'sentimental affectation' and sexual innuendo.[7] In newspapers, books and films, as in magazines, television and theatre, 'permissiveness' involved pushing into territory that had previously been forbidden. Royalty came into the firing-line as part of a bran-tub of topics that had previously been hemmed around with prohibitions. Resistance was merely an incitement. There was also a market incentive. While writers and directors experimented in the name of art, popular press editors discovered that in the new atmosphere which the arts had helped to create, the mass public had shed its inhibitions about material previously considered unprintable.

There were many test cases, as the popular papers descended the scale of taste, and discovered that they gained readers, rather than lost them, by doing so. One occurred in October 1968, when the *Daily*

Express published a family snap of the Queen in bed with Edward as a baby, taken four years earlier. The picture was harmless, but it was a private one, not intended for publication. When Buckingham Palace protested, the paper justified its action on the grounds that the picture had already appeared in *Paris Match*, had been bought by *Life*, and so would in any case be seen world-wide. In vain, the Palace appealed to the gentlemanly code of Fleet Street. An attempt was also made to put pressure on W. H. Smith not to distribute *Paris Match*. But the problem was insuperable. The magazine's London editor simply threatened (in a month of student protest) to pay students to sell copies of the offending issue in the streets instead.[8]

EARLIER the same year, Commander Colville retired after more than twenty years in his post, as press secretary first to George VI and then to his daughter, having fought rearguard actions to the last. 'It is no use ringing up the Palace,' had been the Fleet Street truism, if a royal story cropped up.[9] 'He hated the press,' reflects one of his successors.[10] 'He was an "anti-press" officer,' says a former royal private secretary.[11] His departure was greeted with joy by his adversaries, and precipitated a revolution in the relations between Monarchy and the media.

The Commander's retirement came at a critical moment. In a rare speech, shortly before he left, he spoke of royal lives being 'progress-ively more exposed to public scrutiny,' and of an unending conflict between 'what may be properly termed "in the public interest" and what is private'.[12] The conflict raged in the late 1960s as never before. From the point of view of journalists, the proposition could be inverted. Jonathan Dimbleby later formulated it as a rhetorical ques-tion. 'If the public's "right to know" was inviolate, why should the institution of the monarchy be exempt?'[13] Colville had not been able to offer an answer, but he knew where he stood, and so did the press. Yet by the late 1960s it was clear that the Royal Family, no longer the automatic focus of admiration and reverence as in the past, needed the media as much as the other way round. The problem was taming the beast, without getting bitten in the process. This was the task that William Heseltine, Colville's replacement, set himself.

The appointment of Heseltine was something of a revolution at Buckingham Palace. Not only was he non-aristocratic; he was, by any standards, untweedy. An Australian who had worked as private secretary to Sir Robert Menzies as prime minister, Heseltine had been seconded to the Palace in 1960 for a short period. In 1965 he was appointed assistant press secretary, and worked with Commander Colville for three years. This apprenticeship, however, had not turned him into a second Abominable No Man. On the contrary, his philosophy differed fundamentally from that of his former boss. Where Colville did everything in his power to keep the press out, Heseltine saw it as his job, wherever and whenever possible, to let them in. Heseltine was the first press secretary who recognized a need to sell royalty to the public and, if necessary, to shape its behaviour accordingly.

The impact started to be felt before Heseltine took over Colville's job. During his period as assistant, royal events began to happen for the benefit of, instead of regardless of, the press. One example was the decision in July 1967 that the Queen should bestow a knighthood on the around-the-world yachtsman, Francis Chichester, not at a private investiture as with all other knights, but at a public ceremony at Greenwich, with the same sword that Elizabeth I had used to knight Francis Drake after his circumnavigation in the *Golden Hind* in 1580. The occasion showed the Queen in an unexpected mode, tying her own and the nation's heritage to a present-day enthusiasm. The result was a media spectacular. Opinions varied, however, about whether it was a proud and moving moment, or a blush-making attempt to be trendy. Critics pointed out that there was no analogy between the achievements of the two Francises, and to link them in such a way was demeaning to non-sporting knights, and a demonstration of how marginal royalty had become.[14] However, the Chichester investiture was an indication of the way minds at the Palace were moving: over the next few years a variety of other invented or elaborated traditions evolved, mainly in order to meet the demands of the cameras.

Television, of course, was key. Left to himself, the old Commander had regarded it as the work of the devil. His assistant, however – with some encouragement from the Queen's consort – began to engineer a change of view. While the BBC relaxed its rules on jokes and comments about royalty, Buckingham Palace unbent a little in its relationship with the Corporation. In 1967, the Christmas broadcast was shown in colour for the first time – hitherto, the BBC had held back from even suggesting such an innovation, for fear of a rebuff.[15] The following summer, cameras were invited to televise a royal banquet, during the state visit of the Italian President. 'As you know, there is a distinct wind of change at the Palace,' the General Manager of the BBC Outside Television Broadcasts told colleagues in July. 'It has been growing in momentum over the past few months.'[16] In 1968–9 the wind became a hurricane with the recording, and then the showing, of a film for television which provided a behind-the-scenes portrayal of what Commander Colville had dedicated his career to keeping hidden – the Queen's off-duty family life.

This film, called *Royal Family*, emerged from discussions that involved the Queen's private secretary and Uncle Dickie's film-director son-in-law, Lord Brabourne, who suggested it to Prince Philip when they were both staying with Aubrey (now Lord) Buxton at his home at Stiffkey, in Norfolk. 'The film arose out of John Brabourne and Bill Heseltine feeling that the Royal Family was almost too dull, and one ought to lift the curtain of obscurity,' says an ex-courtier.[17]

According to Heseltine, part of the rationale was a desire to meet television on its own terms, at a time when misleading reports were increasing. 'There was nothing between the Court Circular and the gossip columns,' he recalls.[18] Brabourne suggested Richard Cawston, head of the documentary department of the BBC, as director of the film. As yet the principal actor had not been consulted. 'Talk to the Queen,' said Prince Philip, when the idea got serious. She was cautious. 'You can do it,' she said, 'and then we'll see what it looks like.'[19] The BBC was happy to accept this condition, and was given free on and off-duty access.

It was an extraordinary turnaround. Previous attempts even to nibble at the edges of royal domesticity had been firmly rejected. In 1958, the BBC had asked permission to take interior shots of the royal train, for a children's programme on royal trains. Predictably, the Commander replied on that occasion that 'Her Majesty does not wish to alter the existing custom whereby the interior of Her Majesty's apartments once they have been lived in should remain private.'[20] A relaxation of this policy had occurred in 1966, when cameras had been allowed to explore state apartments – but no member of the Royal

Family was shown in them. Now, Cawston and the BBC were invited to spend a whole year recording the everyday activities of the Queen and her family at home and abroad, and in all situations, recording unrehearsed conversations. A joint BBC-ITV advisory committee was set up, chaired by Prince Philip. The Palace press office was actively involved – helping, instead of creating barbed wire. 'It couldn't have happened without Heseltine,' says Brabourne. 'He understood the point of the film completely.'[21]

The point of the film was to create a favourable impression of the Monarchy, by letting the public in on some of its secrets. 'In the late 1960s the Monarchy was falling behind the times,' says Ronald Allison, a Court correspondent who – poacher-turned-gamekeeper – later joined the Palace press office and subsequently became press secretary. 'There was a need for a positive exercise, and there was a realization that the way you did it was by television.'[22] But if it could not have happened without Heseltine, it also could not have happened without the Duke. 'There was a view that the Queen needed to sell herself a bit,' says a former courtier. 'She did not initiate it. However Prince Philip initiated quite a lot. He took the view "We are fighting an election every day of the week." The Queen took the view "I'm the Queen, I'll do what I have to do. If they don't like it, it's their fault." She is above it all – an icon. Prince Philip never liked being an icon.'[23]

The idea of the film was to shatter the iconography as conclusively as a brick heaved through a stained-glass window. The film was passed off to hesitant royals, and to the sensation-hungry press, as a response to media requests for facilities in the run-up to the Investiture of Charles as Prince of Wales.[24] It could also be presented as a natural outgrowth of past practice. 'There were family clips of film in my father's time,' says Princess Margaret. 'There had always been regular visits by newsreel people.'[25] What made this film different, however, was the freedom given to the camera team to shoot at will. The result was a production that contrasted sharply with even the most extravagant of previous royal documentaries, such as the Coronation film – or indeed any film about an already well-known group of people. The formerly mysterious Royal Family became as visible as the family next door – more so, because of the eavesdropping of private conversations. This, at any rate, was the illusion.

Private Eye, 4th July, 1969

For the Queen, it was not an entirely comfortable film to have made. Sometimes she was disconcerted by the shooting. 'I hadn't realized this would be happening in a private thing like this,' she said at a Commonwealth Prime Ministers' function, when she looked down and suddenly saw a microphone. But she got used to it. 'Cawston had a touch which relaxed them,' says Allison. 'There was a good team who fitted well together, and faded into the wallpaper.'[26] 'Quite early on,' says Brabourne, 'she suddenly discovered it was something she could do.' Cawston showed her the rushes, and she liked what she saw, including her own performance. 'It wasn't a soap,' insists Brabourne. 'It was a matter of conveying these people as human. Before *Royal Family*, the public had no idea what they were like.'[27]

There were key editing decisions. Should the Queen be shown with her husband and children on a picnic? Should she be shown talking to the American ambassador in a way that made him sound insufferably pompous? The Queen did not censor or veto. Obviously, the presentation of the film as *cinema verité* or the 'whole truth' was misleading. Cawston exercised a self-censorship as rigorous as the Palace would have applied if it had been left to them. Nevertheless, the film included footage that could never have been conceived, let alone screened, in the days of the Commander.

The film was distilled from forty-three hours of footage to a one-and-a-half hour programme. It was shown by the BBC on 21st June 1969, and by ITV eight days later. After a preview at the National Film Theatre on June 19th, few doubted the objective. 'It was an attempt to buy popularity,' admits an ex-courtier, simply.[28] It certainly bought public attention and interest. After a huge, orchestrated, press build-up – again, with the unusual feature of the Palace taking the initiative – only the very infirm, the very young, and the very indifferent, failed to see it. According to BBC Audience Research, sixty-eight per cent of the British population watched one of the two showings.[29]

This was the more remarkable because it was a seriously informative, even didactic, film. Seldom, indeed, had so many people sat through so much detailed discussion of constitutional minutiae for so long. Constructed around the device of a year in the life of the Sovereign, it described, season by season, what the Queen did, with a commentary by Anthony Jay explaining why she did it. What made it controversial was the mixing of formal and informal behaviour, so that the private, family life merged with the public performance. Though much was made of the casual nature of private conversations, there is a stiff, camera-conscious feeling to many of them, with only the small children oblivious to what was going on. All the same, it offers a persuasive and compelling essay on the experience of being royal.

The film starts by describing the soon-to-be-invested twenty-year-old Prince Wales as Heir to the 'thirteen thrones' of the Commonwealth. A highlander is shown playing a bagpipe outside the Queen's window as an early-morning alarm clock – a foible of Queen Victoria's which had happened ever since. Robert Graves is given the Queen's Medal for Poetry, with a lot of bowing. Prince Philip is shown as pilot, conservationist, and – at his desk – as patron of charities. The Queen has a conversation with Bobo MacDonald about clothes and jewels she might wear. A sequence on *Britannia* reveals a more relaxed Sovereign, in trousers, cardigan and slippers, in the company of the ubiquitous Uncle Dickie. Red boxes arrive by helicopter. The Monarchy's role, we are told, is changing. 'The Royal Family spend a lot of time encouraging industry,' says the commentary, '. . . the balance has shifted from armies to defend the Empire to exports to defend the pound.'

At Balmoral, Philip appears with his youngest son, aged four, by a boat at the edge of a loch. Edward says 'Get in'. His father says 'Coming'. Red boxes are delivered every morning, and we are reminded that even on holiday, the Queen is 'not off duty'. An elderly, white-haired, toothbrush-moustached Adeane shows the Queen Foreign Office telegrams and remains standing in the royal presence as he does so. The Monarch goes into the local shop on the Balmoral estate with Edward, and is served like an ordinary housewife, buying an ice lolly, asking for bulls-eyes, handing over coins to a non-curtseying old lady behind the counter.

Then comes the most famous scene in the film – the barbecue by the loch. Billed as 'natural,' to the twenty-first century viewer it looks very strained. There is a scrunching of newspapers, and somebody says, 'the fire's not going to work'. Anne lights it, while Charles mixes salad dressing in a reversal of gender roles. The Duke busies himself self-consciously with some sausages. A small child attention-seeks on the landrover roof. There is one moment – the most significant of the sequence – of tender eye-contact between the Queen, making salad, and Charles, whisking the dressing.

A royal tour of South America is covered in tones reminiscent of *Pathé News* in the 1950s. In Rio, dignitaries are invited onto the Royal Yacht, which is described as 'a tiny bit of Britain'. A spectator waves an image of the Queen on a flag which makes her look like a Brazilian. On to Santiago. Before she gets off the plane to inspect troops, the British ambassador comes on board and she asks, 'Are they ready?' as if she was going on stage. We are told that during a fortnight in the continent, she has had fourteen guards of honour, eighteen 'God Save the Queens,' nine speeches, four wreath layings, twelve journeys by air, seventy-nine by road, 2,500 handshakes, twenty-three receptions, lunches, dinners and banquets, a total of 104 engagements in all.

Back in Britain, the Queen, as Head of State, receives the US ambassador, who hands her his credentials. She thanks him, anti-climactically, as if she were getting a not very exciting box of chocolates from a dinner guest. There are a few moments of small talk. 'You're not living in the embassy at the moment?' The ambassador is over-come, or perhaps he always talks like this. 'We are in the embassy residence,' he says, 'subject of course to some of the discomfiture as a result of a need for elements of refurbishing, rehabilitation'.

After that, we are relieved to get out into the fresh air, to see the Queen and Anne watching riders in the early morning mist on the Berkshire Downs, with a trainer. The Queen makes an expert remark. All the Royal Family attend a drinks party at the Palace: Queen Eliza-beth in a purple feathered hat, talking in a much more normal voice than her daughter; Charles speaking awkwardly about the history essay he has to write to a group who, realizing he has made a joke, respond with polite laughter; the Queen, by contrast, losing herself in an animated and cheerful conversation with a circle of appreciative women athletes.

Christmas at Windsor brings in fringe royals (Angus Ogilvy 'a businessman,' the Duke of Kent 'a serving soldier'). Lord Snowdon addresses his mother-in-law as 'Ma'am,' Queen Elizabeth refers to her late husband as 'the King'. The family decorates a huge tree in a vast, empty hall. Four days at Windsor are followed by the annual move to Sandringham, 'a commercial farm, and private home,' which George VI had to buy from his brother. 'Sandringham means winter, Balmoral means summer.' Edward and Andrew throw snowballs, Philip paints a snowscape, the Queen says 'I have done my red boxes today,' like a teacher saying she has marked the week's essays, and drives the children in a landrover to look at hounds and puppies. The royals, we are told, 'try to preserve holidays as a time when the whole family can be together'. To prove it, we are shown them all sitting round the television laughing at an American sit-com.

A scene (which must have delighted Harold Wilson) shows the Prime Minister on his way to a Tuesday audience, 'the moment when Democracy and the Monarch meet'. Wilson is driven down the Mall and is welcomed at the Palace by Sir Michael Adeane. Another courtier says, 'Her Majesty will receive you, Prime Minister,' and then announces him. Wilson bows. You get the impression that he loves bowing. The Queen says, in her strange voice, which the public were not used to, except when reading from a script, 'When do you actually set orf?' The premier replies, in Yorkshire, 'Tuesday morning, crack of dawn.' Then comes the Commonwealth Conference, with the prime ministers and presidents – Milton Obote, Julius Nyerere, Indira Gandhi – ushered in one by one. President Nixon visits, and there is more agonizing small talk. 'You sound as if you're going to have a really busy few days – and the world problems are so complex now,' says the Queen, struggling. 'I was just thinking how much more complex they are than when we last met,' ventures Nixon. They swap signed photos of themselves.

Spring comes, bringing more pageantry, and also the best private glimpse. The Queen, Duke and the two elder children sit round a table together over a meal, and talk about the difficulty of stopping yourself laughing when funny things happen at a solemn public event. Forgetting the cameras, the Queen becomes relaxed and witty. She talks about Queen Victoria who on all occasions had perfect self-control, but was once seen to be 'trembling the slightest bit'. She describes an incident involving herself. Her timing is clever, and wry. 'The Home Secretary said, with his hand over his face, "There's a gorilla coming in". I thought this was a very unkind thing to say about anybody. I pressed the bell, and the door opened – and in came a gorilla! – terribly short body, long arms. I had the most appalling trouble keeping a straight face'. Philip follows with a story about George VI in a rhododendron bush. Charles tries to join in with his own contribution, which gets ignored. The film ends with Charles fishing. 'If he needs help,' concludes the commentary flatly, 'there is a thousand years of family history to draw on.'

The most striking feature of the film, even when viewed more than a quarter of a century later, is the dramatic emergence of members of the Royal Family as personalities. Philip seems imaginative, caged, less extrovert than previously believed, Anne matter-of-fact and confident, Charles gawky and uncomfortable – though happiest with his brothers, who do not disregard him like everybody else. The Queen is small, neat, bird-like. There is a contrast between her glassy look when on show, with which everybody was already familiar; her stiff conversations with dignitaries on formal occasions, or on informal ones when she remembers she is being watched; and the unexpected brightness and humour she displays during the relatively small number of shots of her fully at ease. For all the limitations of such a project, the sense of the family as individuals, and as a group, is powerful. You sometimes find them irritating, but you like them by the end.

At the time, the propaganda seemed to work. People are said to dream about the Queen coming to tea. It was as though she had. Yet if the film smashed icons, it did not destroy the stereotypes. In 1968, before Cawston embarked, a profile-writer presented the Monarch as an engaged mother who liked to 'talk on level grown-up terms' with her elder children, while the smaller ones 'wander in and out of her sitting-room, so far as a diligent nanny and state business allow,' leaving their toys around the sleeping corgis, although occasionally 'the Queen likes to put on an apron to give them their bath'. Though Philip had 'bouts of frustration', the Queen liked nothing better than an evening at home, in front of the television, with shoes kicked off – when not striding the Scottish moors, or doing something with horses.[30] So far from painting a completely different picture from this, the film picks out its features, one by one, and illustrates them – as if the director's concern was to avoid disconcerting either the Royal Family or the public with new ideas, and to reassure them by confirming old ones.

The film received ecstatic notices. It was heralded as a milestone, which it undoubtedly was. Julian Critchley wrote that it was 'devoted to the proposition that the Queen is a human being'.[31] Everybody agreed that it succeeded. 'I think it is quite wrong that there should be a sense of remoteness or majesty,' said Philip, when asked about the film in an interview. 'If people see, whoever it happens to be, whatever head of state, as individuals, as people, I think it makes it much easier for them to accept the system or to feel part of the system.'[32] *Royal Family* got people talking, mainly favourably, about the cast, and made them appreciate that the Monarch did more than ride in coaches and wave. The star herself was pleased, and proud. Shortly after the British showing, she talked to Tony Benn (of all people), about the programme, during a visit to the Steam Generating Heavy Water Reactor at Winifrith, where Benn, now Industry Minister, was her host. Only one scene worried her. 'She said it might have to be cut for showing in the United States,' Benn noted; 'the American Ambassador had used very long words and made himself look rather ridiculous.'[33]

However, there were also longer-term considerations. What if 'accepting the system' – as the Duke put it – was no longer what people were content to do? Was there not a hard logic, and a realism, to the negative approach of the No Man? 'The film showed that the Royal Family was made up of ordinary people like the rest of us,' says a close friend of the Queen and Prince Philip, who had doubted the wisdom of the enterprise. 'But when you discover they are ordinary people you have different expectations of them.' He remembers it being talked about in the presence of Uncle Dickie. 'It was typical Mountbattenism.'[34] Mountbattenism meant a conscious, persuasive courting of public opinion – something which the film achieved, with great artistry. Yet the very artistic success of the documentary begged many questions about an institution which, if it looked ahead, had to think not about five-yearly elections but in terms of decades and generations. Above all, there was the question of whether, once the Royal Family got into the business of revealing secrets, it could pick and choose. 'To those who say "it started the rot,"' says Allison, 'it is possible to reply, "how long could the curtains be held in place?"'[35] But the imagery of pulling back the curtains was false in the case of a film which, though given exceptional licence, still presented the Monarchy as it wished to be seen.

The Palace expected the press to feel grateful. This was naïve. Appetites were whetted, that was all. Indeed the rest of the media simultaneously felt scooped by the BBC, and challenged by Buckingham Palace. Commander Colville had devoted his life to preserving the notion that it was not in the public interest for the public to know the things about royalty that most interested them. Even Heseltine, as newly-fledged press secretary, had made a fuss about the publication of innocuous family photographs. Now the Palace had used a Corporation trusty, and its own privileged access to the medium, to declare public curiosity legitimate and to try to satisfy it, in its own way, with a direct appeal. Editors, rival television producers, publishers were impressed: but they also saw it as a nose-thumbing exercise. The Queen had sometimes authorized lawsuits against former servants who did a Crawfie, and disclosed information acquired in the royal service. Yet, as one writer pointed out, the film 'disclosed more homely facts than servants could ever tell'.[36]

There was a professional issue here, as well as a commercial one – or perhaps a commercial one that could be dressed-up as professional. *Royal Family* had been designed, by the best film-makers and public relations people in the business, to boost the image of a 'model family,' busily engaged in dutiful activities and wholesome recreations. Was it right for a fourth estate worth its salt, to accept such a calculated piece of media manipulation as a given? If royal 'privacy' was no longer sacrosanct, why should its exposure be strictly on royalty's own terms? As if to rub in the point that royalty was now actively engaged in a deliberate campaign of self-projection, the Prince of Wales was interviewed on the radio – something which never happened to his mother at an equivalent age, or at any other time. The interviewer was a friendly presenter called Jack de Manio, who offered pat-ball, sycophantic questions, to which the Prince struggled to give sensible answers. Once again, the Palace was able to use the BBC as its privileged and co-operative mouthpiece.

It was difficult, once the genie of this kind of publicity had been let out of the bottle, to put it back in again. Through the 1960s, the press had been shedding, bit by bit, its former reticence on royal topics. The film – by offering an intimacy never before provided – encouraged the discarding of any remaining restraint. 'The sight of Prince Philip cooking sausages meant that after that people would want to see the dining room, the sitting room, then everything except the loo,' says Kenneth Rose, who subscribes to the 'started the rot' thesis. 'And whereas at that stage you could still keep the British press under control, you couldn't stop the paparazzi.'[37]

THE KNIGHTING of Sir Francis Chichester was one re-invented tradition, which television made available to a mass public. The Prince of Wales's Investiture was another, grander in scale and conception: the first ever major royal ceremonial specifically tailored for the cameras. It took place on 1st July 1969, at Caernarvon Castle, against the background of a long controversy. *Royal Family* had been devised in the royal circle as a piece of self-promotion. The politics behind the Investiture were more complicated. Like the film, it was a Court event, in this case using ceremonial theatre to focus the attention of British subjects and the Commonwealth on the self-renewing Mon-

archy, while pointing to the Royal Family's interest in and identification with each and every part of the United Kingdom. At the same
time, however, it related – in a way that the film did not – to current
concerns at Westminster. Some saw it as 'a project a good deal less
near to the Queen's heart than to Mr Harold Wilson's and Mr George
Thomas's'[38] – a crude Labour Party antidote, at a time of plunging
electoral fortunes, to the rise of Welsh nationalism, which threatened
Labour's hold on the Principality.

The attack, however, was not merely directed at an apparent piece
of party political opportunism. There was also, more worryingly for
the Monarchy, a linkage in the minds of many people in Wales,
between royalty and Englishness. Charles had been created Prince of
Wales in July 1958, at the age of nine, since when he had had little to
do with his titular nation. Before that, there had been a twenty-two-
year gap. Perhaps if George VI had overcome his scruples about Heirs
Presumptive as opposed to Apparent in the 1940s, there might have
been a stronger sense of continuity, and of the Monarchy as a Welsh
institution. As it was – despite a late decision to send the Prince to
University College, Aberystwyth for a term to learn a smattering of
Welsh – the connection felt tenuous, there was resentment at the
imposition of what was seen as a Westminster and Buckingham
Palace-inspired event, and opponents dismissed the whole performance as a symbol, not of historic royal feeling for Wales, but of historic
English oppression. At a time when anti-monarchical protests were
unusual, except from fringe bodies, the Council of the Welsh League
of Youth – a large and generally non-political body – only narrowly
decided against boycotting the occasion altogether. There were also
threats of direct action by extremists.[39]

The only modern precedent for a Prince of Wales Investiture was
not entirely a happy one. This was the presentation of the eldest son
of George V to the people of Wales in 1911 – a ceremony which was
itself a concoction, pressed upon a reluctant Heir by an artful Lloyd
George, with an eye (according to the Duke of Windsor in his
memoirs) 'to what would please his constituents,' and also with a
view to healing wounds caused by plans to disestablish the Welsh
Church. On that occasion, the future Edward VIII had protested
vociferously but in vain at the indignity of having to wear 'a fantastic

costume' consisting of white satin breeches and a mantle and surcoat of purple edged with ermine. Prince Charles suffered a fate similar to that of his great-uncle. Sartorial and ceremonial features were included in the 1969 Investiture, not because there was a precedent for them, but because they were felt to add style to the event, enhance its Welshness or add to its appreciation by an international armchair audience.

The event was organized by the Earl Marshal in conjunction with Lord Snowdon, who had designed the aviary at London Zoo and knew about camera angles, and who had been given the mainly empty title of 'Constable of Caernarvon Castle' by the Queen six years earlier. An attempt was made to revive the atmosphere of the Coronation. The 1953 event, however, had been a religious service of genuine antiquity, with television reluctantly tacked on. The Investiture was little apart from an Arthurian pantomime, with mock-medieval pageantry and Gothic revival words. To that extent, it copied the Lloyd George example. This time, however, it was mixed up with state-of-the-art studio technique.

In place of the discreet crusader's tent in which the previous Investiture had taken place, Snowdon created an ingenious stage set in the middle of the Castle courtyard, composed of three slate thrones under a clear perspex canopy – constructed with the principal aim of giving the cameras a good view. At first it had been intended to dangle 'the largest perspex object in the world' from balloons. The idea was abandoned when it was pointed out that a well-aimed shot from a distant Welsh marksman would cause havoc. Undangled, the canopy was a fitting symbol of the new Monarchy – an institution which, as it now seemed, was prepared to allow its intimate moments to be observed in the living rooms of the entire world, yet believed it would be protected from the consequences. At the same time, the Investiture gave a new twist to the Cawston revolution. Where the BBC team had used modern technology to display the domesticity at the heart of a private mystery, the Snowdon fantasia re-shaped a public ceremonial in order to meet the requirements of modern technology.

Even after the perspex object had been brought down to earth, anxiety about terrorism remained, and there was talk of abandoning the whole venture. The Government, however, felt committed to it, and so did the Palace. So the event went ahead – against a background of bomb scares and minor explosions, and intense security. Crowds lining the procession route were sparse, sometimes outnumbered by police.[40]

The ceremony itself had a quaint *son et lumière* charm, despite the incongruity of the hand-bag holding Queen, and her son dressed as an Edwardian medieval prince. The climax involved the Monarch commanding Garter King of Arms to fetch her purple-clad son who had to kneel on the platform while she put a gold coronet on his head. 'For me', Charles wrote in his diary, 'by far the most moving and meaningful moment came when I put my hand between Mummy's and swore to be her liege man of life and limb . . .'[41] Not only moving and meaningful, but also funny: luckily the humour of the situation, if not of the ridiculous words, did not escape the principal performers. Careful witnesses might even have observed them, like Queen Victoria, to tremble. A few weeks later, the Queen told Noël Coward, over lunch with her mother, that she and Charles 'were both struggling not to giggle because at the dress rehearsal the crown was too big and extinguished him like a candle-snuffer!'[42]

Afterwards, there was a sigh of relief. The Investiture was not a disaster or even a failure. In many ways it was a success. The television audience was colossal, the plaudits keen. A few years later, Christopher Booker detected in the public reaction 'signs of a returning enthusiasm for the Monarchy that would have been unthinkable five years before.'[43] Perhaps there should have been more unease than there was. If it was successful, there was the question of who it was successful among, and whether it was a success of the right type. According to a poll conducted by Opinion Research Centre, about half the population of Wales thought the Investiture was a waste of time. Viewers in England were more appreciative. However, there was a general tendency to merge the Investiture, which followed so swiftly after the *Royal Family* film, with other media extravaganzas. It was also fair to ask whether 'success' was an appropriate criterion to apply to a ceremony which, if it had any significance at all, was supposed to be patriotic, constitutional and spiritual. Moreover, the 'success' – if such it was – had to be qualified by the ambiguity that surrounded the whole occasion. A milestone had been past, of an unfortunate kind: the

1969 Prince of Wales Investiture was the first major royal ceremonial of the century about which it was politically respectable to argue that it should never have taken place.

Indeed, if there was a royalty revival at the turn of the decade, helped by *Royal Family* and the Investiture, it had a very different kind of basis from the quiet swelling of interest that occurred in the 1940s and 1950s. During the reign of George VI and the early years of the present reign, royal popularity – reflecting, in part, the psychological needs of a fragile and threatened Empire – had appeared to grow spontaneously. It had come from outside the institution, responding to a display of traditional virtues, and the absence of obvious vices, on the part of the dynasty, but not requiring active stimulus. This time, much of it was generated from within – the product of an intelligent exploitation of the opportunities the media provided. Such a change involved a new relationship with the public.[44] In the past, royalty had been a barely questioned part of the natural order. Now, it appeared to be seeking a new social contract.

What else could the Monarchy do? A key initiator and searcher after a practical, rather than a merely symbolic, justification for the Monarch – in short, a modern purpose – was the Monarch's husband. At the end of the year, Prince Philip visited North America. When he was in Canada, he spoke again of the Monarchy as if it were a non-mysterious, workaday, democratic institution, and its principal figure somebody who was just doing a job. 'If you don't want us, then let us end it on amicable terms and not have a row about it', he told a press conference in Ottawa. 'The future of the Monarchy depends on the national community, and if at any stage the community decides it is unacceptable then it is up to that community to change it. It is up to the people themselves.'[45] He was talking about Canada and the Commonwealth, not Britain. But his remarks seemed to apply, with equal force, at home.

CYNICS detected another motive behind Buckingham Palace's sudden interest in raising the Monarchy's public profile: money. The *Royal Family* film and the Investiture both happened in a year in which royal finances became an issue for the first time since the fixing of the Civil List after the Accession. Perhaps there was no direct connection.

However, the arousing of sympathetic public interest in the activities of the institution, and in the personalities of those who were part of it, was undoubtedly well-timed.

The royal cash problem was scarcely new. Since the Tudor period, the narrative of the relations between Crown and Parliament – and, through many reigns, the amount of independence permitted to the former – had turned on the matter of tax-derived royal revenues. There had been a principle, which changed little over the centuries: Kings and Queens who asked Parliament for a bigger subsidy faced awkward questioning, if they did not have to give or concede something in return. Inflation had always been the enemy of monarchical government. This was no less true since the evolution of a constitutional monarchy. In the twentieth century, the Civil List had been set at the beginning of reigns, in the expectation that it would last for the whole of them. The immediate aftermath of an Accession – when the new King or Queen had popular support, and a clean slate – was a good time for securing a generous long-term settlement. Hence the arrangement was a satisfactory one, from the Crown's point of view, provided the reign turned out to be short, or the pound maintained its value: so satisfactory, indeed, that not only had recent Monarchs managed to make ends meet, every Sovereign from 1830 until 1952 had made a net profit out of the Civil List in the course of his or her reign.[46] In George VI's case, though his 1937 Civil List arrangements had been hard-hit by inflation, the effect had been counteracted by reduced opportunities for spending, and expectations of hospitality, in the wartime and early post-war years.

For a monarch who wished to avoid a financial clash with Parliament, the moral was thus to accede late or die early, and to reign during a time of price stability or, alternatively, of belt-tightening austerity. It was becoming clear that Elizabeth II would fail on every count. By the end of the 1960s, she had already reigned longer than her father, prices had risen at an accelerating pace and – in an age of affluence – wage and salary bills had grown disproportionately. However, there was also another side. If the Queen's ability to meet official expenditure out of Civil List funds had been impaired, the expanding economy, and her immunity from tax, had greatly increased her private fortune. The second aspect was to become a matter of increasing contention, especially as estimates of the royal fortune varied widely.

The Civil List crisis, if it can be so described, became public the same autumn. On 5th November 1969, *The Times* reported that the Queen was overspending her allowance – partly, it pointed out, because of the Labour Government's Selective Employment Tax, which had been designed to make businesses and other organizations cut their work-forces, and which was levied on the labour-intensive Household staff. As a result of such pressure, the Queen's three hundred full-time staff had been cut by fifteen per cent since the Accession. ('My heart bleeds', responded the republican MP, William Hamilton.) For a couple of years it had apparently been necessary to draw on the private income to pay Palace bills. A Court official was quoted as saying that 'it might be time for the situation to be reviewed'.[47]

Perhaps the matter might have been settled quietly if it had been left there – or it might have been ignored. What ensured that it become headline news of a kind that forced the Government to sit up was a series of off-the-cuff remarks by Prince Philip, still in North America, who responded to the less inhibited style of transatlantic questioning during an NBC 'Meet the Press' recorded interview by saying that the finances of the Royal Family would go into the red in 1970. 'We may have to move into smaller premises, who knows?' he said. He had already been forced to sell a small yacht, he pointed out, and he expected that he would have to give up polo.[48]

If the Royal Family was going to make a public complaint about its straitened circumstances, asking for sympathy about having to cut back on luxuries was scarcely the best way, and a foreign television programme hardly the best place, to do it. Nevertheless the suggestion from such a source of imminent penury was embarrassing to the Labour Government, which was fighting to get through a vital piece of prices and incomes legislation, and was concerned about labour movement repercussions if it exempted the Monarchy from restrictions it was seeking to impose on ordinary workers – yet did not want to appear anti-royal in the run-up to a general election. A few Labour MPs could be found to take the Duke's side. 'If we want a monarchy we have to pay them properly', said Emmanuel Shinwell, a former minister in the Attlee Government, echoing Bevan in 1947. 'We can't have them going round in rags.' Trade unionists hostile to the Government's incomes policy, however, were less solicitous.

Fearing another internal party row if he did something, and public outrage if he didn't, the Prime Minister raised the matter at a meeting of the 'Inner' Cabinet of key ministers on November 11th – revealing the extent of Government help to the Crown that was already taking place. The Chancellor, he explained, had already arranged to transfer some royal spending to various departments, so that, for example, the Ministry of Works now carried the cost of royal castles. A brisk discussion showed colleagues united on one thing – the need to get the Government off the hook as expeditiously as possible. Richard Crossman noted that it was the 'working-class' ministers who were sentimental about the Monarchy, and included both Wilson and Callaghan in this category. 'The nearer the Queen they get the more the working-class members of the Cabinet love her and she loves them,' he noted.[49] He might have added that a love for the Monarchy among proletarian Cabinet ministers was nothing new: between the wars, the railwayman politician Jimmy Thomas had been famous for his special friendship with George V. However, Barbara Castle, similar in background to Wilson, and also a personal admirer of the Queen, was a sharp opponent of giving her an easy time over the Civil List. She demanded an investigation of the private fortune. Crossman heartily agreed. 'The Queen pays no estate or death duties,' he observed, 'the monarchy haven't paid any since these taxes were invented and it has made her by far the richest person in the country.' Despite Crossman's suspicions, Wilson (in this company) seemed to assent – saying to his colleagues that, while most rich people gave generously to charity, the royals felt no obligation to spend any of their private income on seeing themselves through their public life.[50]

The Prime Minister's main public concern, however, was to take the issue out of politics: and, to the extent that it remained inside it, to help the Queen as much as he could. He therefore adopted a bipartisan approach, securing the agreement of Edward Heath, the Opposition Leader, to a new Select Committee on the Civil List – but not until after the general election, when whoever was in office would set one up. In the Commons the same afternoon, he explained to MPs that the List had been incurring increasing deficits since 1962;

mentioned the progressive transfer of Royal Household expenditure to departmental votes; and said that resources built up in the first years of the reign were expected to be exhausted by the end of 1970. The announcement took the heat out of the situation, which was the aim. The Government front bench was relieved. 'If Harold had mishandled it,' wrote Crossman, 'we should now be in a long unpopular row in which we would lose votes by seeming to be mean to royalty.' To this extent, Heseltine's consciousness-raising over preceding months had had its effect.

Wilson's emphasis was on restrained loyalty. When Crossman congratulated him, he replied sagely that, 'I am really looking back to what Baldwin did in the Abdication'. What Baldwin did was to help the Monarchy through a crisis by keeping calm. However, he also took decisive action. Wilson's tactic got Labour out of its immediate predicament, while throwing a lifeline to the Palace. But it did not protect the Monarchy from the argument that, at a time of national anxiety about pay, an individual – or an institution identified with an individual – believed to be extremely rich who asked for more money out of public funds, could not expect to be given it without some searching questions being asked. When a Labour MP said that the promised Select Committee would need to have a much wider ambit than the equivalent body in 1952 – meaning that the House of Commons would wish to go more deeply into the intricacies of royal finance – there was no answer the premier could give, except to agree.

17

A NOTHER ANTIPODEAN tour was planned for early 1970. The Queen began to think about it while she was at Sandringham just after Christmas. Hardy Amies was preparing her dresses. 'You sound as though you are going to have a very busy time at the beginning the this year,' she wrote to him on New Year's Day. 'I am relieved not to have to come up to London for fittings too soon, having only just got here! I shall look forward to wearing my new clothes very much in New Zealand and Australia.'[1] The visit, her first to the Pacific Commonwealth since 1963, began early in March. The Queen flew to Canada, stopping overnight at Vancouver, where she picked up her husband, who had been in Mexico, and then crossed the Pacific, visiting Fiji and Tonga en route, before arriving on 12th March in Wellington. It was an extended trip, with a fortnight in New Zealand, followed by nearly five weeks in Australia.

Royal Family had had its impact. Crowds were unexpectedly large. 'That's how the walkabouts happened,' says a friend.[2] Heseltine was once again the instigator. 'There was a clear policy of making her much more accessible,' says Allison, who was covering the tour for the BBC. 'The preparation for the walkabouts was the film. Suddenly the lady on the schoolroom wall, on the postage stamp, was a real person, who drove cars, barbecued, had a bit of a sense of humour.'[3] On their way to Wellington City Hall for the two-hundredth anniversary celebration of Captain Cook's voyage, the Queen and Duke took an apparently casual, unscheduled walk along the street, talking and shaking hands with onlookers. A *Daily Mail* reporter, Vincent Mulchrone, applied a word previously used to describe the wanderings of Australian aborigines in the bush, and 'walkabouts' became part of the new Monarchy's repertoire.[4] As a result, as Philip Howard pointed out, the Queen became the first Sovereign since Charles II to mingle comparatively naturally among her ordinary subjects.[5]

The visit was followed by a political upheaval in Britain. Shortly after the Queen and Duke got home in May, Harold Wilson seized the opportunity which an upturn in the opinion polls seemed to present, and asked for a dissolution. The election took place on 18th June. The polls were confounded, and Edward Heath was called to the Palace. 'The courtiers could scarcely conceal their delight,' noted Benn, after handing in his resignation, ' – Sir Michael Adeane, the equerries, the ladies-in-waiting – were obviously thrilled at what had happened and were being polite to the "little Labour men".'[6] Crossman, however, formed a slightly different impression of the Queen's own feelings. He asked her if she minded elections. 'Yes,' she replied, 'It means knowing a lot of new people'. He concluded that she did not discriminate much between the parties and 'for her, all this simply means that, just when she had begun to know one, she has to meet another terrible lot of politicians.'[7]

There was certainly no question of a simple return to the aristocratic country-weekend Toryism the Palace had taken for granted before Wilson. Heath's leadership of the Conservatives and premiership marked a decisive shift in the mood and mores of the Party of the Right. His appointment as Prime Minister was a direct consequence of the 1963 muddle over the succession to Macmillan, for which the Queen could be held partly responsible, and which had led to the adoption of a system of leadership election. It was the first time the Monarch had not been involved in the choice of a Tory leader since Austen Chamberlain became leader of the Conservative Party in the House of Commons in 1921. Perhaps it was not entirely a coincidence that Heath was also the first premier since Ramsay MacDonald whose roots were in the manual working-class. Unlike MacDonald, however, the new Prime Minister seemed little interested in, or excited by, either his audiences with the Sovereign or the rituals of Monarchy. The Queen was used to gallantry from her premiers: gallantry was not Heath's style. He had neither the ease of manner and urbanity of his grander predecessors, nor Wilson's delight in tradition and eagerness to please. He could be abrupt to the point of rudeness, and had no small talk. 'Harold was fine, because he loved her and treated her marvellously,' says an ex-courtier. 'But Ted was tricky – she was never comfortable with him.'[8] As a result, though he was correct in his behaviour towards both the Monarchy and the Monarch, the closeness that had existed between the Palace and Downing Street under Labour vanished under the Conservatives.

Where Macmillan had regarded the Queen with admiration and sentimentality, Heath treated her as a piece of necessary business. He did not reverse the one step taken by Wilson which threatened the principle on which monarchical succession was based: the Labour premier's decision not to add to the stock of hereditary peers in the House of Lords. After the invention of life peerages, Macmillan and Douglas-Home had created hereditaries and lifers in roughly equal proportions. It was open to Heath, as a Conservative, to revert to the old practice. He chose not to do so; and the notion that accident of birth was a sufficient qualification for participation in law-making was effectively abandoned by the party that had once been its staunchest protagonist.

More important as a factor in Queen–premier relations, was the Prime Minister's downplaying of the Monarch's overseas role: a touchy subject that was to dog exchanges between the Palace and Tory occupants of Downing Street for decades to come. Heath's 'undisguised disrespect' – as his biographer has put it – for the Commonwealth in general and especially for its African leaders, reflected a widely felt impatience within his party. In 1971, he even effectively prevented the Queen from going to the Commonwealth conference in Singapore, because of member-state attitudes on the question of arms to South Africa. Two years later, he agreed only reluctantly, and after some behind-the-scenes debate, to her attendance at the next meeting in Ottawa. Heath's impatience with the Commonwealth stemmed partly from his anxiety to reduce non-European commitments in preparation for entry into the Common Market. His successor as Tory leader did not need such a motive: and the difference in attitude between Monarch and Prime Minister towards the post-imperial association became a continuing source of embarrassment on both sides.

THE COURT did have some ground for relief at the outcome of the election. It ensured that the Select Committee on the Civil List, which began its deliberations in May 1971, would have a Conservative chairman – the new Chancellor of the Exchequer, Anthony Barber – and a Tory majority, at a time when Labour was moving to the Left. Indeed, the Palace had good reason to be pleased by the composition of the Committee, which included such friends of the Monarchy as William Whitelaw, and the ultra-royalist Norman St John Stevas. However, the Labour contingent was a strong one. In addition to Harold Wilson, as Leader of the Opposition, Roy Jenkins, Joel Barnett, Douglas Houghton and the republican, William Hamilton, were members. If Labour had won the election, some of these would have had bigger things on their minds than the Monarch's finances. As it was, they were able to give it their keen attention.

The same was true of Opposition back-benchers not on the Committee, who regarded some of its Labour members with suspicion. Indeed, Buckingham Palace became a convenient whipping-boy for Labour people who, for one reason or another, wished to discomfort, not just the Tories, but their own leadership, and who found in the Civil List debate an opportunity to denounce them as excessively Establishment-minded. Richard Crossman, who had left Parliament at the election and become editor of the *New Statesman*, led the forces of irreverence. Before the election, he had delivered a lecture at Harvard entitled 'Bagehot Revisited' in which he had described the British taste for Monarchy as 'a universal addiction of the whole nation,' and a deeply rooted myth, 'which canalizes and purges the emotions of a mass democracy exposed to mass media in an irreligious age'.[9] Now, he attacked the Queen for the 'truly regal cheek' of her pay claim, arguing that she was seeking to have her cake and eat it, by asking that the Civil List should take price rises into account, while not accepting that the growth in her non-taxed private wealth should be considered at the same time. 'Money,' he pointed out, 'is an eternal dispute about which one monarch lost his head.'[10] At Lambeth Town Hall, flagship of the new municipal socialism which local election results had recently launched, Labour councillors took the point almost literally. The more Cromwellian among them removed a portrait of the Queen from the main staircase and put it under the sofa. 'It might seem very flippant,' declared Councillor Tony Banks, one of the iconoclasts, 'but these gestures are, I hope, going to be symptomatic of the more positive things Lambeth Council is going to do.'[11]

Buckingham Palace won an immediate victory on the most important issue, the relevance of the Queen's private fortune and income. As Committee chairman, Barber defended her right to keep secret the details of her personal wealth, and also the extent of her resources which resulted from tax immunities. As a consequence, speculation raged in the press about the sum she was concealing, with newspapers vying with each other to produce the most astronomical totals. Figures as high as £50m and £100m for the Queen's private assets were mentioned, the size of the sum depending on the prejudices of the estimator, and on definitions of 'private'. Jock Colville – who had become a director of Coutts, the royal bankers – wrote to *The Times* in support of Buckingham Palace (declining to mention that, as an ex-courtier, he was *parti pris*). He suggested that £2m was a more realistic total than some of the figures being bandied about. The Palace, which normally avoided any comment on such matters, agreed that this was 'more likely to be accurate,' than bigger estimates which included inalienable possessions and treasures, like the Royal Collection, which the Queen was not at liberty to sell.[12] Yet why, people asked, if the royal wealth was so small, did she not take the opportunity provided by the Select Committee to clear the matter up? It was not an edifying exchange. The Queen's resistance on this question was one reason why the atmosphere on the Committee, even among the Conservative members, was one of interrogation and bargaining more than of co-operation.[13]

'The House of Commons has inquired into most things,' wrote Bagehot, 'but has never had a committee on "the Queen". There is no authentic bluebook to say what she does.'[14] The 1971 Select Committee did not provide a bluebook, but it went some way towards defining, with the help of Sir Michael Adeane, the Queen's official duties. These it listed under four main heads: work arising from the normal operations of government, involving the receipt of information and the signing of documents; receiving 'a large number of important people privately,' including in this category Privy Councils and Investitures; attending State occasions such as the Opening of Parliament, Trooping the Colour and religious services, together with many visits to hospitals, army units and so on; and state visits, both as host and tourist.

The Committee put the Crown more seriously on the defensive than at any time since 1936. Although it accepted, in the words of its report, that there was 'no question in any ordinary sense of a "pay increase" for the Queen,'[15] the emphasis, more than ever before, was on justifying, not merely expenditure, but also the need to incur it. It was no longer enough, as one writer has put it, to see the Monarchy 'mainly as a *tableau vivant*, for which the people should pay handsomely.'[16] The Queen, through her close advisers, had to present a convincing case that she gave value for money.

There were a number of questions to be examined: in particular, the appropriate level at which royal activities should be pitched, how far the practice of shifting expenses from the Civil List to department votes could and should go, without a sacrifice of royal discretion, and (the key one from the Palace's point of view) how the Palace could best be protected from inflation.[17]

Sir Michael Adeane was the principal witness. He outlined in words what *Royal Family* had provided in television images, stressing the unfavourable nature, as he saw it, of the Queen's conditions of service, and how unrelentingly she worked. Her job, he said, was continuous, and she could not even look forward to a period of retirement. She received one hundred and twenty letters a day, and spent three hours daily reading Foreign Office telegrams, reports of parliamentary proceedings, ministerial memoranda and Cabinet minutes. She had to devote care to the management of Buckingham Palace, Windsor Castle, Holyrood House, Sandringham and Balmoral. In fulfilment of her wish 'to stand much nearer to her people in all her realms,' she had travelled more extensively than any of her predecessors. She also had domestic responsibilities as a mother. A mass of detail was provided which showed, in almost every case, how much busier the Monarch had become since the Accession. Thus it emerged that the number of centenarians to whom royal telegrams had to be sent had risen from 225 per annum in 1952 to 1,186 in 1970.[18]

While St John Stevas congratulated the Monarch on how much she did, Wilson helpfully drew attention to the extent to which the Queen was always on call, Jenkins wondered whether some of the younger royals might not earn their own living, and Hamilton wondered whether the Monarchy was necessary at all. A *pointilliste* portrait of the institution built up, that was often revealing in unintended ways. For example, Adeane defended the Queen's practice of holding audiences with each British ambassador before he left to take up a posting on the grounds that it made 'a great difference' when he got there 'not only that he has seen The Queen, but that his wife has seen The Queen, because she meets the ladies the other end and it helps her'.[19] He also described how stressful the Monarch found public appearances, despite the many years in which she had made them. The strain of a long day in a provincial town, he declared, 'taking a lively interest in everything, saying a kind word here and asking a question there, always smiling and acknowledging cheers when driving in her car, sometimes for hours, had to be experienced to be properly appreciated.'[20] The Committee's Report was delivered to the House of Commons on 2nd December. 'Nothing in the Crawfie genre has ever revealed so much that really matters about the Queen and all the principal members of her family,' observed *The Times*. What it did not reveal, of course, was the financial information critics most wanted to obtain.

Adeane's advocacy succeeded in its basic aim. The Committee recommended a rise in the Queen's income from £475,000 to £980,000, with substantial rises for other members of the Royal Family as well, constituting an average increase of four per cent per annum since the Accession. The report accepted that the scale and style of royal functions should not be reduced, that there was little further scope for economies, that Palace employees were not overpaid, and that published estimates of the royal fortune were widely exaggerated. It rejected a proposal by Douglas Houghton, a respected Labour elder statesman, who suggested a full separation of the expenses of the Crown as an institution from the provision for the Queen personally, giving the Household a status similar to that of a department of the House of Commons. The Committee concluded that this would be more expensive, not less.[21]

While the Queen awaited Parliament's verdict, she busied herself, appropriately, with details of her personal expenditure. 'I meant to ask you today and stupidly forgot, a question of the account,' she wrote to her dress designer on 8th December. 'Do you think it would

'. . . and treble time for informal garden party handshakes
makes it exactly 980,000 . . .'

Sun, 3rd December, 1971

be possible to have the new clothes and the purchase tax on one bill,
and the other alterations on a separate one? I cannot get the Privy Purse
to accept my word for the purchase tax, as the item is not put separately
on the account.'[22] If she was feeling nervous, she had cause. The sharpness of the debate in the Commons showed the sharpness of the climactic change, not just since 1952, but since 1970. Roy Jenkins, opening for
the Opposition, argued in favour of legislation, if necessary, to deal with
the question of taxing the Queen's private income. There was strong
support from Liberal as well as Labour MPs for variations on the
'Houghton solution'. Houghton himself picked out Princess Margaret,
who – it was claimed – had spent only thirty-one days outside London
on official engagements in 1970, for special castigation. 'Why, oh why,'
he asked, 'are we giving this expensive, kept woman that kind of salary
increase for doing what she is doing – £700 a week?' Joel Barnett, also a
member of the Committee, refused to vote for the new Civil List without
information about the extent to which the Queen's private fortune had
increased since 1952 as a result of tax exemption. The Government
obtained a majority of 121 for its no-longer-bipartisan formula. Most
Labour MPs abstained. Forty-seven MPs, including the former Liberal
leader Jo Grimond, voted against.

If it was a generous settlement, this was partly because the Chairman of the Committee did not simply have to rely on Tory support. The transcript of the evidence contained in the report showed, as *The Times* put it, that the Leader of the Opposition had gone out of his way 'to be protective towards the Queen and her interests'.[23] The Palace privately agreed. 'When it came to re-doing the Civil List,' an ex-courtier remembers, 'Wilson was frightfully helpful. He used all his political skills and knowledge to get her what she wanted.'[24]

The acceptance of the report saved the Monarchy from the need for an immediate overhaul, and preserved the essential features of the status quo. However, the deal was not as open-handed as it appeared at first sight. There were important changes in the way the financial arrangements were organized. To avoid frequent references to Parliament because of inflation, the Civil List Bill provided for the appointment of Royal Trustees – to include the Prime Minister and the Chancellor – to keep the Civil List under annual review and report to Parliament every ten years, when the Treasury might make an order increasing the allowance. This altered the relationship between the Crown and Parliament in one key respect. Before, the Monarch had accepted the Civil List as – in effect – a Coronation gift, unrelated to performance. Now, the List was to be continually scrutinized, and future additions to it were likely to depend on the reputation of the Royal Family, the mood of the nation, and the political colour of the House.

The Palace's public bid for more cash also had another effect. It stimulated a public controversy. 'Earlier monarchs' attempts in 1904, 1905 and 1920 to increase the Civil List in mid-reign had remained secret,' points out Philip Hall, in his study of royal finance, 'nipped in the bud by ministers who pointed out the consequences of the parliamentary debate that would be required.'[25] The 1971 Select Committee Report complemented the Cawston film by filling in the actuarial details. However, the report and the subsequent debate also provided the perilous spectacle of a Sovereign having to justify her activities over the preceding nineteen years, and their continuation on the same scale. For the first time in the reign, the Queen appeared tight-fisted. Although her private fortune was kept out of the calculations, the issue of its existence was highlighted. So was the suspicion that the Monarch was personally opposed to the idea of forfeiting her immunity. 'Her father had forewarned her not to allow it to happen,' says a former aide. During the Select Committee hearings, one critic of the tax immunity suggested to Sir Michael Adeane, over lunch, that the Queen would benefit greatly in public esteem if she seized the opportunity to declare that the scale of the royal immunity should be taken into account in assessing the Civil List. The courtier smiled politely. 'I don't agree,' he replied. 'But even if I did, she wouldn't do it.'[26] The nation, which tended to absolve the Sovereign of responsibility for anything, came to form the same impression. As a result, the Monarchy ceased to be a topic ignored by serious politicians, and entered the mainstream of political debate. Support for the Houghton proposal was strong. So was support for a reduction in the level of 'flummery, protocol and antiquated tradition,' as the *Guardian* put it.[27]

There was a notable stirring in the tabloids, which were beginning to discover that criticizing royalty could sell as many copies as saccharine support. On 3rd December, the *Sun* devoted a double-page spread on the topic of how hard the Queen worked. But when it asked its readers whether she deserved a pay rise, four out of five who replied, did so in the negative.[28] More important, the issues of the size of the undisclosed fortune and income, the tax immunity, and the large annuities to not very active minor royals became firmly lodged in the public consciousness. It was this, above all, that made the 1971 'Committee on the Queen' a watershed.

EARLY IN 1972, the Queen set out on an extended trip to south-east Asia and the Indian Ocean, accompanied by her husband and daughter. 'I find every time I read a new programme for the Far East Tour, I get hotter and hotter at the prospect of six weeks in that climate,' she wrote to Hardy Amies, who – in an attempt to outflank Bobo MacDonald – gave her a white handbag for Christmas.[29] She returned in time to host a visit to Britain by Queen Juliana and Prince Bernhard of the Netherlands, before setting out, mid-May, on a five-day state visit to France.

The French trip provided an opportunity to see the Duke of Windsor, terminally ill with cancer and near the end. The meeting was diplomatic, more than personal – a well-thought-out gesture of for-giveness, much publicized. The Duke was so close to death as the tour approached that the British ambassador, Sir Christopher Soames, had to find out if he would live long enough for the meeting to take place. Though Soames reported favourably, there was an element of the macabre about the actual encounter. Preparing the Duke for the visit took hours, involving the removal of all tubes, apart from a carefully hidden intravenous drip. The Queen, Philip and Charles spent the early afternoon of 18th May watching the races at Longchamp before arriving at the residence of the Duke and Duchess at 4 Route du Champs d'Entraînment at 4 p.m.

The Queen had not seen her uncle for several years. Charles, how-ever, had visited him privately the previous autumn. On that occasion, the Duke had been expansive, talking – as the Prince recorded – 'about how difficult my family had made it for him for the past thirty-three years'. Now the old man was almost beyond speech. The Duchess, 'like a strange bat, flitting to and fro,'[30] greeted the royal party on the steps. She curtsied deeply to each in turn, before leading them to the drawing-room for tea. Then she took the Queen upstairs to see her husband, confined to a wheelchair and weighing barely six stone, but wearing a blue blazer. 'As Her Majesty came in the Duke stood up,' his nurse recalled, 'a great effort for him, said "My dear," made a slight bow and kissed her on both cheeks.' The Queen asked him to sit, sat beside him, and asked him how he was. 'Not so bad,' he replied. He died ten days later.[31]

The Royal Family felt little private grief – least of all Queen Eliza-beth, who had known him best. The Queen herself had barely seen him since her childhood, and she grew up avoiding the mention of his name. He had never, as some originally feared, been a pretender. But his life of brooding idleness and cocktail decadence had been an intermittent source of tension. Stories of the royal home in exile, with the liveried footmen, medals, gold snuff-boxes, and rattle of Manhattan conversation at the dinner table, reminded the world of another side of the model family. The Duke had grumbled freely, especially about the Duchess's ever-denied HRH. 'I did a bloody good job for my country,' he was apt to say, in his half cockney, half-American accent, 'and all I got was a good kick in the ass.'[32] His death tied up a loose end. But there was the problem of the proprieties.

How should a dead, disgraced ex-King be treated by his reigning niece? The problem was to avoid appearing callous, bitter, or hypocritical, all at the same time. 'He had been a threat,' according to Lord Charteris. 'The Queen wanted to play things down.'[33] He was no longer part of the nation over which he had once reigned. Yet, he remained – even in death – royal.

There was much discussion at Buckingham Palace. One difficulty was Trooping the Colour, marking the Sovereign's official birthday, which was due to take place two days before the funeral. To cancel the ceremony seemed excessive, but to continue with it as if nothing had happened might be taken as the perpetuation of an old feud. The Queen settled the matter. 'She seldom took the initiative,' says an ex-courtier. 'But on this she did. She said "Somehow work it out that I can have Trooping the Colour anyway".'[34] There was more discussion. Then Charteris came up with a compromise. The Trooping went ahead, but included the playing of the Lament by the pipes and drums of the Scots Guards, which was felt to provide just the right level of respect.

The general principle was to err, but only a little, on the side of magnanimity. A carefully worded telegram was sent to the Duchess, the product of much drafting. 'I know that my people will always remember him with gratitude and great affection and that his services to them in peace and war will never be forgotten,' it declared. 'I am so glad that I was able to see him in Paris ten days ago.'[35] The Duke had expressed a personal wish to be interred in the family burial ground at Frogmore. His body was flown back to England by the RAF, attended by a party of senior officers. For two days, the coffin was displayed at St George's Chapel, Windsor. Sixty thousand people, out of respect for a once-loved Prince and King, or simply from morbid curiosity, filed past. But there was no lying-in-state in Westminster Hall.

The Duchess was painfully accommodated at Buckingham Palace. 'The Queen didn't want to have much to do with Wallis,' says a former courtier. 'Dinner was given in the Chinese room – with anybody else, it would have been in the Queen's own dining room. She preferred to go down to where Wallis was set up.' The occasion was stiff and awkward. The candelabra had been taken away. Queen Elizabeth was pointedly absent. 'It was OK – everybody behaved decently,' says the same source. 'Charles was there, and helpful. But there was certainly no outpouring of love between the Queen and the Duchess of Windsor, or vice versa.'[36]

THE PALACE was better able to cope with tricky situations like the Duke of Windsor's death because of a series of staff changes that took place at the beginning of the year, just after the acceptance of the Select Committee Report. Having secured the settlement, Sir Michael Adeane retired after nineteen years as the Queen's private secretary. Martin Charteris, private secretary to Princess Elizabeth and then assistant private secretary to the Queen, succeeded him. He only did so after a battle. The Lord Chamberlain, Lord Cobbold, preferred the other assistant private secretary, Philip Moore, and proposed to the Queen, as an interim measure, a joint appointment. At first, the Queen seemed ready to accept Cobbold's advice. Charteris was indignant. Moore, a former diplomat, had only been at the Palace for five years, and Charteris felt that he had trained him up. He saw the Queen, and stated his case, which she accepted. As a result, Charteris got the private secretaryship, and Moore was given the new post of deputy private secretary. Charteris continued to feel, however, that she ought to have seen the merit of his claim in the first place, without his needing to draw attention to it.[37]

The change from Adeane to Sir Martin Charteris (as he became) had as big an impact on the atmosphere at the Palace as the replacement of Commander Colville by William Heseltine. It marked the end of a long era of 'hereditary' private secretaries. Adeane – who had taken over from Sir Alan Lascelles just after the Coronation – had provided a thread of continuity that went back to the beginning of the previous reign, maintaining academic and antiquarian traditions that dated from the last century. Sir Derek Mitchell, a former private secretary to two Prime Ministers, recalls Adeane as an imposing Burghley-like courtier – civilized, intelligent and conveying an impression that you might, at any moment, commit an unpardonable solecism.[38] Charteris brought a very different style. 'Tall, bony, bald,' as Tony Benn described him,[39] he was in some ways as much a traditionalist as his predecessor. In Altrincham's sense, he was undoubtedly 'tweedy'. The grandson of an earl and son-in-law of a Conservative whip, he had the manners and interests of an aristocrat. But he was also a realist. He was fond of saying that the Monarchy should never be ahead of the times or even abreast of them, but it was in trouble if it fell far behind them.

What made Charteris different from either Lascelles or Adeane was that he was a romantic. Partly, this was personal. 'He really loves the Queen, and has done for years,' according to a lady-in-waiting. He had worked for her since she was a very young woman, and his deep devotion, of which he made no secret, never dimmed. But he also had a vision of the institution which was gaier and more colourful than ever allowed by the cautious constitutionalism and slavery to precedent of his predecessors. Where previous private secretaries had been, to a degree, *contra mundum*, Charteris seemed to belong to, and enjoy, the outside world. Jaunty, flamboyant, contagiously enthusiastic, were terms used to describe him. So was amusing. Court correspondents soon noted that, after the retirement of Sir Michael Adeane, royal speeches became unexpectedly funny. Charteris's training was military rather than intellectual – like the Monarch, he had not been to university. But he had a feline intelligence that enabled him to bridge the gap between royalty and politics. 'He was much more instinctive than Michael Adeane,' says one ex-mandarin. With the Monarch, 'it helped that he came from the same drawer socially'.[40] The Queen was as much at ease with him as she ever was with any private secretary.

This change was buttressed by others. Despite their different points of origin, Charteris was much in sympathy with the approach of William Heseltine, who now moved over to become assistant private secretary. Lord Cobbold retired as Lord Chamberlain, and was replaced by the less interventionist (and less effective) Lord Maclean. Heseltine was succeed as press secretary by Robin Ludlow, manager of the Promotion and Research Department of the *Economist*, who was quietly replaced, eighteen months later, by Ronald Allison – a professional journalist who belonged to the Heseltine, as opposed to Colville, school. Where Heseltine had understood public relations from the angle of somebody who had worked closely with politicians, Allison saw it from a Fleet Street point of view – and could talk the same language as the people who rang him up.

'The Palace press secretary must never be seen to be lying,' was his firm principle. 'If there was something brewing, and the journalist asked, "If I were to speculate that there is to be a royal engagement, will I have egg on my face tomorrow morning?" I would simply reply "No",' he recalls. 'I used to say I don't know, I do know but I can't tell you, or yes. If somebody had a scoop, I wouldn't spoil it. If a journalist said he was going for the first edition, I might say, "hold it back to the second to check your facts". I didn't say "Oh, if you've got it, I'll release it to everybody." '[41] The Charteris, Heseltine, Moore, Allison team was a powerful one with a range of talents, helping to make the 1970s a comparatively serene time for the Monarchy. The suspicious, introverted Court of the age of Adeane and Commander Colville had turned into a remarkably extrovert one. There was also a decisive social shift: of the four key courtiers, only Charteris had been educated at Eton.

The changes took place at a time of royal anniversaries – the twentieth of the Accession in February, the twenty-fifth of the Queen's wedding in November – and hence of plaudits. Newspaper profiles, though routinely congratulatory, also showed how perceptions of the Monarchy had moved on, with a decline in emphasis on grandeur and remoteness, and an increased stress on domesticity and accessibility. Grigg gave the Monarch a good mid-term report, noting a shift from the flat public image of the 1950s, to the human and pleasant one of the 1970s, with *Royal Family* as the turning point. However, he criticized the Queen for failing to take the lead in racial integration within the Commonwealth by including members of ethnic minorities on her staff.[42] Louis Heren argued in *The Times* that of Walter Bagehot's five reasons for the continuing strength of the British Monarchy – its intelligibility to ordinary people, the idea of a family on the throne, a strengthening of Government with the force of religion, the ceremonial function, and the Royal Family's role as the head of a nation's morality – only the religious factor had worn thin. Like Grigg, he detected an increase in sympathy for royalty since the 1960s, with the Cawston film as catalyst of the change of mood.[43]

One journalist even suggested that, fifteen years on, a modern, sturdier Monarchy was better placed to shoulder criticisms than it had been in the brittle days of Altrincham and Muggeridge.[44] Nevertheless, it was still the convention for would-be critics to pull their punches. Royal business (as over the Civil List) could now be freely and openly discussed. Royal persons, on the other hand, continued to enjoy relative immunity. Another writer pointed out that Britain was the last great Monarchy in Europe apart from the Papacy – but with the difference that even the best Popes were often written about in the most scurrilous terms, while the Queen, the Duke, the Prince of Wales, Princess Anne and the rest of the Royal Family were not. 'Indeed the public insists on seeing them as paragons, and leading public figures insist on not being quoted even if what they have to say about the Monarchy is unashamedly flattering, as almost all of it is.'[45]

One reason for a surviving and reviving respect for the Monarchy was the symbol of calm neutrality it offered in increasingly divisive times. The rapid economic growth and rise in personal prosperity of the 1960s had given way to soaring prices, frequent industrial disputes, and economic stagnation in the early 1970s. Nationalism had become a growing force in Scotland and Wales, sectarian troubles in Ulster were worsening, and 1972 saw a United Kingdom-wide miners' strike for the first time since the year of the Queen's birth. 'Deferential attitudes have practically vanished,' observed one commentator, 'whether between people and government or between work people and employer.'[46] Fears were expressed about a breakdown of social order. 'Perhaps only a few Britons know that in the unlikely event of great national dissension and violence, the allegiance of the armed forces to the Monarchy would be decisive,' wrote Heren, 'but the majority senses the stability this ensures.'[47]

The Monarchy offered an image of stability; the barbecuing Monarch, leading the life of 'a fairly conventional middle-class woman,'[48] one of reassurance. Both were based on the oldest, most established, and longest-lasting asset of the modern institution – its emphasis on family. It was an image which Christmas broadcasts, revamped by Richard Cawston in the 1970s with accompanying film footage, increasingly underlined, as it became the strongest royal theme. In a year that happened not just to mark a milestone in the reign, but also included the Queen and Duke's silver wedding anniversary, Philip Howard in *The Times* described the Windsors as a team that took much of the load off the Queen's shoulders, 'a large, close and remarkably devoted family.'[49] The *Telegraph*, glumly contemplating the nation's moral decline, observed that 'the Queen, the Duke and their children have set a standard of family life and family happiness that everyone must respect and many envy'.[50]

However, respect and envy for the domesticated, embourgeoised Royal Family was not the same as a restoration of reverence. The public appetite for royal details, always strong, became increasingly voracious in the 1970s. Advances in camera technology made it possible to feed it. Meanwhile, a lucrative trade in intimate royal photographs, established in the 1960s, was further stimulated in the 1970s by a raging circulation war among the tabloids.

In November 1972, Ray Belissario – the 'Peeping Tom the Royals Dread' as editors who used his pictures happily dubbed him – published a book of his own photos called *To Tread on Royal Toes* cheekily timed to coincide with celebrations of the Silver Wedding. Belissario, best known of the paparazzi and proud pioneer of the wide-angled lens, was a source of intense irritation to his royal subjects. They could do little to keep him at bay. On one occasion, he rented a nineteenth-storey suite in the Hilton hotel, as a spying platform for shots of the Royal Family in the garden at Buckingham Palace. Good continental contacts meant that he was seldom without a buyer for his pictures. He claimed that when British editors were overcome with scruples, this had the ironic effect of making his scoops seem more exclusive abroad, and hence of upping the price.[51] What is interesting to the jaded modern royal-watcher, however, is not the daringness of Belissario's photography, but the mild nature, even innocence, of his portfolio of photographs, by end-of-century standards. There are fuzzy pictures of female royals in swimsuits (one of Princess Margaret netted £25,000) and a sequence of Princess Alexandra and Angus Ogilvy, during their honeymoon, kissing on a lawn. But there is nothing a present-day *Sun* reader would give a second glance.

The paparazzi did not challenge the 'perfect family' ideal. On the whole, their images of relaxing royals heightened it. So did pictures taken by regular press photographers of busy members of the Royal Family alongside young people who were evidently not as well brought up as Charles and Anne. In the 1970s as in the late 1960s, scruffy students were a favourite target of the popular press. Hence, much was made in October 1972 of a visit by the Queen to Stirling University, in the course of which the Monarch was allegedly jostled by demonstrators. Pictures next day showed a smiling Sovereign walking past students who were giving clenched-fist salutes, or swigging from wine bottles. 'Queen Courageous,' said the satisfied tabloids, contrasting the dutiful Head of State and dissolute, undisciplined youth.

The Stirling story heralded the Silver Wedding, which brought the 'family' excitement to its climax. Palace briefings freely associated royalty with the themes of marriage, family, nation, family of nations. So did royal speeches. 'We had the good fortune to grow up in happy and united families,' declared the Queen, when she addressed guests at the Guildhall on November 20th, following a Silver Wedding thanksgiving service at Westminster Abbey. 'We have been fortunate in our children, and above all we are fortunate in being able to serve this great country and Commonwealth.'

Echoing her own youthful utterances delivered as a young mother to gatherings of 1940s housewives, she elaborated on the social value of strong marriages. A married relationship, she maintained, needed to mature with the passing years. 'For that, it must be held firm in the web of family relationships, between parents and children, between grandparents and grandchildren, between cousins, aunts and uncles. My Lord Mayor' – and here the lighter touch of Sir Martin Charteris was discernible – 'when the bishop was asked what he thought about sin he replied with simple conviction that he was against it. If I am asked today what I think about family life after twenty-five years of marriage, I can answer with equal simplicity and conviction. I am for it.'[52]

The remark received the nation's appreciative laughter. The Queen's immediate family showed the truth of what she said – especially the grown-up children, whose worlds and interests had expanded greatly since the public had become familiar with them, in a domestic setting, in 1969. There had already been a shift of media attention from the older to the younger royals, and in many ways the 1970s had become the decade of Charles and Anne. After tentative schooldays (it was hard for ordinary people to identify with a victim of the strange regime at Gordonstoun), and an active university life, Charles had emerged as a serious-minded, yet hard-playing, young adult who had inherited his father's taste for manly pursuits. Cambridge had been followed by the Royal Navy College, Dartmouth, and then by a brief period at sea. For several years, he was often to be seen, in the news clips, being winched on or off ships, or healthily swinging a polo mallet. Meanwhile, Princess Anne had distinguished herself in competitive equestrian events – so much so that, despite a reputation for being rude to reporters, she was elected the Sports Writers' Association 'Sportswoman of the Year' and the BBC Sports Personality of the Year in 1971. Later she won silver medals in European championships, and competed in the 1976 Montreal Olympics.

There was the question of girlfriends and boyfriends and matrimony. Charles was linked romantically by the press with every royal female of the appropriate age in Europe, and many of the aristocratic ones as well. Anne's range of possibilities was narrower. She took little interest in conventional upper-class debutante life. On the other hand, her unprecedented step into the world of sports events brought her into contact with young men who shared her expertise, but not her background.

The result was predictable. 'We have marriage trouble,' the Queen told a courtier one evening over dinner. 'Anne wants to marry Mark Phillips.' Phillips was a good-looking, but not very bright, army officer and show jumper. 'What do you want?' asked the courtier. 'I think we should do it,' she replied.[53] The wedding – the second to involve a member of the inner Royal Family and a commoner, this time a middle-class one – took place in Westminster Abbey on 14th November 1973. Despite the Queen's premonitions, it was a popular alliance, encouraging the image of a less hidebound Monarchy, and of an ever more democratically accessible Royal Family.

But there was another meaning to 'family,' apart from strong domestic ties: the wider world community. At the end of 1972, the metaphor of the international family had a special poignancy. The previous year, Britain's attempts to enter the Common Market had finally overcome Gallic doubts. In October 1971, the British Parliament endorsed the decision in principle; the following January, the Treaty of Accession was signed; in October, the Royal Assent was given to the European

Communities Act; and at the beginning of 1973, Britain became a member.

In her 1972 Christmas broadcast, the Queen dealt with this rapid sequence of events by employing the ingenious imagery of the Commonwealth family entering, and joining forces with, the European one. The new European links, she assured her listeners, would not replace the old Commonwealth ties, based on historical and personal attachments. These were bonds too sacred to break. 'One of the great Christian ideas is a happy and lasting marriage between man and wife,' she declared, adapting the Silver Wedding message, 'but no marriage can hope to succeed without a deliberate effort to be tolerant and understanding.'

In the case of communities, she acknowledged, tolerance did not come easily. However, it was the key to harmony within the United Kingdom. It was also a key to the success of the 'Community' Britain was joining. 'We are trying to create a wider family of nations,' she concluded.[54]

IN RETROSPECT, it can been seen as a *cri de coeur*. For if entry into Europe was a turning point for Britain and the Commonwealth, it was a moment of crisis for the Monarchy. The idea of the joining of families, even of the impregnation of one by the other, was political and economic nonsense, a desperate bid to evade the reality. The truth about signing the Accession Treaty, as everybody in politics appreciated, was that it constituted the most decisive step yet in the progressive severance of 'familial' ties between Britain and its former Empire which had begun with Indian independence. It reduced the remaining links to sentimental and cultural ones, and legal niceties.

Yet the Queen's own connections with the Commonwealth remained, independent of any decisions taken in London or Brussels. Not only was she Head of the Commonwealth – whatever that now meant – she was also Head of State of a sizeable proportion of its members, and was required to take advice from their governments. The problem of her divided self had arisen before, in particular over Rhodesia. Britain's entry into the European Community made it more acute, as the interests of Commonwealth nations diverged. So far from the Common Market bringing two 'families' together, it precipitated

– if not a divorce – a diaspora, fragmenting the unity of the Queen's present and former realms. In addition, the Treaty dealt a death blow to the traditional doctrine of the constitutional entity known as the Queen-in-Parliament. It raised but did not answer the question of the future role of a British 'Sovereign' in a Europe that was certain to make increasing demands on British sovereignty. Was she to become a totemic local figure within a wider unit – the UK equivalent of an Indian Maharajah, or the King of Buganda? Or might she – as some optimists fantasized – be adopted as constitutional monarch of all Europe?

The Queen did not voice any feelings of perturbation. Indeed she was made to express such enthusiasm about the Community that opponents of entry complained that she appeared to be personally in favour. A speech she delivered at the state banquet at Windsor in honour of the Federal German President on 24th October 1972 aroused special fury. Anti-Marketeers, who regarded the battle as far from over, were surprised and angered by her description of British entry as 'a great achievement'. 'The Sovereign's constitutional role *vis-à-vis* the Government is to be consulted, to encourage or to warn,' noted the *Telegraph*. 'In view of the Queen's speech, MPs will have to discard any supposition that she warned the Prime Minister against taking Britain into the Common Market.'[55]

What good would it have done if she had? It is possible that the Windsor speech, drafted in Whitehall and amended in Buckingham Palace, signified a concern – both in Downing Street and at Court – to counter any suspicion that she was anti-European. At any rate, the reaction showed how narrow was the path a British Monarch had to tread, when speaking on a contentious matter.

18

At the beginning of 1974, the Queen's constitutionally split personality caused the same difficulty as ten years earlier; over the problem of being, physically, in two places at once. In February, Heath called a snap general election, to take place on the last day of the month – a date which fell in the middle of a long-planned royal South Sea tour. In the past, Prime Ministers had built their election plans around royal itineraries. Heath, facing a national emergency over another miners' strike, and hoping to cash in on it, was not prepared to be sentimental. He expected the Queen to fly back.

The royal party had set out for the Cook Islands, where the Queen was due to open an airport, at the end of January. The prospect was more daunting than usual because, for once, she was without Bobo, who had been hurt in an accident. 'With the disaster of Miss MacDonald having broken her collarbone and four ribs,' she wrote to Hardy Amies a few days before leaving, 'my journey is going to be a very much more wearing affair as I really will have to think out clothes for myself this time!'[1] From the Cook Islands, she travelled on to Christchurch for the start of the Commonwealth Games. Parliament was formally dissolved, *in absentia*, on February 8th, the day she left New Zealand. While politicians at home fought a bitter conflict in the difficult conditions created by the coal shortage and the 'three-day week,' the Queen hopped from island to island in the Pacific, visiting Norfolk Island, the New Hebrides, the British Solomon Islands, Papua New Guinea and finally, on the eve of the United Kingdom election, Australia. As British voters slept before going to the polls, the Queen of Australia opened Parliament in Canberra. Less than thirty hours later, a jet-lagged Queen of the United Kingdom was in Buckingham Palace, ready to receive the Prime Minister, or summon a new one.

The morning after the election, a letter appeared in *The Times* from the ex-courtier Sir Edward Ford, defending the whistle-stop Monarch against critics, on the grounds that it was necessary both to take Australian sensitivities into account, and also for the Queen to be back in Britain immediately after the election. If there should turn out to be a hung Parliament, he wrote, 'she may have to take difficult and important decisions for which she is temporarily deprived of ministerial advice.'[2] The precaution turned out to have been wise. Heath had been expected to win. Instead, Labour obtained the largest number of seats, but without an overall majority.

For four days, the Prime Minister vainly bargained with the leader of the Liberals, Jeremy Thorpe. No attempt was made to dislodge him. The main Opposition party was happy to wait and watch. 'A Government was in existence,' wrote Harold Wilson later, defending the constitutional principle which provided him with his second term of office, 'and until it resigns, following the election results, or a defeat on the Queen's speech, the Palace can only observe the classical doctrine, "We have a Government".'[3] For as long as Heath chose or was able to stay in office, the Palace regarded itself as a mere spectator. 'The Prime Minister is Prime Minister until he resigns,' according to Lord Charteris. 'Only when he resigns, must the Queen act.'[4] However, the Queen's close advisers kept in touch with Whitehall. 'During Ted's awful weekend, when he was trying to stitch up a deal with Jeremy Thorpe,' recalls a former mandarin, 'Martin Charteris rang Sir John Hunt [the Cabinet Secretary] a couple of times, in effect to ask what was he going to do. The question was probably something like, "What is the scenario the Queen is going to be confronted with?"'[5]

On Monday, March 4th, Heath was finally persuaded to give up his attempt to hold onto his office, and he tendered his resignation. In theory, the Queen now had several options. Since no single leader or party could automatically command a House of Commons majority, it was constitutionally open to her to invite Thorpe or some other prominent figure and ask the question she had put to Lord Home in 1963: whether they could form an administration. In practice, however, it would have been surprising not to have turned first to the head of the party which, though not the biggest in votes, had obtained the largest number of seats. Indeed, to have exercised her theoretical right in this regard would have been seen as a deliberate slight to the Labour

Party – not least because of her consistent policy of taking the course of action that seemed least controversial. Nobody was surprised, therefore, that she immediately called Harold Wilson, who thus became the first (and only) of her Prime Ministers who returned for a second term after an interval. According to Wilson, 'our relaxed intimacy was immediately restored'.[6]

The reinstated premier was cautious in his choice of ministers, and filled his Cabinet with familiar faces. Hence the atmosphere surrounding ministerial visits to the Palace was more matter-of-fact than in 1964, with less of a sense of novelty and excitement. The Queen, according to Barbara Castle, 'played her part as pleasantly as she always does'. But there was a spontaneous revolt of a kind from the hand-kissers. Many newly-appointed ministers broke precedent, and returned to their places normally, instead of feeling their way backwards. There were half-bows and half-curtseys in profusion and, biggest anti-deference gesture of all, a sartorial protest. While Mrs Castle defiantly wore an old coat to the Palace, 'Wedgie and Mike [Foot],' she recorded, 'looked as if they had been camping.'[7] It was supposed, after all, to be a left-wing Government.

The formation of a minority administration resolved the industrial crisis that had precipitated the election. The miners were quickly bought off. However, the parliamentary position was unstable, and there were constitutional questions facing the Queen. If the Government was defeated on the Queen's Speech, and Wilson asked for a dissolution, would she be required to consent – or should she look for a stop-gap Prime Minister from another party? Alternatively, if Wilson asked for a quick second election, without being forced into one, in order to capitalize on his post-victory honeymoon, should the Queen refuse the request on the grounds that it was unnecessary? The matter had been talked about, hypothetically, in the mid–1960s, when Labour had been afraid it might lose its narrow majority through by-election losses. In 1965, some observers had wondered whether, in such an event, the Queen might deny Wilson an election, until she had tried to see if Heath, or Heath with Jo Grimond, the Liberal leader, could form an alternative administration without the need for a poll. The question also arose at the end of 1973, when it was argued that Heath would be exceeding his rights if he demanded an election eighteen months before the end of his statutory term, without any constitutional reason for doing so. At both times, the Palace reserved judgement. When Benn asked Charteris in January 1974 about the rules governing dissolution, the Queen's private secretary would only say 'the Queen has absolute rights' – including the absolute right to consult whoever she chose.[8]

It was the first time the Monarchy had been confronted with such possibilities since the hung Parliament of 1929–31, when George V had taken a strongly interventionist line and had helped to determine the outcome of the 1931 political crisis. However, on that occasion, the question of refusing a request for a dissolution did not arise and, indeed, no such request had been refused since 1832. Some (Roy Jenkins, for instance) argued that a Prime Minister's request to dissolve would have to be accepted under all circumstances. Others insisted that a residual right to refuse existed for use in exceptional conditions. According to the second argument, which was advanced with particular conviction by those who wished to embarrass the Government, the fact that a refusal had been *closely considered* on previous occasions in the twentieth century, counted as a precedent. On this basis, the Sovereign's 'discretionary refusal' might be applied if the request came too soon, if an election seemed unlikely to break the deadlock, or if an alternative governing combination was available.[9]

Like most constitutional riddles, the answer could only ever be discovered by trying it out. If the Prime Minister asked for an early dissolution purely on opportunistic grounds, and was turned down, the point would have been established. In practice, however, this was unlikely. Nothing in the Queen's previous behaviour, or the behaviour of the Court, suggested that she would either wish for or entertain such a constitutional showdown, and the political conflict that would result. However, such a calculation did not dispose of the uncertainty. For the issue was not merely what the Queen would actually do, but whether it would be embarrassing to her, and hence damaging to the Prime Minister, for him to ask. In fact, it was soon taken for granted that a second election would follow either in the summer or the autumn.

A trickier issue concerned the Monarch's response to a request following a Government defeat. Wilson left nothing to chance. Feelers were put out before the Queen's Speech, to discover what might happen if the Government lost the vote. Robert Armstrong, Wilson's private secretary, discussed the question with Charteris. 'There was a clear conclusion that the Queen wasn't bound to act on a request,' says an ex-official, 'and the Prime Minister could not absolutely rely on her doing so.' Wilson thought it would be difficult for her to call Heath, because Heath had already failed once to form a government. 'But there was nothing like a guarantee . . . She certainly wanted to reserve her right.'[10] However, 'reserving a right' and getting an unofficial hint about what would happen, were different things. There were also non-Whitehall channels, and Wilson made use of them. 'Harold asked Elwyn-Jones [the Lord Chancellor] to speak to Charteris,' says Joe Haines, Wilson's press secretary. 'If the Government was defeated on its own programme, would the Queen grant a dissolution? Elwyn-Jones said the Queen said yes, and Harold asked him to let the Conservatives know.' The Lord Chancellor was promptly dispatched to warn Lord Hailsham of the likely consequences of a defeat by an anti-Labour combination.[11] No combination was attempted – partly because neither the Conservatives nor the Liberals had any wish for the immediate election that would almost certainly result.

The hurdle of the Queen's Speech was quickly surmounted, largely because Wilson avoided putting into it anything of importance to which the Liberals might object. There was no defeat, no crisis, and the Monarch resumed her interrupted Far East tour, visiting Indonesia, and then Singapore. However, there remained the possibility of a Government defeat on the Budget, or on a confidence motion. Again, there was the question of whether the Queen was obliged, under such circumstances, to accept a request from the Prime Minister to go to the country. In the House, Liberal and Tory MPs protested against the Speaker's ruling that the only way that matters of this kind which related to the Queen could be discussed was on a motion. Early in April, it was announced that Edward Short, the Lord President, would conduct a 'review' of the position, aided by Lord Crowther-Hunt, Wilson's adviser on constitutional affairs. In May, Short announced that the Monarch retained some discretion. 'Constitutional lawyers of the highest authority,' he declared, 'are of the clear opinion that the Sovereign is not in all circumstances bound to grant a Prime Minister's request for dissolution.'[12]

By this time, however, it had become clear that the matter was unlikely to be put to the test. It was a poker game: as over the Queen's Speech, the Opposition parties preferred the path of prudence. Though the Government suffered defeats because of its minority position, its buoyant standing in the opinion polls discouraged its opponents from combining on a confidence motion. In the autumn, the Queen acceded to a request from Wilson for a dissolution at a moment of his own choosing. The election took place in October. Labour obtained a small overall majority, which resolved the immediate uncertainty. Thus, the Queen's prerogative powers were never invoked. Nevertheless, during the middle months of the year a belief in the possibility that they might be, played a part in political calculations. One consequence of the crisis was a new awareness that, in the multi-party conditions thrown up by a volatile electorate, the Monarchy could not be ignored.

DESPITE desperate Government attempts to keep them down, prices and wages climbed ever more steeply in the early 1970s. After the 1973 oil price rise, hyper-inflation threatened. The Queen, with a pegged public income, felt the pinch. After the October 1974 poll, she began to plan for visits to Mexico, the Caribbean, and the Far East. Hardy Amies worried about dresses, and she worried about their cost. 'I'm sorry not to have replied before now – my brain only copes with a certain amount and the election etc., put your letter right out of my mind!' she wrote to him on October 22nd, a few days after the poll. 'I know there are problems about materials these days and I am grateful to be reminded. I am hoping that perhaps 2 items each for Mexico and Japan will be enough, and make my last year's dresses do the rest.'[13]

At the time of the Select Committee Report, nobody had imagined that the Civil List would need to be revised three years later. The settlement had anticipated that only ten yearly reviews would be necessary. Hence, it was embarrassing for the Palace to have to ask the Prime Minister to raise the matter. This Wilson did in a statement to the House on 12th February 1975 which happened to coincide with the *début* of Mrs Thatcher as Conservative leader. On this occasion, both party leaders were on the same side. Barbara Castle noted that the new Opposition leader's 'not very notable intervention' on the subject of the Queen's income was nevertheless 'one which augurs that she will fight every issue with a populist slant'.[14]

The request for a rise in the Civil List from £980,000 to £1,400,000 to take account of the increased costs, was presented under the procedure laid down by the Select Committee – according to which a report from the Royal Trustees, composed of the Prime Minister, Chancellor of the Exchequer, and Keeper of the Privy Purse, was received by the Treasury Ministers, who laid an Order before Parliament. Though interest in Mrs Thatcher exceeded interest in the Civil List, the timing of the statement had the unfortunate consequence, from the Palace's point of view, of giving the details of the royal claim added prominence. There was also another piece of bad luck. Wilson's statement had been preceded, a few weeks earlier, by the publication of a book, *My Queen and I*, by the Monarchy's most dedicated enemy, William Hamilton.

In the past, the Scottish MP's obsessive republicanism had not been taken seriously either in the Commons, or by the public: indeed his existence even helped the Palace, as a kind of lightning conductor, encouraging sober people to equate republicanism with crankiness. Parts of his book fitted this picture, and an element of self-caricature helped to reduce the impact of its invective. Thus the author concluded with a cheerily predictable hope that 'the Monarchy and all its prostituted entourage will be dumped in the garbage can of history'.[15] However, it was no longer quite as easy to dismiss Hamilton as it had been in the past. A veteran of the Select Committee, he offered facts and figures, and not all his points could be dismissed as specious ones. He produced evidence to support an estimate of the royal private fortune in excess of £100 million. He pointed out that the Commonwealth share of Britain's overseas trade had shrunk by half in twenty years. He drew attention to opinion polls that showed that more and more young people felt the Monarchy was out of touch with the modern world. He also poured withering scorn, from a presbyterian and proletarian point of view, on the 'model family' mythology, at a time when others were beginning to feel uneasy about it. None of the arguments was new. But, at the time of yet another 'pay claim', he gained a hearing. He also roused passions. When he predicted on television that the hold of the Monarchy on the affection of the nation would have slipped by the end of the century, the BBC was besieged with complaints.[16] The capacity of such remarks to cause outrage was one reason why his book received wider coverage than any attack on the Monarchy since Muggeridge. Another reason, however, was that the Monarchy had slipped almost imperceptibly from being an issue on the fringes of, or above politics, to being one within it.

On the Labour Left, Hamilton's accusation that the leader of his own party had a relationship to the Monarchy at least as sycophantic as that of any Prime Minister of the century, struck a particular chord – especially as Wilson, once again, seemed to be proving the point. The newly returned premier did his best for the Queen, on this, as on previous occasions. His efforts were hampered on February 22nd by a scoop in the *Morning Star*, then the daily paper of the British Communist Party, in the form of a leaked letter dated 5th December 1973, from Robert Armstrong (who had been private secretary to Heath before Wilson). This stressed that the then Prime Minister attached 'great importance to arrangements which protect the Queen's private share holdings from disclosure,' and indicated that there had been contact with the Palace on the subject.[17] 'It's a cover-up!' shouted the young MP for Bolsover, Dennis Skinner, in the Commons.[18]

Others, on the right, suggested 'a sinister Russian connection' behind the story.[19] The charge of collusion between the Palace and Downing Street over keeping details of the Queen's money secret, however, was hard to refute. A ragged debate on a Labour back-bench motion that the Civil List (Increase of Financial Provision) Order 1975 be annulled, put the Chancellor of the Exchequer, Denis Healey, on the defensive. Healey tried to assuage left-wingers by arguing that the real issue was whether 'humbly paid men and women, the royal staff' should receive the trade union rate for the job. Not only the Left, but also a significant number of middle-of-the-road MPs, were unimpressed. The latter included Michael Stewart. The former Foreign Secretary, like Hamilton, spoke of the writing on the wall, and warned of the likely future trend of opinion about the Monarchy, if the money and tax problem was not cleared up. Unlike Hamilton, he carried weight with his colleagues. The nation as a whole, Stewart declared, was kept in the dark about the real public cost of the Monarchy. There was 'a steady and growing concern about the royal immunity from taxation'. It was not yet a mass movement, he warned, but it was growing.[20]

In the vote on the rebellious motion, eighty-nine Labour MPs, including Neil Kinnock, PPS to the Employment Minister, Michael Foot, opposed the increase in the Queen's Civil List allowance – almost twice as many as had voted against the acceptance of the Select Committee Report. Another fifty deliberately abstained. Criticizing royal expenditure had become a conventional part of Labour politics. Afterwards, a rising Tory right-winger, Norman Tebbit, commented that, so far from being the Queen's loyal subjects, some Labour MPs were Her Majesty's most soiled objects.[21]

THE POSSIBILITY of a royal intervention in politics receded in the United Kingdom following the October 1974 election. In Australia, however, it arose in an unexpected way in the following year, and became the focus of a major political storm. The crisis drew attention to the anomaly of the surviving royal prerogative in distant countries of which the Queen remained Head of State. Britain's entry into the European Community had encouraged the whittling down of the monarchical connection in the old dominions. In Canada, Pierre Trudeau, who regarded his country's British heritage with little sentimentality, had embarked on what John Diefenbaker, a former premier, called an 'insidious chiselling' at the Monarchy. Canadian Tony Bennhs had been at work: the Queen's head was no longer used on many bank notes and postage stamps, and the letters HM and OHMS were gradually being dropped from government documents.[22] Events had followed a similar course in Australia. In May 1973, Gough Whitlam, the Labour Prime Minister, announced the ending of appeals by Australians to the Privy Council, together with changes in the style and title of the Queen in Australia, and new arrangements for the accreditation of heads of mission by and to the country.[23]

Thus the immediate background to the constitutional dispute in Australia was a sense of the increasing legal and constitutional marginality of the Crown across the Commonwealth. Few envisaged a sudden reassertion of its discretionary powers, which was what occurred. The crisis was the sequel to a storm-in-a-teacup row that blew up in the autumn on 1975 over the behaviour of Sir Colin Hannah, State Governor of Queensland, who had been granted a 'dormant commission' in April 1974 allowing him to take over in the event of the death, incapacity, removal or absence of the Australian Governor-General. In October, 'the Queen' – that is, the Queen acting on the joint advice of the British Foreign Secretary, James Callaghan, the Australian Prime Minister, Whitlam, and the Governor-General, Sir John Kerr – withdrew the dormant commission, because of Hannah's public criticism of the Whitlam Government in Canberra, and his support for Opposition demands for a general election.

This intervention, though 'on advice', provided an important precedent for the view that the Queen could and might intervene in Australian constitutional matters. It was followed by a more momentous one, also carried out in the Queen's name, a few weeks later. On 11th November 1975, after the Opposition leader, Malcolm Fraser, used his majority in the Australian Senate to block the Labour government's Budget Bills, Sir John Kerr, exercising the reserve powers invested in him as Governor-General, sought to break the deadlock by summarily dismissing Whitlam as Prime Minister and appointing Fraser as acting premier in his place, pending the holding of an election. Since the Governor-General was the embodiment of the Crown in Australia – in effect, constitutional vicereine – Kerr's unprecedented move raised the whole question of the Australian Monarchy and its role. Anti-monarchists argued that it would highlight the antiquated and undemocratic nature of the system, and also weaken the link between Britain and Australia.[24] Both predictions were, in a sense, accurate. One effect was to fuel growing calls in Australia for a republic.

From the point of view of the Monarchy, the key questions were what the Queen knew in advance, and how she acted, or should have acted, before and after the event. According to the Palace, Kerr had kept her informed of what was happening over the preceding weeks, but – it was at pains to point out – he had not told her about Whitlam's dismissal until after it had happened. Kerr later recorded his view that to have told the Queen what he was planning to do would have risked involving her in an Australian crisis 'in relation to which she had no legal powers,' and it would have been wrong to have taken this risk. 'Governor-Generals are expendable,' he was supposed to have told her later. 'The Queen is not.'[25]

The Monarch, however, was not the only person kept in ignorance of Sir John Kerr's intentions. So was his victim. 'I was unable to communicate with the Queen,' declared Whitlam, 'as I would have been entitled to do if I had had any warning of the course the Governor-General was to take.'[26] When told of his dismissal, he apparently responded that he would get in touch with the Queen at once – but was told that he was too late, because he had ceased to be Prime Minister.[27] Following Kerr's action, the Senate passed the Budget Bill, and the House of Representatives passed a vote of no confidence in Fraser, demanding that Whitlam should be asked to form a new government, on the grounds that the deadlock was resolved. Instead, Kerr dissolved both Houses.

'Well he may say God save the Queen,' said Whitlam, 'but after this nothing will save the Governor-General.' Nobody doubted that Kerr had taken his own decisions, after consulting the Australian Chief Justice. Yet there was still a question-mark over the royal connection or lack of it. Whitlam's own position on the Monarchy had long been a highly critical one. In the Australian Labour Party, there was a tendency to conflate Kerr, the Governor-Generalship, the Crown, and the Queen, as if they were a single, continuous and contentious entity. The issue arose of whether the Queen, though not to be blamed for Kerr's arbitrary action, should have stated afterwards that he had acted unconstitutionally. Thus, on November 14th, the Speaker of the House of Representatives wrote to the Queen, asking her to intervene personally, on the grounds that Kerr had acted 'contrary to the Royal Prerogative'. The letter contrasted the legitimacy derived from the Crown in the form of the Governor-General, and legitimacy derived from the people. 'It is my belief', wrote the Speaker, 'that to maintain in office a Prime Minister imposed on the nation by the Royal Prerogative rather than through parliamentary endorsement constitutes a danger to our parliamentary system and will damage the standing of your representative in Australia and even yourself.'

Here was a Morton's fork. If the Governor-General – though appointed by the Australian Prime Minister – represented the Queen, then arguably he should have behaved like the Queen, and should not have departed from precedent on such a matter. But for the Queen to respond to the Speaker's invitation to intervene after he had done so would be, precisely, to exceed the role she had come to accept. Either to act by reinstating Whitlam, or to accept the *fait accompli*, could appear partisan. She decided, as usual in constitutional matters, to take the line of least resistance. Her private secretary replied to the Speaker that the prerogative powers of the Crown were firmly in the hands of the Governor-General. Only he was competent to commission an Australian Prime Minister.[28] The 'written and accepted constitutional conventions' of Australia precluded the Queen from intervening personally after a Governor-General had been appointed, except on advice from the premier.

There was some semi-serious speculation about what might have happened if Whitlam had anticipated Kerr's decision to sack him by advising the Queen, in the nick of time, of his own decision to sack Kerr. Kerr later claimed that Whitlam had said to him in jest, a few weeks before the axe fell, 'It could be a question of whether I get to the Queen first for your recall or you get in first with my dismissal'.[29]

The crisis had several effects. As in Britain, following the appointment of successive premiers and, conclusively, of Lord Home in 1963, the decision not to risk asserting the reserve power of the Monarchy effectively ensured that it could never be used in future. The Australian Labour Party was confirmed in its prejudice against the Monarchy: Whitlam himself indicated that, if re-elected, he would ensure that neither the Crown nor its representatives could dismiss a government again; and the case became a landmark, psychologically as much as constitutionally – often to be cited by republicans. In 1986 any remaining legal doubt was ended by the Australia Act which removed residual powers of the British Government to intervene in the politics of Australia or its states. However, the memory of the Kerr incident remained, providing ammunition for those who wished to say that the existence of a Monarch, and her representative, was anomalous.

In Britain, there were echoes of the dispute. Just as the possibility of the Queen using her reserve power to appoint a Prime Minister in conditions of parliamentary deadlock in 1974 had reminded British politicians that such a right still existed, so the Governor-General's use of similar powers in Australia reinforced the same message. In

April 1976 the Labour Government in Westminster was reduced, once again, to minority status, raising some of the same questions as in 1974. Hopeful or anxious glances were cast across the oceans. Meanwhile, the Home Policy Committee of the Labour Party National Executive – a powerful and increasingly left-wing body – issued a report arguing that the Sovereign's power of dissolution should be removed, 'to take the Crown out of politics'. The document cited the recent Australian example.[30]

ON 16 MARCH 1976, Harold Wilson announced his retirement at the age of sixty. The same day, the artist Michael Noakes was painting the Queen's portrait in the Yellow Drawing-Room at the Palace. Noakes said he was surprised. The Queen replied that she wasn't. 'I expected he'd go at about this point', she said.[31] Most of Wilson's colleagues had been kept in the dark. So had the press. It had never happened before that a Prime Minister, under no political pressure, had left office simply because he wanted to give up the job. There was soon speculation about the possibility of a secret reason behind the apparently sudden departure.

In fact, the retirement had been planned months in advance, and the Monarch had been one of the first to be told. Whereas Churchill and Macmillan had talked in audiences about resigning and then put it off, much to their colleagues' frustration, Wilson told the Queen precisely when he intended to go, and then, much to the world's – but not apparently the Queen's – amazement, had gone at the prescribed moment. According to his own account, the message was conveyed at Balmoral the previous September in a characteristically Wilsonian way, as if the Queen had temporarily been recruited, for the purpose of receiving such earth-shaking news, to the lower-middle-classes. Leaving their detectives behind, she drove the Prime Minister and his wife to a small chalet on the Balmoral estate, a mile away from the Castle. When they got there, the Queen filled the kettle, and Mary helped by laying the table. After tea, she gave Mary an apron, put on one herself, and they washed the dishes. While all this was going on, Wilson told the Sovereign of his decision to resign.[32]

During the same visit, he informed Sir Martin Charteris that he intended to submit his resignation six months later. He confirmed this in his weekly audience on December 9th, when he told the Queen that March 11th, or thereabouts, would be the date.[33] It later became clear that his reason for these forewarnings was not just a sense of constitutional propriety, or as a personal courtesy. It was also for the historical record: so that nobody could suggest that he was pushed, and went in a hurry.[34] It did not work: so complete, by this time, was the assumption by the press both of Wilson's ambition and of his deviousness, that the obvious explanation – that he had had enough – was the hardest to accept. What had been intended as a dignified exit became muddied by rumours, compounded by a row over Wilson's mysteriously ill-judged 'lavender list' resignation honours.

The Queen was sorry to see him go, for she had liked him. Their 'relaxed intimacy' had been genuine, and so had a warm feeling between the Queen and Mary Wilson who – anti-pomp, often anti-politician, and intensely private – seemed able to identify with the Monarch as a fellow victim. One of Mary's most interesting poems contrasts the rigid, public, crown-bearing, Monarch, the symbolic figure, with the country woman, alone on the moor, 'walking free upon her own estate / Still in her solitude, she is the Queen'.[35]

The Queen expressed her own feeling for the departing premier by accepting Wilson's invitation to a farewell dinner at No. 10 – the only precedent was the retirement party for Churchill, twenty-one years earlier. With Charteris's help, her speech at the dinner surprised some of the party apparatchiks present by its wit.[36] In reply, Wilson tried his best to be Churchillian. He spoke with sentimental loyalty of the Queen's role, using old-fashioned turns of phrase. He declared himself 'utterly confident of the future destiny of that nation over which you reign'. British institutions, and especially the constitutional Monarchy, were more firmly based on popular support and affection than at any time in the century. He warned his successor 'not to be taken in too easily by Bagehot's distinction between the "dignified" and "efficient" parts of the constitution'. The dignified component, he said, 'can lay strong claim to efficiency'.[37]

It was a quip. The truth was that, in Bagehot's sense of the word, the Monarchy was considerably less 'efficient' – that is, powerful – than it had been at the beginning of the reign. The point was demonstrated, in a little noticed but significant way, by the manner of appointing Wilson's successor as Prime Minister – the first mid-term transfer in which the Monarch was only peripherally involved. Although Labour MPs had elected their own leader since the post had first been established in the 1920s, this was the first time the choice of a new one had taken place while the party was in office.

There was a small technical problem, which exercised the Palace: the interregnum. If a Prime Minister of a leader-electing party resigned or died, there was the question of whether the Queen should ask somebody to act temporarily as her first minister, pending the holding of a leadership contest, or do without one. The matter had been considered during the first Wilson Government. According to the secretary of the Parliamentary Labour Party at that time, a contingency plan had been drawn up to avoid a politically dangerous vacuum in the event of the Prime Minister's death, and agreed with the Palace. The plan had specified that if Wilson died in office, a PLP meeting would be called within twenty-four hours if the House was sitting, or forty-eight hours if it was in recess. At this meeting nominations would be received, ballot papers would be duplicated on the spot, and the Party would proceed to a vote. The result would immediately be conveyed to the Palace. The Queen had apparently been told that she must not summon anybody else in the meantime, and Sir Michael Adeane, her private secretary, had indicated that this was understood.[38] However, such a dramatically rapid process of replacement only applied in the event of a death. There was no plan for dealing with a vacancy created by a premier who merely wished to stand down.

Wilson's advance notice to his own officials and to the Palace was helpful. It gave them time to think. 'How does a Labour Prime Minister resign mid-term, in office?' Kenneth Stowe, Wilson's No. 10 private secretary asked Charteris in September 1975, when both knew that a Prime Minister would shortly do so. There were two sides to the question: an orderly transfer (Whitehall's priority) and preserving the last shreds of the royal prerogative (the Palace's). Charteris came up with a formula. 'He doesn't resign as Prime Minister but as Leader of the Party,' he suggested. 'The party should then go through the process of electing a new Leader.'[39] This meant that instead of the rushed schedule, there could be a period of reflection and campaigning, lasting several weeks, in which the Government could carry

on as usual, before the new Leader was chosen and then summoned
to the Palace.

A variation on Charteris's proposal was adopted. Wilson gave notice
of his resignation as Party Leader, while retaining the post, between
the announcement on March 16th of his intention to stand down,
and the election of James Callaghan as his successor on April 5th.
After the PLP ballot, it was Wilson himself who informed the Queen's
private secretary, by telephone, of the result, before proceeding to the
Palace two hours later to tender his resignation as Prime Minister. At
this final audience, Wilson – as retiring premier – was careful not to
advise the Queen to call for Callaghan. Instead, he said to her, according to his subsequent account, 'that she was already aware of the
voting figures I had sent her'[40] – thus paying dutiful lip service to her
constitutional rights, and to the notion that she had some choice.

The reality, as everybody knew, was that she had no choice, and
the appointment of Callaghan brought home the point – which had
been true since 1965, when the Conservatives elected their Leader in
Opposition – that the Queen's discretionary power in the choice of
a Prime Minister in normal circumstances had, for practical purposes,
ceased to exist. The passing gave rise to a ripple of constitutional
comment. While the right-wing National Association for Freedom
called the Labour Party's assumption that Callaghan should automatically become a premier a 'constitutional impertinence,'[41] Lord Blake,
the Conservative historian and constitutional authority, argued nostal-
gically that the two remaining 'efficient' powers of the Crown, to
choose a Prime Minister and to dissolve Parliament, should somehow
be preserved.[42] The issue had become a party-political one: Labour's
Benn-influenced National Executive used the occasion to press that
the Queen's vestigial powers should be transferred to the Speaker of
the House of Commons.

The National Executive, however, did not speak for the parliamentary leadership, and the Queen soon found that, in Callaghan, she
had acquired as devoted a monarchist as his predecessor. Callaghan
and Wilson had little in common as personalities and, for much of
their careers, they had been wary rivals. Their styles in dealing with
the Monarch also differed. Callaghan's approach was more formal,
and less cosy. Nevertheless, as Crossman had observed, he was also

an unapologetic devotee. 'Jim enormously enjoyed his audiences,' says Tom (now Lord) McNally, his former political secretary. 'They were important to him.' He seemed to find them a useful discipline, and an opportunity to gather his thoughts together on what he had been doing during the week.[43] 'Conversation flowed easily,' Callaghan himself later recalled, 'and could roam anywhere over a wide range of social as well as political and international topics.'[44] Veteran of the Exchequer, Home Office and Foreign Office, Callaghan was better known to the Queen than Wilson had been in 1964. He slid into an easy, friendly relationship with her, based on a confidence in each other's absolute discretion about what was said, and a camaraderie derived from the sense of each as the principal figure in a separate sphere. There was even a flirtatious *frisson* – the Prime Minister would compliment the Monarch on her clothes, and she would respond with banter.[45]

Like Wilson, Callaghan found the Queen a good listener and sounding board. She did not directly criticize the Government's plans. But she measured her response to them. She would often express, or hint at, her own opinion by asking a leading question, or referring to somebody else who held an alternative view. If she approved, she would say so, positively. Disapproval was indicated by a significant failure to comment. The 'roaming' of audiences, however, covered other things, apart from policy – including Cabinet personalities and family matters.

In particular, Callaghan – as a former seaman – took an interest in Charles's naval career. When the Prince was a midshipman, he had corresponded with him. As Prime Minister, Callaghan tried to persuade the young man to gain experience by working in Whitehall – perhaps taking a job in the Cabinet Office, at Principal or Assistant Secretary level. Alternatively, he suggested that the Prince might work as a member of the Commonwealth Development Corporation. The Queen, however, was not keen on the Cabinet Office idea; and the Prince was only interested in a Commonwealth job if he could enter at the top. So the attempt to give the Heir to the Throne a practical training came to nothing. Instead, the Prince spent a symbolic day at No. 10 Downing Street. 'We had to do ridiculous things like standing beside the Prime Minister,' McNally recalls, 'giving him a piece of advice on something banal, while Prince Charles watched.'[46]

ON THE SAME DAY that Wilson announced his resignation, Buckingham Palace released the news of Princess Margaret's legal separation from Lord Snowdon – the first time that the breakdown of the marriage of a member of the inner Royal Family had been officially acknowledged in the twentieth century. Was it coincidence, or collusion? It was later claimed that Wilson had fixed that the two headline-grabbing items should be made public at the same moment, by arrangement with the Palace, and as a favour to the Queen. The Palace denied it. According to Wilson's press officer, however, the Queen consulted the Prime Minister about timing. 'He told her his resignation on the same day would blanket the separation, which wouldn't get the same publicity.'[47] In fact, as Haines points out, Wilson did not understand the tabloids. It was the separation that blanketed the prime ministerial resignation, not the other way round.

For some time there had been rumours that the Snowdons could 'no longer support life together'.[48] When the announcement was made, the Palace tried to soften its impact by saying that there were no plans for divorce. Even as it stood, however, the news destroyed the conventional image of royalty. Lord Harewood, though royal, had been little known to the public – indeed, barely at all, until his marriage problems gave him a fleeting prominence. Princess Margaret was somebody people had grown up with. Although marriage break-ups were, by now, ten-a-penny in the outside world, the revelation that the perfect family suffered from the same tensions as many imperfect ones came as a shock.

Who was responsible? The question dominated articles and features on the subject. Quality newspapers blamed popular ones. 'Almost since the day of their marriage the press, fed by bitchy society gossip, took a prurient and intrusive interest in their private life,' noted Philip Howard. The Queen's private life, he suggested, was 'generally considered inviolable by such malice,' as well as being too worthy and dull for it. But the Princess was reckoned fair game 'for our national hypocrisy masquerading as morality'.[49] Howard's comment contained an echo of Malcolm Muggeridge's, almost twenty years before. 'Each

time that the Princess acquires a new escort the gossip writers set to
with a will,' wrote the pioneering castigator of the royalty industry,
in the aftermath of the Townsend affair. 'Once more the cameras click,
the typewriters tap, the wires hum . . .'[50] But even such 'responsible'
comments, from respected journalists, came out of a gramophone
groove. Making copy out of the hypocrisy of others who made copy
out of Princess Margaret's embittered love life (or out of any other
royal gossip) was a long-standing strategem.

Cameras had clicked and type-writers hummed throughout the
Snowdon marriage. The couple guarded an area of privacy, and Snowdon continued a professional life which gave him a status in the outside
world that was unique among those who had married members of
the Royal Family. However, the Snowdon set, involving show business
personalities who were often indiscreet, provided a steady flow of
stories. Rumours of marital trouble began to appear as early as 1967.
'The problem was two large egos,' says a friend. 'Both were rather
spoilt. They competed with each other in a funny way. They were
dotty about each other in the beginning, but they were only really
happy for about two years.'

Snowdon had formed a relaxed, friendly relationship with his sister-
in-law, and with other members of the Royal Family. In their early
married life together he and his wife had thrown themselves into
joint enterprises, like the re-organization and redecoration of their
apartment at Kensington Palace. However, Snowdon – with no background of royalty, and with ambivalent feelings about what being
royal involved – became increasingly frustrated by the restraints the
status entailed, and by the ersatz fame. 'Part of the problem was
that this ghastly infidelity crept in, which is always corrosive to a
relationship,' according to one source. 'He used to humiliate her in
public, she nagged and got peeved. He behaved badly – he used to
do things like leaving early at dinner. They used to fight and shout
when it went wrong. She used to say "I can't talk to him, he won't
listen".'[51] There was press discussion about a 'structural fault' in the
marriage, and about 'clashes of temperament, reflected occasionally
in manifest and semi-public rows'. Part of the structural fault was
that Snowdon wanted to pursue his independent, non-royal career
and found that despite the initial advantages, being royal got in the

way.[52] Eventually neither he nor, in the end, his wife was prepared – for the sake of duty, patriotism, or Church dogma – to live out the marriage as a sham, once it had become irretrievable. It was agreed that the two children – Lord Linley, aged fourteen, and Lady Sarah Armstrong-Jones, aged eleven – should stay with their mother.[53]

The Monarch kept out of it. 'There has been no pressure from the Queen,' stressed Allison, her press secretary, 'on either Princess Margaret or Lord Snowdon to take any particular course.'[54] The break-up was conducted with dignity, and lack of recrimination. Nevertheless, it was a double blow to the Monarchy as an institution. Princess Margaret was remembered both for her dutiful renunciation of Peter Townsend, and – by older people – as a member of the 1930s and 1940s quadrilateral Family which had stood as the Empire's ideal. The effective end of her marriage cracked the glass, throwing doubt on comforting images of the past, as well as of the present. At the same time, it carried the savage message that the Archbishop, the editor of *The Times*, the Cabinet and other moralizers who had advised the Queen about Peter Townsend's suit had, in human terms, been wrong; and that the Queen might have done better to have stood up to them.

As far as the popular press was concerned, the separation was as much a beginning, as an ending. If Margaret, now forty-five, had decided to become a nun (Prince Philip's mother had made such a decision, under similar circumstances), the result might have been different. However, it was not in her nature. The press was quick to sense it. 'When my sister and I were growing up, she was made out to be the goody-goody one,' Margaret was later quoted as saying. 'That was boring, so the Press tried to make out I was wicked as hell.'[55] Alongside the semi-canonized little Princess, there had always been – in the eyes of professional observers – an alter ego, the naughty minx, the wilful younger sister. Reports of the separation, though couched in sepulchral tones, referred elliptically to Roderick Llewellyn, a twenty-eight-year old trainee landscape gardener.

The references were not new. For some time the adventures of the Snowdons, hinted at in the popular papers, had been honing down the conventions which had hitherto made taboo all references to royal entanglements. Margaret's matrimonial difficulties, and her friendships, became the highway to a new, more raucous kind of press voyeurism, which combined the snobbish, the coy, and the explicitly sexual – encouraged by a new generation of less gentlemanly editors, and by competition between the faltering middle-market *Daily Mail* and *Daily Express*. The *Mail's* success in using a more aggressive style of royal reporting had incited the *Express* at about the time of the Snowdon separation to follow suit. It did not take long for the big-selling tabloids to join in.[56] Rumours became blazoned scandals, and what was left of the old sanctimonious reticence was transformed into competitive ribaldry, couched in the language of homily.

The story of the last days of the marriage tumbled out. Nigel Dempster, doyen of the gossip columnists, described how 'Margaret and Tony blithely seemed to tolerate each other's liaisons' – until the appearance of Roddy Llewellyn and of Lucy Lindsay-Hogg, the young woman Snowdon eventually married. A paparazzi picture in the *News of the World* of Margaret and Llewellyn sitting at a table in beach clothes in Mustique, where Margaret owned a house, had apparently precipitated Snowdon's departure from Kensington Palace.

After the split, Snowdon's private life was, to some extent, left alone. The same was not true of Princess Margaret's, and the supposed incongruity of her relationship with a man much younger than her who relished the publicity his affair had given him, was irresistible to the media. As soon as the separation was announced the press laid siege to Llewellyn, who accepted £6,000 from the *Daily Express* for arranging a photograph of his friends.[57] From Buckingham Palace's point of view, the seven-year Roddy affair became a public relations nightmare – even though other members of the Royal Family seldom if ever met him, and only knew of his activities from the press. From the media viewpoint, however, Llewellyn's meetings and holidays with Princess Margaret provided a rich seam of the scandalous, the scurrilous and the absurd.

When people dreamt about the Royal Family, as one journalist put it a few years later, 'women dream that the Queen comes to tea – and men dream that Princess Margaret falls in love with them'.[58] Margaret's unusual friendship was the stuff of fantasies. It was also the stuff of music-hall jokes. Soon, 'Roddy for PM' tee-shirts were for sale in London boutiques, and royal frolics became daily tabloid entertainment, with a mixed message – the allegedly dissipated life style of the idle rich, the embarrassment to the Queen, and the squandering of Civil List money. In April 1978, an ORC poll showed that seventy-three per cent of the public thought that Margaret had damaged her standing as a member of the Royal Family.[59] She had been a butt of press attacks before the separation. Now she was pilloried in a way that had never happened to a member of the Royal Family in the twentieth century. Critics noted that her public engagements had halved between 1977 and 1978, and that a large amount of her time was spent in the Caribbean. MPs spoke of letters from their constituents, clerics of the moral example. 'Princess Margaret's personal life cannot remain purely a family matter,' said Dr Graham Leonard, Bishop of Truro, in a sermon, 'because what the Monarchy does affects society.' Dr Mervyn Stockwood, Bishop of Southwark, however, declared – with greater Christian charity – that recognizing the Princess's record of service to the Church was far more important than censoring her private life.[60]

Contrary to the impression given in the press, Princess Margaret did not go to pieces. Indeed, she even seemed at times to revel in the attacks, as if, at long last, she was able to get her own back on the Establishment that had destroyed her happiness more than twenty years before. Though distressed by the collapse of her marriage, she was relieved when it was over, and enjoyed her husband's replacement. 'Roddy was like Tony without the vice,' says a friend. 'Tony was amazingly entertaining, but very wicked about getting at people in public. Roddy, by contrast, was a sweet character, very easy and giggly.'[61] She did little to conceal her relationship – or to encourage Llewellyn, who happily capitalized on it, to do so either. 'There is no mystique about Mustique,' as the *Mirror* inevitably put it. 'Every time she holidays there with Roddy it is in the full public glare.'[62] Instead of fending off the paparazzi, she now pretended they did not exist. She also became defiantly rude to dignitaries if they failed to amuse her. 'I did not find her an easy person to talk to,' Paul Martin, the monarchophile Canadian High Commissioner recorded after sitting next to her at dinner in May 1977. His wife, he noted, 'thinks she is quite sad and perhaps that is the reason'.[63]

Sad, glad, or *espiègle*, she gave splendid fuel to the Monarchy's opponents, as the Privy Purse prepared for yet another delicate negotiation over the Civil List, and the nation faced a new crisis over pay norms. William Hamilton had never had so much attention. Soon, he and Roddy became tabloid sparring partners. 'There would be a marvellous response from working people if she were told that she could get on with her private life and that the Government couldn't go on supporting her,' said Hamilton, at the height of Llewellyn's notoriety. 'I would like to see Willie Hamilton . . . do all the jobs in the marvellous way she does,' Roddy gallantly but unwisely responded. Hamilton replied that £140,000 for eight public engagements in three months was not a bad rate of remuneration.[64] Hamilton did not only highlight the cost, *pro rata*, of a Princess who was not much in demand for ceremonial occasions. He also attacked at the most vulnerable point: the relationship between public funding and private behaviour. As a person well rewarded out of public funds, he declared, the Princess was expected to have higher standards than other citizens. 'That has always been part of the case of pro-monarchists'.[65]

Thus, there began – and it was to be a long road – the shift away from the justification for the Monarchy on 'model family' grounds. For Hamilton's view was no longer regarded as eccentric: on the contrary, it had become part of a new orthodoxy, echoed by the most sober voices. 'For better or worse,' as another Labour MP put it, 'the Monarchy is justified as a symbol of the social and family life of the nation.' If it abdicated this symbolic role, it would suffer, 'and its political role will change'.[66] But if the Royal Family was no longer to be regarded as 'model', what did it offer? The traditionalist Peregrine Worsthorne suggested – and this was later to become a fall-back position – that it should be seen as 'normal'. Acknowledging 'a sad lack of private decorum' on the part of the Queen's sister, Worsthorne argued that royalty was bound to have occasional black sheep, and from time to time there would be 'royal broken marriages, merry widows, disorderly divorcées, delinquent teenagers'. The closer to the people the Royal Family became, the more affected it would be by the changing standards of a permissive society.[67] The point was made in semi-jest. However, it was an argument upon which, with the passage of time, it became increasingly necessary to rely.

The *Sun*, enlivened by the 'working people' versus 'social gadfly' angle, claimed that the Queen had told her sister to choose, Duke of Windsor-style, between her royal duties and her relationship. 'Give Up Roddy Or Quit' it summarized.[68] Undoubtedly, the Queen was concerned. 'She talked to me about her sister during the bad patch,' recalls an ex-courtier. 'She asked "How can we get her out of the gutter?" She was worried about her.'[69] 'The Queen sometimes found it hard to cope with Princess Margaret,' says one of the Princess's friends. 'She wondered "What am I going to do with her?"' There were a number of meetings involving No. 10. At one point, a Whitehall paper was composed about the options, including the suggestion that Princess Margaret should be taken off the Civil List and allowed to lead a private life – in effect, the ultimatum issued to her over Townsend in the 1950s. 'The Queen was very resistant to this,' recalls a close Callaghan aide, 'and Jim was very supportive of the Queen.'[70]

At the beginning of May 1978, Margaret was taken ill, and diagnosed as suffering from gastroenteritis and alcoholic hepatitis.[71] On May 10th, it was announced that she was seeking a divorce. It was another rubicon. '. . . [I]f she divorced', predicted Philip Howard, before the announcement, 'her example would upset the established principles of Christian family life of the Church of which her sister is head, and attract the disapproval of influential Church leaders.'[72] This was a fear. 'Mindful of the teachings of the Church . . .' Margaret had written in her devout little essay of renunciation, composed by her divorced would-be fiancé, in 1955. However, times had changed, and the Church of England on this occasion treated her with gentleness. Dr Coggan, the Archbishop of Canterbury, expressed his sympathy.[73]

The Roddy tragi-comedy took some of the edge off public reaction to the divorce, especially when it became clear that there was no prospect of Llewellyn becoming a member of the Royal Family. 'I am saying categorically,' he declared, in answer to the obvious question, 'that I will never marry Princess Margaret.' That was a relief to practically everybody. However, the blushes continued. In October 1978, Llewellyn launched a pop record, 'Roddy,' at the night-club Tramp, in the presence of twenty photographers. Even *The Times* printed a picture of the event, whose newsworthiness – as the debutant singer modestly admitted – had more to do with the company he kept than with the quality of his music. The record did not sell many copies.

In December, Lord Snowdon re-married. In 1980, Princess Margaret's relationship with Llewellyn ended when he, too, married somebody else.[74]

19

PRINCESS MARGARET was not the first member of the Royal Family to have an unsuitable companion. She was the first, however, to be treated with such public derision because of it. The Roddy affair, a topic of international prurience and hilarity for many months, signalled the direction in which royal media coverage was moving. 'Permissiveness' – as the Palace was discovering – had two sides. If one was a greater tolerance of deviance in private behaviour, the other was a greater freedom in discussing it. Before the war, people talked about Mrs Simpson behind cupped hands. In the 1970s, Roddy Llewellyn found that he could turn his royal relationship into a cottage industry.

Though the Queen was not held responsible for her sister's behaviour, she was inevitably involved, both because of the Princess's call on public funds, and also because – as critics pointed out – royalty had presented itself as a collective unit, setting a moral example: the 'model family' could scarcely be sold as a curate's egg. The result was a new kind of difficulty. The switch from sugary accounts of public appearances and ceremonies to a narrative of rumour and scandal as the dominant form of royal reporting, tended to obscure the conventional activities of royalty – to the point where it was easy to forget that they were taking place. Reminding people what members of the Royal Family actually did, as well as what they were really like, had been the purpose of the Cawston film. The public taste for novelty, however, quickly becomes jaded. In the 1970s and 1980s, royal misbehaviour became the circulation-raising topic, arousing far greater public curiosity than barbecues or visits to Brazil.

One ground for concern about Llewellyn at Buckingham Palace was that some of the most excruciating stories threatened to downpage the run-up to the 1977 Silver Jubilee, which marked the twenty-fifth anniversary of the Accession. If the Jubilee took time to get airborne as a focus for enthusiasm, part of the reason was rivalry from the Roddy sub-plot, which intermittently provided copy alongside it. In the end, however, the Jubilee triumphed – succeeding in a way that other royal celebrations since the Coronation had not, and providing a thread of public interest in royalty and the Monarchy which lasted much of the year.

A Jubilee year of official festivities was not inevitable, and the anniversary might have been passed over with a minimum of fuss. Yet there were more solid precedents for celebrating the quarter-centenary than there had been for the Investiture in 1969. 'Jubilees' in the past had marked different milestones within the longer reigns. The fiftieth anniversary of the Accession of George III in 1809 had been celebrated with a grand fête and fireworks display at Frogmore, together with a service at St Paul's and dinner at the Mansion House. Late nineteenth-century jubilees had been more ambitious. Victoria's Golden Jubilee in 1887 was attended by more than thirty kings and foreign princes, together with the heads of government of colonies and dominions, and there had been a huge procession through London. There was also a Diamond Jubilee ten years later. The Jubilee that had the greatest impact and the example on which the 1977 one was based, was the Silver Jubilee of George V in 1935, an imperial celebration whose splendour had presaged that of the 1953 Coronation, with which it was often compared. In 1935, there had been a procession, as well as a month of receptions, loyal addresses and street parties throughout the country.[1]

Precedents, however, can lead to anti-climax. Could the George V euphoria be repeated? The very triumph of the 1935 Jubilee was a reason for hesitancy. 'Jim Callaghan and Roy Jenkins were dubious at first,' recalls one ex-courtier.[2] 'The Government didn't want the Jubilee,' says another.[3] The late 1970s was a fragile time, politically and economically. Remembering the Investiture, some ministers were afraid that the ceremonies would seem artificial and the public response would be half-hearted. It was the Court which pushed for it, and won. The formal announcement was made by the Home Secretary in August 1975.[4] Sir Martin Charteris was the key initiator, but he was strongly backed by his colleagues. 'Martin, Bill and I felt that this was the time to celebrate,' says Ronald Allison.[5] There was a fight over the itinerary. The Government was opposed to a national royal tour on financial grounds, but was eventually persuaded. 'I made a plan in my head,' says Charteris. 'The Queen ought to go round this country, and go to all the countries of which she was Queen.'[6] She did both.

Though the Accession took place in February, the main Jubilee celebrations were scheduled for the summer. In the first half of the year, from mid-February to the end of March, there was an Australasian and Pacific tour, with visits to Western Samoa, Tonga, Fiji, New Zealand, Papua New Guinea and Australia. In October, the Queen and Duke went on a Canadian and Caribbean tour, visiting the Bahamas, the British Virgin Islands, Antigua and Barbados. During the intervening months, there was a build-up of events at home, culminating in the main celebration on 7 June. On 4 May, both Houses of Parliament presented loyal addresses. Then the United Kingdom tours began, starting in Glasgow. At the beginning of June there was a 'London week', which culminated in a river progress up the Thames, ending with a fireworks display, and a procession of lighted carriages taking the Queen back to Buckingham Palace.[7]

However, the ambitious Jubilee programme got off to an uneven start. In the spring, a minor row about royal money diverted attention embarrassingly. In April, it was announced that the Queen's share holdings were to be exempted from a provision of the 1976 Companies Act, which enabled companies to require disclosure of the true owners behind nominees' holdings of their capital. The Queen was affected because her extensive share holdings 'by long custom' were not held in her name. Section 27(9) of the Act provided that a person exempted by the Secretary of State for Trade would not be obliged to comply with a notice from a company requiring disclosure.[8] The news revived memories of the leaked Robert Armstrong letter in 1973 – and produced a flutter of criticism from those who opposed loopholes for the rich. 'The exemption widens still further the gap between the Head of State and her poorest subjects,' declared Frank Field, director of the Child Poverty Action Group.[9]

A more serious Palace worry, however, was the slow initial response to the Jubilee plans in the country. For a time the sceptics seemed to have been proved right. There were reports of street parties cancelled, local authorities refusing to help, and lack of demand for souvenir trinkets. The Queen was criticized for failing to take a personal lead, and for neglecting to make the kind of symbolic Jubilee gesture that had popularized the celebrations of her forebears, like an amnesty for prisoners, or even the dispensing of Jubilee mugs to school children.

In some areas, the most visible evidence of the Jubilee was provided by the efforts of Marxists and other agitators to discredit it. While the Communist Party organized its own 'People's Jubilee' at Alexandra Palace, the Trotskyist Socialist Workers' Party dispensed a large quantity of 'Roll on the Red Republic' stickers. The *New Statesman* prepared an 'anti-Jubilee' issue, which prompted the *Sun* to comment in its inimitable style, 'out of the woodwork they crawl, the termites of the Left.'[10] In the lavatory of the Middle Temple, meanwhile, an anonymous graffiti writer summed up the position of the anarchist movement: 'Sod the Jubilee. The Ersatz Orgasm of the Silent Majority.'[11] This, at least, was intended to be funny. Unintended humour was provided by Sir John Betjeman, who wrote a Silver Jubilee hymn for school children to sing at the Albert Hall. Set to music by Malcolm Williamson, Master of the Queen's Music, the Poet Laureate's work was judged to be outstandingly dreadful in a competitive field. 'From that look of dedication / In those eyes profoundly blue,' it went, 'We know her Coronation / As a sacrament and true.'[12]

Although interest grew, as the main events approached, there was still hostility in some quarters. Part of it was political. The Queen's Silver Jubilee speech to Parliament on 4th May demonstrated the difficulty a constitutional Monarch found, on such a supposedly unifying occasion, in voicing sentences bland enough to avoid giving offence to anybody. The occasion was mainly symbolic. Tony Benn attended as a penance, 'to remind himself how totally undemocratic British democracy is'. He was duly reminded.[13] Mrs. Thatcher, in a sea of dark grey and pinstripe, was clad resplendently in a pink gown identical in colour to that of the Queen, and looked, according to the *Guardian's* reporter, 'like a large shrimp'.[14]

The Queen's speech to Parliament, however, turned out to be more than ceremonial. Included among the platitudes were a couple of sentences which ruffled the Scottish Nationalist MPs. 'I cannot forget that I was crowned Queen of the United Kingdom of Great Britain and Northern Ireland,' she said, adding, riskily, 'Perhaps this Jubilee is a time to remind ourselves of the benefits which union has conferred, at home and in our international dealings, on the inhabitants of all parts of this United Kingdom.' Was this the Government putting inappropriately political words in the mouth of the Sovereign, or the Sovereign expressing her own, independently political thoughts? The Prime Minister's office insisted that – though passed for approval to No. 10 – the speech was entirely the product of the Palace. There was discussion of the constitutional propriety of the Monarch saying anything that anybody might disagree with. For her to adhere to the consensus, it appeared, was not enough. What she said constituted a 'personal statement,' and, as such, clearly stood outside (as *The Times* put it) 'the convention that the Sovereign does not descend to the arena of party political controversy.'[15] The press, and Scottish opponents of the union, concluded that she was speaking her mind. Angrily, Donald Stewart, leader of the mainly monarchist SNP, declared that if it came to a choice between independence and the Monarchy, 'we would choose independence'.[16]

The Jubilee celebrations began to acquire momentum during the United Kingdom tours that followed the loyal addresses. In Lancashire, there were more spectators than ever before for a royal event.[17] 'I am simply amazed, I had no idea,' a Lady of the Bedchamber recalls her saying over and over during her tour, at the affection of the crowds.[18] However, it was the June ceremonies which transformed the Jubilee into an excitingly modern visual display, in contrast to the dank theatricals of the Investiture. On 6th June, the Queen climbed Snow Hill, near Windsor Castle, where – surrounded by thousands of children – she lit a bonfire as the signal for the lighting of a hundred other fires across the country. Next day, a million people, as many as at the Coronation, filled the Mall to see the State Coach take the Queen and her husband from the Palace to St Paul's Cathedral, followed by the Prince of Wales on horseback in the scarlet uniform and black bearskin of a Colonel of the Welsh Guards.

After the cathedral service, the Queen and Duke went on a choreographed walkabout through the City, along Cheapside and into King Street, talking to spectators as they walked. The remarks were everyday,

BARON GRADE presents:
Britain's MOST POPULAR FAMILY GROUP
THE WINDSORS greatest TOP OF THE POPS
SINCE THE OSMONDS!!

FRANKLIN

♫ "Singing in the Reign . . ." ♫

Sun, 30th December, 1976

bus-queue ones, mainly related to the weather. 'Oh dear, did you get awfully wet?' the Monarch said to well-wishers who had camped all night, or 'Are you frozen?' The 'most successful Royal Walk ever' – as the *Daily Telegraph* banally called it,[19] ended at the Guildhall, where she addressed a luncheon in her honour.

In her speech, the Queen renewed her Cape Town promise, though with a significant change of wording. 'When I was twenty-one,' she declared, 'I pledged my life to the service of our people and I asked for God's help to make good that vow. Although that vow was made in my salad days when I was green in judgement, I do not regret or retract one word of it.' In 1947, however, the dedication had been to Empire. Now she spoke of the Commonwealth – likening it to an iceberg, the tip of which was represented by occasional meetings of Heads of Government and the Secretariat, but with nine-tenths of the Commonwealth's activity taking place beneath the surface. The submerged, unseen element consisted of friendship and communication between peoples who had been brought together 'by the events of history'.[20]

The central, televised part of the Jubilee, however, was by no means the whole, or even the most important bit of it. The Coronation had focused on an Abbey service and a procession, with local festivities as a joyful echo. The Jubilee, by contrast, became (as had been intended) primarily a community celebration. The street parties some had feared might not happen sprang into life everywhere – with 4,000 in London alone.[21] The celebrations continued with provincial tours which lasted into August. The most contentious was a visit to Northern Ireland. For the Queen to go was to take a physical risk. Not to have gone would have excluded part of the United Kingdom from the celebration. 'The Home Office asked "Does she want to go or not?"' according to Lord Charteris. 'They said "We can get her out of it."' He put the same question to the Queen. It was like Ghana in 1961. 'Since we've *said* I'm going,' she replied, 'I want you to say that I'm going.' The trip went ahead. There was a small bomb, but no disaster. 'It felt wonderful sailing away from Londonderry,' recalled Charteris.[22]

By the time the domestic tours ended, 'literally millions' of people, according to *The Times*, had been out on the street to see and cheer the Queen, while the Palace had received 50,000 letters of greeting.[23] It was impossible not to see the Jubilee as a spectacular success, vindicating its advocates, even though much of the merriment was only tangentially related to the Monarchy. 'My liver is damaged beyond repair, my waistline has disappeared,' wrote Jilly Cooper. 'I've been sabotaged by street parties, but I've never enjoyed a summer more.'[24]

Anti-monarchists, who earlier in the year had spoken disparagingly of the 'sycophantic bonanza' which they believed would never get off the ground, now complained of 'Jubilee fever'.[25] At the beginning of the year, there had been talk of royalty in the doldrums, in the wake of the Margaret separation. By the autumn, the papers spoke of an exceptional period of popularity and security. Did the advance of socialism in western Europe pose a threat to the British Monarchy? a foreign journalist asked the Prince of Wales, early in 1978. 'Last year's celebrations of the Queen's Silver Jubilee in Britain showed there was not a great deal of fear about such a possibility,' the Prince was able confidently to reply.[26]

What were people celebrating? As always with royal festivals, there was a mystery at its heart which the most determined flag-wavers and street-party organizers were the least able to solve. To say, conventionally, that the focus was on 'Queen and people' scarcely explained crowds bigger than at the Coronation or on VE-Day, or local parties as happy as anybody could remember. Dedication to the Monarchy was weaker in 1977 than in the reigns of Victoria or George V, when the institution had a greater influence and significance. Indeed, in most other respects, apart from the Jubilee, it was a nondescript year in a mediocre decade – at the end of a quarter of a century of decline, underlined by the financial crisis and IMF visitation of the year before. All that could be said on the positive side was that 1977 was a little calmer than the period that preceded it, much as 1935 had been a year of recovery, compared with the early 1930s. At the time of the George V Jubilee, however, nation and Empire had been strong themes. In 1977, the United Kingdom was fractured by Celtic nationalism and by the trouble in Ulster, while the 1975 referendum, which confirmed British membership of the European Community, sealed the fate of the Commonwealth in its old form.

Lord Charteris had a simple explanation. 'She had a love affair with the country,' he suggested.[27] Those who accompanied her during the tours came back with a strong sense of the popular emotion – as well as of her own pleasure in the response of the crowds, and their delight in her obvious enjoyment. Among the public at large, whether they turned out to see her or not, there was personal respect and affection for the Queen. In politics, there is the cynic's response, cited when Members of Parliament in safe seats boast about the size of their majority, that if a donkey with a red or blue rosette had been put up it would get as many votes. Up to a point, the same is true of monarchs. It does not take much to make a king or queen popular. The Silver Jubilee, however, seemed to reveal a deeper regard, a warmth for the individual, partly based on a sense that, though seldom revealed, the feeling existed on both sides.

George V was supposed to have said, confronting his own popularity in 1935, 'I am beginning to think they must really like me for myself'.[28]

The Queen might have made a similar remark forty-two years later. But who and what was she? The profiles that proliferated on such occasions showed little change from a decade before – reminding people of what they had long found reassuringly familiar. The portraits were tinted water-colours, not dazzling oils – passive, conservative, middle-aged and settled. She had 'reigned for twenty-five years without putting a foot wrong,' claimed Sir John Colville. She had, he suggested, the qualities of patience, courtesy, a sense of dignity, judgement, self-control and wisdom.[29] Others ticked off the checklist of her known habits and recreations. There were her mainly aristocratic friends who shared her interest in horses, dogs and field sports; her fifty horses, some at Polhampton, near Kingsclere, others at her two studs at Sandringham, with twenty-one of racing age that were in training; her dozen annual visits to the races, often accompanied by her friend Lord Porchester. Her 'normal' pleasures (that is, the ones normal people shared) included doing jigsaw puzzles, playing scrabble, and watching low-brow comedy on television. Her abnormal ones were riding, stalking and walking across the moors at Balmoral. One journalist calculated that she lived in the country about four months a year – most of January at the Sandringham estate, most of August and September at Balmoral and spending April and most weekends at Windsor.[30] She ate and drank little, did not smoke, and had – so it was confidently claimed – 'no psychological hang-ups'.[31]

In the past, the glamour of the throne had been set against the 'model family', with its everyday domestic virtues, as a way of highlighting each. Now, in an equalizing era, the Queen's lack of shining qualities or talents was celebrated as a virtue in itself. Jean Rook, in the *Express*, saw her as 'the same tidy, dedicated, undramatic, magnificently "dull" woman' she had been when she was a tidy, white socked and dull, little princess.[32] The *Daily Telegraph* took the theme a lighthearted stage further. Fashion editors might deplore the Queen's dress sense, it acknowledged. They 'can jump in the Seine.' Aesthetes might deplore her philistinism. 'If she would rather go to Ascot than peer at a lot of dirty nappies in the Institute of Contemporary Arts, what is wrong with that?' However, it concluded, any honest republican could see that she was serious, conscientious, dignified, patriotic, unaffected and wise.[33]

It was John Grigg – ever the shrewdest of royalty watchers – who offered the most perceptive sketch (as well as one of the most flattering). It was not dullness he saw but, on the contrary, a sound, if unimaginative regality:

> She looks a queen and obviously believes in her right to be one. Her bearing is both simple and majestic – no actress could possibly match it. Wherever she may be in the world, in whatever company or climate, she never seems to lose her poise.
>
> These outward graces reflect the exceptionally steady character which is her most important quality. Through a period of fluctuating fashion and considerable moral disintegration, she has lived up to her own high standards and, in doing so, has set an example which has been grudgingly admired even by those who have not followed it. In particular, she has shown how much family life means to her, and has stood rock-firm for all that it represents ... No breath of scandal has ever touched her ... She behaves decently because she *is* decent and it is almost impossible to imagine her causing pain to anyone close to her for the sake of gratifying a selfish impulse.[34]

The Jubilee also celebrated the institution itself, which (it was agreed) had altered little, while all around was bewildering change. The *Observer* noted that, at a time when virtually everything else – Parliament, the Civil Service, the party system, the trade unions, even the integrity of the United Kingdom – was under scrutiny, scarcely anything was being said about the Monarchy.[35] The *Sunday Times* contrasted the continuity and inevitability of what it saw as the cornerstone of the British Constitution, with the Watergate-ridden elective head of state in the United States.[36]

There was, however, an added ingredient to this immutable package, almost as significant as *Royal Family*. The Monarchy itself might still appear a reassuring bedrock in tumultuous times. But the way of discussing it was undergoing as great a transformation as at the end of the previous decade. Then, there had been an attempt, from the inside, to give the royal icons flesh and blood. Now – in a climate of political questioning – the impetus came from outside, and focused on the institution. In January, a hitherto unknown reporter, Robert Lacey, published a book called *Majesty*[37] which changed the written representation of the Monarchy almost as much as the Cawston film had previously changed the visual one. Many reviewers were dismissive. 'I am prepared to believe that they are dull,' wrote Richard Boston in the *Guardian*, 'but surely no one could be as dull as that.'[38] What helped to turn the book into a best-seller was an unexpected matter-of-factness in its tone. Gone was the reverence of the past, the arch or coy way in which royal subjects were generally handled, and also the willingness to take official information on trust. The author treated royalty as if it was any other aspect of British life, which merited serious journalistic inquiry.

Majesty marked the end of the era of sycophantic reporting of the Monarchy. At the same time, and as important, it showed the commercial possibilities of investigative books about royalty that succeeded in bridging the serious–popular divide – demonstrating that tabloid style 'revelations' could be packaged for the non-tabloid, book buying public by combining them with sober analysis. Much of *Majesty*, like *Royal Family*, described the day-to-day routines of Buckingham Palace. But the book also contained new details about the Snowdon marriage, tastefully slipped into a chapter about the Monarchy's constitutional role.

At the start of the Jubilee year, the book was taken as a good omen by loyalists, who cited its instant success as evidence of a new public interest in a phenomenon which, a decade earlier, had apparently gone out of fashion. In retrospect, however, it can also be seen as a time bomb. In due course books between hard covers were to damage the Monarchy much more than a brigade of paparazzi.

ON 14TH OCTOBER, the Queen and the Duke set out for Ottawa. Sir Martin Charteris stayed behind, to clear his office in preparation for his own retirement. The Silver Jubilee had been a final service, and a labour of love, which he regarded as the principal achievement of his private secretaryship. To mark the anniversary, and also his own departure, close helpers since Clarence House days – including Charteris, Bobo and Bennett the butler – presented the Queen with a napkin ring, with their names engraved on it. Charteris said good-bye after she returned from the Caribbean in November. She had Princess Anne with her, but that did not stop him weeping. She gave him items of antique silver, as a present. She said, 'Martin, thanks for a lifetime'.[39] It was a poignant moment for the Monarch, as well as for her retiring secretary. Her staff was changing: tweediness, and with it a set of shared assumptions, was on the wane. Two years earlier Lord Plunket, her closest friend and retainer at the Palace since adolescence, died at the age of fifty-one. 'The greatest tragedy of her life was the death of Patrick Plunket,' says a Lady of the Bedchamber. 'He was the one person who could talk to her on equal terms.'[40] According to another friend: 'She minded when he died. It changed the drift of her life'.[41] After the death of Plunket, and the departure of Charteris, some of the jauntiness, the sense of a continuous party that had begun with the Coronation, went out of Palace life. The now firmly middle-aged Monarch became a less romanticized and more conventional employer.

Charteris was replaced by Sir Philip Moore, the first non upper-class private secretary of the reign. Moore's style contrasted with that of his predecessor, and seemed to reflect his civil service background. Views of him were mixed. Some found him cautious, and liable to stand on his dignity. The old guard were lukewarm. 'Darling old Philip Moore was a bit stuffy,' says one ex-courtier. 'He was very talkative,' says another, 'and he bored the Queen stiff.' There was a theory that he had been taken on by the Palace because of his non-top drawer origins as a sop to the Labour Government. Whether or not this was true, his Whitehall experience provided good lines of communication to prime ministerial private secretaries and Cabinet secretaries, whose language he spoke. There were no bold ventures, like *Royal Family*, or the Jubilee, during his period of office. However, Moore's diplomatic background helped in the non-governmental task of steering the Monarchy through major constitutional changes in the two old dominions, which culminated in the 'patriation' of the Canadian constitution in 1982, and the passing of the Australia Acts in both British and Australian Parliaments in 1986.

The Queen's 1977 trip to Canada had a particular importance. The Jubilee had been a Commonwealth as well as a national celebration, marked in similar style in those countries which the Queen visited during the year as Head of State. A Commonwealth Heads of Government meeting was timed to coincide with 'London Week'. In the case of Canada, however, the Palace took particular care, because the Jubilee happened to occur during a period of national re-evaluation, similar to the one in Australia but with the complicating factor of Quebec.

For some time, Canada had received disproportionate royal attention. In 1976, the entire Royal Family had been present for the opening of the Olympic Games in Montreal, where Princess Anne was competing in the equestrian events. In 1977, Prince Andrew – in a parallel gesture to Charles's Geelong visit – spent six months at Lakefield College, Ontario. Meanwhile, in addition to a five-day Jubilee tour of Ottawa by the Queen and Duke, the Prince of Wales attended centennial celebrations in Alberta. The following July and August, the Queen and Duke were back again, this time for the Commonwealth Games at Edmonton, accompanied by their younger sons. The spate of royal visits reminded the Canadian public of a connection which distinguished the country from their giant neighbour to the south. However, it did not halt the process of change.

In 1978 Pierre Trudeau, as Prime Minister, put forward a new constitution which proposed, *inter alia*, that the Westminster Parliament should surrender its residual constitutional role in Canadian affairs as defined in the 1867 British North America Act, and that in future the Queen would be described simply as Queen of Canada, without reference to the United Kingdom. At the same time (as in Australia, but with a different emphasis) the Governor-Generalship became a focus of attention. According to the new rules, the Governor-General would have to be a Canadian citizen, appointed on the recommendation of the Canadian Prime Minister, though with strengthened powers of dissolution. Once again the real issues were domestic ones. The Canadian debate concerned the balance of power between provincial and federal governments and between the traditionalist majority and a French-speaking, often republican, minority. As in the Kerr case, the Monarchy, peripheral and powerless, got caught in the cross-fire.

Buckingham Palace's reaction was mixed. Remembering the Australian experience, it had little desire to preserve vestigial power which it could not in practice exercise, but whose survival could still cause embarrassment. On the other hand, it did not wish Canada to go the whole way, as some feared might happen, and make the Governor-General Head of State. The cause was not lost, and the Monarchy was able to mount a behind-the-scenes rearguard action – relying on its continued hold on much of Canadian opinion, and on the desire of Canadian politicians not to offend this section by upsetting the Queen.

It helped that the Monarch spoke good French – and also that she had on her side Paul Martin, the ardently pro-royal High Commissioner in London. Her main asset, however, as Martin's diary reveals, was the way that she handled the discussions in which she was involved – conveying the sense that, while appreciating Canadian loyalty and naturally wishing, if possible, to retain it, she had no ambitions other than to help her North American subjects to sort out their constitutional difficulties. 'The Queen has a capacity for relaxation in these matters,' noted Martin, after she had been briefed in July 1978. The diplomacy was delicate. 'She had to be fully involved,' says a British official. 'On this sort of thing, she was invaluable as the Head of State here and in Canada.'[42] Martin contrasted her calm approach with the private anxiety on the same topic recently displayed by the Prince of Wales.

The briefing meetings involved Ron Basford, the Canadian Minister for Justice, and Don Jamieson, the Foreign Minister. 'The Monarch went through those portions of the bill concerning the Crown in Canada imperturbably,' wrote Martin. 'She fully understood what was provided and sought information rather than imposing any impediment in the government's decision to present the bill.' While Sir Philip Moore did not conceal the Palace's displeasure at Trudeau's brusqueness in presenting his proposals, the Queen dealt with the matter pragmatically. Afterwards, the Canadian ministers expressed their relief and gratitude at the approach of 'such a sensible woman;' and what might have been the basis for a quarrel, never became one. At a reception given at the High Commissioner's London residence on 17th July, Martin – choosing words used by Trudeau in a radio broadcast – welcomed the Queen as 'the Head of our Constitutional Monarchy'. Smiling benignly, she spoke of how well the constitutional meetings had gone.[43]

Four years later, following the passage of the British Parliament's Canada Act, the Queen flew to Canada for the proclamation of the country's new constitution – which completed the process of transferring to the Governor-General those functions that had previously been discharged by the Sovereign, and virtually ended the constitutional link with Britain. Henceforth, the Canadian Monarchy was scarcely more than a title – yet it was still a significant one, partly because of the way the negotiations had been handled. 'The Queen remains Queen of Canada,' as *The Times* reassured British readers, 'all the easier for Canadians to accept because she will no longer be burdened by identification with the constitutional issues.'[44]

British ministers were not much involved in the discussions between the Monarch and her servants on the other side of the Atlantic. In any case, there was much to preoccupy them at home. The Silver Jubilee had taken place in the nick of time. If it had been celebrated in 1978, not 1977, the festivities would have been tangled up with an industrial crisis which paralyzed the country almost as severely as the troubles of 1973–4 and which proved fatal for the Callaghan administration. In the autumn, the Government's pay policy collapsed, precipitating the so-called 'Winter of Discontent'. In January 1979, lorry drivers stopped work, followed by local government and other public employees, and in February by civil servants. Pictures of uncollected rubbish in the streets, and stories of bodies unburied, dominated the nation's consciousness.

One cause of the crisis was the rise in oil prices six years earlier, with its knock-on impact on inflation. Concern about oil lay behind a royal trip to the Middle East in the second half of February 1979, involving visits to Kuwait, Bahrain, Saudi Arabia, Qatar, the United Arab Emirates and Oman, with the specific purpose of reinforcing Anglo–Arab ties, and to provide reassurance, following the recent revolution in Iran.

Arrangements for the trip were delicate. Saudi Arabia was the most important country to be visited. Here, local customs presented a special difficulty. During the preparations, the Saudi royal family made it clear, as one British ex-official puts it, that 'they would welcome the Queen as an honorary man,' but they did not wish those who came with her to include women journalists. Such an exclusion was unacceptable in Britain, and the Palace successfully resisted it. However, it agreed to a request that all women taking part in the tour, including the Queen, should obey local conventions of dress. Her designers were asked to produce dresses which did not reveal the royal arms and legs. 'I'm told "no bare flesh" is the main concern!' she wrote to Hardy Amies in anticipation of the Gulf visit.[45] A member of the party recalls the visit as a discomfiting one, for other reasons. Saudi Arabia was an authoritarian country with savagely puritanical laws. A flavour of the trip was provided when the king, as host, marked the occasion by granting an amnesty to a number of Britons held in Saudi prisons for offences related to the absolute ban on the sale or consumption of alcohol. Then, in front of the British party in the royal palace, a leading Saudi clapped his hands, and a servant opened a cabinet containing a range of whiskies, which were offered to the guests.[46]

The Queen returned to Britain at a critical moment. The minority Callaghan administration, approaching its statutory expiry date, was faced by a combination of its opponents on the issue of devolution. On a motion of confidence, the Government was defeated by one vote, and the Prime Minister asked for a dissolution. Here was the situation which many had anticipated years before. Technically, the Queen was entitled to seek an alternative Prime Minister, without an immediate poll. However, an election was due within a few months in any case. The Queen dissolved Parliament on 7th April, and the contest was fixed for 3rd May.

The poll was a watershed. Labour had held office for all but three and a half years since 1964 and – despite the minority status of the Callaghan Government – it did not seriously lose popularity until the Winter of Discontent. Then support for it collapsed, and in the election, Labour suffered a massive defeat. With a substantial Conservative majority behind her, Margaret Thatcher was summoned to Buckingham Palace, where the Queen asked her to form a Government, and to become the first woman ever to hold the office of Prime Minister. 'We were all much more excited and nervous than we tried to appear,' recalls Lord Howe, then Sir Geoffrey, who was appointed Chancellor of the Exchequer. 'The Queen herself was reassuringly matter-of-fact.'[47]

In 1970, Tony Benn had suspected the Court of secret pleasure at the change of Government, on the grounds that in their politics and social assumptions, Palace officials and especially the ladies-in-waiting, were more in tune with Conservative ministers than with Labour ones. Whether or not this was true, the Queen herself faced the same paradox in 1979 as nine years earlier. The Tory victory meant exchanging a Prime Minister who headed a party which was sharply critical of inherited wealth, privilege and position, for one who accepted such things as part of the natural order. Yet it also meant swapping a leader she had come to know and like for one she did not know so well and found much less sympathetic.

In the Queen's relations with Mrs Thatcher, even more than with Heath, there was a rigidity that never softened. The point can be exaggerated. 'Mrs Thatcher's views were very supportive of the Queen's institution,' acknowledges a former senior Tory minister, and frequent private critic of the Prime Minister. 'She had an instinctive respect for its dignity.' Apart from weekly audiences when they were both in the country and Parliament was sitting, and the annual visit to Balmoral, the Prime Minister and Monarch seldom had to meet except on formal occasions, and did not greatly impinge on each other's lives. Moreover there was never – in Mrs Thatcher's eleven years at No. 10 – an example of a public clash between them, or clear evidence of a private one. Both guarded their words. If the Queen made a profession of being discreet, so did the Prime Minister. 'Mrs Thatcher never spoke about her meetings at the Palace,' says an aide, 'and never spoke about the Queen, except in the most dutiful terms.'[48] 'If the Queen offered views on any subject,' says a civil service adviser to Mrs Thatcher in the early years of her premiership, 'she would have taken them seriously.'[49] The notion that they did not enjoy each other's company, however, was not imaginary. Indeed, had it been false, it could easily have been dispelled by either side.

The tales of a stiffness between them began early, before Mrs Thatcher became Prime Minister. Haines remembers Harold Wilson gleefully passing on a story told him in an audience shortly after Mrs Thatcher became Leader of the Opposition, about her fainting during a Palace function. According to Wilson, the way the Queen told it was revealing. 'She doesn't like her,' he confided.[50] An elaboration of this story was also spread by a leading churchman, among his fellow prelates. According to this version, fainting at the Palace was a habit. On one occasion, Mrs Thatcher felt so faint at dinner that she had to retreat to the lavatory. A short time later, at a similar event, the same thing happened. 'She's keeled over again,' said the Queen to fellow guests, as soon as the Tory Leader was out of the room.

It was after Mrs Thatcher formed a Government, however, that the degree of incompatibility became widely apparent. In private, both the Queen and her husband gave the impression that the Prime Minister was 'not their favourite woman,' as one close friend of the royal couple puts it.[51] 'More business-like than warm,' was one description of the Head of State–Head of Government relationship, after the first couple of years.[52] 'The weekly meetings between the Queen and Mrs Thatcher – both of the same age – are dreaded by at least one of them,' wrote Anthony Sampson, who had good Palace contacts, in a book published in 1982. 'The relationship is the more difficult because their roles seem confused; the Queen's style is more matter of fact and domestic, while it is Mrs Thatcher (who is taller) who bears herself like a Queen.'[53] The queenly, even imperial, style of the Prime Minister, strengthened by the Falklands War, seemed to grow with the passage of time, as her electoral triumphs made her appear invincible. 'She got grander and grander,' recalls a Whitehall adviser, 'and I would have thought this would have gone down badly with the Queen.'[54] Another official points to 'a curious gender relationship,' confirming Sampson's sense of two personalities with little in common between them. 'They were very different kinds of women. Margaret Thatcher made her way by hard work and bullying. The Queen was handed it all on a plate.'[55]

Gradually, the two got to know each other better. But there was never any equivalent of the male gallantry the Queen was used to, or of the mutual letting-down of hair, that had been characteristic of earlier premierships. According to a former head of Mrs Thatcher's No. 10 Policy Unit, meetings between the Queen and Prime Minister were stiff and awkward. Audiences ceased to be intimate occasions, and became brisk, formal ones. 'Why does she always sit on the edge of her seat?' the Queen once asked a Tory peer. 'I think Margaret was scared of the Queen,' says an ex-minister, who was close to the premier in the early years. 'She was affected by the aura, the trappings but she was slightly nervous. I think she was in awe of the position.' 'Mrs Thatcher would have thought it impudent to have tried to establish a close relationship,' suggests a former Whitehall adviser, 'and would have expected the Queen to make the first move.' But in fact the Queen did not do so.[56]

There was also a kind of mutual condescension. The Palace seems to have regarded Thatcherite fervour as vulgar, while the Thatcherites considered the Palace irrelevant and effete. It was part personal, part political. 'These were two women who registered different vibrations,' as Hugo Young, Lady Thatcher's biographer, put it.[57] There was irritation among Mrs Thatcher's staff about what one aide calls 'the upstairs-downstairs' aspect, the feeling that pervaded everything of 'them and us' at Court, which the new-right revolutionaries considered snobbish and fuddy-duddy. The Thatcherites, for their part, identified the Court with old style *noblesse oblige* paternalism and social deference, which it was their mission to sweep away. As a result, the mood at No. 10 was dismissive, and the Monarchy was given bottom priority. 'The Palace was on a mental check list,' says one former Thatcher adviser. 'It was mainly a matter of kicking yourself to remember about its involvement, of saying "For God's sake, get the Palace's permission," if we were going abroad, or "For God's sake get the agenda ready for the Audience". It was always riding its high horse about things like the merging of regiments, cap badges and so on. But Palace–No. 10 dealings seldom involved anything the premier was concerned about.'[58]

Downing Street found the Palace helpful about things like Cabinet reshuffles, which had to be conducted with maximum dispatch; and the Palace found No. 10 co-operative on matters like the erection of a statue of Lord Mountbatten on the Foreign Office green, which greatly concerned the Queen. Otherwise, contact was mainly routine. 'Although Mrs Thatcher was enormously punctilious about curtseying,' says a Whitehall official who advised several Prime Ministers, 'I am not sure how important she thought the Queen was.'[59] Preparation for audiences consisted of the Prime Minister's private secretary handing her a card with three topics for discussion on it, which she would read on the way to the Palace.

The Thatcherite attitude of busy impatience also applied to the life-style. Where Wilson and Callaghan unashamedly enjoyed it, Mrs Thatcher treated royal visiting as a tedious waste of time. She regarded trips to Balmoral as purgatory. One former Whitehall official recalls witnessing Monarch and consort cooking sausages for the disconcerted premier and her husband on a windswept hillside, each couple trying desperately to be informal. 'I don't think they got beyond the Ma'am and Prime Minister stage,' he says. 'The idea of a large country house and going across the moors in high heels wasn't her thing,' says a former close adviser. 'She was not at ease with it. It was symptomatic that, on the last day of the obligatory visit, she would arrange to leave at 6 a.m. She couldn't get away fast enough.'[60]

All this, however, was comparatively minor. What mattered much more, and lay beneath the resentment and irritation which characterized the attitude of No. 10 staff (and which may have been reciprocated), was the feeling that – in a way that had not been true during the premierships of Callaghan, Wilson or Heath – Buckingham Palace was alarmed by some of the things the Conservatives were doing. It was not, of course, entirely new for a constitutional monarch to be at odds with his or her own ministers on political matters. George VI's 'gnashes' had sometimes focused on the Labour Government's attacks on private property, and the Queen Mother continued happily to talk to all comers about the misdeeds of communists and left-wingers in the Labour Party or at the BBC. What made the Thatcher era different was an aspect that transcended domestic politics, or even international policy in the normal sense. The Queen never commented openly. However, speculation began, which grew into an assumption, that the Queen and her Palace advisers had a greater concern for the welfare and preservation of the Commonwealth, and hence a greater concern to accommodate Commonwealth opinion, than did her Government.

Perhaps it was an area of difference that was bound, sooner or later, to develop – for the interests of Britain, and the scattered interests of Commonwealth nations, had long ceased to be identical. If the Queen had seen her duty as a purely domestic one, this would have caused little difficulty. However, the Commonwealth, and Commonwealth delegations, honours, rituals and requests continued to take up much of the time and attention of Buckingham Palace – proportionately much larger a share than was true for Government ministers, including the Foreign and Commonwealth Secretary. It was natural, therefore, that the Queen should regard her role as Head of the Commonwealth and as Head of State of her various realms, with a seriousness that did not diminish just because of the changed direction of Westminster policies. '. . . [M]y whole life,' Princess Elizabeth had said in 1947, 'whether it be long or short,' would be devoted to 'the service of our great Imperial family to which we all belong . . .' Her vow had been given religious sanction after she acceded. 'When she took the Coronation Oath and was anointed with holy oil,' according to Lord Charteris, 'she meant it. She has a sense of destiny. She accepts it, however bloody awful it may be.'[61] Her promise, frequently updated in Christmas broadcasts and Commonwealth Day speeches to take account of the changing character of the 'Imperial family', did not become less binding, just because one Prime Minister took Britain into Europe, and another regarded black African leaders as Marxist. Nor was her sense of destiny reduced because she happened to have a Prime Minister whose even bigger sense of destiny clashed with her own.

The Queen had visited every Commonwealth capital, and had been welcomed by the crowds of every Commonwealth state. There were some Commonwealth leaders she had known for decades, since the earliest day of independence. She was, first and foremost, Queen of the United Kingdom – when she spoke for the Commonwealth, she generally did so on the advice of the British Prime Minister, though the text was sent in advance to other governments. Buckingham Palace did not, however, accept the right of the British Government to impose a view of the Commonwealth upon her, and it would have been difficult constitutionally for it to have done so. Though primarily beholden to her ministers in London, she was required to listen to the Prime Ministers of some Commonwealth countries, and needed to take notice of the Heads of Government of others, if she was to maintain the reality and trust of her position.

As the political scientist Vernon Bogdanor puts it, it is 'difficult to imagine the Commonwealth continuing to exist in its present form without the King or Queen as head.'[62] By the 1980s, however, it was also hard to imagine the Commonwealth continuing in its present form without the particular Monarch who had presided over it since its emergence in its modern form. The Queen had been a symbol, but also – in a way that had seldom been true in domestic affairs –

an active force. 'More than any single person,' says a key Whitehall figure of the 1970s and 1980s, 'she is entitled to feel that, whereas she just inherited the title of Queen of England, her Headship of the Commonwealth is something she has striven for and earned.'[63]

The extent of direct Commonwealth links needed to be kept in perspective. By the 1980s, the 'dominion' Commonwealth was small. Of those countries of which the Queen remained Head of State, Britain was by far the largest and most powerful. The smaller realms counted their populations in thousands rather than millions. In the two most substantial 'dominion' states, Canada and Australia, the Queen's status had become or was becoming little more than titular. Of the others, only Papua New Guinea, New Zealand and Jamaica had more than two million people apiece. However the 'republic' Commonwealth was still huge. Taken together, the whole association of forty-nine states accounted for only about thirteen per cent of UK trade in the mid 1980s. Nevertheless, it included more than a billion people.[64]

The association was loose, and interests were divergent. But it was not moribund. Indeed, in some ways it was strengthening. In 1965, when independent states were rapidly being formed, a Commonwealth Secretariat had been set up with a permanent base in London, charged with a range of cultural and aid roles, including the organization of what became, from the early 1970s, the biennial meetings of the Commonwealth Heads of Government (CHOGMs). Held in different capitals, these established a major international importance. They were regarded differently, however, by the Queen and by her ministers in London. To the Monarch, they were occasions of pleasure and reinforcement, offering the world a reminder of her continued global role. Embers of the 'Imperial family' were stoked at these events, wherever they might be held. However, to the British Prime Minister, often the whipping-boy of one Third World grievance or another, they were frequently a nuisance and sometimes a serious embarrassment. To some extent, there was a reversal, or at any rate, a change of roles: at a CHOGM, the British Prime Minister became just another Commonwealth premier, and had an audience with all the rest. It was in this difference of perspective – and in the Queen's divided self, which was more overt at CHOGMs than anywhere else – that lay the seeds of Downing Street–Buckingham Palace dissension.

The Queen did not attend the opening ceremony of CHOGMs, and did not play any formal part in their proceedings. Yet she was a familiar, and spirit-raising, feature of them. She attended a reception and a dinner. She also saw each Commonwealth leader in turn, for an individual audience. Before these meetings, she would be briefed about each country by the Foreign Office – in the case of 'non-realm' states – and by the national governments of 'realms' of which she was Head of State. Sir Sonny Ramphal, a British Guyanian lawyer and politician who became the Secretariat's longest serving and most influential Secretary-General, regarded her role as a crucial one. According to Ramphal:

> First the Queen brought an understanding that it was a post-colonial Commonwealth, something even senior members of the Foreign Office didn't understand. Second, she brought a new quality of caring, a sense that it was an important dimension of her reign, and not just tacked on to being Queen of England. Her success in Commonwealth countries has derived from an awareness that she cared – that they mattered in a sense beyond the British Government. This was a quality that developed very strongly over the years. Third, she was a young woman growing into international life along with young leaders of the Common-wealth. This was not true with those on the way out at the beginning of her reign – Nehru, Menzies, Diefenbaker. But it was of Kaunda, Nyerere and later Indira Gandhi. She grew up with them, understood them and related to them. They could talk with her and she wasn't talking down. She got to know them very well. Even at the times when the British Government was at odds with many of these leaders, she was able to understand their point of view without taking sides, and managed to convey to them that she did.[65]

Others confirm the Queen's close interest in the affairs of every Commonwealth state, the care she had always taken to be briefed before her twenty-minute audience at each CHOGM, and the visible delight and satisfaction the assorted premiers and presidents derived from them. 'They came out of their audience on the balls of their feet,' according to Lord Charteris.[66] 'They tell her all their troubles and worries,' says one lady-in-waiting.[67] 'She's like a mother confessor,' says another. 'They all troop in to listen to her, even if they're from some tiny Pacific island with a few thousand people on it.' 'She used to talk to Hastings Banda as if he were a long lost friend,' says a close observer.[68] Prince Philip was fond of describing her role as that of Commonwealth psychotherapist.[69]

'The Queen attracts a personal loyalty in the Commonwealth context that is complex,' says a former leading Whitehall official, '– but it exists.'[70] It was a unique opportunity for one, well-briefed and reliably discreet individual to obtain an overview of Commonwealth concerns. 'You'll see them getting up and slipping away in the middle of the meeting,' Ramphal told an interviewer in 1986, '. . . Mugabe, Kaunda, Seaga, Lee Kuan Yew, for a private meeting on *Britannia* or at the Governor-General's house . . . It's very friendly, but it's not small talk. She always knows the political situation in the country, the key issues confronting it and where the shoe is pinching economically.'[71] A senior minister at the time, with a different view of the Commonwealth from that of the then Prime Minister, recalls that the Queen was very conscious of the sense of the Commonwealth, not just as a post-colonial institution, but as a genuinely multi-national one – and that she put across that impression at the meeting. 'They all responded with deference,' he says, 'and with an affection that was returned. She liked to regard them as part of the extended family.' Margaret Thatcher, by contrast, did not find it easy to regard them as 'one of us' – she always found it hard to appreciate anybody else's patriotism.[72]

THE PERSONAL loyalty of Commonwealth leaders – an extraordinary aspect, in view of the ideological attachments of some of them – had a practical significance at the CHOGM held in Lusaka, Zambia in August 1979, the first Mrs Thatcher attended. The main topic was Rhodesia which – almost fourteen years after UDI and despite a growing guerrilla conflict – maintained its isolated, white-dominated independence, and provided a permanent affront to the Commonwealth majority. The persistent complaint of Asian and African Commonwealth members, and especially the so-called front-line states, was that Britain's commitment to ending the rebellion was insufficient. Mrs Thatcher – who defined Nkomo and Mugabe as 'terrorists' – was unwilling to attend a conference which she believed would be used as a platform against her policies. 'At first she was absolutely refusing to go to Lusaka,' says a former senior official. 'She said that Peter Carrington [Lord Carrington, the Foreign Secretary] should go instead.'[73] Not only was she unwilling to attend, she threatened to follow the example of Heath and stop the Head of the Commonwealth going as well, on the spurious ground of concern for her personal safety. 'The position is that the Queen will go unless we advise her not to,' the premier declared, in answer to a question, adding, 'the decision we have to make is a very difficult one.'[74]

Some felt it was an occasion for the Monarchy to exercise its constitutional rights. Though it was not the first time the Queen's safety had placed a question mark over a royal Commonwealth visit, it was the first occasion on which this had been offered as a blatant ploy. On 2nd July, the Palace responded to speculation by saying that previously announced state visits to Tanzania, Malawi, Botswana and Zambia including four days in Lusaka for the CHOGM, would take place as planned. 'It is the firm intention,' it was stated, 'that the Queen will be going.'[75] Whether or not the uncompromising nature of this announcement reflected the irritation of a Monarch at being used as a pawn, the suggestion that she was irritated helped to encourage the leaders of the front-line states to believe that the Queen would give them a sympathetic hearing. In the end, Mrs Thatcher decided to go, and the Queen's tour was allowed to proceed.

Ramphal later maintained that the Queen 'brought to Lusaka a healing touch of rather special significance.'[76] Kenneth Kaunda, who was both president of a front-line state and chairman of the conference, expressed a similar view. The British Prime Minister arrived in the Zambian capital expecting little; the front-line leaders expected less. Somehow, and to the surprise of both sides, a bridge was formed between them. According to Ramphal, Kaunda and others, the Queen – fresh from her African tour, and aware of the strength of feeling – played a part in building it.

A key No. 10 adviser watching events from London, is dismissive. 'She was never briefed to do anything other than exchange knowledgeable pleasantries with Commonwealth Prime Ministers,' he says.[77] Pleasantries, however, can serve a function. A former British minister recalls that her detachment from the details of the issue was critical. 'The British were in the dog house because of Rhodesia and Britain was looked on with the greatest possible distrust,' he says. 'The Queen held the whole thing together. People came to her and she couldn't be more friendly or forthcoming. She was turned to, on the grounds that she made less objectionable remarks about these things. They saw the Queen as way above it all – she didn't take any view.'[78] One of the Queen's own staff witnessed an exchange that went beyond 'knowledgeable pleasantries' and which, he believes, provided the catalyst. Kaunda of Zambia, Nyerere of Tanzania and Banda of Malawi were talking to the Queen in a small group at the official reception at the presidential palace. He heard her say something like: 'Far be it for me to get involved in your discussions over this, but I've known you all longer than you've known each other, and isn't it better to talk about it?' After this, he claims, the tide began to turn.[79]

Whether the Queen's role was large or small, most witnesses agree that her presence was, to some degree, an emollient – as a figure outside politics, but with some understanding of, and feeling for, both sides of the argument. 'She talked to Mrs Thatcher and to Kaunda,' says Ramphal. 'The fact that she was there made it happen. Kaunda felt that he'd have let her down a little if he hadn't pulled it off.'[80] A senior Whitehall official gives a less simple picture. 'Mrs Thatcher went to Lusaka in an unconstructive, angry mood,' he says. 'But gradually the atmosphere began to change. The Queen possibly played a part in this.' He sees a process in which the British premier started to 'become slightly fascinated' with a couple of the African leaders, and to see the possibility of agreement. 'At first it was a gleam in her eye, then she worked hard for it, and that led to the Lancaster Gate Meeting.' In this version, the main hero was Mrs Thatcher. 'Nevertheless, it may be that the Queen had some influence. Certainly, the attitudes of some African leaders began to change.'[81]

If so, it was a case of consulting, encouraging and warning several Prime Ministers or Presidents simultaneously. Perhaps it was also a case of nudging attitudes in a constructive direction, 'knocking peoples heads together without appearing to do so,' as one writer described her technique a few years later. No single person was responsible for the outcome which, however, seemed to vindicate both the value of CHOGMs and the British decision to attend this one.

Lusaka – which had threatened to be a disaster, with the Commonwealth breaking up – ended with the Lusaka Accord, and agreement for a new Constitutional Conference to be held in London. As a result, the various groups in Zimbabwe–Rhodesia met at Lancaster House in London later in the year and agreed proposals for a new constitution. The settlement led to an ending of the war, the restoration of legality, free elections and the launching of the new independent state of Zimbabwe within eight months of the Lusaka meeting.[82]

20

D ISCUSSION ABOUT the Queen's safety in Africa contained, in retrospect, a savage irony. The risk to the Royal Family was from another quarter. On the 27th August 1979, Lord Mountbatten was assassinated by the IRA, while on a holiday fishing trip with his family at Mullaghmore, near his home in Sligo, in the Republic of Ireland. A bomb placed under the planks of his boat was detonated by terrorists on the lake shore. Mountbatten was accompanied by his daughter Patricia and son-in-law Lord Brabourne, their fourteen-year-old twin sons, and Lord Brabourne's mother. One of the Brabourne boys and an Irish boy who had been crewing were also killed. The Dowager Lady Brabourne died a few hours later. The other passengers were seriously injured. John and Patricia Brabourne were rescued from the water with broken legs and multiple lacerations, and their surviving son was picked up some distance from the boat. Lord Mountbatten was found floating face downwards in the water, killed instantly by the blast.[1]

The Queen was at Balmoral when she heard the news. It was a devastating personal blow to her whole family. The Brabournes were among their closest friends – in Patricia's case, since childhood. Mountbatten himself – vain, clever, incorrigible and devoted – had been more important to both the Queen and Prince Philip than anybody of his generation apart from their parents. He had often been exasperating. 'He was always trying to organize people, and it was jolly difficult at times to answer him back,' says a former courtier. 'The Queen's attitude was that he was her Uncle Dickie and she was very, very fond of him, but sometimes she wished he'd shut up. Once she said: "I always say yes, yes, yes to Dickie, but I don't listen to him".'[2] In practice, however, both she and her husband listened, and valued his experience, more than they admitted. To Philip, he had been friend, mentor, benefactor and surrogate parent. He had also been a loyal and thoughtful supporter of the Monarchy through all its vicissitudes, and the single individual of greatest personal distinction who had been a member of the Royal Family, or closely related to it, since Prince Albert. 'Life will *never* be the same now that he has gone,' Prince Charles wrote in his diary when he heard the news.[3] In addition to the shock of bereavement, the murder – as horrific an outrage as any yet carried out by the IRA – brought home the unlimited nature of the war that was now being conducted against anybody who could be connected with the British presence in Northern Ireland. The daily threat, to the Queen and to all the members of her family, became terrifyingly apparent. From August 1979 a backcloth of physical risk, and especially of fear for children and relatives not present, was a part of the royal way of life.

Uncle Dickie's counsel was sorely needed in the next few years by the younger members of the Royal Family, as much as by the older. One reason was a bewildering new attitude to royalty. For if the 1970s had been a decade of revived interest in the Monarchy, the 1980s rapidly became a time of royalty worship that bemused the Windsors, irked the more discerning section of the public, and perturbed the shrewder courtiers. 'Worship' no longer necessarily involved respect. It meant, instead, heightened celebrity. From Buckingham Palace's point of view, the most worrisome aspect of the new mood was the treatment of the Royal Family as if they were indistinguishable from show business personalities with the difference that – unlike people who had made their way through the film and television worlds – they had no particular talent to justify the status.

Attention focused on the romantic interests of the Queen's sons, and especially the Heir to the Throne. Since Charles's teens, the press had fixed on one young woman after another as a potential Princess of Wales. It had become clear that he liked women; that they were flattered by his attentions, and sometimes liked him back; but also that he found it hard to form a serious relationship – or, alternatively, young women he courted had reservations about what becoming his wife would entail. 'Every working day of my five years at the Palace,' says Ronald Allison, who was press secretary from 1973 to 1978, 'there was a questioning of who Prince Charles would marry.'[4] Candidates

were analysed, dissected and pursued by the press before the appearance, in 1980, of Lady Diana Spencer, youngest daughter of the seventh
Earl Spencer, and sister-in-law of Robert Fellowes, assistant private
secretary to the Queen. 'Until then,' recalls Allison, 'I don't think
anyone had mentioned her as a possible bride.' It did not take long,
following the Prince's initial overture, for tabloid sleuths to add Diana
to their list, and then to deduce that she was a serious contender. At
first, the Court found it hard to take her seriously. 'I remember seeing
Diana as a bridesmaid in the Guards Chapel,' says one former royal
adviser. 'If somebody had said, "That is the next Queen of England",
I'd have thought them mad.'[5] Within a few months, however, Diana's
face had become one of the best-known in Britain, and within a year
or so, one of the most famous in the world.

At first the newspapers had difficulty in constructing a profile of
Diana Spencer because she seemed, and was, an entirely typical
member of her caste. The product of an aristocratic broken home, and
victim of the upper-class belief that girls did not need an education, she
belonged to the vulnerable world of well-off teenagers who shared
flats in smart districts of central London, did menial female jobs, went
to weekend house parties in the country, and looked for boyfriends
among others of their kind. What helped to make her available as a
potential recruit to royalty was a family connection with the Windsors
which, for at least two generations, had placed the Spencers on the
fringe of the courtier world. As well as the close link with Buckingham
Palace through her sister Jane, Diana's grandmother had been a
Woman of the Bedchamber to Queen Elizabeth for twenty years; her
father had been an equerry both to George VI and to Elizabeth II,
and had accompanied the Queen and Duke as Acting Master of the
Household on their 1953–4 tour; and five other female relatives had
held positions in the Queen Mother's household. In addition, much
of Diana's fractured childhood had been spent at Park House, near
Sandringham, where her father, as Viscount Althorp, had been a
tenant of the Queen.

With such a heritage, Diana was steeped in Royal Family lore, and
was often at gatherings at which royalty were present. 'She had grown
up on the estate and knew them all perfectly well,' says a close friend
of the Queen. 'She knew what it was like to be at Sandringham. She

was not one to be over-awed.' In addition to courtier-like links, her family origins as the daughter of an earl were the same as those of the last woman to marry a future king – though with the possibly significant difference that the Bowes-Lyons were Tories, with a tradition of loyalty to the Crown, while the Spencers had been Whigs with a tradition of individualistic independence.

Not only did Diana know members of the royal circle, she was known by, and liked by, them – although so far, there had been little enough to like or dislike, apart from a chubbily pretty face and an intriguing smile. She seemed, however, a regular member of the tribe. 'We all thought she was charming, terrific fun,' says Lord Carnarvon, 'and she was a great friend of my children.'[6] A relative of the Queen recalls that 'everybody was taken in by this beautiful, unspoilt child'.[7] That was one way of putting it. Another would be to say that, to everybody, including Charles, she seemed eminently suitable. The Queen was aware, because a courtier had felt bound to tell her, of Charles's relationship with Camilla Parker Bowles, wife of a fellow officer.[8] The knowledge of this prospectless liaison, and the desire that he should put it behind him, may have encouraged hopes that Charles's friendship would lead to a marriage. There was certainly a feeling, which the press encouraged, that at thirty-two he needed a bride. The result was a fateful collusion, which drew the royally connected adolescent and the Prince, under pressure to find a 'virginal, Protestant aristocrat,'[9] into a marriage of convenience that was disguised to everybody, including themselves, as a love match.

The Queen played a part in the collusion. In the autumn of 1980, she asked Diana to Balmoral. Who could blame a nineteen-year-old for confusing delight at the glamour of such an invitation with other feelings? It is also hard to blame Charles for being captivated by 'a sort of wonderful English schoolgirl,' as one of his friends recalled Diana Spencer, 'who was game for anything, naturally young but sweet and clearly determined and enthusiastic about him, very much wanted him'.[10] Charles spoke of her to friends as somebody he would like to fall in love with, rather than somebody he had. Diana seemed also to have formed an ambition to fall in love with the Prince. Perhaps, given time, they would have discovered what they actually felt. However, the possibility of allowing the relationship to take its natural course – or as natural as the romance of an Heir could ever be – was quickly removed. As soon as the media discovered his interest, naturalness was out of the question, and pressure either to announce or to renounce became extreme.

An incident known to the tabloids as the 'royal train tryst' was the turning-point. In November 1980, the *Sunday Mirror* ran a story about an alleged secret meeting between the Prince of Wales and Diana Spencer in the royal train in a siding at Holt, in Wiltshire. Reports of this kind were usually ignored by the Palace. This time, however, Michael Shea, who had taken over from Allison as the Queen's press secretary, was authorized to demand a retraction. The paper's editor, Robert Edwards, was unrepentant. Instead of retracting, he dug in his heels, claiming an 'impeccable' source.[11] More interesting to the *Sunday Mirror's* rivals, however, than the story itself was the fact that it bothered the Palace. Shea's denunciation of the 'clear innuendo' in the tabloid report, intended to damp down speculation, had the opposite effect: the news that the denial was made on the personal instructions of the Queen implanted the firm conviction that a marriage was pending.

A siege began. It was like the hounding of Peter Townsend in the 1950s, only worse, because Diana was less able to cope. 'May I ask the editors of Fleet Street whether, in the execution of their jobs, they consider it necessary or fair to harass my daughter daily, from dawn until well after dark?' wrote her mother, Frances Shand-Kydd, reasonably but hopelessly, to the press. 'Is it fair to ask any human being, regardless of circumstances, to be treated in this way?'[12] Other members of the Royal Family were also put under surveillance, in the hope of catching a chance remark or a give-away facial expression. At Sandringham, the Queen was provoked to snap at reporters, 'Why don't you go away?' At the beginning of January, the Palace let it be known that she was 'very distressed' at the harassment she and her family had received during their New Year holiday. Shea warned of 'steps' that might be taken, but it was unclear what these might be.

The Prince of Wales proposed marriage to Lady Diana Spencer at Windsor Castle on 6th February 1981. She immediately accepted. Both treated the engagement like a prize, to be displayed as quickly as possible, in case anyone should have second thoughts. Charles rang his mother. According to the account given by Andrew Morton, Diana rushed home to tell her flatmates, who were eager for news:

> She flopped down on her bed and announced: 'Guess what?' They cried out in unison, 'He asked you.' Diana replied: 'He did and I said "Yes please".'[13]

The engagement was officially announced on February 24th. Diana moved first into Clarence House, and then she and her mother moved into Buckingham Palace to prepare for the wedding. Initial euphoria soon passed. Lonely and missing her friends, she became suspicious of the role Camilla Parker Bowles continued to play in the life, or at least the imagination, of her fiancé.[14] She also got thinner.

On 27th March, the Queen gave her formal approval to the match under the 1772 Royal Marriage Act, at a meeting of the Privy Council. Afterwards, Diana posed with Charles and her future mother-in-law in the Music Room, for the first official photographs. Then the couple flew to Gloucestershire, where they were due to make a visit to the headquarters of the county police. The helicopter landed in the grounds of Dean Close, a boys' public school. A prefect who was scarcely younger than Diana offered her a daffodil and asked: 'May I kiss the hand of my future queen?' 'You will never live this down,' she said, blushing and laughing as he lifted her hand.[15] The incident was captured by the press, and flashed round the world – the start of a complicated relationship with the media of which neither they nor Diana would ever tire, despite protestations on each side to the contrary.

There is the interesting question of whether Diana Spencer was objectively beautiful, or whether – like Marilyn Monroe or Brigitte Bardot – the fascination she aroused shifted the idea of female beauty to fit her style and looks. Early accounts described her as an 'English rose,' attractive and handsome, rather than beautiful, with a fresh, country, point-to-point complexion. Soon, however, she was being called a star, and she became one. 'Young and far more glamorous than any other royal lady,' the *Sun* was observing in April, 'Diana is both an asset and an obvious scene stealer.'[16] There was a dangerous truth in the assertion.

What had changed? It takes time to fall in love. The British public – and also the American, French, German, and Japanese – took a few weeks. Very quickly, however, Diana's shy yet coquettish, gauche yet graceful, approach to the cameras pleased practically everybody. Women identified with her, men found her erotic. Her way of dealing with the public and the press was quite different from that of established members of the Royal Family, who had experienced the attention of the media all their lives. Waif-like, she gave herself to an audience, leaving it momentarily unclear which side of the royal–ordinary divide she was on. One clip of film taken early in the marriage illustrates well the contrast between Diana and her in-laws. It shows a royal group entering a room for a formal banquet. While the Windsors glide in with eyes straight ahead, Diana pauses for an instant to pat her hair, and give the waiting cameramen a half-flirtatious, half-apologetic 'we're all in this together' look. The style – that of an actress or a politician – transformed royalty from dignified-but-dowdy into fashionable for the first time since the early days of Princess Margaret's marriage. The 'Lady Di' effect reached all strata. There was a proliferation of page-boy hair cuts among debutantes and shopgirls. It became a truism that an image of Diana on the cover of a women's magazine would raise sales by twenty per cent, whatever the content.

In June 1981, the Monarch briefly regained the limelight. On June 13th, the Queen attended Trooping the Colour – mounted, for the eighteenth time in a row, on her black Canadian mare, Burmese. During the ceremony, a spectator pointed a pistol at her, and fired six shots. The Household Cavalry had a drill to protect the Queen if she was in danger, and they immediately turned towards her. Burmese reared up. The Queen controlled the horse expertly, and the ceremony was not interrupted. Afterwards, she explained to courtiers what she believed had happened. People imagined her mount had shied because of the shots, she said, but actually they had barely been audible. The mare's reaction was to the movement of the other horses. 'Burmese felt that the Household Cavalry was going to attack me,' she said, 'so she attacked them first'.[17]

The shots turned out to have been blanks. The assailant, a seventeen-year-old boy, was sentenced to two years in prison under an 1842 Act. There had been no danger. Twenty months after the Mountbatten murder, however, it was an alarming incident, which stimulated criticism of the police. It also brought praise for the Queen. Morals were drawn. *The Times* ruminated, not for the first time, on the family-on-the-throne. The target, it philosophized, had not just been the Queen, 'but also a wife, a mother, a grandmother, doyenne of a dozen cousins whose collective endeavours give the British Monarchy its unique breadth and stability.' Thus, the attack on the Queen was an attack on the nation as a whole.[18] The tabloids, meanwhile, indulged in kitsch patriotism. In every pub and club, declared the *Daily Express*, the verdict was the same. Her Majesty had shown 'guts, courage, pluck, bravery or bottle,' and had struck a blow, in the process, against the anti-Monarchy left, 'tinpot little republicans,' who would have 'been diving in all directions for cover if anyone fired what looked like a lethal hand gun at *them*.'[19]

The Queen's display of guts, pluck and bottle helpfully stirred monarchist emotions in the populace a few weeks before the wedding. The ceremony was due to take place on July 29th in St Paul's Cathedral. During July, feelings of loyalty grew into a passion, mixing a love of pageantry with a delight at the romance. Incited by television and the popular press as never before, and by the human interest of the first marriage of a Prince of Wales since the reign of Victoria, public excitement soared. Enthusiasm was not reserved for the mysterious, delicate newcomer to the royal scene. There was also a welling of admiration and affection for the Prince of Wales who – most people agreed – was splendidly equipped for future responsibilities. Enhanced by his betrothal, he had become, in the eyes of commentators, the 'consummate prince,' and everything anybody could wish for in an Heir to the Throne – athletic, good-humoured, dutiful, intelligent without being highbrow, wise beyond his years. Not only, according to one observer, was he 'handsome, jug-ears notwithstanding, and a smashing dresser,' he was 'charming beyond belief, and has acquired completely the requisite royal art of always appearing to be interested in whatever is being shown'.[20]

The trouble, however, with media approval when it became overheated was that, in the cut-throat competition for a new angle, there was a strong inclination to destroy the thing it loved. 'Relations between Palace and press reached a nadir in 1981,' wrote Donald Trelford, editor of the *Observer*, a few years later.[21] That was optimistic – they were to get a lot worse in the 1990s. However, the early 1980s was certainly a trough. Tabloid appetites, voracious at the best of times, passed all bounds. Scruples were abandoned. Shea recalls briefing a young woman journalist on one occasion, on the strict understanding that their conversation should not be recorded. He only discovered that she was secretly taping him with a hidden tape-recorder when it got to the end of the tape, and bleeped.[22]

At first, the Palace tried to resist the ever more strident media pressure to extract or confirm personal information about the couple, and about other members of the Royal Family. A dozen years of royal display since the Cawston film, however, made it unrealistic to imagine reverting to the techniques of Commander Colville. The alternative seemed to be appeasement. Diagnosing much of the interest as loyal and harmless, and in the hope of obtaining trust and co-operation, the Palace therefore embarked on a policy of ever wider access and ever greater informality.

It is impossible, however, to cure an addiction by feeding it. The effect was to sharpen the public profiles of the Royal Family members and inflame still further the demand for news about them. 'It was Bill Heseltine who rolled back the carpet on royal publicity,' says one former courtier. 'I think he went too far in allowing unbridled licence. At one stage all the young royals had been on *Wogan*.'[23] The problem was the logical outcome of a process that had begun years before, perhaps as long ago as *Royal Family* and the Investiture. 'The more the Queen is seen on the screen,' Kenneth Rose noted at the time of the Jubilee, 'the more she is urged to concede another segment of her life to the public gaze.' The royal wedding – and the incessant interest it aroused – intensified this process. The temptations were strong. So long as the latest segment of royalty to be exposed met with public approval, it was easy to fall in with the idea of a public right-to-know. However, there was the danger, as Rose warned, that excessive familiarity and availability would reap a whirlwind if and when the genetic lottery ceased to turn out good princes and princesses.[24] The fate of Margaret, the Diana of her day, should have provided a warning. To expose the Sovereign and her family to unlimited scrutiny, and to expect to find nothing but perfection, was to challenge fate.

Any kind of foreboding seemed out of place, however, as the royal wedding approached. In a climate of total adulation, every aspect of the couple's lives was ruthlessly, caressingly examined. Critical faculties were suspended, praise overflowed. How could the Palace–media nexus be questioned, when royalty succeeded in attracting such support? Articles appeared, congratulating royalty on, among other things, the brilliance of its public relations. In *The Times*, David Wood applauded the surrender of Bagehotian 'mystery' by the Royal Family through a 'calculated exposure' of their private lives. It was, he suggested, 'an astonishing non-stuffy achievement.' Princess Anne deserved particular praise for saying to camera that pregnancy was boring, and that there were limits to maternal dedication. 'When,' Wood rhapsodized, 'had royalty ever before spoken with such candour?'[25]

The reality was of course significantly, and riskily, different – not candour, but its similitude. In fact, the interviews with sympathetic presenters which members of the Royal Family (apart from the Queen), now eagerly indulged in, revealed little about what was going on in their lives. So far from being candid, Princess Anne's remark was an obfuscating pleasantry of the kind any sensible reserved person might make, including one who – as in her own case – was experiencing a difficult marriage. Television created an illusion of intimacy, and not the real thing. The same was true with Charles and Diana. Politely questioned before the adoring and unsuspecting millions, they spoke happily of love and marriage like any other young couple, and gave no inkling of the ambivalence that was already affecting them both.

After the marriage collapsed, people close to them claimed to have seen it coming. There had been an alarming gulf, they said, between the Prince, for whom the wedding was just another royal event, like the Investiture, in a life studded with them, and his fiancée, facing the crisis of her life, whose disturbing manifestation of nervous symptoms was dismissed as stage fright. One ex-courtier remembers travelling with her, before the marriage, in the back of a car, across Vauxhall Bridge, past a huge hoarding with the words: 'Diana, My True Love'. She collapsed and wept and said: 'I can't stand it any more.' [26] 'It was obvious that they were incompatible,' says another. 'He loved music. She loved Duran Duran.'[27] A friend of the Queen recalls Charles bringing Diana for a visit, as any young man might bring his fiancée, and being disturbed by the sense of her ordering him about, apparently trying to humiliate him.[28] As the day approached, the Queen – trying to join in the spirit of things – broke with her usual formality and rang up the Archbishop of Canterbury, Robert Runcie, about hymns for the service.[29] Yet there was already a feeling that the momentous and inescapable event – the cause of celebration for millions of anonymous people – was fraught with terrible implications. The night before the wedding, Diana stayed at Clarence House with her sister Jane, and was sick. 'I felt I was the lamb to the slaughter,' she told a friend. Looking at the crowds camping in the Mall, chatting and singing in cheerful anticipation, she began what she later described as 'the most emotionally confusing day of my life'.[30]

It had been a summer of ominous riots in London, Liverpool, Bristol and elsewhere as urban ghettoes exploded, the anger and frustration of the poor ignited by a sudden rise in unemployment. The wedding offered a glitteringly romantic contrast. It also provided an opportunity for moralizing. Street violence could not be magicked away with a royal wand, acknowledged *The Times*. The occasion was, however, symbolic of the nation's unity. The throne was identified with 'exemplary family life,' and the public gratification reflected pleasure at the prospect of the royal couple carrying this into the next generation. Archbishop Runcie saw it, not just as a symbol of unity, but also as an assertion of the nation's deepest convictions. 'The service insists on the ideal of marriage as a life-long partnership, nourished by shared joy and by hardships faced together,' he observed. He pointed to the alarming statistics of marital breakdown. Nevertheless, when Charles and Diana took their vow, 'they will be doing so as representative figures for the nation'.[31] The press bulged with royal supplements. On the wedding morning, a brief letter appeared on the correspondence page of what was still the leading newspaper, from the travel writer Jan Morris. 'I would like to put on record, in *The Times* of July 29, 1981,' she wrote, 'one citizen's sense of revulsion and foreboding at the ostentation, the extravagance and the sycophancy surrounding to-day's wedding of the heir to the British throne.'[32]

It was a brilliant, theatrical event. With the Prince in naval uniform, and Diana in an ethereal dress, there was a similarity to the Queen's marriage in 1947: but it was superficial. That had been a grand, national celebration of victory, peace, survival and hope for the future. This was, from start to finish, a televisual spectacular: modern popular Monarchy *in excelsis*. Six hundred thousand people lined the route, comparable to the crowds a third of a century earlier. In addition, however, a world audience of a billion watched both the procession and the service at home. The climax was the famous balcony kiss. It was hard not to be moved by the apparent spontaneity and by the youthful charm of the wide-eyed, swan-necked Princess, or touched by the pleasure and pride of her husband. 'The Royal Family of England pulls off ceremonies the way the army of Israel pulls off commando raids,' observed an admiring *Boston Globe*.[33] Afterwards, the Prince and Princess left for the first stage of their honeymoon – spent at Broadlands, the Mountbatten family home – and for a marriage that immediately began to go wrong.

The media cannot be held solely responsible. Others should be blamed for not protecting Diana, or failing to train her to deal with

"I love red—but NOT red carpets!"

Daily Express, 31st July, 1981

its destructive force. This had become incomparably greater than at the beginning of the Queen's married life, when Philip – an older, more worldly-wise consort, but equally new to the sudden pressure of public recognition – had been able to walk, unmolested, from Buckingham Palace to his office in the Admiralty. Eventually, Diana achieved a rapport with the media, based on a kind of secret notion that she was a fifth columnist and, unlike the family she had married into, remained human. However, nothing in her previous existence had equipped her to deal with being door-stepped almost every day of her life.

There was no remission, over the summer months, or in October and November. If public interest ever seemed likely to flag, it was revived in the late autumn by the announcement that the Princess was expecting a baby the following June. The pregnancy, combined with Diana's evident anxiety, finally stirred the Queen and Court into a defensive action. In November, Michael Shea took the unusual step of asking the editors of all the national daily and Sunday papers as well as of television and radio news, and the Press Association, to a special briefing, followed by drinks, at Buckingham Palace. Of those invited, only Kelvin MacKenzie of the *Sun* did not attend. At the briefing, which took place early in December, Shea made a plea for mercy. There was concern, he maintained, that photographers were failing to distinguish between public and private lives. He also declared – and the remark revealed the worries already felt about the Princess's state of mind – that Diana was 'increasingly despondent' at the discovery that she could not leave the front door without being photographed. Afterwards, in a vain hope of reinforcing the moral pressure which it had been the purpose of the whole event to exert, the editors were introduced to the Queen, who circulated among them, moving from group to group.[34]

Yet the psychology was faulty. Once Shea's direct approach might have worked. There was a precedent: twenty-five years earlier, Commander Colville had successfully asked for privacy for Charles at Cheam, after the Prince had suffered exceptional harassment from photographers. Now, however, inter-tabloid rivalry had become so intense – and indifference to the British Monarchy among proprietors so absolute – that appeals to editorial good nature had no impact.

Deference was dead, and some editors were well aware that the Palace had little regard for them. If they were not, the reception helped to make it plain. When the Queen came to the group that included Barry Askew of the *News of the World*, the editor of the Murdoch-owned Sunday paper put a question to her. If the Princess wanted privacy, he asked, why did she go out to buy sweets at shops, and not send a servant? 'That was a pompous remark Mr Askew,' the Queen replied, tartly.[35]

Not only pompous, but symptomatic of an ever-uglier tabloid mind set. In February, the *Sun* – unrepresented at the Palace get-together – and the even lower-market *Daily Star*, published pictures of the Waleses on holiday in the Bahamas, taken with powerful telephoto lenses, which showed Diana wearing a bikini, and visibly pregnant. When Shea issued a statement that indicated the Queen's extreme displeasure, the two papers responded by expressing regret that she should be displeased, and republishing the pictures that had caused offence.[36] So far, indeed, from offering an apology, they continued to regard the photographs as a scoop. James Whitaker, the reporter who tracked the royal couple down to a deserted beach, described the stalking of his prey as if it had been a big game hunt. 'When she turned up in a bikini,' he proudly related, 'it was too good to be true.'[37]

Shea criticized the editors for breaking the 'spirit' of the December meeting. It was rapidly becoming clear, however, that the December meeting had been a tactical error. Now that the basest of the tabloids had shown that requests from the Palace could be ignored with impunity, there was no holding their rivals back. The rat-tat exchange of press 'revelations' and Palace condemnations of them, became a media routine. Meanwhile, replenishments to the Civil List because of high inflation served as a justification, or excuse, for those who wished to argue that a family so heavily supported out of public funds, in order to perform a public role, had little right to personal privacy anyway.

The Queen herself remained largely exempt from criticism, except on the tax issue. Most commentators used the thirtieth anniversary of the Accession in February 1982 to give her a favourable report, and to contrast the supposedly smooth operations of the Monarchy, at the height of a devastating industrial collapse, with the disintegration to be seen in other aspects of British life. At a time of social unrest, suggested *The Times*, when politicians seemed intellectually mediocre and judges out of touch, the Monarchy was 'perceived as the only institution of state which is working as it was intended.'[38] Norman St John Stevas, one of its keenest advocates, defended it as the only 'truly popular institution' at a time when the Commons had lost esteem and the position of the Lords was controversial. Anthony Sampson reflected, more soberly, that the Monarchy was as narrowly upper class and insulated from the urban lives of most subjects as ever. However, he acknowledged that it had increased in prestige in the course of the reign, as one of the few British institutions not battered by economic decline, the retreat from Empire, and the nation's social divisions.[39] Others wondered whether, in the not too distant future, the Queen might take a well-earned rest from public life, and encourage her eldest son and his new wife to deputize for her.[40] The possibility of a retirement – in the form of a voluntary abdication – became the subject of discussion.

However, the grand, constitutional, historic aspects of royalty were no longer the parts the public wished to see – or at any rate were allowed to know about by the popular press. The Queen, embodying the traditional Monarchy, was respected; but she aroused much less interest and received far less coverage than the younger generation of royalty who, familiarized and stripped of dignity, provided the nation's daily fare. Indeed, talk of the Queen stepping down or taking a back seat was partly a reflection of the shift, and of a sense that, in the crude currency of tabloid celebrity, she had already been usurped by her daughter-in-law. For in the febrile yet expectant climate left behind by the royal wedding, nobody was the subject of a greater popular curiosity and longing than the Princess of Wales.

It is often said of victims that they participate in their own abuse. In the case of Diana, though in many ways a victim, her treatment cannot simply be seen as a persecution. It was more complicated. Though she hated the relentless nature of the attention, the staring eyes wherever she went, she had no wish for seclusion. Being Princess of Wales, after all, was a career choice she had made for herself, as well as a marriage. There were aspects of the limelight – appearing at great occasions, being greeted by adoring crowds – which she liked. Challenged over interruptions to the Waleses' skiing holiday in Liechtenstein at the beginning of 1983, Harry Arnold of the *Sun* responded indignantly that Diana did not seem to appreciate that she was 'the world's number one cover girl.'[41] In fact, she had begun to appreciate it very well – and her thoughtfully expensive clothes, ever-changing hairdos, and defiant hats indicated that becoming a star was not involuntary.

Meanwhile, a new borderline was being crossed in the 'privacy' debate. So long as royal 'private' lives were irreproachable, it was possible to defend 'privacy' in general from a high moral platform. It was much more difficult, however, to reject the argument that it was in the public interest to discover what was going on, once this ceased to be the case.

A leader in the field of freer sexual morals was the Queen's second son, aged twenty-one at the time of the Waleses' wedding, and increasingly seen as the late twentieth-century equivalent of a regency buck. The popular press in the early eighties was full of Prince Andrew's exploits, about which he did not bother to be particularly reticent. Unlike his elder brother, whose female relationships had tended to be upper class, Andrew's liaisons were more democratic, adding to the tabloid *frisson*. He acquired an inevitable nickname. 'Randy Andy's highly publicized friendship with actress Koo Stark and Katie Rabbett, and his alleged affair with former model Vickie Hodge deeply upset the Queen,' Audrey Whiting, the *Sunday Mirror's* veteran royalty watcher, confided in June 1984. 'She has made it clear she will not tolerate any more "indiscreet behaviour."'[42]

Actually, the opposite was the case. The Queen made little attempt to curb the activities of her children, especially the younger ones. 'She should have told them off more,' considers one ex-courtier. 'The trouble is that the Queen hates dictating to the family,' says another. 'Because she is Queen, she has always been reluctant to stop her children doing anything.' 'I think she's terrified of her children', says a former adviser to the Prince of Wales. 'She's afraid they won't do what she tells them.' If she was not a hugging mother, she was also a far cry from a censorious one. She treated Andrew with a special indulgence. 'She was happy about his relationship with the very nice, gentle girl Koo Stark,' says a former courtier.[43] One reason, after the summer of 1982, was the outbreak of the Falklands War, in which Andrew took part as a serving Royal Navy helicopter pilot in the Task Force sent to recapture the islands from Argentina.

THE QUEEN was directly involved in the South Atlantic War of 1982, which had been precipitated by the Argentinian annexation of the British colony in April, in four distinct ways: as Sovereign of the country whose sovereignty had been breached by the invasion, and whose Government had declared its intention of regaining the islands; as Head of the Commonwealth and of the remaining fragments of Empire, which included the Falklands; as Head of the Armed Forces; and as the mother of a combatant. Although her role was largely symbolic in the first three cases, it was more than titular. The symbolism of the Queen of Britain and the Commonwealth, whose realms had been violated, and whose forces were set on recapturing them, was powerfully invoked as a weapon in the psychological side of the war.

There was some similarity to the use of the Monarchy at the time of Rhodesian UDI sixteen years earlier. Then, Harold Wilson had persuaded the Queen to send messages which were intended to remind white Rhodesians of their overriding loyalty to the Crown. After the Argentinian invasion of the Falklands, the Queen was also deployed as an icon of British legitimacy. The difference was that, on this occasion, colonial loyalty could be taken for granted, and the purpose was not to detach subjects from a rival authority, but to reassure them of Britain's continued support. The messenger was Rex Hunt, the ousted Governor, who on 7th May broadcast a special message from the Queen, which underlined the point that the Falklands remained a colony of the Crown. The message was highly personalized, and Hunt conveyed, in particular, the Sovereign's 'warm appreciation' of the birthday greetings her Falklands subjects had sent her.

At the same time there was a national and world-wide appreciation that the Queen would not countenance the idea of Prince Andrew being exempted from active service because of his royal status. 'Prince Andrew is a serving officer,' declared a statement from Buckingham Palace on April 1st, in response to inquiries about his mother's attitude, 'and there is no question in her mind that he should go.' What gave the war, and royalty's involvement in it, a special poignancy was that the outcome was not predictable: as the Task Force approached its destination, severe British naval losses as a result of the Argentinian use of Exocet missiles threatened the success of the whole operation. For all those involved in the Task Force, the hazard was real. The anxiety of the Queen and Prince Philip was the same as that of any parents of a young man involved in a perilous action and who, day by day, witnessed the progress of the war on television, sometimes in horrific detail – except that, in the Queen's case, she also received bulletins from Downing Street. Hence, when on May 26th, she spoke for the first time about the Falklands battles, six days after British forces landed on West Falkland, her words were felt to have a special meaning. 'Before I begin I would like to say one thing,' she declared at the opening of the Kielder Dam in Northumberland, 'our thoughts today are with those who are in the South Atlantic and our prayers are for their success and a safe return to their homes and loved ones.'

By this time, Britain had gained American support for a military response to the invasion. However, it was still vitally important to strengthen the bond, and the Queen was uniquely placed to help do so. A few days after the Queen's Kielder speech, President Reagan and his wife visited Britain, and became the first American presidential couple to stay at Windsor Castle. The aim was to buttress Reagan's ideological sympathy for Mrs Thatcher with a personal relationship between the elderly, not overly-involved, Californian monarch and the British one. It seemed to work. The Reagans, sentimental to a fault – though also with an eye to American public opinion – were delighted to be royal guests. The President let it be known that he found the British Head of State 'charming, down-to-earth'. Luckily, there was also a common interest that was more substantial than drop scones. The Queen and Ronald Reagan both enjoyed horses, and went out riding – posing for the cameras. 'It's called the forward seat,' said the President, commenting on the Queen's style, 'the modern riding, and you know she was in charge of that animal.'

In a speech to Parliament on June 8th, President Reagan confirmed his firm backing for the United Kingdom over the Falklands. That night, at a banquet in the President's honour at St George's Hall in Windsor Castle, the Queen spoke, in reply, of drawing comfort 'from the understanding of our position shown by the American people'.[44] Once again, though the words were composed by others, her listeners took them to have a directly personal meaning.

Six days later, Port Stanley was liberated, the war ended, and Andrew telephoned home. 'My mother was in – it was about the right time in the evening,' he told reporters. 'She was surprised to hear from me. She asked [me] to pass on how proud she was of everyone and to say how marvellously all the troops had done.'[45] On June 25th, she visited some of the casualties of the conflict. One young private, injured at Darwin by a sniper, asked her to congratulate the Prince and Princess of Wales on the birth, four days earlier, of a son. Her response was dynastic. 'Thank you, yes,' she was reported as saying. 'I am very pleased that we have another heir.'[46]

DESPITE its Lilliputian scale, and the imperial pretensions of the Prime Minister, the Falklands War offered a brief reminder of the historic role of the British Monarchy – including a timely demonstration of a connection between royalty and the services that was important to those who belonged to them, and which was much more than formal and ceremonial. The key fighting service in the Falklands conflict happened to be the one with which the Royal Family was most closely linked – Philip, Charles and Andrew had all been regular naval officers. Mrs Thatcher's No. 10 advisers might be supercilious about Buckingham Palace's interest in service and regimental traditions. They mattered, however, to the men themselves: and at time of war – even a small one – the Monarch became, as in the past, a focus of loyalty and patriotism. This role was not diminished when the Prime Minister invoked the Queen's name – embarrassingly to many – after the recapture of the island of South Georgia on April 25th; or when Mrs Thatcher appeared to usurp the Sovereign's position by taking the salute at the Falklands Victory Parade in the City.

For a time, Andrew was fêted as a war hero, and royal reporting acquired a respectful tone. Koo Stark was a particular favourite with the tabloids, partly because she was American, partly because of the extraordinary name, and partly because of the discovery that she had once appeared naked in the lesbian shower scene of a soft-porn movie. In February 1983, the *Sun* published the unremarkable revelations of a former Palace storeman, which described the behaviour of Koo as a royal guest. 'Queen Koo's Romps at the Palace,' it announced misleadingly. The accompanying article wrongly claimed that Miss Stark had felt so at home at Buckingham Palace that she had given orders to the staff, raided the pantry, and helped herself to the Queen's favourite chocolates.

Royal patience snapped. Shea had spoken of 'steps'. The Palace now attempted to take one. Faced with this trivial but embarrassing story, the Queen ordered an injunction to be sought to restrain the paper from publishing further details. In addition, her lawyers made a claim for damages for breach of confidence based on the profits the ex-storeman and the *Sun* had received. The action was intended as a deterrent, as well as a punishment. Yet again, however, it served to demonstrate how powerless the Monarchy had become in the face of newspapers which had abandoned the old code. Not only was there a question-mark over whether the Sovereign was able to sue in her own courts. The action also revealed the depth of the Queen's anger and, in consequence, sold more copies of the *Sun*. When news of the writ reached the tabloid, a whoop of joy went up in the editor's office. A champagne cork popped, and people started singing 'Happy Days Are Here Again'. 'Queen Gags the Sun' declared the front page the next day. 'It was the first time the Queen has ever taken legal action against a newspaper,' the paper boasted proudly.[47]

It was a struggle the Palace could not win. Neither the attempt to gain co-operation, nor the decision to fight back, stood any chance against a fourth estate that was aware of an apparently insatiable public demand. In vain, Michael Shea – who was himself becoming a familiar media performer – put a brave face on it. 'Even the more sensational stuff has been covered in a happy, pleasant, unmalicious way,' he told an interviewer, hopefully. He distinguished between the provincial press, where coverage was 'one hundred per cent nice' and the national press, where it was 'ninety-five per cent pleasant'. Unfortunately it was the five per cent that reached the largest number of readers, setting the agenda, and carving out a new, cruder way of viewing royalty. It was partly that the lives of younger royals had become more frivolous and less discreet. It was certainly also true that newspapers, diagnosing a restless public mood after a surfeit of 'niceness,' had become aware of circulation possibilities which previously did not exist. Whatever the main reason, in the mid–1980s the tone of royal reporting decisively and permanently changed, led by the ever-pioneering *Sun*.

A cheapening process involved the picking up of casual, off-the-record remarks, of a kind that would have been ignored if uttered by politicians or ministers, as part of the code that governed the relations between politicians and the lobby, and treating them as news. For example, when Princess Margaret refused to appear at a musical award ceremony with a transvestite pop singer called Boy George she was quoted as saying that she did not want 'to be photographed with that over-made-up tart'. Margaret's son, Lord Linley, was reported to have said that dinner with Princess Michael of Kent was the gift he would give his worst enemy[48] – and so on. But there was also a new kind of royal story. The flirtations of Edward VII and Edward VIII, and the agonies of George VI, were tactfully concealed from the public by editors who knew that their loyal proprietors would object if they were used. In the 1980s neither editors nor proprietors felt any such inhibition. Rumours began to be printed about the Princess of Wales of a kind which, had they reached editorial offices in any previous decade, would have been quietly spiked. It was reported that Diana had fallen down stairs while pregnant; that she was believed to be suffering from the eating disorder, anorexia nervosa; that she and her husband had been witnessed having an out-of-doors quarrel; and that she had arbitrarily sacked members of staff at Kensington Palace. There were also stories of a rift in Princess Anne's marriage, and suggestions that Anne's short temper was responsible.

But the Queen herself was seldom the subject of this kind of reporting. Her exclusion was not a matter of loyalty. It was more that, unlike some of her relatives, the Monarch did not talk to the press, did not row in public, and even in private kept a closely guarded tongue. Years of tight self-control had taught her the art of gliding off subjects she did not wish to discuss or turning away from a remark she did not wish to deal with, as if she had not heard. 'The Queen doesn't pull the curtain back on what she is thinking and feeling,' says a friend, 'even at her funniest and most outspoken.'[49] It could be claimed on the Queen's behalf that, virtually alone among the Royal Family, she did not seek to have her cake and eat it as far as publicity was concerned. There was no question of welcoming attention for some aspects of her private behaviour while resisting it for others.

THE PERCEPTION of the Queen as a deeply private person helped to increase the public shock when, in the summer of 1982, her privacy was dramatically breached by an intruder whose ability to penetrate Buckingham Palace demonstrated the weakness of its security. Early in the morning of July 9th, the Queen was disturbed in her bedroom by a man who had apparently climbed into the gardens, shinned up a drainpipe, and wandered through corridors unchallenged. The intruder, Michael Fagan, drew the curtains, waking the Queen up, and began talking about his family. It took two calls by the Queen to the police switchboard before a chambermaid and a footman arrived and escorted him out. Afterwards, she told a courtier that, confronted by Fagan sitting on her bed with a bleeding hand, holding a broken ashtray, 'I got out of bed, put on my dressing gown and slippers, drew myself up to my full regal height, pointed to the door, and said "Get out!" and he didn't.'[50] She told a friend, 'He just talked the usual sort of bilge that people talk to me on walkabout, I can handle that.'[51] But she was not entirely nonchalant about the incident. 'I have never heard the Queen so angry,' said her footman, who was with her when she spoke to the police on the telephone from her study, after Fagan had been taken away.[52]

Everybody agreed that she had shown courage and good sense. 'It didn't surprise me a bit to hear how she handled that intruder,' said President Reagan, still glowing after his visit to Windsor.[53] But there was also a certain public hilarity, at the incompetence of the police, the clown-like character of Fagan – who enjoyed a fleeting career as a television celebrity – the incongruity of the scene, and the discovery (which should not, however, have come as a surprise to readers of John Dean's memoirs, published twenty-eight years before) that the Queen did not share a bedroom with her husband. One wag observed that, even so, it must have been pretty crowded. There were two

Ladies of the Bedchamber, one Extra Lady of the Bedchamber, four Women of the Bedchamber, and three Extra Women of the Bedchamber, making ten in all – not counting the Mistress of the Robes.

The lapse in security caused embarrassment to the Government, especially as it coincided with an IRA campaign of violence on the mainland. A few days later, it was overshadowed by two terrorist attacks which killed and injured soldiers of the Queen's Household Cavalry as they rode to the Changing of the Guard, and musicians of the Royal Greenjackets on the bandstand in Regent's Park. At the Palace garden party on July 20th, the day after the bombings, the Queen looked 'pre-occupied and uncharacteristically severe'.[54] Early in August, the press noticed a reduction in the number of her private engagements and concluded that a combination of Fagan, the resignation of her personal detective after he had admitted a long term relationship with a male prostitute, the IRA killings, the removal of a wisdom tooth, and the death of an old friend, Lord Rupert Nevill – on top of the danger to Andrew earlier in the year – had placed exceptional strain upon her.[55]

There were, however, no major cancellations. That autumn, the Queen and her husband set out on a tour of Australia and the Pacific Islands, starting in Brisbane, to open the Commonwealth Games, 'which will be hot,' as she wrote to Hardy Amies.[56] The following February, the heat – if judged by the pressure of media attention – increased, as the royal couple embarked on yet another trip, this time to the Caribbean, Mexico, and the West Coast of the USA. On the last leg, they visited Hollywood, before joining the Reagans at their ranch. World interest exceeded itself. At one point, the press corps reached 3,300. Michael Shea addressed press conferences of a thousand, in front of forty television cameras. Local television channels devoted up to seven hours a day to the visit.[57]

However, the interest in British royalty did not just focus on the Queen. Almost as much attention was paid to what *Time* magazine called 'Palace Dallas' – Andrew's romance with Koo, 'Her Royal Rudeness' Princess Anne, and the Waleses who were reported to be at each other's throats. Pride of place went to 'Shy Di, the radiant, misty darling of the tabloids' who, only seven months after the birth of

Prince William, was being called a spoilt brat, a fiend and a monster; and to reports that Charles was 'desolate' that divorce was not possible for a future King.[58]

21

1983 was a politically decisive year. In June, a general election produced the largest Conservative majority for more than half a century. It was an extraordinary turnaround for Mrs Thatcher who, only eighteen months earlier, had been the most unpopular Prime Minister on record. Now, in the wake of the Falklands victory and with the Opposition split and marginalized, the supremacy of the Conservative Party, and the apparent invincibility of its Leader, provided scope for a centralized use of power far more autocratic than at the time of Lord Hailsham's famous Dimbleby lecture in 1976, when he had warned of an 'elective dictatorship.'

For a Monarchy that wanted to stay outside the political arena, it was not a comfortable situation. One of the classic justifications for an hereditary Head of State was that he or she could provide a base of neutral common sense – performing the role, as the constitutional expert Sir Ivor Jennings put it at the beginning of the reign, of the 'good solid citizen'. Thus, the Monarch was supposed to be part of the system of checks and balances, the more valuable because royal restraint could be applied behind the scenes. 'To have such a person at the centre of affairs, cool, calm and judicious is a great advantage,' explained Jennings, 'especially with a brilliant but wayward Prime Minister'.[1]

But what if the brilliant but wayward leader obtained a resounding mandate from the people? And what if the threat of waywardness came from the right? The conventional account had been based on an assumption that any radical disturbance to the equilibrium would be left-wing. When the possibility was discussed, people thought fondly of the calming effect George V was imagined to have had on Labour after the First World War, or of George VI after the Second, even perhaps of Elizabeth II and Harold Wilson. Conservative waywardness was a new proposition. How should a Monarchy that abhorred any kind of involvement in controversy respond to a sharp, confrontational shift in favour of the better off? The question troubled the Queen's advisers on a number of occasions over the next few years, as royal attitudes that had previously been assumed to be consensual were challenged, and new, radically reforming doctrines rocked the established order.

At first it was just a feeling, but one that increased in strength after the second Tory victory; that Monarch and premier did not chime. Tales of a 'bad relationship' between Sovereign and Prime Minister, which circulated at this time, need not be given much credence: the Queen did not have bad relationships with people. Indeed, in her memoirs, Lady Thatcher is at pains to dismiss such a notion (before ignoring the Monarch in the rest of her book almost entirely).[2] However, throughout the longest premiership of the reign so far, it was never possible to detect the slightest degree of warmth on either side.

In some ways, this was surprising. For the first time, the Queen had as her Prime Minister somebody who was not only the same sex, but also the same age as herself. One event, moreover, early in Mrs Thatcher's second term, pointed sharply to an aspect of the lives of both of them – their vulnerability to terrorist attacks – that seemed to provide an area of mutual understanding.

On 12th October 1984 an IRA bomb exploded at the Grand Hotel, Brighton at the time of the Conservative Party Conference. Mrs Thatcher, obviously the main target, escaped, but five people were killed, and others were terribly injured. The Queen was out of the country – on a private visit to the United States, in the company of the Porchesters, inspecting American studs. It was several hours before she was able to talk to the Prime Minister. When she was eventually put through, the first thing Mrs Thatcher said was: 'Are you having a wonderful time?'[3] The story, told in Palace circles, had a double meaning. It demonstrated the Queen's solicitous concern at the outrage, about which she had every reason to feel shock and personal sympathy. It also seemed to show the stiffness of the premier, who could not express her real feelings even at a moment of life and death.

The Brighton atrocity forged a kind of bond. In addition to the shared experience of losing close friends or relatives at the hands of a common enemy, there was the reminder of the daily danger to each of them, and their kin. Yet it was an exceptional moment, and there were other things that pushed them apart. Not just the style, but also the priorities, of the uncompromising premier raised questions at the Palace. The 'welfare Monarchy' as Frank Prochaska has described it,[4] did not find it easy to embrace a leader and an administration that treated welfare policies as soft. When the Queen did refer to the Prime Minister on private occasions, her remarks were not critical: but they did tend to be quizzical, as if there was something about the first female premier which she found difficult to fathom. 'Do you think Mrs Thatcher is a religious person?' the Monarch asked Dr Runcie after the publication of *Faith in the City* – a report by the Archbishop of Canterbury's Commission on Urban Areas, published in 1985, which expressed concern about the urban unemployed, and was dismissed by Thatcherite politicians as Marxist. Runcie replied that he thought the Prime Minister was interested in the ethical side of religion, but he did not imagine that the doctrine of Grace, and concepts like the Body of Christ, meant much to her. 'The Queen listened,' Lord Runcie recalls, 'but didn't take part in the conversation.'[5]

On Commonwealth matters, the gap that existed between the Queen and her Government in the United Kingdom was more overt. There was never any doubt that the interests of Commonwealth countries, including poorer ones, concerned the Monarch much more than they did British ministers. A minor, but significant example of this difference occurred after the 1983 election, at the time of a short-lived crisis involving Grenada, a Caribbean island with a population of less than 100,000, of which the Queen happened to be Head of State. During the crisis, the Queen became concerned at a failure to tell her what was going on.

In one sense the problem, which arose in October, was well handled. Following an upheaval in which the Grenadian Prime Minister was killed, the Governor-General of the island, Sir Paul Scoon, asked the US Government, together with neighbouring Caribbean states, to send troops to restore order. An invasion was quickly and efficiently mounted and the objective was achieved. However, the Grenadian Head of State had been neither consulted nor informed, by Scoon or anybody else.

The Queen was reported to be furious – as much with Mrs Thatcher as with Scoon or the Americans – about being deliberately or carelessly ignored. Buckingham Palace let it be known (or did not effectively deny) that, as *The Times* put it, she disapproved of 'the notion that foreign powers may walk into member states' of the Commonwealth, especially without prior warning. 'There was no difference of opinion,' insists a close Thatcher aide. 'Both the Queen and Mrs Thatcher were highly indignant.' The two indignations, however, had a different emphasis. 'We were unsettled by the American deceit,' recalls a member of the British Government at the time, 'but torn in the public presentation of it, while also concerned not to be humiliated by appearing not to have been in the Americans' confidence: at the same time, we were torn about whether we ought to keep up the pretence and shelter under the notion of the special relationship.' The focus of the Queen's anger, on the other hand, was the apparently casual way in which one of her realms had been treated, without any consideration of her role as Sovereign. 'This fortified our own dismay with the Americans,' says the same source, 'and in a curious way an independent attitude from the Palace was helpful.'[6] Part of the 'independent attitude' was believed to be irritation at the Prime Minister for letting the Americans get away with it. A legend grew up around the incident: there was speculation that a regular Tuesday audience had been postponed because of the Queen's displeasure, and there was a story that, when it took place, the Prime Minister was not invited to sit down. 'The two women may not like each other over much,' suggested the *Observer*.[7]

It could be argued that the Queen's ignorance was a blessing in disguise. If Scoon had told Buckingham Palace about the invitation to invade, she would have been in an embarrassing position. She would have had either to betray the secret of an independent country of which she was the Head of State or else have withheld important information from the British Government (which had also been kept in the dark).[8] However, it did not seem a blessing to be casually ignored, and the possible 'divisibility' problem felt less important than the sense that big governments – including the British one – simply forgot that the Queen's role as Head of State of little countries existed. Moreover, against the blessing-in-disguise argument, there can be set a legal one. Some expert opinion held that although Scoon was not obliged constitutionally to seek the Queen's permission before exercising his residual powers in her name, it was incumbent on him to inform her of his intention to request an intervention, and his failure to do so could be held to render the request constitutionally invalid.[9]

The Queen's supposed reaction over Grenada was seen as an instance of her protective interest in Commonwealth countries and of the seriousness with which she regarded her Commonwealth functions – and also the lack of sympathy between her and her British Prime Minister, who did not seem sufficiently concerned about the same issue. A further symptom of her Commonwealth-mindedness was provided a few months later. It was a year of foreign visits. After the USA, came Canada, with Zambia in March, Sweden in May, and Kenya, Bangladesh and finally India in November, culminating in the Commonwealth Heads of Government Meeting in New Delhi. These exhausting yet exhilarating travels provided the Head of the Commonwealth with a rather different view of world problems, and especially those of the parts of the world which fell within her sphere of interest, from that of her Prime Minister in London.

An indication of the difference was presented in the 1983 Christmas broadcast, closely following the CHOGM, which showed the Queen reflecting on her recent experiences – and especially her visit to India. To the Head of the Commonwealth and her staff, it seemed natural to highlight current developing-world concerns. Hence the programme echoed the recent report of the Brandt Commission, which had drawn attention to the danger of global inequalities. 'The greatest problem in the world today,' the Queen declared, 'remains the gap between rich and poor countries, and we shall not begin to close this gap until we hear less about nationalism and more about interdependence.' One of the main aims of the Commonwealth, she went on, was 'to make an effective contribution towards redressing the economic balance between nations'.[10] In an attempt to liven up a programme whose customary blandness had become the despair of its producers, the Queen's remarks were accompanied by some film taken during the royal tour of India, which showed Mrs Gandhi apparently being interviewed by the Queen about technological co-operation and development.[11]

A few years before, such a display of royal interest in the Commonwealth might have been passed without comment. However, times had changed, and the Palace had failed to take account of post-election triumphalism on the British Right. The combination of Mrs Gandhi and the suggestion that rich countries had economic responsibilities towards poorer ones produced an explosion of protest.

Who had induced the Monarch to voice such dubiously socialistic sentiments, while apparently endorsing a highly controversial political figure in an Indian election year? Redistribution had an obvious appeal to poorer Commonwealth countries. But it was not, critics pointed out, the policy of Her Majesty's Government in London. Nor had the principles of Brandt been top of the United Kingdom delegation's agenda at the CHOGM. Indeed, as the Prime Minister's biographer later put it, 'the entire British effort was devoted to resisting declarations for greater justice between the countries of the rich north and the poor south'.[12] The proposition that economic inequality was the biggest problem in the contemporary world was not exactly the kind of rhetoric currently emanating from Downing Street.

The Times, in high Thatcherite mode, warned that too independent an interpretation of the title 'Head of the Commonwealth,' unsanctioned by ministerial advice, could threaten the stability of the Monarchy. The same point was made with particular force by Enoch Powell, who – though no longer in the Conservative Party – had a strong following among the Prime Minister's supporters. In a speech on January 20th, Powell attacked unnamed 'ministers' for putting in the mouth of the Sovereign 'speeches which suggest that she had the interests and affairs of other countries in other continents as much or more at heart than those of her own people,' and for implying that even in the United Kingdom she was more concerned with the view of 'a vociferous minority of newcomers' than with the great mass of her subjects. The protest harked back to the origins of the modern Commonwealth – to the Nehru compromise, and to the idea, which Powell had always considered contentious, that a British Monarch might speak for nations other than Britain. His attack, however, was not really directed at ministers. Since the Christmas broadcast was a rare occasion on which the Sovereign spoke without advice, he was effectively criticizing the Buckingham Palace staff, and the Queen herself.[13]

Powell's objection was not just to the content of the Queen's message. It was also to what he saw as the danger of a 'divided' Monarchy obscuring the painful truth of Britain's reduced world status. By voicing independent opinions as Commonwealth Head, he suggested, the Queen allowed herself to be the vehicle of a damaging myth. 'The tension between her role as Queen of England and Queen of other countries or Head of the Commonwealth', according to Powell later, 'is resolvable only by the enduring humbug of the Commonwealth, which is the British people humbugging themselves, persuading themselves they're still large – a bullfrog mentality.'[14] Powell's warning linked the Queen, the Commonwealth, new Commonwealth immigration, sentimentality towards ex-colonial peoples, and national decline. It was seized upon with enthusiasm by right-wingers who had previously defended the (old dominion) Commonwealth as a bulwark against Europe, but who now regarded the (Third World dominated) Commonwealth as, at best, a distraction, at worst, an association of left-wing mendicants.

There was also something else. Enoch Powell was a critical friend of the Monarchy, a loyalist with a sense of history but also – as he believed – of realism. Others, especially among younger 'New Right' radicals, saw less to be loyal about. Thus, they began to link an impatience with the political priorities of the Commonwealth, and even a feeling that the Commonwealth had outlived its usefulness, with an asking of questions about the Monarchy itself – its trappings, cost, and constitutional role – and its place in the new, post-consensus order.

Here was an irony: a probing of hallowed constitutional principles, and of the institution that lay at their core, from the most zealous element within the party which, for centuries, had been its most devoted defender. The argument, however, was not just constitutional: it related to the broad ideological aims of the New Right. The old Conservatism had drawn inspiration from the sense of a stable social hierarchy, with the Queen at its pinnacle. The neo-liberal version was socially egalitarian. In the Prime Minister's New Model Army, it was a point of doctrine that social Darwinian toughness towards the poor and unsuccessful should be combined with a rejection of unearned privilege. The old Conservatism had been led by aristocrats. Thatcherism, by contrast, drew its vigour from a lower-middle-class work ethic. It regarded aristocracy as decadent and – a Thatcher word – 'wet', and tended to see the Royal Family as composed of, and advised by, upper-class people who were unproductively wealthy. The objection, indeed, was remarkably similar to that of the traditional Left since the nineteenth century.

'Wetness' meant, among other things, having a paternalist attitude towards the badly-off, and holding a sentimental belief that in a morally healthy and united society the well-off should be asked to give the badly-off a helping hand. The new Conservatives, noting Mrs Thatcher's indifference to the Queen's role, and observing the Queen's sympathy for poorer Commonwealth countries, concluded that wetness was rampant in Buckingham Palace itself. Thus the fashionable view developed that the Monarchy – like the episcopacy, and the House of Lords – was part of the problem which it was the mission of radical Conservatism to solve. The political point was linked to a moral, and puritanical, one: as Cannadine put it a few years later, 'many Thatcherites regarded the Monarchy as just another vested interest, an unacceptable amalgam of snobbery and frivolity'.[15] Stories of the spendthrift, juvenile behaviour of the younger royals – the Princess of Wales's colossal shopping bills, or Prince Andrew spraying journalists with paint during a trip to California – caused almost as much indignation among the new Tory zealots as among the supporters of Tony Benn.

However, it was not just Marxians and Conservatives. To some extent the new attitude towards royalty among Tory intellectuals reflected, as well as led, the public mood which, in the harsh 1980s, was shifting seismically. The Royal Family did not become unpopular. On the contrary, if Charles and Diana, Andrew and Fergie had been real soap-opera stars instead of their simulacrum, they would have had excellent grounds for self-congratulation. It lost, however, its previous immunity. In a climate of free market fervour, urban decay and industrial collapse, the tinsel adulation that accompanied the 1981 wedding dissolved. It was replaced by a fascinated, lip-smacking envy and lust, with the Queen's daughters-in-law – new recruits who had acquired everything that status, money and fame had to offer – as the prime focus of both. Never had royalty been so glamorous, and never more visible. But the price of exposure was the loss of the last vestiges of traditional deference across the political spectrum.

David Wood had written of the special 'tone of voice' journalists had once been required to adopt when writing on a royal topic.[16] The tonal change, when it came, was profound. In place of the cadences of chivalry and awe, the new royal reporting was mocking and familiar. Altrincham had courted ostracism and jeopardized his career with a few loyal criticisms: now, articles about royalty without a sting did not get published. Those that did, reflected a right-wing iconoclasm in chic journalism that was as careless of the old bourgeois values as it was contemptuous of socialist ones. Formerly, royalty had been as fenced around with as many taboos as sex. Now, as with sex, anything went.

To be modern in the world of Wapping was to be no respecter of persons. 'Life imitating soap imitating life,' was how Julie Burchill, queen of the neophytes, described the Royal Family in 1984. Burchill threw in a kind of punk republicanism, couched in the yuppy vernacular, which – in a popularized version of the Enoch Powell and Adam Smith critique – identified royalty with the British disease. 'The monarchy is a tranquillizer', she wrote:

> it makes a population stolid and fatalistic, undynamic, unbelieving in a meritocracy – the kiss of death to a country – to see a group of people, under-educated . . . , inbred, possessing neither intelligence nor beauty . . . ruling all it surveys. Only the deeply dull drop-out countries of the world have monarchies, countries for whom *a major victory* means coming second in the Eurovision Song Contest: Spain, the Netherlands, Great Britain . . . Monarchies are not a hallmark of classiness, but a brand of lack of confidence.[17]

Here was a pincer: a millenarian new establishment that regarded the Monarchy as an irrelevance or even as an obstacle to its aims, in alliance with hip, brat-pack nihilism. Thus, during the difficult, divided, societally-threatening middle years of the decade, as mass unemployment and job insecurity became chronic aspects of national life, Britain's royalty obsession came full circle: from 1950s 'Shintoism,' through 1960s dullness and 1970s accessibility, to the ravening 1980s, when media hunger had turned the bemused, half-resisting, half-co-operating, ill-equipped dynasty into a circus – and finally to the point at which the only remaining possibility was outright rejection.

WHAT IF the Queen's loyalties as Head of Commonwealth, and her duty as British constitutional Monarch, pulled in diametrically opposite directions? Few, even in the Palace, doubted the answer: she would have to ditch the Commonwealth. Arguably, however, she was entitled to put up a fight before doing so.

Although such a dilemma never presented itself in quite so brutal a form, in 1986 a crisis arose in the Commonwealth which once again seemed to threaten its very existence: and the Queen was given the choice of appearing to accept the full implications of the policy of her Government in London, or of indicating – in some way – that, though constrained, she was not impervious to the representations of Commonwealth leaders.

The issue was sanctions against South Africa. These had long been demanded by a majority of Commonwealth states, especially the African ones, and had been resisted by Mrs Thatcher and her ministers on the grounds that they were an ineffective instrument against apartheid, and inimical to British interests. The question had not only isolated Britain within the Commonwealth; it had also hardened the Prime Minister's already myopic view of other member states. 'Mrs Thatcher saw the Commonwealth entirely through pragmatic eyes,' says one of her closest aides. 'She saw it almost solely as an organization for putting pressure on her over South Africa.'[18] Eventually, it became an automatic reaction – instinctive, more than pragmatic. 'Anything the Commonwealth preferred,' as her biographer puts it, 'was likely, on her analysis, to demand British opposition.'[19] In the run-up to a Commonwealth summit in August, Mrs Thatcher repeatedly made clear her contempt for the views of a multi-racial organization dominated by representatives of the Third World – apparently believing that her attitude was shared by much of the British electorate. By the summer, the dispute, and the heavy symbolic weight it carried, seemed about to tear the association apart.

This was the nightmare Buckingham Palace had always feared, for it placed the Queen in an intolerable dilemma. The advice she had consistently received from her courtiers, and been happy to take, was to avoid controversy on all matters and to remain passive. Indeed, on South Africa and the Commonwealth anything except passivity would have been unconstitutional, and seriously damaging to the Monarchy. On the other hand, to remain entirely passive in such conditions could easily be seen as actively taking sides. Where – people inevitably asked – did her personal sympathies lie? There was much speculation. Her sincere interest in the poorer Commonwealth states was well known; so was her long standing relationship with several Commonwealth leaders. Neither was denied in Palace press briefings, or public addresses. 'The Queen on more than one occasion conveyed the impression that on the South African issue she was concerned to keep the temperature down,' says a former minister, who had a similar aim.[20] People put two and two together, and decided that – in the interests of her own role, if nothing else – she hoped for a compromise. In June, with a Commonwealth conference approaching, speculation was reinforced by reports, of unknown provenance, that she was seriously if privately opposed to the position taken by the United Kingdom Government.

There was a groundswell of rumours, building up over a period of weeks. In April, Henry Stanhope wrote in *The Times* that the fact that the Queen 'stays above the fray is a modern political miracle,' in view of her heavy Commonwealth involvement. An interview with Sir Sonny Ramphal drew attention not only to the part played by the Queen in Lusaka in 1979, but to her 1983 Christmas broadcast, with its rich-and-poor nations theme. Additional evidence of her sympathies, Ramphal suggested, had been provided by her performance at the Nassau CHOGM in 1985 – when, on the divisive sanctions question, she had studiously avoided any implication that she was on Britain's side against other Commonwealth members. 'Not for one moment,' the Commonwealth Secretary-General maintained, controversially and a little mischievously, 'did anyone suspect that she might enter the arena or do anything else but try to bridge the divide which existed, in the interests of the Commonwealth.'

By this time, some countries were threatening to boycott the Commonwealth Games in Edinburgh, because of Britain's attitude. Against such a background, the *Sunday Times* – edited by the rumbustious Andrew Neil – decided to take up the question of the Queen's split personality. On June 8th, it reported, unremarkably, that the Monarch had been 'sickened' by television pictures of clashes between security forces and black Africans in the South African townships. The following week it reported that the Prime Minister intended to tell the Queen about a proposed minimal sanctions package, designed by Downing Street to concede to the Commonwealth derisorily little, while protecting British interests in the republic. At the same time, the paper claimed that the Monarch was 'increasingly concerned' about the danger of the Commonwealth disintegrating over the issue; and it cited reports (whose source seems once again to have been Ramphal) that the Queen had expressed her concern to Mrs Thatcher in an audience. Other papers took up the theme. In July, *The Times* reminded readers that Elizabeth II was 'seventeen queens in one person and more besides,' which necessarily involved her in saying contradictory things. In so far as the Commonwealth existed as a political entity, with a collective position, she embodied and expressed it. On this occasion, it pointed out, such a position differed from that of the United Kingdom.[21] Strict constitutionalists reached for their Bagehots. The Victorian seer, however, could not help on the 'seventeen queens' (let alone forty-nine) conundrum.

In the *Financial Times* Malcolm Rutherford considered where such a complicated status might lead, in the case of a Queen who seemed happier in the company of African and Asian leaders than of the English middle classes. He also posed the key question which the crisis had presented: 'Will she, will she have to, can she blow the whistle if divisions within the Commonwealth get out of hand?' He located the source of potential trouble as the Commonwealth Secretariat in London. Because the Queen received advice on Commonwealth matters directly from the Secretary-General, he pointed out, and not simply from the Foreign and Commonwealth Office, she was likely, sooner or later, to be caught in the middle of a Britain versus Commonwealth clash.[22]

Media interest was heightened by the knowledge that the Cabinet was itself divided on the issue – and that the Foreign Secretary, Sir Geoffrey Howe, was pressing Mrs Thatcher to give ground, but without any effect. 'That to me is immoral,' the Prime Minister told Hugo

Today, 16th July, 1986

Young, when he asked her about sanctions in an interview on July 9th. 'I find it repugnant.' The remark deeply embarrassed Howe, who was flying to Zambia for talks with Kenneth Kaunda as she spoke.[23] Rival campaigners joined in the debate from predictable standpoints. While Enoch Powell insisted that 'Head of Commonwealth' was a meaningless title and the Queen's sole duty was to accept the constitutional advice of her Prime Minister in Downing Street, John Grigg agreed that if she believed a compromise was desirable, she was entitled to make her views known. 'Certainly, in what she chooses to say about the Commonwealth as such,' wrote Grigg, 'she is not bound by the "advice" of her UK ministers.'[24]

In the *Sunday Telegraph*, Peregrine Worsthorne accused the Queen of a leftist, going-native-on-the-Commonwealth stance. Echoing some of the Prime Minister's close advisers, he compared the Common-wealth great-and-good she seemed now to find congenial, to the aristo-cratic courtiers she had once been accused of listening to too exclusively. The Monarch, he suggested, had 'simply replaced one unrepresentative and undemocratic lot of sycophants with another, thereby ending up even more isolated in an ivory tower than she was before'.[25] On June 16th, the *Guardian* reported that there had been tension at the Prime Minister's regular audience at the Palace.

In fact, there was tension all round – between Mrs Thatcher and the Commonwealth, Mrs Thatcher and the Foreign Secretary, as well as between the two halves of the Queen's constitutionally divided personality. With the public increasingly intrigued by suggestions that strained relations must, before long, reach breaking point, the press tried to extract clues from Buckingham Palace – and began to have some success. Early in the summer, it got back to No. 10 – to the great annoyance of the Prime Minister's staff – that a senior courtier had made critical remarks about the sanctions policy at a gathering of royal officials from across Europe.[26] In July, the new tabloid *Today* published a story about a Thatcher-Queen quarrel – based on infor-mation acquired by the editor from the Palace press office, which was apparently authorized. Because it was not an established newspaper, however, the rest of the media treated it with scepticism.[27]

It was against such a background of rumour and controversy that the *Sunday Times* exploded its bombshell. On July 20th, it boldly announced the most fundamental disagreement between a British Monarch and the Prime Minister of the United Kingdom for fifty years. 'Sources close to the Queen,' wrote Michael Jones, the paper's respected political editor, and Simon Freeman, another journalist, had the previous day exclusively disclosed to the *Sunday Times* Her Majesty's dismay at the policies of the Prime Minister – a dismay which went far beyond the current crisis in the Commonwealth over South Africa. Describing the revelation as an 'unprecedented disclos-ure of the Monarch's political views,' Jones and Freeman claimed to have irrefutable evidence that the Queen considered the whole approach of her Prime Minister to be 'uncaring, confrontational and socially divisive'.

Usually, stories that purported to describe royal attitudes were vague about their point of origin. This one was precise. It was based, the two journalists explained, on several briefings by advisers to the Queen who were fully aware that the information would be published, and were in no doubt about its likely impact. The information was also specific. The same sources were quoted as saying that the Queen believed the British Government should be more caring towards less privileged people; that she had feared during the 1984 miners' strike that serious long-term damage was being done to the social fabric of the nation; that she had had doubts about the Prime Minister's decision to allow the Americans to use British airbases for a raid on Libya in April 1986 (doubts which had, indeed, been rumoured in the press at the time); and that she was concerned that the whole direction of Government policy threatened to undermine 'the consensus in British politics which she thinks has served the country well since the second world war'.

Thus, the Queen's unhappiness by no means simply related to the current controversy over sanctions. Yet, apparently, it was not an accident that the revelation took place while these were under discussion. The explanation for the Palace's disclosures at such a time, according to the journalists, was the Queen's deep concern that the Commonwealth might break up on the issue. While she herself was not necessarily an advocate of the pro-sanctions position, she believed that a compromise was essential if the association was to be saved.

To sceptics who still wondered why the Queen should suddenly end a lifetime's discretion and favour the *Sunday Times* exclusively with her innermost thoughts, the paper offered a startling new image of the Head of State. 'Far from being a straightforward countrywoman, a late middle-aged grandmother who is most at ease when she is talking about horses and dogs,' it asserted, 'the Queen is an astute political infighter who is quite prepared to take on Downing Street when provoked.' Furthermore, provocation was much more likely to come from the right than from the left. Contrary to what might have been imagined, on a whole range of issues, the Monarch's thinking was left of centre. Like her eldest son, she was worried about race relations and inner-city decay in Britain – and shared many of Charles's ideas about the Government's duties towards less privileged people. Indeed, her outlook on such matters placed her, in effect, among the Conservative Party's ultra-wets, or even alongside the SDP-Liberal Alliance. In sum, the Queen was a moderate, a Mountbattenite, who – according to an unnamed close adviser – was, above all, 'concerned that nothing detracts from the Commonwealth'.[28]

If this story had been presented merely as inspired speculation, it would have received little attention: rumours of differences between the Queen and Prime Minister, as we have seen, were long-standing. Indeed, the *Sunday Times* played down suggestions of a personality clash, in order to stress the policy points. What made the account a sensation was its combination of a detailed rundown of the Queen's supposed anti-Thatcher opinions; the declaration that they had been very recently reaffirmed; and the repeated insistence, by a quality newspaper, that the information came from what an accompanying editorial called an 'unimpeachable' source who, moreover, had expected and intended what was said to be published. According to the *Sunday Times* the following week, its journalist had spoken to the key source no less than five times before publishing the story, which had also been discussed with No. 10 Downing Street, and the Palace had at no time asked for it to be withheld.

Immediately the hunt was on for a name. Faced with a barrage of demands for authentication, Andrew Neil quickly declared that the informant was at Buckingham Palace. This narrowed the field to the three courtiers who dealt with political matters – the Queen's private secretary, Sir William Heseltine, her assistant private secretary on the political side, Robert Fellowes, and her press secretary, Michael Shea. On July 27th, the *Observer* pinpointed Shea. The following day there was a limited Palace admission in the form of a letter published in *The Times* from Sir William Heseltine in which the Queen's chief adviser acknowledged that the press secretary had spoken to Simon Freeman several times before the story appeared.

Heseltine disputed the account of the remarks that was published. Nevertheless, the *Sunday Times* story, and the identification of the press secretary as the source, raised several questions. Given that Shea was the Queen's official mouthpiece, had a good working relationship with his employer and was known to be in contact with her two or three times a week, how did he come to be talking on such a delicate topic in the first place? Was the Queen herself in any way responsible for the disclosures, if they could be so described? Did they – despite Heseltine's disclaimer – give a broadly accurate picture of her views? Finally, what were the political and constitutional implications?

Despite the private secretary's disclaimer, most other newspapers assumed that – allowing for a bit of literary licence – the *Sunday Times* account of the Queen's opinions was essentially correct. *The Times*, sister paper to the *Sunday Times*, suggested that the letter from Heseltine, which it had itself published, was disingenuous.[29] Others, more generously, saw it as an exercise in damage limitation. Attention focused on whether the remarks had been authorized by the Monarch (it was soon accepted that they had not); and on the ideological slant of the commentator. Ian Aitken, in the *Guardian*, expressed alarm at the notion of the Queen, or the Palace, seeking to rally public opinion against an elected government – even an objectionable one.[30] Generally, however, the Left rejoiced at finding an ally in an unexpected place.

In Downing Street, there were pained faces, and stoicism, with aides resisting the temptation to hit back: it would scarcely help the Prime Minister a year or so before an election for her staff publicly or even obliquely to criticize the Palace. 'There was a lot of dismay around, a lot of shaking of heads over the *Sunday Times* material,' says Sir Bernard Ingham, then the Prime Minister's Press Secretary. 'It was a cross we all had to bear. No. 10 sought to calm it down as best we could.'[31] Another close aide to the premier puts it more pithily. 'The idea that the Queen was pissed off with Mrs Thatcher was the last bloody thing we needed,' he says. However, not everybody in the Government was equally dismayed. According to one report on the Tuesday after the initial story – as the nation relished the thought of the day's regular audience (who would be telling off whom?) – the Foreign Office, which took a more conciliatory view of the Commonwealth than Downing Street, was positively cheerful. 'In a way, I was quite pleased', admits a senior Foreign Office figure at the time, 'because the Palace seemed to be intervening on our side of the argument against the Prime Minister.'[32] At the Commonwealth Secretariat, meanwhile, there was unashamed delight. 'I was very glad about the Thatcher row,' recalls Sir Sonny Ramphal. 'What was in the *Sunday Times*, what Michael Shea was saying to the press, was what we knew to be the reality, and it needed to be said.'[33]

The row continued meanwhile over what had actually been said. Heseltine's letter had insisted that Shea 'said nothing which could reasonably bear the interpretation put upon it,' and it repeated the Palace's consistent denial that the *Sunday Times* report represented the Queen's opinion of Government policy. It also claimed that the only reason for not asking the paper to refrain from publishing the story was that the Queen's private secretary knew such a request would be refused. In his reply, Neil effectively accused Heseltine of lying. He also added a new allegation. For some time, he declared, 'unattributable briefings and guidance' had been given to various journalists by Buckingham Palace, 'which clearly distance the attitude of the Royal Family from the Thatcher Government.'[34]

In the end, the question turned on the difference between his own interpretation and that of Freeman. Today, Shea recalls that he had regarded his conversations with the *Sunday Times* reporter (whom he had never met) as informal briefings for an article Freeman claimed that he was preparing about the Monarchy in the distant future. When Freeman asked questions like 'Mrs Thatcher is not very keen on the Commonwealth – what does the Queen feel about it?' Shea would reply, as he thought, routinely, 'Yes, you would be right in thinking the Queen, as Head of the Commonwealth, is naturally very keen on the Commonwealth,' 'Yes, she's concerned about a divided nation,' and so on. 'In response to journalists' questions,' he says, 'I would never say she was right-wing or left-wing on any specific issue.' There had been no prior briefing by the Queen, and he had never heard the Queen speak critically about the Prime Minister, or indeed any of her Prime Ministers.

The issue turned on the Monarch's discretion, as much as on Shea's. Was it really plausible to imagine that she would not only let slip critical remarks about UK Government policy but encourage them to be released to a Sunday newspaper? 'The fact is that the Queen does attach more importance to the Commonwealth than Lady Thatcher,' according to another Palace source. 'But to think that the Queen or the Prime Minister were sufficiently unprofessional as to allow this to be the cause of a collision is absurd.'[35]

Yet this was, precisely, the claim made by the *Sunday Times*. According to Simon Freeman, Shea had taken him by surprise by discussing the Queen's political opinions, after he had rung the Palace to ask for background material. 'He started saying things like "on race and social division she is well to the left of centre",' according to the *Sunday Times* reporter. In a second conversation, Shea had allegedly made even more revealing disclosures about the Queen's personal opinions on the miners' strike, the raid on Libya and division within the Commonwealth.[36] 'Michael Shea couldn't resist the persuasive power of Simon Freeman, who had been courting him,' suggests another ex-courtier, who points out that the *Sunday Times* had recently printed a flattering profile of the royal press secretary. 'Freeman seduced, tricked and caused him to be indiscreet.'[37] According to Michael Jones – brought in as an experienced senior journalist to give authority to the story – 'We were absolutely sure about it.'

What made them sure was that when they gave notice to Buckingham Palace of what they were intending to print, the Palace could have stopped it, but did not do so. Jones was not only convinced that the picture of the royal establishment's view of a radical Tory Government was true. He was also convinced that the Palace knew what to expect. 'There were repeated calls,' he says, 'and they knew we were splashing it.' It was an indication of how seriously he himself regarded the story that he rang up Downing Street.[38] Sir Bernard Ingham remembers taking the call. 'Michael Jones, who I knew extremely well and trusted, told me what he was writing,' he recalls. 'I said I was not commenting. I got onto the Prime Minister's Private Secretary, Nigel Wicks. He alerted Mrs Thatcher, who said, "Don't say anything at all". She was dismayed that this kind of thing could come between her and the Queen.' Ingham also spoke to Shea, who confirmed that he had spoken to the *Sunday Times*. Ingham's reaction was not entirely one of surprise. 'There was a feeling around Buckingham Palace that people there were amused by Mrs Thatcher,' he reflects, 'people who derived amusement from Mrs Thatcher's passion, unspecified people who looked down their noses at her, as a kind of Johnnie-come-lately.'[39]

In short, what took place was a double breakdown in communication: between Downing Street and the Palace, whose drifting apart over many months lent plausibility to the story, and between the Palace and the *Sunday Times*, each of which had its own reason for understanding what was said in a particular way. Such reporting mishaps, a product of the system of unattributable briefing, were not uncommon, though this was the first one involving Buckingham Palace. Undoubtedly Neil, Jones and Freeman believed themselves to be in possession of a scoop. It is equally clear that the Palace did not intend to provide one. One courtier remembers speaking to Shea after the telephone call to Freeman, and being told by the press secretary that he expected the article to be a helpful piece about the Queen's constitutional role.[40] Indeed, it is hard to give credence to the most serious accusation against him, that he had spoken to the press as if he had the Queen's authority when he did not have it – if only because such behaviour was certain to rebound, both against the Palace and against him personally. Nevertheless, a degree of wishful thinking on one side may have compounded an element of imprudence on the other.

Once it became clear that the Queen herself was not involved, talk of a constitutional crisis faded. David Owen, leader of the Alliance, urged the Monarch to 'give the same anti-racialist lead at home as she gives abroad' – and suggested that the conflict between the two women was real.[41] But the Labour leader, Neil Kinnock, declined to exploit the mutual embarrassment and instead allocated blame even-handedly to 'loose-lipped courtiers' and 'wide-eared reporters'.[42] According to one source, the Prime Minister was 'knocked sideways by it, she was very down in the mouth'. One reason for concern was that the report of a Palace–Downing Street rift heightened her difficulties in a Cabinet divided on the sanctions issue. 'She was distressed by the stories,' according to a close adviser, 'because she thought they would be damaging to her.' If so, she kept her feelings under control. 'She went out of her way not to appear to be irritated,' says a senior ministerial colleague. 'She was reluctant to show her irritation.' According to another aide, the Queen apologized to her in an audience, 'but Mrs Thatcher was so respectful of her that she would have immediately put it behind her and considered that the Queen had been badly served.'[43]

Mrs Thatcher treated the luckless Shea with kindness. All three were at Holyrood when the story broke. Sir John Riddell, private secretary to the Prince of Wales, was also in the party and remembers coming down in the morning and picking up a newspaper with huge headlines about the Queen's rift with the Prime Minister. 'Mrs Thatcher was there, made up to the nines,' he recalls. 'I realized it wasn't going to be a very jolly breakfast.' Later, however, the Queen deliberately placed the press secretary between herself and the Prime Minister at table. Shea apologized for what had happened. 'Don't worry, dear,' the premier replied.[44]

Others were less magnanimous, and felt that the press secretary had been seduced into saying more than he should. 'There's no doubt that he had his hair firmly washed for the episode,' says a former civil service adviser to Mrs Thatcher.[45] When Shea left the Palace a few months later, the press credited him with a highly successful tenure of his post, praising him for professionalizing media access and facilities for foreign trips, and for enhancing the popularity of the Royal Family.[46] Some believed, however, that his departure was connected with the incident. Yet the *Sunday Times* story did not come out of the blue, and only aroused interest because it confirmed what many people had come to think.

In the Commonwealth, the much denied report acted as a tonic. When Sir Geoffrey Howe made a second visit to Zambia and faced the cameras for a televised meeting with Kenneth Kaunda on July 24th, he found the veteran leader vigorous in his denunciation of Mrs Thatcher (who, the Zambian leader said, 'has been kissing apartheid'), but appreciative of the British Head of State. He was prepared to welcome the Foreign Secretary, Kaunda gravely informed the Zambian press party, 'because of his "love and respect" for Her Majesty the Queen . . .'[47]

At home, the public belief that the Monarchy, the Church and the Lords provided the only significant opposition to an over-mighty government was strengthened, along with the notion that the Queen stood to the left of her Prime Minister. Whether, or how far, the belief was accurate, remains an enigma: though there has never been a political row of any consequence about the Monarch standing to the right of her Government to redress the balance. The Queen herself remained unfailingly discreet. But the occasional raised eyebrow, conversation brought abruptly to a close, or expression of concern about a state or group of people who Mrs Thatcher considered of little account, conveyed a feeling to those who met the Queen, and through them the public, that the *Sunday Times* disclosures – even if they were nothing of the kind – were not far from the mark.

In November 1988, the issue came up again in a less dramatic form, over a reported exchange between the Queen and Neil Kinnock. 'The people of Govan,' the Monarch allegedly said to the Leader of the Labour Party over dinner, 'have got nothing. I know because I have sailed *Britannia* there'. Many commentators blamed Kinnock for reporting a private conversation, and allowing it to get into the press.[48] Others, however, also noted the observation – and linked the story to a widely-publicized refusal by the Prime Minister to allow the Queen to accept an invitation from the Soviet leader, Mikhail Gorbachev, to visit Moscow. 'The conclusion is inescapable,' wrote Robert Harris in the *Observer*; 'the Sovereign and her heirs are old-fashioned "wets" who would find no place in the present Cabinet.'[49] The theme did not go away: and a new generation of radical Conservatives found less and less reason to link their political commitment to an automatic support for the Monarchy.

THE COMMONWEALTH might have become a tenuous association, its ties to the mother country weakened by British hostility to Third World regimes, and by a declining share of British trade, compared with Europe. But the umbilical chord that linked some mother states constitutionally to the Monarchy continued to give Buckingham Palace a different perspective – and to produce lines of diplomacy which sometimes appeared to be separate from those of the Foreign and Commonwealth Office. This was especially so in the case of smaller, poorer states where the recognition of the Queen offered a kind of security, as well as a connection with the wider world. One of these was Fiji, another island state where the Palace suddenly found itself unwittingly embroiled. In Grenada, the problem had been that the Queen was ignored. In Fiji, the Queen found herself the object of an appeal.

In May 1987, the Fijian Governor-General, Ratu Ganilau, asked the Queen for her support, following a military *coup d'état* on the island, which he claimed would result in undemocratic changes. The Queen responded positively, declaring that Ganilau remained the 'sole legitimate source of executive authority in Fiji,' and expressing the hope that 'the process of restoring Fiji to constitutional normality might be resumed.'[50] Her stance contained the paradox that, for sound legal and constitutional reasons, the Fijian Head of State was opposing her normal supporters on the island. The coup had been carried out by Melanesians, traditionally devoted loyalists of the Crown, in a country where more than half the people were Indians, who were not. Thus the Queen was placed in the position of refusing to endorse the constitutional entrenchment of her own followers in order to uphold a constitutional principle.[51]

In September there was a second coup. This time, the military ousted the Governor-General himself, an action which the Queen declared illegal. In October, the coup leader on both occasions, Lieutenant-Colonel Sitiveni Rabuka, revoked the 1970 constitution and deposed the Queen as Head of State. The Palace responded by repudiating the step; insisting that the Queen continued to regard the Governor-General as the 'sole legitimate source of executive authority'[52] in Fiji; and – in a second message – declaring that she was 'sad to think that the ending of Fijian allegiance to the Crown should have been brought about without the people of Fiji being given an opportunity to express their opinion on the proposal'. Such communications had little material effect. However, Fiji's former status as a Monarchy had one consequence which Rabuka had not envisaged. By making the island a republic, he had automatically taken the country out of the Commonwealth. The rules required republics to reapply to join, and be accepted by the other member states. Fiji reapplied, and was refused.[53]

This got the Queen off the hook: she had no responsibility, constitutional or otherwise, for a country of which she was not Head of State and which had ceased to be a member of the Commonwealth. In practical terms, her involvement had never been much more than notional anyway. Yet the exchange was relevant to the Queen's fragmenting multiple-persona, because – as a result of the revolutionary situation in Fiji, and the lack of a properly constitutional government – her messages had been issued without binding ministerial 'advice,' either from Fiji or London. The limbo this placed her in did not escape the attention of the ever vigilant Enoch Powell, who denounced as an absurdity the notion of a Monarch who was British but not solely British, and of two lines of communication from London, governmental and royal. He dismissed the idea that the Queen might act 'personally, and not on binding advice,' or that 'some curious entity called "Buckingham Palace"' was entitled to make statements about the situation in a remote country. Such a proposition, he wrote, was 'constitutionally unsound and fraught with disagreeable consequences'. The only issue was who was in control in Fiji: if there were no 'responsible' ministers from whom she could take advice as Head of State, she had no role – and it was dangerous to the general principle of the Crown acting only 'on advice' to imagine otherwise.[54]

Powell's analysis, however, left the human aspect out of account. The fact remained that to many Commonwealth citizens around the world the Queen continued to be seen as a person with interests and emotions, and not just as a constitutional automaton. Occasional messages and interventions, however slight, gave the impression of a watching brief. They also highlighted the Queen's stubborn refusal to accept that the Commonwealth, though no longer a political or economic bloc, was withering away. If the death of the Commonwealth was often predicted, but never quite took place, this was partly because of its Head: who upheld a model of the association which she had inherited from her father and grandfather, and which she referred to at every opportunity. Though the Commonwealth had changed greatly from the 'Empire' to which she had dedicated her life in Cape Town in 1947, it remained – in her imagination – a family.

It was in this 'familial' concept – involving the idea of a continuing organic growth, and of an intuitive mutual understanding – that her greatest difference from Margaret Thatcher lay. While the British Government treated the Commonwealth as a tiresome obstacle to a realistic foreign policy, the Queen saw her own role in quite other terms. Thus at the end of September 1986, two months after the *Sunday Times* row, she spoke to a meeting of Commonwealth parliamentarians about the Commonwealth's 'family relationship' from which came 'the capacity to disagree without breaking up'.[55] Four years later, she spoke again as if she were the matriarch, rather than just the symbolic head, of a billion-strong 'family'. In her 1990 Commonwealth Day message, she likened member states to individuals who varied widely in age, appearance, tasks, talents, temperament and, from time to time, opinions. Despite such differences, she suggested, 'members of a family have no difficulty in recognizing each other as relations, and in putting a value on their kinship. They are able to sum one another up with both realism and affection. They appreciate each other's special qualities. Above all, they have learned to feel at home with each other. So have we in the Commonwealth.'

It was not entirely fanciful to imagine that she was speaking of Charles and Anne, Andrew and Edward, when she said that Commonwealth countries could develop in many directions, and even earn each other's disapproval, and yet still be held together by the family bond:

> In the last resort, there is no compulsion to conform. If we are sometimes critical of each other, or disappointed, it is because we expect more of members of our family than we do of others. Now and then a member may even feel constrained to go off on their own. Some years ago this happened to Pakistan, for example. Yet today we have the joy of having Pakistan back in the family. This illustrates perfectly the nature of the underlying bond which distinguishes the Commonwealth from all other international organizations.[56]

But was it still true? If there remained a connecting link between the countries of the former Empire, based on language and a common heritage of British institutions and administration, it was stretching meaning to talk of it as an 'underlying bond'. Indeed, sceptics could argue that to the extent that such a 'bond' continued to be acknowledged in the Commonwealth, it was because the association had lost most of its significance, and it was scarcely worth the effort to break free. In short, 'family' relationships had become so open as to have little surviving value.

If this was right, however, the metaphor – ironically – was not entirely redundant. For in the years that followed, the Queen's own extending family began to develop in ways that seemed almost to reflect those of the Commonwealth at large.

22

THERE WAS A SEQUENCE to the rapid change in the public perception of royalty that occurred in the mid and late 1980s. Criticism
of 'frivolity' – largely confined to the younger royals – came first.
Then came the suggestion that the Royal Family was overpaid and
undertaxed, and did not give value for money. Finally – after 'frivolity'
and tax complaints had eroded much of what was left of traditional
respect – the idea took root that the central myth of royalty was,
indeed, no more than that. The Royal Family, it came to be said, was
not a model of domestic virtue and private happiness but, in the
modern jargon, dysfunctional. Much of the 'anti-royal' reporting
reflected the unhappy failure of some of the younger members of the
Royal Family, especially the newer ones, to discover publicly approved
roles which they found satisfying. But it was also a product of public
prurience, and of a press which now had almost no incentive to give
the Royal Family the loyal protection it had enjoyed since the nineteenth century.

Occasionally, Prince Philip was targeted. One notable media assault
on him occurred during an historic royal tour of China, the first ever
by a British Head of State to the mainland, which took place in the
autumn of 1986. Nearly a hundred and fifty journalists flew out from
the United Kingdom alone, to accompany the royal party – all conscious that their editors wished for something more exciting than
reports of polite exchanges of goodwill, or of the royal couple standing
on the Great Wall. The tour was arduous, taking in Beijing, including
the Forbidden City, Shanghai, the south-west city of Kunming and the
central city of X'ian with its army of terracotta warriors.[1] According
to one member of the party, during a trip to an industrial installation
in the south-west, Prince Philip's restlessness got the better of him.
After they had climbed a hillside to get to an observation point, Philip

'kept making environmentalist noises' about smoke that was billowing over the lake – so insistently that British officials were worried that the Chinese would overhear them.

However, it was not Prince Philip's concern about the environment that threatened to cause diplomatic damage, but a chance comment he made in X'ian. Chatting to some British students, he cheerily remarked that they would get 'slitty eyes' if they stayed too long in China. The words were picked up by the grateful media, and flashed around the globe as evidence of royal racial insensitivity, making headlines everywhere – except in China itself, where no slight was apparently felt. 'Chinese fury at royal clanger,' said the British press. 'Duke insults Chinese.' Sir Geoffrey Howe, the Foreign Secretary felt called upon to apologize to his Chinese opposite number, Wu Xuequian, who seemed singularly uninsulted.[2] It was a significant comment on world news values that so innocent and trivial a joke could cause such a fuss.

In Britain the incident largely obliterated any political impact that news of a royal unfreezing of Sino-British relations might have had. Nevertheless, those who took part in the trip were impressed by the Queen's reception. Lord Howe, recalls 'an extraordinary reverence and respect' for the Monarch as an institution. He particularly remembers in Shanghai 'driving along the barely lit streets to the Royal Yacht Britannia, and seeing millions of Chinese faces peering at us'. He came away with the sense that the Queen's office carried great authority.[3]

At home, the 'slitty eyes' affair became part of the profile of the royal figure who was famous for gaffes and minor gaucheries stretching back nearly forty years. They were not particularly held against him, and even helped to define him as a regular fellow, close to the man in the street. In any case, the older royals were ceasing to be at the centre of the media's attention: *faux* by the Queen's consort, though still a source of entertainment, were yielding ground to the behaviour of the younger generation. In the 1980s, the supreme ruffler of feathers – mainly British Establishment ones – became the Prince of Wales, who had inherited some of his father's interests, as well as his father's willingness to speak out of turn. The sense of Charles as a man of strong opinions was greatly strengthened in 1984 when – with magnificent affrontery – the Prince told an audience of distinguished

planners and architects, who had invited him to utter the usual com-
plimentary pleasantries, that, in his own considered opinion, 'some
planners and architects have consistently ignored the feelings and
wishes of the mass of ordinary people in the country'. Relishing the
storm that broke out about his head, and also the role of tribune of
popular aesthetics, the Prince continued to make speeches on a variety
of topics in which he took a layman's interest – indicating, as he
approached middle age, a desire to occupy the role of Sir Ivor Jennings'
'good solid citizen' against the obfuscations and obscurantism of the
professionals.

In the quality newspapers, his speeches attracted a good deal of
attention, much of it angry. For a time he was seen as the voice of a
new kind of opposition – traditionalist yet communitarian, on the
side of plain speech, good English, preserving what was best, team-
work, and self-help, and against bureaucracy, self-appointed authority,
and artistic pretension. As a controversialist, he had a predictable
effect: arousing the sympathetic if bemused interest of ordinary people,
and the extreme irritation of the experts in the fields he made his
own, who felt that he had taken advantage of his public position, and
treated them unfairly. In the tabloids, however, there was less interest
in what the Prince had to say about Shakespeare, housing, and urban
renewal. Instead of his public life, increasingly, as the decade progressed, the private life of the least frivolous of the young royals
became the focus of the most intense and intrusive scrutiny.

It did not take the press long to discover that something was seriously wrong. Bit by bit, the jigsaw of the Waleses' failed relationship
was pieced together. 'Separate breakfasts, separate timetables, separate
friends,' wrote an acute royalty watcher called Andrew Morton in
1987. 'These days the Prince and Princess of Wales are leading active,
interesting, but totally independent lives.'[4] Here was a story, editors
quickly realized, with limitless scope.

At the major tabloids, Monday morning headlines about the Royal
Family became a routine – regardless of whether there was any news
to justify them. 'Give me a Sunday for Monday splash on the royals',
Kelvin MacKenzie of the *Sun* would say to his staff. 'Don't worry if
it's not true – so long as there's not too much of a fuss about it
afterwards.'[5] In this kind of marketplace, the Queen was pushed aside.

She continued to offer quiet reassurance, and her Christmas broadcast – now directed by Sir David Attenborough – drew a United Kingdom audience of fifteen million. It was possible to pronounce the Monarchy in good shape. 'It can preach moral sermons without hypocrisy', wrote the journalist Simon Jenkins in 1986. 'It can still have us sitting, every year, listening to what it has to say.'⁶ But only once every twelve months: in between, it was the younger royals, and increasingly, the habits, moods, sulks and tantrums of the younger royal spouses, that provided newspaper copy.

If the Queen, her husband, and some of the other state-subsidized descendants of George V led lives that combined traditional royal and upper-class recreations with dutiful public service, the same had ceased to be true of all of them. The 1986 'revelations' affair had provided one kind of turning-point in the way people understood the Monarchy, reminding them that it could not simply be seen as a ceremonial accompaniment to the Government of the day. A television show in 1987 called *It's a Royal Knockout* provided another – making the public stunningly aware that a sense of decorum was not an automatic quality in the Royal Family, and even that some members of it might be more deserving of their Civil List incomes than others. It was a critical moment in the altering image of British royalty, with a new osmosis: from the widely admired, disciplined, trim, happily expanding but still essentially nuclear family (in the eyes of the media and public) into what one historian would describe, a few years later, as 'an over-extended, multi-generational dynasty, devoid of any cultural direction, purpose or justification'.⁷ It was a change of perception as much as of substance: a flicking from a benign distortion to a malign one.

Stories about the life of Prince Andrew – generally of a happy-go-lucky character – had been brought to a satisfactory conclusion (it was felt) in March 1986 when the Prince became engaged to Sarah Ferguson, an exuberant young woman who was the daughter of Prince Charles's polo manager, and who worked for a publishing company. The wedding was preceded by a joint television appearance before journalists, and by much media admiration of a very large, very expensive ruby engagement ring. The Prince became Duke of York, a title previously held by both the Queen's father and grandfather. The couple were married at Westminster Abbey on July 23rd – three days after the *Sunday Times* published its 'revelations' about the Queen's opinions. The ceremony was cheerful, theatrical, hugely publicized, if somehow lacking in civic point. The day reached its climax with a Buckingham Palace kiss which replicated the Charles and Diana one and seemed to establish it as an obligatory part of the royal wedding ritual. Afterwards, the couple occupied an apartment at Buckingham Palace before moving into a sprawling, ranch-like mansion built for them at Sunninghill Park, site of what had originally been intended as the country home of Andrew's parents in 1947.

The Duchess – privately, and now universally, known as 'Fergie' – was a new kind of addition to the Royal Family. Neither beautiful nor talented, she was, to the delight of early observers who discovered a member of the clan it was easy to relate to, outgoing and extremely jolly. The popular press quickly identified her as one of their own: her barmaid looks, bouncy style and lack of old-fashioned stuffiness (it was reported and counted as an advantage that she had a 'past') appealed to their readers. It also helped that she was believed to be the Monarch's favourite among her children's spouses. 'The Queen was very fond of Fergie,' says a friend. 'She liked the way she used to sit with her legs apart, making jokes.'[8] Comparisons were soon being drawn. 'The relationship between the Queen and Princess Diana is strictly one between mother-in-law and a new wife, cordial but distant,' wrote Morton, 'in sharp contrast to the warm chatty friendship the Duchess of York has quickly built up with the Chairman of the Family Firm.'[9] The Duchess rapidly developed chatty relationships with everybody, including the Princess of Wales (who became her close friend) and newspaper reporters. As a result, she was seldom out of the news – upstaging her husband almost as much as Diana upstaged Charles.

Only the youngest of the Queen's children now remained single. Prince Edward was also the least well known. Academically the brightest of the four, he had spend three years at Jesus College, Cambridge, studying history and involving himself in university and college drama. After graduating, he had followed a parentally-approved path by joining the Royal Marines and, for a time, seemed set in the same mould as his father and brothers. Then he rebelled. In January 1987, he surprised both his parents and his commanding officer by announcing that he was leaving the service with the intention of pursuing a career in the theatre. The following year, he took up full-time employment as a production assistant in the West End. In the meantime, with time on his hands, and keen to make a mark, the twenty-three year old Prince turned his attention to television. His interest was especially aroused by the slapstick series *It's a Knockout*, which provided a spectacle of show business and sporting personalities taking part in light-hearted and often ridiculous games before a live audience. In theory, the object was to raise money for charity – though the participants also gained free 'human interest' publicity in the process.

What could be more entertaining, and the source of more harmless pleasure to the public, than a 'royal' version of the programme? What could be a better joke, public and private, than the sight of royal celebrities showing what a colossal sense of humour they had, by joining in the fun? Delighted by the prospect, Prince Edward persuaded not only Andrew and Fergie, always good for a laugh, but also Princess Anne to take part. The idea was for a special mock-Tudor *Knockout* with royals alongside some fifty celebrities all in fancy dress. It was put forward by a student friend of Edward, and seized with enthusiasm by John Broome, the owner of the castle-cum-pleasure park Alton Towers, near Birmingham. 'Both the BBC and John Broome positively drooled at the idea,' recalled Edward,[10] as well they might. What was good for TV ratings and for business, however, was less good for the Monarchy.

Before it could happen, permission had to be obtained from the Queen. At this point, wiser counsels might have prevailed. 'It was a terrible mistake,' says one of the Monarch's friends. 'She was against it. But one of her faults is that she can't say no.' Sir William Heseltine was also dubious, and did his best to prevent the programme from happening. His colleagues supported him. 'There was not a single courtier,' one recalls, 'who did not think it was a mistake.' He was defeated by youthful enthusiasm and the Queen's maternal indulgence. 'It was an awful idea', reflects another former aide. 'How could you not appear undignified in that set up? But Prince Edward was determined it would happen.' With his mother's consent, the programme went ahead. The only condition was that the royal participants should act as team leaders and not take part in the rough-and-tumble of the games.[11]

The programme was screened on June 19th, following much advance publicity. Set in Broome's Staffordshire folly, the show parodied royal ceremonial, with Rowan Atkinson, Barbara Windsor and Les Dawson making 'olde worlde' speeches. Anne, Edward, Andrew and Fergie waved and shouted at the sidelines at the antics of the non-royal celebrities, who did silly things. Four non-royal dukes – whose only point in the programme seemed to be their titles – also took part. The royal team leaders were interviewed by the comedians, with a great deal of mock deference and mock bowing. Gary Lineker cavorted in women's tights. The royals wore brightly coloured cloaks, and did a lot of raucous shouting. 'Give us a *B* . . . give us an *L* . . .' bellowed the Duchess of York, leader of the 'Blue Bandits' team.

The performance raised a million pounds for charity, and enabled Princess Anne to brandish a shield advertising the Save the Children Fund. It was meant to be funny. For most people watching at home, however, it was the most excruciating episode of an (at best) plodding series. Part of the problem was the confusion of roles. It was unclear why the royals should lead teams of people who, in general, were famous because of their achievements, rather than their rank; and attempts by the royals to behave like celebrities and be witty fell flat. People who liked to see the Royal Family being natural, changed their minds. The audience felt as if it had stumbled in on an under-rehearsed private charade, and was left wondering why so much attention had been paid to such galumphing performers. 'The atmosphere throughout was one of a massive weekend party and organized much like one,' wrote Prince Edward, with revealing candour.[12] But that was not all. What might have been passed off as a regrettable mistake was turned into a public relations disaster by the inexperienced Edward, who – confronting a press conference of fifty weary journalists at the end – was so upset by their lack of enthusiasm that he walked petulantly out of the press tent, with the cameras on him. 'It's a Walkout,' said the inevitable headlines next day. 'Edward Storms Out After Game Show.'[13]

In a way, the Grand Knockout Tournament was the *reductio ad absurdum* of a process that had begun with *Royal Family*. Perhaps it was even a logical outcome. The Monarchy had started by trying to make itself less remote. It had sought to come to terms with modern informality, and to display its own off-duty character. In *Knockout*, it did so – with appalling, regrettable frankness. If this was what royalty was really like, what was there to look up to? How could subjects of the Crown be expected to snigger at Les Dawson's mock-obsequiousness one moment, and bow to royalty out of genuine respect the next? The trouble, as the columnist Helen Mason put it, was that the royals wanted to be seen as ordinary, when they were not.[14] From the path-breaking vignettes of the Cawston film – 'peep-shows into a rarefied world' – to the bawdiness of *Knockout*, there had been a creeping debasement. Before Cawston, the Royal Family had accepted public attention stiffly and bravely. Now the over-exposed dynasty were unavoidable, appearing not only to take media interest as their due, but to relish every moment of it they could get.

One of the mistakes of *Knockout* was that it gave the impression of the Royal Family using their privileged access to the media to sell themselves. That had been a complaint in 1969. Shifting conventions in the intervening seventeen years, however, meant that it had ceased to be possible for royalty simply to receive the publicity it wished for. Some of the young royals might enjoy the ersatz glamour of constant television appearances: but the embrace was a perilous one. With public fascination undiminished, the tabloids no longer merely searched for intimate glimpses. In the circulation war of the late 1980s, a premium was attached to stories and pictures that revealed anybody who was a member of, or was remotely linked to, the Royal Family, in an unfavourable light. The race was on for dirt: and spotlights were shone into the murkiest corners to see what could be unearthed.

An early sufferer was Major Ronald Ferguson, father of the Duchess of York. At the end of 1987, the Duchess became pregnant; her first child, Princess Beatrice, was born in August of the following year. As the event approached, the media concentration on Fergie and her family led to the discovery that her father had frequented a West End massage parlour. Major Ferguson was not royal, though he was in royal employment in a minor sporting capacity. But for the fact of his daughter's marriage, his life would have remained entirely obscure. His slender links with the Royal Family, however, were enough for the tabloids. Pillorying Ferguson, they sought to tarnish his in-laws by association. The stories got grubbier: there were lurid accounts of a 'rift' between the Queen and the Duchess, in which the Monarch was alleged to have told Fergie not to give public support to her father. The *Sun*, caricaturing its own moralistic prurience, criticized the Queen for shaking hands with the unfortunate Major.[15]

However the tabloids were not the younger royals' only persecutors. After *Knockout*, the qualities joined in too – often taking their cue (and their information) from downmarket rivals. Leading the field was the *Sunday Times*. Bruised by the 'revelations' affair, and by accusations that he had over-reached himself, Andrew Neil responded defiantly – adopting the role of scourge of a dynasty of which, as his editorials made clear, better things were expected. Over the next few years the *Sunday Times* played an important part in establishing the idea of a 'royal problem' in the minds of a middle-class readership. The tone was not cheeky, as in the tabloids, but admonishing. The paper acknowledged that there were 'barely any individual republicans of note' in Britain. Nevertheless, it maintained, there was a need for the Queen to sort out her family.

Though some of its arguments were specious, not all of them were. Thus it pointed to what had undoubtedly become a major contradiction: the Royal Family's place in a class structure that few defended. Echoing Malcolm Muggeridge thirty years before, it declared that a modern Monarchy, 'should not be seen as an apex of a hierarchical, aristocratic society; it should be set apart from all classes, something distinctive and unique that exists because the British people want it to exist'. The paper went on to argue that the younger royals needed more to do. Charles should be given greater responsibility, the others should be encouraged to take jobs. Most important of all, the Monarchy 'must never become the hereditary branch of the show-business industry'. With some hypocrisy (the Murdoch press, including the *Sunday Times*, had been the major culprit) it attacked the eagerness of the media to feed the public's 'currently grotesque appetite for all things royal,' and the willingness of the young royals to co-operate with it. Finally, it predicted – and once again, the *Sunday Times* scored a first – that such tendencies, if unchecked, would eventually lead to a republic.[16]

If there was an element of mischief-making in this assault, others with less of an axe to grind also expressed their irritation or disgust at the indifference of the young royals to the consequence of making fools of themselves. Later in the year, the respected Tory columnist T. E. Utley carefully spelt out the case for royal reticence. The royals, he wrote, 'are there to supply a perennial pageant of virtue – the virtues of family life, of civic obedience, of respect for the arts, of care for the poor and afflicted'. In view of the paradox that Monarchy needed to uphold standards it could not possibly meet, it was desirable to keep what really went on discreetly hidden. The function of the Queen, and by derivation her family, was to represent the national ethos in idealized form. Otherwise, what was the point of having an hereditary Monarchy? The answer, Utley concluded, was that there would be no point, 'if the present ridiculous exercise continues'. The *Sunday Times* saw present trends leading to a republic. Utley inverted Bagehot's claim that Britain's constitutional system was already a disguised republic, and suggested that through the degrading of the Monarchy, republicanism was being introduced by the back door.[17]

Thus it was that the dreaded word, previously the mark of a crank or a revolutionary, entered respectable and even Conservative discourse; and, once the word had been uttered, it became inevitable that a debate that had been avoided for a hundred years would ensue. On the Right, republican talk was mainly in the form of a warning of what might transpire, if the Monarchy failed to adapt. On the Left, it began to emerge as an aspiration, or even a proposal. Encouraged by a discussion of constitutional reform to which the Thatcherite dominance had given rise, and by the impact of Celtic separatism, the role of royalty began to arouse interest in circles that had previously disregarded it. Early in 1988, the radical essayist Tom Nairn published *The Enchanted Glass: Britain and its Monarchy*, a brilliant polemic which fundamentally altered the parameters of the left-of-centre debate.

Hitherto, the convention of the Marxist and democratic socialist Left had been to treat the British Monarchy as objectionable but trivial, at worst a mere symptom of a rotten system. *The Enchanted Glass* stood this on its head. Nairn was almost as scathing about the 'idiot-theory', as he called it, that the Monarchy had no importance, as he was about the institution itself. Instead of seeing the Monarchy as a marginal part of British life, he placed it at the heart of the 'British problem' of social conservatism, nostalgia for Empire, and what he labelled 'Ukania', defined as 'the Geist or informing spirit of the UK,' involving an artificial and exploitative pseudo-nationalism.

Earlier anti-monarchists like William Hamilton had focused on the cost, pretensions, supposed affront to democracy, and irrationalism, of the institution. They wrote as if it were separable from the political system as a whole. Nairn not only saw it as integral. He looked broadly at the 'mystique' of Monarchy, whose power – he argued – was real. It was wrong, he suggested, to treat media interest in royalty and in film stars as the same thing. Royals were 'persons and symbols ordinary in appearance but quite super-ordinary in significance'. Far more than was true of royal families elsewhere in Europe, the Windsors in Britain were 'like an interface between two worlds, the mundane one and some vaster national-spiritual sphere associated with mass adulation, the past, the State and familial morality.' The precise nature of royal mystique remained, itself, mysterious. Yet it was a serious misconception to see popular royalism as mindless and passive, or simply the product of media manipulation. On the contrary, it contained 'an apparently inexhaustible electrical charge . . . People enjoy the Monarchical twaddle, and show very little sign of being robotized or "brain-washed".'

Nairn repeatedly returned to the point that, while the orthodox account of the Monarchy binding the state together was in a sense correct, that by no means described the whole of its influence. 'Europe's greatest living fossil, the enchanted glass of an early modernity which has otherwise vanished from the globe' deserved attention because of its colossal influence on civil society. The author called for a 'new republicanism' as the *sine qua non* of socialist change. But his argument was not a simple abolitionist one. He acknowledged the psychological, as much as political, difficulty. He also saw little sign of a trend. Even Labour voters were overwhelmingly pro-Monarchy, and as yet there existed 'no serious republican campaign or movement, no republican press, and no recognized or avowable anti-Monarchic stance in everyday argument . . .'[18]

The Enchanted Glass was not a book about which anybody could be condescending. Even ardent monarchists were impressed by the informed passion and Paine-like elegance of Nairn's invective. It was hard to read without being persuaded of at least one of its tenets: that the idea of Monarchy retained an immense symbolic and psychic hold. Even the author's most radical arguments could no longer be considered as eccentric: indeed, much of his analysis did not differ from that of the newly irreverent right. Many neo-liberals found themselves nodding in agreement, for instance, at the suggestion that the Monarchy embodied the 'glamour of backwardness' and was the upholder, not of capitalism as such, but of reaction. The book received little immediate attention, confirming its author's judgement about the intelligent public shying away from a serious discussion of the topic. Over the next few years, however, its textured messages became the currency of a growing argument, emboldening other writers.

Opinion was flowing fast. At the beginning of 1989, one right-wing commentator noted in the *Daily Telegraph* that despite the continued popularity of the Monarchy, the Royal Family was subject to more criticism than at any other time in the century. The reason, he suggested, was not just the behaviour of the young royals. It was also because the Queen reflected the unchanging, aristocratic, Tory-paternalist consensus mentality which it was Mrs Thatcher's mission to attack.[19] The following year, Frank Vibert, deputy director of the Institute of Economic Affairs – an influential think-tank which had helped to inspire the neo-liberal revolution – included in a paper the suggestion (which he was persuaded at the last moment to withdraw) that the Queen should be given a purely symbolic role as 'an emblem of historical continuity,' while her residual powers should be transferred to an officer appointed by Parliament.[20] A strikingly similar proposal had been made by Tony Benn, many years before.

THE QUEEN's income and wealth aroused new interest at the beginning of the 1990s. One of Mrs Thatcher's last actions as Prime Minister (ironically, in view of the supposed lack of sympathy between Downing Street and the Palace) was to put the Civil List on a sounder footing than it had had for a generation. In July 1990, the Government announced an increase of more than fifty per cent in the Queen's Civil List income as part of a ten-year agreement – assuming an annual seven-and-a-half per cent inflation rate, a figure that was based on the average for the previous decade. The object was to remove the need to set the amount of the Civil List each year, which high inflation had made necessary in the 1970s and 1980s – producing headlines every Budget Day about the Queen's 'pay rise' which had been embarrassing to the Government and Palace alike. The new deal meant that the Queen and her family would get more than they needed at the beginning of the decade, but less at the end – and they would be expected to put the early surpluses into reserve. The total was set at an annual £7.9 million from 1st January 1991.[21] The Prime Minister justified the new system as 'appropriate for the dignity of the Crown,' and received Opposition support. 'The overwhelming majority of people in this nation,' said Mrs Thatcher in response to a left-wing attack, 'are agreed that the Royal Family is the greatest asset the United Kingdom has.'[22]

The settlement was the culmination of a reorganization of royal finances that followed the appointment of the Earl of Airlie, formerly chairman of Schroeders, as Lord Chamberlain in 1984. During the negotiations, the Court was able to exploit the Government's desire not to appear stingy towards the Monarch with whom it was reported to have had differences. 'Lord Airlie was pressing very hard on salaries,' a former Downing Street official recalls, 'and for giving particular people permanent secretaries' salaries when their level didn't in the least justify it.' However, the sums were small, and the policy was appeasement. 'There was never any inclination to seek out rows,' says the same source.[23]

'The aim was to make the Palace master of its own destiny,' says a courtier. 'However, at the time, Lord Airlie had sleepless nights.' He need not have worried. The 1990 Civil List arrangement worked out well for the Palace, partly because forward guesses of inflation were once again off target, this time over-estimating the level of price rises, and removing (so far) the need for further recourse to Parliament. Indeed, the package was looking so favourable after the first year that some observers asked why such an approach should apply to the Queen's Household, and not to the NHS.[24]

Airlie had been introduced as a new broom, after the thirteen-year term of Lord 'Chips' Maclean, twenty-seventh Chief of Clan Maclean and a former Chief Scout who (according to one observer) 'played his part with distinction and dignity at all great royal ceremonial events,'[24] but whose ceremonial ardour had exceeded his business or administrative competence. Maclean had perpetuated a distinctly tweedy atmosphere in some parts of the Royal Household into the 1980s. 'There was a breed of yobbo aristocrats floating around the Palace,' recalls one ex-courtier. 'The Lord Chamberlain's office with all its protocol was from another world, straight out of the 1920s. People came in at 10 a.m. and had dry martinis at noon. But you couldn't fault them on state occasions, banquets, parades and so on.' Airlie was also a traditional courtier – in some ways, tweediness personified. Grandson of Queen Mary's close friend and retainer, he had a conservative view of the Monarchy. He also shared his predecessor's taste for flummery. 'He is immensely grand,' says a former royal aide, 'with hundreds of thousands of acres in Scotland and a castle. He looks wonderful when dressed up in his ceremonial garb. Cecil B. de Mille would describe him as being a bit too much.' But he was also a successful and experienced banker, and his appointment precipitated a quiet revolution. Confronting what one courtier calls 'a Heath Robinson way of organizing things' he called in the firm of Peat Marwick McLintock, already auditors to the Queen, for an exhaustive study of the creaking royal business, bringing both the occupied and unoccupied palaces into its ambit.

The result of the inquiry was a 1,500 page report completed in 1986, which called for sweeping changes. A Lord Chamberlain's committee made up of heads of department was set up to cover all aspects of the Queen's affairs and to implement recommendations. There was a small but notable input from the Monarch. 'Why,' she would ask, 'have I got so many footmen?' The report took some time to absorb. 'Lord Airlie gave bits of it to the Queen,' says a courtier. The result was a rationalization of royal management, with improvements to business practices and cost effectiveness. The reforms, in parallel with a tightening of financial controls throughout the public sector, provided a basis for the 1990 Civil List arrangements. The settlement was in the nick of time. For public and political opinion, already strained by reports of the extravagance of the younger royals, was losing sympathy with the Royal Family on the money question. The tax-free income the Queen derived from her personal fortune had been a taken-for-granted part of the system at the beginning of the reign, when everything to do with the Monarchy had been treated as part of the natural order. Even in the 1970s the pressure for change had been small. Although Labour had declared its intention to take away the immunity, the Wilson and Callaghan governments did nothing to alter the status quo between 1974 and 1979, and a financial assault on the Palace had never been part of the Conservatives' agenda. Yet lack of action did not mean that the point had been forgotten. During the 1980s, objections grew louder on all sides. The annual Civil List 'pay rises,' the young royal spending sprees, and the new climate of royalty appraisal in the media, meant that even the most monarchist sections of the Tory press questioned the exemption.

A contributory factor was the persistent refusal of Buckingham Palace to discuss the Queen's private assets, or what they were worth – a coyness which might have seemed reasonable if these were purely private but, in view of their privileged status, seemed particularly hard to defend. The result was a damaging guessing game – involving a range of estimates often based on the principle that a large figure had a greater news value than a relatively small one. In 1989, the American business magazine *Fortune* placed the Queen's personal wealth at £7 billion, a total which would have made her the world's richest woman and fourth richest person. According to the magazine, this colossal sum was increasing at a rate of £3 million a day.[26] The sense of a Queen not only fabulously rich but also getting rapidly richer with the taxpayers' help, was increased by a *Harpers and Queen* survey of wealthy people at the beginning of 1991. This not only placed the Queen ahead of Imelda Marcos in the 'richest women in the world' stakes, but claimed that shrewd investment had raised her untaxed income by twenty per cent in the preceding twelve months. Such astronomical totals had a particular tabloid appeal at a time of national belt-tightening. On the basis of such figures, suggested the *Sun* glee-fully, taxing the Queen at forty per cent would yield more than £200 million a year, 'enough for a dozen hospitals.'[27] The *People* placed the extent of public loss even higher. 'By the time you have read this paper, Her Moneybags the Queen will be about £7,000 better off, give or take the odd thousand,' it leered on February 10th. 'The chill wind of the recession won't be blowing under the carpets of Buckingham Palace, not when you're saving more than £256 million on income tax!'

It was a touchy and confusing subject. What was 'private' wealth and what was not? Wearily, the Palace pointed out – yet again – that the Queen owning something did not necessarily mean that she could sell it and pocket the cash nor that it necessarily yielded any income. Sensational calculations of the Queen's fortune in the headlines included assets which she technically possessed but which she kept in trust for the nation and were not disposable, such as the Royal Palaces, the Royal Collection, the Crown Jewels and Royal Jewellery. Old Master drawings in the Royal Collection, for example, were treated as part of the national heritage, and could not be sold for the Queen's own personal purposes or given or left to anybody other than her successor as Sovereign.[28] To many ordinary taxpayers, however, the distinction between disposable and inalienable wealth mattered less than the fact that, by any measure, the Queen was extremely rich and getting richer at the public expense – while simultaneously obtaining an increase in the Civil List.

By the time the new arrangement came into effect, feeling on the royal finances was running high. According to one opinion poll at the beginning of 1991, for the *Sunday Times*, the proportion of people who thought the Royal Family 'an expensive luxury the country cannot afford' had risen from twenty-four per cent the previous year to forty-two per cent. Another poll, for the *Independent on Sunday*, found that seventy-nine per cent of a 1,090 sample believed that the Queen should be taxed on her income.[29] Why, people asked, did she need the Civil List at all? 'There is a feeling of unease about their enormous wealth,' declared the then Conservative MP, Emma Nicholson, expressing a cross-party and cross-nation sentiment. 'It would be enormously nice if she would consider living off her own income.'[30]

THE PROBLEM of the Queen's wealth and non-tax payment was bound up with the question of value for money, and – since they had become the Monarchy's most vulnerable point – the young royals. In 1991 the issue of young royal behaviour became more prominent, partly because of the short-lived Gulf War.

In August 1990 the Iraqi leader Saddam Hussein invaded neighbouring Kuwait, and announced its annexation. It was the first test of the 'new world order' since the collapse of Soviet-based communism the previous year. After the UN Security Council had passed a resolution demanding the immediate withdrawal of Iraqi troops, the governments of the United States, Britain and other countries sent forces to Saudi Arabia and the Persian Gulf in the hope that the threat of retaliatory force would persuade Saddam to abide by the decision. When he failed to do so, the United Nations authorized the use of 'all necessary means', setting 1st January 1991 as the deadline.

Meanwhile, in Britain, the foreign crisis had been overtaken by a domestic one. For some time, Conservative MPs had been alarmed by their party's poor rating in the polls – and by evidence that this was linked to the strident style and uncompromising policies of Mrs Thatcher, particularly over the new local government 'poll tax'. It was the premier's hubris, and insensitive attitude towards members of the Cabinet who disagreed with her, however, that caused her downfall. The alienation of Sir Geoffrey Howe – for nine years one of the chief props of the administration – proved to be the last straw. A final insult involved the Queen. On October 5th, Howe flew to Balmoral for a Privy Council meeting – and was startled to discover from the Monarch that she had been told that Britain had joined the ERM, before he himself had been consulted or informed. Four weeks later, furious at repeated humiliations, Howe resigned from the Government. When he formally took his leave at the Palace, he found the Queen 'full of discreet sympathy'.[31]

Howe's departure, and a forensic speech in the Commons explaining it, triggered a long-anticipated challenge to the leadership. In the ensuing contest, Michael Heseltine obtained enough votes in the first ballot to force a second. Faced with the defection of most of her Cabinet and almost certain defeat, Mrs Thatcher reluctantly stood down – the first premier to have resigned as a result of political pressure since 1963, if not since 1940. This time, however – and it was a significant moment – the Queen was not called upon to resolve the difficulty. The Prime Minister did not formally leave office until the completion of the electoral process that had been established in the wake of the Macmillan–Home *débâcle*, in order to meet just such an eventuality.

The outcome caused some surprise. The second ballot contest was a three-way one, with Douglas Hurd, the Foreign Secretary, John Major, the Chancellor of the Exchequer, and Michael Heseltine, who had resigned from the Cabinet over the Westland affair and had long been the main pretender, as candidates. Tory MPs chose John Major – Mrs Thatcher's own preferred successor – partly because his non-controversial rise had earned him fewest enemies. But there was also something else: of the three, Major was the candidate with the humblest background. It was a symptom of the change that had overtaken a party formally dominated by old Etonians and infused with a belief in social hierarchy, that one of the candidates, Douglas Hurd, felt it prudent to apologize for having been at Eton.

On 28th November, John Major kissed hands at Buckingham Palace as the Queen's ninth Prime Minister. At forty-nine, he was the first who was younger than the Head of State, who soon discovered in him a more relaxed and congenial visitor than his predecessor. Mr Major did not lack critics or opponents during his premiership. During his six and a half years at No. 10, however, there was never any hint of the tension that was reported to exist between the Palace and Downing Street in the 1980s.

Major's political inheritance included the growing crisis in the Middle East, where allied forces were preparing for conflict. Action began with an aerial bombardment on 16th January. A ground offensive was launched on 24th February. Four days later the war was over, after a battle that resulted in a large loss of life on the Iraqi side, and only a small number of casualties for the Allies. British forces suffered twenty-four dead, mainly through 'friendly' fire, and forty-three wounded. The victory succeeded in its primary aim of removing Saddam Hussein from Kuwait, but not in its secondary one of toppling him from power in Baghdad.

As far as Britain was concerned, the Gulf was a minor affair compared to the Falklands. British participation was small, and mainly token. There was neither the affront of an attack on sovereign British territory, nor the challenge of a nation standing alone. Nevertheless, the Iraqis were a serious enemy, and there were fears that the Allied forces might get bogged down in a desert conflict. Public opinion was united in support of Britain's stance, and – with eager media help – public interest in the war became intense.

The Gulf War also differed from the Falklands in another way: royalty was not directly involved. Prince Andrew's presence on HMS *Invincible* during the South Atlantic expedition had provided a link between Monarchy, Commonwealth and the war effort which had been helpful to all of them. There was no equivalent nine years later. The point was not ignored by the press, especially as news about the Gulf War happened to coincide with fresh stories about the allegedly irresponsible behaviour of the young royals.

Here was a new formula, mixing royal gossip, anti-royal criticism, jingoism, and heroic tales from the front. In January 1991 the tabloids, which had put them there in the first place, began complaining about the royals being on the front pages at such a time. In February, the *Sunday Times* took up the campaign, rebuking some of the Queen's relatives for their life-style, and expressing regret that there were no members of the Royal Family on active service. True, declared a leader, whose tone suggested the hand of the paper's editor, Prince Andrew was still in the Navy. 'This time, however, his ship is far enough away from the war to allow him recently to enjoy a couple of days' golf on a sunny Spanish links'. The Royal Family as a whole, it concluded, were much to blame for not setting a better example at a time of national emergency, and for painting 'a mixture of upper-class deca-dence and insensitivity which disgusts the public and demeans the Monarchy'. The Queen, it declared, should put a stop to it. Others joined in, including the *Guardian* which objected to 'Viscount Linley in drag' at a party, and 'Fergie spending £5 million on a house that's always empty'.[32]

According to the *Sun* the Queen had told her family to avoid an appearance of frivolity.[33] The attacks – in which the Royal Family was collectively accused of negligent insensitivity – echoed a criticism directed at the Palace after the Lockerbie air disaster in 1989, when the Queen had not been represented by any member of her family at the memorial service. 'Where are the Royals?' asked the *Sun* on that occasion, above a picture of a weeping Pan Am stewardess and an inset of photos of nine royals and what they were doing instead (the Queen: horse-riding, Diana: sunbathing in the Caribbean, Anne: skiing in the Alps, and so on).[34] This time, the *Sunday Times* carried a similar list of members of the Royal Family and what they were doing in place of unspecified war work. Other papers, meanwhile, connected the royal non-involvement, or irresponsible behaviour, with the taxation issue. It was the first open criticism of the Royal Family in wartime of the century. Buckingham Palace responded with disdain. However, a spokesman let it be known that the Queen had requested a series of briefings from the military which went beyond constitutional requirements; and that, through her new private secretary, Sir Robert Fellowes, who had taken over from Sir William Heseltine the previous year, she was closely in touch with the Prime Minister and Foreign Secretary about the conduct of the war.[35]

The successful outcome of the conflict gave the Monarchy a temporary boost, with some American help. In May 1991, the Queen became the first British Head of State to address a joint meeting of the US Congress in Washington. The special relationship was briefly made to seem real. In her Government-crafted speech, the Queen looked beyond the Gulf War, and thanked the American people for 'their steadfast loyalty to our common enterprise throughout this turbulent century'.[36] It was a curiously triumphant moment, which a mere Prime Minister – or elected figurehead – might have found it hard to capture. Basking in the sentimental benignity of a Congress steeped in the mythology of Churchill, Dunkirk and D-Day, the British Monarch – long in the American people's consciousness – was able to underline the continuity and uphold the legitimacy of the Allied peace-keeping effort. In a full house, her speech was often interrupted by clapping.

But the value of the Queen as a ceremonial ambassador did not distract her domestic critics for long. North of the border, she began to be identified as an English Sovereign. 'The Monarchy is less important and popular in Scotland and Wales', Nairn observed in 1988.[37] Celtic nationalism, in the form of outright separatism, had receded. Nevertheless a MORI poll at the beginning of 1991 showed more Scots in favour of an elected president (forty-eight per cent) than of retaining the Queen (forty-three per cent), should Scotland ever become independent.[38] In England, the focus in a gathering recession was on money. The war against Iraq was over: the guerrilla war over the Queen's finances was just beginning. In June 1991, the case of the pro-tax insurgents was powerfully strengthened by an ITV *World in Action* programme, in which a careful researcher, Philip Hall, convincingly demonstrated that the royal tax immunity was not an historic right but, on the contrary, had only been acquired in the twentieth century.

According to Hall's evidence, Queen Victoria and Edward VII had each paid income tax: the exemption had been acquired thereafter, in stages, over a period of forty years, by George V and George VI. Income tax had been paid by George V on investment revenue. It was not until the reign of the present Queen's father that the Inland Revenue had waived this as well. Hall's detailed study of the subject, *Royal Finances*, published at the beginning of 1992 – on which the programme was based – placed the Queen's private wealth at £341 million, a more modest total than the inclusive figure given by *Fortune* and *Harpers and Queen* but big enough to fuel the pro-tax campaign. What also fuelled the campaign was the discovery that there were almost no opponents. Alongside evidence of the history of adept Royal accounting, *World in Action* was able to produce keen supporters of the Monarchy, like Lord St John of Fawsley (the former Conservative minister, Norman St John Stevas), to argue that the exemption had become hard to defend and would eventually have to be modified.

Royal warnings that if the Queen paid tax she might have to sell Balmoral did not dampen discussion. Some even wondered whether reducing the number of royal residences might not be a sensible economy. Nor did the continued resistance of the Palace to requests for hard information about the royal fortune. By keeping silent, the Queen's advisers hoped to keep critics at bay. Instead, shyness on the topic had the opposite effect, adding – not just to wild speculation about what the Palace had to hide – but also to the sense of the Monarchy as an unaccountable vested interest. 'When the royal fortune is computed at anything between £100 million and a figure sixty times greater than that,' despaired the *Guardian*, 'how can a sensible reckoning be made between the Queen's rights and responsibilities?'[39]

The campaign continued through much of 1991. In July, the Liberal Democrat MP Simon Hughes introduced a ten-minute rule Bill which

called for equal opportunities in regard to the Throne, to give princesses the same chance of succession as princes. Hughes linked this
proposal to the now familiar demand that the Queen should pay tax
– which, because the Palace refused to respond, provided a licence to
criticize the Monarchy across a wide front. Even those who defended
the Queen's position felt constrained to do so whimsically, as if pro-
Monarchism with a straight face would appear pompous. There was
a self-consciously young fogey aspect to the argument of the journalist
Charles Moore, for instance, that Conservatives had forgotten what
the Monarchy was about. 'Many of the most republican newspapers,'
he wrote ' – the *Sun* for example, and the *Sunday Times* – are strongly
Tory and see no inconsistency in this.'[40]

By the beginning of 1992, there were more questions being asked
than ever before, and more caveats. 'To speak in rude and general
terms,' William Gladstone wrote after Prince Albert's death, 'the
Queen is invisible and the Prince of Wales is not respected.'[41] The press
began to study the history books, and draw a comparison. '. . . [T]he
Invisible Monarch,' one tabloid called Victoria's great-great-
granddaughter, '. . . apparently a victim of her own dullness.'[42]
Anthony Sampson recalled a conversation with Sir Michael Adeane
twenty years earlier, in which the then private secretary had reflected
on the hazards of 'the long reign ahead, like Queen Victoria's, when
a fickle public could tire of an ageing monarch and large family.'
Other courtiers, Sampson noted, had recently started to mutter about
'the problems of the QVS, the Queen Victoria Syndrome'.[43] With a
rise in talk of republicanism or – a familiar proposal, going back to
the 1940s – the 'Scandinavianization' of the British Monarchy, parallels
were drawn with the republican clubs of the late nineteenth century,
the huge anti-monarchist demonstration in Hyde Park in 1871, and
Charles Bradlaugh's protest, in the week after Victoria had asked
Parliament for financial provision for her son Arthur, against 'any
more grants to princely paupers.'[44]

There were other points of similarity. The 'Widow of Windsor,'
who virtually disappeared from public life, had been the butt of savage
populist humour. The same seemed to be happening to Elizabeth II.
At the beginning of the reign, it was forbidden to represent the Queen
on the stage, any kind of impolite caricature of the Monarch was

Above Syringa princess, 8th July 1941

Below Princess Elizabeth with her mother at the Derby, 4th June 1948, the day her pregnancy was announced

Previous page Detail of portrait by Michael Noakes, 1973, from the Collection of the Prince of Wales

Scene from *The Royal Family*, 1969

Children's Palace in Canton, October 1986

Above 'Give us a B . . .' Duchess of York as TV star, June 1987

Below The Queen with bride and bridesmaids, June 1981

Wet look. Diana the ambassadress, New York 1995

ASSOCIATED BRITISH-PATHE Present

WELCOME THE QUEEN! 'U'

IN TECHNICOLOR

Commentary written by JOHN PUDNEY · Narrator EDWARD WARD
Produced by HOWARD THOMAS   Associate Producer TERRY
ASHWOOD   Distributed by ASSOCIATED BRITISH-PATHE LTD.

The March "WELCOME THE QUEEN"
specially composed by Sir Arthur Bliss.
additional music by Malcolm Arnold.

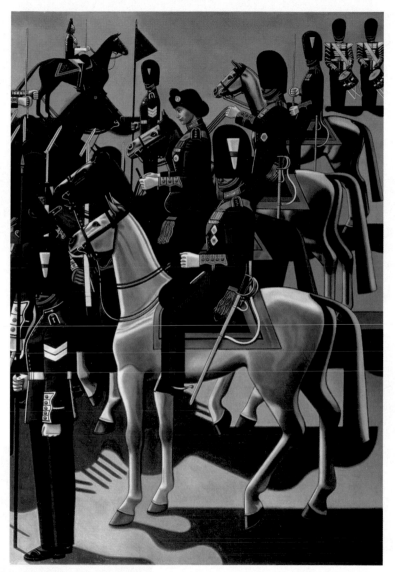

Detail of William Roberts *Trooping the Colour*, 1959

Opposite Iconography. *Top* Poster for a film marking the return of the Queen and Duke from the 1953–4 royal tour. *Left* Andy Warhol *Queen Elizabeth II of the United Kingdom*, 1985. *Bottom left* 'God Save the Queen' banned design for the Sex Pistols record sleeve, 1977; *bottom right Spitting Image* 1985

Top Queen Anne touching Dr Johnson, when a boy, for scrofula.

Middle Diana meets a resident of Lord Gage Centre, Newham, 1990.

Right 'The Apotheosis of Princess Charlotte Augusta', by Henry Howard, 1817.

unpublishable, and cartoon representations that appeared in obscure foreign newspapers provoked diplomatic incidents. By the 1990s, lampoons of the Queen were everywhere – in newspapers, in the theatre, on tee-shirts. On television, the Head of State and her family were portrayed as grotesque *Spitting Image* puppets – the Queen herself satirized, as one paper put it, 'as a dotty granny presiding over a loony soap opera'.[45]

However, the nineteenth-century comparison fell down on a number of points. Not only had Elizabeth inherited a more solidly based throne than her ancestor, she was not 'invisible'. Moreover, the contemporary Prince of Wales – despite tales of a disintegrating marriage – commanded enough respect for some to regard him as a more positive figure than his mother, and even as a possible substitute. Indeed, the vigorous public profile of Prince Charles – busying himself with community projects, and firing off strongly-worded speeches at various sections of the Establishment – helped to revive stories of an imminent abdication by the Queen in his favour, along the lines of the dignified retirement of Queen Juliana of the Netherlands in 1980. At the beginning of 1990, one poll showed that nearly half the population supported an abdication in favour of Charles 'at some stage'. At the end of 1991, the story became more concrete. It was widely predicted that the Queen would use her Christmas broadcast to declare her intention to step down on February 6th, the fortieth anniversary of the Accession.[46] The rumour, however, had no substance. In the broadcast, the Queen spoke pointedly of her hope to serve the nation and the Commonwealth 'for some years to come'. Allegedly, the words seriously upset the Prince of Wales.[47] There has been no need to repeat them.

Few celebrations accompanied the anniversary. The sense that the reign was not at its highest point discouraged any festivities, like those of the Silver Jubilee. A plan to erect a fountain in Parliament Square was dropped at the request of the Queen herself. Newspaper profiles registered the date with sympathy, more than with congratulations. *The Times* noted that the Monarchy was 'suffering the effect of the decade of Diana,' which had resulted in an unremitting focus on royal private lives – a development for which some Royal Family members were themselves responsible.[48] In the *Sunday Times*, Robert Harris

"I PREFERRED IT WHEN SHE JUST USED TO SHAKE HANDS!"

Sun, 20th August, 1992

wrote of the Monarchy's 'increasingly anomalous position.'[49] The *Observer* chivalrously acknowledged that it would be hard not to respect 'this level-headed, devoted, plain-speaking, commonsensical woman who inspires affection.' Then it got down to the business of taking the Monarchy apart – suggesting that the Queen should look for ways of 'reinforcing public confidence.'[50]

News or rumours of rending royal marriages added to the anomaly of the 'family on the throne' idea. The Waleses' difficulties had been known for some time. Evidence of the breakdown of the marriage of the Duke and Duchess of York, who officially separated the following March, seemed part of a pattern. The shock was small. Stories of the Duchess's flirtations, money-making activities and frequent holidays made it almost a relief, and few contemplated the possibility of her leave-taking as a national disaster. The question was where it would lead. If the Royal Family was still a model, what was it a model of? David Cannadine reflected the opinion of a new breed of 'constitution-alist' intellectuals when he denounced the Monarchy as 'passive, philistine, bewildered, anachronistic, obsessed with protocol and tradition and smothered in a courtly embrace redolent of quarter-deck attitudes and saddle soap.'[51] The ITV programme *This Week* claimed that the

Monarch herself was discriminatory to boot: only nine out of 891 royal employees, it revealed, came from ethnic minorities. Who was responsible? 'I don't blame the household for that', commented John Grigg, 'I blame her. I think you have to blame the boss.'[52]

Yet the marriage that had first been rumoured to be in difficulties, wasn't. The Queen and her husband had travelled a long way since the 'rift' stories, intermittently revived, of the 1950s. Much of their time was spent apart, because of separate engagements, interests and holidays, and there was a sense of them operating as separate royal units, with different interests and different if overlapping circles of friends. Nevertheless, those who saw the royal couple together regularly did not doubt the affection and regard they had for one another.

People continued to be startled by Philip: his brusqueness caused alarm, especially in an environment saturated with politeness. Some continued to feel that he had a grudge against the world. There were indelible images: one visitor to Balmoral vividly recalls the Queen's consort opening a door at the castle and – irritated by the sudden entry of two yapping dogs – setting about them vigorously with a stick. The incident seemed to symbolize how he dealt with people, including his family. 'The Duke has occasional snaps,' said a former aide, 'and he can be very intemperate and wounding without thinking.' With the Queen, however, there was a respectful and appreciative understanding. A leading courtier for twenty years, who does not mince his words about the younger royals, speaks of 'an amazingly successful' marriage – amazing partly because of the extent to which they lived their own lives, but also because of the sense of mutual dependence, after nearly half a century together. There was a reserved, yet visible, fondness. A friend who spent a few days on holiday with them alone, recalls 'an extremely relaxed relationship' between them. 'The only things they argued about were trees, or about their memories – and they did so without rancour or the remotest sense of animosity.' The Queen teased her husband in a laughing, uxorious way about something he had said or done – usually implying that he had been irrational or impulsive.

In the fourth and fifth decades of her reign, she was firmly settled in her routines. As a young woman, she had leant heavily on her courtiers, the starched shirts with encyclopedic memories. Now it was often the other way round: her aides, often a generation younger than her and with little knowledge of the functions of royalty, came to expect and rely on her long experience and judgement. Yet her instincts were against innovation, the deep conservatism of her temperament if anything growing with the passage of time. Tradition, the rhythm of the royal seasons, doing things the way they had always been done, were her best comfort. She remained uncompromisingly regal: when people contrasted the British monarchy with the Scandinavian ones, they generally had in mind the personal style of the Windsor incumbent, more than the difference in constitutional role.

She was the object of fantasy, but not the creator of it. The concreteness she applied to her rural pursuits she applied also to politics which, after horses, remained her major interest and about which she had become – surprisingly, to those with low expectations – highly knowledgeable. She conveyed no sense at all of Britain's relative decline, or – in her conduct of the office – of a loss of sovereignty within the tightening European Union. She took an interest in older people who had lived through or fought in the Second World War, and in the regiments with which she was associated. On state visits, she was a source of pride to accompanying British ministers and diplomats who valued her practised ability to show interest in everything, and to disguise exhaustion or boredom: this was in contrast to her husband, who frequently needed diversion. In domestic politics, she showed more interest in the people than the policies, and politicians who explained to her what they were doing, sensed a two-dimensional approach. 'The Queen never got engaged in a topic to the extent that she would mind becoming disengaged,' reflects one ex-minister.

'She doesn't weave fancy images about anything or anybody,' says a former aide. 'She accepts things as they are, enjoys them, but doesn't get excited by them – in the way that her sister might.' She lacked the gift – or perhaps, in a royal setting, the snare – of imagination. The countryside provided her aesthetic: appreciating beauty in nature, she made little pretence of valuing it in art or music, and she continued to take scant interest in her Collection. The gardens at Buckingham Palace – a dazzling parkland of trees, lawns and flowers – contained no work by the great British sculptors, the Moores, Frinks and Hepworths, of her reign, let alone foreign ones. Although by 1990s she had become so highly practiced – and had been through so many computations of the royal role – that public appearances held few remaining terrors, she continued to avoid making even the smallest off-the-cuff speech: her public jokes were always scripted ones. Her dealings with politicians and officials were appropriately friendly and courteous, and most of those who had worked closely with the Palace valued her – as they might a colleague who was not a rival – as somebody they could rely on and trust. But there was seldom much more. She was so used to asking polite, sensible questions to keep people happy, that she found it difficult to do so for any other purpose. 'It was her business to have a good relationship with the Prime Minister,' says a former senior mandarin. 'She never went beyond that in my experience.' One former Tory politician likens her, not unkindly, to a highly competent chairman of his constituency association women's committee. The mandarin puts it higher. 'She is a very cool, professional lady,'[53] he suggests.

TED HUGHES, the Poet Laureate, marked the fortieth anniversary of the Accession with a bleakly unsentimental poem that cut through fashionable criticism and described how many ordinary people related to the Queen – linking his own memory with what he saw as a shared experience. For many, he indicated, the Monarch was inescapably part of their lives:

> Just come of age
> I met her eyes
> Wide in surprise
> To have been
> Just made a Queen
> On a front page
> Forty years later
> Looking at her
> All see the Crown
> Some their mother
> One his wife
> Some their life

The date was also celebrated by a BBC documentary, *Elizabeth R*, made by Edward Mirzoeff, which showed the sixty-five year old Monarch at work and play, and included a voice-over commentary by the Queen herself. Like the Cawston film, this was the product of a year's shooting, in which the director and his team trailed their subject, with few restrictions on access. Though scarcely an informal glimpse it was a sensitive one, and – with the Queen soliloquizing about her role – constitutionally as important as any predecessor. It showed the Monarch meeting foreign Heads of State, preparing speeches, sifting through red boxes, making an official visit to Northern Ireland, meeting staff and patients at a hospice. One sequence covered at the CHOGM in Harare, Zimbabwe – and showed her first meeting with Nelson Mandela, recently released from prison.

The film includes frequent shots of the Queen having her portrait painted, wearing Garter Robes in the Yellow Room, talking incessantly about tourists she could see through the window ('Yes, yes, yes, yes,' replies the painter). Philip is a shadowy figure (in contrast to the prominent part he plays in *Royal Family*) with barely a walk-on role, and the Queen is presented as a woman alone. The most animated scene is at the Derby, when she suddenly darts forward, bird-like, to watch the race, before winning £16 in the Royal Box sweepstake. 'That's very good, a very nice mare,' Porchey, standing beside her, is heard to say. The Queen's own comments on being Monarch are mundane but believable. Of Prime Ministers she remarks 'they unburden themselves if they have any problems ... occasionally one can put one's point of view and perhaps they hadn't seen it from that angle.' Of herself, she says: 'In this existence, the job and the life go together – you can't really divide it up.'

The overall impression is of alert, practised, but not effortless, professionalism. When she talks to people she does so attentively and pleasingly: showing just the right degree of detached interest before passing on to the next person. 'You have to work out in your own mind the hard work and then what you enjoy in retrospect from it,' she reflects. 'I have a great feeling that, in the end, probably the training is the answer to a great many things. You can do a lot if you are properly trained – and I hope I have been'. It is as if she speaks of herself, not as the owner of the Royal Stables, but as the occupant of one of the stalls. Discussing the need for the next generation to commit themselves to the family business, she expresses trepidation.

'I think that this is what the younger members find difficult,' she says, '– the regimented side.'[54]

Some commentators complained that the film blandly ignored the controversy now raging round the Royal Family, and that it was revealing almost in spite of itself: the Monarch showing herself as old-fashioned, even antiquarian in her attitudes, and out of touch with the lives of her subjects. Others felt that, despite the strange world of castles and ceremonials she inhabited, the personality conveyed was sterling and even likeable. 'Most public comment on the film was indiscriminately favourable,' observed Grigg, 'which surely was an unhealthy sign.'[55] There was none of the shock-of-the new of *Royal Family*, first shown twenty-three years before.

The Cawston documentary had been a fly-on-the-wall account of a busy working life. *Elizabeth R* was closer to a self-appraisal, looking back. Alexander Chancellor, former editor of the *Spectator*, saw it as a propaganda film dedicated to the task of presenting the Queen as a dutiful public servant. He reckoned that up to a point it worked: the Monarch seemed to be 'an engaging and rather quirky character, but also a woman who is curiously detached – perhaps even a little cold.'[56] There was also a disconcerting sense of peering into a mausoleum. 'The Queen came across as having an enormous sense of humour,' observed Alan Hamilton of *The Times*. 'She needs it in a job like that.'[57]

B AD PUBLICITY did not stay within the confines of the United Kingdom. It was one of the Queen's misfortunes that what the *Guardian* called 'the soapy glamour of beautifully groomed young people doing expensive things'[1] was almost as fascinating to Americans and Germans as it was to Britons. In a very immediate sense, royalty was the public face of Britain abroad. Often, the only news about the United Kingdom the editors of foreign newspapers deemed worth reporting concerned the behaviour and misbehaviour of the Royal Family. The point was underlined in February 1992, when the Queen visited Australia for the 150th anniversary celebrations of Sydney City Council. On her arrival, she discovered not only that talk of the young royals had preceded her, but that it had become embarrassingly mixed up with the latest battle over the future of the Constitution. The change of attitude to the Queen was made disconcertingly apparent by Paul Keating, the Labour Prime Minister, whose party was pledged to make Australia a republic by the year 2001. In his welcoming speech, Keating emphasized the importance to Australia of its strengthening ties within the region. His words were directed at his own constituency of republican supporters, and he seemed almost to treat his guest as an irrelevance.

The republican movement had crept up on Australia in a way that served as a warning to the Monarchy at home not to take the popular support it might receive, at any particular moment, for granted. At the time of the Coronation, monarchism had been almost as universal in Australia as in the United Kingdom. Only fifteen per cent, according to polls, favoured the idea of a republic. Thereafter, the figure gently drifted upwards. In the mid 1980s the proportion of the population wanting to keep the Monarchy, against those who wished to dispense with it, was still two to one – although pro-monarchists were showing a declining level of commitment.

A number of factors contributed to the gradual disengagement. One was the weakening of economic ties, especially following Britain's entry into the European Community. Another was the reduction of strategic ones, following British withdrawal 'East of Suez.' A third was the fast increase in the proportion of the population of non-British descent, accelerated by the dropping of a 'whites only' immigration policy. To many Australians, especially younger ones, the British Royal Family had come to be seen, in the words of the author Thomas Kenneally, chairman of the republican movement, as no more than 'intriguing relics . . . of a world which has almost gone.'[2] In 1981, the Australian Labour Party incorporated a republican objective into its platform – almost casually, and apparently as a result of a slow and cumulative erosion of sentiment, rather than because of a crusade.[3]

In the 1980s, the last remnants of the constitutional link with Britain were eliminated, apart from the Crown itself. In March 1986, the Queen had visited the country to sign the Proclamation of the Australia Act, which abolished the right of Australians to appeal to the Privy Council. The following year, a constitutional commission set up by the federal attorney-general, Lionel Bowen, recommended that the Queen's residual powers to veto legislation should be abolished. Other symbolic changes included the replacing of 'God Save the Queen' as the national anthem by 'Advance Australia Fair'. In 1990, Queensland, the most royalist state, voted to end the honours system. Meanwhile Bob Hawke, as Prime Minister, appointed a committed republican, Bill Hayden, as Governor-General. The Queen's lukewarm reception in 1992 compared with earlier visits was thus part of a process which most observers accepted would eventually lead to a complete severance.

The antics of the younger royals, in this context, fuelled the arguments of republicans and embarrassed the defenders of the Monarchy. They were also a distraction at home, where a public preference for royal gossip over the latest trade figures or white paper, threatened to obscure the political debate, as Parliament approached the end of its longest term since 1964. In the spring of 1992 the private problems of the Duke and Duchess of York took up more and more space in the newspapers, swamping discussion of party policy. The dissolution took place on March 16th, shortly after the Queen's return from her tour. The general election, fixed for April 9th, promised to be the most hard fought since Mrs Thatcher had been elected to office almost thirteen years before, and – for the first time – Labour had a good chance of winning. The tabloids, however, were full of Fergie and her relationship with a Texan oil millionaire, Steve Wyatt – a topic which, the papers' editors believed, would sell more copies that the latest speech by Major or Kinnock.

The stories were accompanied by hints that more would follow. It did. On the same day as the dissolution, Buckingham Palace briskly announced that the Duke and Duchess of York were to separate. The statement indicated that the decision had been made by the Duchess, and that its exquisitely self-centred timing was her responsibility. It also made clear that the Queen was displeased by the behaviour of her daughter-in-law, and that she blamed her for leaks to the press. Those who spoke to Palace officials were surprised by the degree of irritation the Duchess had caused, and by the openness of criticism of her, including the suggestion that she was unfit for royal or public life.[4] 'Vulgar, vulgar, vulgar,' was how Lord Charteris, the Queen's former private secretary, later described her in a *Spectator* interview, not intending his words to be published. At least one member of the royal staff cheerfully acknowledges the almost physical difficulty he experienced when required to bow to the Duchess. A close friend of the Queen refers to her as 'muck'.[5] At the annual Holyrood House garden party in Edinburgh that summer, Anthony Sampson heard courtiers 'talking unusually candidly about some of their concerns: about the relentless siege by the world's media, the inexhaustible appetite for scandals, the over-extended family, and the impossibility of answering back.'[6]

In the reputable press, there was still a tendency to separate the difficulties of the Royal Family as a whole from the Monarch herself, 'a great panjandrum,' as Christopher Wilson described her in the *Daily Express*, 'above the vulgar gossip which billows round the feet of the young royals.'[7] However, this habit – the last relic of traditional deference – soon became impossible to sustain. The Palace statement

about the Yorks, intended to end speculation during an election campaign, was accompanied by a widespread feeling of relief, of good
riddance, and by an absurd hope that, with a disagreeable business
out of the way, things might get better. In fact, they got worse. Every
passing month of the fortieth anniversary year of the Accession seemed
to bring a new embarrassment, humiliation, error, or accusation, with
the Queen, as head of both the institution and the family, inextricably
involved. The sequence of events was like a list of battles in the rout
of a once proud army: in January the publication of photographs of
Fergie with Steve Wyatt on a Mediterranean holiday, in February the
image of 'Diana alone' on a trip to the Taj Mahal during a visit by
the Waleses to India, in March the Yorks' separation announcement,
together with claims in a book by Lady Colin Campbell of Diana's
close relationship with four men, in April the divorce of Princess
Anne and Mark Phillips, in May the departure of Fergie from Sunninghill Park taking her daughters with her.

The main course was provided by the problems of the Prince and
Princess of Wales. In retrospect – in view of the episodes apart, semi-
public quarrels, and heart-to-hearts with garrulous friends – the
remarkable thing is that the details remained secret for so long. The

Sun, 29th February, 1992

Queen and Prince Philip chose not to notice. When Diana turned up late for meals, or left them early without explanation, her behaviour was ignored. According to friends, Charles blamed his parents for not being more supportive. 'He felt very let down by his unsympathetic mother and father,' says a confidante. 'When his marriage went wrong, he felt criticized by them.' Perhaps they were more concerned than they seemed. 'The Queen was aware of stresses and strains,' says a courtier from the period. 'She was wholly sympathetic towards Charles – in fact rather one-eyed in her approach.' On one occasion the Queen and her husband dined *à quatre* with friends whose own children also had troublesome marriages, for the specific purpose of 'wondering together where they went wrong'. To others who knew the couple well, the gap between the gauchely reflective Prince and the sharp, whimsical, brittle Princess was obvious within a year of their wedding. 'The only thing Charles wanted,' says a relative, 'was a happy marriage.'[8] Friends of his wife said much the same about Diana. Wanting a happy marriage, however, and being happy in the company of the person you are married to are not the same thing: and to be locked into a famous and visible union in which neither party felt comfortable, yet whose most intimate moments had a public importance, was a very special form of suffering.

The difficulties of the Prince and Princess had long been the subject of rumour – but little of it backed by hard fact, and most only half-believed by non-tabloid readers. This position changed in June 1992, when the *Sunday Times* began the serialization of *Diana: Her True Story*, by Andrew Morton, a young journalist who had for some time taken a close interest in royalty. The book was a breakthrough, and its impact stunning. Not only did it substantiate its account with carefully checked evidence and authenticated quotation. Any doubt that the core of Morton's information came from friends of one of the main characters with her encouragement or connivance was dispelled when the Princess, given the opportunity to reject the account, declined to do so. In a way, it was the logical outcome of the trend towards openness, ending a century and a half of royal reserve on personal matters and replacing it with the opposite: royal exhibitionism.

Readers were intrigued to be told, and the Royal Family was horrified for the world to be informed, that while pregnant with a potential future king, the Princess of Wales had deliberately thrown herself down the wooden staircase at Sandringham; that she had slashed her wrists with a razor blade; and that, in an attempt to rescue her from the terrible psychic consequences of becoming one of the most admired women in the world, she had been dispatched to a succession of therapists. The important point about the book, however, was that much of it – including the account of the Waleses' unhappy marriage and the Princess's psychological disorders, hitherto unknown or only guessed at – rang true.

It was a new kind of book, for a new generation: although its style was that of a romantic novel, it could not be dismissed as scandal-mongering. It did not belong to the kiss-and-tell genre that began with Crawfie, or even the Insight Team approach that started with Robert Lacey. The story was a moral classic about a young woman who had entered the legendary world which millions dreamt about, and who found that the 'model family' was, indeed, a myth. Its power derived, not just from a voyeuristic interest in well-sourced details about people everybody already had in their imagination, but from the narrative skill of the author. Morton wrote with sensitivity of the Princess, but he also revealed the bleakness of the milieu from which she came, and the sorry deprivation of her background, disguised by class and money.

People who had half-envied recruits to the Royal Family, but also, with their other half, been appalled by the prospect, had their more rational feelings confirmed. Perhaps it was this, more than anything, that fascinated: the transition from kindergarten teacher (albeit a posh one) to the idol of billions, a leap which anybody could make, provided the right person fell in love with them. What was it like? 'One minute I was nobody,' Morton quoted Diana as saying to friends, 'the next minute I was Princess of Wales, mother, member of this family and it was too much for one person to handle.'

There was also another aspect of the book. If it presented the Princess as vulnerable and unable to cope, it also took up cudgels on her behalf – painting a hostile portrait of her husband, and blaming him both for his lack of understanding and for his continuing relationship with Camilla Parker Bowles. At the same time, Morton presented the Royal Family not as a haven of domestic virtue but as unhelpful and self-absorbed. The strongest theme of the book – and the strongest theme of the Princess – was a juxtaposition of warmth and coldness. On the one hand, there was Diana, 'tactile, emotional, gently irreverent and spontaneous,' who was quoted as saying 'I hug my children to death and get into bed with them at night. I always feed them love and affection, it's so important.' On the other, there was the picture of the icy Windsors, with their unfriendly mansions where the Princess found the atmosphere so dispiriting that it was liable to bring on a bulimia attack. There was little direct criticism of the Queen, either by the author, or by Diana, who declared that she had 'a deep respect' for the Queen's work, and had told her 'I will never let you down'.[9] However, the impression conveyed by the book was of a family whose emotional temperature was low, and in which relationships were strained, distant and did not work. It was a tale which, after a surfeit of young royals for a dozen years or more, the public was ready to hear. By early the following year, the book had sold four and a half million copies world-wide.

'Just a little reminder, Charles,' teased the *Sun*, not a tabloid to refrain from kicking a man when he was down, on July 28th, '. . . it's your wedding anniversary tomorrow, and heaven knows you've had problems.' The problems, however, were not just visited on Charles. The resounding journalistic and commercial success of *Diana: Her True Story* made it inevitable that more would follow. A couple of decades earlier, a seriously negative report about the Queen's family would have been unprintable. Now, the opposite was the case: a bounty hunt for worse revelations, grimmer details, wider scandals, began in earnest. At a time of what the *Guardian* called a 'simmering circulation war'[10] between the major tabloids, the Morton book released all inhibitions. In August, the *Daily Mirror* scored a spectacular coup when it published a picture of the Duchess of York – who, though separated, was still married to the Duke – bare-breasted beside a pool, with another friend, John Bryan, who was kissing her toes. The simmering war became total: editors ransacked attics for old material which, in the past, had seemed too damaging to use.[11] One sensational scoop deserved another: the *Sun* retaliated against its rival with the two-and-a-half-year-old tape recording of a telephone conversation, apparently picked up on New Year's Eve 1989 by a radio ham, in which the Princess of Wales spoke with great affection to a friend, James Gilbey, who referred to her as 'Squidgy' or 'Squidge'. In it, she described her marriage as 'torture,' and gave an account of the Royal Family that fitted the version her friends (including Gilbey) had given Morton. She also spoke of the Royal Family distancing itself from her, supposedly out of jealousy, because of her success with the public. 'The distancing will be because I go out and – I hate the word – conquer the world,' she was heard to say. She also spoke of the strange way the Queen Mother, another Royal Family recruit, looked at her ('It's not hatred, it's sort of interest and pity'), of her depression, and of her difficulty at family meals at Sandringham, where she was staying. 'I was very bad at lunch and I nearly started blubbing,' said the Princess's voice. 'I just felt really sad and empty and thought "bloody hell, after all I've done for this fucking family" . . .'[12]

More tapes followed – raising the question of whether the eaves-dropping, always presented as an accident, was actually the product of an undercover operation. Dianagate was followed by Fergiegate – consisting of tapes of conversations between the Duke and Duchess of York, which revealed the Duchess's disappointment with married and royal life, as early as 1990. In September, it was reported that another friend of Diana, Major James Hewitt, issued a High Court libel writ against the *Sun*, following reports about his relationship with her. In November – while tabloid photographers tracked every facial muscle for a symptom of mutual hostility whenever the Prince and Princess of Wales appeared in public together – the transcript of yet another illicit recording, the 'Camillagate' tape, was published. In this, the most sensational recorded conversation so far, the Prince of Wales spoke to his mistress touchingly and absurdly, and with reckless indiscretion. 'Your great achievement is to love me,' the Prince was heard to say. 'I'd suffer anything for you. That's love. It's the strength of love,' Mrs Parker Bowles was heard to reply. Diana had used the word 'fucking' on her tape; Charles made a harmless (until the whole world got to hear about it) joke about a tampon. The *Sun* asked its readers whether it should publish the conversation in full, and called on them to ring a printed number. Some 21,000 were prurient enough to do so.

*   *   *

THE MOMENTS when the 'toe-sucking' and 'Squidgy' stories became public were not comfortable ones at Balmoral, where much of the Royal Family was assembled. 'What do you all do?' Princess Margaret said to a friend later. 'We all had to come down to breakfast anyway.'[13] The Queen kept off the topic, and guests did not raise it. People in bus queues, or on television comedy programmes, imposed no such self-restraint. The sheer indignity of the way in which Fergie had been caught *in flagrante* became a national joke, while the current focus of Diana's romantic interest was turned into a national guessing game. In addition to the marital difficulties and careless behaviour of the younger members of the Royal Family, there was also the perennial issue of money, which – because it touched the Queen directly, and also touched the public in their pockets – mattered as much, if not more. Of course, the two were linked. When the Monarchy was at its most popular, the question of how it was financed could be dealt with comparatively easily, by a grateful Government and Parliament. Vulnerability on one aspect of royal life, however, increased vulnerability on the other.

In August 1992, there were hints that the Queen, long under pressure over the tax exemption, was 'voluntarily' considering paying income tax. The Royal Household, led by the Lord Chamberlain, had been asked to examine the problem. Against a background of opinion polls which showed eighty per cent of the population in favour of such a move, there was reported to be strong support for it in the Palace, and especially from Prince Charles. 'It looks like a convenient smoke screen at a time when the Royal Family is being battered,' said Andrew Morton, in his role as scourge of the Monarchy.[14] In fact, discussions had been going on for some time. 'It was partly reactive,' acknowledges a leading member of the Household. 'However, the decision to pay tax was actually taken before the two broken marriages and the tapes.' A working party with the Treasury on royal tax had been set up in February – the month before the Yorks' official separation. The Queen was neither in favour, nor opposed. But she no longer resisted. 'Her line was that she accepted it, if that was the recommendation and it was felt appropriate,' says the same source.[15] The process of discussion, however, took an unconscionable length of time: in retrospect, the Palace would have done better to have pre-empted speculation by making an early announcement. Its failure to do so meant that when the announcement eventually came, it looked as if it had been forced.

In September, the Murdoch-owned press, sensing a popular theme, launched a new attack on the Queen for her failure to pay tax. 'The *Sun* is not amused,' announced the tabloid, adding, 'we can no longer sit in silence while the royals self-destruct.'[16] In addition to the tax issue, there was the question of the 1990 Civil List deal, which was working out better than either the Government or the Palace had expected. On September 13th, Robert Sheldon, the Labour Chairman of the Public Accounts Committee, called on the Queen to make a 'voluntary adjustment' to the current arrangement, in view of falling inflation. He also suggested that, for good measure, she might say something about taxation on her own personal income at the same time.[17] Sheldon's appeal was backed by Tory backbench calls for the Civil List to be cut. One newspaper, observing the bi-partisan nature of the criticism, claimed that 'a wave of anti-royal feeling' was sweeping the country.[18] A fortnight later it was reported that the Prime Minister was planning to limit the Civil List to three members of the Royal Family, instead of eleven, as part of a constitutional settlement under which the Queen would begin to pay tax.[19] The report, however, was not confirmed.

Both Government and Palace were shortly overtaken by events. On 20th November, a fire broke out at Windsor Castle. It was not the first time such an accident had occurred. Six years previously, Hampton Court had been devastated by a fire that killed an elderly widow who lived in a grace-and-favour apartment, and destroyed several state apartments and much of the roof. Nobody died in the Windsor fire, but the damage it caused was much worse. It started in the private chapel in the north-east part of the Castle, and spread. Although most of the furniture and paintings were in store, the state dining room and three drawing rooms were badly damaged, and several roofs collapsed.

While the fire was still burning, Prince Andrew held an impromptu press conference, describing his mother as 'shocked and devastated'.[20] Philip, in Argentina for a conference, spent hours on the phone, trying to console her.[21] At home the 'anti-royal feeling' was replaced by a wave of sympathy, encouraged by images of the bent and distraught

Monarch as she watched firemen fighting the blaze. However, sympathy was sharply reduced when the Heritage Secretary, Peter Brooke, in what he imagined would be a popular move, declared that as the Castle was uninsured, the Government would pay the repair bill, estimated at between £20m and £40m. In another era, such an announcement might have seemed fitting. In the current climate, and in the context of discussions about the Queen's wealth and tax exemption, the bland announcement that the taxpayer should subsidize what was still largely a private palace, caused uproar.

Polls showed an overwhelming dissatisfaction with the Government's decision. There had been minor protests in 1987, when it was announced that the Department of the Environment would pay a £2m bill for the rebuilding of Frogmore House.[22] This, however, was a different proposition. Not only was the amount much larger. There was also a feeling that the same standards ought to apply to the Queen as to her subjects. People who paid insurance premiums on their own houses could relate to the Queen's predicament, but could see no reason why she should not have shared their prudence. Thus, the Windsor fire – which might have revived awareness of the historic role of the Monarchy, and brought a rallying of support for it – led to a huge revolt of public opinion on the topic of royal wealth and privilege in general.

On November 24th, four days after the fire, the Queen used the opportunity of an anniversary speech at the Guildhall to respond to the growing chorus of criticism, on a range of issues, and the implications for the institution she embodied. Perhaps it was an indication of the past success of the Monarchy, or of its hidebound nature, that such a thing had never happened before in the four decades of her reign. Speaking in a voice that was still hoarse, as one commentator noted, from a cold exacerbated by visits to the fire,[23] she departed from the platitudes expected at such an event, and referred to her own recent experience. '1992 is not a year on which I shall look back with undiluted pleasure,' she said – a wry understatement that suggested her own involvement in the drafting. 'In the words of one of my more sympathetic correspondents, it has turned out to be an *annus horribilis*.' This was the phrase that was remembered. The important part of the speech, however, was elsewhere, when she made a well-considered retreat from the position that had existed since the nineteenth century, effectively acknowledging that there could be no holding back the debate that had already begun. 'No institution,' she declared '– City, Monarchy, whatever – should expect to be free from the scrutiny of those who give it their loyalty and support, not to mention those who don't.' It was a bold move. Yet there was a bleakness about the speech, as well as the delivery of it, that made it seem more of an appeal for forbearance and understanding than an invitation to discuss reform. 'Forty years is a long time,' she ended, flatly. 'I am glad to have had the chance to witness, and to take part in, many dramatic changes in life in this country.'

The speech was noted as a political one. 'She is entitled to defend herself,' said the new Labour Leader, John Smith, who was among the guests, 'and she did it rather wittily and rather charmingly.'[24] Others felt that it offered too little, too late. 'Please be kind to us,' interpreted the *Daily Mail*, while the *Sun* – in a coarse pun on 'Annus' – translated it into 'One's Bum Year.' To Hugo Young, a Catholic, it 'sounded like an act of penitence. Appealing for decency, it relinquished command . . .' He blamed successive Prime Ministers since 1952 for ducking the question of monarchical reform.[25] There was a recession: some critics pointed out that, if the Queen had had a bum year, so had many of her subjects.

It soon became plain that the speech was intended as a prologue. On November 26th, the question of reform was partially answered – or, at least, a basic step was taken. In a statement to the House of Commons, the Prime Minister announced that the Queen and the Prince of Wales would pay tax on their private income from 1993, and that £900,000 Civil List payments to five other members of the Royal Family would be ended. John Major told the House that the initiative had come from the Monarch herself, and that the decision had been made the previous summer.

According to Lord Airlie, at an unprecedented press conference when the full details were announced, three months later, the Queen 'asked me in February last year' to look at the feasibility of paying tax.[26] 'We had been working on the Queen's tax for months,' says a leading courtier. 'When the fire came, we weren't actually finished, though it was nine-tenths done. It was very bad luck. The plan had been that it would take effect from April 1st 1993, and it would have been announced in the New Year. Then this thing overtook us, we needed to move fast, and it looked as if we had been pressurized.'[27] In politics, however – even royal politics – appearances matter, and getting the timing right is critically important. It was impossible to present the tax decision as a spontaneous gesture at a time when demands for the Queen to be taxed had become almost impossible to resist. Airlie half admitted as much in his statement. The inquiry, he declared, was conducted because of an 'increasing emphasis on wealth, tax and the Civil List, and against the background of the increasingly severe recession,'[28] which was tantamount to acknowledging that political criticism was a factor.

'The whole business was badly handled,' says a former adviser to Prince Charles. 'Effectively, the Queen agreed to pay tax as a result of a tabloid campaign'.[29] That was the overwhelming impression. The Queen's offer, wrote Alexander Chancellor, a former editor of the *Spectator*, voicing the assumption of Right as well as Left, 'was announced so late that it could only seem a panicky response to mounting public indignation over the behaviour of her children and the tendency of her palaces to catch fire.'[30] The *Sun* which had been campaigning for such a change, was in no doubt about who deserved credit for it. 'The Queen pays tax and it's victory for people power,' it boasted.[31]

The change when it came, was more than a token one. It constituted not only a major concession to demands that had been growing since the Select Committee more than two decades before, but also a revolution in the financing of royalty.

'The Queen is a very pragmatic person,' as Michael Peat, who had been recruited from the Queen's auditors to become the Household's Director of Finance and Property Services, put it in a television interview. 'She appreciates that there is a general feeling that she should pay tax.'[32] The terms of the 'voluntary' deal spelt out by the Prime Minister in February 1993 detailed the full extent of the reform. Tax would not be paid on what were regarded as public assets, or on the use of the royal yacht, the royal train and the Queen's flight; money paid by the Queen to her mother and husband as expenses would be tax deductible; and no inheritance tax would be paid on bequests to the next Sovereign. But tax would be paid on private assets; bequests to the Queen's other children would not be exempt from inheritance tax; the Queen would return to the Treasury the Civil List money voted to all members of her family except herself, her husband and her mother. Adjustments would also be made to the contributions made by the Prince of Wales to the Treasury from the profits of the Duchy of Cornwall.

If the Palace hoped for media gratitude, it was disappointed. The response of much of the press was, at best, grudging – with a suggestion that the Monarchy had offered too little, too late. The *Daily Mirror* claimed that the exemptions were excessive, and accompanied its report with a front-page cartoon of the Queen as a scrooge-like miser – the cruellest picture, as one observer remarked, ever printed outside the underground press – beside the headline HM THE TAX DODGER.[33] Others complained about a lack of clarity over the distinction between 'public' and 'private' royal wealth. ('Are both Sandringham and Buckingham Palace really so vital to the Queen's public duties,' asked the *Guardian*, 'that they each deserve to be exempted from inheritance tax?') There was also dissatisfaction that neither the amount of tax paid, nor the size of the fortune, would be revealed – even though the Lord Chamberlain was at pains to play down high estimates of the latter. The Queen had authorized him to say, he declared, that an estimate of £100m (one of the lowest) was 'greatly over-stated'.[34] Nevertheless, the package took the sting out of the major complaint which had done significant damage to the standing of the Monarchy over a period of years and which, if left unrectified, would certainly have done more.

The settlement did not resolve the Queen's other difficulties. Indeed, *annus horribilis* was not yet over. On December 9th, Buckingham Palace announced the separation of the Prince and Princess of Wales, a decision which may have been hastened by the Morton book and subsequent revelations but which, most people agreed, had long been inevitable. Unlike the two previous marriage breakdowns among the Queen's children, it raised immediate and serious dynastic issues. In a House of Commons statement, the Prime Minister insisted that there was no question of a divorce; and that, moreover, in the event of Charles becoming King, Diana would automatically become Queen.

But there was also the matter of access to the children, and decisions about the education and upbringing of the second and third in line to the Throne. As if to emphasize the problems that lay ahead for the Waleses' fractured family, it was revealed that the Princess had turned down an invitation to spend Christmas with the Royal Family, and so would not be seeing her children on Christmas Day.

Annus horribilis had one final kick. After a year that had seen the divorce of one of the Queen's children, the separation of two others, and the burning of her favourite official residence, together with a level of adverse comment on the Monarchy never before known, it was natural that the Queen's Christmas Day broadcast should arouse particular media interest. In it, the Monarch dealt with her own private difficulties with dignity, downplaying without avoiding them. She referred to the inspiration she had drawn from the courage of Leonard Cheshire, in his terminal illness. Her meeting with him, she said 'did as much as anything to help me to put my other worries into perspective.' She also spoke of her own, and her family's 'commitment to your service in the coming year'. The impact of the message, however, was reduced by another tabloid scoop. Ignoring normal embargo rules, the *Sun* coolly published the text of the broadcast two days before its delivery. The Queen, officially described as 'very, very distressed' by the *Sun's* action, sued for breach of copyright. At first, the paper seemed set to fight. Then it climbed down, apparently on orders from Rupert Murdoch. In a rare victory for the Palace, it agreed to pay legal costs, and £200,000 to charity.[35]

The *Sun's* capitulation may have reflected a feeling at the top of the Murdoch empire that the Queen herself retained a modicum of public sympathy, whatever people might feel about her children and their spouses. However, the cheekiness of the tabloid, and quality, press did not diminish. Calls for a slimmed down Monarchy became widespread, and the Queen, who had no critics who dared to reveal themselves early in her reign, now seemed to have few defenders among journalists and politicians. Though party leaders and other prominent members of the Establishment avoided joining in the chorus of detractors, few chose to give the existing system an open endorsement. One prominent member of the Government who did rally to her support, was Douglas Hurd, the Foreign Secretary, who

– in a thoughtful speech to the Foreign Press Association just after the tax announcement – argued that the Monarchy would continue to have an important role as a bulwark of British independence within the European Union. He also pointed to the danger wanton attacks could cause to the institution, and the individual, at the heart of the British political system. The constitutional monarchy, he declared, was 'not some trifling toy which can be tossed about in public controversy as if damaging it did no harm.'[36] His speech was politely reported, but little noted. Fashion was moving fast the other way.

IF THE MONARCHY was at the heart of the British system, it had by now become peripheral to the Australian one. Indeed domestic Australian opinion appeared to be flowing rapidly towards republicanism, for reasons largely unconnected with the behaviour of the Royal Family. To the swelling population of non-British descent the Monarchy meant virtually nothing. 'We have to become our own nation,' declared Malcolm Turnbull, Chairman of the Republican Advisory Committee, voicing what had become an increasingly conventional opinion, 'no longer defined by reference to another country.'[37]

At the beginning of 1993, Keating won an election, with an increased majority, fighting on a republican platform. One of his first acts after the poll was to set up a constitutional commission to prepare the way for a referendum. 'The Queen of Australia is not Australian and however conscientiously and skilfully she performs the role of Australian Head of State, she cannot symbolise or express our Australianness,' he declared in August.[38] The speech could be taken as a vindication of the Altrincham proposal, more than thirty-five years before, that the Queen should establish residences in countries of which she was Head of State. John Grigg, writing in May, did not exactly say 'I told you so'. But he did write that if, following Keating's victory, Australia became a republic, it would be largely the Queen's fault, for allowing herself to be known there only as an occasional visitor.[39] However, by the time that Keating visited Britain in September, partly to prepare the way, British opinion was well adjusted to the idea of Australia's evolution, and considered it, in the words of the *Guardian*, 'a perfectly natural one for a distant and mature democracy'. The Queen's own attitude appeared to be one of calm acceptance of what increasingly looked inevitable.

Yet predictions that the Queen was about to become a 'Britain only' monarch were premature. In Australia, the pro-Monarchy lobby still had some resilience, and a constitutional card to play. While royal portraits came down in town halls all over the country, Queensland announced a review of every reference to 'the Crown' in its procedures, and surveys showed that eighty per cent of eighteen to twenty-year-olds wanted a republic. But most people did not care: or care enough to make it worth the while of politicians to break down the barriers to reform. To produce a republic required not only a majority in a referendum, but also the support of four out of six states – which was likely to depend, in the end, on the current standing of any government that tried to push through such a change. In 1996, Keating's ambition to achieve a republic by the first year of the next century received a major setback when his government was defeated in a general election. Yet even strong monarchophiles accepted that the election result merely delayed what was bound eventually to come. One former courtier suggested that the Queen would do well to seize the moment, with pressure reduced, to indicate privately to the present Prime Minister, John Howard, 'that they should move forward with her blessing'.[40]

The Australian movement raised the possibility of a chain reaction. Republicanism had been the norm, since the beginning, among 'new' Commonwealth states, with only some of the smaller independent nations deviating from the pattern. In recent years, however, those countries which had kept the Queen as head of state had felt little inclination to change. In the wake of the Australian movement, talk increased. At the Commonwealth Conference in Cyprus in October 1993, the Queen anticipated possible pressures by declaring her willingness to accept a severance wherever that was the popular wish.[41] In addition to Canada, where the Queen now had a status that was little more than nominal, possible 'defectors' included New Zealand, Jamaica, and Papua New Guinea – that is, all the remaining countries with a population greater than a few hundred thousand. If these became republics, the Queen's constitutionally divided status would virtually end, applying only to a few scattered islands and territories.

The anomalous position of Hong Kong was due to end on 1st July 1997, when China recovered sovereignty.

However, there was no stampede. Whilst Australians confronted the constitutional complexities that shedding the Queen entailed, Canadians found in the Monarchy a part of their national identity which distinguished them from Americans, and New Zealanders saw it as something that differentiated them from disloyal Australians. Meanwhile, the Commonwealth itself showed no sign of incipient disintegration or a desire for a different Head. In Cyprus, the Queen reflected that she would have been surprised, at the beginning of her reign, to know how many Commonwealth countries there would be forty years later – and, as a racing woman, she would not bet on how many there might be forty years hence. In fact, there was shortly to be an important addition. The day after South Africa officially became a democracy, President de Klerk, en route to Oslo to collect his joint Nobel Peace Prize, visited the Queen – the first South African leader to do so since the country left the Commonwealth, to avoid being expelled, in 1961.[42] The subject of South Africa's return was discussed. The following year, it was re-admitted. In March 1995, the Queen returned to the country for the first royal visit since she had travelled there, with her parents and sister, in 1947 and made her extraordinary vow, which she had kept.

She was welcomed by President Mandela and by the African population with whom she had kept faith even, as many believed, against her own Prime Ministers. 'I expect hundreds of people will come limping forward saying I remember dancing with you nearly fifty years ago,' a close relative said to her just before the trip. 'You were quite right,' said the Queen when she got back, 'they did'. But it was the response in the townships that took the British party by surprise. Here, too, the memory and the context was 1947 – but also the decades in between. Black Africans of all ages lined the streets, as for no other foreign visitor, shouting their welcome, and waving banners saying 'Thank you for coming back'.[43]

THE QUEEN'S Guildhall challenge was largely ignored by politicians. However it fed into an intellectual debate about the Monarchy which had begun in the 1980s, and had been vigorously stoked by the Murdoch-owned quality newspapers. While there was no conclusive evidence of Rupert Murdoch's republican sympathies, there was plenty of the Australian-turned-American proprietor's indifference to the Monarchy's fate; or, alternatively, of his willingness to give the editors of his British papers their head on a circulation-boosting topic.

In a way, the most striking symptom of the way the world had turned upside down on the royalty question was the behaviour of *The Times*, traditional thunderer on behalf of Establishment values, which had taken a keen, protective interest in the Royal Family's marital intentions, and had blacked Altrincham's criticisms of the Queen and Buckingham Palace in 1957, on the grounds of their impertinent disloyalty. Now the same paper sponsored the first ever major conference on the Monarchy, organized by Charter 88, a left-of-centre reform group which advocated a Bill of Rights and a written constitution, and included outspoken republicans among its leading members. The event took place (appropriately) at the Elizabeth II Centre in Westminster and gathered political, legal, journalistic, theatrical and literary personalities from across the spectrum, as well as members of the royalty-interested public.

Despite the Guildhall gauntlet, there was still a sense of derring-do, of breaking through a final barrier, about such an unprecedented event, as anarchist poets mingled with ex-courtiers and ate Mr Murdoch's lunch. There were token defenders. Charles Moore, representing the *Daily Telegraph* right, made a withering comparison between anti-monarchy constitutional reformers and enthusiasts for a public building recently erected at St Pancras. 'The new British Constitution could so easily become a political version of the new British Library,' he warned, '– expensive, unnecessary, unpopular, ugly, slow to come into use and out-of-date before it is even constructed.' For most contributors, however, the once-untouchable institution was in the dock. Some suggested a clipping of the Civil List, and of the last vestiges of the Monarchy's constitutional power. Others gave no verbal quarter. The playright David Hare was even prepared to offer the tabloid press two cheers for its excesses. 'Newspapers, led by the Murdoch group, have begun the project of putting the Royal Family in such a state of tension that their lives will become unliveable,' he declared. This, he acknowledged, did nobody any credit.

Nevertheless he saw it as the only available tactic against a Royal Family which people were still unwilling to confront head on. 'We shall mock them,' the playright concluded, 'till they wish they had never been born.'[44] The conference concentrated on the recent financial and sexual misfortunes of the Royal Family. Yet it was also a direct response to Tom Nairn's call to the Left, four years earlier, to take the Monarchy seriously both as a British institution and as an idea – and, indeed, Nairnism suffused many of the discussions.

There had been other echoes of Nairn, not just from socialists. In a study of the British Constitution published in 1992, Ferdinand Mount, formerly head of Lady Thatcher's Policy Unit, pointed to what he saw as 'a bizarre truncation' in almost all modern writings on the subject: namely their failure to give the Monarchy more than a passing mention, and – when they did discuss it – their slavery to Bagehot's nineteenth-century interpretation. Basing his view partly on his own (possibly untypical) Downing Street experience, Mount concluded that there was little evidence of Prime Ministers taking any notice of royal advice, that audiences had become little more than a charade, and that what mattered much more was the residual role of constitutional arbitration. If there was an area that needed criticizing, he suggested, it was not the Monarchy's failure of moral leadership, but the tendency of members of the Royal Family to voice their opinions publicly and privately on politically contentious issues.

Mount's account raised the question of whether the Monarchy and Royal Family were becoming more important rather than less, in a system whose other checks and balances had declined. 'Would anyone have expected in 1945,' the author asked, 'that, nearly half a century later, the Royal Family would be playing a far more prominent part in public affairs than George V or George VI and their families would have dreamed of essaying?'[45] The cry was taken up by the novelist and biographer (and tongue-in-cheek devotee of Diana) A. N. Wilson, who asked: 'Is this the taste of things to come – a Monarch who will not be content to be consulted, to encourage and to warn?' It was a question, Wilson suggested, that mattered much more than whether the Prince of Wales 'talked dirty' on the telephone to the wife of a fellow officer.

Whether any increase in the public role of the Royal Family was to be applauded or deplored, depended – of course – on whether the royal influence was felt to be a benign one. Wilson quoted Bagehot: 'George III interfered unceasingly, but he did harm unceasingly.'[46] However, some of those who attacked royalty for a 'something must be done' attitude on social matters, were simultaneously – and without any sense of contradiction – prepared to value the potential role of the Monarchy as a bulwark against Brussels bureaucrats. 'By far the biggest present assault on our rights comes not from the Crown of the House of Windsor,' argued the Eurosceptical Charles Moore, 'but from the strong diadem of European Union.'[47]

The argument could be turned around: the very existence of an unreformed Monarchy, symbol of an outdated doctrine of sovereignty and cluttered with imperial memories, stood in the way of European integration. Thus the historian Stephen Haseler, who – a decade earlier – had predicted the demise of the Labour Party, now declared with equal conviction that the current Queen would be 'Elizabeth the Last,' and that a British republic would swiftly follow the establishment of an Australian one. Urging as much speed as possible in this direction, he pressed the half-Thatcherite, half-Eurofanatic argument that the Queen's personal attachment to the 'ramshackle multi-national institution' of the Commonwealth was a foreign policy distraction that got in the way of the European ideal.[48]

But how was a republic to be brought about? Some suggested a referendum. Others, like Tony Benn, called for a simple House of Commons Bill. There remained, however, Tom Nairn's point. The Monarchy was not just an institution: it was a state of mind. It was sociological, as much as political, 'not just a golden bauble on the top of a stone pyramid,' as Wilson put it, but 'more like the golden thread running through an entire tapestry' – hard to unstitch and perhaps not worth the attempt. Bearing this in mind, some of the Monarchy's more sophisticated critics had a fallback position. As the *Guardian* columnist (later editor of the *Observer*) Will Hutton put it at the 1993 Monarchy conference, effective reform of the British state did not necessarily mean a republic, 'but it does mean a republican attitude to the Constitution.'[49]

According to its advocates, a 'republican attitude' to the Constitution meant an end to royalty deference and to the notion of subjection to the Crown. Yet the idea of Britain as ceremonially a monarchy while in practice a republic was scarcely new. Indeed, the book on which most interpretations of the British Constitution had rested for a century and a quarter was based on it. In his wrily pragmatic chapter on the Monarchy in *The English Constitution*, Bagehot had, precisely, dismantled the clockwork of what he described as Britain's 'disguised republic'. How could the Constitution be re-shaped at the end of the twentieth century, to make it appear more 'republican' than the system had appeared to a shrewd, conservative commentator in the mid-nineteenth?

A North London buzzword of the 1990s was 'citizenship' – in some ways comparable to 'meritocracy' and 'scientific planning' thirty years earlier, and with many of the same implications. So powerful had this idea become, that the Conservative Government itself had picked it up, offering a 'Citizens' Charter'. Where meritocracy in the Gaitskell-Wilson era had been heralded as the key to an efficient, fast growing economy, citizenship had become the *sine qua non* without which, in the words of Anthony Barnett, Charter 88's co-ordinator, 'there is no avenue to economic revival, social cohesion or modernising our democracy.'[50] Citizens had common rights and duties: they could not fulfil them, it was argued, if they remained within a social hierarchy with the mentality and legal status of 'subjects' of the Crown. Some went further, regarding the existence of an hereditary Monarchy, along with hereditary law-makers in the House of Lords, as a psychological brake to economic progress, and an affront not just to citizenship, but to democracy itself.

It could be pointed out, however, that those who, in the past, had seen Britain as a haven of political liberty, or who had sought to extend citizens' rights, had seldom regarded the Monarchy as any kind of obstacle, and – moreover – that reforms recently proposed to strengthen rights did not undermine the Monarchy's position.[51] The Monarchy, it could be argued, had lost the characteristic which had made it most dangerous when it was at the height of its prestige: its social power. The very pillorying of the Monarchy was, in one way, a healthy sign that it had largely ceased to operate as a fount of snobbery. Yet if the accusation that the Monarchy had caused current economic problems, threatened civil liberties and continued to underpin the class system was difficult to sustain, so was a defence of it on anything like the traditional grounds that had been advanced at the beginning of the reign. The Monarchy was no longer a focus for imperial loyalty; the Commonwealth had ceased to require a royal Head (however good the Queen might be at doing the job); few apart from hereditary peers supported the retention of an hereditary House of Lords, or of the hereditary principle for anything except the Monarchy; a constitutional arbitration role might be performed as well by an elected president or, perhaps, by the Speaker of the House of Commons; and if there was a need for a model family, the Windsors for the time being were unable to provide one.

There remained the 'golden thread' argument, which the abolitionist Nairn saw as a problem, but which could also be seen as a strength: the Monarchy continued to provide a reminder of the nation's history and traditions, and of the origins of things, from postage stamps to cathedrals. To get rid of an institution, recently fallen on hard times, that had been in almost continuous existence since the reign of King Egbert – and whose role and functions had evolved continuously – required a very good reason. Finally, in a political system frighteningly described as an 'elective dictatorship,' the existence of one ancient, non-executive institution which retained a hold on the imaginations of most ordinary people and could represent them to a potentially overbearing Prime Minister, was not necessarily worse than having an elected, and almost certainly party-political, presidency. It was absurd to regard a Monarchy as essential to British democracy, because the majority of well-functioning democracies did without one. But there was no need to abandon it either, unless there was something unquestionably better to put in its place.

IN BRITAIN, the fortieth anniversary of the Coronation produced a confused reaction: bewilderment at the continued disarray of the Royal Family, and criticism of the way in which the Monarchy's affairs were conducted, but also respect for the Queen as an individual. In April, the decision was announced that parts of Buckingham Palace would be open to the public during the summer, and the precincts of Windsor Castle would also be opened, to help pay for the Windsor repairs. In June, an ICM poll showed that despite such measures, and the tax changes, two-thirds of the population felt that the Monarchy was too big a drain on taxpayers' money. Yet there was also a spate of articles acknowledging that the Queen herself performed her duties well, and deserved both the admiration and the thanks of the nation.

Most people who were old enough had vivid memories of the Coronation. Some commentators re-evoked them, drawing contrasts between the society over which the Queen had reigned when she was crowned and the one that existed four decades later. Lynda Lee-Potter, in the *Daily Mail*, recalled the material differences. In 1953, she observed, few ordinary families had a car or a fridge, and 'most of us had never heard of an avocado or the Costa del Sol'.[52] In the *Guardian* Richard Gott wrote that, for all its sentimentality, the Coronation in 1953 had been a real celebration, 'long before the invention of heritage culture overlaid such occasions with candy floss and false display'. It had been, he reflected, 'a genuine Old Testament moment,' with Monarch, Church and State locked into 'their age-old unequal compact with the people – keeping them at arm's length as observers, not participants.' Gott's view of the Queen forty years later was of an archetype who remained true to herself – 'dull, unimaginative, unoriginal, uninspired, dutiful – a typical and recognisable representative of the rural landed class from which she springs . . . a dead ringer for those hundreds of scarved Tory women who used to be on view most days of the rural year, at horse shows, point-to-points, race meetings . . .' In the 1990s, however, this type no longer existed. Scottish castles had been traded for country cottages in the Dordogne, *Country Life* for *Hello*. 1953, and the Queen who was crowned in that year, seemed to belong to another century.[53] Yet it could also be argued that being behind the times had been a defining feature of the Monarchy, in good times as well as in bad. Although peripheral members of the Royal Family – siblings or in-laws – might be fashionable and modern, such a quality had been carefully avoided by Sovereigns. Indeed 'belonging to the previous century' was a description that fitted every monarch since the reign of George IV – with the single exception of Edward VIII.

Constitutionally and ceremonially, the British Monarchy continued to function, despite financial or domestic travails. However, an important part of its imagined role remained hypothetical. The 'reserve powers' – often referred to, but never invoked – were still assumed to exist, despite lack of usage. It was generally agreed that the Queen's prerogative in the event of a prime ministerial request for a dissolution was still intact, and that she was entitled to refuse such a request if it were made in 'irregular circumstances': for example, early in a Parliament. The journalist Simon Heffer noted in an essay on the Constitution published in *The Times* in July 1994 that if such a crisis occurred, the Queen would take soundings from among a cast of distinguished public figures and constitutional experts. Heffer's list of such experts, presumably Palace-derived, included only two members of the Labour Party, against five Conservatives.[54] Nobody minded or probably even noticed, because the possibility of such a consultation seemed so remote. Yet the question of what the Queen might do if the Government was unable to carry on was not entirely academic, in view of serious divisions on the Conservative benches, and it became even less so as the Major Government's majority was whittled away by by-elections and defections.

Meanwhile, the Monarchy's domestic problems became part of its evolving image: no longer a model family, but an all too common one – although, as it was also frequently pointed out, three failed marriages out of four children was above the national norm. There were plenty of shocks and embarrassments still to come. In May 1993, old stories about Prince Philip's friendships with women appeared in the serialization of a book by Lady Colin Campbell, and it was rumoured that Kitty Kelley, relentless investigator of American superstar private lives, had sent her team across the Atlantic to unearth the secrets of the British consort. In the autumn of 1994, a book of rather greater substance appeared called *The Prince of Wales*, written by the journalist and broadcaster Jonathan Dimbleby.[55] Unlike Morton's work, this was an 'authorized' biography, for which the author was given full access, both to Charles's papers and diaries, and to the Prince, who allowed himself to be taped at length, voicing his intimate thoughts. Its publication was preceded by a lengthy ITV interview, in which the Heir to the Throne openly admitted his own adultery.

Royal reticence by now had gone full circle – from the days of the Abominable No Man, when the breakfast menu of the Royal Family was a tightly guarded secret, to the musings-aloud of the future Monarch. Dimbleby's book took the Prince seriously, and to some extent at his own valuation, as a thoughtful but misunderstood public figure, with ideas and schemes which ranged from the eccentric to the creative. It described how, in the absence of the 'proper' role which some (including Lord Callaghan) had hoped to give him, the Heir had put together a portfolio of trusts, charities and personal institutions; and the way in which he had come to be identified with a back-to-nature environmentalism, a concern for people least able to look after themselves and – in his habit of telling the Establishment home truths – his father's gruff populism. The author also chronicled Charles's involvement in the 'unofficial opposition' of the harsh early 1980s, when the Prince had helped to draw attention to the void created by the collapse of manufacturing industry and the Government's failure to respond to it. In the process, he pointed to the problem highlighted by Mount: the thin line between the taking of imaginative social initiatives, and political campaigning.

It was not this part of the book, however, that seized the attention of the media, and the nation, when *The Prince of Wales* was published. Dimbleby had learnt from Morton the questions to put to modern royalty and its friends: and they did not shrink from answering them. As a result, the book told the story of the Waleses' marriage from the other side, with many corroborating witnesses. Particular interest was aroused by Dimbleby's full account of Charles's relationship with Camilla Parker Bowles, which both confirmed and added to what had already been said during the ITV interview; and by an alternative account of Diana's behaviour before and after the marriage, that presented her as quixotic, self-obsessed, and paranoid. Though Dimbleby disagreed with Morton on some matters, reflecting the different bias of his witnesses, his account lent weight to *Diana: Her True Story* in others: in particular, the extent of the mismatch, and the ghastly charade as Diana gained in mega-stardom, radiantly compensating in public for what was tragically missing in private.

The book also aroused interest because of the discussion it contained (in which again Dimbleby appeared as the Prince's amanuensis), of Charles's childhood and upbringing, including how he saw his relationship with his parents. Morton had painted the Queen as an aloof mother, not unkind, but disengaged – encouraging speculation that the problems in the Waleses' marriage might have been the product of maternal deprivation not just in the case of Diana, but of Charles as well. Reviewers of *Elizabeth R* had earlier noticed a curious air of detachment in the principal character, and suggested that this might help explain her children's difficulties.[56] Others had commented on the Queen's reported inability to show physical affection, and tendency to put her children after her duty.[57] Dimbleby's references to the Queen and Prince Philip were brief. Since, however, they were assumed to come from the Prince of Wales, they helped to establish a new legend. The Queen was presented as cold, Philip as a bully. The Monarch and her husband, formerly set in the nation's imagination as the ideal mother and father, became indifferent parents, who caused the marriages of their children to break down by starving them of love.

The main impact of the book was to stir, yet again, public interest in the Waleses' still technically existing marriage, and to raise the question, relevant to the future of the Monarchy, of whether the Prince was fit to succeed. The Coronation chant 'May the Queen live forever,' became the fervent invocation of some of the Monarchy's strongest supporters. Other members of the Royal Family – Prince Andrew and, mercifully, the Duchess of York, with her Budgie books and thirst for publicity – were sidelined. The world divided into two camps: those who sided with the Princess of Wales, who included many feminists and constitutional reformers, identifying her with the plight of oppressed women, or with a modernist critique of the Monarchy – and supporters of the Prince.

The following summer, the Queen returned to public attention with the anniversary, not of a royal event, but a national one. The celebration of VE- and VJ-Day, brought the Queen, Princess Margaret and the ninety-five-year-old Queen Elizabeth out onto the balcony at the Palace in a happy, non-militaristic reminder of the end of the Second World War. The festivities – in which royalty was not the reason for celebrating, yet was able to play a fitting part – seemed to revive the bond between Monarchy and people. The sight of the three elderly women, in contrasting colours, standing together as they had stood fifty years earlier, was deeply affecting to all those with a sense of the nation's history and achievement. 'Queen Elizabeth was in tears,' says a lady-in-waiting to the Queen. 'As they left the balcony, the Queen's eyes were brimming, but she was absolutely determined that nobody should see. When they got back inside, she quickly took a large gin and knocked it back.'[58] The Palace was worried that not enough people would turn up. In fact, the crowd was huge, good natured and appreciative – its evident pleasure marred only by the entertainer Cliff Richard who, for some reason, had been employed to lead the singing of a pop song called 'Congratulations' of which only he seemed to know the words. However Vera Lynn, who also sang, successfully evoked the 1940s, there was a flypast of wartime aircraft, and the Royal Family, minus its currently problematic members, was reassured, as well as moved, by the public response.

During 1994 and 1995, a number of important but non-sensational – and therefore comparatively unpublicized – books appeared, which underlined the continuing role of the institution. Peter Hennessy in *The Hidden Wiring* and Vernon Bogdanor in *The Monarchy and the Constitution* examined the constitutional role, Frank Prochaska, in *Royal Bounty*, drew attention to the importance of royalty's tradition of patronage and support for voluntary causes,[59] while the socialist historian Raphael Samuel argued in *Theatres of Memory* that a respect for the past, and for traditional ways of thinking and behaving, need not be equated with a conservative or backward-looking desire to return to them. Samuel pointed out, in particular, that early post-war Britain had been a highly progressive society which drew strength from a pride in the nation's history: orange juice for babies and the Festival of Britain had co-existed happily with state theatricals and the national anthem. He attacked the fashion for crude 'heritage baiting' as a poor man's modernism.[60]

Then the Princess returned to the offensive. 'There is a studied casualness in her relationship with the Royal Family,' a friend of the Queen reflected. 'She has a "What the hell, I'll show them" sort of attitude.' This became apparent in November 1995 when, bitterly stung by Dimbleby's suggestion that she was psychologically unstable and a 'problem' – and still craving public attention, like a drug – she agreed to take part in an hour-long interview on the BBC's *Panorama*. It was a mark of the collapse of the old relationships that once existed within the British Establishment that such a programme could be

"Orff with her ring" . AFTER TENNIEL .

Guardian, 22nd December, 1995

arranged, not only without consulting the Palace, but without its knowledge. Even the chairman of the BBC, Marmaduke Hussey, was kept in ignorance – presumably because of his proximity to the Household, through his wife, Lady Susan Hussey, a lady-in-waiting to the Queen. So was the Monarch. The day before news of the forthcoming interview became public, the Princess telephoned her mother-in-law and asked if she could spend Christmas at Sandringham – but did not mention the broadcast. The Palace, and the Queen, were not informed of their impending humiliation until an hour and a half before the BBC announced its scoop – apparently at Diana's own insistence. At the time, the feeling of betrayal at the Palace, which still felt it had a special relationship with the Corporation, was palpable. 'They could have found a way to tell us this was happening,' maintains one source.

Delighted with its prize, the BBC abandoned any pretence at objectivity, restricting the interview to the gentlest of questions, and retaking shots indefatigably to produce a fluent, and undeniably engrossing, package. Twenty-three million people in the United Kingdom alone watched the programme, screened on November 20th –

the largest national television audience ever – as the Princess answered her husband's admission of adultery by herself confessing to adultery with James Hewitt, and unravelled the narrative of her marriage along Mortonian lines, contrasting her own healing approach to her family and the public with the alleged coldness of her husband. 'You will never be King', she had told Charles, according to one of his friends. 'I shall destroy you.'[61] On television, she merely indicated that she did not expect him to succeed, and offered her son as an alternative.

She did not speak of the Queen directly. Of herself, she said, 'I would like to be queen of people's hearts'. Nicholas Soames, a member of the Government and friend of the Prince, reacted seconds afterwards by saying that Diana 'seemed on the edge of paranoia'. Polls showed that many people disagreed. A majority of viewers were impressed by the performance, and sympathized with the performer.[62] At first, the Palace's only response was to make it clear – indeed, it had little choice, in view of the position of the Waleses' children – that it intended to continue to help the Princess as best it could. The Monarch herself seemed able, as always, to keep her life in compartments: Diana belonged to the public, rather than to the private sphere. After the *Panorama* broadcast had been announced, but before it had taken place, a friend of the Queen and Duke who spent a weekend with them was struck by how little they seemed to be showing the strain. Nothing came up in conversation except the rural pursuits that always interested them, with plenty of jokes. While the whole world was arranging to be at home to watch *Panorama*, the subject of the day was not even hinted at.

However, the Queen did not let her daughter-in-law have the last word. After the *Panorama* interview in which the Princess had spoken of their marriage being a bit crowded, she consulted the Prime Minister, the Archbishop of Canterbury and senior Household staff. Then she made a pre-emptive strike – writing letters to both the Prince and Princess (which somebody, possibly in Prince Charles's circle, leaked) giving it as her own opinion, with her husband's support, that an early divorce was desirable. The tone of the letters was more measured than she felt. According to one close source, they came out of a deep exasperation, and of a desire to state her position in incontrovertible prose because, as she had learnt, 'bulimics re-write history in 24 hours'.[63]

When the contents of the letter became publicly known, the Palace indicated in a statement that the Prince of Wales took the 'same view' as his mother. At first, the Princess of Wales seemed taken aback. Then her lawyers began negotiating a divorce settlement in earnest. 'Despite the fulminations of moralists and sentimentalists,' declared *The Times*, which had once fulminated against the prospect of Princess Margaret marrying the divorced Peter Townsend, 'a divorce carries no constitutional implications.'[64] Most agreed that the move was a wise and necessary one, and the Palace was at pains to stress that the initiative for it came from the Queen herself. The Duke and Duchess of York paved the way, divorcing in April. In July, a settlement was reached between the Prince and Princess of Wales, and in August their fifteen-year marriage ended. The same summer, the Palace announced that the Queen's Christmas broadcasts, which had been the monopoly of the BBC since George V delivered his first Christmas broadcast to the Empire in 1932, would be rotated with ITV on a two-yearly cycle, starting in 1997 – a redistribution of favours which the BBC had successfully resisted nearly forty years earlier, at the time of the Altrincham–Muggeridge row. The Palace denied that it was punishing the BBC for the Diana interview – but indicated the extent of royal anger by letting it be known that the decision had been 'accelerated' by the affront.

In mid-1996, there were more British republicans, and more monarchist critics of the Royal Family, than at any time in the twentieth century. The change had been swift. 'Today in 1986,' Philip Ziegler had written, only ten years earlier, '[the Monarchy] stands for essentially the same values as it stood for sixty years ago and as it will do sixty years ahead.'[65] After a sixth of that time, the question had become, not whether the Monarchy would mean the same, but whether it would survive at all. Yet there was a paradox: a pilloried Family, a much criticized institution, even a widely questioned role – and yet, a valued incumbent. As the *Independent* pointed out, the Queen's seventy-three per cent approval rating might be below its peak: but it was still one many elected presidents would be delighted to enjoy at any time, let alone after forty-four years in office.[66] Most serious politicians, as always, shied away from the topic of the future of the Monarchy. When Labour's Welsh spokesman, Ron Davies, remarked that the titular head of the principality was unfit to be King, he was sharply slapped down by his Leader. The reason was simple. As the *Guardian* observed, ministers and would-be ministers were afraid that 'any party which gets itself into this debate will only lose'. In one sense, discussion has been freer than ever before in the last few years. In another, it had not properly begun.

As for the Queen, she carried on. She led a more solitary existence than in the past. The number of intimate friends among her contemporaries was declining. Patrick Plunket had died in 1975, Rupert Nevill in 1982. Her mother, one of the pillars of her life, had a successful hip operation in 1995, and seemed immortal. However in September 1993, Bobo MacDonald – nursemaid at 145 Piccadilly, and then royal dresser for sixty-seven years, scourge of designers and milliners, relentless custodian, daily companion, confidante, and friend – died at the age of eighty-nine.[67] With her husband often away, the Queen frequently dined on her own. If she was lonely, she did not say. But she was not immune to the recent strains and humiliations suffered by the Royal Family. 'The problems of her children have preyed on her mind,' says a close friend. 'She can't bear to watch programmes like *Panorama* and she won't read the tabloids.' She was prepared to show her feelings more than in the past, talking about family difficulties quite openly to at least one member of the Cabinet. She also seemed to take comfort from her mailbag, many times larger than at the start of the reign, and from letters written by ordinary people expressing concern, which often affected her more than the polite or embarrassed sympathy of friends. 'You see,' she would say, turning them over, 'they really do understand.'[68]

In public, she did her duty and – especially at times of grief or crisis – people continued to relate to her. On Mothering Sunday, she and her daughter visited Dunblane, and her tears were shared by the nation. A few days later, she was in Poland, and then Czechoslovakia. In July, President Mandela paid an historic return state visit. Though he had uncompromising words to say about past government policies towards South Africa, he gave every sign of personal pleasure at his public, and royal, reception.

At seventy, Elizabeth was not a triumphant Queen. Unlike her long reigning predecessors as female Monarch, Elizabeth I and Victoria, her period on the Throne had not coincided with a time of rising national power and comparative wealth. Instead, some of the nation's sense of failure and decline unfairly attached to her. It was difficult to point to major achievements; yet it was equally hard to think of many mistakes. She continued to do what was expected of her – not much more, but certainly no less – taking pleasure in the routines and customs of a regulated life: reading and signing the papers that were sent to her, delivering the speeches others prepared, reacting to suggestions from advisers, meeting dignitaries, visiting, touring, taking part in ceremonies. She did not seek to be queen of people's hearts. But to watch her at work on a walkabout, in a hospital, or at a garden party was to see a woman who both knew and enjoyed her business. Though the last few years had visibly aged her, she was in good health, and resilient. She carried out more engagements in 1996 than twenty years before. She did not complain, or vary her habits. 'The Queen's strength,' in the words of one of her aides, a friend for half a century, 'is that she doesn't change very much.'[69]

In her reserve there was a vein of sadness: some claimed to see beneath the surface a hint of passion, though for who or what it was impossible to tell. Yet she remained self-sufficient, and did not lose her grip. The pressures of a lifetime of excessive praise, and ridicule, had not destroyed her. Nor had the effects of her singularity. The stilted addresses, gracious handshakes, dutiful pleasantries, acknowledging waves belonged to her nature. But so did an amused appraisal of the society in which she played her unique, unchosen part: the sole non-subject of her realms. She did not question, but she did observe.

After the guests had left, the door would shut. Then the eyes would brighten and the face light up – flashing with feline humour at the expense of those who had just paid her court.

24

D URING THE PERIOD of the Royal Family's troubles, most people seemed to think that the Monarchy needed to change and – in an all-purpose word – to modernise. There was less clarity about what that might mean. Functionally, huge changes had already taken place. In the preceding generation, Buckingham Palace had moved a long way from the 'tweedy' Court criticised in the 1950s. In place of ageing aristocrats, it was staffed by men and women in mid-career on secondments or short-term contracts, either from the civil service or the private sector. Many were specialists, in press or public relations, or in arts administration. Financially, too, the Palace was now incomparably more streamlined. Yet the future direction of the one public organisation for which the elected Government was not responsible remained undefined. A question hung in the air: what should a modern Monarchy be like?

Some critics argued that it should be turned into an entirely ceremonial institution, divested of its discretionary and advisory roles – as indeed it had become, or was in the process of becoming, in the Queen's other realms. The 'Houghton solution', involving a minister for the Crown answerable to Parliament on matters relating to royalty, remained on the table as another possibility. For the time being, however, root and branch reform was ruled out, and the starting point of discussion within or involving the Palace was the need to preserve a distinctive royal sphere. Meanwhile prime ministers saw little advantage in tampering with an institution from which they derived authority and which, in practice, offered little constraint, and they did their best to protect it from parliamentary buffetings. But they were not able to protect it from the press. Nor were they able to defer, indefinitely, a fundamental constitutional debate.

The institution was becoming vulnerable on a number of counts.

To the allegedly hidebound Monarchy and the non-accountable and 'undemocratic' Monarchy, had been added in the 1990s the Royal Family composed of people who had become figures of fun. Historians, casting around for parallels, drew attention to the behaviour in the early nineteenth century of the Prince Regent, later George IV, and Caroline – labelled by contemporary wags 'the Queen of Hearts'. In some ways, the position was worse. The Hanoverians did not have to contend with media which had either the global range or the rapaciousness of the press and television at the end of the millennium. In other respects, however, the prognosis was better. By 1996, the greatest humiliations appeared to be coming to an end. Indeed, if the Windsor fire and Andrew Morton's book had opened a period of royal crisis, the divorces of the Prince of Wales and the Duke of York four years later seemed to close it. The ending of the marriages did not halt the feuding which had changed the role of royal adviser from haughty guardian to despairing apologist. But it did mean that the behaviour of the Princess and the Duchess was no longer strictly royal business – except where it affected the children.

'Both myself and the Respondent recognised there were irreconcilable differences and that accordingly we could no longer live together,' Prince Charles wrote on the pre-printed affidavit form, as the main reason for his separation.[1] There was little more to be said about the most celebrated marriage of the last half-century, which had so conspicuously and publicly failed. For the 'model family' it was a solemn moment. For the public, it was disorienting. As well as ending the legal agreement with the Prince's consort, the divorce tore up an unspoken contract with the people of the Queen's realms, which did not make any provision for a split Royal Family. 'There is no place,' according to the cultural historian, Marina Warner, 'in the conceptual architecture of Christian society for a single woman who is neither a virgin nor a whore.'[2] Equally, there was no place in the imagery of European royalty for an ex-wife. Faced with the untidiness of Diana's post-marriage position, the press sought to redefine her as a whore. In any case, it soon became apparent that the marital conflict was not over. Editors who had hoped for a continuing saga were not disappointed, as the bruised and isolated Princess made her fury plain. 'Diana: I'll run rings round Charles,' scooped the *Mirror*. 'The *Sun* captures the mood of the nation: BYE-BYE BIG EARS!' exulted its rival.[3] A new (or rather very ancient) narrative was launched: two royal courts exchanging salvoes. 'Women leave the Royal Family in only one mode,' the Duchess of York was fond of saying '– with their heads cleaved from their shoulders.'[4] Aided by 'friends of Prince Charles,' a media execution of the Princess of Wales began.

At the same time, a rumbling civil war raged within the Monarchy itself, between Buckingham Palace and St James's Palace. It had familiar aspects. 'There had been endemic friction between Monarchs and Princes of Wales for centuries,' as one ex-courtier puts it, wearily. There was a schizoid aspect. Privately, relationships were easier than the press often allowed. Charles continued to spend several weeks in the summer with his parents at Balmoral. 'He always had masses to talk about with his father and they fell on each other when they met,' says a former royal aide. 'With the Queen it was "Mummy, don't be so silly" – that kind of thing.' In their public lives, however, there was a kind of delegated rivalry. The middle-aged Heir wanted to be independent of his parents, while the retainers of the Sovereign wanted to rein him in. There was a pattern: if the Prince's office felt rebuffed in its attempts to pursue a particular reform or pet scheme, Charles would signal his resentment by refusing to under-study the Queen for engagements. There would be rival briefings, enabling journalists to set the two palaces against each other, adding to the impression of clashes between royal personalities. The situation was made harder by differences over the Prince's official handling of the Princess of Wales and Camilla Parker Bowles. The Prince found Buckingham Palace interfering and patronising, the Queen's advisers found the Prince's office unpredictable and maverick, and difficult to deal with because (in their own view) the mere fact of working at Buckingham Palace 'counted as a minus' at St James's. The Queen's deputy private secretary, Robin Janvrin, was sometimes detailed to provide emollience. Advisers recall that members of the Royal Family were 'strangely uncommunicative' with each other, even on non-official business, preferring to use courtiers as a human postal service. 'A member of the family would say, "Could you have a word with so-and-so",' according to one. 'They should have just picked up the phone.'[5]

Meanwhile the icy details of the Charles–Diana break-up cast a pall over other royal business. The divorce occurred in the same year as the Queen's seventieth birthday. For some time, her employees had been contemplating the approaching anniversary glumly. For fear of a backlash, state-led celebrations were kept to a minimum. Some of the Queen's overseas realms issued commemorative postage stamps. Britain did not. Neither was there any repetition of the festival of flowers of ten years before, when six thousand daffodil-waving school children had serenaded the Monarch outside Buckingham Palace. 'Everybody is entitled to spend their seventieth birthday how they wish,' declared a Palace spokesman, 'and what the Queen's wishes are at seventy may be different to what they were at other ages.'[6] There was no official explanation, but everybody knew the reason: royal popularity was at a low ebb.

While the Court closed down hatches, the press greeted the approaching milestone in more textured terms than at the conclusion of previous royal decades. There were a number of themes. The first was the duration of an Elizabethan age which had spanned most of the second half of the twentieth century. In June, the Queen was due to become the fifth longest reigning monarch in English history, overtaking her sixteenth-century namesake, and leaving only Henry III, Edward III, George III and Victoria left to beat. Observers recalled that when the Queen came to the throne, Winston Churchill had three more years as Prime Minister, and the British monarch reigned in most of Africa. Since that time, the position of the United Kingdom in the world had altered out of recognition, and so had the lives, values and expectations of a majority of its citizens. A solitary fixed point was the Queen. A second, counterveiling, theme was that the radiant young Sovereign was now an old lady, albeit a remarkably sturdy one – and that the institution over which she presided had not moved with the times. For how many years should she continue as Head of State? In the past, Nature could generally be relied upon to pass the baton. On recent Bowes-Lyon form, however, Elizabeth II might rule another thirty years, by which time – as one analyst pointed out – Diana would be in her sixties, possibly re-married with a grown-up glamorous daughter.[7] On the other hand, if the reign ended prematurely, there could be a downside. 'The Queen well knows,' reflected the *Daily Express*, contemplating this aspect, 'that she has no choice but to soldier on till her last breath.'[8] Yet if the Queen stayed, would the Monarchy meet the challenges facing it?

Lord Deedes saw the Sovereign as a force for steadiness in stormy social seas, while the historian Frank Prochaska argued that, so far from being a reactionary ruler, she was in effect a 'social democrat' who gave more than £200,000 annually to good causes.[9] All agreed, however, that the institution over which she presided was in flux. Even newspapers traditionally associated with the Establishment tempered their congratulations. The *Telegraph* observed in the Head of the Royal Family a melancholy air that had been absent when she first sat on the throne, while *The Times* noted 'a strong mood today,' that only the Queen's person sustained the Monarchy, and that without her, there would be a republic.[10] The journalist Stephen Glover commented that she seemed to belong to another age, 'her voice, accent, intonation, idiom and mannerisms marking her out as someone of a different time'.[11] It was left to the *Guardian* to sound a horn for North London Jacobinism. 'Does she realise yet just how terrible the crisis of the Windsors has become?' asked the paper's political columnist. 'That her heir has become a national joke? That the failure of three out of four marriages contracted by her children is a source of despair? That they have swapped majesty for the status of international soap stars?'[12]

Once such questions had been the preserve of cranks and Communists. Now they reflected not only a middle-bourgeois puritanism about the antics of the upper classes, but a growing liberal critique of the institutional order. A general election was approaching, which Labour seemed certain to win. Avoiding economic commitments, 'New Labour' had put cost-free constitutional changes on the agenda, offering the prospect of devolution for Scotland and Wales, regional assemblies in England, entrenchment of human rights, proportional representation in general elections, and the abolition of the hereditary principle in the House of Lords. The Palace was not included in this list, but it could scarcely escape the atmosphere in which other reforms were being promulgated. Criticisms of the Monarchy that had been on the margins had entered the mainstream.

Politicians held back. It was one thing for the chattering classes to hold a widely shared opinion. It was another for office-seekers to state it publicly. In the mid-1990s, the Labour leadership was not in a mood for unnecessary risks. Open reformism was left to the other ranks. A sign of growing interest in the issue lower down the hierarchy was provided in a Fabian essay, *Long to Reign Over Us?* by Paul Richards, published in August 1996, which proposed the abolition of the Civil List, the transfer of Royal Prerogative powers to the Speaker, the creation of a rotating Commonwealth presidency, the transformation of the Royal Household into a Department of the Crown answerable to Parliament (the 'Houghton solution'), a decennial referendum on the Monarchy, and a new national anthem.[13] There was little in such a package that had not already been put forward by Hamilton, Benn and others, over the preceding thirty years. What had changed was the climate, the timing, and the provenance. Though Fabian publications did not represent any official or collective view, the Fabian Society was sufficiently close to the Establishment-in-waiting for the utterances of its authors to be an embarrassment. Tories rejoiced. 'The views in this pamphlet are shared by many within the Labour Party,' declared Michael Portillo, the Defence Secretary.

Hurried consultations produced a swift assurance from the Labour leadership ruling out the possibility of a new administration seeking to alter the political role or status of the Queen. 'Tony Blair is a strong supporter of the Monarchy and believes the existing arrangements work extremely well,' a discomfited party spokesman declared, denying that the essay would have any influence on policy-making.[14] Thus, before it had even taken office, Labour had defined its position in terms which were identical to those of every previous left-of-centre administration of the century. 'In Britain,' Peter Riddell had recently pointed out, 'it is regarded as bad form and displaying a lack of seriousness for any leading politician to discuss the Monarchy . . . most Labour MPs keep quiet, whatever their private views.'[15] The argument for change remained in aspic – and seemed destined to stay there, unless and until something arose that would shift public expectations.

Those who queried the official Labour position were offered a simple and apparently watertight syllogism. The actual powers of the Monarchy presented no threat to Labour's plans; whatever people might feel about individual royals, public support for the Monarchy was real; any whisper of a threat to the Queen's position risked losing more votes than it could conceivably attract; therefore it was bad politics even to consider an alteration to the status quo, and any reform would have to come, of her volition, from the Monarch herself. Since the Conservatives usually had even less reason or desire to interfere, the New Labour logic effectively extended the Sovereign's unconditional lease – offering an immunity that threw back onto an increasingly nervous and isolated institution an immense, and argu- ably unfair, responsibility for its own future. Given the outlook of the incumbent, the effect was to hold up progress which even the Queen's staff increasingly favoured. 'Ducking this issue is something that the Labour Party has managed particularly well in its ninety-six-year his- tory,' Richards pointed out. 'No serious attempt has been made by any Labour Government to reform the Monarchy, nor has any serious suggestion been made of reform while in Opposition.'[16] It was a fair and damning assessment, which highlighted a pusillanimity on Labour's part that could turn out to be a much greater threat to the survival of the institution than programmes of modernisation.

Nevertheless, the Monarchy itself was not entirely unresponsive. Its defenders could point to a royal reflectiveness that had not had existed in the past. In particular *annus horribilis* had led to the setting up of the so-called 'Way Ahead' group, an informal council of inner royals, senior courtiers and other royal officials. The group first met in Sep- tember 1994, and re-assembled a couple of times a year when the Queen was at Balmoral or Sandringham, flying the constitutional kites which party politicians had shied away from. The Queen's deputy private secretary was seen as the instigator. 'Robin was very much one for turning ideas into hard action,' says a former royal adviser, adding: 'A sea-change was happening in the 1990s – the reform process was coming in any case'.[17] In August 1996, the agenda of a forthcoming Way Ahead meeting in Balmoral was leaked. Items discussed included giving female royals the same rights of succession as males, abolishing the ban on heirs to the Throne marrying Catholics, ending the Mon- arch's position as Supreme Governor of the Church of England, and a reduction of the 'Royal Family' to include only the consort, children and grand-children directly in line.[18] Even though it was strongly asserted that the discussions were in-house, and details would only be submitted to ministers if they wanted to hear them, the meeting raised eyebrows. Kenneth Rose diagnosed panic, while Tony Benn suspected the Monarchy of plotting to consolidate itself – something, he suggested, that was beyond its remit. Others saw a positive side. One effect of equal rights for royal girls and boys would be to reduce the chance of the Duchess of York ever becoming Queen Mother.[19]

The Duchess, however, was not the main problem. In October 1996, the Queen, accompanied by Prince Philip, embarked on a state visit to Thailand, to celebrate the golden jubilee of King Bhumibol Adulyadej, who had reigned for even longer than she had. It did not go unnoticed that the Thai royal family also had marital difficulties – the heir to the throne was divorced from his first wife, and his second wife was living in London *in cognito*. It also did not go unnoticed that the ex-wife of the heir to the British throne had chosen the same week to visit Sydney to support her good causes. While the Queen and Duke watched 1,500 actors and four elephants play out the birth of the Thai nation, the Princess of Wales publicly danced with 'Shifty Nifty' Neville Wran, a former New South Wales premier and noted anti-monarchist. Meanwhile, Prince Charles toured the Ukraine and other ex-Soviet republics. The Queen travelled with the Foreign Secretary and a retinue of thirty-nine, the Prince with seventeen, the Princess with only two. 'Of course,' observed a journalist who flitted between the three parties, 'the Princess's tour attracted by far the largest media contingent.'[20]

In the meantime, Dianagate had nudged the Palace into some practical steps. In keeping with the announcement made after the *Panorama* interview, the 1996 Royal Christmas broadcast was the last to be made by the BBC under an exclusive contract. Once, loss of the exclusive rights would have been regarded by the Corporation as a catastrophe. The previous few years, however, had seen a slide in audiences. In 1996, the total number of viewers dropped by three million to barely eleven million, partly because of a rival Channel 4 Rory Bremner impersonation of Princess Diana running at the same time.[21] But as television receded in importance, other media came on

Guardian, 20th August, 1996

stream. On 6 March 1997, Buckingham Palace went onto the Net. The Queen herself unveiled the royal website at Kingsbury High School in North London. 'This is the official website of the Monarchy in Britain,' the screen declared, offering details of royal personages, royal finances, even royal corgis. Surfers quickly noted that while the formerly-royal Duchess of York rated only a passing mention, a whole page was devoted to the Princess of Wales. The site was an instant success, with 12.5 million hits in the first two months, and 50,000 registrations in the visitors' book.[22] Two months later, the Palace announced plans to set up an e-mail system, which would make the Monarchy interactive.[23] Shortly afterwards, the Queen made her live debut, when her speech at the opening of a Tyneside factory was broadcast across cyber-space.[24]

In May 1997, a general election produced the biggest landslide since the Second World War – a victory that reflected disenchantment with the Conservatives, rather than a deep-rooted desire for change. Tony Blair was called to the Palace and accepted the Queen's invitation to become her tenth Prime Minister. Although Labour had been out of office for even longer than in 1964, there was little of the culture shock that had been experienced when Harold Wilson took over from Sir Alec Douglas-Home. It was a sign of the political and social times: the Queen's third Labour premier was also the first of any party for more than thirty years to have attended a public school. Indeed, the transition stood the textbook version of Britain's class divide on its head: an Oxford-educated High Anglican Labour prime minister replaced a religiously-indifferent lower middle class Tory who left grammar school at sixteen. There were other novelties. The age gap between Monarch and premier was growing. At forty-three, Blair was the first of the Queen's prime ministers to have been born during her reign. In style and social attitude, he was closer to junior members of the Palace staff than to many of the politicians the Monarch had been used to. He was the first premier since Ramsay MacDonald to kiss hands without having previously held any office. He was also the first male prime minister with a professionally success-ful spouse, or with one who was reportedly 'a quite passionate republican'.[25]

If this was an accurate interpretation, Mrs Blair kept prudently quiet about it. One historian identified the new administration as 'the most anti-monarchical government Britain has ever had,' with a Cabinet containing a majority of closet republicans, and a press secre-tary similarly inclined. From the start, however, the doctrine of collec-tive responsibility precluded open expressions of disloyalty, and the new premier himself displayed not a flicker of criticism. In Opposition, Blair had defended the Queen's role. As Prime Minister, he accepted it – as his predecessors had done – unreservedly. The Queen had received Winston Churchill in audience as if he was her uncle, or even grandfather. In age, Blair might easily have been her son. 'She gets on well with him,' claims a Labour insider. Courtiers judge such matters by the clock. Tony Blair's audiences, they observe, go on longer than those of any previous premier in recent memory. 'There is clearly something working there,' suggests one.[26] However, other hardened observers reflect that getting on with prime ministers is one of the Monarch's well-honed skills.

*   *   *

DURING THE MONTHS after the divorce, it became *de rigueur* to regard Prince Charles as an unsuitable future King. Various points were held against him – his appearance, style, mannerisms, hobbies, private affections and public obsessions. The substantial objection was his divorced status and supposed marital intentions. As the reaction to the Prince's adultery 'confession' made clear, members of the public applied standards to members of the Royal Family that were different from those applied to each other. However, the matter was more than a question of secular morality. Whatever stand might be taken by the population at large on moral grounds, the question of the Heir's relationship to Mrs Parker Bowles had become inextricably tied to the Monarch's symbolic headship of the established Church.

The Church of England hierarchy faced a dilemma. The Prince of Wales appeared irrevocably committed to the third member of his once-crowded former marriage. Although he and Camilla did not share a roof, there was little doubt that both saw their partnership as permanent. A statement by the Prime Minister at the time of the divorce that the Prince had no plans to re-marry convinced nobody that he did not wish to do so. In 1936, Church and State had united in insisting that occupying the Throne and marriage to a divorced person were incompatible. Edward VIII had chosen to renounce, marry and be damned. Now the Heir was seeking, in effect, to nullify the pre-war verdict. Should the Church condemn and seek to end the arrangement, or condone and agree to sanctify it? Condoning would constitute a shift on divorce which many clergy were not ready to make. To condemn, on the other hand, would place the Church in an awkward position (to put it mildly) in relation to a future Supreme Governor who not only refused to repent, but continued to sin, albeit in a way which – in practice – most clergy accepted among their non-royal parishioners.

On the day the Waleses' decree became absolute, a Gallup poll showed that fifty-six per cent of all full-time Anglican clergy were opposed to a divorced Prince who re-married becoming King. Most senior clerics kept silent on the issue. Eventually, however, they were goaded into expressing a view. As always, the Monarchy was delicately poised on religious matters: not only did it need to avoid partisanship in any internal Church of England dispute, it sought to avoid giving offence to members of other sects and faiths. Ecumenicism was a movement of which it instinctively approved. In December 1995, the Queen visited Westminster Cathedral and became the first Sovereign since the seventeenth century to attend a Roman Catholic service in the British Isles. Protestant extremists shouted 'betrayal' and 'the Pope is anti-Christ'.[27] A few months later, however, the accusation of betrayal was levelled not by Protestants within the Church of England but by Catholics outside it. In July, a columnist on the influential *Catholic Herald*, William Oddie, accused the Queen of having a flexible conscience. In 1955, he reminded her, Princess Margaret had ended her relationship with a divorced man after declaring that she had made her decision 'mindful of the teachings of the Church'. Four decades later, the Monarch was in danger of being less 'mindful' in relation to her son. Oddie was backed by the *Herald*'s editor who declared that by not only consenting to Charles's divorce but actively encouraging it, the Queen had 'betrayed the ideal of marriage'.[28]

At first, the Church of England ignored this challenge. Then it put up the Dean of St Paul's, the Very Reverend Eric Evans, to reply to a criticism that was aimed as much at Anglican fudge as at the Monarch herself, and which was particularly difficult to answer, because there was no unified opinion. Attitudes in the established Church split three ways: between hard-liners, liberals and those who accepted what had happened but rejected the idea of a second wedding as the next logical step.[29] Evans placed himself in the last category. He made a nice distinction. 'The Church of England has always believed that divorce is possible,' he maintained. 'What our Lord condemned was marrying again, which was really committing adultery. Re-marriage is the difficulty.'[30] Evans's stance (Jesus would have put up with the divorce, but would have balked at a second marriage) became the new orthodoxy. As a leading advocate of Church disestablishment put it, the Anglican communion felt entitled 'to believe that the new Monarch *means* the Declaration and the Oath' in the Coronation Service – including the promise to 'maintain and preserve inviolably' Church teaching.[31] Thus, for the time being, the Church felt more comfortable with a fornicating Heir than with one who regularised his relationship, and was thereby committing canonical adultery. So, according to polls, did his future subjects. The result was a state of

limbo, with nothing resolved. 'Compared with this', as David Cannadine aptly remarked, 'the abdication of Edward and its aftermath were
a garden party.'[32]

Charles's one hope was that public opinion might change. What
common sense objection could there be, in the long run, to a match
which, if it had not involved royalty, would have seemed obviously
desirable? Though the polls showed disquiet, they also indicated little
concern about legal or theological niceties. The difficulty was the
public's continuing sympathy for the Prince's aggrieved first wife.

The Princess could not simply be ignored. A key factor was her
unalterable status as the mother of children who were public property.
The divorce settlement reflected this reality. Diana was not left penniless. In addition to a £15 million lump sum, reckoned to yield an
income of £1 million per annum, she was granted an additional
£350,000 for her private office, and an apartment at Kensington Palace
to provide, in the words of an official, a 'central and secure home'
for herself and her children.[33] The provisions that most interested the
public were those that related to her familial and 'royal' position. She
was granted equal responsibility with her husband for the children's
upbringing. Armed bodyguards were to be assigned to her on police
advice, and when she was with her sons.[34] However, while technically
remaining a member of the Royal Family she was required not only
to give up her military service appointments but also the title 'Her
Royal Highness' – a decision which seemed to echo Windsor vendettas
against Wallis Simpson.

The settlement solved the short-term problem of how the Princess
would live, and how the children – in whom the nation had a long-
term investment – should be brought up. But it did little to mollify
the Princess or to smooth the path to a re-marriage. Legally, a Prince
of Wales could only marry with the permission of the Monarch who
– in such a case – would certainly have to take the advice of the
Prime Minister who, in turn, would be mindful of public opinion.
Unfortunately for the Prince and Mrs Parker Bowles, polls consistently
showed a state of opinion that would have made it foolhardy for
either to allow a marriage to take place. Repeated surveys pointed to
the same conclusion: that Diana was overwhelmingly regarded as the
wronged party; and that Camilla had become a lightning conductor

for public unease about royal behaviour in general. It was symptomatic that when Carlton Television screened a debate on the Monarchy with 3,000 randomly-selected participants, any mention of Camilla was greeted with booing and hissing.[35] In the face of such opposition, the Prince had little choice – short of renouncing either Camilla or his own right to the succession – but to relegate his companion to a domestic *demi-monde*. However, this could only be a short-term expedient. It still left open the question of the role she might play if Charles succeeded to the throne.

Determined to retain both Camilla and the succession, the Prince at first adopted a tactic perilously similar to that of his great-uncle. He sought simultaneously to keep his affair discreet, while making implicitly clear his own unshakeable commitment to the person he wished to keep from view. While the Princess of Wales 'flashed her gold, sapphire and diamond wedding and engagement rings for the cameras in a gesture of defiance' at the English National Ballet, within hours of losing her HRH, the Prince sought to rehabilitate Mrs Parker Bowles. The result was a media bounty-hunt. In August 1996 the *News of the World* scooped its rivals – with the alleged connivance of St James's Palace – by publishing the first photograph for twenty years of the couple together.[36] Rumours abounded: that the Prince had promised the Queen he would not marry; that Charles and Camilla had come to a secret accord to the same effect[37]; that they would marry morganatically, and Camilla would become plain Lady, not Princess or potential Queen. A game of cat-and-mouse with the press evolved, developing into a protocol. Mrs Parker Bowles would be kept out of sight. She would not accompany the Prince on any public functions or at traditional Royal Family gatherings. But there would be no attempt to hide the existence of the relationship.[38]

The notion of an acknowledged-but-not-proclaimed affair was of course a finely balanced one. Because it was acknowledged, there was no longer a need for the tight secrecy that had been required in the days when St James's Palace pretended it was not happening. On the other hand, the fact that the Prince did not wish it to be publicised, raised the value to newspapers of any gossip or photographs that related to it. Moreover, when such items appeared, it was automatically assumed by rival newspapers that they were part of a subtle game played by the Prince's advisers.

Could the situation allow for any movement? As the first anniversary of the divorce approached, there was a testing of the water. The tactic involved showing, not only the Prince's and his partner's mutual devotion, but also Mrs Parker Bowles's publicly-useful virtues. New Labour was felt to take a relaxed and encouraging view of such an approach. However, the Prince faced a potential trap. On the one hand, those least bothered on the marriage issue (New Labour, the liberal broadsheets) included people who were ideologically most antagonistic towards the Monarchy. On the other, traditional defenders of the Monarchy – bishops, the old-fashioned middle-class and patriotic working-class – were those most likely to be hostile to 'Queen Camilla'. The danger was of making enemies of both at the same time.[39]

Nevertheless, Charles continued gingerly but purposefully to bring his companion out of the closet. During the first half of 1997, he developed a plan with the precision of a military campaign, aimed at acclimatising the public to the romantic reality. The climax was to be a party at Highgrove, his country residence, to celebrate Mrs Parker Bowles's fiftieth birthday. It was an act of defiance fraught with danger, comparable to the behaviour of his great-great-grandfather, Edward VII, who as Prince of Wales had thrown parties for Mrs Parker Bowles's great-grandmother Alice Keppel, as a similar mark of devotion, although in the case of Victoria's Heir marrying his mistress was never a possibility.[40] In some ways it was bolder. Charles and Camilla did not drink wine out of gold cups on the royal yacht like their forebears,[41] but the semi-public intimacy of the Highgrove event was in the same spirit. The party, for eighty friends, was widely and no doubt accurately seen as 'a tentative move towards the ultimate elevation of Mrs Parker Bowles to the rank of consort'.[42] Beforehand, there was speculation about a 'Camilla Group', led by the Tory politician Nicholas Soames, dedicated to protecting Mrs Parker Bowles from ungallant slurs.[43] There were also hints on the Labour side that the Prince's strategy might be working. On the day of the party, Tony Wright, PPS to the Lord Chancellor, told BBC's *Today* programme that 'most people would rather have a happy Monarch than an unhappy monarch,' and that he did not believe that a marriage 'would cause the sky to fall in'.

Mrs Parker Bowles was not a princess, but she was beginning to be seen as one. On the evening of the party on 17 July 1997, she arrived at Highgrove dressed in pink and smiled at reporters with uncustomary geniality, as she was driven through the gate.[44] At the same time, proprieties had to be maintained. There were calculated distinctions. No pictures of the couple together were permitted. But photographers were allowed on to the estate to get a better view of the guest of honour, while a police officer briefed waiting journalists on the names of other guests. Among the latter was Camilla's ex-husband – but notably not the Prince's mother, or his ex-wife. It was by all accounts a magical night. Those present included carefully selected writers and publicists. 'Camilla looked absolutely radiant,' wrote Jilly Cooper. 'The most striking memory I have is of the full moon which arrived early and stayed late. I think it's a sign.'[45] Charles led his partner to the strains of *Dancing Queen*. Next day William Hill cut the odds against a marriage by the turn of the century from 6–1 to 3–1. All agreed not only that the Prince and his partner were happier than they had ever been, but that they deserved to be so.

Or almost all. Across the Channel, in St Tropez, where the real, ex-HRH, Princess was on holiday, there were disconsolate splashings. If the Court of Queen Camilla was one focus of press attention, the Court of Princess Diana was another. The Princess had not been asked. What was her reaction? Ubiquitous cameras studied her demeanour for clues, reporters pressed for comments. 'Wouldn't it be funny if I suddenly came out of the birthday cake?' she allegedly remarked.[46] The tenor of press coverage was less than magnanimous. On Camilla's birthday *The Times* royal correspondent noted that discretion was not the Princess's watchword as she 'frolicked in the water in full view of the paparazzi' – before going night-clubbing until 4 am.[47] At home, there was amusement at behaviour that was deemed typically quixotic. Having induced police to chase away British cameramen, she posed for French ones by swinging on the ropes of her host's motor cruiser. Photographs sold for a reputed £30,000. On another day, wearing a leopard-print swimsuit and designer sunglasses, the Princess gave an impromptu press conference. 'You are going to get a big surprise with the next thing I do,' she told reporters.[48]

What might that turn out to be? There was a good deal of pleasurable anticipation, much of it about whether, and how, she might try to stand in the way of a re-marriage. Many now believed an announcement to be imminent. 'Public opinion seems to be shifting, gradually, from "not that woman!" to "why shouldn't they?",' wrote the columnist William Rees-Mogg in the aftermath of the Camilla party.[49] Fired by the Highgrove success, the Prince and his partner pressed ahead with the next stage of their phased strategy. This was to be a fundraising event on behalf of Mrs Parker Bowles's favourite charity, the National Osteoporosis Society, to be held on September 13th, and billed as Charles and Camilla's 'first public outing together'.[50] Mick Jagger, Emma Thompson and Eric Clapton were among those expected to attend, both to raise money for osteoporosis and to help along the steadily advancing rehabilitation of the Prince's friend. 'Consultants are already circling around her court,' wrote Simon Jenkins, predicting that Highgrove was a prelude to a concerted public relations offensive.[51]

The prospect of a marriage continued to be anathema to the Archbishop of Canterbury, Dr George Carey, who declared on August 5th that such an event was likely to 'create a crisis for the Church'.[52] It remained anathema to many Catholics, such as the convert Ann Widdicombe, who ominously warned: 'I hope we don't end up with an abdication.'[53] Others, however, were becoming more tolerant, according to a *Times* survey of leading 'opinion formers', which indicated that elite attitudes had changed. 'Senior members of the Privy Council are also now convinced that there is no real objection to the Prince remarrying,' wrote the paper's Whitehall editor on August 8th. A sensible arrangement had been reached over custody, and the two young princes were in any case fast approaching an age at which it would cease to be relevant. As the summer advanced, the countdown to a second wedding had apparently begun.

However, an area of difficulty remained. While Charles's private life seemed settled, his ex-wife's was not: and, as long as this was the case, her behaviour was likely to be a distraction. The people might, as Bagehot observed, prefer a royal marriage to a ministry: but their enjoyment of a second marriage would be greatly reduced if clouded by the knowledge of – and media focus upon – a disgruntled former spouse.

What kind of life was the Princess now expected by the Royal Family and loosely-defined 'Establishment' to lead? Was she to be used or ostracised? The Palace policy, reflecting a vacuum at the top on the issue, was to have no policy. The Monarch preferred not to get involved. According to one view, the Princess and the Queen had an unspoken regard for each other's qualities. 'The Queen, knowing that Diana was ill in a bulimic sense more often than not, made allowances,' according to one insider.[54] Others maintain that the relationship between the Monarch and her daughter-in-law was largely non-existent. According to Diana's former private secretary, Patrick Jephson, dealings in the run-up to the divorce were characterised by mutual nervousness. 'Between the two women, there seemed to be no substantial communication.' The Princess discovered that support from some sections of the press did not protect her from the 'Hanoverian implacability of her in-laws' which radiated from the royals whenever they met her.[55] Other witnesses maintain that the implacability hardened: after the divorce, the Princess was given no advice and was left to sink or swim. 'There was a failure to embrace her in an understanding manner,' suggests one ex-courtier. 'There was a clear determination to get rid of her off the face of the earth. She was seen as a destructive force. The attitude was "go away".' The subject of the Princess and her future became a non-subject – something not to be raised. 'The attitude was just: get off the patch – she's a pain, pest, get her out of the family.' Yet the Queen also appeared as much bewildered as angry. A guest at Sandringham on Boxing Day around the time of the divorce recalls being told that Diana had come to church with the royal party the day before, then left after lunch, refusing to stay. Using the excuse of taking the guest aside to look at the array of family Christmas presents, the Queen unburdened herself. 'I don't know what it is,' she said. 'She hates us. She doesn't want to be with us. It is so sad. It doesn't have to be like that.'

Though they could be guessed at, the Queen did not make her own feelings public. By contrast, the Princess felt no need for reticence. As she sought restlessly to adjust to her post-royal life, she was happy to fuel, by word and gesture, the tabloid demand for evidence of her hostility to the Windsors. Editors – also feeling their way – alternated between a woman wronged and glamour tarnished. Public sympathy for Diana's plight was mixed with a sense that she had brought it upon herself. In the months following the divorce, she found herself with a new script, and uncomfortably in danger of acquiring a new identity: the banished ex-royal who, like the Duchess of Windsor, had become a functionless, thrill-seeking appendage to the Royal saga, and was expected to pay the price. Thus the Princess became mawkish fare for continental magazines, while in the mainstream British press, writers adopted a quizzical, slightly amused tone in describing somebody who, they implied, craved the attention they gave her.

Diana, however, was not Wallis. She had little interest in the trappings of royalty and, indeed, impatiently rejected them. At the same time, she had acquired a taste, not just for public attention, but also for exercising her undeniable ability to draw public attention to the good causes she espoused. Commentators viewed her philanthropy in varying ways. Admirers identified her as a new kind of high-profile patron, who saw that there were better ways of helping to raise money or highlight a social problem than by shaking hands with dignitaries and making stilted speeches. Detractors, on the other hand, suggested that she was as interested in the photo-opportunities – and the irritation caused in St James's Palace – as in the sufferers. Palace staff believed there was a tit-for-tat approach. Following the divorce, Diana got her office to take on engagements in retaliation to the engagements Charles took on. 'After the Dimbleby book she told me, "One day, I'll get back at him. I'll pick a moment and clean him up",' recalls one former royal aide. 'They were at each other's throats.' Whatever her motives, perhaps partly because of the conflict observers could detect in them, she remained a scene-stealer, 'a dazzling public performer'.[56]

Here was the central irony, painful to both St James's and Buckingham Palace. 'The Court is a separate part,' wrote Bagehot, 'which stands aloof from the rest of the London world, and which has slender relations with the more amusing part of it.' Diana had rejected aloofness, yet remained leader of the amusing part. 'To state the matter shortly,' according to the Victorian writer, 'Monarchy is a Government in which the attention of the nation is concentrated on one person doing interesting actions. A Republic is a Government in which that attention is divided between many, who are all doing uninteresting actions.'[57] Diana's presence in the Royal Family had made the Court more interesting. 'They were thrilled when she arrived,' according to a former aide, ' – to have this happy boisterous creature in their midst.' Her exclusion made it more dull – and moved the focal royal story away from the family proper, to wherever she happened to be. The truth was that for some time the 'one person' had not been the Queen, or her Heir, but Diana: her departure took away the pageant's savour.

What amused a public audience, however, appeared arid and lonely to those closest to her. The Princess's friends at this time found her witty, whimsical, impulsive and fey – and, at the same time, angrily relieved to have broken free of those she contemptuously referred to as 'that lot'. Yet they were also aware that she had entered a twilight world, outside the Establishment yet not belonging anywhere else, increasingly cut off from the possibility of normal relationships. 'She was like a racehorse,' says one, not unfriendly, ex-courtier, who knew her well at this time. 'Unreliable, highly strung, unpredictable, very erratic. She was very good with people at arm's length – if you were a leper she could bridge the gap on the basis that she would be going home in the evening.' After the separation, and especially after the divorce, she had fewer engagements, partly from choice – she 'wanted to get out of the royal madness,' as she put it. The downside was that it deprived her of things to do during the day. 'All she ever did was shop, go to the gym, spend hours on the phone.'[58] At weekends, she was often alone in her Kensington Palace apartment. Her genuine friendships, in any case, were declining in number. 'She was charming and foul by turns,' maintains her former private secretary. Latterly, 'it always seemed to be the foul that came out on top'.[59]

There was a bleakness, compounded by lack of education and the constraints imposed by her celebrity status. 'She loved her children dearly,' according to a source, 'though I detected that the boys had her measure. When she was banging on about the press, they rolled their eyes, meaning "She's at it again".' The arrangement with her ex-husband was that in the holidays the children spent equal time with each parent. 'She had nothing much to do when she was with the boys except to go out and get a Big Mac or video in Kensington High Street. When they were with the Prince of Wales there was hunting, shooting and other interests to share. When she made trips away with them, for example to Disneyland, they turned into media circuses. By the end she had no hands left to play.'[60] 'Diana the hunted,' as the journalist Suzanne Lowry had called her in a book published more than a decade earlier[61] was a technically accurate description. Not only could she not go to the gym without being photographed. The impossibility of keeping her romantic life secret raised question marks about anybody with the temerity to be seen in her company. One relationship that at first seemed to have staying power was with Dr Hasmet Khan, a Pakistani surgeon she had met at the Royal Brompton Hospital in 1995. It was a mark of the difficulty of the life she was now leading that she had to adopt disguises in order to visit his hospital accommodation.[62] At one point in the liaison, she confided to a member of the Household that she wanted Khan to come and live with her in Kensington Palace.[63]

Some royal advisers regarded her as dangerously unstable. 'Nicholas Soames's view of her mental state was widely shared in Palace circles,' claims Jephson.[64] A member of the Royal Family who held it was her ex-husband. 'The Prince took the attitude: "she's completely off her rocker and has to be written out of the script",' according to a former royal aide. 'Diana was terribly, terribly mentally sick,' Charles told an informant, after the Princess's death. 'She was quite mad. She used to throw things.'[65] In March 1996, the Princess was involved in an accident when she was driving in the Cromwell Road. Concern was expressed about the lack of care she showed over her own safety. 'As to whether she would actually take an overdose,' a psychiatrist was quoted as saying, in a speculative 'psychological' study of her problems published at the time of the divorce, '. . . I don't think she would. But she could do something that would get her killed by somebody outside, or put herself at danger in some other way by being reckless . . . there is nothing Diana would like more, in a sense, than to go out as a martyr.'[66] Among the more responsible media commentators, there was unease at the pressure she was under. 'Are we not turning the lives of people like Diana and Charles into what amounts to a snuff soap opera?' asked Matthew Parris, in defence of both of them.[67]

Cummings

"I'm having a ghastly nightmare that the photographers stopped invading my privacy!"

The Times, 16th August, 1997

During the hot, politics-filled summer of 1997, the pressure seemed to slacken. For a few weeks, the Princess appeared less often on the front pages, and there was talk of the divorce having marginalised her. The respite was brief and ended, predictably, with evidence of a fresh entanglement that promised to stimulate the jaded public palate. To the existing list of suitors was added a new name: Dodi Al-Fayed, son of Mohamed Al-Fayed, the owner of Harrods. Comment was pillorying, harrassing and flippant. Was this a genuine romance, or merely an attempt to raise hackles by linking the Windsors to the most inappropriate dynasty available? There was little doubt among some members of the Household. 'Diana going off with him,' suggests one, 'was cocking a snook at her husband and all his works.'[68] On August 10th, the *Sunday Mirror* published photos, for which they paid a quarter of a million pounds, of Dodi and Diana on holiday in France, apparently kissing. The press sought a Buckingham Palace reaction but did not get one. The dalliances of the Princess were no longer an official concern.

The Queen was in Balmoral surrounded by members of her extended family, including the Prince of Wales and his sons. At home there was no royal news. An ICM poll conducted at the beginning of August offered the Princess some consolation, giving the Monarchy its lowest rating ever, with the proportion of people who answered that Britain would be 'worse off without the Royal Family,' slipping below fifty per cent for the first time, and showing hostility to the prospect of Queen Camilla at a new peak.[69] Otherwise, the press was reduced to reporting that dozens of the Queen's swans had been killed by blue algae, caused by the August heat.

Those looking forward to Diana's 'next thing', however, did not have long to wait. The day after the algae story, British newspapers carried reports of an interview with the Princess published in *Le Monde* under the heading 'La Princesse au Grand Coeur'. Questioned by a French journalist, Diana presented herself as a dedicated campaigner against injustice. She praised New Labour for its stance on landmines, and dismissed the former administration led by John Major as 'hopeless'. But her main targets were the media, and her former in-laws. 'The press is ferocious,' she was quoted as saying. 'It never forgives anything, it is only interested in mistakes. Every good intention is diverted, every gesture is criticised.' As for the Windsors, she contrasted the lack of spontaneity of the Royal Family (where 'nothing, of any sort, could be done naturally') with her own impulsiveness. 'I work by instinct,' she told the reporter, 'that is my best adviser' – adding in words that were to resonate later:

> I feel close to people whoever they are . . . that is why I annoy certain circles. Because I am much closer to people at the bottom than at the top, the latter do not forgive me. Because I have a real relationship with the most humble people. Nothing gives me greater pleasure than to try to help the most vulnerable people in society. This is an aim and henceforth an essential part of my life. A sort of destiny. I will run to whoever calls in distress, wherever they are.

The Princess was cruising with Dodi in the Mediterranean when the interview appeared in the British press on August 27th, causing a doubtless half-intended row. It was not a big story, and might have received scant attention had it not been high summer, with newspapers understaffed and little else going on. An obscure Tory front-bencher was found to express his dismay, and the historian Lord Blake called it 'quite the most extraordinary thing I have heard from a member of the Royal Family'. From the Al-Fayed yacht, Diana denied criticising the former Tory Government. The French journalist denied her denial. Meanwhile Robin Cook, the new Foreign Secretary, defended the Princess's frankness and welcomed her landmines campaign. *Le Monde*, pleased by the fuss, called the interview the most important since her 'televised confession to Dimbleby' – mixing up Dimbleby and Martin Bashir.

Next day, the press took note of the first anniversary of the royal divorce. St James's Palace, ready with a counter spin, issued a statement announcing that Mrs Parker Bowles intended to open a London office to deal with her voluntary work for the National Osteoporosis Society. On August 29th it was reported that Diana, still on the yacht, was expected to return to Kensington Palace the same day.[70] On the 30th, *The Times* noted that the Princess had been criticised for failing to wear a life-jacket while zooming about off the Sardinian coast on a two-seater jet-ski – unlike the pursuing paparazzi, who had taken the required precaution.

At Balmoral, it was a summer like any other, minus the Princess of Wales. As well as Charles and his sons, the party included Princess Anne with her husband, Captain Lawrence, and her daughter Zara Phillips, and a number of members of the Household, together with Mabel Anderson, the former nanny. A few friends also gathered. Talk at dinner on August 29th was about what they were up to, what the grouse were like, days spent on the hill. A source of amusement or alarm was Zara who had a silver stud in her tongue. 'Every time she laughed, you saw this flashing.' Philip arrived in the evening, in the driving rain. The Queen was playing patience at a card table in the drawing room, talking to her mother and sister. The Duke went up to his wife, stroked her head and said: 'Lovely to see you'. Next morning, the boys were 'larking around' in the nursery, asking Mabel where their clothes were. They were going shooting. 'Are these socks right?' shouted one of the princes. 'It was all so happy,' according to an informant.[71]

Despite expectations, Diana did not return to England on the 29th or the 30th. Later, it was suggested that she delayed her departure to avoid becoming embroiled in further controversy over her 'Conservatives are hopeless' remark.[72] Instead, she and Dodi Al-Fayed travelled to Paris on August 30th, apparently planning to return to Britain next day. They arrived at the Ritz hotel at 11 pm, to be greeted by about forty photographers. Shortly after midnight, the couple left the building by a rear entrance hoping to avoid them. The hope was disappointed. They were seen, and there was a chase. Pursued by photographers on motor cycles and in cars, Dodi's driver took them towards a house in western Paris where they intended to spend the night. They never reached it. In a tunnel beneath the Place de l'Alma, the car went out of control and collided with a pillar. The driver and Al-Fayed were killed instantly. The Princess and a bodyguard were seriously injured. It was a commonplace accident, with a commonplace cause: the driver, under the influence of alcohol, was driving at excessive speed.[73] It soon became the most famous accident in the world.

Ordinariness was combined with Boschian horror: underground, at night, surrounded by the voracious media. Witnesses recall smoke billowing from the engine, and the blare of the horn echoing out into the street. Photographers were at the scene within seconds. 'Whether or not the paparazzi helped cause Diana's death,' in Martin Amis's words, 'they undoubtedly defiled its setting.'[74] Most accounts agree that they immediately began taking pictures, and only then offered or attempted to get help. Some observers remember a group of between ten and fifteen, their cameras going off like machine guns. 'It's true, we didn't help the wounded,' one later admitted. 'Maybe it was through a sense of modesty (*pudeur*) . . . It shows a lot of arrogance going to help the people that we were following just a few minutes earlier.'

The first doctor on the scene had been travelling through the tunnel in the opposite direction. When he examined the victims, he found that the Princess was still breathing. He called the emergency service, and put an oxygen mask on her face. The police arrived shortly afterwards and had to fight their way through a crush of photographers who were still shooting the wrecked car and its occupants. One policeman recalled that the Princess's eyes were open, and that she muttered in English, 'My God' – apparently at seeing Dodi dead beside her. By the time the emergency services were on the scene, she had become incoherent. While she was being moved to the ambulance, she suffered a heart attack, and was given a cardiac massage. The ambulance drove slowly towards the Pitié-Salpetrière hospital, stopping on one occasion so that she could receive further attention. X-rays at the hospital showed extensive internal bleeding. After a second heart attack, her chest was opened and she received a manual heart massage followed by electric shock treatment.[75] But no spontaneous heart beat was resumed and at 4 am she was pronounced dead. Downing Street received the news a few minutes later. 'This is going to be a monster event,' said one adviser.[76] At 4.41 am the world was told in a brief newsflash: 'Diana, Princess of Wales has died, according to British sources, the Press Association learnt this morning.' The British Ambassador, Sir Michael Jay, made the official announcement at a press conference at the hospital at 5.45 am. 'Tonight's accident is a terrible tragedy', he said. 'The death of the Princess of Wales fills us all with deep shock and deep grief.'[77] 'Over the wires the electric message came,' a Poet Laureate wrote, describing how the world learnt of the illness of Queen Victoria's eldest son. Electric messages seemed to travel faster and further at the end of the twentieth century. The news that the Princess had been injured, then that she was dead, reached Americans first, starting on the West Coast. Britain woke to it. The universal reaction was disbelief.

25

NOBODY CAN ASSESS, because nobody can possibly know, the impact of private grief. The public reaction, on the other hand, was manifest: though open to different interpretations. Swift, vocal, unexpected, the wave of emotion that followed the accidental death of a recently-rejected princess has been taken as evidence of the fragility of modern British Monarchy. This, in a way, it was. But it can also be seen as a powerful expression of the continuing grip of the idea of royalty on the popular imagination.

How can Diana week be diagnosed? Four years later, it is impossible to know whether what became known as 'the public grief' was unique, or should be seen as a symptom of a wider malaise, heralding other as yet unimaginable convulsions. In the wake of the terrorist outrage of 2001, when the grounds for worldwide grief were incomparably more profound, yet public mourning was comparatively restrained, it is especially perplexing. A few observations can nevertheless be made.

First, despite the temptation to dismiss it as banal, the collective emotion was an objective reality. Second, the grief was hysterical in the sense that it was disproportionately greater than feelings expressed following other, frequently as tragic, losses and disasters. September 1997 was not a good month, as one commentator put it, for those who imagined that human society was governed by reason.[1] Third, the grief was fanned and exaggerated by the very force initially blamed for the tragedy – the press and electronic media, whose fixation on the Princess to the exclusion of any other kind of news had a self-fulfilling aspect, making it impossible for people to discuss anything else, even if they had wished to do so. Fourth, the gushing and excited tone of much of what was said at the time, embarrassing to read at a cool distance, was actually a symptom of the pathology it was describing and, indeed, feeding. Fifth, although mass hysteria occurs from time to time, the global reach of this particular manifestation was something that had not previously been known. Purely parochial explanations of what occurred, in terms of the relationship of the British to authority, fail to take account of the enormous interest aroused by the tragedy in the United States, Germany, South America, and many other countries without either a royal family, or strong ties to the United Kingdom. 'Floral fascism and an explosion of almost medieval irrationality'[2] in the early autumn of 1997 were by no means a purely Anglo-Saxon phenomenon.

After the announcement, there were two sequences of events. One involved the Spencers, the Windsors and royal advisers. The other, the press and public. The Government adopted the role of broker. In the process, the Monarchy – which had spent the twentieth century trying to keep out of politics – was placed at the centre of a political storm.

The royal response to the tragedy began when Robin Janvrin, at Balmoral, received a call from France shortly after the ambulance reached the hospital. He woke the Prince of Wales. Mohamed Al-Fayed was also contacted, and immediately arranged to fly by helicopter to Paris. The Prime Minister, in his constituency, took a call at around 3.30 am.[3] A call to Balmoral shortly afterwards conveyed the news that the Princess had died. On hearing it, according to one account, the Prince broke down. Shortly after 7 am, the Prince told his children.[4] Harry was later heard asking if they were sure she was dead – whether they were certain they weren't making a mistake.[5] Buckingham Palace issued a simple statement: 'The Queen and the Prince of Wales are deeply shocked and distressed by this terrible news.' No further announcement was made. In a breakfast conversation with the Prime Minister, the Queen made it clear that no member of the Royal Family would speak publicly about the tragedy. The job of articulating the nation's feelings would be left to him.[6]

Charles immediately made the decision to fly to Paris to collect the body. However, there was initial uncertainty about what would happen next. An institution that functioned on tradition had no experience of the sudden death of a central player, let alone one whose official status was so ill-defined. It was an added difficulty that the accident occurred at a moment of royal diaspora. Members of the Queen's staff on duty were divided between Balmoral and Buckingham Palace, while several key courtiers were on holiday – Geoff Crawford, the Press Secretary, in his native Australia, and Mary Francis, the Assistant Private Secretary, in Greece. Charles's private secretary, Stephen Lamport, was in London. The duty press officer at Buckingham Palace was the Deputy Press Secretary, Penny Russell-Smith. Crawford heard the news on the radio, about five hours after the death. There was no immediate instruction for either him or Mary Francis to return. 'It's all under control, it could just be a family funeral,' was the message. 'When I rang up,' says one ex-courtier, 'there was genuine uncertainty about whether it was going to be public or private. If it had been private, guidance wouldn't have been needed.' Thirty-six hours later, a different message came through: 'There's been a huge change. The funeral will be on Saturday, please get back.' Crawford arrived in London early on the Thursday morning. When he left Sydney, Australians were laying flowers in the streets.

At Balmoral, the atmosphere, as one witness puts it, was 'what you would imagine any family to be going through'. The tragedy was experienced first and foremost (and perhaps always) as a private loss. There was a desire to protect the princes – and to do so by keeping them in Scotland, out of the limelight. Up to a point, the aim was realised. 'Balmoral,' suggests one source, 'creates this unworldly feeling – calm, sedate. It cuts you off. The attitude was "we're here looking after the boys in their grief".' The rhythms of life went on, and it was possible on the estate to imagine that nothing outside was happening. It was necessary to turn on the radio or television to be aware of the turmoil raging in London and the rest of the United Kingdom.

The turmoil, however, had to be addressed. Caught between the private and the public, the Queen's response was to fall back on what had always been her defence in times of stress: routine and protocol. There should be no departure from how things had always been, no abandonment of custom. Unfortunately, routine and protocol were designed to deal with normal events, or abnormal ones that happened to other people. They offered little solace in a crisis of such unpredicted and uncontrollable magnitude. At Buckingham Palace, there had been a sense of the Princess as a diminishing problem, with the peak of damage passed. 'Her coverage was reducing in the media – the story was coming off the boil,' according to a former aide. 'The Queen had been protected from the reality of what the Princess's standing in the world was like,' says a New Labour insider. 'She didn't recognise what was going on out there.' According to a former royal aide: 'The Royal Family were like rabbits in the glare of a headlight. The family had no conceivable idea of how the whole thing was being perceived.'

August 31st was a Sunday. A royal party, including the Queen, the Prince of Wales, the Queen Mother, and Princes William and Harry, attended morning service as usual at Crathie Kirk, near the castle. According to a member of the Royal Family in conversation later, the boys were given the option of going or staying. The Queen said something like: 'We're going to church. Do you want to come? You don't have to.' They said yes they did, they did not want to be left behind. Going was better than sitting alone. Members of the church party wore black. Charles's eyes were reported to be bloodshot. Otherwise, there was no visible acknowledgement of the calamity. 'The extraordinary thing is, the boys haven't even cried,' the Queen Mother said later in the day. 'It must be the shock.' During the service Diana was not mentioned, and the minister delivered his original sermon, including jokes, without any reference to the tragedy. Afterwards, Charles drove himself to Aberdeen airport. In Paris, the Prince and Diana's two sisters were greeted at the hospital by President Chirac. Just after 5 pm, the coffin was carried from the hospital by four pall-bearers. The French President was seen to wipe away a tear as the cortège left. Meanwhile, people had been laying flowers at Balmoral, and outside the gates of Buckingham Palace and at Kensington Palace. They began before dawn. 'The public expected the Royal Family to react like film stars,' says a former courtier, 'with a public display of private grief.'[7] Nothing would have been more out of character: yet nothing in the circumstances was more required.

The mass emotions were not invented. 'When a leader dies,' according to an authority on bereavement, 'particularly if the death was unexpected, the survival of the group itself is threatened. Its members feel personally threatened because a leader is each member writ large.'[8] As soon as the death was known, the sense that people Diana had never met strongly identified with her as a symbolic leader, was poignant and palpable. Many of the bouquets were accompanied by handwritten messages, as if the writer needed to explain why he or she was affected. 'I could not weep when my mother died,' according to one, typically. 'You have taught me how to weep.' Another wrote:

I can't understand this feeling of pain,
For someone who never even heard my name.[9]

It was the spontaneous gathering of crowds that made the media aware that the story was not just the death, but the reaction to the death. On television, mourners were shown openly weeping. Reporters began interviewing some of them. People remembered her beauty, her impulsiveness, the precision of her wit, her lack of social distance, her tactile quality. Comfort was taken in clichés. 'Diana was in everybody's life,' said one mourner. 'Britain has lost the jewel in the crown of its Royal Family. It is as though the fairy tale has finally come to an end.' Older people related the tragedy to royal events in the past. 'I was a little kid when King George VI died,' said a middle-aged man. 'I was down here with my mum. It was a freezing cold day and I remember the same crowds, except most people wore black.'[10]

Tributes from foreign leaders showed that the Princess, often the cause of mixed feelings at home, was a less complicated symbol in other countries. Nelson Mandela described her as 'an ambassador for victims of landmines, war orphans, the sick and needy throughout the world'.[11] Mother Teresa – whose death a few days later was barely noticed because of the Princess mania – promised to pray for her.[12] Across the Atlantic, Diana was swiftly adopted as 'America's Princess'. 'From the moment she danced with John Travolta, she became an honorary American,' wrote the former editor of the New Republic, Andrew Sullivan. '. . . In that early act alone, and in countless other gestures in subsequent years, Diana tapped into . . . suburban American dreams, and more than fulfilled them.'[13] Wracking their brains for an analogy, journalists on both sides of the ocean placed Diana alongside stars and politicians who shared the characteristic of shocking the world by being struck down in their prime – Lennon, Monroe, Luther King. Soon she belonged to everybody. The Prime Minister was in his constituency for the Bank Holiday weekend without political

Daily Express, 1st September, 1997

staff. Somebody found him a black tie.[14] Facing the cameras, and doing what in retrospect the Queen should have done, he made a carefully-rehearsed, but nevertheless moving statement that encapsulated a feeling widely shared. 'She was the people's princess', he said, 'and this is how she will stay.'[15]

Obituaries appeared in the British press on September 1st, by which time everything that conceivably might be said about Diana had been, press stories had begun cannibalising each other, and a posse of reporters was roaming the capital looking for a new angle. 'A great virtue could have been made of the family's reaction,' says a former aide. 'What happened was a disappearing into a bunker.'[16] 'Not since the Abdication has the Palace needed sound heads as it does today,' reflected *The Times*.[17] Disasters generally invite blame. On this occasion, because of the presence of the paparazzi at the scene, the first target was the press. Recriminations against the media began from the moment of the announcement of the death. When journalists assembled at La Pitié-Salpetrière to cover Prince Charles's arrival, there were shouts of 'assassins' from the crowd. On the day after the tragedy, the Princess's younger brother, Earl Spencer, fuelled public feeling against the media by reading a statement saying that every editor and proprietor who had published intrusive pictures of Diana had blood on their hands. In London, photographers and cameramen were jostled and insulted. Then the search for culprits widened. For the Queen, a dangerous period had begun.

If Diana belonged to the people, who or what had taken her away? The answer was a nebulous 'Them', who increasingly cropped up in scribbled notes attached to bouquets. 'They' – who lacked understanding, who had no spontaneity, who excluded Diana, who pushed her out in the cold – were the Establishment, the anonymous bureaucrats, above all the icy, insensitive, surviving Windsors. The mood expressed in the written messages hardened. Diana, they declared, was the 'true' royal who understood ordinary people. On the tributes and epitaphs, the Princess began to be accompanied by Dodi – a comfortingly mysterious martyr of whom, until a few weeks earlier, nobody had heard – while the Windsors were presented as remote and out of touch. The press amplified the theme. By their silence, 'They' were revealing themselves in their true colours. 'A lot of people held the Prince of Wales responsible for his ex-wife's sorry end', diagnosed the *Independent* on the Tuesday, ' – not directly responsible, but somehow culpable because the death and its manner seems as if it is an extension of the sadness of her life'.[18] The message was quickly picked up by roving interviewers and bounced back into the crowds, intensifying into a series of contrasts: Diana's warmth, the Royal Family's coldness; Diana's spontaneity and accessibility, the Royal Family's stiffness and aloofness; the Princess's modernity, their stuffiness – and so on.

Outside Balmoral, mourners noticed that the Royal Standard was not being flown at half-mast. A Palace spokesman explained that the Standard accompanied the Sovereign, wherever he or she happened to be. It was never flown at half-mast – not for the death of the Queen's father, or after the death of any Sovereign, or after the death of Winston Churchill. 'Are we really saying that the Princess was more important to the nation than Churchill?' asked a royal defender.[19] 'The Queen's attitude,' according to one courtier, 'was "why after a hundred years of history should we do it differently?"'

This, indeed, was the nub. What to the public, and to journalists who took it up, seemed the simplest gesture of respect, was regarded by the Monarch as a matter of tradition and family custom, on which it would be both demeaning and ridiculous to give way. 'The Queen was very upset by the accusations of not caring, and not coming to London,' says one source. 'She was very annoyed by the criticism over the Royal Standard.'[20] One psychological view of grief suggests that the first stage of the mourning process is denial. The second is anger.[21] After Diana's death, anger seems to have struck the crowds and the Queen at about the same time. According to various accounts, her intransigence on the issue of flagpoles was greater than on any other.

The tabloids detected a chink. If not at Balmoral, what about London? At Buckingham Palace, the flagpole stood insensitively bare: symbol of the unfeeling royals' hostility to the Princess and of their indifference to public opinion. A spokesman responded: flags were only flown over royal residences when the Sovereign was residing in them. The crowds were unpersuaded. 'With hindsight,' reflects a former member of the royal staff, 'we should have settled on a better pattern of key decisions. You must have something every day for the media.' As it was, the media had to find something for itself. A story was gaining momentum: the Royal Family did not share the feelings of the crowd, or sympathise with them. In the Palace, there was alarm. 'We had a grim recognition,' says an insider, 'of reaping a whirlwind.'[22]

The tabloids hesitated, conscious of the anti-paparazzi and anti-media climate, and as bewildered as anyone. Then they picked up and led the attack on the uncaring Monarch. 'Let her flag fly at half-mast,' demanded the *Daily Mail*. 'The Final Insult,' said the *Sun*. 'Show us you care,' appealed the *Express*. The *Mirror* begged: 'Speak to us, ma'am, please speak.' The humbug contained in these attacks was not lost on everybody. The American singer, Madonna, who had some experience of media overheating, was asked about her own thoughts on Diana. 'You were never allowed to make mistakes without being hanged in the public square,' she observed. As for the press, 'if you co-operate they say you are being manipulative. They were constantly doing that with Diana ... They were so awful to her and now ... they are putting her on a pedestal and saying she is so great and fabulous, yet two weeks ago they were ripping her to shreds.'[23]

'There was a bit of a black hole,' acknowledges a former royal aide. Why was the Palace so slow? The real problem, the press began to perceive, was not the Court, but its employer. The point had become difficult to deny. 'If she had made an early and personal statement saying "we are all in shock – she was a wonderful woman", that would have stopped the rot,' reflects an ex-courtier. 'Her refusal meant that

Blair had open season. In the old days, the PR person appeared on television. Today it is the Managing Director. You have to do it.' But the Managing Director did not stir. Should the Monarch have appeared in person? 'There was the dotty idea,' says another former aide, 'that the Queen should abandon her grandchildren and make some public declaration of grief.' But not everybody thought it so dotty. 'The great public emotion needed a reaction,' according to a third adviser. 'A slicker PR machine would have been out there saying things on the Queen's behalf.'[24] Staff were put on the defensive. 'The Princess was a much-loved national figure, but she was also a mother whose sons miss her deeply,' pleaded the now-returned Queen's press secretary, echoing the line taken in Balmoral.[25] 'Thank goodness we're all together,' said the Queen Mother privately, expressing her daughter's view. 'We can look after them' – meaning the boys.[26] However, the argument that the Queen was so preoccupied at 'the great haven of Balmoral' comforting her grandchildren that she was unable to speak to the nation, no longer seemed adequate. A private crisis had become a public one, even though nobody knew what it was about.

Stories leaked of confusion and uncertainty over the funeral arrangements – Spencers pressing for a private ceremony, and the Queen initially supporting them, before agreeing to the formula of a 'unique funeral for a unique person,' neither state nor private. Meanwhile, there were rumours of a battle between the Prince of Wales and his mother over where the body should rest before its internment. According to one version, each palace had its own agenda – Buckingham Palace defending the Monarchy, St James's defending Prince Charles and Kensington defending the memory of Diana. One issue was whether Elton John, a friend of the Princess, should be invited to sing. The Palace became embroiled in a discussion over the practicalities of John moving his own piano into the Abbey and rehearsing on it. 'At the moment it will be a pretty formal affair,' a pro-John advocate was quoted as saying. 'We want to incorporate the spirit of Diana.'[27] The question of whether or not the singer should be allowed to perform – the Palace denied that it was opposed, but the press ignored the denial – encapsulated the division between those who saw the ritual as a way of evoking the past, and those who wanted to use it to express current feeling. Mixed in was the role of the Monarchy itself. By the Wednesday, it had come directly under fire.

The broadsheets divided between the royalist but sharply critical *Times* and *Telegraph*, and the insurrectionary *Guardian* and *Independent*, which began hopefully to identify the crowds as progressive and even potentially republican. However, as the days passed, it was not just the liberal press that perceived the need for an intervention that would take the heat out of the situation. On the Thursday, *The Times* reported 'increasing public disquiet' at the failure of the Queen and her relatives to respond to the tide of sympathy.[28] By this time, there was a checklist of grievances: the 'unfeeling' attendance at church on the Sunday with the boys, non-existent or unlowered flags, the unresolved nature of the funeral service and – above all – the Queen's apparently stubborn refusal either to speak, or to return from Scotland and face her people (that is, her people in London) who, for the first time in her reign, were calling her to account. Understaffed and regrouping, the Palace fought a rearguard action – with one hand tied, because of the Queen's resistance. Frustration among advisers became difficult to hide. 'The Royal Family was clearly out of touch,' considers an ex-courtier. 'It felt as though they were on another planet.'

There were other problems. Despite long experience of dealing with the press in difficult circumstances, the Palace scarcely had the resources to handle the hundreds of journalists currently in town. The Government, fresh out of an election, was in a position to fill in the gaps. It was also in a position to make use of, and add to, its post-victory prestige. There was a speedy assessment within the Blair entourage. Then, in widely-noted contrast to the Queen, the Prime Minister travelled south as quickly as possible, and allowed himself to be seen greeting mourners at the gates of Downing Street. Buckingham Palace did not cede control, and remained in charge of the funeral arrangements. Over the wires the message came, however, that Blair, not the Royal Family, was sensitive to the feelings of the people.

At the Palace, the Lord Chamberlain, Lord Airlie, assembled a team to put together the 'unique' ceremony, for which no contingency plans existed. This included key courtiers, members of the Windsor and Spencer families, together with Government advisers. Meetings were held each morning, with a telephone link to Scotland. Royal staff worked, on a daily basis, with Alastair Campbell and Anji Hunter from No.10. 'The Palace was all over the place in the first two days,' says a New Labour insider. 'They didn't know what modern public relations was about. They were keen to get advice on what became a mega communications strategy.' There were tensions. 'Charlie Spencer was not easy,' says a Palace source. 'Robert [Fellowes] did not find him easy. He had his own views and a long-standing attitude towards the Royal Family. There were fairly direct discussions about what would happen. In times of stress, people do talk directly.' There was a disagreement over asking newspaper editors to the funeral. Buckingham Palace sent out invitations; the Spencer camp expressed its bitterness against the media by effectively cancelling them. Yet participants agree that the key decisions came from the Palace. 'The Government attended planning meetings every day,' according to an ex-courtier. 'But they were at one remove. There was some spinning going on, aligning the Prime Minister with the Diana camp, versus the Palace. However, there was very close co-operation and working together. It was not the case that the Government or political machine was forcing the Palace to act in various ways.' According to a Government adviser, what the Palace needed – and what it got – was a 'reality check': the benefit of the advice of people who fully understood the press–public opinion nexus. But control, he acknowledges, remained in royal hands.[29]

In politics, however, the reality that matters is the perception. By mid-week, the press view had firmed up: Buckingham Palace was at sixes and sevens, the Prime Minister's office was making the running and mediating judiciously in family quarrels. 'People are being insensitive to what is a difficult time for them,' a senior Government official replied, not entirely helpfully, to criticisms of Buckingham Palace. 'It is unfair to characterise them as not knowing how to respond.'[30] The implication was noted. 'Blair instrumental in people's funeral plan,' said the newspapers. As one, anti-New Labour, commentator put it, 'That was Mandelson-speak for: "The Court, stuffy as ever, cannot be trusted to reflect either the grief of the nation or the debt it owes to the charismatic Diana".'[31] Later, it became the received wisdom that while Buckingham Palace had been overwhelmed by the tide of events, Downing Street had emerged with credit for effectively taking over the operation. Meanwhile, politicians out of the front-line were voicing their non-attributable opinions. 'In the early part of the week we were frustrated by the stuffed shirts and deadbeats at the Palace,' an anonymous minister was quoted as saying.[32] According to one investigation, the stuffed shirts included the Queen herself whose conversations with the Prime Minister had become strained. Allegedly, 'There was not much natural empathy between them' at any rate on this topic.[33] Blair's conversations with the Prince of Wales appeared to be more productive. All in all, it was a good few days for the fledgling administration and a rotten one for the Palace which, hampered by lack of guidance from the top, lacked direction.

At first the attitude of the Windsors to the 'public grief' – including its wilder and more threatening manifestations – was one of vexation. There was a feeling that it was all absurd, a distraction put up by the tabloids, and the crowds would soon snap out of it. 'It was so *un-British*,' says one retainer. 'They thought they knew the British public, thought they had a rapport with it,' says another insider, 'but it had suddenly deserted them.' An institution that prided itself on understanding the nation, no longer did.[34]

One un-British – or at any rate, novel – manifestation was the floral displays, made possible, as has since been pointed out, by a new market-place in cut flowers, wreaths and bouquets borne of increased public affluence.[35] Fortunes were made in Diana week. Wholesale prices rose by 25 per cent, with some customers reported to be spending £100 a time. Later it was estimated that £25 million had been spent on 1.3 million bouquets – a figure widely quoted to indicate that flower-laying in memory of dead princesses was not eccentric, but had become a national custom, 'both enormously touching and deeply unsettling'.[36] Two recently invented traditions were spontaneously combined to produce it: flowers to celebrate liberty (as after the fall of Communism, or of Fascism in Southern Europe) and the practice of placing flowers by the roadside at the site of an accident or murder. The effect was to transform urban centres. Cenotaphs and town halls all over the country acquired mountains of colour and cellophane, flickering eerily in the early autumn sunlight. There were also other, stranger, monuments. In Kensington Gardens, beyond the bouquets that covered an acre of land shoulder-high, every tree and stump in the park became an altar, decorated with candles, toys, letters, photos, drawings and prayers.

In the Mall and Birdcage Walk, a huge crowd constantly mingled. Many queued. At St James's Palace, the waiting time to sign books of condolence grew to five hours, and eventually to eleven. By Friday, the number of books had grown to forty-three. It was pointed out that when George VI died there had been just five. People wrote in the books that the light had gone out of their lives. According to a recent study of Diana messages, many of the entries were written in semi-biblical language, and described a Damascus Road-type 'conversion experience' involving a physical collapse or fit that occurred when the mourner heard the news of the tragedy ('the presence of God was so strong on me that I could hardly get up').[37] The Salvation Army organised free teas for people queuing. In St James's Street, close to the chapel where the coffin lay, people were to be seen in huddled groups, kneeling and praying. Who were they? Some reports suggested a large number of people from ethnic minorities, and of homosexual men. An ICM exit poll of St James's Palace book signers, however, showed that only ten per cent had an 'ethnic' background (roughly in line with the South East England norm) and only four per cent described themselves as gay. On the other hand, there was a large preponderance of women (80 per cent), and disproportionate numbers of younger people (68 per cent were under 45), middle class people (56 per cent) and readers of the *Daily Mail* (27 per cent).[38]

How much was the product of hype? To some extent, people preceded press – despite the Balmoral view to the contrary. At first, the media were almost as much taken aback as the Palace by the public response. Like an army preparing for war, the world's press organisations take time to mobilise: crews have to be assembled, planes boarded. Once the media had arrived, however, their presence in the British capital guaranteed primacy for the story until it had run its course. The full scale of the phenomenon began to be apparent on the Tuesday. By the Wednesday, the whole world's press corps had decamped to London and for the rest of the week there was nothing else to report. Across continents, assemblies postponed debates, politicians stopped issuing statements, correspondents ceased filing. All interest focussed on the United Kingdom, and on British handling of a mood nobody understood but everybody seemed to share. Within a couple of days, signing books at British embassies and consulates had become a world-wide craze, and by the fourth day, more than 100,000 people had left messages of condolence on the newly-installed Princess of Wales obituary website. Outside the royal palaces, international news teams erected shanty-towns of scaffolding and camera equipment, topped by Babel's towers designed to get the best backdrop to whatever grief-stricken member of the public happened to be being interviewed. Elsewhere in the capital, television crews hunted for anybody with the remotest royal connection or knowledge. A festival air reigned in the streets. The highly-charged mood combined ecstasy and sadness. 'I spent hours during the night in the grounds of Kensington Palace,' Diana's mother recalled later, 'witnessing thousands of people so thoughtfully choosing where to put their flowers and light their candles, seeing tears pour down the faces of every age, race and creed.'[39]

Although the crowds brought the media, rather than the other way round, the media became a means for the crowds to talk to themselves. Television coverage was so continuous that it became impossible to tell press and crowd apart: any rumour or sentiment picked up from among the mourners was immediately fed back and, if it struck a chord, given universal currency. Non-stop vox pop on radio and television meant that people interviewed, searching for something to say, repeated what they had heard other people say on the same media a few hours earlier. Selective editing of responses could be seen, according to one view, as 'exploiting interviewees, calling up artificial emotions, constituting an artificial consensus with formulaic responses . . .' Alternatively, it could be seen as a democratic opening up of a matter of legitimate public debate.[40]

By the Thursday, there was a sense of siege: an empty Palace, a bare flagpole, a Royal Family aloof, an ocean of cellophane and flowers, and a populace, encouraged by the press, demanding acknowledgement. People were waiting – much, a medieval scholar might have observed, as the peasants had waited for Richard II outside the Tower in 1381. The moment was not, in a literal sense, revolutionary: yet it felt closer to a revolutionary moment than the British Monarchy had experienced for a long time. The Princess had become a symbol, not just of love and generosity, but of hope and freedom. When the Queen's representatives declared that the Royal Family was 'touched by public support,' it did not ring true. Out of touch with public sentiment, was the feeling.

Faced with the non-response of the Queen, the press directed its offensive against her servants. The *Guardian* led in tones that evoked *sans culottes* and tumbrels. 'Everything that we hear from Buckingham Palace suggests that [the Queen] is surrounded by stupid, blind, stuffy, self-promoting, rivalrous, gin-drinking courtiers, who haven't realised that a modern constitutional Monarch exists no longer by right but only by consent and free will,' wrote an incendiary Simon Hoggart. 'You fly a flag at half-mast on Buckingham Palace because the public craves it and the public will demand it, in spite of the fact that Elizabeth I or Walter Bagehot might have disapproved.'[41] Then the attack shifted to the person of the Monarch herself. *The Times* quoted Auden ('Stop all the clocks, cut off the telephone . . .'), and observed that a great national drama was unfolding. 'Many are bemused by this outpouring of raw emotion,' it noted, 'a few even sneer at it, as alien or vulgar.' However it was impossible for anybody to ignore it, least of all the head of an institution which had so far made no visible change to its routine, expressed itself only through spokesmen, and had made no personal gesture of significance. What was the nation to make of silence and absence 'at a time of vocal and visible lamentation?' In Diana, claimed a newspaper that had once thundered in defence of stiff upper lips and Establishment values, 'the world glimpsed a new Monarchy, spontaneous and responsive, careless of protocol but caring about people.'[42]

'Your Majesty, Please Look and Learn,' said a message laid outside Buckingham Palace on September 4th.[43] At last, under the most intense pressure, she did. 'Until mid-week,' according to one adviser, 'the attitude was "You mustn't be bullied by what the press says". It changed because of the realisation that the press reflected a very profound public attitude.'[44] Following consultations between Fellowes, Janvrin and Airlie, concession was made on all the main points. Eating its words of a few hours earlier, the Palace announced that to meet the concerns of large numbers of people who had expressed sympathy for the Princess and her family, a union flag would be raised to half-mast at Buckingham Palace; the Queen would fly to London, forthwith, instead of taking the overnight train; the length of the funeral procession route would be doubled, to increase the opportunity for spectators; and the Queen would personally pay her respects at the Princess's coffin at St James's Palace, and meet the crowds waiting to sign books of condolence. Most important concession of all, the Queen would speak on television to her people and the world.

The same evening, the Monarch – accompanied by her husband, eldest son and Princes William and Harry – left Balmoral to attend a special church service. On their way back, they stopped to look at floral tributes outside the castle gate. The Prince of Wales was seen as instigator of the change of tack, influenced – or so Downing Street spin-doctors keenly proclaimed – by conversations with the Prime Minister. 'The hand of Tony Blair, who favoured a public event, is very much behind the arrangements, made in consultation with the Palace and the family,' considered *The Times,* expressing the Government version.[45]

The royal capitulation reduced the pressure on the Royal Family momentarily, but at a cost. 'Diana, breathless, hunted by her own quick hounds,' the poet Andrew Motion wrote of the dead Princess.[46] Since the tragedy, the dogs had turned on the survivors. The sense of a Monarch flushed out, a Monarch on the run, a Monarch with nowhere to turn, was palpable. Where would it end? Some who had been fiercest in their criticisms wavered. 'There is something profoundly distasteful about the way she has been brow-beaten into all this,' wrote Paul Vallely of the *Independent.*[47] The decision to appease her attackers could have gone badly wrong. Courtiers were understandably nervous about her broadcast, promised for September 5th – the delivery of which, more than any other public performance of her reign, seemed to put her in the dock, facing accusers. When No. 10 suggested that the broadcast should be live into the six o'clock news, they were at first told 'the Queen doesn't do live'.[48] Then the point was put to her directly. 'She agreed to do the broadcast live, without hesitation,' says an ex-courtier.[53] As a result, she was inserted live into the top of the bulletin.

There was little time to prepare either the speech or the details of the Queen's long-awaited journey to Buckingham Palace. Crawford composed a handwritten plan. Some of the bunches of flowers were moved, to allow the royal party to walk up and down and read the messages before going into the Palace. Fellowes wrote a draft of the speech, Crawford adding to it. A key question was the phrasing of the Queen's admission that the Royal Family could benefit from the Princess's example. Crawford and Fellowes talked over key phrases in the first draft and there was some adjustment of the grammar. Janvrin, Mary Francis, the Prince of Wales's office, No 10 were all given copies. 'There was a draft,' says an ex-courtier. 'We were all involved in discussing it. The draft was sent around, including No. 10. There was no major Downing Street input – it was a Palace thing.' The Prime Minister's contribution – via Alastair Campbell – was to suggest that she might say, 'speaking as a grandmother,' which was immediately incorporated.

Cameras were set up in the Chinese Drawing Room with a background of the Victoria Memorial and the crowds – the same view that the world's television stations had been showing all week, but from the opposite angle. First, the Queen had to run the gauntlet of spectators and photographers. She arrived in London by plane with her husband, mother and sister. When they reached the Palace, she and the Duke left their car to look at the flowers and other offerings on the railings. It was a nerve-wracking moment and a seminal one. According to an aide, 'she didn't realise the reaction of the public until she got back to London, when she saw all the messages including those about the awful Royal Family. At Balmoral, she hadn't taken it in. You never know what it is like until you are actually there. All the remarks and people hugging each other, sobbing – the whole nation seemed to have gone bananas. The Queen and Prince Philip felt utterly bewildered.'[49] Looking at the messages, the Queen shook her head. The crowd burst into spontaneous applause, and an eleven-year-old girl handed her five red roses. Taking them, the Queen said, 'Would you like me to place them for you?' The girl replied, 'No, Your Majesty. These are for you,' thrusting them into her hands.[50]

'We were not confident,' says one ex-courtier, 'that when the Queen got out of the car, she would not be hissed and jeered.' 'There was genuine fear that if members of the Royal Family walked from St James's Palace to Buckingham Palace they might be booed, attacked or have things thrown at them,' according to another former aide. 'The turning point was the arrival at Buckingham Palace,' recalls a third. 'As the car came along, you could hear the crowd begin to clap. I remember thinking "Gosh, it's all right".' There was just time for the Queen to read through the speech a couple of times before she was on air. 'She went through it word for word in London when she got back,' according to another source. 'She made sure that what was in it, she believed in. We kept on fine-tuning it.' Fellowes talked to her and said, 'Can you say this and believe in it?' She said, 'Yes, I can believe in it very clearly.' She changed very little. 'Robert understands the Queen emotionally,' suggests a former colleague. 'He is very close to her instincts'.[51]

Politically the broadcast was a triumph. Agreeing to do it – having previously refused – had been a risk. After days of mounting pressure for a personal appearance, there was a danger that a televised statement might appear grudging or apologetic, an exercise in damage limitation. It came across as none of these things. The Queen spoke directly to camera, confidently and with little impression of reading from an autocue. She spoke with dignity. Making her own tribute to Diana as 'an exceptional and gifted human being,' she reminded the audience of the Princess's sense of humour, warmth and kindness. She described her as somebody she admired and respected, 'for her energy and commitment to others, and especially for her commitment to her two boys'. She did not say that she had loved her former daughter-in-law, and there was no admission of error. However, in a much-quoted passage, she acknowledged that there were 'lessons to be learnt' from the Princess's life and from the 'extraordinary and moving reaction to her death'. She added: 'I share in your determination to cherish her memory.'[52]

The instant effect of the broadcast was to change the world's view of the hitherto perplexingly reclusive Monarch. What was achieved, as one writer has since put it, 'was a dissipation of the hostility to the Windsors'.[53] A Gallup poll taken immediately afterwards found two-thirds of UK respondents reacting very, or somewhat, favourably with only nineteen per cent reacting unfavourably.[54] The impact was

Sunday Times, 7th September, 1997

reinforced by a series of choreographed walk-abouts among the people and the flowers outside the three palaces. The appearance of William and Harry at Kensington Palace had a particularly powerful effect on onlookers.[55] Some newspapers were not so ready to retreat. The *Observer* continued to see the public mood as not only political, but radical.[56] However, the peak of resentment against 'Them' had passed. On Friday evening, Diana's coffin was taken from St James's to Kensington Palace. The route was lit up by flash-bulbs, and the way was strewn with flowers. By Saturday, the day of the funeral, national sympathy seemed once again to embrace the surviving Royal Family, rather than to be directed against them.

'No one is bothering to ask each other what they are going to be doing at the weekend', wrote the journalist Suzanne Moore. 'No one needs to. If we are not going to line the route of Diana's funeral we will be watching it on TV.'[57] The world-wide audience was estimated at 2.5 billion – far greater than watched the 1981 wedding.[58] In every continent, the streets were empty, shops and businesses closed. From Calcutta to Soweto, traffic came to a standstill. It was impossible to escape the collective mood – a feeling described by one hard-headed and republican writer as 'sorry, confused, sympathetic, fascinated, appalled'.[59] People shook themselves. Many were puzzled and disturbed to have a sensation they regarded as ridiculous about somebody they never knew and in whom they had taken little interest. Those who were unmoved themselves, could not fail to observe the behaviour of other, normally sceptical people who were swept up in an emotion which, however it might be objectively regarded, had never been experienced on such a scale before.

The funeral was a hasty improvisation. It was not the first time in British royal history. When Queen Victoria died in 1901, Palace officials were startled to find how little had been prepared, and how much had to be made up.[60] On this occasion, the pooled knowledge and imagination of courtiers, the Prince of Wales, No.10 advisers and Earl Spencer overcame the Queen's caution and produced a tone of informality and inclusiveness.[61] There was some following of precedent. The decision that William and Harry should accompany the Duke of Edinburgh, the Prince of Wales and Earl Spencer on foot behind the cortège in the procession from St James's Palace to Westminster Abbey, repeated a practice adopted at the funeral of Lord Mountbatten in 1979, the first occasion on which adolescents had been included in a walking group. However, the Diana ritual fell into none of the recognised official categories of 'state funeral', 'ceremonial royal funeral', or 'private royal funeral'.[62] Instead of the soldiers who normally marched behind a royal coffin, there were five hundred members of Diana's charities. The Monarch provided her own innovation. During the procession, other members of the Royal Family, including the renegade Duchess of York, were invited to cluster by the gates of Buckingham Palace. As the cortège passed, the Queen gave a quick, solemn, unscripted but clearly pre-meditated head bow in the direction of her dead ex-daughter-in-law. 'We said "you can't sit at Buckingham Palace",' recalls a royal adviser. 'It was agreed that the family should go out as the coffin went past. They went down to the gate. The Queen hadn't said anything about bowing. She did it on her own initiative. Earlier, her instincts had deserted her. But not then.'[63] In Westminster Abbey, the world's royalty and statesmen rubbed shoulders with pop super-stars and anonymous social workers. Tom Cruise, Nicole Kidman, Tom Hanks and Steven Spielberg arrived in a group.[64]

The funeral service itself was a ritual of cathartic simplicity and power. Music by Verdi was followed by Elton John singing and accompanying himself on the piano. Lessons were read by Diana's sisters and by the Prime Minister. Any danger of mawkishness was removed by Earl Spencer's oration which combined a tender description of his sister, and a biting denunciation of those he blamed for her unhappiness. He spoke, in particular, about the Princess's ability to empathise with outsiders, about the savagery and cynicism of the press ('at the opposite end of the moral spectrum'), and about the alleged coldness of the family she had married into. 'Diana explained to me once that it was her own innermost feelings of suffering that made it possible for her to connect with her constituency of the rejected,' he told the congregation, '. . . for all the status, the glamour, the applause, Diana remained throughout a very insecure person at heart.'

The climax came when Spencer identified his sister with ordinary people, picking up the 'people's princess' theme that had dominated the week, and giving a side blow to the Windsors with their supposedly outmoded values. Diana, he said, was somebody 'with a natural nobility, who was classless and who proved in the last year that she needed no royal title to generate her particular brand of royal magic.'[65] According to one report, the remark was greeted with 'audible gasps from the pews occupied by the Royal Family, and from Hillary Clinton'.[66] The crowd watching the service on a huge screen in the Park broke into applause, which could be heard – first far away, then growing closer – in the Abbey, where the congregation joined in: a new breach of precedent. The critique of royalty, however, was not quite over. Speaking directly to his royal nephews, and on behalf of his mother and sisters, he pledged

> that we, your blood family, will do all we can to continue the imaginative way in which you were steering these two exceptional young men so that their souls are not simply immersed by duty and tradition, but can sing openly as you planned.[67]

At the end of the speech, Harry and William took part in the general clapping.

Like many of the most memorable speeches, it was full of illogicalities and non sequiturs. In particular, the Windsors were as much the princes' 'blood family' as the Spencers – more so, in the sense that they included a parent and two grandparents still living. Nevertheless, there was a sense of listening to history, and to phrases that would not be forgotten. In addition to the Bardic romance of an earl challenging his Sovereign in her own Abbey, the attacks on the media and on the Establishment were in tune with what people were feeling. Spencer later claimed to have written the speech quickly, at a single sitting. 'I woke up very early, at 4.30 on the Wednesday morning between her death and the funeral,' he told a South African interviewer. 'I just sat at my desk and I had finished it by 6 o'clock. That was it, I didn't change anything . . . I was just speaking as a brother to a sister and on behalf of a sister.'[68]

After the service, the coffin was carried out of the church and driven through North London, then up the motorway to the family estate at Althorp Park in Northamptonshire for burial on an island in the middle of a lake. Spectators lined the route, throwing flowers from bridges onto the hearse. At the beginning of the motorway, the driver had to stop to remove petals from his windscreen.

26

PEOPLE WERE TAKEN ABACK by Diana week. That so much emotion and prurience should have been expended on the former daughter-in-law of a non-executive head of state, not only defied reason. It gave a glimpse of a collective state of mind that might, in different circumstances, express itself in less innocuous ways. There were memories of the death of Kennedy. However, that had been an event of political importance, whereas this – apart from the reaction – had none. Indeed, an alarming feature of the Diana 'public grief' was that there was no previous manifestation with which it could be compared. Yet this was not quite true. In terms of sheer volume of mourning, it beat all rivals. But in other respects, it was not entirely new.

A distinction needs to be made here between the natural response to a sudden death, and a reaction which appears unreasonable. The death of a prominent, well-loved public figure, especially if it is premature, may be expected to arouse a high degree of collective sympathy. Thus the early death of George VI, the first Sovereign for centuries to die before his sixties, was experienced as a particular shock. So was the death of the greatly and justly admired Prince Consort in 1861. People spoke of the latter event as a catastrophe, and wondered at a loss that had made 'thoughtful men and maidens, with unrestrained tears exhibit such emotion'.[2] A case of a rather different order, on the other hand, is presented by the otherwise obscure Princess Charlotte Augusta, 21-year-old daughter and only child of the Prince of Wales (later George IV), who died in childbirth in 1817, in the first year of her marriage to Prince Leopold of Saxe-Coburg. Thirty years later, Harriet Martineau wrote that 'never was a whole nation plunged in such deep and universal grief. From the highest to the lowest, this death was felt as a calamity that demanded the intense sorrow of domestic misfortune.'[3]

Grief for both Albert and George stayed within bounds which seemed (and seem, given the contemporary climate) normal and appropriate.* In neither case was it hostile, or directed politically against a target. The same was not true of Charlotte, whose story – in life, and in death – bears comparison with that of Diana. With both women, there was a background of royal controversy. With each, an early death was followed by a spontaneous and angry outpouring that went beyond a mere feeling of loss, and seemed to express a wider sense of injustice, as if some unidentified force had left the public orphaned. Before the tragedy, Charlotte had been much in the public eye because of her pregnancy: when the news was announced, bonfires that had been prepared for the expected birth were quickly dismantled, church bells tolled, public functions were cancelled, shops and theatres shut and mourning was worn by aristocrats and labourers alike. Memorial sermons were preached in every church, and on the day of the funeral, all commercial activity closed down. The procession at Windsor was lined by Royal Horse Guards to keep back the crowds, and lit by thousands of torches.

The most remarkable manifestation of the Princess Charlotte grief was literary. Poets vied with each other to compose the most moving elegies. 'Those who weep not for kings shall weep for thee . . .', wrote Byron, incorporating the event into *Childe Harold's Pilgrimage*,

The fair-hair'd Daughter of the Isles is laid,
The love of millions![4]

The outpouring of grief spread across Europe, and rulers of Continental countries published condolences. For a time, the death seemed to encapsulate a mood that had revolutionary undertones. Contemporary accounts suggest that enthusiasm for the Princess and unhappiness at her death derived partly from the contrast people drew between her own supposedly stainless character and the tainted characters of those

---

* Two European tragedies also merit attention. In 1898, the Empress Elizabeth of Austria was stabbed by an anarchist on the shore of Lake Geneva; in 1935, Queen Astrid of the Belgians died in a car crash. Both events produced great national (and imperial) outpourings of grief – although neither, apparently, had the impact of the deaths of Charlotte Augusta or Diana. (I am grateful to the Rev. Peter Galloway for drawing my attention to these examples.)

closest to her and partly from a recognition that she came from a disturbed background. As second in line (after her father), she was seen as the best hope for the nation, and after her death there were rumblings about the mental and moral inadequacy of surviving members of the Royal Family.

There was more. Not only was Charlotte Augusta considered superior to those who survived her, she was regarded as a people's princess, on the side of society's outcasts. 'The people came ... to see in Charlotte's plight – as a victim of the Regent and by extension of the Government and of the *status quo* generally – a measure of their own,' according to the historian S.C. Behrendt.[5] Like Diana, Charlotte was renowned for her empathy and for her deep feelings of 'alliance with the universal family of the earth'. There were anecdotes about her kindness to the destitute, and she was felt to have narrowed the social distance between rich and poor. During her adolescence and brief adulthood, her development and prospects had been closely followed in the public prints. People were aware of imperfections – she had a reputation for being headstrong, with a violent temper. However, allowances were made because of the difficult life she had led, and the provocations she had suffered. There was also sympathy for her as a woman, and as the victim of an affliction visited on women.

Not everybody shared the popular mood, which some felt to be over-blown. In particular, Shelley wrote a pamphlet contrasting the death of the Princess on 7 November 1817 with the unmourned execution of three politically-dissident Derbyshire labourers the next day. 'She had accomplished nothing, and aspired to nothing,' the poet declared, 'and could understand nothing respecting those great political questions which involve the happiness of those over whom she was destined to rule.'[6] However, such an opinion went against the tide of an extraordinary outpouring of elegiac literature.

The link between the princesses cannot be pushed far. Diana at 36 was a well defined personality; Charlotte, barely more than a child, was sufficiently a *tabula rosa* to have any characteristic pinned upon her that suited the myth-makers. Nevertheless the parallel between the two episodes, separated by nearly two centuries, is close enough to arouse curiosity. In each case, grief was combined with grievance:

the death of a cherished female, identified as champion of the have-nots, sparked an apparently inexplicable popular protest dispro-portionate to the nature of loss. Most notably of all, the mourned victim – deceased fantasy leader of the masses – had the distinctive quality of being 'royal'. It is, indeed, impossible to understand either the 1997 or the 1817 eruption without taking account of this last – easily neglected but persistently emotive – factor.

DIANA DIED less than two years after the *Panorama* interview, and exactly a year after the divorce. What alternative next chapter could have kept up the pace? Some saw a kind of inevitability. 'She was in orbit,' Prince Charles told confidants afterwards, expressing the view of many. 'She was going round like a top and something had to snap and it did.'[7] Since Diana was not driving the car, she can scarcely be blamed for the accident that killed her. Nevertheless, the story seemed to end appropriately – a people's death which might, in a less expensive vehicle, have happened to anybody.

It was critical that Diana was ordinary. After the death, some obitua-rists hailed her as the greatest member of the Royal Family since Victoria. There were references to her 'extraordinary combination of gifts'. Yet at the heart of the Diana cult was the lack of a discernible talent: the image was of a social air-head, page-three girl with clothes on, Cinderella bride with a sad childhood. 'Madonna sings. Grace Kelly acted,' as one writer put it. 'Diana simply breathed.'[8] It was important to the story that it was a non-story built onto a domestic narrative with a gothic quality, inviting horror and pity: her parents' divorce when she was six, the grandmother testifying against her mother, the custody award to her father who allegedly beat his wife and neglected his children, the unloveable step-mother, the rambling mansion 'like an old man's club with lots of clocks ticking away,'[9] confirming the popular belief that stately homes were all right to look at but not to live in. Such a heritage made Diana's scholastic in-adequacy (five failed 'O' levels) comfortably explicable, while her pre-marriage career as 'Sloane cleaner, a Sloane baby-minder and kindergarten helper, and a Sloane skivvy,' became something millions of women were not threatened by, and millions of men looked for in their partners. Morton's book with its (as it turned out, justified) tone of authenticity, popularised the plot and filled in the gaps – adding to the drama everybody carried in their heads the idea of a heroine who was victim both of an unfriendly Establishment and of her own insecurity. It was a non-story: but one for which the public could provide details made up of its own projections and desires.

The narrative became a feast for theorists. One interpretation, drawing on both feminism and psychoanalysis, presents the Princess (much as Charlotte had been presented) as an archetype of female suffering, in Diana's case violated both by her husband and the world. Thus, Beatrix Campbell turns Diana's ivory silk wedding-dress into a shroud, covering an object of perverse desire for millions of people who fantasised about virgin brides even though (as the writer wryly pointed out) virgin brides were now rather hard to come by.[10] It is not necessary to engage fully in this kind of debate in order to take from it one key point, starkly threatening to the modern monarchical idea: the clash between the public fairy story surrounding marriage of a royal heir, and the actual pressures on a young couple hoping for a happy life. Viewed in such a way, the post-natal depression, the bulimia and suicide attempts, the lovers, the quack therapies, the silent telephone calls – became cries of help which the public had failed to heed. At the dark core of Diana's nightmare could be seen a mismatch between ancient belief (virginity, selflessness) and contemporary reality – and at the root of the public reaction to her death, collective guilt at having placed an ingenuous teenager in a gilded cage.

Another aspect linked to Charlotte Augusta. It was a key ingredient that the lonely Princess appealing for sympathy looked out for, and understood, the suffering of others: Diana the searcher for love was also Diana the empathiser, the toucher, the healer. To the unhappy woman who by a smile or embrace could fill thousands of strangers with delight, was added the woman who 'worked by instinct' and was 'closer to the bottom than the top', whose aim and destiny – as she herself said in her final interview – was to help those who, in different ways from herself, were also defenseless. Thus we find the mature Princess, not only suffering, but appreciating and seeking to alleviate the extreme suffering of others.

In 1987, the year her marriage effectively ended, Diana accepted an invitation to open the first dedicated AIDS ward in Britain at the

Middlesex Hospital, and made the then startling gesture of shaking hands with an HIV sufferer. It was the beginning of a new persona, central to the posthumous cult. Her willingness to be seen in physical contact with those afflicted by one much-feared disease was soon extended to the victims of another, leprosy; and then to the victims of land mines, a man-made blight that plagued many war-torn zones, especially in Africa. In each of these missions, she displayed an ability to relate the pain of others to herself. Contrasts played a part: health and malnutrition, beauty and deformity, privilege and deprivation. The most important element, giving power to the imagery, was the sense conveyed of shared exclusion.

Cynics called her a polished performer. There was undoubtedly a trade-off. If the causes benefited from her presence, so did the Princess. As Jephson, who accompanied her on many of her missions, pointed out, Diana was able to obtain a reputation for saintliness, 'just by turning up'. Like a former Prince of Wales, who famously remarked, on visiting out-of-work Welsh miners, 'Something must be done,' she had a facility for making quotable remarks that crossed barriers of wealth and culture. Emerging from a hut in a poverty-stricken village in Nepal, she was heard to say, 'I will never complain again'.[11] Part of the performance, however, lay in believing in the part in a way that other public figures could not manage. At the same time, her lack of squeamishness helped the charities she patronised directly by shifting public attitudes towards disturbing or unsightly disorders. As the poet Maya Angelou put it after the tragedy:

> Her hands which had held bright tiaras and jewelled crowns,
> Also stroked the faces of pain along Angola's dusty roads,
> She was born to the privilege of plenty
> Yet, she communed with the needy without a show of pompous
> piety.[12]

A tremulous, half-apologetic trust in her own feelings gave immediacy to her way of dealing with people. 'Harry appeared by a miracle, but then it just went bang, our marriage,' she told the Panorama interviewer.[13] Nobody had ever talked like that from behind a royal rampart. On public platforms, other royals made little scripted jokes which audiences appreciatively tittered at. By contrast, Diana could raise laughter by speaking from the depths of her own despair. Her speciality was a kind of debutante self-deprecation. 'Ladies and Gentlemen,' she began a speech at a fund-raising event for Birthright, an organisation that sponsored research into post-natal depression:

> you are lucky to have your patron here today. I was supposed to have my head down the loo for most of the day. I'm supposed to be dragged off in a minute by men in white coats. If it's all right with you I thought I might postpone my nervous breakdown.

Such measured outbursts were not just self-centred – or refreshingly open departures from the royal norm. They placed the speaker on the same side as her audience, against an enemy: the heartless press in alliance with an anonymous authority, the opponents of spontaneity and of the pursuit of happiness. It was such feisty performances that had turned Diana, in some circles, into an icon of female assertiveness, 'one of the great success stories of contemporary psychotherapy' – whose triumphant resort to alternative remedies had enabled her to achieve her independence against the odds.[14]

The Princess's anti-land mines campaign was in a different category from her interest in AIDS and leprosy sufferers. It involved a degree of radically-tinged political involvement, and arose from her role as patron of the International Red Cross, which in 1995 sought to focus world attention on the topic. The problem had been particularly severe in Angola, where much of the country had been sewn with mines, killing or maiming thousands of people, including children, and wrecking the economy.[15] When Diana was persuaded to visit the country, the media descended as never before in its troubled history. As with her other causes, principle and narcissism seemed to mingle. 'No-one has looked more fetching in a bomb-proof vest and visor,' as one television commentator remarked.[16] Diana was photographed and televised in danger zones wearing protective gear and hugging limbless children. At the same time, the footage drew attention to royal flesh more starkly than at any time since the 1981 wedding: a body to be desired, accessible to those in need, yet vulnerable. What the children made of it (or whether there was any follow-up) nobody troubled to find out. From the militant Red Cross's point of view, however, the trip was a triumph. Images of Diana's empathy turned the issue into a global talking-point, and implicitly criticised the Tory Government for failing to act.

Here was a nice constitutional point, stirring old embers. The episode could be taken in two ways: as yet another example of the Princess's indifference to proprieties, and a further nail in the dignified Monarchy's coffin; or as a significant revival of still-existing royal influence, reminding other members of the Royal Family of a potentially powerful function. What the Monarch herself could or could not do in politics was nowhere laid down. The great Victorian constitutionalist, A.V. Dicey, wrote of a 'sphere' for royal influence, adding that the rules and actions regulating the personal action of the Crown 'are utterly vague and undefined.'[17] Since the accession of Elizabeth II, if not since the trauma of the 1936 Abdication, the prevailing Palace view had been to interpret such a 'sphere' in the most limited way possible, seeking on all occasions to preserve the Sovereign from the expression of any controversial opinion except on prime ministerial advice. The Princess of Wales's behaviour raised the question of the legitimate range of political activity of somebody who, though formally detached from the institution of the Head of State, continued to be associated with it in the public mind, and to be the recipient of royal subsidy. Prince Philip and the Prince of Wales had sometimes caused irritation by making speeches that trod on the toes of professionals. They had avoided statements, however, that were openly partisan. The land-mines issue was one on which political parties had differing points of view. By taking sides, the Princess, not elected and with no authorisation from those who were, showed that a maverick member of the Royal Family could make use of Dicey's 'sphere', without incurring any penalty.

At the time of the divorce, there had been talk of 'ambassadorial' visits by the Princess in the future. Ambassadors, however, are people who stick strictly to the policy of their employer. Diana's impact depended on her readiness to depart from a script. Some suggested that she might stand for Parliament. Whether her self-declared destiny to 'run to whoever calls me in distress, wherever they are,' would have tempted her – or others – to widen her political role, is impossible to know. The important point about her destiny, however, was that it existed in a context. She was able to move public opinion on matters in which she took an interest, not just or even primarily because her beauty or empathy or vulnerability brought her close to ordinary people, but because of something which other beautiful, empathetic and vulnerable women did not have. It was an attribute, linking mind and body, whose significance had diluted remarkably little since the early nineteenth century. Indeed if, as Campbell suggested, the cult of Diana had as much to do with the Princess's physicality – unmarked limbs caressing maimed ones, and so forth – as with her soul, what invested her physical being with special importance was the strange attribute, shared with Charlotte Augusta, of being royal.

WHAT DID 'royal' mean, at the end of the twentieth century? Liberals and socialists took little interest in a category which they saw as no more than a rank in the social structure; conservatives, who gave little thought to it either, saw royalty as a buttress to Church, State and the established order. Nobody, however, could deny that it continued to exist in the minds of the majority of people, including many who were indifferent to most aspects of the political system. Diana week demonstrated the point. On the face of it, the public grief was a dramatic rejection of what had apparently been taken for granted since the Enlightenment. It was as if a whole history book – about the Glorious Revolution and Act of Settlement, containing the clear understanding that kings and queens derived their authority from Parliament not God – had been torn up. The fever was all the more startling, because it occurred at a time of declining social deference, and more open criticism of royalty than had existed for generations. Those who perceived the mood as incipiently republican stood the evidence on its head. Anybody who visited Kensington Gardens – glittering, candle-lit wonderland – was aware of emotions that were much more primitive.

To identify royalty as a 'survival' is merely to re-state the question: even though its longevity, from pre-history to the present, has been notably greater than that of any other political category yet devised. 'Royal' is not a general characteristic, and it defies a simple definition. 'Regal' describes a style, 'royal' a perceived essence that is religious, sacred, familial, dynastic, traditional. It receives reverence and commands authority because of a combination of these features. Above all, it is personal: linking the well-being of the tribe to the flesh and blood of an individual. In some societies, indeed, the body of the king and the body politic have been seen as the same. Thus in Nepal, injury to one was tantamount to injury to the other, with the king's ministers likened to his limbs. The slogan 'hail the realm, hail the king' – still to be seen stencilled across bus and lorry windscreens – is a way of saying the same thing twice over, and of affirming the king as a 'cosmic person'.[18]

In western Europe, kingship and the physicality of the ruler were similarly connected. Indeed, the concept of the Crown as the embodiment of the State, arguably contains the same idea.[19] We have seen how, in the English monarchical tradition, the physical act of anointing with holy oil – which can be traced to Mercian practice in the eighth century – played an important part, along with kneeling, hand-kissing and crowning.[20] Anointing bestowed upon the monarch priestly powers, linking the temporal and the spiritual, and it remains the prime ritual of the Abbey Coronation service. The anointed king was equipped with a unique authority that derived from his physical being.

How was that authority made manifest? One answer – surprisingly relevant to modern Monarchy, as exemplified by Diana – was by touching. Royal anointing gave the king power. Royal touching showed that he had it. Nobody today believes, or would admit to believing, that the touch of a monarch can perform a miraculous cure. The belief that it could do so, however, was once so universal and persistent that for many centuries it was almost a defining quality of monarchy itself – inseparable from the very concept of a physical, hereditary, royal bloodline, institution. It therefore merits inspection, if we are to understand the feelings 'royal' people continue to arouse among human beings who regard themselves as rational.

The idea of monarchs (as opposed to deities, saints and magicians) as healers is to be found in classical texts. Suetonius and Tacitus both related that the Emperor Vespasian restored eyes to the blind and limbs to the lame. The Emperor Adrian was also supposed to have cured blindness by his touch.[21] In northern Europe, by the time of the coming of Christianity, royal curative powers were already well established. A pagan ruler was expected to purify his people, employing a divinely acquired ability to preserve their health. Thus, it was the function of the priest-king and his Christian successor to exercise his 'thaumaturgic power'.[22] In France, where royal touching paralleled the rite in England, the first identifiable practitioner was Robert II of the Franks (996–1017). The first English Christian king to whom such a power was ascribed was Edward the Confessor, to whose 'healing Benediction' Shakespeare referred (more than five centuries later) in *Macbeth*.

WE DO NOT know exactly what conditions Edward, and later kings, were imagined to be able to cure, but it may be significant that they were unsightly ones. Later, royal curative powers were specifically applied to 'the king's evil', the name given for scrofula, or tuberculous adinitis – inflammation of the lymph nodes due to the bacillus of tuberculosis. This condition was frequently confused with a variety of the ganglia that were typically unpleasant and disfiguring, involving suppurations which made the face putrid with sores that gave out a foetid odour. It remains unclear why they, in particular, were supposed to be amenable to the royal touch. One hypothesis is that 'scrofula took the place of leprosy as a disease specifically under the control of priestly medicine', when leprosy in Europe became less common.[23] At any rate, a significant aspect of the disease was that – like the biblical leprosy – scrofula made the sufferers repugnant, and thus enhanced the charity of the touch.

Modern medical knowledge has removed the element of risk involved in physical contact with disfiguring ailments. Nevertheless there is at least a similarity of form between Diana's 'touchings' and the Confessor's. Thus, in one eleventh-century incident, vividly described by William of Malmesbury, a woman with unsightly sores was sent to Edward's bathroom, where:

> the pious king, dipping his hands into the water and stroking her neck, soon restored her to a happy state of health; the tumours that were filled with worms and corrupt blood bursting and disappearing. But as the sores left wide and disgusting cavities, he ordered her to be supported at the Crown's expense till perfectly cured. Before the seventh morning a beautiful new skin appeared, so that no vestige of the disease could be perceived. A year afterwards she had twins, which added greatly to the sanctity of Edward.[24]

This almost technical account of touching may be set against the many crudely written poems written after Diana's death, in which the writers express appreciation of the Princess's generosity in physically touching the afflicted. A book published a year later containing some 1,600 'demotic' Diana poems by different authors, provides striking evidence of the centrality of this theme in the public grief. 'Her small hands touched people,' begins one called *Diana's Common Touch*,

> The sick and the lame
> Her warm hands touched victims
> Of war mines in pain.

The theme of touching and healing is often linked to simple Christian imagery, in which Diana is likened to a celestial being, Mother Teresa, the Virgin Mary, even Christ. 'God gave us an angel, sent from heaven above,' is an opening that often occurs. So do variations on:

> Like the Messiah you touched the lepers
> Embraced the sick and the dying.

In the poems, the Princess variously holds, caresses and strokes. References to her 'gentle touch' and 'A Princess with a loving touch' and lines like 'This lady's hands were dedicated to healing' crop up time and again. The phrase 'touchy-feely' to describe the Diana style may contain the same idea. One author wrote, 'those who met her felt they were made whole'. Some of the poems implied that 'real' or 'true' royalty know how to cure with a touch, unlike the non-tactile Windsors – others that Diana's touch had a contagiously spiritual quality:

> You touched the sick and you held their hand
> Healing emotions rippling round every land.[25]

We have suggested a link between nineteenth- and twentieth-century princesses, excluded friends of the destitute. Is it possible to see in such writings a much more ancient heritage? We may note, at any rate, the remarkable history of a popular belief. For the Confessor's miracle presaged a period of at least six centuries in which the ability of rulers to perform cures by touching was a taken-for-granted attribute of monarchy in England and France – so much so that, in later years, claimants sought to display their healing touch as evidence of their fitness for the throne. The historian Marc Bloch points out that typically it is the royalty, not the saintliness, of the king that accounts for the miracle: 'God alone is their author, who chooses appropriate channels, regardless of piety or moral worth. Bad kings touched just as successfully as good ones'.[26] The monarchs themselves tended to regard their powers with good humoured generosity, making charitable use of them without relating them to any other quality.

The tactile miracle could take an indirect form. In addition to the king's touch, there were cramp rings. From the time of the Plantagenets, coin presented at the altar on Good Friday by an English King or Queen was fashioned into rings for the cure of diseases including muscular pains or spasms, and especially epilepsy. In a special ceremony that continued until the mid-sixteenth century, the Monarch intoned a prayer which declared that those raised to 'the heights of royal dignity' had been made 'instruments and channels' of divine gifts. The ceremony involved the royal personage rubbing the rings with his or her hands, thereby turning them into miraculous charms.[32] But the best results were achieved by hands-on physical contact.

Touching did not die out at the Reformation. On the contrary, it seems if anything to have been enhanced by it. In Tudor times, direct royal touching became so routine that there was a fixed procedure. Following a royal proclamation announcing the appointed day, a service took place involving the hanging of a gold coin (a 'touch-piece' or 'angel') around the neck of the sufferer. Huge ceremonies were held, and crowds grew to such a size that it became necessary to ration supplicants to one touch each. In the seventeenth century, 'touching' played a significant part in the theology of the Civil War. On the royalist side, faith in it increased, and belief in the King's miraculous gift became one of the dogmas of the Crown – rejected by the supporters of the Long Parliament, according to Bloch, 'but still alive in the hearts of the common people'. When Charles was brought south by parliamentary commissioners in February 1647 after being handed over by the Scots, sick people flocked to him, bringing coins for the ritual. Embarrassed by the persistence of the miracle-belief, Parliament later issued a Declaration 'concerning the Superstition of being Touched for the Healing of the King's Evil'.

Following Charles's execution, special powers were attributed to handkerchiefs dipped in his blood.[28] During the Commonwealth, an enterprising travel agent organised sea tours for English and Scottish scrofula sufferers to visit the future Charles II at his court in the Low Countries. After the Restoration, the new King continued to perform the ceremony much as in his father's time, though using a specially-minted token, valueless as currency, in place of a gold or silver coin. Between May and September 1660, no fewer than 23,000 people were touched – Samuel Pepys records one particular session in 1661, in the banqueting hall. Although essentially monarchical, the power could also be exercised, in certain circumstances, by royal relatives. Thus Charles II's illegitimate son the Duke of Monmouth touched at least once for scrofula in 1680, and again during the 1685 rebellion – as a way of establishing his claim. The posthumous Bill of Indictment against the Duke listed the rite of healing as one of the charges. James II touched. The Calvinistic William of Orange, on the other hand, declined to do so, and the 1701 Act of Settlement reinforced a rational-ist, law-based view of the Monarchy. However, when Anne became Queen in the following year, she resumed the rite. In the words of Bagehot, 'there was a change of feeling; the old sacred sentiment began to cohere around her'.[29] The infant Samuel Johnson, who contracted scrofula from the milk of his wet-nurse, was famously touched by Anne at St James's Palace in 1712, after being brought to London from Lichfield on medical advice for the purpose. Though only two-and-a-half at the time, he later recalled 'a lady in diamonds and a long black hood'. Dr Johnson wore the touch-piece the Queen gave him on a ribbon round his neck for the rest of his life. Queen Anne continued to touch until the year of her death in 1714, six years after the last occasion on which the Monarch exercised the right to refuse the Royal Assent to a parliamentary bill.[36] Swift expressed belief in the rite, and a patriotic card-game of the time showed on the nine of hearts a picture of 'Her Majesty the Queen touching for scrofula'.

Thereafter, the rite was discontinued by the Hanoverians, whose claim to the throne was only tenuously based on descent. Nevertheless, until the reign of George III the prayer book included the liturgical service for the healing of the sick by the King. Writing in 1791, James Boswell dismissed 'the superstitious notions . . . as to the virtue of the regal touch', while acknowledging the extent of the credulity attaching to it.[30] Meanwhile, the Stuart Pretenders continued to touch in exile. An account of Charles Edward (Bonnie Prince Charlie) touching a seven-year-old girl in the Picture Gallery at Holyrood during the '45 rebellion, vividly illustrates the surviving power, and romance, of the ancient belief. The child was stripped naked and placed on her knees in the middle of a circle of the Prince's attendants. A clergyman said a prayer. Then Charles

> approached the kneeling girl, and, with great apparent solemnity, touched the sores occasioned by the disease, pronouncing at every different application the words "I touch, but God heal".

The ceremony ended with another prayer. The girl was then dressed, and passed around the circle, each member giving her a small sum of money. Charles Stuart was last observed touching for scrofula and giving out small silver medals in Italy in 1786. His successor as Stuart Pretender to the English throne, Henry, Cardinal Duke of York, continued the practice until the first years of the nineteenth century – shortly before the death of the Prince Regent's 'people's princess' daughter caused such widespread distress.[31] In France, the rite fell out of use before the Revolution but was briefly revived by the restored Charles X in the early nineteenth century. The last French 'touching' occurred in 1825. By then, the superstition had apparently died out in England, but there were traces. In parts of Scotland during the reign of Victoria, ordinary gold coins were held to be universal panaceas, because they bore 'the image of the Queen'.[32]

Such beliefs had long since left the mainstream of political or religious understanding. Yet the mystery remains. Why did the 'king's touch' legend retain its romance for so long – in England, roughly from the eleventh to the eighteenth century? Unlike one-off miracles in the New Testament, or those attributed to medieval saints, which were regarded as proof of exceptional holiness and were generally not replicated, the royal miracle was performed routinely by successive generations of English and French kings (and queens) regardless of their moral standing. The touch, moreover, was a specifically *royal* capacity. Although it was performed by monarchs as a priestly function, there is no comparable tradition for priests, of whatever elevation. At its peak, exercises of the touch were mass events, comparable to the rituals performed at holy shrines. There is plenty of witness testimony as to their supposed efficacy. Some historians have accepted that cures were indeed brought about, advancing psychological explanations for the phenomenon; others have dismissed the reports as the 'optimism of believing souls'.[33] What concerns us here, however, is the persistence of the popular belief, and the light it may shed on the continuing concept of 'royalty' itself.

'Kings are justly called Gods,' wrote James I in 1616, 'for that they exercise a manner or resemblance of Divine Power.'[34] This inflammatory doctrine led James's son to the scaffold, and the restored Monarchy wisely did not seek to revive it. Yet divinity is so close to the universal concept of kingship that it is, arguably, impossible for politicians and constitutionalists to separate the two, however much they try. Certainly one of the defining features of the British Monarchy – its 'royalty' – is powerfully dependent on meta-human origins. From earliest times, membership of a 'royal' caste or clan was a taken-for-granted qualification. Thus the Woden-sprung monarchs of the Anglo-Saxon kingdoms possessed, according to the early medievalist Professor William Chaney, 'a charismatic power' that permeated not just the king himself, but the king's extended family, or 'royal race'. So far from being 'democratic' as some have believed, the process of choosing an Anglo-Saxon king involved selection exclusively from members of the royal race, who alone possessed the key quality of hereditary *mana*, or semi-divine luck, providing a vital link between the tribe and the divine, on which the tribe's well-being depended.[35]

Modern constitutional monarchy in Britain officially eschewed any notion of divine right, while maintaining the role of 'Supreme Governor' of the established Church. The popular concept, however, may not always have been so rigorously secular. We have seen that 'touching' survived the Civil War, the Bloodless Revolution and even the Act of Settlement. A vague religious sentiment surrounding the physicality of the Monarch undoubtedly lasted a good deal longer. Thus the 'Royal Maundy' ceremony – which until the Hanoverians involved the Monarch washing the feet of the poor, as well as handing them gifts – has continued, without the washing, to the present day.[36] Before, indeed, we dismiss completely the notion that the modern rationalised

Monarchy has been something more than 'symbolic', we should note at least one shared characteristic with its magical forebear: the continuation of a concept of 'royal' that is widely understood as specifically familial.

Monarchy *per se* does not have to be hereditary: it has not been, for example, in Tibet, or the Vatican. In the British case, however, heredity is an essential part of the concept. Awe is accorded to a Monarch's relatives, as to no other grouping. In 1688, strict adherence to royal primogeniture was abandoned, and since the Act of Settlement, the law has specifically disqualified from the throne categories of people who, whatever their degree of consanguinity, are deemed unsuitable. There has even been recent talk of 'skipping a generation'. But there has never been any serious suggestion, since Oliver Cromwell, that the Monarch should not belong to the 'Woden-sprung' line, or that the Monarchy might pass to another family altogether. Thus in Britain, and in other European countries, the idea of Monarchy has been so closely linked to the idea of a royal family, that it is actually impossible to envisage the first without the second.

Like everything else to do with the British Monarchy, the hereditary principle can be varied at will by Parliament, and has been from time to time. The fact remains, however, that it is still there: apparently retained because of feelings towards it that are scarcely more rational than a belief in the king's touch. Even in the twentieth century, as Bogdanor puts it, the Sovereign 'seemed to be a magical figure, a human being, yet possessing qualities which set him or her apart from others.'[37] In sum, it is hard not to conclude that the British idea of constitutional Monarchy – however much it is wrapped up in rationalist explanations – has popular superstition as its base. Similarly, reference to the alleged 'redemptive powers'[38] of Monarchy deriving from a royal right to authority outside the mechanisms of the political system, presupposes a widespread non-rational state of mind.

'Monarchical Government,' wrote the historian of kingship, A. M. Hocart, early in the twentieth century, 'has a psychological value we are not yet in a position to understand.'[39] It is possible to turn the proposition around. Monarchy, rather than having a value, could be presented as an opiate, an answer to David Cannadine's fundamental question: 'how are people persuaded to acquiesce in a polity where the distribution of power is manifestly unequal and unjust, as it invariably is?'[40] As such, it could be argued, it has so far served its purpose well. Yet to take this kind of a view of constitutional Monarchy is to deal solely with function. It does not explain the hold on the public imagination that has enabled the function to be exercised. That hold cannot be attributed in any direct sense to the Anglo-Saxons. Nevertheless, it remains true that long after 'mature' opinion had abandoned any such sentiment, the general public had its own view on the 'right' by which Monarchs reign.

THE POINT lies behind the chapter on the Monarchy in Bagehot's *The English Constitution*, which is contemptuous in its dismissal of a 'right' that comes from anywhere except Parliament. The author, however, dismissed the belief in such a right, not the sociological fact that people held it. To Bagehot the superstitions of the masses were a factor that needed to be taken seriously. 'If you ask the immense majority of the Queen's subjects by what right she rules,' he observed, 'they would never tell you that she rules by Parliamentary right, by virtue of 6 Anne, c.7. They will say she rules by "God's grace": they believe that they have a mystic obligation to obey her.'

Usage, moreover, was firming up such a belief:

> When [Victoria's] family [i.e. the Hanoverians, in 1714] came to the Crown it was a sort of treason to maintain the unalienable right of lineal sovereignty, for it was equivalent to saying that the claim of another family was better than hers: but now, in the strange course of human events, that very sentiment has become her best line of support.[41]

By the end of the twentieth century, the Monarchy – shorn, not only of divine right, but also of almost all remaining political influence – had become a different kind of institution, in a different political system. Yet it is possible still to recognise the concepts both of 'mystic obligation' and 'the unalienable right to lineal sovereignty' in the modern polity. Of course, some of the legitimacy that attaches to other ancient institutions – Parliament, the Law Courts – also contains an element of 'unalienable' right, that can only be explained in terms of antiquity and tradition. As the constitutional historian John Neville

Figgis once put it, any believer in natural rights is an inheritor of a doctrine of divine right.[42] In neither of these cases, however, is the obligation or right personalised, as it is in the case of a Monarch. Nor is it 'mystic'. What makes the public relationship to the Monarchy and royalty peculiar in the present, as in the past, is the real or imagined relationship with individual personalities, and the feelings of entanglement that accompany it.

In the twentieth century, little conscious superstition clung to the Monarch – remarkably little in view of the survival of many quasi-religious beliefs, especially in relation to faith-healing, in which Diana herself dabbled. Unconscious feelings, however, were another matter. Of course, unconscious feelings can be as reciprocal as conscious ones. 'Diana could touch and feel,' writes Martin Amis, 'perhaps she believed she could heal.'[43] Maybe she did. 'Her touch was almost a spiritual thing ... she had this magic effect on people she had compassion for,' her ex-husband has been heard to say. 'People felt that if they touched her, they would be cured of what they had – and sometimes they were. It may have been auto-suggestion'.[44] Or perhaps the rapport with Diana's public was achieved simply through her emotional response to what they sought in her. At any rate, the persistence of the belief in the special access of Monarchs and by extension other royals to divine grace, alluded to by Bagehot, may indeed point in the direction in which we should be looking. The rise, flourishing, and decline of the 'king's touch' legend in western Europe closely shadows a belief in witchcraft, suggesting that the two reflect a similar pattern of credulity. However, while witches ceased to be identified by the beginning of the eighteenth century, Monarchs – re-packaged and modified – continued to reign, carrying with them half-remembered associations. Thus it may not be fanciful to see, attaching to the political construct of royalty as to the fairy-tale mythology of magic princes and princesses, a wistful hope for the miraculous kiss and the healing touch. It may not be fanciful, either, to imagine that in linking herself physically with sufferers from horrifying and unsightly ailments, as well as in her interest in alternative treatments like aromatherapy (with its 'royal' anointing), the Princess was unwittingly associating herself with a very ancient belief.

There was in any case an additional element, which helped to unite the charismatic and the traditional. The decline of overt reverence for Monarchy in the twentieth century was combined with a rise in public visibility. Photography, the newsreel and then television were largely responsible for the change from a remote iconography to a popular familiarity with the faces, bodies, gestures of royal personalities, that was greater than for any other category of public figure.

The shift from distant reverence to drawing-room exposure accelerated in the years following the *Royal Family* documentary, and especially after the Waleses' marriage. Of course, Diana was not the first to be admired for her looks, or to be subject to a voyeuristic scrutiny. Almost every prominent member of the Royal Family, male and female, since the 1930s had been coyly presented, at some stage in their life, as an object of desire. It was, however, the Princess's fortune to be exposed to a process of what may be called 'iconic sexualisation' at a time when the pressures on famous people generally had reached an unprecedented intensity.

Diana was not the first to be sexualised: she was, however, the first to have been presented in openly erotic terms. When the Queen Mother and the Queen, at about the same age, had been people's princesses, the media imagery had been contained within an antiseptic code of Establishment-determined convention. The interval between Princess Elizabeth and Princess Diana saw a revolution both in public mores and in the behaviour of popular newspapers. Thus, from the moment of the *Daily Mirror*'s through-leg shot of a gullible kindergarten teacher, there was a media race to catch Diana in suggestive or smouldering poses. Over the years from engagement to divorce, the erotic imagery evolved. 'At the outset,' according to the journalist Suzanne Lowrie, a few years after the royal marriage, '. . . she was the innocent, the virgin, the old-fashioned sweetheart, wooed and wed . . . according to the best, most romantic book. She was thus a sexual prize, a social asset and object of competition, almost at times a quarry to be chased.'[45] In the wake of Charles's search for a suitable bride, 'innocent' and 'virgin' were words much explored by the tabloid press, and widely discussed in the pubs and clubs. But so was a sense of her responsiveness, not just to her husband (displayed in the wedding-day kiss), but to the world.

'La Princesse Sexy' was the cover-line name *Paris Match* gave her, three years after she had theoretically been put out of reach. Discovering how much was wishful-thinking, and how much the accurate perception of loneliness, became a game which the tabloids and their photographers played with the public – and, competitively, with each other. 'They loved looking at her,' according to Beatrix Campbell, 'they loved chasing her, frightening her and, simply, staring at her. Their work also revealed a determination to dominate her.'[46] Stories circulated that conveyed the sense of a Princess, if not obtainable, then in search of reassurance, while the message apparently delivered by her clothes and grooming indicated a desire for appreciation. Feminists saw her as the victim of male fantasies. She could also be seen, however, as the model or mirror for female ones – defining fashion, make-up, dress codes and an ideal of physical perfection.

Thus royalty superstition, press exploitation, and sympathy came together. Within a few years of the royal marriage, comparisons began to be made with earlier world sweethearts, whose outward glamour had belied an inner torment, trapping them 'between the isolation of reality and their own images.' Diana, suggested Lowrie, combined 'the glamour of the movie star with the power of the madonna: sexual yet untouchable.' At this early stage, the 'endlessly viewable heroine of an obsessively viewing age' met the demands made of her as a model royal in an age that still put royalty on a pedestal. The Princess had to be presented as an ideal of love, beauty, youth and sexuality, while at the same time appearing as a quintessentially happy mother and wife. She achieved all this, wrote the author (before anybody realised how badly things had gone wrong), 'by appearing and gesturing and saying almost nothing.'

So far, it was simply a matter of doing well what royalty had always tried to do. However, it was important that Diana on a pedestal – Diana the icon, sex object, female role-model – also longed for communion with those who had put her there. 'It is part of Diana's success,' as Lowrie noted, 'that she seems closer to the High Street than any temple of *haute couture*.' She could be seen as a force for conservatism. 'Simply by slimming, and dressing beautifully and conventionally, and by having two children and a rich husband, she represents the reactionary dreams of her generation.'

That was in the Thatcherite, yuppified mid-1980s, when fashion models had only two looks, 'sulky and very sulky'.[47] Later, when Diana fell from the pedestal and was characterised as somebody who was not only sexually interesting but possibly interested in sex, she became a different kind of symbol: the condonable harlot. While Diana as the Virgin was unspotted and untouchable, Diana as Mary Magdalene, the forgiven prostitute, offered a different kind of looking-glass, 'a comforting mirror,' as Marina Warner has written, describing the biblical saint, 'to those who sin again and again, and promise joy to human frailty.'[48]

The metaphor ends sacrificially. Untouchable, iconic, yet touching and communicating, Diana the royal whore with her open adultery and succession of lovers had apparently embarked on a campaign to expose the hypocrisy of constitutional Monarchy. So successfully destructive had she become that the damage was beginning to look irreparable. The crisis shook the institution to its foundations. But it also revived a part of the public imagination which it had become conventional to ignore: if not 'mystic obligation' then a relationship to royalty revealed as a more universal and more rousable feeling than what remained of the public's other traditionally collective loyalties – to faith, party, class.

27

WHAT HAD THE PEOPLE'S POMP, the formal informality, been for? Great funerals are always about more than grief. They carry messages – about nation, power, victory in war, world influence. They also contain statements that point to the future: reaffirmations by a ruling élite of its grip on the existing order:

> O ceremony, show me but thy worth!
> What is thy soul of adoration?
> Art though aught else but place, degree and form,
> Creating awe and fear in other men?[1]

Diana's funeral was unusual – particularly unusual in Britain – because it was a political event but not a reaffirming one. Rather than a demonstration by the powerful of their power, it was a response to a popularly declared need. It was also unusual because, unlike previous royal ceremonies, it was one in which British or Commonwealth identities played little part. The Princess was seen as above nation.

Who or what did she represent? Everybody had a theory, nothing was ever more exhaustively written about, never was there more literary indulgence. Some expressed cynicism. 'How often do you see a royal funeral on television, especially one with Elton John singing at it?'[2] replied one young interviewee, asked if he had enjoyed the show. Some observers noted how it had been turned to the Prime Minister's advantage. 'What is remarkable,' wrote Kenneth Rose, 'is the speed with which the Government managed to associate itself with Diana once she was dead.'[3] For the Government and new premier, it was certainly a rite of passage. One journalist suggested that managing the public grief would come to be seen as one of the most important political episodes of Tony Blair's career, comparable to the Falklands War in Margaret Thatcher's.[4]

Other commentators took it as a sign of the political weather that the causes the Princess had supported were left-wing ones – inner-city squalor, the excluded, landmine victims – and that the Tories, in normal times the natural ally of the Monarchy, had been almost completely excluded from the week's passions.[5] The Archbishop of Canterbury suggested that not only the Palace but also the Church could learn lessons from the spectacle of millions of people expressing their spiritual yearnings.[6] Meanwhile, morals were drawn, often of a *mea culpa* kind. It became a commonplace to observe that what the public built up and loved, it inevitably destroyed. 'We could not get enough of her,' admitted the *Independent on Sunday*.[7] 'I killed her', wrote an anonymous obituarist, quoted in the *Guardian*:

> I hounded her to death. I followed her every movement. I gave her no peace. For I bought the papers. I read the stories and I looked at the photographs. They did this for me. How can I live with that?[8]

The continuing royals were widely felt to have had a narrow escape. One writer called for 'a ruthless audit of palace protocol in which a wide range of outsiders should participate.' A typical shopping list of reforms for the 'People's Monarch' included the winnowing of royal ritual, a redeployment of royals from duties involving the armed forces to visits to inner-city estates and state schools, an assessment of the length of royal holidays, and a re-consideration of the size of royal pay packets.[9] For a time, hyperbole reigned. The *Sunday Times*, describing the Princess as 'a bigger phenomenon than the Royal Family itself,' declared that Charles now faced the same options as Edward VIII – the Monarchy, or a private life with the woman he loved.[10] The *Observer* called the previous seven days 'the most extraordinary week in recent history,' and Spencer's tribute 'surely the most moving speech ever made at a funeral in Westminster Abbey' – as devastating for the Monarchy as Sir Geoffrey Howe's speech had been for the Thatcher premiership. It concluded that British society could no longer sustain a constitutional Monarch, in view of Charles's alleged inadequacies and desire to marry, unless the throne passed directly from the Queen to Prince William.[11] One paper considered that the Princess had been 'loved throughout the world as no other woman in the century',[12] yet another that she had exposed the Monarchy as dysfunctional and out-of-touch[13] – although, as one writer bravely pointed out, the recent history of the Spencer family did not suggest that it was notably less dysfunctional than the Windsors.[14]

The media took time to adjust. At first, a variety of rumours circulated. There was speculation, fuelled by Dodi's father and widely aired in the Middle East, about secret service involvement in the accident: 'They' supposedly wanted to be rid of the turbulent Princess. There were also tales of royal entourage rows, including the story that Charles and Sir Robert Fellowes had engaged in a furious altercation on the royal train. Neither the French court of inquiry, nor anybody else, produced evidence to support the first conjecture and the second was hotly denied.

There were direct effects. In addition to a fund in aid of the Princess's good causes, which raised a remarkable £94 million in sixteen months, attempts to perpetuate the Princess's memory included Diana hospital wards, Diana streets and Diana babies – though not nearly as many as had once been called Albert. An early international agreement on landmines was directly attributed by commentators to the post-tragedy climate. In Britain, large municipal bills were incurred for the operation and clearing up an estimated 10,000 to 15,000 tons of 'grave gifts' – mainly rotting vegetation; and the Institute of Psychiatry reported a statistically significant increase in suicides among depressed women. At Althorp, the Princess's brother invested the grave with a maximum degree of Arthurian romance. Tourists were not allowed onto the island where Diana was buried, and had to contemplate a memorial urn on the edge of the water instead.[15] The sense of homecoming was strengthened by Mrs Shand-Kydd, the Princess's mother, who recalled the nine months before her daughter was born, 'that time when she was completely mine'.[16] However, contrary to the wishful thinking of one or two newspaper editors, Althorp did not become a Canterbury for reproachful pilgrims, nor Diana a Thomas à Becket to the Queen's Henry II. An ICM poll conducted in the week after the funeral showed that an overwhelming majority thought the Palace was out of touch and should modernise. But only twelve per cent were in favour of a republic, with little difference between age groups.[17] The most extraordinary legacy was a series of breast-beating announcements by tabloid newspapers, led by the Murdoch press, renouncing the use of intrusive paparazzi photographs, and promising to respect the privacy of William and Harry. Unblushingly, the *News of the World* pledged its determination 'that yobs with cameras masquerading as photo-journalists will be cut off forever from the respectable newspaper world'.[18]

For a few weeks – especially in the United States – Diana news continued to lead. Then fashion moved on. The public grief was replaced by public amnesia as people who had apparently been inconsolable got on with their lives. Royalty interest shifted to the survivors – for whom there emerged a shame-faced, guilty sympathy – and especially to the young princes, rightly seen as the tragedy's real victims. A year later, the first anniversary of the death was marked by a hasty scaling down of Diana commemorative events in the media, due to a lack of interest on the part of a fickle public.

When Prince Albert died in 1861, the Royal Household observed deep mourning for twelve months, after which Queen Victoria permitted her servants to wear white, mauve and grey. Armbands continued to be worn for eight years.[19] Six years after the Consort's demise, Bagehot recorded that the Court was still in a state of suspended animation.[20] In 1997, by contrast, Buckingham Palace tried to get back to normal as quickly as possible – except that one of the main characters in the disturbed normality of the recent past was missing. 'There was some sense of "she's gone, now life will resume its measured tread"', says one ex-courtier. At the same time, there was a recognition that the royal world had changed for ever. The feeling, unexpressed, was strongest at the top. 'The Queen was overwhelmed,' says a Palace source, closely involved at the time, 'like a stunned fish'.[21]

Among staff, there was a mixture of amazement at what had occurred and chastened relief at having got through it. Courtiers also felt a quiet sense of achievement at having pulled off the funeral in six days against a barrage of unhelpful criticism and in the glare of a global spotlight. 'At the beginning of the week it was a case of the Monarchy not working,' says an aide. 'At the end of the week it *was* working'.[21] The day itself – marked by dignity and restraint, as well as by a smooth-running operation – was felt to have been unifying, and the ceremonial both inside the Abbey and outside was a source of pride. But it was a close-run thing. Everybody was aware how near the institution had come to a reverse that might have been irretrievable. For the Palace, there was now an unmistakable project.

RETURNING TO NORMAL meant not cancelling appointments. It also meant performing duties in a way that took account of the new, post-crisis reality without being unbalanced by it. The Monarch's programme for the autumn of 1997 did not make this easy. It was a year of half-centenaries for Queen and Commonwealth. The most pressing fixture – long planned, and much discussed before the tragedy, because of its delicacy – was a double state visit by the Queen and Duke to mark the fiftieth anniversary of the independence of the Indian sub-continent.

Billed in Britain as 'the Queen's first set of public engagements since the death of the Princess,' the two-week tour had a different significance in Asia, primarily because of Kashmir. The aims of the trip were to strengthen ties with India and Pakistan, to close a still-tender chapter of colonial history and – most delicate of all – improve relations between giant, and intermittently warring, neighbours. At a time of near-anarchy in Pakistan and continuous artillery exchange along the Kashmiri border, the last of these missions turned out to be a perilous one. The Head of the Commonwealth, noted the *Daily Telegraph*, 'will be particularly careful to avoid any gesture which might be seen as favouritism in one direction'.[22] Unfortunately, the speech-writers were not careful enough: almost any formula of words that expressed friendship towards one nation, was liable to be interpreted suspiciously in the other.

At first, the visit went well. In her opening address at a state banquet in Islamabad, the Queen showed signs of lessons learnt. She spoke of net surfers in Rawalpindi accessing the Buckingham Palace website, of the world moving too fast for some of her own generation, and of 'the work in Pakistan during the life of Diana, Princess of Wales'. She also sought to underline the emergence of a new Commonwealth culture. Once, the idea of a mixed British-Asian identity would have been not so much embarrassing as unthinkable. Now, the modernising Head of the Commonwealth turned it into a progressive aspiration.

She spoke of the British Muslim, for whom 'being British and Pakistani is a way of life'. Her comments received interested and favourable attention. The Asian press, however, was much less engaged by high-minded generalities primarily directed at people of immigrant stock in the United Kingdom than by remarks that had a regional relevance. In the context of the anniversary celebration she spoke of the need for Pakistan and India to 'renew efforts to end historic disagreements',[23] an apparent reference to Kashmir. In Pakistan, this was calmly received. In India it caused outrage. Indian newspapers and politicians expressed fury at an allegedly impertinent interference in their country's internal affairs.

For the rest of the sub-continental tour fall-out from the row became virtually the only issue. In an attempt to rescue the situation, Palace officials pointed out that everything the Queen said had been on Foreign Office advice – then hastily added that this was not meant as a criticism of the Foreign Office. 'It is unreasonable to criticise Her Majesty for calling for reconciliation between the two countries,' defended the Foreign Secretary, Robin Cook. Indians did not agree. The call for a middle way, uttered on Pakistani soil, sounded in India like a demand for a concession. By the time the Queen left Pakistan for India, the tour had degenerated into a competition among regional newspapers to denounce the royal visit in the most emphatic terms.[24]

'Queen will echo Diana's work with poor in India,' announced the British press, as the Palace hopefully unveiled plans for the Head of the Commonwealth to receive a garland from a female untouchable, and to meet voluntary workers from the urban slums. What made the news, however, were altercations between courtiers and Indian officials on the tarmac. 'The British are peeved that their Queen has been insulted by these uncouth natives,' declared an Indian civil servant, capturing the end-of-tour mood, 'and the Indians are upset by perceived racism and insensitivity.' In Britain, the former Conservative Government (which booked the trip), the two Asian Governments, the British Foreign Office, and the new Foreign Secretary, were variously blamed. Nobody blamed the Queen for her 'fortnight *horribilis*', in which, according to one British commentator, 'she has been humiliated, misinterpreted and misused'.[25] Nevertheless, the trip's failure raised the issue, at a tender moment, of whether yet another of the

Indian Express, 12th October, 1997

Monarchy's dwindling functions – royal state visits – had become obsolete.

There was a lucky contrast: the Queen's Asian visit was not the only royal trip that autumn. Charles had long been booked for a Southern African tour. Unexpectedly, this turned out to be a public relations success. If the Queen's tour fell flat because of the politics of the region she visited, Charles's succeeded for the same reason. Indeed, both trips curiously echoed the Royal Family visit to South Africa in 1947, devised to revivify an Empire in transition. Princess Elizabeth's Cape Town speech had been directed almost as much at the Indian sub-continent as at Africa. Nevertheless, Africa had listened closely, just before the shutters of apartheid closed. One effect had been to forge a bond – which the Queen continued to feel – between the Head of the Commonwealth and liberal opinion in the southern part of the continent. In welcoming Charles half a century later, modern black and white Africans acknowledged British royalty's steadfastness.

At the same time, the 1997 visit – so soon after the Diana tragedy – aroused personal sympathy. The Prince's decision to take William and Harry recalled 1947, when the King and Queen had travelled with their young daughters. The post-war trip had been accompanied by speculation about Princess Elizabeth's romance. The 1997 visit gave the world an opportunity to inspect her teenage grandsons in the company of their single-parent father. As it happened, it also provided an opportunity for blood families to meet on Spencer territory: Cape Town's residents included Diana's brother. Addressing a state banquet hosted by President Mandela, Prince Charles spoke with feeling about Diana and her public concerns, especially land mines. Afterwards, sealing the truce, he and Earl Spencer were seen warmly shaking hands. During the visit, observers were touched by the evident strength of the bond that existed between the Prince and his children. The tour seemed to turn a corner. Sensing a shift in the public mood, the British press reduced its attacks on the Heir, and his popularity ratings began to rise accordingly.

The Queen's South Asia tour was swiftly followed by a celebration that could have become an even greater embarrassment: the fiftieth anniversary of the other royal event of 1947, the Elizabeth–Philip marriage. A few months earlier, the Palace had been expected to use the occasion to repair damage done to the 'family Monarchy'. The tragedy set back such hopes, and put the Queen's advisers in a dilemma. On the one hand, the nation's mood was scarcely cele-bratory, especially on the topic of royal unions; on the other, the Monarch's Golden Wedding could not be greeted with official silence. Royal chroniclers pointed out that it was the first time since 1811 that a reigning Sovereign had reached such a landmark. On the last occasion, in view of George III's mental state, 'festivities were thin on the ground'.[26] This time, the Court sought to rise to the challenge, and – with help from Downing Street – set about re-moulding the Monarchy's image for a post-Diana world.

The Asian tour had been the Queen's first important public per-formance after the funeral. The Golden Wedding was to be her first major personal one – designed to indicate change without surrender. The emphasis was on continuity, adaptability, survival, permanence. Glamour and mystery were shelved. As in the end-of-Second World War anniversary celebrations, the Palace focussed on what had become the Monarch's greatest asset: through good times and bad, she had always been there, in the words of one of her aides, 'the benign Great Mother'.[27] Profile-writers responded politely, turning around the alleged faults that had been the cause of complaint a few weeks earlier. There was an appreciation that the Queen's life had been hard, especially recently. No longer cold and remote, she was presented as iron-willed, disciplined and orderly, and stoically resistant to expressions of emotion. 'Sometimes you see a muscle working in her cheek,' observed one writer, 'but not more than that.' The model family was re-cast once again as the recuperating post-traumatic family, in which the Queen and Duke could be seen as 'joint pillars', in a royal sea of discord.[28]

The Golden Wedding was on 20 November 1997. On the 19th, the Duke of Edinburgh set the tone in a Guildhall luncheon speech, in which he dwelt on the subject of marriage. Tolerance, he declared, was the essential ingredient. 'You can take it from me that the Queen has it in abundance.' He added that people in her position 'have to learn to accept certain constraints ... but they also discover that it gives them exceptional opportunities.'[29] Next day, a special service at the Abbey – pale shadow of the splash of colour that had entranced the world in 1947 – was followed by a lunch hosted by the Prime Minister. This event, inevitably dubbed a 'people's banquet,' turned out to be a cleverly understated piece of New Labourism and New Monarchism which (like the people's funeral) mixed celebrities and people from all walks of life, including a small contingent that could be defined as 'ordinary'. In her speech, the Queen returned her husband's compliments. She spoke briefly of the tragedy. She also acknowledged the difficulty royalty experienced in reading the message of public opinion. 'But read it we must,' she said, with modulated emphasis. In reply, Blair bent the rule that the contents of a Prime Ministerial audience are a tight secret, and recalled the Queen's closing words in their last meeting: 'Please don't be too effusive.' Ignoring this injunction, he described her as 'the essence of dignity . . . a dignity that is very much down to earth. Unstuffy, unfussy, indeed unfazed by anything.' Distancing himself from republicans within his own party, and using a phrase designed for the headlines, he concluded: 'You are our Queen. We respect and cherish you. You are, simply, the Best of British.'[30]

The speech received a mixed response. One commentator accused the premier of drowning her in treacle, and of implying that the Monarchy now endured on his own terms. That was one interpretation. Another was that Blair did not so much rescue the Monarchy as give due acknowledgement to its still-existing power over public opinion. His speech could be seen as support for the old judgement that governments had nothing to gain from interfering with an institution which, despite misadventures, continued to be regarded as outside and above politics. At the time of the tragedy, there had been talk of No. 10 nudging an un-modernised Buckingham Palace into the 21st century. Blair's speech could be seen as a reminder that – for all the constitutional reform agenda and republicanism of the Cabinet – the Monarchy and a monarchical zone remained inviolate. 'Tony Blair delivered the national verdict on Diana's death in August 1997,' in the words of one assessment of the 1997–2001 administration, 'but about the institution she had forced into such public scrutiny he had no public thoughts to offer.'[31]

The Golden Wedding signalled the end of the mourning period and – together with Charles's Southern Africa visit – the start of a tentative recovery. Blair might have indicated his intention not to intervene. However, among Palace staff there was a sense of urgency. There had been little doubt about the need to adapt, when the Princess was still alive. The question was how much change the newly receptive Queen would now accept. 'Lessons to be learned' was the key. 'The broadcast altered everything,' says a former aide. Though reforms had begun before the tragedy, Diana's death was seen as a catalyst, opening the way to more. 'Before the Princess died, there had been thought about change', says another ex-courtier. 'However, nothing much had in fact changed. The finances were in a better state, but the way the money was used hadn't greatly altered. You knew what you wanted to do, but couldn't do it. For example, there had been an imbalance of visits – to manufacturing industry, rather than the service sector, to City livery companies rather than foreign banks – that reflected tradition rather than the pattern of employment.' Following the death, the Palace became more imaginative in soliciting invitations. 'After the Queen's broadcast, little was explicit,' according to the same source, 'but the private secretaries began to propose more vigorous ideas, and they were accepted. It made us bolder, and Royal Family members bolder as well'. Staff looked at things they felt the Queen was capable of coping with psychologically. 'The Queen is quite incapable of verbalising her opinions,' explains another ex-adviser. 'The only progress that can be made is by how she reacts to suggestions. After the broadcast, we found it easier to convince her about doing things, and easier to push things through.'[32]

Taking the public's temperature became a Buckingham Palace obsession. In addition to commissioning focus groups and private polls, the Household appointed a highly-paid communications director to take strategic control of the royal image.[33] There was also a review of the way royal engagements were chosen, with gaps left in the Queen's diary for emergency or 'topical' visits. At the same time, regular visits began to be grouped, with a day devoted to a particular industry or profession. In the months following the Princess's death, themed days included a City tour involving lunch at the *Financial Times*, visits to the American bank Merrill Lynch and the Bank of England in the course of which the Monarch sat in on a Monetary Policy Committee, and a meeting with the oldest newspaper vendor in the square mile. In March 1999, another tour encompassed theatre-land, taking the Queen to the Lyceum for a rehearsal of a youthful favourite, *Oklahoma!*, and to the Almeida in Islington, where Klaus Mann Brandauer was preparing for the role of Albert Speer.[34]

There was a choreographed change of style. 'The Queen's instincts were always towards incremental evolution,' as one insider puts it, diplomatically. 'There was no question of a radical shift in the way she did business.' A significant shift occurred, nonetheless. Before the tragedy, if the Queen visited a school, she would stand in the doorway and listen to the teacher. Now she made a point of sitting down with the children. 'This sort of thing was discussed in advance,' according to a courtier. 'She was taking a leaf out of the Princess's book'.[35] Taking leaves from the Princess's book, of course, could be risky. There was a triple bind. If the Palace did not respond to pressure it was accused of conservatism; if it did and moved too eagerly, it was accused of panic; if it moved forward with due caution, Peter Mandelson and Alastair Campbell were likely to get the credit. Thus, the Palace press office found itself insisting that Diana's death had not caused a sudden change of tack, while seeking also to demonstrate that a change of tack was taking place. Eventually, a formula was arrived at. Those who asked were told that the Palace had been mod-ernising before the accident. It was continuing to doing so, if anything, at an even faster pace.

Alongside 'listening' and 'modernisation', 'informality' became a buzz-word, as the Palace sought to dismantle the buttresses of protocol that had sustained the Monarch since her childhood. Visits to work-ing-class homes became stage-managed photo opportunities, fed to cooperative cameramen, eager to demonstrate the Diana effect. Before long, the Queen was to be seen perched on a sofa with an elderly pensioner in a flat in Hackney, meeting people outside a drive-in McDonalds, visiting an out-of-town shopping centre, and having her hand massaged by an aromatherapist at a health centre.[36] 'In the touchy-feely era of the New Royals', as the *Daily Mirror* put it, 'the gloves are well and truly off.'[37] There was a flurry of media excitement when the Queen visited a pub, a gesture immediately seized upon as yet more evidence of the Monarch loosening up. 'The fact that the

Queen first visited a pub in 1954,' observes an ex-courtier dryly, 'made no difference.'

Meanwhile, press access to behind-the-scenes activity at Buckingham Palace and Windsor Castle was extended (to help display the Queen as a busy Head of State). Protocol changes included the abolition of bare flagpoles: after 1997, an unoccupied royal residence automatically had the union flag hanging over it. In February 1998, Lord Lieutenants were sent a letter telling them that bowing and curtseying to royalty was optional (it always had been, but the public apparently needed reminding). In April 1998, a pink-haired female rock singer, Julie Thompson, was shown chatting to a smiling Queen at a Buckingham Palace reception during the European-Asian economic summit – a result of allowing photographers to mingle more freely. In May, cameras were invited to record a foreign ambassador presenting his credentials to the Head of State.[42] There was also talk of the Monarch spending 'quality time' with people she met on royal visits, instead of being whisked past them.

There were slips. At the ceremonial de-commissioning of the Royal Yacht *Britannia*, after forty-four years in service, eagle-eyed cameramen caught the Queen and the Princess Royal dabbing their eyes. Perhaps it was the biting wind: the royal demeanour, however, invited the comment that a family that had been conspicuously dry-eyed on other occasions, was moved to tears at the passing of 'an old, dear and trusted friend' which happened to be a lump of metal. Nevertheless, the shift in royal attitude from treating critics as enemies to be deflected, to acknowledging them as voices that needed to be heard, was detectable to outsiders: and for the time being, the media gave the Court the benefit of the doubt.

As the first anniversary of the tragedy approached, the Palace felt confident enough to brief the press that the Queen had, indeed, been taught by Diana. 'The Princess was very good at picking issues, and we have to learn from that,' a spokesman was quoted as saying. 'She was very good at keeping abreast of topics of public concern. That was one of her strengths, and a lesson that could be learnt.' One immediate public concern was how to mark August 31st in an appropriate way. The Prime Minister was due to be in Balmoral. Would the New Labour team seize the opportunity to portray the Blair

Government as the driving force behind the post-Diana reforms? To outflank a possible line of attack, the Palace asked that flags should fly at half-mast on all public buildings – for one anniversary only. But there was no compromise on the Royal Standard, which flew at Balmoral to mark the Monarch's residence there, and was not lowered for Diana or anybody else.[38]

In September 1998, the Queen and Duke went on a state visit to Brunei, and then to open the Commonwealth Games in Kuala Lumpar, where hopes of what one paper called 'an all-singing, all-dancing people's state visit' were not realised. However, the British Monarch was photographed travelling in a Kuala Lumpar commuter train; and words like 'change', 'challenge', 'modernisation' and 'keep pace' peppered her speeches. 'We are not seeing a new Queen,' observed the *Sunday Telegraph*. 'What we are gradually noting is the same Queen reflecting the changing society around her'.[39] Previously, she had avoided making off-the-cuff comments. Now reports of them sprinkled press accounts of her engagements. Topicality became a feature of the adapting Queen. In Brunei, she remarked to the Sultan's family: 'I can't write any more. I can only write on computers. You can rub things out. It's so simple.' In Kuala Lumpar, modernisation took the form of signing footballs for members of the Malaysian Manchester United fan club. Afterwards, the two visits were judged a success, and a show-case for the Monarch's new 'hands-on' approach to public engagements.[40] 'Her Majesty,' the *Sun* concluded, in a conciliatory mood, 'has shown she really can be the People's Queen.'[41]

Meanwhile, there were a series of changes at Court. The Australian Geoff Crawford had already replaced Charles Anson as Press Secretary before Diana's death. After the tragedy, Lord Camoys took over from Lord Airlie as Lord Chamberlain, and early in 1999 Sir Robin Janvrin followed Sir Robert Fellowes as the Queen's Private Secretary. At the end of 2000, Crawford took up a private-sector public relations post in Australia and was replaced by Penny Russell-Smith, his deputy, and the first woman to be appointed to the position. There was a newly emerging pattern. In the past, senior courtiers had tended to remain at the Palace until retirement. Now a period of royal service had come to be regarded as a staging post in a career, and even a launch pad. One result was to dilute the tribal instinct of the Monarch's entourage, which had been a source of strength. Another was to normalise the Court within the civil service and corporate worlds.

The departure of Sir Robert (now Lord) Fellowes to take up a senior post in banking, and the succession of Janvrin, were symptomatic. The decade of Fellowes had seen a revolution in the business and conduct of the Private Secretary's office. At the same time, the post had moved from the shadowy world of the *eminence grise* into the centre of controversy. Formal duties had stayed the same: running the Queen's official programme, providing a constitutional link between Crown and Downing Street, advising the Monarch on matters that concerned her as Head of State of the seventeen countries of which she was Sovereign. The Home Office advised on technical and legal matters, although (according to a former courtier) 'an awful lot is common sense, guided by what the public think these days'. There had always been a political aspect. In the past, the political role had been kept as much as possible behind the scenes, with the Queen's Press Secretary tackling the media. In recent years, however, the Private Secretary had become a public figure in his own right, better known than the permanent secretaries of important Government departments, or than some Cabinet ministers.

Meanwhile, it had been a decade of rapid, less visible, evolution in the Palace as a whole. The Airlie-Peat reforms had put the Household's finances on a firm business footing, the Palace had been opened to the public, the Queen had 'voluntarily' agreed to pay tax, the Civil List had been rationalised. Fellowes had been a cautious broker of change, seldom the instigator, but skilled at putting ideas to his employer, who trusted his judgement. As a courtier, his position had been difficult. Some of the younger royals resented his influence over the Queen, and St James's Palace resented his closeness to the Princess. 'Diana would go to Robert and squeal,' was an established view in the Charles camp. Some of the Prince's friends accused him of turning the Queen against Camilla. Others, however, considered that his ability to understand the Monarch had been critical in recent storms, and that he gave her what she most needed – clear opinions and reassurance.

He had taken her seriously as a person, and had been prepared to argue with her. 'She is not an idiot,' was a particular Fellowes theme. 'She has a mind of her own.' According to an insider: 'There was no

Sunday Telegraph, 7th September, 1997

servility in his disposition.' Another former colleague recalls him as a 'heartland Englander, with heartland values,' a man who had sought to manage change at an exceptional moment. 'To keep your head when all around lose theirs . . .' Kipling's lines seemed apt. His departure ended an aspect of the Court that – almost incestuously – linked business and family ties. But it also removed a loyal friend and stout adviser.

The change of Private Secretary introduced a new style. Fellowes belonged to the stratum of rural gentry and aristocracy that was part of the Queen's own background: Janvin naturally related to the urban, mandarin upper-middle-class. 'Robert is more the Queen's type, Robin's approach is more bureaucratic,' says one former courtier. 'Both were nice to work with, but were very different colleagues,' says another. 'Robert likes to get through his in-tray as fast as possible,' according to the same source. 'He likes quick answers – he is not wedded to great strategy sessions. Robin moves more slowly. He likes to mull over complicated things before deciding what advice to give.' Instinctive, passionate, open-minded were adjectives used to describe Fellowes. Cerebral, diplomatic, quizzical were applied to Janvrin.[42] If Fellowes was a careful moderniser who was wary of the latest whim, Janvrin saw a need to redefine the institution.

WHICH EMPHASIS was more appropriate? The Monarchy was self-consciously modernising: but it was doing so at a time when people outside were least inclined to notice. This was because the Constitution over which the Queen presided was changing at an even faster rate. So far, the Blair Government had not shown itself to be as radical socially or economically as its Labour predecessors. Yet constitutionally there were significant changes. The Freedom of Information Act, curtailment of the hereditary principle in the House of Lords, devolution of powers in Scotland, Wales and Northern Ireland, establishment of a London Assembly and elected mayor, partial incorporation of the European Convention on Human Rights, and a green-light to European integration, did not amount to the re-modelling of Britain demanded by the most vehement constitutional campaigners. Together, however, such reforms altered the political system more radically than at any time since 1918. In the context of such a shake-up, reforms at Buckingham Palace that would have appeared sensational a decade earlier, seemed modest. Meanwhile, the impact of the constitutional upheaval had repercussions for the Monarch's own role.

The most visible impact was on the Queen's relationship with the newly-devolved Scottish Government, and with its so-called 'first minister'. Who was to be formally responsible for appointing such a person – the Queen of Scotland, or some other individual or body? The new rules did not unpick the United Kingdom, or remove the ultimate sovereignty of the Queen-in-Parliament: to this extent, the status of the Queen north of the border remained the same as south of it. However, the prescribed relationship of the Monarch to the first minister included a notable innovation. In the United Kingdom, the Queen appointed the Prime Minister, with an accepted degree of royal discretion in hypothetically uncertain circumstances. In the new

Scotland, such discretion was formally removed, and the Monarch was required to accept the recommendation of the Speaker of the Scottish Parliament, whatever that recommendation happened to be.

This did not appear a radical variation, because politicians and the public had ceased to expect the Monarch to exercise her discretionary power in the UK context, except in circumstances which had so far not arisen. However, in Scotland the circumstances were no longer so hypothetical: the establishment of a proportional representation voting system for Scottish parliamentary elections meant that there was a high probability of a 'hung' Assembly occurring. At the same time, the little-noticed decision not to give the Queen the same discretionary power in relation to a Scottish appointment as to a UK one, raised the issue of whether Scotland, or the United Kingdom, was now the anomaly. If proportional representation was ever introduced for Westminster, would the same principle apply – or would Parliament accept the increased likelihood of the Sovereign being called upon to play a political role? As often occurred, a change to one aspect of the Constitution, for one set of reasons, had implications for other aspects that had not been intended or thought through.[43]

In addition, there was the question of royal involvement in birth-of-nation ceremonial arrangements for the first, historic opening of the Assembly. Scottish opinion was divided, between those who saw the Queen's participation as a visible sign of nationhood, and those who saw it as a relic of Englishness on an otherwise Scottish occasion. Eventually it was agreed that the 'royal' aspect should not only be low on pageantry, but on content as well. The Scottish Queen would travel in the Scottish landau in a horse-drawn procession from the Palace of Holyroodhouse up the City's Royal Mile. But her part in the opening ceremony would be limited to a few formal words.

Scottish coolness towards an essentially British Head of State might have ended the Queen's role here: as a minor ceremonial actor. However, there was a conflict. A wish to play down the visible participation of the British Monarch was combined with an equally powerful desire to emphasise that the free Scottish nation had independent access to the Queen of Scotland. It was important to the concept of Scotland as a self-sustaining country that the Sovereign should not appear to marginalise her relationship to Scottish institutions: privileges extended to a Westminster premier, went the argument, should also apply to an Edinburgh one. Hence it was stressed that the Monarch would meet regularly (though comparatively infrequently) with Scotland's first minister, thereby giving the latter a status not granted to any mere member of the Cabinet in London, who only had audiences in exceptional circumstances. The Scottish audiences would take place with nobody else present, and with no written record – as for the Prime Minister of the United Kingdom. Crucially, the Queen would not divulge to the British premier the content of the conversation.

The first Scottish audience, with Donald Dewar, took place at Holyroodhouse on 17 May 1999 in the Morning Drawing Room. It lasted twenty minutes, appropriately shorter than for a Westminster premier, but establishing the principle that the Monarch would have a relationship with her devolved Scottish kingdom that was separate from her relationship with the United Kingdom as a whole. The Queen opened the Scottish Parliament six weeks later, wearing a green and purple *ensemble* created by a Hebridean designer. Fears of absent guests and apathy were banished in the national euphoria, and crowds lined the Edinburgh streets ten deep. Official business was rounded off with a visit to Glasgow's Craigdale estate, which produced a memorable picture of the Queen of Scotland having tea and chocolate biscuits in the parlour of a council bungalow.[44]

IN THE COMMONWEALTH the trend was in the same direction as in Scotland – towards a reduction in the Monarch's direct role. The end, however, was not yet in sight. A nine-day, three-nation, African tour by the Queen in November 1999 signalled the changing climate in a year that also saw the ending of Britain's nominal role in Hong Kong, the last populous colony, and with it a significant reduction in the number of the Queen's subjects. Yet the Commonwealth itself, so far from fading away, was more buoyant than for many years past. Indeed, there was even a queue to join it. Though Nigeria had been suspended in 1995, the Republic of Cameroon had joined in the same year. Meanwhile, Palestine, the Yemen and Rwanda were all exploring the possibility of membership. At the same time, a revival of historiographical interest in the former British Empire, and the rise of the

English-language 'Commonwealth novel' reminded citizens of member nations of a deep and lasting cultural bond. An Australian economist, Katherine West, wrote of the business connections provided by the 'multi-diaspora' Commonwealth, with everything from company law to accounting technologies closely related, because of the historic British link.[45] Post-colonial hostility to the Commonwealth seemed to be on the wane, superseded by a new generation of voters and leaders who saw advantages to the surviving connection.

The Queen, seldom happier than when she was in Africa, threw herself into the tour with a special energy. In Ghana, the national press congratulated her on appearing to know more about President Nkrumah, her host in 1961, than most Ghanaians. In another recently admitted Commonwealth recruit, Mozambique, she was greeted by Africans in FRELIMO tee-shirts.[46] In Durban, she addressed the fiftieth anniversary Commonwealth Heads of Government Meeting. Looking back, she recalled her twenty-first birthday speech in which 'I committed my life to the service of the Commonwealth.' (In fact, the word used had been 'Empire', but nobody corrected her). Looking forward to the twenty-first century, she spoke of computers, the internet, e-mails and globalisation.

Nevertheless, some of her listeners wondered whether she was modern enough, and whether the time was approaching to cut the royal umbilical. The Queen had succeeded her father as head of a very different Commonwealth in 1952 – but by appointment, not heredity. She had made an impressive job of it for almost half a century. Not only had she provided a calming influence, and occasional mediation between nations. She had achieved the remarkable feat of retaining the loyalty and sentimental attachment of the leaders of member states, even when they had been bitterly opposed to United Kingdom policies. In many countries, however, the concept of a British-led organisation had come to seem an anachronism.[47] Don McKinnon, a New Zealander newly-elected as Commonwealth Secretary-General, defended her on the grounds that she did not interfere, and that her headship was a powerful symbol. 'The Queen does not impose herself nor set policy,' he pointed out. 'She is very much a figurehead. A proposition to get rid of her is rather juvenile.' Smaller states, he suggested, saw 'the linkage to the British crown more importantly than the larger states.'[48] It was significant, however, that the defence had to be made.

Headship of the Commonwealth was one thing, being Head of State was another. Whatever might have been true of smaller countries, in which she still reigned, opposition to a 'foreign' Monarch as national symbol in the bigger ones was growing. In Australia, the Queen's second largest non-British realm, matters were coming to a head. Following the election of the monarchist John Howard as Prime Minister in 1996, the Queen might have taken the initiative to bow out of Australian politics gracefully and thereby cheat the executioner, at a time when she was not under immediate pressure. She chose not to do so. Neither did she fight to retain her throne. It was left to the people of Australia to decide, which – as it turned out – they found singularly hard to do.

The Howard victory slowed, but did not halt, a seemingly inexorable trend. The Queen had already suffered several stages of what republicans liked to call her 'civic death' – including the removal of her name from the ministerial oath of allegiance, the removal of her portrait from Sydney Town Hall, and the announcement that the Government would no longer endorse any future applications for the 'royal' prefix by Australian organisations.[49] By the end of 1996, the proportion of Australians favouring a republic had reached 55 per cent, with only 38 per cent opposed.[50] The very lack of resistance to such a change, however, created its own difficulties for those opposed to the status quo. Confident of victory on the main issue, republican campaigners shifted the debate from whether the Monarchy should be abolished, to the kind of system that should replace it. The result was a battle of great significance for those facing the same dilemma elsewhere.

The question was when and how: but it was also what. In particular, was the removal of the Queen merely to be a cleaning-up operation, aimed at producing a tidier constitution that remained, in all essentials, the same – or was it to be the occasion for a radical shift in balance, giving an Australian President a degree of authority the British Sovereign never had? There was the matter of specific powers – for instance, whether these should include the right to dismiss a prime minister, as the Governor-General had dismissed Gough Whitlam in 1976. But there was also the question of the method of choice. This

posed a problem of a kind that would certainly arise in similar circumstances in Britain, or any other country seeking to replace a near-
powerless figurehead. Was Australia seeking to move from a distant,
unelected Monarch to a home-grown president who could claim a
popular mandate? Polls showed that ordinary Australians wanted a
say in picking their head of state. Politicians, however, were anxious
that they should not have one. Paul Keating, ardent in his republicanism, was equally ardent that a plebiscite to elect a president would be
a mistake – and that it would lead to a French-style system, shifting
power from prime minister, cabinet, and parliament 'to that single
person' who would have a unique authority.[51]

In February 1997, the Howard Government announced the setting
up of a 'people's convention' to consider such issues, and promised
a referendum on the Constitution by 2000, if the convention produced
a consensus in favour of change. A year elapsed between the announcement of the convention, and the holding of it. In that time, positions
hardened. The first and central issue was the future of the Crown.
On the one hand, monarchists defended the existing system, arguing
that the Crown in Australia was Australian, not British, and that the
Governor-General was not a stand-in for the Queen but exercised the
limited powers invested in the office as constitutional Head of State.
On the other, republicans argued that the Monarchy was an anachronism, and proposed a non-executive presidency on the German or Irish
model. In so doing, the Australian republican movement was careful
to avoid making the issue personal. Few doubted, however, that recent
blows to the Monarchy's prestige had helped to give the campaign
momentum.

At first, the monarchists, characterised by Keating as 'a dedicated
Zimmer-framed Dad's Army of true blue Royalists,'[52] were on the
defensive. The glitterati ridiculed their position. So did the new Establishment, composed of the most globally-orientated sections of the
business and corporate community. However, the very hopelessness
of the cause was gradually turned to the monarchists' advantage as
attention shifted from the republican issue to the failure of the republicans to agree among themselves. Internecine wrangles caused delay,
precluding reform in time for the millennium, and the monarchists
gained fresh heart. Meanwhile, excitement engendered by the visit of

the Princess of Wales in the autumn of 1996 provided a reminder that, however much they might reject Monarchy with their heads, emotionally Australians were as riveted by royalty (or at any rate, some royalty) as ever. They were good at self-mimicry. 'This hoop-la about Diana's visit to our shores would make a brown dog weep,' wrote Peter FitzSimons, a Sydney columnist. 'Here we are, a country moving resolutely to becoming our own free-standing republic, simply going ga-ga because this 35-year-old refugee from the House of Windsor is now among us. Strike a light and hold the hell-fire, but what is the big deal?'[53] When Diana died less than a year later, the response was confused. Australians shared the general grief, reacting against the Windsors. At first, surveys showed a boost to the republican cause. However the impact was not clear-cut. Some republicans discovered feelings they did not realise they had,[54] and a poll at the end of October showed that half the population remained undecided on how to vote in a referendum.[55]

In November 1997, advocates of change launched a big advertising campaign, focussing on the hereditary principle. 'If you're not related to the Queen,' posters declared, 'you'll relate to the Australian Republican Movement.' Monarchists found it increasingly hard to sustain the argument in favour of a foreigner as a national symbol. Some retreated into a degree of agnosticism that came close to acceptance of their opponents' case. There was 'monarchist' talk of removing the Queen's head from the currency and coinage, even of re-naming the Governor-General President. 'I'm extending a great big olive branch to the republican movement,' declared Tony Abbott, a key figure in Australians for Constitutional Monarchy. 'I'm conceding the emotional incongruity of sharing a Head of State with another country'.[56] Such acts of appeasement did not stem the pro-republican tide, and the convention, part elected and part appointed, which met on 2 February 1998, already had a built-in republican majority.

However, the real argument was only just beginning, and the divisions in the republican camp enabled monarchists to mount an effective rearguard action. There was no attempt to make a sentimental case. In a battle over the role of the Queen, the Queen seldom came into it. Both sides held to an unspoken agreement that personalities were best avoided. 'We're not talking about her,' insisted Malcolm

Turnbull, leader of the Australian Republican Movement, 'we're talk-ing about an institution.'[57] While republicans were anxious to avoid appearing disrespectful, monarchists were afraid that the obvious Eng-lishness of royal personages would damage their case. Howard himself presented retention as the least-bad option, among a plethora of presi-dential systems currently on offer.[58] 'I oppose Australia becoming a republic,' the Prime Minister declared simply, 'because I do not believe that the alternatives so far canvassed will deliver a better system of Government.'[59] For the republicans, on the other hand, the issue was identity, and 'cultural cringe' – the national inferiority complex about Britain, and the ambition to eliminate it.[60]

The convention sat for two weeks. The verdict – 46 delegates in favour of getting rid of the Monarchy, 27 in favour of retaining it, with three non-aligned – caused no surprise. What mattered was the formula on offer. In the end, delegates voted for a compromise devised to bring together 'direct election' and parliamentary camps on the republican side, but in practice rejecting direct election. The voters were to be offered a straight Yes-No choice between a 'Keating's republic,' with a president elected by a two-thirds majority of parlia-ment, and keeping the Queen. Rank and file republicans rejoiced. Some imagined that all that was now required to make 'Keating's republic' a reality was a brisk popular vote. In fact, there was much for monarchists still to play for.

The referendum was due in November 1999. The delicate issue of an impending visit by the Queen to Australia was resolved by postpon-ing the tour till 2000, after the poll but before the Olympics which she would not be asked to open in case by then she had ceased to be Sovereign. However, the republican campaign, bitterly divided over the presidency issue, began to slip badly as the vote approached. In a country that regarded its own political elite with a high degree of suspicion, defenders of the Crown were able to raise doubts about the idea of a political cabal scheming in smoke-filled rooms. 'What the hell do these politicians think they are, that they can choose the president?' asked Malcolm Mackerass, a leading monarchist.[61]

Other constitutional spectres were raised. Experts began to discuss the possibility that some states might secede from the federation, rather than obey a pro-republic vote. In the case of Queensland, where monarchist feeling was strong, there was a particular complication. A nation-wide vote for a republic might still leave the state as a Monarchy, because the state recognised the Queen as its own head, separately from the Commonwealth of Australia as a whole. By July, the 'No-to-a-change' campaign was ten per cent ahead – largely because of doubts about the republican system on offer. In October, one poll showed that less than a third of voters wanted to retain the status quo. However, only fourteen per cent supported the republican model available.

As referendum day approached, worried republicans tried to raise a last-minute 'Charles III and Queen Camilla' scare. It had no effect. There was no sudden burst in popularity for the Queen. However, the opinion-poll gap between Yes and No supporters widened to fifteen per cent, with a large group of 'don't knows'. Indifference became the fashionable mood. One (no longer Australian) figure who did voice an opinion was Rupert Murdoch, who surprised nobody by declaring himself a committed republican. Monarchists replied that if the issue was Australian independence, the house of Murdoch posed a bigger threat than the house of Windsor. In the United Kingdom, most of the press followed the Murdoch lead. The British public, staunchly monarchist at home, expressed little alarm at the prospect of an Australian republic. Just before the referendum, ICM showed only 34 per cent of UK voters in favour of Australia keeping the Queen, and 40 per cent in favour of it getting rid of her.[62] Elsewhere in the Commonwealth, the contest was watched with interest, especially in the countries where the Monarch still reigned, and where a 'Yes' vote would strengthen republican movements.

On 6 November 1999, six years after Keating had launched the republican debate as Prime Minister, Australia voted 55 per cent to 45 per cent against the new constitutional package. For the change to go through, the rules required an overall majority in the country as a whole, and in four out of six states. In fact, only Victoria – by a tiny margin – backed the republican scheme. 'The world will look at Australians as a pack of ninnies,' said Thomas Keneally,[63] when the result was known. The world was certainly perplexed. For the monarchists, it was an astonishing triumph. It was an equally remarkable humiliation for Malcolm Turnbull. Yet everybody knew that the vote

Sunday Times, 7th November, 1999

was against a president chosen by the politicians, not an endorsement of the Queen, whose street-wise Australian Press Secretary in Buckingham Palace had kept as discreetly silent as possible during the campaign. One poll, just before the referendum, showed only nine per cent of Australians wishing to retain the Monarchy.[64] After the result, the opposition Labor leader, Kim Beazley, renewed a promise to put the issue to the electorate again, this time offering the direct election model. Most observers agreed that, though it had suffered a setback, Australian republicanism had not gone away.

THE QUEEN WAS in Ghana when the referendum was held. Her face next day offered no sign of emotion. 'If she had achieved a normal political success,' wrote Matthew Engel in the *Guardian*, 'she would have raised both fists skywards, and punched the air in delight.'[65] Privately, however, the voters' decision was the cause of Palace relief and wry royal satisfaction. It was, after all, the first time in history that the British and Commonwealth Monarchy had been put directly to a democratic or electoral test. The Queen had not chosen, as she might have done, to withdraw from the lists to avoid embarrassment. Though not vindicated, she had survived: her people had spoken. As one paper pointed out, Australia now had, in effect, an elected hereditary Monarch.[66]

From the Monarchy's point of view, the outcome provided a breathing-space. It ended a phase of royal history in which every major item of news affecting the throne seemed to diminish its authority, and showed that the institution still had some strength. It also removed the danger of an immediate chain-reaction, with copy-cat referendums elsewhere, and deprived British republicans, in particular, of the fillip they were looking for. During the long drawn-out Australian contest, there had been stirrings in realms around the world. In Canada and New Zealand, small but active republican movements had secured a foothold, and in most of the Caribbean islands republican sentiments were increasingly voiced. In the Bahamas, a constitutional commission had been set up in 1998, and in Barbados the election of a republican Prime Minister, Owen Arthur, early in 1999 seemed to herald reform. At the end of the same year, the *Observer* reported that only in a handful of realms, mainly the smallest – Belize, St Christopher and

Nevis, and (in the Pacific) the Solomon Islands, Tuvalu and Papua New Guinea – was there no significant demand for a republic.

The Australian 'No' vote deprived nascent movements of a model, and also reminded politicians of the complications that a republican road could entail. In Britain, the main lesson for politicians – currently embroiled in complex legislation to reform the House of Lords – was that reform or abolition of a single historic institution could not be taken in isolation. Any major change in constitutional rules – however irrational the existing rules might seem to be – was likely to alter the balance of the whole system, in ways that might not be intended. At the same time, the Australian debate had highlighted the potent symbolism of the Crown, exposing issues of identity much deeper than the divide (in Australia's case) between an 'Anglo-Celt' racial aristocracy, and other, newer groups. A Pandora's Box of unresolved cultural differences had been opened, raising the question posed by the historian Stuart Macintyre: 'Who are we now?'[67] Tom Nairn had asked the same question, in a United Kingdom context, more than a decade earlier. Thus, the Australian experience provided a setback to Commonwealth republicanism, but also a marker, reminding the movement's activists (and opponents) in the countries where the monarchical tradition had been strong, that while a path to change existed, reform would not necessarily be easy or painless.

It was too soon to tell whether the referendum would come to be seen as a dress rehearsal for a decisive showdown a few years hence. 'In Australia, the debate is along the lines of: after the Queen, Charles – no way,' according to one observer.[68] For the time being, however, there was a restoration of the *status quo ante*. Normal relations between Australia and its distant Head of State, always good, were resumed. Once again, it was open to the Queen to follow her victory with an antipodean abdication: accepting the implicit verdict of the poll, and inviting warring republican factions – as her last piece of constitutional advice – to settle their differences. Such an act might have been a political master stroke. Once again, it was not in her nature to make it. Instead, she carried on as if nothing had happened. In March 2000 she embarked on a two-week Australian tour – her thirteenth, though the first since 1992 – blandly reiterating her established position, which was, in any case, the constitutional reality. The fate of the Australian

Monarchy was for Australians to decide. 'Whatever the future may bring,' she declared in a keynote speech, crafted by Sir Robin Janvrin, 'my lasting respect and deep affection for Australia and Australians will remain as strong as ever.'[69]

28

I N THE YEARS before the Queen's 2002 Golden Jubilee, the crisis
that had beset the Monarchy in the early and mid 1990s softened.
The frenzied atmosphere had gone, and a more sedate pace resumed.
Some attributed this to the removal of the Diana problem. They
pointed to Australia, where monarchists led more composed lives now
their message was no longer confused by a wayward ex-royal star.

After the tragedy, the Prince of Wales saw more of his children and
the easy affection that existed between them helped to answer the
accusation that he was emotionally cold.[1] Meanwhile, after a short
interval, the process of acclimatising the public to Camilla Parker
Bowles resumed, helped by her own reticence and discretion. Although
the prospect of a marriage had receded, polls began to indicate a
more tolerant attitude to the possibility of one eventually taking
place. No post-Highgrove 'coming out' was proposed. However, in
2000 the two Palaces allowed it to be known that the Queen and
the Prince's companion had met and spoken to each other at an
informal gathering.

As a royal dissident, Diana had no immediate successor. Press interest in a previous generation of rule-breakers – Princess Margaret and
Princess Michael of Kent – had faded, while Prince Andrew's ex-wife,
'Fat, frumpy, feckless, free-loading Fergie . . . the Duchess of Pork,'
also had a declining media appeal, at least in the United Kingdom.
The postscript to the Yorks' divorce showed, indeed, how rapidly and
completely the mystique of royalty could be diluted. After it became
absolute in 1996, the tally of grievances against Fergie mounted, as
she embarked on a new career as an American television chat show
host, cashing in to the best of her ability on her failed marriage. In
March 1997, she moved back into Sunninghill, her former marital
home, where she resumed a complicated but friendly relationship with

the Duke. The tabloids feasted on a humiliating interview with Ruby Wax, and on public exchanges with the Duke of Edinburgh. However, like the defrocked Rector of Skiffley who sought to make a living by putting his head in the mouth of a lion, she lost her ability to shock. In an interview in August 1999, the Duchess claimed that she had only divorced for commercial reasons, and simultaneously blamed courtiers she called 'the Grey Men' for the marriage break-up. She also hinted at a half-belief in Diana assassination theories, claiming that she felt 'frightened' after the Princess's death.[2] But Fergie – slimmed-down, high spending, irrepressibly buoyant – now belonged to the *Hello* magazine world of the merely notorious, and had ceased to be somebody whose remarks could do damage.

After the divorce, the Duchess was treated with weary tolerance by her ex-parents-in-law, who allowed her to keep an office at Buckingham Palace with two staff, to 'look after the children's interests'. When economy-minded courtiers raised the matter, Philip accused them of being 'bureaucratic'. Meanwhile the Duke of York, semi-ironic and semi-affectionate, referred to his former wife as 'Her Royal Highness'. 'That's Andrew for you,' said the Queen, when staff took it up.[3]

Another potentially harmful critic also lost his sting. At the time of the funeral, Earl Spencer's speech had the ring of a declaration of dynastic war. Some imagined that the people's peer, expressing the mood of the nation, would offer himself as role model to the young princes, and even seek a part in their upbringing. There were obstacles, however, in the way of either possibility. Spencer lived in South Africa, and was therefore only intermittently available for avuncular duties. There was also another reason. At the time of his sister's death, he had been embroiled in a marital dispute which culminated in a Cape Town divorce less than three months later. During the court hearing, he was accused of treating his own severely anorexic wife with greater cruelty than had ever been attributed to the Prince of Wales. The British press, still smarting from the Earl's well-aimed barbs in his funeral oration, back-lashed against a young aristocrat who, according to one writer, had been tutored in the art of 'exhibiting elegance and correct manners in public while behaving quite appallingly in private.'[4]

When Spencer took part in a lengthy television interview in June

1998, there was a mixed reception. The programme gave him an opportunity to reminisce about Diana but also – sceptics claimed – to advertise the opening of Althorp to the public. One suggested that Charles Spencer had become in his press relations the 'male mirror of Diana,' who had described tabloids as 'evil' while feeding the public appetite.[5] As guardian of his sister's grave and head of the alternative dynasty, Earl Spencer retained a place in the public imagination. A Diana Memorial pop concert at Althorp at the end of June 1998 attracted a huge audience. However, a rival event in Hyde Park on 5 July organised by Capital Radio in aid of the Prince of Wales Trust – the 'Party in the Park' – drew even more. Charles's appearance on the platform was greeted with unexpected warmth. At least one poll, which had placed the Heir at a nadir of popularity the previous year, now put him higher on the 'are you satisfied with how he does his job' table than the Prime Minister.[6] Meanwhile, the Prince's teenage sons showed little inclination to take up their uncle's offer of emotional guidance.

In January 1999, the announcement of the engagement of Prince Edward to Sophie Rhys-Jones, a public relations consultant, strengthened the impression of the Royal Family settling down after a bad patch. There was an irony here. At one time, Edward had presented a problem – if not the black sheep, the member of the family who had broken the mould and flouted his father's wishes, abandoning the Marines in order to work in the world of theatre and television. In competition with people of every class, he had mixed fortunes. The *Knockout* débâcle was not easily forgotten, and – despite a limited success in the production and presentation of documentaries – he had difficulty in establishing himself as an independent talent. Yet there was respect for his determination to make a non-traditional career outside the royal compound.

Edward had avoided the danger of a broken marriage, but not of giving rise to gossip, by remaining obstinately single. Was he homosexual? There were plenty of jokes on the theme that his orientation was common knowledge. At a dinner in 1990, a journalist approached him and brazenly put the question. The Prince's denial provoked 'Edward: "I'm not gay"' headlines, which did not dampen speculation. Gradually, however, the rumour was overtaken by the accurate story that he had embarked on a 'trial marriage,' a new form of Windsor courtship that involved his partner moving in to Buckingham Palace, and occupying an adjoining room.[7] It was a mark of the nation's altered mores that a set-up which once would have been considered scandalous received little press attention during the years in which the tumultuous marital and romantic lives of Edward's siblings were under constant scrutiny. The arrangement was also an indication of royal realism. Indeed, not only did it have the approval of the Queen, who reportedly wanted 'to ensure that this relationship should be allowed to move at its own pace and not in the confines of Victorian protocol.' It appeared to have her enthusiastic support. For several years before her marriage, Sophie regularly took part in Royal Family gatherings at Balmoral and Sandringham. However, the announcement of the engagement presented a problem that had not occurred before in the Queen's reign. The public might once have cared more for a marriage than a ministry. But how could it now be expected to celebrate another indissoluble royal union?

The wedding was fixed for 19 June at St George's Chapel, Windsor. The choice of venue signalled a scaled-down, more private event, and the arrangements pointed in a low-key, Scandinavian direction. The service was to be conducted by a bishop, not the Primate, and there would be no Guard of Honour. As the day approached, press attention focussed on Edward's choice of a partner who was not only untitled, but 'the lowliest commoner to marry into the Royal Family for centuries.' Before the marriage, Sophie was keen 'to get the Queen to set up parameters about what she should and should not do,' according to a former royal aide. However, nothing happened.[8] Despite the reservations that now surrounded any royal match, the auguries were good. Julie Burchill wrote of 'the balding prince and his bovine bride-to-be.'[9] But most observers calculated that Edward had chosen well, and that Sophie could have done worse than marry the only one of the Queen's children to have made a career of his own. Sophie's announcement that she would continue to work for her public relations business, and would not carry out engagements in her own right, which once might have seemed a dereliction of duty, was taken as a sign of promise. 'This is clearly a robust union of two self-confident equals,' observed a hardened student of royal form, after the couple had undergone a ritual interview. The service was televised live by the BBC, and relayed to 6,000 ticket-holding members of the public in Windsor grounds. The wider public responded with approval, relief, and less curiosity than at any royal wedding since the nineteenth century. One commentator observed the day before that not a single person of his acquaintance had 'displayed the slightest interest in tomorrow's wedding, still less any excitement or happiness at the prospect of it.'[10]

Edward's wedding closed a chapter. In particular, it seemed to end the primacy in the public imagination of the Queen's children, and passed the baton to a rising generation that had grown to, or was approaching, adulthood – especially William, whose looks, physical grace and diffidence resembled his mother's, and who was reaching an age at which the media would cease to feel constrained by its own post-Diana undertakings. The new 'younger royals' offered a different style, carrying with it the expectation that they would seek to live normalised, non-royal lives. Of the descendants of George VI, only the Queen herself and her eldest son had married into the world of royalty or aristocracy. Through marriage or parentage, the rest could claim a background or environment (though not a standard of living) that was as much commoner as Windsor.

THE REPUBLICAN DEFEAT in Australia did not close down discussion of the Monarchy in the Commonwealth. It merely postponed a debate which, sooner or later, would have to take place in all the Queen's remaining realms. The proposition seemed simple, although in practice it was not always so. Should a liberal democracy have as its symbolic head a hereditary British Monarch who, like medieval rulers curing the king's evil, exercised authority because of accidents of history and birth, rather than on the basis of election or attainment? Nowhere was this debate more overdue at the beginning of the new millennium than in the United Kingdom itself.

To some extent, in a quietly British, incremental way, it had already begun. There were no mass republican rallies, as in Victoria's reign. However, the old taboo surrounding the topic – the Right regarding it as improper, the Left as not worthy of consideration – had largely been shed. The peeling away of inhibitions had occurred in stages,

Top Floral fascism, Kensington Palace, September 1997.

Above left Bowing Queen.

Above right Mourners in Hyde Park.

Above Last rites for *Britannia*, December 1997.

Below Queen of Scotland. With Donald Dewar, Scottish First Minister, after the opening of the Edinburgh Parliament, 1st July 1999.

Above Tea with the Queen. At home on the Castlemilk estate, Glasgow, July 1999.

Below Maundy money. With pensioners at Westminster Abbey, April 2001.

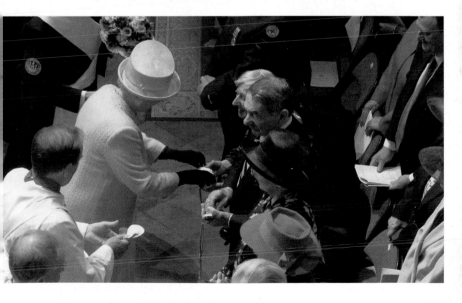

Pheasant strangler. Sandringham Estate shoot, November 2000.

Opposite: Above Monarch on the boards. Sue Townsend's 'The Queen and I',
Haymarket Theatre, Leicester, 1994.

Right Queen in waiting. Mrs Parker Bowles at a party hosted by
the Press Complaints Commission, February 2001.

Above 'I've met a lot of Popes in my time.' Exchanging gifts with John Paul II, Vatican, October 2000.

Below 'Moon Against the Monarchy.' Protest outside Buckingham Palace by the Movement Against the Monarchy, June 2000.

Above State Opening.

Right Gap year. Prince William on his Raleigh International Expedition in Chile, December 2000.

Overleaf Modernising Monarch. Launching the royal website, 1997.

roughly paralleled in other areas of permissiveness. Bit by bit, the Monarchy had shifted from a part of the Constitution and social landscape that was generally considered to be beyond reproach to one whose *raison d'être* was widely felt to be in need of examination. The issue was not, or not yet, whether Britain should dispose of the Monarchy altogether. Committed republicanism was still the province of a small minority. In any case, as Vernon Bogdanor pointed out, republics do not usually come about through adherence to republican doctrines.[11] The issue was how to make greater sense of an institution and part of the national culture of such visible significance, yet one which for the time being seemed poorly integrated into the society it formally led. Some continued to shy away. Everybody knew, however, that the issue, once raised, would not simply fade, partly because it was so closely linked to wider questions of national identity and purpose.

Although it had started, the discussion had not progressed far. Indeed, the arguments remained traditional ones. Opponents or critics pressed Tom Nairn's points about the Monarchy giving rise to the 'glamour of backwardness,' underpinning inherited privilege and contributing to economic decline. Defenders insisted that Britain's economy was now stronger than that of many of its republican rivals, and that the transmission of privilege had much more to do with inherited property than with the continuation of a single hereditary institution. Only occasionally did observers consider the wider question of what the complex relationship between the British and their titular ruler signified, or what the writer Christopher Hitchens jestingly called the non-questions: 'Is the Monarchy too remote? Is it remote *enough*?'[12] In a two-dimensional debate, it was as if monarchists were embarrassed by the textured heritage of royalty, and republicans could not cope with it.

The opening of the debate did serve the purpose, however, of drawing attention to aspects that had either not been present, or not noticed, when the reign began. At that time, people had spoken of the institution as if it was frozen in time, a kind of constitutional mammoth, unaltered while the rest of the political system changed around it. Indeed, its supposed immutability was counted as a strength – notwithstanding Sir Henry Marten's lessons about the need to adapt.

By the end of the century, the proud claim to be what its opponents now called a 'living fossil' had become a reputation it urgently needed to lose.

Yet a conundrum remained. What was the Monarchy supposed to do, supposed to be like? There was no mission statement, or consensus. The contemporary lexicon of audit, accountability and transparency was difficult to apply. The absence of rules made it difficult to check achievement against goals. The question of function, when applied to any other organisation, demanded a logical, secular response. In the case of the Monarchy, it was almost the other way round. It was a matter, not of justification, but of reconceptualising something whose existence and obligations had long been assumed.

For the time being, there was a sense of an institution on probation: recovering in prestige, applauded if it did not get into trouble, but ever at risk that a new wave of bad publicity would catch it unawares. It was accused of being trapped in the past: in fact it was obsessed by the future. 'The Princess's death threw up all sorts of nasty questions,' says an aide. 'Why are we here, how does the Monarchy enhance lives, what value does it have? Do we have a strategy for ten year's time? What do we want to be in Jubilee Year?'[13] The questions defied easy answers, partly because the institution had not been set up, like a bank or a school, to meet a consumer need, and partly because an understanding of its role had always lagged behind the reality. There were also contradictions that made it impossible simply to tail public opinion. Thus, the public simultaneously celebrated the Monarchy as curator of tradition, and criticised it for being too tradition-minded.

One difficulty was a lack of scriptural authority. The only durable attempt to justify the British Monarchy had been written in the nineteenth century, in defence of the established order, and as a blast against the new-fangled demand for democracy. Walter Bagehot's *The English Constitution* was often quoted (for example, on the Monarch's right to be consulted, to encourage and to warn) as if it was itself a codification of what it described, rather than an opinionated appraisal. Modern justifications of the Monarch's role which drew heavily on Bagehot ran up against the problem that almost none of what he wrote could still be sustained.

Bagehot began by describing Monarchy as more intelligible than republican Government: most people a century-and-a-third later found it a good deal less so. He argued that it strengthened Government 'with the strength of religion,' meaning the Church of England: in the course of the twentieth century, the Church turned into a minority sect. He described the Queen (Victoria) as 'the head of society,' meaning aristocratic society: by the turn of the millenium, the application of such a title was an anachronism. He declared the 'family on the throne' an interesting idea: the point struck at the heart of the contemporary angst. He celebrated the Monarchy on the grounds that it 'acts as a *disguise*' for the benefit of 'the coarse, dull, contracted multitude' who 'really believe that the Queen governs': in the New Labour era, there was a commitment to openness.[14]

But if the writings of Bagehot, standard fare in late nineteenth- and early twentieth-century royal school-rooms,[15] no longer offered comfort to monarchists, what was there left? Part of the difficulty was, precisely, that the role did not stand still. Between Bagehot's 'disguised republic' and the limited national symbol of the late twentieth and early twenty-first centuries, lay several generations of 'imperial' Monarchy, which did not fit either into Bagehot's conspectus, or into a modern one.[16]

One reason for the paradoxical resilience of the Bagehotian model was that attempts to revise it were quickly superseded. *The English Constitution* might be out-of-date: but attempts to replace it were overtaken by events. Thus, at the beginning of Elizabeth II's reign, the constitutional writer Sir Ivor Jennings tried to put the Queen and her role into four boxes: first, as 'the Crown', impersonally providing 'the cement' that bound the Constitution; second, as a person whose name 'similarly binds the units of the Commonwealth'; third, as an individual who performs 'political functions of the highest importance' personally; fourth, as 'a social figure exercising important functions outside the political sphere'.[17] For several decades, Jennings's analysis was taken as a classic account. But by the end of the century, only the last of his boxes held more than tenuously. What, then, was the continuing role? The most fundamental surviving characteristic was the hereditary principle. We have seen how in Western pre-Christian culture, royal heredity was linked to the concept of *mana*, or tribal luck. Like the authors of the Act of Settlement, Bagehot had seen how *mana* could be harnessed to provide stability and legitimacy in a law-based state. In practical terms, the hereditary qualification had (and has) the advantage of removing an element of uncertainty over the succession. This was a point noted by Machiavelli, who observed that an hereditary principality presented fewer difficulties than other states.[18] However, strict adherence to heredity did not deal with the potential problem of an immovable Head of State with a diminishing ability to perform appropriate duties; or of a restless and underemployed Heir, doomed to a lifelong apprenticeship. Moreover, there was a circularity about seeing the principle as a constitutional safeguard. It could only serve this purpose if there was a widespread acceptance of its legitimacy, and this was itself at issue in the Monarchy debate.

Yet the story did not finish there. 'How is it,' wrote Dicey in 1885, 'that all the understandings which are supposed to regulate the personal relation of the Crown to the actual work of Government are marked by the utmost vagueness and uncertainty?'[19] One answer was that the very vagueness of the Monarchy's role meant that, even or especially when it was most valued, its actual function was not recognised. 'History notoriously takes wing at dusk,' as Raphael Samuel has put it.[20] Roles can often be seen most clearly when they are over. Or, to put it another way, the image of the Monarch was a miasma: just as it looked like one thing, it became something else. Thus, it could not be assumed that because a set of functions that once glittered from the royal diadem – imperial splendour, pinnacle of society, model family – had been lost, others might not be found to replace them.

This was scarcely a satisfactory answer to those who argued that the Monarchy had outlived its usefulness. A thriving institution does not have to justify itself: one whose value is widely questioned, does. Once, it had been possible for the Monarchy serenely to exist, decorously bestowing its favours, and looking to posterity for gratitude. That time had evidently passed, and there was an immediate need to demonstrate its value. A critique that pointed to possible abolition had more or less taken over the whole of the Labour and Liberal Democratic parties; the number of newspaper editors and proprietors, not to mention industrialists, bankers or even civil servants prepared to defend it was diminishing; and, although polls showed no collapse of public support, they indicated a gradual dilution which, if not reversed, could alter the calculations of political leaders. 'A visceral dislike of the whole monarchical business is widespread among younger voters,' wrote the political analyst Andrew Marr, after the Waleses' marriage had fallen apart in the mid 1990s.[21] A few years later, polls continued to show a correlation between age and support for the Monarchy, with younger people indicating the greatest disaffection. 'The use of the Queen, in a dignified capacity, is incalculable,' wrote Bagehot.[22] If, however, the Sovereign appeared as no more than a mannequin for the heritage industry, then the institution seemed in danger of disappearing, not necessarily in a moment of republican fervour, but because no powerful body of opinion existed with the will to preserve it.

Nevertheless, though the questions were difficult, they were not necessarily insurmountable. Indeed, the vagueness and uncertainty surrounding the institution could be defended on the grounds that it gave flexibility. Although the Monarchy could not be pinned down to a single purpose, it was certainly not out of work. Rather, it was busier and more in demand than ever before. Those who defended it used words and phrases which were old-fashioned but not necessarily redundant – service, duty, continuity, a nation representing itself to itself, encouraging good causes, celebrating achievement.

How should it give encouragement, and to whom? For royal staff there was a tightrope act: having to move with the flow of public opinion, and gain the approval of politicians in doing so, while retaining the Monarch's right to a discretionary sphere within which decisions were not taken 'on advice'; needing to show that changes were taking place, while insisting that they had been taking place anyway and there was no question of being pushed. In the constitutional sphere, anything the Queen's advisers did took them into a minefield. On the one hand, inertia on matters of public concern allowed surviving powers to wither, and amounted to slow constitutional suicide; on the other, almost any kind of unilateral or non-routine action risked over-stepping the limits of democratic propriety. The institution could be compared to a long-established newspaper facing critical readers and a loss of circulation. What should it do –

change the logo? Try to go upmarket or down? Alongside the common criticism that the Palace was stuck in a time warp, there was the danger of the Monarchy devaluing itself by following the latest fashion. More than ever in the past, the Court paid attention to its public image. Yet the truth was that no strategy would make much long-run difference unless there was a need for what the institution had to offer.

Meanwhile, the Court continued to exist: it was not impossible to imagine it as an institution holding itself in reserve, ready to handle some future national crisis or exigency that had not yet arisen. Arguably, however, such a role could best be adopted by standing back from the public clamour. In the twenty-first century, the Monarchy was not 'popular' in the way that it had been for most of the twentieth. In this respect, its experience was similar to that of other institutions that depended on public support. Membership of political parties and church attendance, for example, showed a parallel decline. But popularity was not the only measure of the success of an institution. Indeed, unthinking adulation could turn out to be a greater danger than a climate of critical scepticism.

Different roles had been performed, according to the social and political times. Which had been a 'success' and which a failure? Retention of office – a key test for politicians – was not at issue. Laying seed corn, to assure the dynasty's indefinite survival, was. 'The point about the Monarchy,' as one ex-courtier puts it, 'is that it is looking at endlessness.'[23] By this litmus it was not clear that the two episodes of over-heated enthusiasm – the 1950s, and the fifteen years following the BBC *Royal Family* documentary – were necessarily the best. Indeed, so far from seeking popularity, the Court might have been more fruitfully employed attempting to flatten out the curves of a manic-depressive cycle, by concentrating on areas in which it could be unobtrusively effective.

The Empire had gone, aristocracy was out of fashion, the 'model family' idea was an embarrassment, the Anglican Church scarcely needed a Supreme Governor, and royal reserve powers were likely to be exercised with decreasing frequency. However, there was one taken-for-granted role that had acquired a new twist, and which, in its way, was the logical sequel to centuries of touching for the king's evil. It could be called 'making good the democratic deficit'.

In a famous 1992 essay, J.K. Galbraith pointed to the devastating impact of affluence on those who did not share in it.[1] In the United States, competition for the votes of the comfortably-off, who now formed a substantive majority, would leave the poor with their demands unmet. 'Were one permitted one confident prediction,' wrote the American economist, 'it would be of the likelihood of an increasingly oppressive authority in areas of urban deprivation.'[24] A decade later, Galbraith seemed well vindicated. Despite periods of left-of-centre government, prison populations were bigger than ever on both sides of the Atlantic and the author's distopian vision of an increasingly divided, stockade society, in which politicians had an incentive to punish but not to help the weak and marginal, had come alarmingly closer.

Putting it simply, politicians attend to those who elect them, and pay less attention to minority groups which are either too listless to vote, or whose interests appear to be opposed to those of the comparatively affluent mass. For royalty, however, the picture was different. In the words of the Buckingham Palace website, 'The Monarchy is a focus for national unity,' symbolising 'the permanence and stability of the nation, which transcends the ebb and flow of party politics.'[25] In the end, of course, the Monarchy was as much the creature of public opinion as the politicians. However, it could afford to take a longer view and indeed needed to do so. Its concern was for the nations of the United Kingdom as a whole, and for their social cohesion. 'The Monarchy provides a third way between Government and people,' as one royal adviser puts it.[26] Thus, it was ideally placed to take an interest in the plight of those without political champions who, like sufferers from scrofula in the past, fell outside the normal philanthropic safety net – for humanitarian reasons but also to avoid the kind of social disintegration Galbraith feared and which any Monarchy had an incentive to prevent.

Royal good works had a long pedigree.[27] As we have seen, touching for the king's evil was historically associated with the giving of alms. In the nineteenth century, alms-giving gave way to association with, and patronage of, specific charities. In the twentieth, George VI had his King's Camp, Prince Philip pioneered the Duke of Edinburgh Awards, Anne championed the Save the Children Fund. The Sovereign's charity became both a symbolic echo of mystical or religious functions – as in the distribution of Maundy money – and practical. Royal patronage continued to be a cherished accolade in the voluntary sector – a modern illustration of the continuing efficacy of the royal touch.

In recent years, however, royal patronage had become less decorous. Charles and Diana, in their contrasting and competing ways, had shifted the royal focus away from the long-established mainstream charities, and directed attention at the social margins. While Diana raised the profile of desperate people by being photographed in their company, Charles interested himself in self-help schemes through his Prince's Trust, first established in 1976. Diana's 'touchings' had an impact which was dramatic and immediate, putting her causes in the headlines and on the agenda. The Prince's schemes took organisational form, concentrating on launching young men and women who stood the least chance of finding work: the disabled, people from ethnic minorities, adolescents who had been in care, under-achievers, ex-offenders.[28] It was a mark of the scope for this (in reality, highly political) approach that the Prince's Trust developed into an innovatory social think tank, from which both major parties harvested ideas. Monarchy, as Bogdanor points out, rested on a social base: if that changed, so would the institution.[29] The Trust had, precisely, identified a new constituency of the dispossessed, and a royal focus on the gaping hole in the political system was able – in the grandest of historical ironies – to help make the Palace's website claim come true.

The 'Galbraithian' Monarchy presented a new kind of challenge that was, in reality, very old. It was possible to imagine that, alongside its formal duties, the institution might build on its historic role as protector of the unrepresented. At the same time, there was a heritage that went beyond the activities of individuals. The Monarchy had a cultural significance that was difficult to unravel and possibly dangerous to seek to unstitch. Here we encounter a bewildering set of contradictions unnoticed by a cultivated elite that equated royalty and royal taste with kitsch. No doubt it was a factor that twentieth century

Sovereigns took scant interest in the arts, preferring the excitements of the turf and the grouse moor. As a result, Monarchy had largely been expunged as the subject matter of art or literature. The American Andy Warhol and the Italian Pietro Annigoni were the only painters to have produced familiar images of royalty in the present reign, and the predicament of royalty seldom featured in serious fiction. Recently, royalty had been the subject of satire and comedy, comparable to the lampoons of the early nineteenth century. However, a visiting Martian could be forgiven for wondering why a phenomenon so continually in the minds of the public was so little reflected in artistic expression.

That royalty had not only been supremely visible, but central to our culture throughout the twentieth century could not be doubted. Uninterested in culture, yet part of it: but what kind of culture?

The philosopher Roger Scruton has identified three ways in which 'culture' can be understood: culture as the defining quality of what nations are (common culture); culture, not as a possession of a whole nation, but as the possession only of its educated members – so-called 'high' culture; and – in addition to 'common culture' and 'high culture' – the comparatively new phenomenon of 'popular culture,' replacing the former folk cultures that once defined the tribes and nations of the world. The concept of common culture, Scruton maintains, 'leapt fully-armed from the head of Johan Gottfried Herder' in the mid-eighteenth century.[30] By contrast, popular culture was a phoenix arising from the ashes of the common cultures Herder identified, spreading its plastic wings over them all. Scruton's framework is relevant to the contemporary 'cultural' context of present-day British royalty.

Arguably, royalty used to be the essence of Herder's 'common culture' – part of the national zeitgeist. It continued to be identifiable in this way, although less so. It had little part in high culture, which did not know what to do with it. Where it found a resting-place was in popular culture, with its capacity to homogenise, export, and ring the globe. One of the striking features of the present Queen's reign has been royalty's own role as an agent of the transition from common to popular. Thus, the last fifty years of consumer-led capitalism and galloping improvements in communications has seen an astonishing coalescence of traditions, myths, narratives. If in some respects national identities retained their separateness, there were also a set of life patterns, economic demands, clothes, food, drink, images, personalities, that were globally shared, and mediated by a widely understood language.

At the beginning of the twenty-first century, it was appropriate neither to celebrate nor to bemoan this change. Nevertheless, it had become important to note it: whether or not it subsumed individual cultures, its impact was bound to grow. For the moment, the essence of the popular culture was simplicity. Communicated principally by visual images – television, magazines, the internet – it had reached the maximum audience (and hence the maximum profit of whoever its sponsors happened to be), by reducing everything to a lowest common denominator, if not of blandness, then of ease of appreciation. Part of the essence of the popular culture was its sparse landscape: only a few stories, faces, products, could fill the shared consciousness at any one time. Since the advent of television, the British Royal Family had been one of them.

Thus, the reasons why members of the Windsor family had a unique place in the world's collective consciousness begin to be apparent – including the extraordinary case of the Princess of Wales and the 'public grief'. The 'royalty' concept, with its magical origin, continued to exercise a fascination in many countries without monarchies or plausible royal families. At the same time, the Windsor Royal Family remained, despite declining political power, the premier dynasty in a Europe where other monarchies reigned over smaller states, and in a world containing many countries that still related to the British Monarchy, through their own history, through the Commonwealth or as surviving 'realms'. Meanwhile, because of the continuity of their line and the political stability of their country, the Windsors have provided a multi-generational saga, which people have grown up with, and continue to follow.

A shared experience of ever-present media images accounts for an extraordinary universality. According to this view, Diana – most interesting member of the group – was mourned by everybody because in every country, courtesy of 'the ferocious global media', she had long been part of everybody's daily experience. Arguably, the communications revolution of the 1990s created conditions in which an emotional explosion of some kind was waiting to happen, given the right prompt. 'Many of us saw images of Diana more frequently than our own parents or siblings,' points out the American writer, Andrew Sullivan. 'She penetrated our lives more fully than many of our friends.' People found themselves thinking about Diana in spite of themselves: simply because, under constant bombardment from a megaphone, they had no choice. Diana's personality had become a part of their mental baggage, and its abrupt, unscripted removal was a shock for which they did not have the defences to cope. Looked at as an artefact of international popular culture – one of a handful of tunes the whole world can hum, and whose joys and disasters are common currency to Thai taxi-drivers in Bangkok and Zulu herdsmen in the South African veldt – the continuing story of Elizabeth II and her family thus falls into place: as a drama that has continued to play a part in people's lives, whether they like it or not; and hence as a phenomenon with a possible future, as well as a past.

AT THE BEGINNING OF the new millennium, a traditional area of difficulty for the Monarchy lurked, just as sex scandals were beginning to recede: money. Criticism of state provision for royalty was no longer as fierce as it had once been. The Civil List arrangement established by Margaret Thatcher had worked to the Monarch's advantage because of low inflation, while the tightening of the Palace's finances reduced the scope for indictment on grounds of profligacy or inefficiency. Meanwhile, the decision to pay income tax drew the sting of the 'money bags' kind of attack. Nevertheless, the Royal Family had not shaken off its accusers. Previously criticism had focussed on the level of public subsidy, or the scale of the private wealth. Now there was a new claim. It was suggested that some recipients of public subsidy were making use of their royal status for commercial gain.

In relation to staff, the problem was not new. Since Crawfie, the temptation facing former royal employees had often proved impossible to resist. In 2000, Diana's former private secretary, Patrick Jephson, joined the list of those who gave in to it, publishing memoirs against the wishes of the Palace. But governesses and courtiers were one thing, family members another. As younger royals tried to make their way in the non-royal world, the question arose of the use that could be made of their link with a 'firm' whose standing and profile depended on the taxpayer, without tarnishing the 'dignified' aspect of the institution, or appearing to take private advantage of a public trust.

The royals most involved in the business world were Prince Edward and Sophie, now the Earl and Countess of Wessex. At the end of 2000 the press started to take an increased interest in their activities. In November, the *Guardian* reported that Edward's TV company Ardent was showing nearly £2 million losses over the seven years of its existence. It also asked questions about the refurbishment, and use, of his 50-room home, The Stables, and referred to 'unease' about the way in which the Prince and the PR company run by Sophie appeared to be using their connections[31]. For the time being, the matter went no further. In the spring of 2001, however, the press returned to the attack.

Was it or was it not the case that the Queen's daughter-in-law had been trading on her name? The *News of the World* determined to find out, using time-honoured methods. In April, it was revealed that the Countess of Wessex had been set up, in a classic tabloid sting, by a reporter armed with a tape recorder, and masquerading as a 'sheikh' and possible customer. Although the paper was at first persuaded not to publish the results, some of the material appeared in rival Sunday tabloids instead. The latter included comments on public figures, allegedly made by Sophie, of a kind that would have been innocuous over a dinner table, but seemed inappropriate when directed at a potential client. The press dwelt, in particular, on descriptions of the Prime Minister's wife as 'horrid, absolutely horrid', of the Leader of the Opposition as 'deformed' and of the Queen as 'the old dear'. Palace blushes were also caused by the Countess's reported prediction that Charles and Camilla would marry after 'the old lady' (the Queen Mother) died. The *News of the World* followed up with the transcript of an unsavoury conversation between the reporter and Sophie's business partner, in which the latter appeared to be offering to procure young men.

Long-term effects were hard to gauge, short-term ones were predictable. Sophie's indiscretions involved courtiers in a familiar exercise in damage limitation, which almost inevitably backfired. 65 MPs signed a

'So Sophie. After that absolutely abysmal performance, you are the weakest link – goodbye.'

Daily Mail, 9th April, 2001

motion calling on the Royal Family to set up a register of royal interests, setting out their business affairs for public inspection. More ominously for the Royal Family, several members of the Government felt emboldened publicly to break the silence that normally accompanied such a mishap. Chris Smith, Culture Secretary with responsibility for the media, reminded a BBC audience of the necessity for everybody 'be we MPs, or indeed, members of the Royal Family', to operate with the highest degree of probity.[32] Meanwhile one newspaper divided the New Labour elite into those it considered roundheads (critics of the Monarchy) and cavaliers (defenders), placing nine members of the Cabinet in the former category.[33] The scandal quickly blew over. However, it was widely seen as the most serious royal embarrassment since the Diana tragedy, undermining the reputation of the Countess as a sensible, down-to-earth exception to the rule that royal spouses could not be relied upon. Evidence of the immediate damage was provided by an ICM poll at the end of April, which indicated that 34 per cent thought Britain would be better off without the Monarchy – the highest proportion yet recorded.

Meanwhile, the 'old lady' was in excellent spirits. Queen Elizabeth's hundredth birthday had been marked the previous July not only by a congratulatory telegram from her daughter but also by a pageant which both she, and the public, seemed greatly to enjoy. Afterwards, Roy Hattersley accused the nation, accurately, of 'treating her with something approaching idolatry' following a display, which attracted huge summer crowds and the largest television audience for an early evening slot for years.[34]

The Queen Mother was one star. Her second-in-line great-grandson was in the process of becoming another. In August 2000, Prince William secured a place at the Scottish University of St Andrews, on the basis of better 'A' level results (A, B and C) than his father – thereby ending Cambridge's long monopoly on royal heirs, and also ending the tradition of sending members of the Royal Family to universities which their exam results did not justify. In December, in a calculated publicity move, Buckingham Palace released photographs of the Prince mucking-in during his post-Eton gap year in South America – including one shot that showed him cleaning a lavatory.[35] The press treated the pictures with suspicion, but also a grudging respect at the professionalism of the Palace operation. While the tabloids pondered William's romantic prospects, the broadsheets hoped they were not being misled. 'We look at these photographs', wrote Alison Roberts in the *Evening Standard*, contemplatively, 'and see a handsome, surprisingly well-adjusted young man doing what thousands of middle-class British teenagers do every year, travelling the world and trying to help less privileged people in poorer countries – or rather, this is what we're supposed to see'. Behind the Windsor family's decision, she reflected, lay 'the immensely patronising assumption that the entire country wants to look at glossy pictures of its teenage offspring'.[36] The fact remained, however, that it did.

In October, the Queen embarked on a four-day state visit to Italy, taking in a visit to the Vatican and her first meeting since 1982 with the Pope – another long-reigning monarch. The encounter was about symbolism, not the exchange of views. His Holiness spoke of ecumenicism and the Anglican Supreme Governor spoke about Northern Ireland, thanking him for his help in the peace process. The Queen had met Pius XII in 1951, before her accession, and John XXIII a decade later. She was reported to have told advisers: 'I have met a lot of popes in my time'. The tour also included Milan, where the royal suite at the Principe di Savoia Hotel allegedly included an extra room for the sole purpose of housing the Queen's shoes, an unlikely story but one that allowed a waggish Francis Wheen – who nevertheless was to be seen at a Buckingham Palace party a few months later – to compare her to Imelda Marcos.[37]

Meanwhile, an era seemed to be drawing to a close. The Queen Mother began to falter, while the health of her younger daughter deteriorated sharply. In 1998 Princess Margaret suffered a stroke, and in the following year scalded her feet badly in a bathroom accident. In March 2001, she suffered her third stroke in three years, before making a partial recovery. 'I'm determined to beat it', the Princess told visitors. But she could no longer read properly, or write.

The Duke of Edinburgh, who in the past had not always been easy for the Court to manage, seemed closer to the Queen than in the past. He celebrated his eightieth birthday in June 2001. Still fit and physically erect, and keenly engaged in his esoteric sport of carriage-driving, he was ageing benignly. Friends suggested that he had mellowed, and become less irascible, especially with his wife. The bantering style remained. He would criticise her for wearing unsuitable clothes on a shooting expedition ('Oh, shut up', she would reply), or if she attended to her animals, not him. 'For goodness sake listen to me,' he said on one occasion, 'don't talk to the dogs'.[38] But their alliance was stronger than ever, and she relied heavily on his judgement. Meanwhile, the Prince of Wales continued his lonely campaigns, which occasionally caught their moment. In July 2000, he warned of 'a growing divide' between those with rural lives and town-dwellers, and reiterated his opposition to genetically-modified farming. A few months later, he drew attention to his own continued defiance of political and parliamentary opinion on the subject of foxhunting by falling off his horse in the company of the Meynell and South Stafford-shire hunt, and injuring his shoulder.[39] Though the incident provided ammunition for critics, it did him no harm with the countryside lobby, or with the rurally-sympathetic general public.

Early in 2001, the royal link with agrarian Britain was highlighted in an unexpected way, by the first serious outbreak of foot-and-mouth disease since the 1960s. A rigorous culling policy failed to eliminate the epidemic. Both the Queen, as a countrywoman, and the Prince of Wales, with his interest in organic farming, were identified as friends of the livestock owners and handlers. One mid-April poll showed that the electorate considered the Prince to be more in touch with public views on farming than the Prime Minister.[40] Meanwhile, the Queen let it be known that she favoured the cancellation of Cheltenham races. They were duly cancelled. She was also believed by some to favour the postponement of the expected general election until the crisis eased. Nobody knew what she said to the Prime Minister. However, the poll was postponed. It was eventually held on June 7. Tony Blair's victory with a large working majority opened the possibility that he would become the second of the Queen's prime ministers to serve two full terms.

It was the thirteenth general election of a reign that had now encompassed the greater part of the United Kingdom's democratic history. The Queen, who had presided over a quiet revolution in the nation's international standing, economy, and values, showed no signs of intending to step down before the fourteenth, or at all. In the run-up to 2002, Elizabeth II's Golden Jubilee year, retirement was not on the Palace agenda. 'The only time', according to a friend, 'I ever heard her refer to the subject was after a rough voyage up the West Coast of Scotland in the Royal Yacht, when they were all sick. She said: "I lay on my bunk and thought: I'll have to abdicate". Instead of planning a withdrawal, she looked forward to going on – and on.

Through crises and controversies, she continued to perform her ritual duties at an age when most people who had taken a prominent part in public life had left it. She took pride in her doggedness. 'Among my contemporaries', she remarked at a private gathering, 'I am reckoned to have weathered rather well.' It was a justified assessment. In appearance, she was remarkably the same at 75 as five or ten years before – a small, sturdy figure with a mask-face that suddenly lit into a smile, a flash of beauty, before falling back into dourness.

Her energy and determination to carry out her duties were undiminished. She enjoyed the sense of doing the job she was required to do efficiently and well. 'The word thank-you is not in her vocabulary', an aide once ruefully said. Nevertheless she was 'one of the most efficient and easy to deal with people I'd ever worked with,' according to an ex-courtier with a civil service background.

She was strong, but passive. In her public life, she listened to what she was told. In her domestic life, she remained affectionate but remote. In both, she did not like or expect to have to take the initiative. She enjoyed her children's company, especially away from London. But the family was not close, and informal meetings were sporadic. Though head of the nation, she was disinclined to act as head of her kin. 'There was no family leader', says an ex-courtier. Prince Philip, who came closer than his wife to such a role, had his own interests. 'He dips into family matters, then off he toddles', according to a source.

Where private and public mixed, the Queen was at her least effective. She did not easily praise her children, and she was equally unwilling to pass judgement on them. When asked by advisers to intervene in personal matters with a public bearing, she backed away. Courtiers sometimes despaired of her insistence that it was 'up to them' – that is, her children, or in-laws – even when their behaviour impinged directly on her own ability to carry out her work. She continued – and continues – to find it hard to confront the Prince of Wales. Once, when her advisers were eagerly hoping that she would use the opportunity of a rare visit to Highgrove to discuss urgent matters with Charles, she returned to the Palace saying that she 'didn't have a chance' to talk to him.

Relations between the two offices eased in the early 2000s, and some of the weight of official and ceremonial business began to shift to St James's Palace. Imperceptibly, the Prince began to take a larger role. Yet co-operation remained sporadic, and it was difficult to bring off joint engagements. Monarch and Heir worked with their separate entourages, carried out their separate programmes, pursued their own interests, and seldom met except at family events and during occasional state visits. There was fondness and a kind of detached, impatient, mutual regard. But there was distance. Among her children, the Queen was closest to her youngest son, who had stayed for longest at Buckingham Palace.

Sense of duty, high degree of professionalism, doing her job well, being on top of it – these were words and phrases her loyal employees (and ex-employees) used to describe her. So were shyness and stubbornness and – surprisingly, after so many years – nervousness and frayed temper at public occasions and before speaking engagements. At the same time, a lifetime's experience of extraordinary events gave her a sense of proportion. 'She is not greatly exercised by any rigmarole in the great tapestry of life', as one former courtier puts it. She was inured to the press which, on the whole, she did not read. She was far more disconcerted by physical intrusions on her privacy – for example, by a photographer catching her unawares on a country path – than by a tabloid front page.

Sangfroid carried dangers: a lifetime of being shielded from, and filtering out, criticism made it difficult to adjust when flexibility was called for. Advisers were frustrated and exasperated by a reluctance to confront the most pressing problem facing her. Yet she did not make commitments lightly. She took seriously 'lessons must be learnt', much as she had taken seriously her Cape Town pledge and, for that matter, the Coronation Oath. After the 1997 broadcast, there had been a conspicuous change of direction. She was prepared to address her mind to the matter of a new royal style in the way that she had not been beforehand.

Yet she did not try to be liked. One journalist, referring to a 2000 *Daily Mirror* photo of a head-scarfed Sovereign ending the life of an injured bird at a shoot, described her as 'the level-headed old pheasant-strangler'. The description seemed oddly appropriate for a woman, ever in the public eye, who put up no show or front. At the same time, a consciousness of her role never deserted her, and her demeanour fitted the occasion. If she was opening Parliament, she was solemn and impassive. At other formal events, her style was notably different from that of her husband. Going down an introduction line, the Duke would make fun of the event, trying to lighten it with buffoonery. She did not: she would ask stilted little questions, taking each person seriously, as part of a professional job.

Socially, she had a brittle charm, an under-stated sense of humour, a startlingly loud laugh, and a powerful sense of the ridiculous. People described her liking for jokes as Hanoverian: she had a good ability to laugh at herself. She enjoyed cartoons, however barbed. 'She doesn't mind if they present her as a daft old frump', according to a former adviser. At the same time, she was a shrewd observer, and lampooned others. She kept herself informed about people. 'The Queen always knows everything', says a source. 'She never gossips, but keeps her ear close to the ground. She always knows'.[41] She was aware, through constant use, of the psychological power of being Sovereign. Nobody who met her for the first time ever forgot the experience. Most also enjoyed it. This was because of her position, and because of the excitement people feel when they see in the flesh somebody whose face they have known all their lives. But it was also because of the straightforwardness of her approach, and – curiously – because of its lack of spontaneity. For the Queen, meeting new people was always hard work. She was appreciated for her efforts, and her apparent fragility in social situations made those who met her feel protective.

Straightforward meant that she did not mince her words. She answered questions abruptly if that was all they required. Her female retainers described her as having a 'man's mind', meaning that she was more interested in male talk about upper-class rural pursuits than in children or where to buy hats. In conversation, she was cautious – both temperamentally and from training. She did not like to discuss feelings, and did not bare herself emotionally. She pulled back from talk that became too deep. Her eyes would dart around, fixing her interlocutor with a stare, looking not so much at you as through you, flitting from topic to topic, nervous about resting on any one subject for too long.

She was most relaxed in her private, animal-and-retainer-filled worlds at Windsor, Sandringham or Balmoral. She remained committed to her pleasures, which did not change – racing, breeding, shooting, and working her dogs. She kept a diary, a paragraph a night, like her father and grandfather. It was a routine, like brushing her teeth, not (though time will tell) an imaginative exercise. She led a life that was at once both gregarious and increasingly alone. She had never had a wide circle of friends, and the number of intimate ones was diminishing. On 11th September 2001, day of catastrophe across the Atlantic, 'Porchey' – Lord Carnarvon, her racing companion since adolescence

– died following a heart attack. At the St Paul's memorial service for the world's dead, private and public grief combined.

She felt affection for the public in the same measure that they felt it for her. She seldom met them, except for semi-official pleasantries – lasting relationships were almost never struck up. She remained the little girl in the big palace, with her nose against the glass. But she liked to think, and she could have been right, that many of her subjects saw in her somebody at heart similar to themselves: prosaic, unpretentious, the kind of person who in the words of a sympathiser goes around the house turning out the lights the children had left on. She liked, too, to think that the reputation for honesty of purpose which made foreigners see in her a distillation of the national identity was one her people were happy to embrace. She looked forward to her Golden Jubilee – the first since Victoria's magnificent imperial celebration in 1887 – without trepidation, or expectations of any kind. She would take it as it came. She was aware of what she thought she had achieved. She was constant, in a shifting world.

Jubilee celebrations were due to reach their climax in June 2002. The opening months of the year, however, were a time of bereavement. Princess Margaret died on 8 February 2002. Queen Elizabeth, the Queen Mother died less than two months later on 30 March, in her 102nd year. Her coffin lay in state in Westminster Hall. Two hundred thousand people waited up to ten hours to walk past. The queue – cheerfully reflective in the spring sunshine – snaked across Lambeth Bridge, and back along the river as far as the London Eye. Elizabeth II was now the only surviving member of the symmetrical Royal Family that had reluctantly invaded Buckingham Palace in 1936 – when the new, dutiful King was so appalled he broke down, and the 'little ladies of 145 Picadilly' had offered the Monarchy an extra lease of life.

NOTES

The following abbreviations are used frequently in the Notes:

BBC/WA	BBC Written Archives, Caversham
BCD	Barbara Castle's diary
CCD	Chips Channon's diary
HND	Harold Nicolson's diary and letters
NCD	Noël Coward's diary
PRO	Public Record Office, Kew
RA	Royal Archives, Windsor
RCD	Richard Crossman's diary
TBD	Tony Benn's diary

Diary references are to the standard published editions, unless otherwise indicated.

Chapter One

1. Ede to Lascelles 22.6.48 RA GVI PS 9091 /1.
2. 22.4.26 *The Times*.
3. R. Churchill *The Story of the Coronation*, London: Derek Verschoyle, 1953, p. 11.
4. Cited in J. Wheeler-Bennett *George VI: His Life and Reign*, London: Macmillan, 1958, pp. 209–10.
5. J. Ellis (ed) *Thatched with Gold: The Memoir of Mabel Countess of Airlie*, London: Hutchinson, 1962, p. 179.
6. 30.5.26 *Sunday Express*.
7. 21.12.26 *The Times*.
8. C. Hardyment *Dream Babies*, Oxford: Oxford University Press, 1984, p. 32.

9. 25.5.26, *Westminster Gazette*.
10. A. Ring *The Story of Princess Elizabeth*, London: John Murray, 1930, p. 100.
11. M. Crawford *The Little Princesses*, London: Cassells, 1950, pp. 18–19.
12. 'X' *Romances of Our Royal Family*, London: Hutchinson, 1936, p. 153.
13. Crawford *Little Princesses* p. 19.
14. 23.4.26 *The Times*.
15. P. Mortimer *Queen Elizabeth: A Life of the Queen Mother*, Harmondsworth: Viking, 1986, p. 103.
16. 'X' *Romances* pp. 149–150.
17. L. Sheridan *From Cabbages to Kings*, London: Odhams, 1955 p. 67.
18. F. Towers *The Two Princesses: The*

Story of the King's Daughters, London: Pilgrim Press, 1940, p. 15.

19. Sheridan *From Cabbages to Kings*, pp. 10–11.

20. Crawford *Little Princesses*, p. 21.

21. Lady Elizabeth Cavendish: interview.

22. Ring *The Story of Princess Elizabeth*, p. 1.

23. Wheeler-Bennett *George VI*, p. 141.

24. B. Baxter *Destiny Called to Them*, New York: Oxford University Press, 1939, p. 28.

25. Cited in Wheeler-Bennett *George VI*, p. 224.

26. 9.1.27, *Star*.

27. Ring *The Story of Princess Elizabeth*, p. 117.

28. Cited in Wheeler-Bennett *George VI*, p. 216.

29. Ring *The Story of Princess Elizabeth*, p. 34.

30. 'X' *Royal Romances*, p. 147.

31. 25.6.27, *Daily Mail*.

32. Ring *The Story of Princess Elizabeth*, pp. 38–9, 20–21.

33. 29.12.27, *Westminster Gazette*.

34. Ring *The Story of Princess Elizabeth*, p. 37.

35. J. Colville *Strange Inheritance*, Salisbury: Michael Russell, 1983, p. 109.

36. 28.10.28, *Sunday Dispatch*.

37. Ring *The Story of Princess Elizabeth*, p. 58.

38. E. Acland *Princess Elizabeth*, Toronto: John C. Winston Co. Ltd, 1937, pp. 24–5.

39. 28.10.28, *Sunday Dispatch*.

40. Ring *The Story of Princess Elizabeth*, pp. 77–8.

41. A. Ring *The Story of Princess Elizabeth brought up to date and including some stories of Princess Margaret* London: Murray, 1932, p. 124.

42. E. Acland, p. 127.

43. 'X' *Romances of Our Royal Family* p. 151.

44. *The Crowning of the King and Queen*, London: Evans Bros. Ltd., 1937, p. 32.

45. Ring *The Story of Princess Elizabeth*, 1932 ed., pp. 124–5.

46. Crawford *Little Princesses*, p. 17.

47. Ellis (ed) *Thatched with Gold*, p. 180.

48. J. Gore *King George V: A Personal Memoir*, London: John Murray, 1941, p. 380.

49. Woods Papers, cited in Kenneth Rose *King George V*, London: Weidenfeld and Nicolson, 1983, p. 389.

50. Crawford *Little Princesses*, pp. 30–1.

51. Rose *George V*, p. 389; Gore *King George V*, p. 380.

52. Rose *George V*, p. 39.

53. 9.2.28, *Daily Chronicle*.

54. M. Crawford *Queen Elizabeth II*, London: George Newnes, 1952, p. 16.

55. H. Nicolson *King George V: His Life and Reign* London: Constable, 1952, p. 433.

56. 15.3.29, *Daily Mail*.

57. P. Townsend *Time and Chance*, London: William Collins & Sons, 1978, p. 145.

58. 23.4.30, *Daily Sketch*.

Chapter Two

1. J. R. Clynes *Memoirs: Vol 2 1924–1937*, London: Hutchinson, 1937, pp. 128–9.

2. 27.10.30, *Evening News*.

3. 22.3.32, 23.3.32, 4.4.32, *The Times*.

4. Crawford *Little Princesses*, p. 22.

5. Sheridan *From Cabbages to Kings*, p. 62.

6. Confidential interview.

7. 7.4.44, *The Times*.

8. Countess Mountbatten: interview.

9. Crawford *Little Princesses*, pp. 16–18.

10. K. Rose *Kings, Queens and Courtiers*, London: Weidenfeld and Nicolson, 1985, p. 86.

11. Unpublished draft obituary, 1957, *Manchester Guardian*.

12. Royal Archives.

13. Churchill *Story of the Coronation*, p. 12.

14. 27.9.36, *Sunday Express*.

15. Crawford *Little Princesses*, p. 22.

16. Ellis (ed) *Thatched with Gold*, pp. 205–6.
17. *The Story of Our King and Queen*, Manchester: Sankey, Hudson & Co, 1937, p. 58.
18. Cited in F. Prochaska *Royal Bounty: The Making of a Welfare Monarchy*, London: Yale University Press, 1995, p. 191.
19. Baxter *Destiny Called to Them*, p. 26.
20. 22.3.34, *Daily Sketch*.
21. 22.4.34, *Sunday Express*.
22. Sheridan *From Cabbages to Kings*, p. 61.
23. 27.9.36, *Sunday Express*.
24. 27.1.30 *Daily News*.
25. 'X' *Romances of our Royal Family*, p. 152.
26. H. Smith *A Horseman Through Six Reigns: Reminiscences of a Royal Riding Master*, London: Odhams Press, 1955.
27. H. Chance *Our Princesses and Their Dogs*, London: John Murray, 1936, p. 5.
28. Crawford *Little Princesses*, pp. 17, 48, 24–25.
29. Countess Mountbatten: interview.
30. Confidential interview.
31. Greatorex *King George VI: The People's Sovereign*, London: R.T.S. Lutterworth Press, 1939, p. 66.
32. Baxter *Destiny*, p. 32.
33. Towers *Two Princesses*, p. 33.
34. 26.9.34, T. E. Evans (ed) *The Killearn Diaries 1934–1946*, London: Sidgwick and Jackson, 1972, p. 45.
35. Nicolson *George V*, p. 516.
36. Towers *Two Princesses*, p. 42.
37. Gore *George V*, p. 437.
38. A. Clark (ed) *'A Good Innings'. The Papers of Viscount Lee of Fareham*, London: Murray, 1974, p. 331.
39. J. Corbitt *Fit for a King, A Book of Intimiate Memoirs*, London: Odhams Press, 1956, p. 182
40. 20.2.36, H. Nicolson *Diaries and Letters 1930–1939*, Collins, London, 1966, p. 245.
41. Dennis *Coronation Commentary*, New York: Dodd, Mead and Co, 1937, pp. 176–7.
42. J. G. Lockhart *Cosmo Gordon Lang*, London: Hodder & Stoughton, 1949, p. 397.
43. 6.2.77, *Observer*.
44. Sheridan *From Cabbages to Kings*, p. 67.
45. Crawford *Little Princesses*, p. 36.
46. Dennis *Coronation Commentary*, p. 175.
47. K. Martin *The Magic of Monarchy*, London: T. Nelson & Sons, 1937, p. 17.
48. Sir Edward Pickering: interview.
49. 19.10.57, *Saturday Evening Post*.
50. Martin *Magic of Monarchy*, p. 11.
51. Crawford *Little Princesses*, p. 39.
52. Wheeler-Bennett *George VI*, p. 276.
53. Alan Lascelles to Joan Lascelles, 23.11.36, D.Hart-Davis (ed) *In Royal Service: The Letters and Journals of Sir Alan Lascelles 1920–1936*, Volume II, London: Hamish Hamilton, 1989, pp. 201–2.
54. J. Bryan and C. V. Murphy *The Windsor Story*, London: Granada, 1979, p. 273.
55. Baxter *Destiny*, p. 50.
56. 6.2.37, Wallis to Edward in M. Bloch (ed), *Wallis and Edward: Letters 1931–1937*, London: Weidenfeld and Nicolson, p. 258.
57. Cited in *ibid*, p. 283.
58. Crawford *Little Princesses*, p. 42
59. Cited in Wheeler-Bennett *George VI*, pp. 286–7.
60. *Ibid.*, p. 288; Crawford *Little Princesses*, p. 39.

Chapter Three

1. 12.12.36 Beatrice Webb Diary, (ed) N. and J. Mackenzie *The Wheel of Life, The Diary of Beatrice Webb*, Vol. 4, 1924–1943, London: Virago, 1985, p. 382.
2. W. Bagehot *The English Constitution*, (first published 1867), Fontana edn., London, 1993, p. 89.

3. Dennis *Coronation Commentary*, p. 196.
4. Martin *Magic of Monarchy*, p. 101.
5. Pine *The Twilight of Monarchy*, London: Burke, 1958, p. 40.
6. Cited in P. Ziegler *King Edward VIII: The Official Biography*, London: HarperCollins, 1990, p. 331.
7. Cited in C. W. Domville-Fife *King George VI and Queen Elizabeth*, London: Rankin Brothers Ltd, 1937, p. 46.
8. Dennis *Coronation Commentary*, p. 201.
9. C. Petrie *Modern British Monarchy*, London: Eyre and Spottiswoode, 1961, p. 178.
10. Domville-Fife *King George VI and Queen Elizabeth*, p. 21–2.
11. Ellis (ed) *Thatched with Gold*, p. 205.
12. 18.5.37, Chips Channon diary, R. Rhodes James (ed) *Chips Channon: The Diaries of Sir Henry Channon*, London: Weidenfeld and Nicolson, 1967, p. 12.
13. 18.12.36, *Sunday Graphic*.
14. Princess Margaret: interview.
15. Ibid.
16. Crawford *Little Princesses*, pp. 39–41.
17. D. Morrah *To Be a King: A Biography of H.R.H Prince Charles*, London: Arrow Books, 1969, p. 28.
18. 6.2.77, *Observer*.
19. Morrah *To Be a King*, pp. 28–32.
20. Towers *Two Princesses*, p. 70.
21. Countess Mountbatten: interview.
22. S. Sutherland *American Public Opinion and the Windsors*, Vermont: Driftwood Press, North Montpelier, 1938, p. 34.
23. Wheeler-Bennett *George VI*, p. 309.
24. Dennis *Coronation Commentary*, p. 216.
25. Martin *Magic of Monarchy*, p. 107.
26. See Rev. R. J. Campbell 'Our Great Inheritance,' in *Sermons for the Coronation of His Majesty King George VI*, London: Skeffington and Son Ltd, 1937, pp. 19–20.
27. Dennis *Coronation Commentary*, p. 217.
28. Bronislaw Malinowski *The First Year's Work*, London, 1938, cited in P. Ziegler *Crown and People*, London: Collins, 1978, p. 46.
29. Martin *Magic of Monarchy*, p. 106.
30. 27.5.37, HND, p. 301.
31. 12.5.37, CCD, p. 124.
32. M. Crawford *Happy and Glorious*, London: Newnes Ltd, 1953, pp. 33, 81.
33. 12.5.37, CCD, p. 124.
34. Towers *Two Princesses*, p. 76.
35. HRH Princess Elizabeth 'The Coronation, 12 May 1937' (Royal Library).
36. *'X' Romances of Our Royal Family*, p. 154.
37. Countess Mountbatten: interview.
38. Lady Elizabeth Cavendish: interview.
39. Countess Mountbatten: interview.
40. 22.12.37, *Daily Sketch*.
41. See for example, 22.4.37, *The Times*.
42. M. Chance *Our Princesses and Their Dogs*, London: John Murray, 1936, p. 26.
43. Towers *Two Princesses*, pp. 86–7.
44. Crawford *Little Princesses*, p. 52.
45. 10.4.38 diary, in R. F. Kennedy *Time to Remember: An Autobiography*, London: Collins, 1974, pp. 207–10.
46. Towers *Two Princesses*, pp. 87, 100.
47. L. Sheridan *Princess Elizabeth at Home* 'Published by Authority of Her Majesty The Queen,' London: John Murray, 1944, p. 2.
48. Royal Archives.
49. Crawford *Little Princesses*, p. 52.
50. 19.11.47 *Daily Telegraph*.
51. Princess Marie Louise *My Memories of Six Reigns*, London: Evans Bros, 1956, p. 313.
52. Confidential interview.
53. 19.11.47, *Daily Telegraph*.
54. Crawford *Elizabeth II*, p. 49.
55. P. Annigoni *An Artist's Life*, London: W. H. Allen, 1977, p. 82.
56. Wheeler-Bennett *George VI*, p. 373.

57. 18.5.39, *The Times*.
58. Towers *Two Princesses* p. 114; Crawford *Little Princesses*, pp. 55–6.
59. Wheeler-Bennett *George VI*, pp. 388–92.
60. Towers *Two Princesses*, p. 112.
61. Greatorex *King George VI*, pp. 120–1.
62. Towers *Two Princesses*, p. 112.
63. Sir E. Miéville to Sir A. Hardinge, 20.6.39, RA GVI PS 2266.
64. Crawford *Little Princesses*, p. 56.
65. Towers *Two Princesses*, p. 117.

Chapter Four

1. Crawford *Little Princesses*, p. 60.
2. Towers *Two Princesses*, p. 127.
3. Corbitt *Fit for a King,* pp. 158–9.
4. Crawford *Little Princesses*, p. 62.
5. Neville Chamberlain papers, NC/7/4/22.
6. Princess Margaret: interview.
7. Ibid.
8. 26.2.53, Harold Nicolson unpublished diary.
9. D. Morrah *The Work of the Queen*, London: William Kimber, 1958, p. 22.
10. Princess Margaret: interview.
11. 19.11.47, *Daily Telegraph*.
12. Mrs Ogden Reid to Sir Ronald Lindsay, 19.1.38, RA GVI PS 2766.
13. Sir R. Lindsay to A. Lascelles, 24.1.38, RA GVI PS 2766.
14. RA GVI PS 2766.
15. F. Ogilvie to Sir A. Hardinge, 13.9.40, RA GVI PS 4970.
16. 14.10.40, *The Times*.
17. RA GVI PS 4970.
18. J. Colville *The Fringes of Power: 10 Downing Street Diaries 1939–1955*, London: Hodder & Stoughton, 1985, pp. 165–6.
19. 19.10.40, RA GVI PS 4970.
20. Cited in Ziegler *Crown and People*, p. 76.
21. Towers *Two Princesses*, p. 118.
22. 'The Domestication of Majesty: Royal Family Portraiture 1500–1850,' *Journal of Interdisciplinary History*, XVII: I (Summer 1986), pp. 155–83.
23. 8.4.42 in G. Payn and S. Morley (eds) *The Noël Coward Diaries*, London: Weidenfeld and Nicolson, 1982, p. 16.
24. *For a King's Love: The Intimate Recollections of Queen Alexandra of Yugoslavia*, London: Odhams Press, 1956, p. 106.
25. 13.1.44 Alanbrooke Diaries, cited in S. Bradford *George VI*, London: Weidenfeld and Nicolson, 1989, p. 416.
26. 21.4.40, *Daily Express*.
27. Queen Alexandra *For a King's Love*, p. 111.
28. E. Roosevelt *This I Remember*, London: Hutchinson, 1950, pp. 210–11.
29. Smith *Horseman* pp. 146–91.
30. B. Curling *All the Queen's Horses*, London: Chatto and Windus, 1978, pp. 16–17.
31. 20.10.42, *Star*, 14.9.41, *Sunday Express*.
32. Smith *Horseman* p. 151.
33. 22.11.43 *Daily Mail*
34. 27.4.41, *Sunday Express*, 25.3.43, Lascelles unpublished diary, LASL 1/2/1.
35. Corbitt *Fit For a King*, p. 179.
36. 21.4.47, *The Times*.
37. Sheridan *Cabbages to Kings*, pp. 93–106.
38. Sheridan *Princess Elizabeth at Home*, p. 8.
39. 14.7.41, 23.8.41, 2.12.41, 25.4.41, *The Times*.
40. 25.5.41, *Sunday Dispatch*.
41. 27.3.41, *The Times*.
42. Cited in D. Laird *How The Queen Reigns*, London: Pan, 1959, pp. 168–9.
43. E. Roosevelt *This I Remember*, p. 209, cited in T. Aronson *The Royal Family at War*, London: John Murray, 1993, pp. 122–3.
44. Smith *Horseman*, p. 147.
45. 19.5.43, CCD, p. 359.
46. Townsend *Time and Chance*, pp. 145, 136.

47. Queen Alexandra *For a King's Love*, pp. 105–6.
48. 22.4.44, *The Times*.
49. 23.9.43, *Daily Sketch*.
50. 22.4.44, *The Times*.
51. 24.4.44, W. Midgeley (John O'London's Weekly) to E. Miéville; 25.4.44 Miéville to Midgeley, RA GVI PS 2870.
52. Sheridan *Cabbages to Kings*, p. 138.
53. E. Miéville to Col. Lord Wigram, 15.4.42, RA GVI PS 5839.
54. 22.4.42, *The Times*.
55. Duke of Norfolk: interview.
56. Sir E. Miéville to R. Bunnelle, 24.4.42, RA GVI 5818; R. V. Machell to Miéville, 28.4.43, A. Lascelles to Machell, 29.4.43, RA GVI 2870.
57. Sheridan *Princess Elizabeth at Home*, p. 38.
58. 23.9.43, *The Times*.
59. 21.10.42, Sir A. Hardinge to E. Iwi, RA GVI 072/126.
60. 18.11.42, RA GVI 072/085.
61. Simon to Churchill, 29.6.43, RA GVI 072/088.
62. RA GVI 072/088.
63. 26.8.43, *The Times*
64. 31.12.43, *Camarthen Journal*.
65. 1.5.43, RA GVI PS 6966.
66. A. Lascelles to Sir A. Hardinge, 1.5.41 RA GVI 222/13.
67. Sir G. Wollaston to A. Lascelles, 6.1.44 RA GVI 222/33.
68. 8.1.44, RA GVI 222/34. See also 8.1.44 Lascelles unpublished diary, Vol.II, p. 156, LASC 1/2/2.
69. 28.1.44, RA GVI 222/45.
70. 25.1.44, Colville diary, p. 468, also 27.1.44 Lascelles unpublished diary, Vol.II, p. 160, LASC 1/2/2.
71. 21.4.47, *The Times*.
72. 31.1.44, *ibid*.
73. 9.5.44, *ibid*.
74. 1.4.44, A. Lascelles to the Town Clerk of Nottingham, RA GVI PS 6891.
75. 1.12.44, RA GVI PS 730. See also 4.12.44 Lascelles to Alexander (A. V. Alexander papers).

76. Crawford *Little Princesses*, p. 141.
77. 3.4.68, Barbara Castle, *The Castle Diaries 1964–1976*, London: Papermac, 1990, p. 213.
78. 5.3.45, *The Times*.
79. 1.3.45, RA GVI PS 7423.
80. Unpublished obituary, 1957, *Manchester Guardian*.
81. Sheridan, *Cabbages to Kings*, p. 115.
82. Smith *Horseman*, p. 150.
83. Sheridan *Cabbages to Kings*, p. 115.
84. 3.12.43, *Daily Mail*.
85. 19.12.43, *Sunday Graphic*.
86. Lascelles unpublished diary.
87. Sheridan *Cabbages to Kings*, p. 115n.

Chapter Five

1. 9.5.45, *The Times*.
2. '8 May 1945 V.E. Day,' Lascelles unpublished diary, Vol.III, p. 87, LASC 1/2/3.
3. Lord Carnarvon: interview.
4. 9.5.95 *Guardian*, Radio 4 interview.
5. 9.5.45, *The Times*.
6. 16.8.45, *ibid*.
7. Curling *All the Queen's Horses*, p. 17.
8. Princess Margaret interview.
9. 8.8.45, 8.5.45, 18.7.45, *The Times*.
10. 8.12.45, 13.12.45, 12.3.46, 13.3.46, 18.3.46, Lord Baldwin to A.Lascelles, RA GVI.
11. 3.11.47, Gaitskell to Lascelles; 14.11.47 Lascelles to Gaitskell, RA GV.
12. 22.3.46 *The Times*.
13. D. Butler and G. Butler *British Political Facts, 1900–1994*, London: Macmillan, 1994, p. 312.
14. 22.4.46, *The Times*.
15. Crawford *Elizabeth II*, p. 33.
16. Lord Charteris: interview.
17. Confidential interview.
18. Ellis (ed) *Thatched with Gold*, p. 227.
19. 2.1.37, *Literary Digest*, cited in C. Higham and R. Moseley *Elizabeth and Philip The Untold Story* London: Sidgwick and Jackson, 1991, p. 55.
20. Crawford *Little Princesses*, pp. 59–60.

21. Cited in Bradford *King George VI*, p. 301.
22. P. Ziegler *Mountbatten: The Official Biography*, London: Collins, 1989, p. 102.
23. See P. Mortimer *Queen Elizabeth: A Life of the Queen Mother*, London: Viking, 1986, p. 215.
24. Preface to H.R.H. Prince Andrew of Greece *Towards Disaster: The Greek Army in Asia Minor in 1921*, London: John Murray, 1930, p.xi.
25. E. H. Cookridge *From Battenberg to Mountbatten*, London: Arthur Barker Ltd, 1966, p. 249.
26. Princess George of Hanover: interview.
27. Ellis (ed) *Thatched with Gold*, p. 227.
28. Cited in J. Pearson *The Ultimate Family. The Making of the Royal House of Windsor*, London: Michael Joseph, 1986, p. 78.
29. Mike Parker: telephone interview.
30. Princess George of Hanover: interview.
31. Mike Parker: telephone interview.
32. Countess Mountbatten: interview.
33. Unpublished obituary of the Queen, 1957, *Manchester Guardian*.
34. HM Queen Alexandra of Yugoslavia *Prince Philip*, London: Mayfair Books, 1961, pp. 53–5.
35. Ziegler *Mountbatten*, p. 101.
36. HM Queen Alexandra of Yugoslavia *Prince Philip*, London: Mayfair Books, 1961, pp. 53–5.
37. H. Cordet *Born Bewildered*, London: Peter Davies, 1961, p. 109.
38. Cited in Wheeler-Bennett *George VI*, pp. 748–9.
39. 23.4.41, Chartwell papers 20/29A.
40. 27.11.93, transcript of interview for Brook Productions *The Windsors*.
41. See R. Allison and S. Riddell *The Royal Encyclopedia: The Authoritative Book of the Royal Family*, London: Macmillan, 1991, pp. 149–52.
42. Mike Parker: telephone interview.
43. Lady Pamela Hicks: interview.
44. Queen Alexandra *For a King's Love*, pp. 68–9.
45. Mike Parker: Brook Productions interview.
46. Queen Alexandra *Prince Philip*, p. 62.
47. Crawford *Little Princesses*, p. 85; Allison and Ridell (eds) *Royal Encyclopedia*, p. 150.
48. 18.11.43, *Evening Standard*.
49. 20.12.43, *The Times*.
50. Sheridan *Cabbages to Kings*, p. 115.
51. 26.12.43, Lascelles unpublished diary, Vol.II, p. 148, LASC 1/2/2.
52. Crawford *Little Princesses*, p. 86.
53. 21.1.41, CCD, pp. 286–7.
54. 4.12.46, Mountbatten to Tom Driberg (Lord Bradwell papers).
55. Lord Charteris: interview.
56. Sir Edward Ford: interview.
57. Mike Parker: telephone interview.
58. 16.2.44, CCD, p. 470.
59. Lascelles unpublished diary, Vol.II, p. 41, LASC 1/2/2.
60. 23.8.44, *Killearn Diaries*, p. 311–12.
61. Ziegler *Mountbatten*, London: Collins, 1985, cited in Bradford *George VI*, p. 421.
62. 27.10.44, CCD, p. 483.
63. 2.3.45, Lascelles to R. A. Strutt, RA GVI 270/01.
64. 7.8.45, Lascelles unpublished diary, Vol.3, p. 148, LASC 1/2/34.
65. 26.10.45, Sir Alexander Maxwell to Lascelles, 2.11.45, Lascelles to Maxwell, RA GVI 270/12.
66. Crawford *Little Princesses*, pp. 98–100.
67. Princess George of Hanover: interview.
68. Crawford *Little Princesses*, p. 100.
69. Corbett *Fit For a King*, p. 187.
70. J. Koumoulides *Greece in Transition: Essays in the History of Modern Greece 1821–1974*, London: Zeno, 1977, p. 204.
71. 18.10.46, Lascelles to George VI, RA GVI 270/16; 27.10.46, Mansergh to Lascelles, RA GVI 270/19.

72. 4.11.46, Mansergh to Lascelles, RA
GVI 270/22.

73. 30.11.46, Lascelles to George VI, RA
GVI 270/20. (Despite the date given,
the context of this note makes it clear
that it preceded Mountbatten's note
of 15.11.46.)

74. 15.11.46, Mountbatten to Lascelles, RA
GVI 270/25; 15.11.46, Mountbatten to
Prince Philip, RA GVI 270/26.

75. 14.8.46 (Lord Bradwell papers.)

76. 4.12.46, Mountbatten to Driberg
(Lord Bradwell papers.)

77. 7.12.46, *The Times*.

78. 27.1.47, Mountbatten to C. Ede, RA
GVI 270/30.

79. 22.11.72 MBI/K200, Mountbatten
papers.

Chapter Six

1. 7.8.45, Lascelles unpublished diary,
Vol.3, p. 148, LASL 1/2/3.

2. Crawford *Little Princesses*, p. 110.

3. See Ziegler *Mountbatten*, p. 457.

4. Ellis *Thatched with Gold*, pp. 225–8.

5. Bradford *George VI*, p. 751.

6. Cited in Bradford, *George VI*, p. 420.

7. Confidential interview.

8. End of August 1947, unpublished
Colville diary.

9. Sir Edward Ford: interview.

10. Confidential interview.

11. End of August 1947, unpublished
Colville diary.

12. Confidential interview.

13. Sir Alan Lascelles was a rare (and
surprising) exception.

14. Confidential interview.

15. Ellis (ed) *Thatched with Gold*,
pp. 225–8.

16. 26.12.43, Lascelles unpublished diary,
Vol. II, p. 148, LASC 1/2/2.

17. Cited in *Daily Graphic*, 10.1.47, *Daily
Mail*, 28.3.47.

18. Crawford *Little Princesses*, p. 112.

19. Unpublished obituary, *Manchester
Guardian*, 1957.

20. Mrs Woodroffe: interview.

21. 13.5.46, Mary Strachey to George
Bishop, RA GVI PE 1039.

22. Mrs Woodroffe: interview.

23. Lord Carnarvon: interview.

24. Sir John Miller: interview.

25. Confidential interview.

26. Lord Carnarvon: interview.

27. Confidential interview.

28. 9.10.46, *The Times*.

29. HM of Yugoslavia *A King's Heritage.
The Memoirs of King Peter II of
Yugoslavia*, London: Casseu, 1995.

30. A. Buxton *The King and His Country*,
London: Longmans, Green & Co,
1955, 3.9.45, p. 77.

31. Confidential interview.

32. End of August 1947, Colville
unpublished diary.

33. Rt. Rev. Simon Phipps: interview.

34. Ellis (ed) *Thatched with Gold*,
pp. 223–4.

35. Wheeler-Bennett *George VI*, p. 416.

36. D. Adamson *Last Empire*, London: I
B Tauris, 1989, p. 110.

37. 21.3.46, RA GVI PSO 8100/01A/15.

38. *Natal Mercury*, cited in 16.3.46 *The
Times*.

39. Confidential interview.

40. J. Dean *H.R.H. Prince Philip, Duke of
Edinburgh: A Portrait*, London: Hale,
1954, p. 38.

41. 12.2.47, Lascelles to wife, LASL 4/4/2,
Lascelles papers.

42. Princess Margaret: interview.

43. 18.2.47, Lascelles unpublished diary,
LASC 4/4/3, Lascelles papers.

44. *Their Majesties The King and Queen
and Their Royal Highness The
Princess Elizabeth and The Princess
Margaret in the Union of South
Africa*, February-April 1947.

45. Townsend *Time and Chance*, p. 171.

46. B. S. Shaw *Royal Wedding*, London:
MacDonald, 1947, p. 66.

47. 19.2.47, *The Times*.

48. 1.4.47, Lascelles to his wife, LASL 4/
4/13, Lascelles papers.

49. Shaw *Royal Wedding*, p. 62–3.

50. S. G. Bocca *Elizabeth and Philip*,

Henry Holt & Co, New York, 1953, pp. 71, 77.

51. Lord Carnarvon: interview.
52. 21.4.47, *Manchester Guardian*.
53. S. Evelyn Thomas *Princess Elizabeth: Wife and Mother: A Souvenir of the Birth of Prince Charles of Edinburgh*, London, 1949, p. 47.
54. 30.4.47, LASL 4/4/17, Lascelles papers.
55. 13.5.47 LASL 4/4/17 Lascelles papers.
56. 22.4.47, *The Times*.
57. 18.4.47, *News Chronicle*.
58. 21.4.47, *The Times*.
59. *Princess Elizabeth: The Illustrated Story of Twenty-one Years in the Life of the Heir Presumptive*, London: Odhams Press, 1947, p. 128.
60. 10.4.47, *News Chronicle*.
61. 4.7.47, Colville unpublished diary.
62. 20.4.47, *Sunday Dispatch*.
63. 19.5.47, 'Royal Engagement', R34/862/5, BBC/WA.
64. 10.7.47, *Daily Telegraph*.
65. Confidential source.
66. Crawford *Little Princesses*, p. 147.
67. 10.7.47, Colville unpublished diary.
68 End of August, Colville unpublished diary.

Chapter Seven

1. 10.7.47, *Manchester Guardian*.
2. 10.7.47, Colville unpublished diary.
3. Wulff *Queen for Tomorrow*, p. 184.
4. 10.7.47, *Daily Telegraph*.
5. See Queen Alexandra's account of her own remarks to George VI at the wedding feast, in *For a King's Love*, p. 162.
6. Dean *H.R.H. Prince Philip*, pp. 36-41.
7. Ellis (ed) *Thatched with Gold*, p. 228.
8. Crawford *Little Princesses*, p. 111.
9. Dean *H.R.H. Prince Philip*, p. 43.
10. 21.9.47, 29.9.47, End of August 1947, Colville unpublished diary.
11. Sir Edward Ford: interview.
12. Confidential interview.
13. 22.10.47, 23.10.47, *The Times*.
14. Shaw *Royal Wedding*, p. 94.

15. 22.10.47, Hugh Dalton unpublished diary.
16. 17.11.47, CCD, p. 509.
17. N. Hartnell *Silver and Gold*, London: Evans Brothers, 1955, p. 113.
18. 10.10.47, Lascelles to Attlee, dep 61, fol. 221 (Attlee papers.)
19. 22.10.47, Hugh Dalton unpublished diary.
20. Note prepared by the Keeper of the Privy Purse, 24.10.47, RA GVI 295/14.
21. 22.10.47, Hugh Dalton unpublished diary.
22. 27.10.47, Lascelles memo RA GVI 295/12.
23. 'Princess Elizabeth's Establishment', Lascelles to Attlee, 25.10.47, PRO PREM 8/652.
24. 27.10.47, Lascelles memo, RA GVI 295/12.
25. 27.10.47, Dalton to Attlee, PRO PREM 8/652.
26. 27.10.47, Dalton to Attlee, PRO PREM 8/652.
27. 31.10.47, Dalton to Attlee, PRO PREM 8/652.
28. 6.11.47, 7.11.47, Lascelles memos, RA GVI 295/26-7.
29. 10.11.47, Lascelles memo RA GVI 295/33.
30. PRO CAB, 128/10/200.
31. 13.11.47, Lascelles to George VI, RA GVI 295/41.
32. 2.12.47, PRO Cabinet Economic Policy Committee minutes.
33. 3.12.47, U. Alexander to Cripps, 5.12.47, Cripps to Alexander and Lascelles, RA GVI 295/55, 59.
34. RA GVI 295/53.
35. 10.12.47, *Manchester Guardian*.
36. 4.10.47, *New Statesman*, cited in E. Wilson *Adorned in Dreams: Fashion and Modernity*, University of California Press, Los Angeles, 1987, p. 226.
37. Ziegler *Crown and People*, pp. 82-3.
38. Crawford *Little Princesses*, p. 113.
39. *Marriage of HRH The Princess Elizabeth and Lieutenant Philip*

Mountbatten, RN, List of Wedding Gifts, St. James's Palace, London, 1947.

40. Ibid, No.1211, p. 114.
41. Ellis (ed) Thatched with Gold, p. 307.
42. J. Colville The Fringes of Power, p. 619.
43. Shaw Royal Wedding, p. 100.
44. 18.11.47, CCD, p. 510.
45. List of Wedding Gifts, p. 72.
46. J.W. Laurie (ed) Dedication: A Selection from the Public Speeches of Her Majesty Queen Elizabeth II, London: Heinemann, 1953, p. 24.
47. Corbitt Fit for a King, pp. 42–5.
48. Wulff Queen for Tomorrow, pp. 173–6.
49. Shaw Royal Wedding, pp. 104–12.
50. Hartnell Silver and Gold, pp. 112–5.
51. Bocca Elizabeth and Philip, p. 79.
52. Colville Fringes of Power, p. 620.
53. Ellis (ed) Thatched with Gold, p. 229.
54. Princess Margaret: interview.
55. Queen Alexandra For a King's Love, p. 32.
56. 26.11.47, CCD, p. 511.
57. Lady Pamela Hicks: interview.
58. Ellis (ed) Thatched with Gold, p. 229.
59. 7.8.47, Jowett to Lascelles, RA GVI 8644.
60. 30.7.47, RA GVI 8644.
61. 18.9.47, G. M. Young to Lascelles, 21.9.47, Lascelles to Young, RA GVI 8644.
62. RA GVI 8644.
63. 30.10.47, Colville unpublished diary.
64. November 1947, Colville unpublished diary.
65. Crawford Little Princesses, pp. 34, 114.
66. Lady Pamela Hicks: interview.
67. 21.11.47, The Times.
68. Wulff Queen for Tomorrow, pp. 166–70.
69. Wheeler-Bennett George VI, p. 754.
70. 20.11.47, CCD, p. 510.
71. Smith Horseman, p. 149.
72. C. Stuart (ed) The Reith Diaries, London: Collins, 1975, p. 204.
73. Carpenter Fisher, p. 273.
74. 10.12.47, cited in H. Vickers Cecil Beaton: The Authorised Biography,

London: Weidenfeld and Nicolson, 1985, p. 320.
75. 10.12.47, cited in H. Vickers Cecil Beaton: The Authorized Biography, London: Weidenfeld and Nicolson, 1985, p. 320n.
76. Queen Alexandra For a King's Love, p. 102.
77. 21.11.47, The Times.
78. Queen Alexandra For a King's Love, p. 162.
79. Crawford Little Princesses, p. 119.
80. 21.11.47, The Times.
81. 20.11.72, Philip Howard in The Times.
82. C. McDonald A Hundred Years of Royal Style, London: Muller, Blon & White, 1985, p. 79.
83. Ziegler Crown and People, pp. 83–4.
84. 21.11.47, 12.12.37, 21.11.47, The Times.
85. Ziegler Crown and People, pp. 83–4.
86. Souvenir Programme, pp. 6–8.
87. 17.6.47, 'Functions of the Prime Minister and his Staff', (PRO CAB 21/ 1638).
88. Wheeler-Bennett George VI, p. 326.

Chapter Eight

1. Bocca Elizabeth and Philip, p. 86.
2. Dean H.R.H. Prince Philip, p. 62.
3. 15.12.47, Colville unpublished diary.
4. 17.11.47, CCD, p. 510.
5. Crawford Little Princesses, p. 125.
6. Dean H.R.H. Prince Philip, p. 112.
7. 18.12.47 Manchester Guardian.
8. 18.12.47, 19.12.47 The Times.
9. 17.12.47, unpublished Colville diary.
10. 17.12.47, CCD, p. 512.
11. Ziegler Crown and People, p. 84.
12. 14.1.48, unpublished Colville diary.
13. 21.12.47, RA GVI PS 3939.
14. 25.1.48, News of the World.
15. 23.1.48, 14.2.48, unpublished Colville diary.
16. E. Roosevelt The Autobiography of Eleanor Roosevelt, London: Hutchinson, 1962, p. 230.
17. 11.5.48, (Lord Bradwell papers.)
18. P. M. Williams (ed) The Diary of

Hugh Gaitskell 1945–1956, London: Cape, 1983 p. 62.

19. 15.5.48, 18.5.48, *The Times*.
20. Reports by Sir Oliver Harvey to the Foreign Secretary and the King, 22.5.48, RA GVI PS 8917.
21. 20.5.48, *Manchester Guardian*.
22. 3.6.48, unpublished Colville diary.
23. Colville *Fringes of Power*, p. 625.
24. 26.5.48, *The Times*.
25. Evelyn Thomas *Princess Elizabeth, Wife and Mother*, p. 5.
26. Crawford *Queen Elizabeth II*, p. 12.
27. 15.1.69 'Obit. Scripta' LASC 1/2/33, Lascelles unpublished diary Vol III, pp. 255–6.
28. Ede to Lascelles, 22.6.48, RA GVI PS 9091 (i).
29. 15.1.69, Lascelles unpublished diary.
30. 29.7.48, 21.8.48, Lascelles to Ed, RA GVI PS 9091 (i).
31. 15.1.69, Lascelles unpublished diary.
32. 5.11.48, Lascelles to George VI, RA GVI PS 9091 (1).
33. 15.1.69, Lascelles unpublished diary.
34. 5.11.48, Lascelles to George VI.
35. Wheeler-Bennett *George VI*, pp. 793–4.
36. 9.11.48 Lascelles to George VI, RA GVI PS 9091 (2).
37. Morrah *To Be a King*, p. 13.
38. 5.6.48, *Washington Post*.
39. Lascelles to George VI, RA GVI.
40. Evelyn Thomas *Princess Elizabeth, Wife and Mother*, p. 8.
41. 15.11.48, 15.11.48, *The Times*.
42. 14.11.48, Hugh Dalton unpublished diary.
43. Crawford *Little Princesses*, p. 127.
44. Dean *H.R.H. Prince Philip*, p. 108.
45. C. Beaton *The Strenuous Year, Diaries 1948–1955*, London: Weidenfeld and Nicolson, 1973, p. 17.
46. Dean *H.R.H. Prince Philip*, p. 110.
47. Corbitt *Fit for a King*, pp. 136–7.
48. Crawford *Elizabeth II*, p. 20.
49. 10.1.49, *The Times*.
50. Wheeler-Bennett *George VI*, p. 765.
51. Sir Edward Ford: interview.

52. Rt. Rev. Simon Phipps: interview.
53. Confidential interview.
54. 10.11.49, 12.4.50, M. Muggeridge *Like It Was*, Collins, 1981, pp. 360, 382.
55. Confidential source.
56. Sir Edward Ford: interview.
57. Colville *Fringes of Power*, p. 625.
58. Dean *H.R.H. Prince Philip*, p. 116.
59. 18.6.49, CCD, p. 439.
60. Dean *HRH Prince Philip*, p. 48.
61. Crawford *Elizabeth II*, p. 54.
62. Mike Parker: telephone interview.
63. 19.10.49, *The Times*.
64. S. Clark *Palace Diary*, London: Harrap, 1958, p. 44.
65. RA GVI 9569.
66. Dean *H.R.H. Prince Philip*, p. 119.
67. 21.1.50, *Sunday Graphic*.
68. Dean *H.R.H. Prince Philip*, pp. 119, 120.
69. Mike Parker: telephone interview.
70. Dean *H.R.H. Prince Philip*, pp 120–3.
71. 13.8.50, 18.9.50, 11.11.50, *The Times*.
72. Dean *H.R.H. Prince Philip*, p. 124.
73. 9.3.50, *Evening News*, 5.3.49, Beaverbrook papers.
74. E. Longford *Elizabeth R*, London: Weidenfeld and Nicolson, 1983, p. 84.
75. 8.10.51, Comptroller to Mr N. Townshend, RA GVI PE99.
76. Confidential information.
77. Crawford *The Little Princesses*, London: Duckworth, 1993, pp.viii-ix.
78. Rose *Kings, Queens and Countries*, p. 60.
79. Sir Edward Ford: interview.
80. 30.3.50, Sir F. Browning to Lascelles, 31.3.50, Lascelles to Browning, RA GVI/6995.

Chapter Nine

1. Dean *H.R.H. Prince Philip*, pp. 117, 130–1.
2. Confidential interview.
3. 1.7.48, Colville unpublished diary.
4. Mike Parker: telephone interview.

5. Lord Charteris interview.
6. Mike Parker: telephone interview.
7. 14.6.50, Brook to Prime Minister RA GVI PS 1231.
8. 20.6.50, PRO PREM 6/1271.
9. 6.6.51, 8.6.51, *The Times*.
10. 27.9.51, Princess Elizabeth to Lascelles, RA GVI 10152 (2).
11. 21.9.51, Attlee papers.
12. Hardy Amies papers.
13. 1.7.48, Colville unpublished diary.
14. 11.7.51, Lord Halifax to Lascelles, 15.8.51, Lascelles to Sir F. Browning RA GVI 10135 (3), (8).
15. Lord Charteris: interview.
16. Lord Alexander to George VI, RA GVI 10135 (8).
17. 19.10.51, Jane Weston 'Our Love to Elizabeth', Canadian Broadcasting Corporation transcript.
18. Lord Charteris: interview.
19. Hartley *Accession*, p. 41.
20. Dean *H.R.H. Prince Philip*, p. 133.
21. Confidential interview.
22. Dean *H.R.H. Prince Philip*, p. 140.
23. 26.10.51, Donald S. Dawson memo, Harry S. Truman papers.
24. Lord Charteris: interview.
25. 6.11.51, RA GVI 10135 (3).
26. 2.11.51, Harry S. Truman papers.
27. 2.11.51, *Washington Evening Star*.
28. 20.7.51, 20.7.51, Sir O. Franks to Foreign Office, RA GVI 10135 (3).
29. 3.11.51, 4.11.51, Harry S.Truman papers.
30. 2.11.51, *Washington Evening Star*.
31. See end of August, Colville unpublished diary.
32. RA GVI 8800/Au/47.
33. 25.10.51, *East African Standard*.
34. Confidential interview.
35. Mitchell to Sir Thomas Lloyd (Colonial Office), RA GVI 8800/Au/49.
36. *Voices Out of the Air*, p. 51.
37. Dwight D. Eisenhower papers.
38. RA GVI 8800/Au/49.
39. 5.2.52, PRO CAB 128 (Cabinet minutes).
40. Princess Margaret: interview.
41. 6.2.52, HND, p. 219.
42. Interview transcript for Brook Productions *The Windsors*.
43. Princess Margaret: interview.
44. Sir Edward Ford: interview.
45. Colville *Fringes of Power*, p. 640.
46. Lady Pamela Hicks: interview.
47. Lord Charteris, Mike Parker: interviews.
48. Hartley *Accession*, pp. 129–30.
49. *The Windsors* interview transcript.
50. 11.2.52, J. Morgan (ed) *The Backbench Diaries of Richard Crossman*, London: Hamilton and Cape, 1981. p. 72.
51. *Political Adventure: The Memoirs of the Earl of Kilmuir*, London: Weidenfeld & Nicolson, 1964, p. 199.
52. H. Macmillan *Tides of Fortune 1945–1955*, London: Macmillan, 1969, pp. 370–1.
53. 9.2.52, *The Times*.
54. Lord Charteris: interview.
55. Lady Pamela Hicks: interview.
56. *The Windsors* interview transcript.
57. 12.2.52, RA GVI PE 946.
58. Lord Charteris: interview.
59. Dean *H.R.H. Prince Philip*, p. 149.
60. Lord Charteris: interview.
61. 8.2.52, *The Times*.
62. 7.8.52, Hugh Dalton unpublished diary.
63. Macmillan *Tides of Fortune*, pp. 372–5.
64. 6.2.82, 8.2.52, *The Times*.
65. Beaton *Strenuous Years*, p. 114.
66. Kilmuir *Political Adventure*, p. 199.
67. 24.2.53, Lord Moran *Winston Churchill: The Struggle for Survival, 1940–1965*, London: Constable, 1966, p. 403.
68. 9.2.52, *Daily Graphic*.
69. 11.2.52, RCD, p. 72.
70. 6.2.51, PRO CAB 128.
71. Hughes *Constitutional Development*, pp. 208–9.
72. P. Mansergh *The Name and Nature*

of the British Commonwealth: An Inaugural Recital, Cambridge: Cambridge University Press, 1954, p. 15.

73. 27.2.52, PRO PREM 11/247.
74. 29.2.52, R. Buchan-Hepburn to J. Colville, Colville to Prime Minister PRO PREM 11/247.
75. March 1952, Colville unpublished diary.
76. Colville *Fringes of Power*, pp. 641–2.
77. 18.2.52, PRO CAB 128.
78. Confidential interviews.
79. Lady Pamela Hicks: interview.
80. March 1952, Colville unpublished diary.
81. *Ibid.*
82. PRO CAB 128.
83. 4.4.52, 9.4.52, Colville unpublished diary.
84. 10.4.52, *The Times.*
85. Lord Moran *Winston Churchill* p. 378.
86. 20.6.52, Colville unpublished diary.
87. Dean *H.R.H. Prince Philip*, p. 153.
88. Confidential interview.
89. 11.3.52, Dwight D. Eisenhower papers.
90. 15.9.52, cited in Longford *Elizabeth R*, p. 147.
91. Beaton *Strenuous Years*, pp. 134–5.
92. Morrah *To Be a King*, p. 29.
93. J. Dimbleby *The Prince of Wales: A Biography*, London: Little, Brown, 1994, p. 19.
94. Dean *H.R.H. Prince Philip*, p. 116.
95. Mike Parker: telephone interview.
96. Dean *H.R.H. Prince Philip*, p. 153.
97. Ellis (ed), *Thatched with Gold*, pp. 236–7.
98. 24.5.52, *The Times.*
99. Cited in Crawford *Happy and Glorious*, pp. 84–5.
100. In the 1992 BBC television programme *Elizabeth R*, 6.2.92, *Guardian.*
101. 11.2.52, RCD, p. 72.
102. 11–14.2.52, Cabinet minutes, PRO CAB 128.

103. Moran *Churchill*, p. 404.
104. 9.7.5, PRO PREM 11/246.
105. 31.10.52, *The Times.*
106. L. A. Nicholls *The Crowning of Elizabeth II: a Diary of the Coronation Year*, London: MacDonald & Co, 1953, p. 10.
107. 4.11.52, HND, p. 230.
108. Beaton *Strenuous Years*, pp. 120–1.
109. L. A. Nicholls *Crowning of Elizabeth II*, pp. 42–3.
110. 26.2.53, Harold Nicolson unpublished diary.
111. 27.10.52, Lascelles to Nicolls, R32/862/13, BBC/WA.
112. 27.5.5, R34/862/12, BBC/WA.
113. Nicholls *The Crowning of Elizabeth II*, pp. 49, 67–8.

Chapter Ten

1. Princess Margaret: interview.
2. 'The British Monarch c.1820–1977', in E. Hobsbawm and T. Ranger (eds) *The Invention of Tradition*, Cambridge: Cambridge University Press, 1983, p. 133.
3. 1.2.7, *Daily Mail.*
4. Sir Edward Ford: interview.
5. Moran *Churchill*, p. 404.
6. M. Gilbert *Churchill: A Life*, London: Heinemann, 1991, p. 911.
7. Nicholls *Crowning of Elizabeth II*, pp. 67–8.
8. Beaton *Strenuous Years*, p. 147.
9. 21.2.52, 29.2.52, R34/862/12, BBC/WA.
10. 15.4.52, 23.5.52, Nicholls to R. Colville, R. Colville to Nicholls, R34/862/12, BBC/WA.
11. 27.5.52, 20.6.52, 3.6.52, Richard Colville correspondence with B. R. Nicholls; 16.6.52, Philip Dorté (head of Television Films) memo, R1234/862/12, BBC/WA.
12. 22.8.52, 27.8.52, 29.8.52, 17.9.52, R34/862/13, BBC/WA.
13. 12.10.53, R34/862/16, BBC/WA.
14. 30.10.52, R34/862/13, BBC/WA.
15. 30.4.60, *New Statesman.*

16. Princess Margaret: interview.
17. Beaton *Strenuous Years*, p. 114.
18. Corbitt *Fit For a King*, p. 194.
19. Princess Margaret: interview.
20. Confidential interview.
21. Sir Edward Ford: interview.
22. Confidential interview.
23. Sir Edward Ford: interview.
24. C. Warwick *Princess Margaret*, London: Weidenfeld & Nicolson, 1983, pp. 58–9.
25. Sir Edward Ford: interview.
26. Townsend *Time and Chance*, p. 309.
27. Petrie *Modern British Monarchy*, p. 219.
28. Townsend *Time and Chance*, p. 199.
29. Of 139 people questioned in a 1953 survey, only 4 said that they thought the Coronation of George VI had been more memorable than that of his daughter (Ziegler, *Crown and People*, p. 48).
30. S. Haffner 'The Renascence of Monarchy', *The Twentieth Century*, June 1953, Vol. CLIII, No. 916, pp. 415–24.
31. P. C. Gordon Walker 'Crown Divisible', *The Twentieth Century*, June 1953, Vol. CLIII, No. 916, p. 45.
32. Adamson *Last Empire*, p. 118.
33. Herbert Agar, cited in *National and English Review*, Vol. 140, No. 844, June 1953.
34. P. Black *The Mystique of Modern Monarchy*, Watts & Co, London, 1953, p. 33.
35. K. and V. McLeish *Long to Reign Over Us . . . Memories of Coronation Day and of Life in the 1950s*, Bloomsbury, London, 1992, p. 113.
36. Confidential source.
37. 7.7.52, PRO PREM 11/34; 30.10.52 BBK H/156 Beaverbrook papers.
38. R. Churchill *Story of the Coronation*, p. 94.
39. 21.10.52, PRO PREM 11/34 (Cabinet conclusions).
40. C. Frost *Coronation June 2 1953*, Arthur Hacker Ltd, London, 1978, pp. 39–40.
41. 9.1.83, *Sunday Telegraph*.
42. 27.10.52, Lascelles to Nicholls, R34/862/15, BBC Written Archives.
43. 22.10.52, PRO PREM 11/34.
44. 24.10.52, Sir N. Brook to Churchill, PRO PREM 11/34.
45. 2.11.52, J. Colville to Duke of Norfolk, PRO PREM 11/34; 6.5.53, R34/862/15 BBC/WA.
46. Frost, *Coronation*, pp. 39–42.
47. 28.9.53, *The Times*.
48. 27.5.53, RCD, p. 236.
49. Mountbatten papers.
50. 6.11.52 'Diary of Coronation Preparations', Vol. 1,2,3,13 Fisher papers.
51. Nicholls *Crowning of Elizabeth II*, p. 85.
52. 31.5.53, Colville *Fringes of Power*, p. 714.
53. Beaton *Strenuous Years*, p. 140.
54. Rose *Kings, Queens and Courtiers*, p. 36.
55. E. Shils and M. Young 'The Meaning of the Coronation', *Sociological Review*, Vol. I, No. 2, December 1953, p. 72.
56. G. F. Fisher *I Here Present Unto You . . . Addresses interpreting the Coronation of Her Majesty Queen Elizabeth II*, London: SPCK, 1953, pp. 15–29.
57. Carpenter *Fisher*, p. 265.
58. S. B. F. Price *Rituals and Power: The Roman Imperial Cult in Asia Minor*, Cambridge: Cambridge University Press, 1984, p. 7.
59. See A. M. Hocart *Kingship*, London: Watts & Co, 1941, Chapter IV.
60. B. Wilkinson *The Coronation in History*, London: The Historical Association, 1953, p. 8.
61. Lord Charteris: interview.
62. Petrie *Modern British Monarchy*, p. 198.
63. Wilkinson *The Coronation in History*, pp. 34–5.

64. J. Grigg 'The Queen's Opportunity', *National and English Review*, August 1952, Vol. 139, No. 834, p. 83.

65. Carpenter *Fisher*, p. 266.

66. Charles Beriot in K. and V. McLeish *Long to Reign Over Us*, p. 138.

67. *Daily Telegraph Coronation Supplement*, cited in T. Grove (ed) *The Queen Observed*, London: Pavilion, 1986, p. 99.

68. Princess Alice, Countess of Athlone, *For My Grandchildren: Some Reminiscences*, London: Evans, 1966, p. 287.

69. Beaton *Strenuous Years*, pp. 143–4.

70. Laird *How the Queen Reigns*, p. 170.

71. Beaton *Strenuous Years*, pp. 144.

72. 4.6.53, Colville *Fringes of Power*, p. 714.

73. Hocart *Kingship*, p. 56.

74. Frost *Coronation*, p. 128.

75. Beaton *Strenuous Years*, p. 148.

76. Frost *Coronation*, p. 134.

Chapter Eleven

1. Petrie *Modern British Monarchy*, p. 26.

2. Cited in E. Carpenter *Archbishop Fisher*, Canterbury: Canterbury Press, 1991, p. 284.

3. 3.6.54, Vol. 123–28, Fisher papers.

4. Curling *All the Queen's Horses*, p. 30.

5. Fisher *Addresses*, pp. 35–8.

6. June 1953, Vol. CLIII, No. 916, pp. 414–5.

7. Fisher *Addresses*, pp. 35–8.

8. Shils and Young 'The Meaning of the Coronation', pp. 63–70.

9. 'Monarchs and Sociologists: A Reply to Professor Shils and M. Young', *Sociological Review*, Vol. 3, No. 1, July 1955, pp. 13–23.

10. T. Nairn *The Enchanted Glass: Britain and its Monarchy*, London: Radius, 1988, pp. 116–23.

11. Lord Harewood *Tongs and the Bones*, London: Weidenfeld and Nicolson, 1981, pp. 136–8.

12. 20.4.81, David Wood *The Times*; 23.10.55, *Sunday Pictorial*.

13. 14.6.53, *People*.

14. Lord Charteris: interview.

15. 29.6.53, Moran *Churchill*, p. 414.

16. N. Dempster *H.R.H. The Princess Margaret: A Life Unfulfilled*, London: Quartet Books, 1981, p. 23.

17. N. Barrymaine *The Story of Peter Townsend*, London: Peter Davies, 1958, p. 132.

18. 16.7.53, NCD, p. 215.

19. 17.7.53, *Daily Mirror*.

20. 16.7.53 NCD, p. 215.

21. 22.7.53, *Evening Standard*.

22. 24.7.53, *The Times*.

23. Townsend *Time and Chance*, pp. 212–3.

24. Confidential interview.

25. 28.6.53, 5.8.53, Moran *Churchill*, pp. 414, 450.

26. 2.8.53, Colville *Fringes of Power*, p. 673.

27. Moran *Churchill*, pp. 450–1.

28. K. Rose *Kings, Queens and Courtiers*, London: Weidenfeld and Nicolson, 1985, p. 14.

29. 5.1.53, Colville *Fringes of Power*, p. 660.

30. E. McDowell *Hundred Years of Royal Style*, p. 129.

31. 21.11.53, 23.11.53, NCD, pp. 222–3.

32. 16.2.54 Ford to D. Pitblado, PRO PREM 11/751.

33. 18.11.53, Moran *Churchill*, p. 498. Also see p. 480.

34. Lady Pamela Hicks: interview.

35. Ziegler *Crown and People*, p. 84.

36. 'New Zealand and the Monarchy', paper presented to the 'Australia and the Monarchy Conference' at Australia House, London, September 1994.

37. D. Lowe '1954: The Queen and Australia in the World', paper presented to the 1994 'Australia and the Monarchy' conference.

38. P. Spearritt, cited in ibid.

39. Lowe '1954: The Queen and Australia in the World'.

40. Lady Pamela Hicks: interview.

41. Confidential interviews.
42. Moran *Churchill*, p. 548.
43. Longford *Elizabeth R*, p. 166.
44. Cited in ibid., p. 166.
45. 21.8.54, R 34/862/16, BBC/WA.
46. 6.10.54, Queen to Eden, AP30A, Earl of Avon papers.
47. 27.3.55, Colville unpublished diary.
48. Gilbert *Churchill: A Life*, pp. 438–9.
49. 27.4.55, *The Times*.
50. 27.4.55, Moran *Churchill*, p. 653.
51. N. Fisher *The Tory Leaders: Their Struggle for Power*, London: Weidenfeld and Nicolson, 1977, p. 69.
52. 19.1.53, Shukburgh diary, cited in D. Carlton *Anthony Eden: a Biography*, London: Allen Lane, 1981, p. 297.
53. Longford *Elizabeth R*, p. 174.
54. A. Eden *The Memoirs of the Rt. Hon. Sir Anthony Eden: Full Circle*, London: Cassell, 1980, p. 266.
55. Cited in Gilbert *Churchill*, p. 939.
56. Cited in Longford *Elizabeth R*, p. 174.
57. Petrie *The Modern British Monarchy*, Eyre and Spottiswoode, London, 1961, p. 204.
58. 3.11.55, NCD, p. 289.
59. Townsend *Time and Chance*, p. 216.
60. Dempster *Margaret: A Life Unfulfilled*, p. 2.
61. 27.10.54, *Daily Express*.
62. 18.11.54, 19.11.54, 20.11.54, *Daily Mirror*.
63. 2.1.55, *The Times*.
64. 11.3.55, *Daily Herald*.
65. 24.4.55, *Sunday Express*.
66. Rt. Rev. Simon Phipps: interview.
67. 1.5.55, *Sunday Dispatch*.
68. Cited in Warwick *Princess Margaret*, p. 72.
69. Lady Elizabeth Cavendish: interview.
70. Rt. Rev. Simon Phipps: interview.
71. Vol.201, Fisher papers.
72. 21.10.55, *The Times*.
73. 23.10.55 Newcastle Chronicle.
74. 19.10.55, *The Times*.
75. Townsend *Time and Chance*, p. 235. There is a confusion over dates. Townsend gives the date of the *Times*

leader as 24 October, though it is clearly the leading article published on the 26th to which he refers.
76. Ibid, pp. 235–8.
77. Cited in Barrymaine *Townsend*, p. 185.
78. 31.10.55, HND, p. 290.
79. 3.11.55, NCD, p. 289.
80. 31.10.55, *Manchester Guardian*.
81. Cited in Barrymaine *Townsend*, p. 183.
82. Sir Edward Ford: interview.
83. Rt. Rev. Simon Phipps: interview.
84. This section is largely based on confidential interviews and information.
85. Confidential interviews.
86. Rose *Kings, Queens and Courtiers*, pp. 239–40.
87. Confidential interviews.
88. Sir Hardy Amies: interview.
89. Hartnell *Silver and Gold*, p. 124.
90. Confidential interviews.
91. H. Amies *Still Here: an Autobiography*, Weidenfeld and Nicolson, London, 1984, p. 104.
92. 24.10.78, Queen to Amies, Amies papers.
93. Sir Hardy Amies: interview.
94. Michael Noakes: interview.
95. C. R. Cammell *Memoirs of Annigoni*, Allan Wingate, London, 1956, pp. 102, 175.
96. P. Annigoni *An Artist's Life*, W. H. Allen, London, 1977, pp. 82, 174, 186.
97. Confidential interview.

Chapter Twelve

1. Clark *Palace Diary*, pp. 186–8.
2. E. Crankshaw (ed) *Khruschev Remembered*, London: Deutsch, 1971, pp. 406–7.
3. W. Clark *From Three Worlds*, London: Sidgwick and Jackson, 1986, p. 283.
4. 2.8.56, ibid, p. 168; Clark, *Palace Diary*, p. 193.
5. Lord Charteris: interview.

6. Confidential interview.
7. Clark *Palace Diary*, p. 194.
8. See Longford *Elizabeth R*, p. 181.
9. Lord Charteris: interview.
10. Sir Edward Ford: interview.
11. Lord Charteris: interview.
12. Confidential interview.
13. Confidential interview.
14. 'Note of a conversation with Lord Mountbatten', 6.6.76, AP 23/18/13a (Lord Avon papers.)
15. Lord Charteris: interview.
16. 15.11.56, PRO PREM 11/1163.
17. Eden *Full Circle*, p. 583.
18. Sir Edward Ford: interview.
19. January 1957, Colville unpublished diary.
20. A. Sampson *Macmillan: A Study in Ambiguity*, London: Allen Lane, 1967, p. 234.
21. Sir Edward Ford: interview.
22. R. A. Butler *The Art of the Possible: The Memoirs of Lord Butler*, London: Hamish Hamilton, 1971, p. 195.
23. H. Macmillan *Riding the Storm 1956–1959*, London: Macmillan, 1971, pp. 180–5.
24. Lord Charteris: interview.
25. Sampson *Macmillan: A Study in Ambiguity*, p. 125.
26. Fisher *The Tory Leaders*, p. 175.
27. R. Rhodes James *Anthony Eden*, London: Weidenfeld and Nicolson, 1986, p. 595.
28. AP 20/33/12 (Lord Avon papers.)
29. Rhodes James *Eden*, p. 595.
30. AP 20/33/12 (Lord Avon papers.)
31. Kilmuir *Political Adventure*, pp. 285–6.
32. Morrah *Work of the Queen*, pp. 158–9. Others consulted by Michael Adeane included Lord Charteris and Lord Waverley (see V. Bogdanor *Monarchy*, p. 93).
33. Kilmuir *Political Adventure*, pp. 285–6.
34. 19.10.57, *Saturday Evening Post*.
35. Cited in D. Laird *How the Queen Reigns*, p. 109. See also Lord Blake *The Office of Prime Minister*, Oxford: British Academy, Oxford University Press, 1975, p. 56.
36. Morrah *To Be a King*, p. 14.
37. Lord Charteris: interview.
38. 16.1.58, Queen to Eden, AP 50 A, (Lord Avon papers.)
39. See Dimbleby *Prince of Wales*, pp. 34–5.
40. Confidential interviews.
41. Curling *All the Queen's Horses*, pp. 11–15.
42. A. Burnett *The Derby: The Official Book of the World's Greatest Race*, London: Michael O'Mara Books, 1993, p 84.
43. Confidential interview.
44. Sir John Miller: interview.
45. Lord Carnarvon: interview.
46. Confidential interview.
47. Sir John Miller: interview.
48. Lord Buxton: interview.
49. Sir Edward Ford: interview.
50. Confidential interviews.
51. Rose *Kings, Queens and Courtiers*, p. 238.
52. B. Boothroyd *Philip: An Informal Biography*, London: Longman, 1971, p. 197.
53. Rose *Kings, Queens and Courtiers*, p. 238.
54. Boothroyd *Philip*, p. 222.
55. Confidential interviews.
56. 11.2.57, *Manchester Guardian*.
57. 18.2.57, *The Times*; 12.2.57, *Daily Telegraph*; 11.2.57, *Daily Herald*.
58. Brook Productions *The Windsors* interview transcript.
59. 12.2.57, *Irish Times*.
60. 12.2.57, *Daily Mirror*.
61. 12.2.57, *Irish Times*.
62. Alistair Cooke, 11.2.57, *Manchester Guardian*.
63. 10.2.57, *Sunday Pictorial*.
64. In 1995, one German newspaper reported that Prince Philip had twenty-four illegitimate children, and that this had been confirmed by Buckingham Palace. It turned out

that the paper had mistranslated 'godchildren'. (Private information.)

65. Confidential interview.

66. 22.2.57, PRO CAB 128, Cabinet Minutes.

67. 16.1.57, AP 30 A, (Lord Avon papers.)

68. 17.1.57, AP 30 A, (Lord Avon papers.)

69. Lord Charteris: interview.

70. See V. Rothwell *Anthony Eden: A Political Biography*, Manchester: Manchester University Press, 1992, pp. 245–6. Keith Kyle's definitive study of the Suez Crisis does not mention the Queen at all.

71. Macmillan *Riding the Storm*, pp. 180–5.

72. H. Macmillan *Pointing The Way 1959–1961* London: Macmillan, 1972, p. 30.

73. Bagehot *The English Constitution*, p. 113.

74. Macmillan *Riding the Storm*,p. 344.

75. Lord Egremont: interview.

76. Sir Edward Ford: interview.

77. See A. Horne *Macmillan 1957–1986 Vol. II of the Official Biography*, London: Macmillan, 1989, p. 168.

78. D. Judd *Empire: The British Imperial Experience, From 1765 to the Present*, London: HarperCollins, 1996, pp. 359–66.

79. Nairn *Enchanted Glass*, p. 213.

80. 22.10.55, *New Statesman*.

81. August 1957, *National and English Review*.

82. *Economic Review*, Vol. 149, No. 894.

83. 6.3.57, 7.3.57, *The Times*.

84. John Grigg: interview.

85. 'Foundation Stones and Things,' *National and English Review*, August 1957, pp. 70–83.

86. 'The Monarch Today', in ibid, pp. 61–7.

87. 6.8.57, *New Statesman*.

88. *National and English Review*, September 1957, p. 121.

89. 15.8.57, *Daily Express*.

90. 3.8.57, *Spectator*.

91. 7.8.57, 8.8.57, *The Times*; Altrincham 'Rumpus and After', *National and English Review*, September 1957, p. 45. *The Times* printed 'boss' in quotation marks, presumably on the grounds that the use of the term to refer to the Queen was disrespectful.

92. 8.8.57, *The Times*.

93. Nairn *Enchanted Glass*, pp. 67–8.

94. 20.9.57, Fisher to Mrs. Alice Brace, Vol.183 ff 66–7, (Fisher papers.)

95. Confidential interview.

96. John Grigg: interview.

97. 17.11.57, *Sunday Graphic*.

98. 11.10.57, Queen to Eden, AP 30 A (Lord Avon papers.)

99. P. Brandon *Ike: The Life and Times of Dwight D. Eisenhower*, London: Secker and Warburg, 1987, p. 349.

100. 11.10.57, Queen to Eden, Ap 30 A (Lord Avon papers.)

101. 16.10.57, *Manchester Guardian*.

102. Confidential source.

103. 14.10.57, *The Times*.

104. Cited in Clark *Palace Diary*, p. 208.

105. 14.10.57, Board of Management minutes No.401, BBC/WA.

106. 'Some Further Points on the Muggeridge Incident', RCONT1, Muggeridge, Malcolm: Talks 1957–62. Grisewood to Jacob 23.10.57, BBC/WA.

107. 11.11.57, Board of Management Minutes, BBC/WA.

108. 20.12.57, memos from Cecil McGiven, deputy director Television Broadcasting, BBC/WA.

109. 'Further Points on the Muggeridge Incident'.

110. 12.8.57, *Daily Mail*.

111. 'Rumpus and After', pp. 106–15.

112. 10.8.57, *New Statesman*.

113. 23.10.57, 15.11.57, *The Times*.

114. 5.2.77, *Daily Telegraph*.

115. 30.5.93, *Sunday Times*.

Chapter Thirteen

1. 19.9.56, Jacob to Sir Robert Fraser, T16/609, BBC/WA.
2. 31.1.57, Norman Collins to Jacob; 8.2.57, S. J. Lotbiniere to Jacob, T16/608/1, BBC/WA.
3. 7.3.57, Jacob memo, R34/1105/1 BBC/WA.
4. 7.3.57, Peter Dimmock (Head of Outside Broadcasts) memo, T16/186/4, BBC/WA.
5. 7.10.57, Peter Dimmock memo, T/16/186/4, BBC/WA.
6. 30.10.57, Jacob to Sir Alexander Cadogan (Chairman of BBC Governors), T16/609, BBC/WA.
7. Cadogan to Butler, 7.11.57, T16/609, ibid.
8. 2.12.57, George Campey memo, ibid.
9. 4.12.57, Jacob memo, ibid.
10. 17.1.58, Anthony Craxton memo, R34/1105/1, BBC/WA.
11. 26.12.57, HND, p. 342.
12. 8.1.58, P. Dimmock to M. Charteris, T16/608/1, BBC/WA.
13. 3.12.58, A. Craxton memo, T16/186/5, BBC/WA.
14. John Grigg: interview.
15. Morrah *The Work of the Queen*, pp. 37–44.
16. Lord Altrincham *The British Commonwealth: Its Place in the Service of the World*, London: Hutchinson, 1943, pp. 100–1.
17. Bagehot *The English Constitution*, p. 98.
18. Morrah *The Work of the Queen*, pp. 37–44.
19. D. Laird *How the Queen Reigns*, p. 24.
20. Sampson *Anatomy of Britain*, p. 36.
21. 20.10.57, Eisenhower to the Queen (Eisenhower papers).
22. 30.8.59, Eisenhower to the Queen (Eisenhower papers).
23. 7.8.59, HND, p. 369.
24. 8.8.59, 3.12.59, *The Times*.
25. 27.1.60, 2.2.60, cited in Howard *Rab*, p. 276; Higham and Moseley *Elizabeth and Philip*, pp. 213–7.
26. Beaverbrook papers, cited in Parker *The Queen*, p. 117.
27. 7.2.60, Macmillan diary, in H. Macmillan *Pointing the Way 1959–1961*, p. 161.
28. 2.2.60, Cabinet Conclusions, PRO CAB 128/40.
29. 2.2.60, cited in Howard *Rab*, p. 276.
30. 24.1.60, Queen to Eisenhower (Eisenhower papers).
31. 4.2.60, Eisenhower to the Queen (Eisenhower papers).
32. 20.2.60, 23.2.60, *The Times*.
33. NCD, p. 168.
34. 22.2.60, Cabinet Conclusions, PRO CAB 128/40.
35. Warwick *Princess Margaret*, p. 97.
36. Dempster *H.R.H. The Princess Margaret: A Life Unfulfilled*, p. 49.
37. 8.5.60, NCD, p. 458.
38. Bagehot *The English Constitution*, pp. 87–8.
39. Macmillan *Pointing the Way*, pp. 193–4.
40. 8.4.60, *Daily Telegraph*; Vickers, *Beaton*, p. 439.
41. C. de Gaulle *Memoirs of Hope*, Weidenfeld and Nicolson, London, 1971, pp. 254–5.
42. Butler and Butler *British Political Facts*, p. 271.
43. Macmillan, *Pointing the Way*, p. 171.
44. 5.4.61, High Commissioner dispatches, MB1/3239 (Mountbatten papers).
45. 5.5.60, Adeane to Macmillan (PRO) PREM 11/5064.
46. 21.1.61, 3.3.61, 18.1.61, 6.3.61, *Manchester Guardian*.
47. Lord Charteris: interview.
48. Macmillan *Pointing the Way*, pp. 459–72.
49. 18.11.61 H. Evans *Downing Street Diary: The Macmillan Years*

1957–1963, London: Hodder and
Stoughton, 1981, p. 171.

50. 4.2.62, Henry Fairlie in *Sunday Telegraph*.
51. 21.11.61, *The Times*.
52. 25.11.61, cited in *The Times*.
53. Horne *Macmillan*, Vol II, p. 399.
54. 24.11.61, Queen to Lord Porchester, Royal Collection.
55. Bagehot *The English Constitution*, p. 100.
56. Macmillan *Pointing the Way*, p. 472.
57. 30.1.60, *New Statesman*.
58. P. Mansergh *The Commonwealth Experience*, London: Weidenfeld and Nicolson, 1969, p. 405.
59. M. Green *A Mirror for Anglo-Saxons*, London: Longmans, 1957, p. 144–5.
60. Morrah *The Work of the Queen*, pp. 48–9.
61. See Z. Cowen *The British Commonwealth of Nations in a Changing World: Law, Politics and Prospects*, Evanston, Illinois: Northwestern University Press, 1965, p. 46.
62. P. Black *The Mystique of Monarchy*, pp. 32–4.
63. F. Underhill *The British Commonwealth*, Durham, NC: Duke University Press, 1956, pp. 82–4.
64. C. J. Hughes 'The Constitutional Development of the British Commonwealth 1945–1954', Sonderdruck aus: "Das Öffentliche Recht der Gegenwart," Tubingen, 1956, p. 42.
65. Lord Altrincham and others *Is the Monarchy Perfect?*, London: John Calder, 1958, p. 1.
66. Petrie *Modern British Monarchy*, p. 300.
67. 15.1.59, *The Times*.
68. See for example Paula Davine in *Daily Telegraph*, 21.4.61.
69. 16.4.63, Adeane to T. J. Bligh, PRO PREM 11/5064.
70. 7.11.62, *The Times*.

Chapter Fourteen

1. 4.2.62, *Observer*.
2. 25 million, according to BBC Audience Research (4.1.61, T16/608/3, BBC Written Archives). Live broadcasting stopped in 1960, at the Queen's request, ostensibly because a recording would allow Commonwealth countries to transmit on Christmas Day, but also because of the strain of a live transmission, and the upset to the Queen's Christmas Day (20.1.60, T16/608/3 BBC/WA).
3. 20.5.62, *Daily Express*.
4. 17.6.58, T16/185/5, BBC W/A.
5. 6.2.62, *Guardian*.
6. 4.2.62, Henry Fairlie in *Daily Telegraph*.
7. 7.3.62, President's Office Files (Kennedy papers).
8. 20.5.62, Queen to Kennedy (Kennedy papers).
9. Cited in A. Horne *Macmillan 1957–1986: The Official Biography*, London: Macmillan, 1989, Vol.II, pp. 554–6.
10. H. J. Harvey 'The British Commonwealth: A Pattern of Co-operation,' *International Conciliation*, January 1953, No. 487, pp. 4–5.
11. Cited in Horne *Macmillan*, Vol. II, p. 358.
12. H. Macmillan *Memoirs VI At the End of the Day*, p. 137.
13. 28.11.62, Queen to Eden (Lord Avon papers).
14. 4.4.63, *The Times*.
15. 3.6.62, Evans *Downing Street Diary*, p. 109.
16. Horne *Macmillan*, Vol.II, pp. 345, 485–6.
17. 11.6.63, *The Times*.
18. 13.3.63, *Evening Standard*.
19. 13.8.63, *Daily Mirror*.
20. 3.5.63, T. Benn *Out of the Wilderness: Diaries 1963–67*, London: Hutchinson, 1987, p. 41.

21. 11.7.63, *Daily Express.*
22. Cited in Pearson *The Ultimate Family*, p. 165.
23. 7.1.63, de Lotbiniere memo, T16/608/3, BBC/WA.
24. 2.6.63, Evans *Downing Street Diary*, p. 270.
25. 13.8.63, T16/608/3, BBC/WA.
26. 16.3.64, Board of Management minutes, T16/608/3, BBC/WA.
27. 12.8.63, Adeane to Swinton, ACAD 174/7/9 (Earl of Swinton papers).
28. Cited in Horne *Macmillan*, Vol.II, p. 533.
29. 30.9.63, ACAD 174/7/9. (Earl of Swinton papers).
30. Macmillan *At The End of The Day*, p. 490.
31. Horne *Macmillan* Vol.II, p. 534.
32. Macmillan *At the End of the Day*, p. 508.
33. 16.9.61, Evans *Downing Street Diary*, p. 160.
34. Horne *Macmillan*, Vol.II, p. 553.
35. Ibid, p. 556. On the same day that Macmillan briefed his lieutenants to make soundings, he told Swinton on the telephone that Hailsham's Conference speech had ruled him out – which seems to indicate that he had prejudged the outcome. (See 13/14.10.63, ACAD 174/7/9, Lord Swinton papers.)
36. See R. A. Butler *The Art of the Possible*, p. 247, The Memoirs of Lord Butler, London: Hamish Hamilton, 1971, R. Bevins *The Greasy Poll: A personal account of the realities of British politics*, London: Hodder and Stoughton, 1965, p. 143.
37. Horne *Macmillan*, Vol.II, pp. 556–8.
38. A. Howard and R. West *The Making of the Prime Minister*, Cape, London, 1965, p. 88.
39. Sir Edward Ford: interview.
40. ACAD 174/7/9, (Lord Swinton papers.)
41. 16.10.63, Swinton to Lady Swinton, ibid.
42. Evans *Downing Street Diary* p. 300.
43. R. S. Churchill *Fight for the Tory Leadership: A Contemporary Chronicle*, London: Heinemann, 1964, p. 137.
44. Lord Hailsham *A Sparrow's Flight*, London: Collins, 1991, p. 354.
45. Macmillan *At the End of the Day*, p. 515.
46. Horne *Macmillan*, Vol.II, p. 565.
47. Transcript of interview, ibid, pp. 566–7. Among the inaccuracies in this account, given many years after the event, is Lord Stockton's reference to the length of the audience, which he said was an hour – double the actual time.
48. Macmillan *At the End of the Day*, pp. 515–8.
49. Lord Charteris: interview.
50. Confidential interview.
51. Enoch Powell: interview.
52. Churchill *The Fight for the Tory Leadership*, p. 125.
53. Enoch Powell: interview.
54. Kenneth Rose: interview.
55. Lord Charteris: interview.
56. Lord Home *The Way the Wind Blows*, London: Collins, 1976, p. 185.
57. K. Young *Sir Alec Douglas-Home*, London: J. M. Dent, 1970, p. 168.
58. Lord Charteris: interview.
59. Churchill *The Fight for the Tory Leadership*, p. 142.
60. Cited in N. Fisher *Iain Macleod*, London: Deutsch, 1973, p. 240.
61. See V. Bogdanor *Monarchy and the Constitution*, Oxford: Oxford University Press, 1995, pp. 93–9 for a different view.
62. 12.3.64 *The Times.*
63. See Varley *Bodyguard*, pp. 76–81.
64. B. Penrose and S. Freeman *Conspiracy of Silence: The Secret Life of Anthony Blunt*, London: Grafton Books, 1986, p. 291. See also Allison and Riddell (eds) *Royal Encyclopedia*, p. 54.
65. C. Pincher *Top Secret Too Long: The*

Great Betrayal of Britain's Crucial Secrets and the Cover-up, London: Sidgwick and Jackson, 1984, p. 367.

66. Penrose and Freeman The Conspiracy of Silence, pp. 411–2.

67. Confidential interviews.

68. 5.2.64, Adeane to Bligh, PRO PREM 11/5062.

69. 14.4.64, PRO PREM 11/5062.

70. 29.4.64, Adeane to Sir Saville Garner, PRO PREM 11/5062.

71. 17.9.64, PRO PREM 11/5062.

72. 16.9.64, The Times.

73. PRO CAB 128/38, Cabinet Conclusions.

74. See Kenneth Rose 'Why the Queen's Christmas Broadcast failed to please', 29.1.84, Sunday Telegraph.

75. 12.10.64, Guardian.

76. W. R. Young (ed) Paul Martin: The London Diaries 1975–1979, Ottawa: University of Ottawa Press, 1988, p. 411.

77. 14.4.64, 29.4.64, PRO PREM 11/5062.

78. 1/2.9.64, PRO PREM 11/4756.

79. 4.9.64, Derek Mitchell 'Note for the Record', ibid.

80. 17.9.64, Agnew to Mitchell, ibid.

81. 4.9.64, ibid.

82. 6.9.64, Adeane to Mitchell, ibid.

83. Douglas-Home to H. Wilson, ibid.

84. 17.9.6,'Note for the Record', PRO PREM 11/5062.

Chapter Fifteen

1. Lord Charteris: interview.

2. D. Mitchell memorandum, 'Deadlock', n.d. PRO PREM II/4756.

3. H. Wilson The Labour Government 1964–1970: A Personal Record, London: Weidenfeld and Nicolson, 1971, p. 22.

4. 18.10.64, 20.10.64, PRO PREM 13/088.

5. Joe Haines: telephone interview.

6. Sir Derek Mitchell: interview.

7. 5.11.65 Daily Express.

8. Joe Haines: telephone interview.

9. Sir Edward Ford: interview.

10. G. Barry Royal Service, p. 88.

11. 5.11.65 Daily Express.

12. 26.8.66, AP30A, (Lord Avon Papers.)

13. 22.10.64, RCD, p. 29.

14. 21.10.64, TBD, pp. 168–9.

15. 20.11.64, TBD, pp. 190–1.

16. 23.10.64, 26.10.64, PRO PREM 13/085/86.

17. PRO PREM 13/5556.

18. 22.10.65, Mitchell memo, PRO PREM 13/556.

19. 27.10.65, Daily Telegraph.

20. PRO PREM 13/556.

21. 10.11.65, PRO DO 183/56.

22. 10.11.65, PRO PREM 13/545.

23. 11.11.65, BCD, p. 33.

24. 27.11.65 Wilson to Gibbs (telegram) PRO PREM 13/621.

25. 18.11.65, D. J. M. 'Note for the Record', PRO PREM 13/553.

26. 19.11.65, Mountbatten to Wilson, PRO PREM 13/553.

27. R. Blake A History of Rhodesia, London: Eyre Methuen, 1978, pp. 386–7.

28. 3.12.65, Smith to Queen, PRO PREM 13/556.

29. 3.12.65, PRO PREM 13/556.

30. Cited in Wilson The Labour Government 1964–70, p. 50.

31. K. Flower Serving Secretly: An Intelligence Chief on Record, Rhodesia into Zimbabwe 1964–1981, London: Murray, 1987, pp. 82, 94.

32. 17.11.65, Daily Telegraph.

33. 27.11.65, PRO PREM 13/621.

34. 29.5.77, Sunday Times.

35. 28.5.64, The Times, PRO PREM 11/8061.

36. 27.4.58, Moran Churchill, p. 739.

37. 27.1.58, 1/137, Chartwell papers.

38. 29.1.65, The Times.

39. 16.3.65, Guardian.

40. 30.1.62, PRO PREM 11/5061.

41. 20.1.62, PM to P. de Zulueta, PRO PREM 11/5061.

42. 28.11.62, Zulueta to PM, PRO PREM 11/5061.

43. 21.4.64, Adeane to Butler, PRO PREM 11/5061.
44. 28.5.65, *Guardian.*
45. N. Henderson *The Private Office*, London: Weidenfeld and Nicolson, 1989 p. 105.
46. Longford *Elizabeth R*, p. 262.
47. 26.5.65, *Guardian.*
48. 23.6.65, AP30A, (Lord Avon Papers.)
49. 13.7.65, BCD, pp. 25–6.
50. 22.12.65, RCD, p. 420.
51. Higham and Moseley *Elizabeth and Philip*, pp. 275–6.
52. Lord Carnarvon: interview.
53. J. Douglas-Home *Horse-Racing in Berkshire*, Stroud: Alan Sutton, 1992, p. 123.
54. Sir John Miller: interview.
55. Allison and Riddell, *Royal Encyclopedia*, p. 431.
56. 25.11.64, 13.1.65, pp. 192, 203; 26.1.65, pp. 166, 210; 11.2.65, p. 211, 26.1.65, pp. 166, 210; 18.2.65, p. 222; 10.3.65, pp. 229–32; 11.3.65, p. 233; 1.7.65, p. 284; 28.7.65, p. 301; 24.10.65, p. 339; 16/18.10.65, pp. 336–7; 21.12.65, p. 361; 31.12.65, p. 364; 5.5.66, pp. 408–9; 15.6.66, pp. 430–1 5.7.66, pp. 445–6; 11.3.74, p. 120, TBD.
57. 9.11.64, pp. 52–3; 27.6.65, p. 257; 20.9.66, RCD, p. 542.
58. 11.3.71, *The Cecil King Diary 1970–1974*, London: Cape, 1976, pp. 89–90.
59. 11.1.67, RCD, pp. 194–5; 29.7.66, RCD, p. 593; 11.8.66, RCD, p. 611.
60. Lord Carnarvon: interview.
61. 11.8.66, RCD, p. 611.
62. 20.9.66, RCD, p. 542; 13.11.67, RCD, p. 570; 20.9.66, RCD, p. 542.
63. 22.8.68, *New Statesman.*
64. 22.5.68, *The Times*; 23.5.68, *Daily Telegraph*; 25.5.68, *Daily Mail*; 25.5.68, *Guardian.*
65. L. Harris *Long to Reign Over Us*, London: William Kimber, 1966, cited in 10.10.66, *Daily Telegraph.*
66. Bagehot *The English Constitution*, p. 99.
67. R. Rose and D. Kavanagh 'The Monarchy in Contemporary Political Culture', *Comparative Politics*, Vol 8, No 4, July 1976, pp. 548–76. The survey was conducted in 1968.
68. 23.8.68, *New Statesman.*
69. Confidential interview.
70. 30.10.66, *Sunday Times.*

Chapter Sixteen

1. Butler and Butler *British Political Facts*, p. 421
2. *The Windsors* interview transcript.
3. Harewood *Tongs and the Bones*, p. 218.
4. 28.7.67, RCD, p. 448.
5. Allison and Riddell (eds) *Royal Encyclopedia*, p. 80.
6. 3.12.65, 29.4.67, 1.5.67, *The Times.*
7. 18.4.66, *Daily Telegraph.*
8. 2.10.68, 3.10.68, 26.11.68, *Daily Express.*
9. D. Thelford 'What the Papers Say: The Palace and the Press' in T. Grove (ed) *The Queen Observed.*
10. Ronald Allison: interview.
11. Lord Charteris: interview.
12. Cited in H. Cathcart *The Married Life of the Queen*, London: W. H. Allen, London, 1970, p. 192.
13. Dimbleby *Prince of Wales*, p. 126.
14. J. Grigg *The History of The Times, Vol VI The Thomson Years 1966-1981*, London: Times Books, 1993, p. 42.
15. 29.4.66, 19.5.66, T16/608/3, BBC/WA.
16. 16.7.68, T16/186/8, BBC/WA.
17. Lord Charteris: interview.
18. Sir William Heseltine: interview.
19. Lord Brabourne: interview.
20. 13.3.58 Colville to de Lotbiniere.
21. Lord Brabourne: interview.
22. Ronald Allison: interview.
23. Lord Charteris: interview.
24. 9.10.86, *Listener*, cited in Nairn *Enchanted Glass*, p. 217.
25. Princess Margaret: interview.
26. Ronald Allison: interview.
27. Lord Brabourne: interview.

28. Confidential interview.
29. Ziegler *Crown and People*, p. 134.
30. 28.2.68, *Daily Mirror*.
31. 20.6.69, *The Times*.
32. 10.11.69, *ibid*.
33. 11.7.69, TBD, p. 190.
34. Confidential interview.
35. Ronald Allison: interview.
36. Cathcart *Married Life*, p. 193.
37. Kenneth Rose: interview.
38. Grigg 3.2.72, *Evening Standard*.
39. Cited in Nairn *Enchanted Glass*, p. 220.
40. Ibid, pp. 221, 225.
41. Dimbleby *Prince of Wales*, p. 134.
42. 27.7.69, NCD, p. 404.
43. 5.2.77, *Daily Telegraph*.
44. A. Duncan *The Reality of Monarchy*, London: Heinemann, 1970, pp. 289, 327.
45. 11.11.69, *The Times*; 3.11.69, *Daily Mail*.
46. P. Hall *Royal Fortune: Tax, Money and the Monarchy*, London: Bloomsbury, 1992, pp. 106−7.
47. 6.11.69, 5.11.69, 10.11.69, *The Times*.
48. 10.11.69, NBC interview.
49. 11.11.69, pp. 22−6; 12.11.69, RCD, pp. 725−6.
50. 12.11.69, *The Times*.

Chapter Seventeen

1. 1.1.70, Queen to Amies (Amies papers.)
2. Lord Brabourne: interview.
3. Ronald Allison: interview.
4. Allison and Riddell (eds) *Royal Encyclopedia*, p. 566.
5. 20.11.72, *The Times*.
6. 22.6.70, TBD, p. 297.
7. 22.6.70, RCD, p. 953.
8. Confidential interview.
9. R. Crossman *Inside View: Three Lectures on Prime Ministerial Government*, London: Cape, 1972, p. 40.
10. cited in 28.5.71, *The Times*.
11. 14.7.71, *Guardian*.

12. 9.6.71, *The Times*.
13. See J. Grigg *The History of the Times, vol VI*, pp. 230−1.
14. Bagehot *The English Constitution*, p. 100.
15. Report from the Select Committee on the Civil List, 1971, pp. ix, xi.
16. J. H. Grainger 'The Activity of Monarchy', *Cambridge Quarterly*, Vol VII, No 4, 1977, p. 305.
17. 20.5.71, *The Times*.
18. 3.12.71, *Daily Telegraph*.
19. 29.6.71, Minutes of Evidence Taken before the Select Committee on the Civil List, p. 32.
20. Appendices to the Minutes of Evidence taken before the Select Committee on the Civil List, 1971, p. 111.
21. 3.12.71, *The Times*.
22. 8.12.71, Queen to Amies (Amies Papers.)
23. 22.12.71, 15.12.71, 3.12.71, *The Times*.
24. Lord Charteris: interview.
25. Hall *Royal Fortune* pp. 106−7.
26. Confidential interview.
27. 3.12.71, *Guardian*.
28. 3.12.71, *Sun*.
29. 7.1.72, Amies papers.
30. Cited in Dimbleby *Prince of Wales*, p. 179.
31. M. Thornton *Royal Feud: The Queen Mother and the Duchess of Windsor*, London: Michael Joseph, 1985, pp 315−20.
32. Kenneth Rose: interview.
33. Lord Charteris: interview
34. Confidential interview.
35. 29.5.72, *The Times*.
36. Confidential interview.
37. Lord Charteris: interview.
38. Sir Derek Mitchell: interview.
39. 26.7.65, TBD, p. 298.
40. Confidential interviews.
41. Ronald Allison: interview.
42. 3.2.72, *Evening Standard*.
43. 21.1.72, *The Times*.
44. 7.2.72, *Daily Mail*.
45. *Sunday Times* 1973.

46. 20.11.72, *Daily Telegraph*.
47. 5.2.72, *The Times*.
48. 7.2.72, *Daily Mail*.
49. 20.11.72, *The Times*.
50. 20.11.72, *Daily Telegraph*.
51. R. Belissario *To Tread on Royal Toes* Aberdeen: Impulse Books, 1972, pp. 62–3.
52. 21.11.72, *Daily Telegraph*.
53. Confidential interview.
54. 27.12.72, *The Times*.
55. 25.10.72, *Daily Telegraph*.

Chapter Eighteen

1. 20.1.74, Amies papers.
2. 1.3.74, *The Times*.
3. Wilson *Final Term: The Labour Government 1974-1976*, p. 11.
4. Lord Charteris: interview.
5. Confidential interview.
6. H. Wilson *Memoirs: The Making of a Prime Minister 1916–64*, London: Weidenfeld and Nicolson, 1986, p. 5.
7. 5.3.71, BCD, p. 427.
8. 13.9.65, p. 319; 21.1.74, pp. 94-5; TBD.
9. 8.3.74, *The Times*.
10. Confidential interview.
11. Joe Haines: telephone interview.
12. 8.4.74, 11.5.74, *The Times*.
13. 22.10.74, Queen to Amies (Amies papers).
14. 12.2.75, p. 562, BCD.
15. William Hamilton *My Queen and I*, London: Quartet Books, 1975, pp. 187–95.
16. 30.1.75, *The Times*.
17. 22.2.75, 25.2.75, *Morning Star*.
18. 25.2.75, *ibid*.
19. 2.3.79, *Sunday Telegraph*.
20. 27.2.75, *Guardian*.
21. 27.2.75, *The Times*.
22. 10.6.73, *Sunday Express*.
23. 2.5.73, *The Times*.
24. 11.11.75, TBD, p. 459.
25. Sir John Kerr *Matters for Judgement*, full details p. 330; R. Lacey *Majesty: Elizabeth II and the House of Windsor*, London: Hutchinson, 1977, p. 300;

cited in Bogdanor *Monarchy and the Constitution*, p. 277.
26. 12.11.75, *The Times*.
27. Bogdanor *Monarchy and the Constitution*, p. 285.
28. 12.11.75, 15.11.75, 25.1.75, *The Times*.
29. Cited in Bogdanor *Monarchy and the Constitution*, p. 277-8, p. 285.
30. 27.4.76, *The Times*.
31. Michael Noakes: interview.
32. Howard and West *The Making of a Prime Minister*, p. 6.
33. Wilson *Final Term*, p. 29.
34. See B. Pimlott *Harold Wilson*, London: HarperCollins, 1992, p. 647.
35. 'The Opening of Parliament,' in M. Wilson *New Poems*, London: Hutchinson, 1979, p. 49.
36. Joe Haines: telephone interview.
37. 24.3.76, *The Times*.
38. 27.5.65, TBD, p. 263.
39. Lord Charteris: interview.
40. Wilson *Final Term*, p. 239.
41. 15.4.76, *Free Nation*.
42. 15.4.76, *The Times*.
43. Lord McNally: interview.
44. 7.2.82, *Sunday Times*.
45. Confidential interview.
46. Lord McNally: interview.
47. Joe Haines: telephone interview.
48. 4.3.76, *Daily Mirror*.
49. P. Howard *British Monarchy in the Twentieth Century*, London: Hamish Hamilton, 1977, p. 145.
50. 19.10.57, *Saturday Evening Post*, republished in Lord Altrincham and others *Is The Monarchy Perfect?* London: John Calder, 1958, p. 139.
51. Confidential interview.
52. 8.2.80, Paul Johnson *Now!*
53. 20.3.76, *The Times*.
54. Ronald Allison: interview.
55. 7.10.84, *Mail on Sunday*.
56. See R. Lacey *Majesty: Elizabeth II and the House of Windsor*, p. 320.
57. Dempster *H.R.H. The Princess Margaret: A Life Unfulfilled*, pp. 126-30.
58. 7.10.84, *Mail on Sunday*.

59. 7.4.78, *Sun*.
60. 3.4.78, *Guardian*.
61. Confidential interview.
62. 4.4.78, *Daily Mirror*.
63. 15.5.77, Young (ed) *Martin: London Diaries*, p. 256.
64. Cited in Dempster *Princess Margaret: A Life Unfulfilled*, p. 149.
65. 5.4.78, *The Times*.
66. 5.4.78, Jeremy Bray in *The Times*.
67. *Sunday Telegraph*.
68. 5.4.78, *Sun*.
69. Confidential interview.
70. Confidential interview.
71. Cited in Dempster *Princess Margaret: A Life Unfulfilled*, p. 149.
72. P. Howard *British Monarchy*, p. 143.
73. C. Warwick *Princess Margaret*, p. 137.
74. Cited in Dempster *Princess Margaret: A Life Unfulfilled*, p. 149.

Chapter Nineteen

1. Allison and Riddell (eds) *Royal Encyclopedia*, pp 287–8.
2. Ronald Allison: interview.
3. Lord Charteris: interview.
4. 8.8.75, *Guardian*.
5. Ronald Allison: interview.
6. Lord Charteris: interview.
7. Allison and Riddell (eds) *Royal Encyclopedia*, pp 288–9.
8. 18.4.77, *Financial Times*.
9. 27.4.77, *Guardian*.
10. Cited in 5.6.77, *Sunday Times*.
11. Ziegler *Crown and People*, p 173.
12. 8.2.77, *Daily Telegraph*.
13. 4.5.77, TBD, p 127.
14. 5.5.77, *Guardian*.
15. 6.5.77, *The Times*.
16. 5.5.77, *Daily Telegraph*.
17. Allison and Riddell (eds) *Royal Encyclopedia*, pp 288–9.
18. Confidential interview.
19. 8.6.77, *Daily Telegraph*.
20. 8.6.77, *Guardian*.
21. Allison and Riddell (eds) *Royal Encyclopedia*, pp 288–9.
22. Lord Charteris: interview.

23. 18.8.77, *The Times*.
24. 10.77.77, *Sunday Times*.
25. 15.8.77 Raymond Fletcher in *The Times*
26. 15.3.78 *Daily Telegraph*.
27. Lord Charteris: interview.
28. Cited in Allison and Riddell *Royal Encyclopaedia* p. 288.
29. J. Colville *The New Elizabethans 1952–1977*, London: Collins, 1977, p. 411.
30. 5.6.77 Anthony Bailey in *Observer*.
31. 5.2.77 Brian Connell in *The Times*.
32. 7.6.77, *Daily Express*.
33. 5.2.77, *Daily Telegraph*.
34. 29.5.77, *Sunday Times*.
35. 6.2.77, *Observer*.
36. 6.2.77, *Sunday Times*.
37. Lacey *Majesty: Elizabeth and the House of Windsor*, p. 49.
38. 22.1.77 *Guardian*.
39. Lord Charteris: interview.
40. 1.9.78 Young (ed) *Martin; London Diaries*, p. 412.
41. 15.6.78, 21.6.78, ibid, pp. 387–9.
42. Ibid, p. 402.
43. 17.7.78, *The Times*.
44. 17.4.82, *The Times*.
45. Queen to Hardy Amies (Hardy Amies papers).
46. Confidential interview.
47. Howe *Conflict of Loyalty*, p. 112.
48. Confidential interview.
49. Confidential interview.
50. Joe Haines: *Daily Telegraph* interview.
51. Confidential interview.
52. 1.2.82 *The Times*.
53. Sampson *Anatomy of Britain*, p. 6.
54. Sir Clive Whitmore: interview.
55. Confidential interview.
56. Confidential interviews.
57. Young *One of Us*, p. 491.
58. Confidential interviews.
59. Confidential interview.
60. Confidential interview.
61. Lord Charteris: interview.
62. Bogdanor *The Monarchy and the Constitution*, pp. 265, 274.

63. Confidential interview.
64. 16.4.86, Henry Stanhope *The Times*.
65. Sir Sonny Ramphal: interview.
66. Lord Charteris: interview.
67. Duchess of Grafton: interview.
68. Confidential interview.
69. 16.4.86 *The Times*.
70. Lord Hunt: interview.
71. 21.2.84 *Guardian*.
72. Confidential interview.
73. Confidential interview.
74. Cited in A. Morrow *The Queen*, Granada, London 1983, pp. 142–152.
75. Michael Shea: interview.
76. Sir Sonny Ramphal: interview.
77. Confidential interview.
78. Confidential interview.
79. Michael Shea: interview.
80. Sir Sonny Ramphal: interview.
81. Confidential interview.
82. 16.4.86, *The Times*.

Chapter Twenty

1. Allison and Riddell (eds) *Royal Encyclopaedia*, p. 564.
2. Lord Charteris: interview.
3. Dimbleby *Prince of Wales*, p. 267.
4. Ronald Allison: interview.
5. Confidential interview.
6. Lord Carnarvon: interview.
7. Confidential interview.
8. A Morton *Diana: Her True Story*, London: Michael O'Mara Books Ltd, London 1992, p. 48.
9. Dimbleby: *Prince of Wales*, p. 280.
10. 22.11.80, *Guardian*.
11. 22.10.80, *The Times*.
12. 3.1.81, *Daily Telegraph*.
13. Morton *Diana: Her True Story* pp. 55–8.
14. Dimbleby *Prince of Wales*, p. 287.
15. 28.3.81, *The Times*.
16. 20.4.80, *Sun*.
17. 15.6.81, *Daily Express*.
18. 15.6.81, *The Times*.
19. J. M. Packard *The Queen and Her Court, A Guide to British Monarchy Today*, London: Robson Books, 1981, pp. 23–4.
20 Confidential interview.
21. 8.3.87, *Observer*.
22. Michael Shea: interview.
23. Confidential interview.
24. 30.1.87, *Sunday Telegraph*.
25. 20.4.81, *The Times*.
26. Confidential interview.
27. Ronald Allison: interview.
28. Confidential interview.
29. Lord Runcie: interview.
30. Morton *Diana: Her True Story*, pp. 63–4.
31. 29.6.81, 28.6.81, *The Times*.
32. 29.7.81, Jan Morris in *The Times*.
33. Sampson *Changing Anatomy of Britain*, p. 5.
34. 9.12.81, *The Times*.
35. 2.6.93, *Guardian*.
36. 19.2.82, *The Times*.
37. 28.2.83, *Time Magazine*.
38. 19.2.82, 1.2.82, *The Times*.
39. Sampson *Changing Anatomy of Britain*, p. 5.
40. 1.2.82, *The Times*.
41. 16.1.83, *Sun*.
42. 3.6.84, *Sunday Mirror*.
43. Confidential interviews.
44. 8.5.82, 27.5.82, 27.5.82, 9.6.82, 19.6.82, *The Times*.
45. 26.6.82, *Daily Telegraph*.
46. Private information.
47. 22.2.83, *Sun*.
48. Cited in P. James *Margaret: A Woman of Conflict*, London: Sidgwick and Jackson, 1990, p. 167.
49. Lord Buxton: interview.
50. Michael Shea: interview.
51. Confidential interview.
52. A. Morton *Inside Buckingham Palace*, London: Michael O'Mara Books, 1991, p. 84.
53. 17.8.82, *Daily Telegraph* citing *Time*.
54. 14.7.82, 21.7.82, *The Times*.
55. 4.8.82, *Daily Express*.
56. 30.3.82, Amies papers.
57. 22.9.86, *Guardian*.
58. January 1983, *Time Magazine*.

Chapter Twenty-One

1. I. Jennings *The Queen's Government*, Harmondsworth: Penguin, 1954, pp. 44-5.
2. M. Thatcher *The Downing Street Years*, London: HarperCollins, 1993, pp. 309.
3. Confidential interview.
4. Prochaska *Royal Bounty*, p. 49.
5. Lord Runcie: interview.
6. Confidential interviews.
7. 30.10.83, *Observer*.
8. Bogdanor *Monarchy and the Constitution*, p. 278.
9. A. Payne, P. Sutton and T. Thorndike *Grenada's Revolution and Invasion*, London: Crown Helm, 1984, pp. 181-2.
10. 21.1.84, *Guardian*.
11. 6.2.84, *The Times*.
12. H. Young *One of Us: A Biography of Margaret Thatcher*, p. 484.
13. 6.2.84, *The Times*.
14. Enoch Powell: interview.
15. 8.2.92, *Financial Times*.
16. 20.4.81, *The Times*.
17. 14.10.84, *Sunday Times*.
18. Confidential interview.
19. Young *One of Us*, p. 484.
20. Confidential interview.
21. 16.4.86, *The Times*.
22. 19.7.86, *Financial Times*.
23. Cited in 22.7.86, *Guardian*.
24. 17.7.86, *Daily Telegraph*.
25. 20.7.86, *Sunday Telegraph*.
26. Confidential interview.
27. Brian MacArthur: interview.
28. 20.7.86, *Sunday Times*.
29. 28.7.86, *The Times*.
30. 21.7.86, *Guardian*.
31. Sir Bernard Ingham: interview.
32. Confidential interview.
33. Sir Sonny Ramphal: interview.
34. 28.7.86, 29.7.86, *The Times*.
35. Confidential interview.
36. 29.7.86, *The Times*.
37. Confidential interview.
38. Michael Jones: telephone interview.
39. Sir Bernard Ingham: interview.
40. Confidential interview.
41. 3.8.86, *News of the World*.
42. 31.7.86, *The Times*.
43. Confidential interviews.
44. Sir John Riddell: interview.
45. Confidential interview.
46. 8.3.87, *Observer*.
47. G. Howe *Conflict of Loyalty*, London: Macmillan, 1994, p. 488.
48. 23.11.88, *Daily Mirror*, 24.11.88, *Guardian*.
49. 27.11.88, *Observer*.
50. Cited in Bogdanor *Monarchy and the Constitution*, p. 287.
51. Adamson *Last Empire*, p. 109.
52. 26.9.87, *The Times*.
53. Bogdanor *Monarchy and the Constitution*, p. 282.
54. 2.10.87, *The Times*.
55. 26.9.86, *Guardian*.
56. 13.3.90, *The Times*.

Chapter Twenty-Two

1. 16.10.86, *Guardian*.
2. Howe *Conflict of Loyalty*, p. 381.
3. Lord Howe: interview.
4. Cited in Dimbleby *Prince of Wales*, p. 316, 391.
5. P. Chippindale and C. Horrie *Stick It Up Your Punter! The Rise and Fall of the Sun*, London: Heinemann, 1990, p. 106.
6. 28.12.86, *Sunday Times*.
7. David Cannadine in 8.2.92, *Financial Times*.
8. Confidential interview.
9. A. Morton *Inside Kensington Palace*, London: Michael O'Mara Books, 1987, p. 91.
10. *Knockout: The Grand Charity Tournament with a Foreword by H.R.H. Prince Edward*, London: Collins, 1987, p. 8.
11. Confidential interviews.
12. *Knockout: The Grand Charity Tournament*, p. 3.
13. P. James *Prince Edward: A Life in the*

Spotlight, London: Piatkus, 1992, pp. 106-9.
14. 21.6.87, Sunday Times.
15. 7.6.88, Sun.
16. 21.6.87, Sunday Times.
17. 2.11.87, The Times.
18. Nairn Enchanted Glass. p. 93, p. 27, p. 53, p. 115, p. 53.
19. 6.2.89, Daily Telegraph.
20. 2.10.90, Daily Mail.
21. Royal Finances, London: Buckingham Palace, 1995, Second Edition, p. 6.
22. 25.7.90, Guardian.
23. Confidential interview.
24. 26.1.92, Observer.
25. Allison and Riddell (eds) Royal Encyclopedia, p. 323.
26. Cited in 24.8.89, Daily Express.
27. 4.2.91, Sun.
28. Royal Finances, p. 6.
29. 18.2.91, Daily Telegraph.
30. 4.2.91, Sun.
31. Howe Conflict of Loyalty, pp. 639, 663.
32. 23.2.91, Guardian.
33. 31.1.91, Sun.
34. 5.1.89, ibid.
35. 26.2.91, The Times.
36. 17.5.91, Daily Telegraph.
37. Nairn Enchanted Glass, p. 84.
38. 24.1.92, Sun (Scotland).
39. 26.11.92, Guardian.
40. 5.7.91, Daily Telegraph.
41. Cited in Nairn Enchanted Glass, p. 327.
42. 5.1.92, People.
43. Sampson The Essential Anatomy of Britain, London: Hodder & Stoughton, 1992.
44. Cited in Nairn Enchanted Glass, p. 328.
45. 30.1.92, The Times.
46. 22.1.90, 24.1.92, Guardian.
47. Morton Diana: Her True Story, p. 137.
48. 30.1.92, 29.1.92, The Times.
49. 19.1.92, Sunday Times.
50. 26.1.92, Observer.
51. 8.2.92, Financial Times.
52. 19.1.92, Sunday Times.
53. Confidential interviews and information.
54. 6.2.92, Daily Telegraph.
55. The Monarchy Revisited, London: W. H. Smith, 1992, p. 22.
56. 19.12.92, Independent.
57. 29.1.92, The Times.

Chapter Twenty-Three

1. 24.1.92, Guardian.
2. 26.2.92, ibid.
3. G. Winterton Monarchy to Republic: The Australian Republican Government, Melbourne: Oxford University Press, 1986, pp. 1-13.
4. 20.3.92, Guardian.
5. Confidential interviews.
6. Sampson Essential Anatomy of Britain, p. 57.
7. 13.7.92, Daily Express.
8. Confidential interviews.
9. Morton Diana: Her True Story, p. 79, pp. 134-8.
10. 12.2.93, Guardian.
11. Sir Edward Pickering: interview.
12. Cited in A. Morton Diana: Her New Life, London: Michael O'Mara Books, 1994, pp. 45-6, 74.
13. Confidential interview.
14. 30.8.92, Sunday Times.
15. Confidential interview.
16. Cited in 12.2.93, Guardian.
17. 14.9.92, Guardian.
18. 14.9.92, Today.
19. 28.9.92, Guardian.
20. 21.11.92, ibid.
21. Lord Buxton: interview.
22. 16.2.87, Sun.
23. 25.11.92, The Times.
24. 25.11.92, Guardian, The Times.
25. 26.11.92, Guardian.
26. Tax and Parliamentary Annuities: Lord Chamberlain's Statement, 11.2.93.
27. Confidential interview.
28. Statement, 11.2.93.
29. Confidential interview.
30. 19.12.92, Independent.

31. Cited in 12.2.93, *Guardian*.
32. 12.2.93, *The Times*.
33. A. N. Wilson *The Rise and Fall of the House of Windsor*, London: Sinclair-Stevenson, 1993, p. 176.
34. 12.2.93, *Guardian*.
35. 5.1.93, ibid.
36. 1.12.92, *The Times*.
37. 12.9.93, *Observer*.
38. 2.8.93, *Daily Express*.
39. 7.3.93, *The Times*.
40. Confidential interview.
41. 21.9.93, 22.10.93, *Guardian*.
42. 9.12.93, *The Times*.
43. Douglas Hurd: interview.
44. A. Barnett (ed) *Power and the Throne: The Monarchy Debate*, London: Vintage, 1994, pp. 57, 209–10.
45. S. F. Mount *The British Constitution Now*, London: Heinemann, 1992, p. 42.
46. A. N. Wilson *The Rise and Fall of the House of Windsor*, London: Sinclair Stevenson, 1993, p. 156.
47. Barnett *Power and the Throne*, p. 59.
48. S. Haseler *The End of the House of Windsor: Birth of a British Republic*, London: I. B. Taurus, 1993, p. 111.
49. Wilson *Rise and Fall*, pp. 201–2.
50. Barnett (ed) *Power and the Throne*, p. 202.
51. Mount, *British Constitution*, p. 101.
52. 2.6.93, *Daily Mail*.
53. 24.9.93, *Guardian*.
54. 5.7.94, 6.7.94, *The Times*.
55. Dimbleby *Prince of Wales*, p. 19.
56. 19.12.92, *Independent*.
57. 2.6.93, *Daily Mail*.
58. Confidential interview.
59. Prochaska, *Royal Bounty*, p. 190.
60. *Theatres of Memory: Past and Present in Contemporary Culture*, London: Verso, 1994, Vol. 1, pp. 259-71.
61. Confidential interviews.
62. 21.11.95, *The Times*.
63. Confidential interviews.
64. 21.12.95, *The Times*.
65. *Elizabeth's Britain 1926-1986*, Twickenham: Country Life Books, 1986, p. 346.

66. 5.3.96, *Independent*.
67. 5.3.96, 24.9.93, *Guardian*.
68. Confidential interviews.
69. Duchess of Grafton: interview.

Chapter Twenty-Four

1. 16.7.96, *The Times*.
2. M. Warner *Alone of All Her Sex: the myth and cult of the Virgin Mary*, Weidenfeld, London, 1976, p.?
3. *Mirror, Sun* 16.7.96.
4. Sarah, Duchess of York *My Story*, Simon and Schuster, London, 1997, p 195.
5. Confidential interviews.
6. 15.4.96, 26.2.96, 20.4.96, *Daily Express*.
7. 21.4.96, Anthony Barnett, in *Independent on Sunday*.
8. 15.4.96.
9. 20.4.96, *Independent*.
10. 20.4.96.
11. 19.4.96, *Daily Telegraph*.
12. 20.4.96.
13. London, 1996, pp. 1–10.
14. 12.8.96, *The Times*.
15. 12.8.96, *Daily Telegraph*.
16. 20.11.95, 12.8.96, *The Times*.
17. Confidential interview.
18. 20.8.96, *Guardian*.
19. 20.8.96, *Daily Telegraph*.
20. 16.10.96, Robert Hardman in *Daily Telegraph*.
21. 27.12.96, *Guardian*.
22. 7.3.97, *Daily Telegraph*.
23. 3.97, *Financial Times*.
24. 20.7.97, *Sunday Times*.
25. A. Rawnsley *Servants of the People: The Inside Story of New Labour*, Hamish Hamilton, London, 2000, p. 66, p. 69.
26. Confidential interview.
27. 28.8.96, 1.12.95, *The Times*.
28. 25.7.96, *Daily Telegraph*.
29. See T. Harrison *Defenders of the Faith: The Church and the Crisis of the Monarchy*, Fount, London, 1996.
30. 27.7.96, *The Times*.

31. C. Buchanan *Cut the Connection: Disestablishment and the Church of England*, Darton, Longman and Todd, London, 1994, p. 137.
32. 14.7.96, *Sunday Times*.
33. 13.7.96, *Daily Telegraph*.
34. See 2.9.97, *Guardian*.
35. 2.9.96, *Sunday Times*.
36. 25.8.96, *News of the World, Sunday Times*.
37. 2.2.97, *Mail on Sunday*.
38. 16.9.96, *The Times*.
39. John Charmley 20.6.97, *Sunday Telegraph*.
40. 20.6.97, *Sunday Telegraph*.
41. See D. Souhami *Mrs Keppel and her Daughter*, HarperCollins, London, 1996, p. 52.
42. 19.7.97, *The Times*.
43. 18.7.97, *Independent*.
44. 19.7.97, 18.7.97, *The Times*.
45. 20.7.97, *Sunday Times*.
46. A. Morton *Diana: Her True Story – In Her Own Words*, Michael O'Mara Books, London, 1997, p. 263.
47. 19.7.97, *The Times*.
48. 20.7.97, *Sunday Times*.
49. 21.7.97, *The Times*.
50. 8.7.97, *Sun*.
51. 19.7.97, *The Times*
52. 6.8.97, *Daily Telegraph*.
53. ?.7.97, *The Times*.
54. Confidential interviews.
55. P.D. Jephson *Shadows of A Princess: Diana, Princess of Wales 1987–1996 – An Intimate Account by Her Private Secretary*, HarperCollins, London, 2000, pp. 290, 337.
56. Confidential interviews.
57. *English Constitution*, p. 96.
58. Confidential interviews.
59. Jephson *Shadows*, p. 372.
60. Confidential interview.
61. *The Princess in the Mirror*, Chatto and Windus, London, 1985, p.55.
62. Martyn Gregory *Diana: The Last Days*, Virgin, London, 1999, pp. 2–3.
63. Confidential interview.
64. *Shadows of a Princess*, p. 372.

65. Confidential interview.
66. C. Hutchins and D. Midgeley *Diana on the Edge: Inside the Mind of the Princess of Wales*, Smith Gryphon, London, 1996, pp. 208–11.
67. 10.6.97, *The Times*.
68. Confidential interview.
69. 21.8.97, *Guardian*; T. Sancton and T. Macleod *Death of a Princess: An Investigation*, Weidenfeld, London, 1998, p. 113.
70. 27.8.97, 28.8.97, 29.8.97, *The Times*.
71. Confidential interview.
72. 7.9.96, *Sunday Telegraph*.
73. Gregory *Diana*, p. 225.
74. In B. MacArthur (ed) *Requiem, Diana, Princess of Wales 1961–1997. Memorials and Tributes*, Pavilion Books, London, p. 194.
75. Gregory *Diana*, pp. 77–8, pp. 66–75.
76. Private information.
77. Gregory *Diana*, p. 75.

Chapter Twenty-Five

1. 13.10.97, *The Times*.
2. 9.11.97, *Independent on Sunday*.
3. J. Rentoul *Tony Blair: Prime Minister*, Little, Brown, London, 2001, p. 344.
4. C. Andersen *The Day Diana Died*, Blake, London, 1999, pp. 203–4, 218.
5. Confidential interview.
6. Rawnsley *Servants of the People*, p. 143.
7. Confidential interviews.
8. J.B. Kamerman *Death in the Midst of Life: Social and Cultural Influences on Death, Grief and Mourning*, Prentice Hall, Englewood Cliffs, 1988, p. 83.
9. Author's observation. H. Killingray, et al, (eds) *Poems for a Princess: In Memory of Diana, Princess of Wales 1961–97*, Anchor Books, Woodston, 1998, p. 259.
10. 3.9.97, *Guardian*.
11. 3.9.97, *The Times*.
12. 3.9.97, *Guardian*.
13. 7.9.97, *Sunday Times*.
14. Rentoul *Tony Blair*, p. 240; private information.

15. Rawnsley attributes 'people's princess' to Alastair Campbell; Rentoul suggests that it may have come from an article by Julie Burchill, months earlier. 'People's princess' was also used in the first edition of this book, published nearly a year before the tragedy to refer, not to Diana, but to the then Princess Elizabeth at the time of her marriage in 1947 (above, p. 126). 'People's Monarchy' had been used by the historian John Charnley, and no doubt other variations were current.
16. Confidential interview.
17. 2.9.97, *The Times*.
18. 2.9.97.
19. 7.9.97, *Sunday Times*.
20. Confidential interview.
21. Cited in T. Lutz *Crying: The Natural and Cultural History of Tears*, Norton, New York, 1999, p. 222.
22. Confidential interviews.
23. Cited 3.9.97, *The Times*.
24. Confidential interview.
25. Ibid.
26. Confidential interview.
27. 3.9.97, *The Times*; Rawnsley *Servants of the People*, p. 65.
28. 4.9.97, *The Times*.
29. Confidential interviews.
30. 4.9.97, *The Times*.
31. Quoted by K. Rose 7.9.97, *Sunday Telegraph*.
32. 7.9.97, *Sunday Times*.
33. Rawnsley *Servants of the People*, p. 66.
34. Confidential interviews.
35. J. Goody *The Culture of Flowers*, Cambridge University Press, Cambridge, 1993, p. 228.
36. 7.9.97, *Sunday Telegraph*.
37. Myers 'Broadcast interviews about Princess Diana', pp. 176–7.
38. 7.9.97, *)bserver*.
39. MacArthur (ed) *Requiem*, p. ??
40. Myers 'Entitlement and sincerity', p. 167.
41. 5.9.97, *Guardian*.
42. 4.9.97, *The Times*.
43. 5.9.97, *Guardian*.
44. Confidential interview.
45. 5.9.97, *The Times*.
46. 6.9.97, *Independent*.
47. ibid.
48. Rawnsley *Servants of the People*, p. 67.
49. Confidential interviews.
50. 6.9.97, *The Times*.
51. Confidential interviews.
52. 6.9.97, *Guardian*.
53. Rawnsley *Servants of the People*, p. 68.
54. 11.9.97, *Daily Telegraph*.
55. 7.9.97, *Sunday Times*.
56. 7.9.97 ??
57. MacArthur (ed) *Requiem*, p. 33.
58. 7.9.97, *Observer*.
59. Simon Hoggart 5.9.97, *Guardian*.
60. O. Bland *The Royal Way of Death*, Constable, London, 1986, pp. 265, 190.
61. Confidential interview.
62. Bland, *The Royal Way of Death*, p. 190.
63. Confidential interview.
64. 7.9.97, *Sunday Times*.
65. 7.9.97, *Observer*.
66. 7.9.97, *Sunday Times*.
67. 7.9.97, *Independent on Sunday*.
68. 8.9.97, *The Times*.

Chapter Twenty-Six

1. 14.9.97, *Observer*.
2. T.W. Aveling *Princely Greatness Yielding to Death: A Sermon*, John Snow, London, 1861, p. 5.
3. Cited in S.C. Behrendt *Royal Mourning and Regency Culture: Elegies and Memorials of Princess Charlotte*, Macmillan, London, 1997, pp. 20, 24–5.
4. Cited in ibid, p. 46.
5. In Behrendt *Royal Mourning*, pp. 1, 20.
6. Sir John Peel, in H.V. Corbett (ed) *A Royal Catastrophe*, Vincent Corbett, Broadway, 1985, p. 56.
7. Confidential interview.
8. MacArthur (ed) *Requiem*, p. 148, 194.

9. Morton *Diana*, p. 77.
10. B. Campbell *Diana, Princess of Wales: How Sexual Politics Shook The Monarchy*, Women's Press, London, 1998, pp. 90, 133–4.
11. Jephson *Shadows*, p. 282.
12. MacArthur (ed) *Requiem*, p. 206.
13. Campbell *Diana*, pp. 152, 172.
14. 6.9.97, *Guardian*, cited in ibid, p.172.
15. V. Brittain *Death of Dignity: Angola's Civil War*, Pluton, London, 1998, p. 69.
16. N. Owen *Diana: The People's Princess*, Carlton, London, 1997, p. 31, 71.
17. A.V. Dicey *Introduction to the Study of the Law of the Constitution*, Macmillan, London, 1885, p. 462.
18. R. Burghart in D. Cannadine and S. Price (eds) *Rituals of Royalty*, Cambridge University Press, Cambridge, 1987, p. 269.
19. Buchanan *Cut the Connection*, pp. 137–8.
20. M. Bloch *The Royal Touch: Sacred Monarchy and Scrofula in England and France*, Routledge and Kegan Paul, London,1973, p. 266.
21. J.S. Billing 'The King's Touch for Scrofula', *Proceedings of the Charaka Club*, Vol.II, 1911, p. 68.
22. W.A. Chaney *The Cult of Kingship in Anglo-Saxon England: the transition from paganism to Christianity*, Manchester University Press, Manchester, 1970, 72–3.
23. N. Woolf *The Sovereign Remedy: Touchpieces and the King's Evil*, British Association of Numismatics Societies, London, 1990, p. 16; Billing's 'King's Touch', p 70.
24. Billing's 'King's Touch', p. 64.
25. Denise A. Johnson, in p. 343.
26. Bloch.
27. Woolf *Sovereign Remedy*, p. 24.28.
28. Bloch *Royal Touch*, pp. 12–13, 207–10.
29. *English Constitution*, p. 89.
30. C.J. Boulton *Erskine and May's Treatise on the Law, Privileges, Proceedings and Usage of Parliament*, (21st ed), Butterworths, London, 1989, pp. 8, 529. N. Page *A Dr Johnson Chronology*, Macmillan, London, 1990, p. 1; C. Hibbert *The Personal History of Samuel Johnson*, Penguin, Harmondsworth, 1984, p. 6; P. Rogers *The Samuel Johnson Encyclopedia*, Greenwood Press, Westport, 1996, p. 354; C.J. Boswell *Life of Johnson* (ed. R.W. Chapman) Oxford University Press, Oxford, 1980, p. 32.
31. Bloch *Royal Touch*, p. 220.
32. Woolf *Sovereign Remedy*, pp. 26–8.
33. Bloch *Royal Touch*, p. 222.
34. *The Political works of James I*, Harvard University Press, Cambridge, Mass, 1918, p. 64.
35. Chaney *Cult of Kingship*, p. 74.
36. P.A. Wright *The Pictorial History of the Royal Maundy*, Pitkin, London, 1973, pp. 3–8.
37. Bogdanor *Monarchy*, p. 305.
38. L. Cleveland 'Royalty as symbolic drama: the 1970 New Zealand tour', Vol.XI, *Journal of Commonwealth Political Studies*, 1973, pp. 28–45.
39. Hocart *Kingship*, p. 36.
40. Cannadine and Price (eds) *Rituals of Royalty*, p. 19.
41. *English Constitution*, p. 91.
42. J.N. Figgis *The Divine Right of Kings*, Harper and Row, New York, 1965 ed., p. 171.
43. MacArthur (ed) *Requiem*, p. 195.
44. Confidential interview. As Marina Warner has pointed out, most pilgrims to Lourdes come away believing that they have seen a miracle while they were there (*Alone of All Her Sex*, p. 310).
45. S. Lowrie *The Princess in the Mirror*, Chatto and Windus, London, 1985, p. 133.
46. Campbell *Diana*, p. 193.
47. Lowrie *Princess in the Mirror*, p. 133, 111.
48. *Alone of All Her Sex*, p. 235.

Chapter Twenty-Seven

1. W. Shakespeare *Henry V*, Act IV scene I.
2. J. Thomas 'A Fairy Story? Popular Attitudes of Lesbians and Gays to the Death of Princess Diana'. Unpublished paper, 2001, p. 8.
3. 7.9.97, *Sunday Telegraph*.
4. 7.9.97, *Independent on Sunday*.
5. 7.9.97, *Sunday Telegraph*.
6. 8.9.97, *The Times*.
7. 7.9.97, *Independent on Sunday*.
8. Cited in B. MacArthur (ed) *Requiem*, p. 16.
9. 7.9.97, *Independent on Sunday*.
10. 7.9.97, *Sunday Times*.
11. 7.9.97, *Observer*.
12. 7.9.97, *Sunday Times*.
13. 7.9.97, *Independent on Sunday*.
14. 7.9.97, *Sunday Telegraph*.
15. *The Diana, Princess of Wales Memorial Fund, Annual Review 1999*, London, p. 13.
16. MacArthur (ed) *Requiem*, p. 183.
17. 9.97, *Observer*.
18. MacArthur (ed) *Requiem*, p. 221.
19. E. Schor *Bearing the Dead: The British Culture of Mourning from the Enlightenment to Victoria*, Princeton University Press, 1994, pp. 251–2.
20. *English Constitution*, p. 27.
21. Confidential interviews.
22. 6.10.97, 8.10.97, *Daily Telegraph*.
23. 13.10.97, 20.10.97, *The Times*.
24. 5.11.97, *Daily Telegraph*.
25. 18.10.97, *Daily Express*.
26. 20.11.97, *The Times*.
27. The phrase is used by Caroline Ellis and Minna Thornton in a book published eight years earlier, *Women and Fashion: A New Look,* Quartet, London, 1989, pp. 152–4.
28. 2.11.97, *Sunday Telegraph*.
29. 20.11.97, *The Times*.
30. 21.11.97, *Daily Telegraph*.
31. P. Toynbee and D. Walker *Did Things Get Better? An Audit of Labour's Successes and Failures*, Penguin, London, 2001, p. 203.
32. Confidential interviews.
33. 1.11.98, *Independent on Sunday*.
34. 5.3.99, *The Times*.
35. Confidential interview.
36. 20.2.98, 28.3.98, *The Times*.
37. 11.12.97, *Daily Mirror*.
38. 20.4.98, 28.5.98, 12.12.97, 28.8.98, *The Times*.
39. 16.8.98, *Sunday Telegraph*, 24.7.98, 20.9.98, *The Times*.
40. 24.9.98, *Guardian*.
41. 24.9.98, *Sun*.
42. Confidential interviews
43. 12.11.98, *Financial Times*.
44. 1.3.99, 9.5.99, 8.7.99, *The Times*.
45. 6.4.96. *Guardian*.
46. 14.11.99, *Observer*.
47. 14.11.99, *Sunday Times*.
48. 15.11.99, *Daily Telegraph*.
49. M. Turnbull *The Reluctant Republic*, Heinemann, Port Melbourne, Australia, 1993.
50. According to an AGB-McNair poll, 8.2.97, *Financial Times*.
51. Transcript of Keating interview with Paul Lyneham, *Special Edition 7.30 Report*, ABC TV, 8 June 1995.
52. 28.1.96, *Sunday Express*.
53. *Sydney Morning Herald*, cited in *Evening Standard*, 31.10.96.
54. 3.J. Duruz and C. Johnson in A. Kear and D. Sternberg (eds) *Mourning Diana: Nature, Culture and the Performance of Grief,* Routledge, London, 1999, p. 143. Kim Beezley, the Labor Opposition leader, remarked that he was surprised how much he missed Diana, given that 'issues affecting the British royal family are not the first thing in my mind every morning'.
55. 2.11.97, *Sunday Telegraph*.
56. 9.11.97, *Observer*.
57. 23.1.96, *Sunday Times*.
58. 7.4.97, *The Times*.
59. 3.2.98, *Guardian*.

60. Christopher Hitchens *Vanity Fair*, September 1998.
61. 22.7.99, *The Times*.
62. 11.10.99, 1.11.99, *Guardian*.
63. 7.11.99, *Observer*.
64. 8.11.99, *Guardian*.
65. 8.11.99, *Independent*.
66. 7.11.99, *Observer*.
67. 5.11.99, *Guardian*.
68. Confidential interview.
69. 18.3.00, *The Times*.

Chapter Twenty-Eight

1. Confidential interview.
2. *Observer*, 18.8.99.
3. Confidential interview.
4. Chris Blackhurst, *Independent on Sunday*, 30.11.97.
5. 21.6.98, *Sunday Telegraph*.
6. 16.7.98, *Guardian*.
7. 13.4.94, *Daily Mail*.
8. 7.1.99, *The Times*; confidential interview.
9. 7.1.99, *Guardian*
10. 14.6.99, 18.6.99, *Daily Telegraph*.
11. *Monarchy* p. 299.
12. C. Hitchens *The Monarchy*, Chatto and Windus, London, 1990, p. 2.
13. Confidential interview.
14. *English Constitution*, pp. 87–98.
15. See Nicolson *King George V*: pp. 61–3.; also K.C. Wheare 'Walter Bagehot', *Proceedings of the British Academy*, Vol. LX (1974), Oxford University Press, London, pp. 18–19. Nicolson found in the Royal Archives a summary of Bagehot's chapter on Monarchy written by George V as Duke of York in 1894, concluding (in the Duke's words) that the institution 'is still a great political force & offers a splendid career to an able monarch'.
16. See Mount *British Constitution Now*, p. 44.
17. Jennings *Queen's Government*, p. 30; See also I. Jenning's, *Cabinet*

Government, Cambridge University Press, Cambridge, 1936, p. 259.
18. R. Samuel, *Theatres Memory* Vol. II *Island stories, unravelling Britain* (ed. A. Light, et al), Verso, London, 1998; N. Machiavelli *The Prince*, Norton, New York, 1992, p. 34.
19. Dicey *Introduction*, p. 461. See also A. Jay *Elizabeth R: The Role of the Monarchy Today*, BBC Books, London, 1992, pp. 62–4.
20. R. Samuel *Theatres of Memory*, Vol. I, p. 203.
21. A. Marr *Ruling Britannia: The Failure and Future of British Democracy*, Michael Joseph, London, 1995, p. 233.
22. *English Constitution*, p. 48
23. Confidential interview.
24. J.K. Galbraith *The Culture of Contentment*, Sinclair-Stevenson, London, 1992, p. 46.
25. The British Monarchy: The Official Website, http://www.royal.gov.uk.
26. Confidential interview.
27. See Prochaska *Royal Bounty*, also F. Prochaska *The Republic of Britain 1760–2000*, Allen Lane, London, 2000.
28. Confidential interview.
29. *Monarchy*, p. 56.
30. See B. Pimlott *Should the Arts Be Popular?*, Lloyds/TSB Forum, London, 1999, pp. 12–15; R. Scruton *An Intelligent Person's Guide to Modern Culture*, Duckworth, London, 1998, pp. 1–5.
31. 1.11.00.
32. 2.4.01, 11.4.01, *Guardian*.
33. 10.4.01, *Daily Mail*.
34. 25.4.01, 17.7.00, 21.7.00.
35. 11.12.00, *The Times*.
36. 12.12.00.
37. 17.10.00, *Guardian*.
38. Confidential interview
39. 25.7.00, 8.1.01, *Guardian*.
40. 10.4.01, *Daily Mail*.
41. Confidential interviews.

SOURCES AND
SELECT BIBLIOGRAPHY

Sources mentioned in the Notes, and some others that have been especially useful, are listed below. The names of people interviewed are in the Foreword and Preface.

PRIVATE AND OTHER UNPUBLISHED PAPERS

Use has been made of the following collections of papers and letters (the current holder is given in brackets):

A. V. Alexander (Churchill College, Cambridge)
Sir Hardy Amies (Sir Hardy Amies)
Lord Attlee (Bodleian Library, Oxford)
Lord Avon (Birmingham University)
Lord Beaverbrook (House of Lords)
Lord Bradwell (Christ Church, Oxford)
Neville Chamberlain (Churchill College, Cambridge)
Chartwell (Churchill College, Cambridge)
Sir John Colville (Churchill College, Cambridge)
Hugh Dalton (British Library of Political and Economic Science)
Dwight D. Eisenhower (Dwight D. Eisenhower Library)
Lord Fisher (Lambeth Palace)
John F. Kennedy (John F. Kennedy Library)
Sir Alan Lascelles (Churchill College, Cambridge)
Lord Mountbatten (University of Southampton)
Harold Nicolson (Balliol College, Oxford)
F. D. Roosevelt (F. D. Roosevelt Library)
Lord Swinton (Churchill College, Cambridge)
Harry S. Truman (Harry S. Truman Library)

PUBLIC AND INSTITUTIONAL RECORDS

1. State Papers

State papers at the Public Record Office, Kew, relating to the Queen and the Monarchy are available, under the thirty-year rule, for the period up to 1965, and are to be found under a number of headings. Papers consulted include: minutes and papers of the Cabinet and its committees (CAB); Ministry of Defence (DEFE); Dominions Office (DOM); the Foreign Office (FO); the office of the Prime Minister (PREM).

2. Other Records

BBC Written Archives (Caversham Park); Royal Archives (Royal Library, Windsor); *The Windsors*: interview transcripts (Brook Productions); unpublished obituary of the Queen, *Manchester Guardian*, 1957 (*Guardian* library); The British Monarchy: The Official Website *http://www.royal.gov.uk*.

3. Published Official Documents

Hansard: House of Commons Debates (HC Debs) Fifth Series; Report from the Select Committee on the Civil List, 1971; Minutes of Evidence, Select Committee on the Civil List, 1971; Appendices to the Minutes of Evidence, Select Committee on the Civil List, 1971.

PRESS AND PERIODICAL LITERATURE

Newspapers

Carmarthen Journal, Daily Express, Daily Graphic, Daily Herald, Daily Mail, Daily Mirror, Daily Sketch, Daily Star, Daily Telegraph, East African Standard, Evening News, Evening Standard, Financial Times, Guardian, Independent, Indian Express, Irish Times, Mail on Sunday, Manchester Guardian, Morning Star, Newcastle Chronicle, News Chronicle, News of the World, Observer, People, Saturday Evening Post, Star, Sun, Sunday Dispatch, Sunday Express, Sunday Graphic, Sunday Mirror, Sunday Pictorial, Sunday Telegraph, Sunday Times, Sydney

SOURCES AND SELECT BIBLIOGRAPHY

Morning Herald, The Times, Today, Washington Evening Star, Washington Post.

Journals and Periodicals

Cambridge Quarterly, Literary Review, Listener, National and English Review, New Statesman, Now!, Spectator, Time Magazine, Twentieth Century.

SECONDARY SOURCES

1. *Autobiography, Biography, Diaries, Letters, Memoirs*

E. Acland *The Princess Elizabeth*, Toronto: The John C. Winston Co. Ltd, 1937.
P. Annigoni *An Artist's Life*, London: W. H. Allen, 1977.
Queen Alexandra of Yugoslavia *For a King's Love; The Intimate Recollections of Queen Alexandra of Yugoslavia*, London: Odhams Press, 1956.
—*Prince Philip*, London: Mayfair Books, 1961.
Princess Alice, Countess of Athlone *For My Grandchildren: Some Reminiscences*, London: Evans, 1966.
H. Amies *Still Here: An Autobiography*, London: Weidenfeld and Nicolson, 1984.
N. Barrymaine *The Story of Peter Townsend*, London: Peter Davies, 1958.
C. Beaton *The Strenuous Years, Diaries 1948–1955*, London: Weidenfeld and Nicolson, 1973.
T. Benn *Out of the Wilderness: Diaries 1963–67*, London: Hutchinson, 1987.
R. Bevins *The Greasy Poll: A Personal Account of the Realities of British Politics*, London: Hodder and Stoughton, 1965.
Lord Blake *The Office of Prime Minister*, Oxford: British Acadamy, Oxford University Press, 1975.
M. Bloch (ed.) *Wallis and Edward: Letters 1931–1937*, London: Weidenfeld and Nicolson, 1986.
S. G. Bocca *Elizabeth and Philip*, New York: Henry Holt & Co, 1953.
B. Boothroyd *Philip: An Informal Biography*, London: Longman, 1971.

743

S. Bradford *George VI*, London: Weidenfeld and Nicolson, 1989.

P. Brandon *Ike: The Life and Times of Dwight D. Eisenhower*, London: Secker and Warburg, 1987.

R. A. Butler *The Art of the Possible: The Memoirs of Lord Butler*, London: Hamish Hamilton, 1971.

J. Callaghan *Time and Chance*, London: Collins, 1987.

C. R. Cammell *Memoirs of Annigoni*, London: Allan Wingate, 1956.

J. Campbell *Edward Heath*, London: Cape, 1994.

D. Carlton *Anthony Eden: a Biography*, London: Allen Lane, 1981.

E. Carpenter *Archbishop Fisher*, Canterbury: Canterbury Press, 1991.

P. Carrrington *Reflections on Things Past: The Memoirs of Lord Carrington*, London: Collins, 1988.

B. Castle *The Castle Diaries 1964–70*, London: Weidenfeld and Nicolson, 1984.

H. Cathcart *The Married Life of the Queen*, London: W. H. Allen, London, 1970.

M. Chance *Our Princesses and Their Dogs*, London: John Murray, 1936.

A. Clark (ed) *'A Good Innings'. The Papers of Viscount Lee of Fareham*, London: Murray, 1974.

S. Clark *Palace Diary*, London: Harrap, 1958.

T. Claydon and P. Craig *Diana: Story of A Princess*: Hodder and Stoughton, 2001.

J. R. Clynes *Memoirs: Volume 2 1924–1937*, London: Hutchinson, 1937.

J. Colville *Strange Inheritance*, Salisbury: Michael Russell, 1983.
—Colville *The Fringes of Power: 10 Downing Street Diaries 1939–1955*, London: Hodder & Stoughton, 1985.

E. H. Cookridge *From Battenberg to Mountbatten*, London: Arthur Barker Ltd, 1966.

H. Cordet *Born Bewildered*, London: Peter Davies, 1961.

M. Crawford *Queen Elizabeth II*, London: George Newnes Ltd, 1952.
—*Happy and Glorious*, London: Newnes Ltd, 1953.
—*The Little Princesses*, London: Cassells, 1950.
—*The Little Princesses*, London: Duckworth, new edn., 1993.

E. Crankshaw (ed) *Khruschev Remembered*, London: Deutsch, 1971.

S. Crosland *Tony Crosland*, London: Cape, 1982.

R. Crossman *The Diaries of a Cabinet Minister, Vol. I Minister of Housing 1964–66*, London: Hamish Hamilton and Jonathan Cape, 1975.

—*The Backbench Diaries of Richard Crossman*, J. Morgan (ed), London: Hamish Hamilton and Jonathan Cape, 1981.

N. Davies *William: King for the 21st Century*: Blake, London, 2000.

J. Dean *H.R.H. Prince Philip, Duke of Edinburgh: A Portrait*, London: Hale, 1954.

N. Dempster *H.R.H. The Princess Margaret: A Life Unfulfilled*, London: Quartet Books, 1981, p. 23.

J. Dimbleby *The Prince of Wales: A Biography*, London: Little, Brown, 1994.

C. W. Domville-Fife *King George VI and Queen Elizabeth*, London: Rankin Brothers Ltd, 1937.

The Memoirs of the Rt. Hon. Sir Anthony Eden: Full Circle, London: Cassell, 1980.

H.R.H. The Duke of Edinburgh *A Question of Balance*, Salisbury: Michael Russell, 1982.

A. Edwards *Royal Sisters*, London: Collins, 1990.

Princess Elizabeth: The Illustrated Story of Twenty-One Years in the Life of the Heir Presumptive, London: Odhams Press, 1947.

J. Ellis (ed) *Thatched with Gold: The Memoir of Mabel Countess of Airlie*, London: Hutchinson, 1962.

H. Evans *Downing Street Diary: The Macmillan Years 1957–1963*, London: Hodder and Stoughton, 1981.

T. E. Evans (ed) *The Killearn Diaries 1934–1946*, London: Sidgwick and Jackson, 1972.

S. Evelyn Thomas *Princess Elizabeth: Wife and Mother: A Souvenir of the Birth of Prince Charles of Edinburgh*, London, S. Evelyn Thomas, 1949.

N. Fisher *Iain Macleod*, London: Deutsch, 1973.

R. Flamini *Sovereign: Elizabeth II and the Windsor Dynasty*, London: Bantam Press, 1991.

C. Frost *Coronation June 2 1953*, Arthur Hacker Ltd, London, 1978.

C. de Gaulle *Memoirs of Hope*, Weidenfeld and Nicolson, London, 1971.

M. Gilbert *Churchill: A Life*, London: Heinemann, 1991.

J. Gore *King George V: A Personal Memoir*, London: John Murray, 1941.

Greatorex *King George VI: The People's Sovereign*, London: R.T.S. Lutterworth Press, 1939.

Lord Hailsham *A Sparrow's Flight*, London: Collins, 1991.

W. Hamilton *My Queen and I*, London: Quartet Books, 1975.

Lord Harewood *Tongs and the Bones: The Memoirs of Lord Harewood*, London: Weidenfeld and Nicolson, 1981.

K. Harris *The Queen*, London: Weidenfeld and Nicolson, 1994.

D. Hart-Davis (ed) *In Royal Service: The Letters and Journals of Sir Alan Lascelles 1920–1936*, Volume II, London: Hamish Hamilton, 1989.

N. Hartnell *Silver and Gold*, London: Evans Bros, 1955.

B. Hawke *The Autobiography of Bob Hawke*, London: Heinemann, 1994.

C. Higham and R. Moseley *Elizabeth and Philip: The Untold Story*, London Sidgwick and Jackson, 1991.

A. Holden *Charles, Prince of Wales*, London: Weidenfeld and Nicolson, 1979.

Lord Home *The Way the Wind Blows*, London: Collins, 1976.

A. Horne *Macmillan 1957–1986 Vol. II of the Official Biography*, London: Macmillan, 1989.

A. Howard *Rab: The Life of R. A. Butler*, London: Cape, 1987.

G. Howe *Conflict of Loyalty*, London: Macmillan, 1994.

C. Hutchins and P. Thompson *Fergie Confidential: The True Story*, London: Simon and Schuster, 1992.

B. Ingham *Kill the Messenger*, London: HarperCollins, 1991.

P. James *Margaret: A Woman of Conflict*, London: Sidgwick and Jackson, 1990.

—*Prince Edward: A Life in the Spotlight*, London: Judy Piatkus, 1992.

P.D. Jephson *Shadows of A Princess: Diana, Princess of Wales 1987–1996: An Intimate Account By Her Private Secretary*, London: HarperCollins, 2000.

D. Kay *Elizabeth II: Portrait of a Monarch*, London: Ebury Press: 1991.

R. F. Kennedy *Time to Remember: An Autobiography*, London: Collins, 1974, pp. 207–10.

J. Kerr *Matters for Judgement*, London: Sun Books, 1988.

D. Kilmuir *Political Adventure: The Memoirs of the Earl of Kilmuir*, London: Weidenfeld & Nicolson, 1964.

C. King *The Cecil King Diary 1970–1974*, London: Cape, 1976.

A. Jay *Elizabeth R*, London: BBC Books, 1992.

R. Jenkins *Life at the Centre*, London: Macmillan, 1991.

J. G. Lockhart *Cosmo Gordon Lang*, London: Hodder & Stoughton, 1949.

E. Longford *Elizabeth R*, London: Weidenfeld and Nicolson, 1983.

S. Lowry *The Princess in the Mirror*, London: Chatto and Windus, 1985.

N. and J. Mackenzie (eds) *The Wheel of Life: The Diary of Beatrice Webb*, Vol. 4, 1924–43, London: Virago, 1985.

H. Macmillan *Tides of Fortune 1945–1955*, London: Macmillan, 1969.
—*Riding the Storm 1956–1959*, London: Macmillan, 1971.
—*Pointing The Way 1959–1961* London: Macmillan, 1972.
—*Memoirs IV: At the End of the Day*, London: Macmillan, 1973.

Princess Marie Louise *My Memories of Six Reigns*, London: Evans Bros, 1956.

K. and V. McLeish *Long to Reign Over Us. Memories of Coronation Day and of Life in the 1950s*, Bloomsbury, London, 1992.

Lord Moran *Winston Churchill: The Struggle for Survival, 1940–1965*, London: Constable, 1966.

D. Morrah *To Be a King: A Biography of H.R.H. Prince Charles*, London: Arrow Books, 1969.

A. Morrow *The Queen*, London: Granada 1983.

P. Mortimer *Queen Elizabeth: A Life of the Queen Mother*, Harmondsworth: Viking, 1986.

A. Morton and M. Seamark *Andrew the Playboy Prince*, London: Severn House, 1983.

A. Morton *Diana: Her True Story*, London: Michael O'Mara Books Ltd, London 1992.
—*Diana: Her New Life*, London: Michael O'Mara Books, 1994.

M. Muggeridge *Like It Was*, London: Collins, 1981.

L. A. Nicholls *The Crowning of Elizabeth II: A Diary of the Coronation Year*, London: MacDonald and Co, 1953.

H. Nicolson *George V: His Life and Reign* London: Constable, 1952.
—*Diaries and Letters 1930–1939*, Collins, London, 1966.

R. Ollard (ed) *Prince Philip Speaks*, London: Collins, 1960.

N. Owen *Diana: The People's Princess*, London: Carlton, 1997.

J. Parker *Prince Philip: A Critical Biography*, London: Sidgwick and Jackson, 1990.

G. Payn and S. Morley (eds) *The Noël Coward Diaries*, London: Weidenfeld and Nicolson, 1982.

H.R.H. King Peter of Yugoslavia *A King's Heritage: The Memoirs of King Peter of Yugoslavia*, London: Cassell, 1955.

B. Pimlott *Harold Wilson*, London: HarperCollins, 1992.

J. Pope-Hennessy *Queen Mary*, London: Allen and Unwin, 1959.

J. Rentoul *Tony Blair: Prime Minister*, London: Little, Brown, 2001.

R. Rhodes James (ed) *Chips Channon: The Diaries of Sir Henry Channon*, London: Weidenfeld and Nicolson, 1967.

R. Rhodes James *Anthony Eden*, London: Weidenfeld and Nicolson, 1986.

A. Ring *The Story of Princess Elizabeth*, London: John Murray, 1930. —*The Story of Princess Elizabeth Brought up to Date and Including some Stories of Princess Margaret* London: Murray, 1932.

E. Roosevelt *This I Remember*, London: Hutchinson, 1950. —*The Autobiography of Eleanor Roosevelt*, London: Hutchinson, 1962.

K. Rose *King George V*, London: Weidenfeld and Nicolson, 1983.

K. Rose *Kings, Queens and Courtiers*, London: Weidenfeld and Nicolson, 1985.

V. Rothwell *Anthony Eden: A Political Biography*, Manchester: Manchester University Press, 1992.

A. Sampson *Macmillan: A Study in Ambiguity*, London: Allen Lane, 1967.

Sarah, Duchess of York *My Story*, London: Simon and Schuster, 1997.

I. Seward *Prince Edward*, London: Century, 1995.

L. Sheridan *Princess Elizabeth at Home*, Published by Authority of Her Majesty The Queen, London: John Murray, 1944.

D. Souhami *Mrs Keppell and her Daughter*, London: HarperCollins, 1996.

The Story of Our King and Queen, Manchester: Sankey Hudson & Co, 1937.

C. Stuart (ed) *The Reith Diaries*, London: Collins, 1975.

M. Thatcher *The Downing Street Years*, London: HarperCollins, 1993.

F. Towers *The Two Princesses: The Story of the King's Daughters*, London: Pilgrim Press, 1940.

P. Townsend *Time and Chance*, London: William Collins & Sons, 1978.

H. Vickers *Cecil Beaton: The Authorised Biography*, London: Weidenfeld and Nicolson, 1985.

C. Warwick *Princess Margaret*, London: Weidenfeld & Nicolson, 1983.

J. Wheeler-Bennett *George VI: His Life and Reign*, London: Macmillan, 1958.

J. Whittaker *Diana v. Charles*, London: Signet, 1993.

P. M. Williams (ed) *The Diary of Hugh Gaitskell 1945–1956*, London: Cape, 1983.

H. Wilson *The Labour Government 1964–1970: A Personal Record*, London: Weidenfeld and Nicolson, 1971.

—*Memoirs: The Making of a Prime Minister 1916–64*, London: Weidenfeld and Nicolson, 1986.

Duke of Windsor *A King's Story: The Memoirs of H.R.H. The Duke of Windsor*, London: Odhams Press, 1951.

L. V. Wulff *Queen for Tomorrow*, London: Sampson Lowe Maston & Co, 1948.

H. Young *One of Us: A Biography of Margaret Thatcher*, London: Macmillan, 1989.

K. Young *Sir Alec Douglas-Home*, London: J. M. Dent, 1970.

W. R. Young (ed) *Paul Martin: The London Diaries 1975–1979*, Ottawa: University of Ottawa Press, 1988.

P. Ziegler *Mountbatten*, London: Collins, 1985.

—*King Edward VIII: The Official Biography*, London: HarperCollins, 1990.

2. Other Books

D. Adamson *Last Empire*, London: I B Tauris, 1989.

R. Allison and S. Riddell (eds) *The Royal Encyclopedia: The Authoritative Book of the Royal Family*, London: Macmillan, 1991.

C. Andersen *The Day Diana Died*: Morrow, New York, 1998.

H.R.H. Prince Andrew of Greece *Towards Disaster: The Greek Army in Asia Minor in 1921*, London: John Murray, 1930.

Lord Altrincham *The British Constitution: Its Place in the Service of the World*, London: Hutchinson, 1943.

Lord Altrincham (John Grigg) and others, *Is the Monarchy Perfect?* London: John Calder, 1958.

T. Aronson *The Royal Family at War*, London: John Murray, 1993.

T.W. Aveling, *Princely Greatness Yielding to Death: A Sermon*, London: John Snow, 1861.

W. Bagehot *The English Constitution*, (first published 1867), London: Fontana ed., 1993.

A. Barnett (ed) *Power and the Throne: The Monarchy Debate*, London: Vintage, 1994.

B. Baxter *Destiny Called to Them*, New York: Oxford University Press, 1939.

S.C. Behrendt, *Royal Mourning and Regency Culture: Elegies and Memorials of Princess Charlotte*, London: Macmillan, 1997.

R. Belissario *To Tread on Royal Toes*, Aberdeen: Impulse Books, 1972.

M. Billig *Talking of the Royal Family*, London: Routledge, 1992.

P. Black, *The Mystique of Modern Monarchy*, London: Watts & Co, 1953.

R. Blake *The Office of Prime Minister*, Oxford: Oxford University Press, 1975.

—*A History of Rhodesia*, London: Eyre Methuen, 1978.

O. Bland, *The Royal Way of Death*, Constable, London, 1986.

M. Bloch, *The Royal Touch: Sacred Monarchy and Scrofula in England and France*, Routledge and Kegan Paul, London, 1973.

V. Bogdonor *The Monarchy and the Constitution*, Oxford: Clarendon Press, 1995.

C.J. Boulton, *Erskine and May's Treatise on the Law, Privileges, Proceedings and Usage of Parliament* (21st ed.), Butterworths, London, 1989

V. Brittain, *Death of Dignity: Angola's Civil War*, Pluton, London, 1998.

J. Bryan and C.V. Murphy *The Windsor Story*, London: Granada, 1979.

Buchanan *Cut the Connection: Disestablishment and the Church of England*, Darton, Longman and Todd, London, 1994.

A. Burnet *The Derby: The Official Book of the World's Greatest Race*, London: Michael O'Mara Books, 1993.

D. Butler and G. Butler *British Political Facts*, London: Macmillan, 1994.

A. Buxton *The King and His Country*, London: Longmans, Green & Co, 1955.

Campbell *Diana, Princess of Wales: How Sexual Politics Shook the Monarchy*, London: Women's Press, 1998.

J. Campbell *The Queen Rides*, London: Lutterworth Press, 1965.

R. J. Campbell *Sermons for the Coronation of His Majesty King George VI*, London: Skeffinton and Sons Ltd, 1937.

D. Cannadine and S. Price (ed) *Rituals of Royalty: Power and Ceremonial in Traditional Societies*, Cambridge: Cambridge University Press, 1984.

Cannadine and S. Price (eds) *Rituals of Royalty*, Cambridge: Cambridge University Press, 1987.

W.A. Chaney, *The Cult of Kingship in Anglo-Saxon England: The Transition From Paganism to Christianity*, Manchester: Manchester University Press, 1970.

P. Chippindale and C. Horrie *Stick It Up Your Punter! The Rise and Fall of the Sun*, London: Heinemann, 1990.

R. Churchill *The Story of the Coronation,* London: Derek Verschoyle, 1953.

—*Fight for the Tory Leadership: A Contemporary Chronicle*, London: Heinemann, 1964.

W. Clark *From Three Worlds*, London: Sidgwick and Jackson, 1986.

L. Colley *Britons*, London: Yale University Press, 1992.

J. Colville *The New Elizabethans 1952–1977*, London: Collins, 1977.

H.V. Corbett (ed) *A Royal Catastrophe*, Broadway: Vincent Corbett, 1985.

J. Corbitt *Fit for a King: A Book of Intimate Memoirs*, London: Odhams Press, 1956.

Z. Cowen *The British Commonwealth of Nations in a Changing World: Law, Politics and Prospects*, Evanston, Illinois: Northwestern University Press, 1965.

R. Crossman *Inside View: Three Lectures on Prime Ministerial Government*, London: Cape, 1972.

B. Curling *All the Queen's Horses*, London: Chatto and Windus, 1978.

N. Dempster and P. Evans *Behind Palace Doors*, London: Orion, 1993.

G. Dennis *Coronation Commentary*, New York: Dodd, Mead and Co, 1937.

A.V. Dicey *Introduction to the Study of the Law of the Constitution*, Macmillan, London, 1985.

B. Donoughue *Prime Minister: The Conduct of Policy Under Harold Wilson and James Callaghan*, London: Cape 1987.

J. Douglas-Home *Horse Racing in Berkshire*, Stroud: Alan Sutton, 1992.

A. Duncan *The Reality of Monarchy*, London: Heinemann, 1970.

C. Ellis and M. Thornton *Women and Fashion: A New Look*, London: Quartet, 1989.

J.N. Figgis *The Divine Right of Kings,* New York: Harper and Row, 1965 edn.

G. F. Fisher *I Here Present Unto You: Addresses interpreting the Coronation of Her Majesty Queen Elizabeth II*, London: SPCK, 1953.

N. Fisher *The Tory Leaders: Their Stuggle for Power* London: Weidenfeld and Nicolson, 1977.

K. Flower *Serving Secretly: An Intelligence Chief on Record: Rhodesia into Zimbabwe 1964 to 1981*, London: Murray, 1987.

F. Fraser *The Unruly Queen: The Life of Queen Caroline*, London: Macmillan, 1997.

D. Friedman *Inheritance: A Psychological History of the Royal Family*, London: Sidgwick and Jackson, 1990.

P. Fussell *Wartime: Understanding Behaviour in the Second World War*, Oxford: Oxford University Press, 1989.

J.K. Galbraith *The Culture of Contentment*, London: Sinclair-Stevenson, 1992.

J. Goody *The Culture of Flowers*, Cambridge: Cambridge University Press, 1993.

M. Green *A Mirror for Anglo-Saxons*, London: Longmans, 1957.

Martyn Gregory *Diana: The Last Days*, London: Virgin, 1999.

J. Grigg *The History of The Times, Vol VI The Thomson Years 1966–1981*, London: Times Books, 1993.

J. Grigg *The Monarchy Revisted*, London: W.H. Smith Contemporary Paper, 1992.

T. Grove (ed) *The Queen Observed*, London: Pavilion, 1986.

Lord Hailsham *On the Constitution*, London: HarperCollins, 1992.

P. Hall *Royal Fortune: Tax, Money and the Monarchy*, London: Bloomsbury, 1992.

T. Harrison *Defenders of the Faith: The Church and the Crisis of the Monarchy*, London: Fount, 1996.

S. Haseler *The End of the House of Windsor: Birth of a British Republic*, London: I. B. Tauris, 1993.

C. Hardyment *Dream Babies*, Oxford: Oxford University Press, 1984.

L. Harris *Long to Reign Over Us*, London: William Kimber, 1966.

N. Henderson *The Private Office*, London: Weidenfeld and Nicolson, 1984.

P. Hennessy *Whitehall*, London: Fontana Press, 1991.

—*Never Again: Britain 1949–51*, London: Cape, 1992.

—*The Hidden Wiring: Unearthing the British Constitution*, London: Gollancz, 1995.

C. Hibbert *The Court of St James's*, London: Weidenfeld and Nicolson, 1979.

C. Hitchens *The Monarchy*, London: Chatto and Windus, 1990.

E. Hobsbawm and T. Ranger (eds) *The Invention of Tradition*, Cambridge: Cambridge University Press, 1983.

A. M. Hocart *Kingship*, London: Watts & Co, 1941.

B. Hoey *All the Queen's Men: Inside the Royal Household*, London: HarperCollins, 1992.

A. Holden *The Tarnished Crown: Crisis in the House of Windsor*, London: Bantam Press, 1993.

A. Howard and R. West *The Making of the Prime Minister*, London: Cape, 1965.

P. Howard *British Monarchy in the Twentieth Century*, London: Hamish Hamilton, 1977.

Hutchins and D. Midgelcy *Diana on the Edge: Inside the Mind of the Princess of Wales,* London: Smith Gryphon, 1996.

W. Hutton *The State We're In*, London: Cape, 1995.

A. Jay *Elizabeth R: The Role of the Monarchy Today*, London: BBC Books, 1992.

I. Jennings *Cabinet Government,* Cambridge: Cambridge University Press, 1936.

—*The Queen's Government*, Harmondsworth: Penguin, 1954.

D. Judd *Empire: The British Imperial Experience, From 1765 to the Present*, London: Harper Collins, 1996.

J.B. Kamerman *Death in the Midst of Life: Social and Cultural Influences on Death, Grief and Mourning*, Eaglewood Cliffs: Prentice Hall, 1988.

A. Kear and D. Sternberg (eds) *Mourning Diana: Nature, Culture and the Performance of Grief*, London: Routledge, 1999.

H. Killingray et al *Poems for a Princess: In Memory of Diana, Princess of Wales 1961–97*, Woodston: Anchor Books, 1998.

S. King Hall *The Crowning of the King and Queen*, London: Evans Brothers, 1937.

Knockout: The Grand Charity Tournament, with a Foreword by H.R.H. Prince Edward, London: Collins, 1987.

J. Koumoulides *Greece in Transition: Essays in the History of Modern Greece 1821–1974*, London: Zeno, 1977.

K. Kyle *Suez*, London: Weidenfeld and Nicolson, 1991.

R. Lacey *Majesty: Elizabeth II and the House of Windsor*, London: Hutchinson, 1977.

D. Laird *How The Queen Reigns*, London: Pan, 1959.

J. W. Laurie (ed) *Dedication: A Selection from the Public Speeches of Her Majesty Queen Elizabeth II*, London: Heinemann, 1953.

J. H. Le May *The Victorian Constitution*, London: Duckworth, 1979.

E. Longford *Royal Throne: The Future of the Monarchy*, London: John Curtis, 1993.

S. Lowrie *The Princess in the Mirror*, Chatto and Windus, London, 1985.

T. Lutz *Crying: The Natural and Cultural History of Tears*, Norton, New York, 1999.

B. MacArthur (ed) *Diana, Princess of Wales 1961–1997, Memories and Tributes*, London: Pavilion Books, 1997.

P. Mansergh *The Name and the Nature of the British Commonwealth: An Inaugural Lecture*, London: Cambridge University Press, 1954.
—*The Commonwealth Experience*, London: Weidenfeld and Nicolson, 1969.

K. Martin *The Magic of Monarchy*, London: T. Nelson and Sons, 1937.
—*The Crown and the Establishment*, Harmondsworth: Penguin, 1963.

A. Marr *Ruling Britannia: The Failure and Future of British Democracy*, London: Michael Joseph, 1995.

B. Masters *Dreams About HM The Queen and Other Members of the Royal Family*, London: Blond and Masters, 1972.

C. McDonald *A Hundred Years of Royal Style*, London: Muller, Blom & White, 1985.

D. Morrah *The Work of the Queen*, London: William Kimber, 1958.

A. Morton *Inside Kensington Palace*, London: Michael O'Mara Books, 1987.
—*Theirs Is The Kingdom: The Wealth of the Windsors*, London: Michael O'Mara Books, 1990.
—*Inside Buckingham Palace*, London: Michael O'Mara Books, 1991.

F. Mount *The British Constitution Now*, London: Heinemann, 1992.

T. Nairn *The Enchanted Glass: Britain and its Monarchy*, London: Radius, 1988.

J. M. Packard *The Queen and Her Court: A Guide to British Monarchy Today*, London: Robson Books, 1981.

A. Payne, P. Sutton and T. Thorndike *Grenada's Revolution and Invasion*, London: Crown Helm, 1984.

J. Pearson *The Ultimate Family: The Making of the Royal House of Windsor*, London: Michael Joseph, 1986.

B. Penrose and S. Freeman *Conspiracy of Silence: The Secret Life of Anthony Blunt*, London: Grafton Books, 1986.

C. Petrie *The Modern British Monarchy*, London: Eyre and Spottiswoode, 1961.

B. Pimlott *Should the Arts Be Popular?*, Lloyds/TSB Forum, London, 1999.

C. Pincher *Top Secret Too Long: The Great Betrayal of Britain's Crucial Secrets and the Cover-up*, London: Sidgwick and Jackson, 1984.

L. Pine *The Twilight of Monarchy*, London: Burke, 1958.

S. B. F. Price *Rituals and Power: The Roman Imperial Cult in Asia Minor*, Cambridge: Cambridge University Press, Cambridge, 1984.

F. Prochaska *The Republic of Britain 1760–2000*, London: Allen Lane, 2000.
—*Royal Bounty: The Making of a Welfare Monarchy*, London: Yale University Press, 1995.

A. Rawnsley *Servants of the People: the inside story of New Labour*, London: Hamish Hamilton, 2000.

Royal Finances, London: Buckingham Palace, 1995, Second Edition.

A. Sampson *The Anatomy of Britain Today*, London: Hodder and Stoughton, 1965.
—*The Changing Anatomy of Britain*, London: Hodder and Stoughton, 1971.
—*The Essential Anatomy of Britain*, London: Hodder and Stoughton, 1992.

R. Samuel *Theatres of Memory: Past and Present in Contemporary Culture*, London: Verso, 1994.
—*Theatres of Memory, Vol.II Island Stories, Unravelling Britain*, ed. A Light, et al, London: Verso, 1998.

T. Sancton and T. Macleod *Death of a Princess: An Investigation*, London: Weidenfeld, 1998.

E. Schor *Burying the Dead: The British Culture of Mourning from the Enlightenment to Victoria*, Princeton: Princeton University Press, 1994.

R. Scruton *an Intelligent Person's Guide to Modern Culture*, Duckworth, London, 1998.

B. S. Shaw *Royal Wedding*, London: MacDonald, 1947.

L. Sheridan *From Cabbages to Kings*, London: Odhams, 1955.

H. Smith *A Horseman Through Six Reigns: Reminiscences of a Royal Riding Master*, London: Odhams Press, 1955.

S. Sutherland *American Public Opinion and the Windsors*, Vermont: Driftwood Press, North Montpelier, 1938.

R. Tomlinson *Divine Right: The Inglorious Survival of British Royalty*, London: Little Brown, 1994.

P. Toynbee and D. Walker *Did Things Get Better? An Audit of Labour's Successes and Failures*, Penguin, London, 2001.

M. Thornton *Royal Feud: The Queen Mother and the Duchess of Windsor*, London: Michael Joseph, 1985.

F. Towers *The Two Princesses: The Story of the King's Daughters*, London: Pilgrim Press, 1940.

M. Turnbull *The reluctant republic*, Port Melbourne, Australia: Heinemann, 1993.

F. Underhill *The British Commonwealth*, Durham, NC: Duke University Press, 1956.

M. Warner *Alone of All Her Sex: the myth and cult of the Virgin Mary*, London: Weidenfeld and Nicolson, 1976.

M. Wiener *English Culture and the Decline of the Industrial Spirit 1850– 1980*, Cambridge: Cambridge University Press, 1981.

B. Wilkinson *The Coronation in History*, London: The Historical Association, 1953.

A. N. Wilson *The Rise and Fall of the House of Windsor*, London: Sinclair-Stevenson, 1993.

E. Wilson *Adorned in Dreams: Fashion and Modernity*, Los Angeles: University of California Press, 1987.

H. Wilson *The Governance of Britain*, London: Weidenfeld and Nicolson, 1976.

M. Wilson *New Poems*, London: Hutchinson, 1979.

G. Winterton *Monarchy to Republic: The Australian Republican Government*, Melbourne: Oxford University Press, 1986.

N. Woolf *The Sovereign Remedy: Touchpieces and the King's Evil*, London: British Association of Numismatics Societies, 1990.

P.A. Wright *The Pictorial History of the Royal Maundy*, Pitkin, London, 1973.

'X' *Romances of Our Royal Family*, London: Hutchinson, 1936.

P. Ziegler *Crown and People*, London: Collins, 1978.

—*Elizabeth's Britain 1926–86*, Country Life Books, 1986.

3. Articles and Miscellaneous

J.S. Billing 'The King's Touch for Scrofula', *Proceedings of the Charaka Club*, Vol II, 1911, p.68.

N. Birnbaum 'Monarchs and Sociologists: A Reply to Professor Shils and M. Young', *Sociological Review*, Vol. 3, No. 1, July 1955, pp. 13–23.

R. Brandon 'New Zealand and the Monarchy', paper presented to the Australia and the Monarchy Conference, Australia House, London, September 1994.

R. J. Campbell, 'Our Great Inheritance', in *Sermons for the Coronation of His Majesty King George VI*, London: Skeffington and Son Ltd, 1937.

L. Cleveland 'Royalty as symbolic drama: the 1970 New Zealand tour', Vol. XI, Journal of Commonwealth Political Studies, 1973.

The Diana, Princess of Wales Memorial Fund, Annual Review, 1999.

J. H. Grainger 'The Activity of Monarchy', *Cambridge Quarterly*, Vol. VII, No. 4, 1977.

J. Grigg 'The Queen's Opportunity', *National and English Review*, August 1952, Vol. 139, No. 834, pp. 81–5.

P. C. Gordon Walker 'Crown Divisible', *Twentieth Century*, June 1953, Vol. CLIII, No. 916, pp. 415–21.

S. Haffner 'The Renascence of Monarchy', *Twentieth Century*, June 1953, Vol. CLIII, No. 916, pp. 415–21.

H. J. Harvey 'The British Commonwealth: A Pattern of Cooperation', *International Conciliation*, January 1953, No. 487, pp. 1–12.

P. Hennessy 'The Monarchy: Britain as Disguised Republic?' *Gresham College Lecture*, London: Gresham College, 1995.

P. Hennessy and C. Anstey 'Jewel in the Constitution: The Queen, Parliament and the Royal Prerogative', *Strathclyde Analysis Paper No. 8*, Glasgow: University of Strathclyde, 1992.

P. Hennessy and S. Coates 'The Back of the Envelope: Hung Parliaments, the Queen and the Constitution', *Strathclyde Analysis Paper No. 5*, Glasgow: University of Strathclyde, 1991.

C. J. Hughes 'The Constitutional Development of the British Commonwealth 1945–1954', Tubingen, 1956.

D. Lowe '1954: The Queen and Australia in the World', paper presented to the Australia and the Monarchy Conference, Australia House, London, September 1994.

Marriage of H.R.H. The Princess Elizabeth and Lieutenant Philip Mountbatten, RN, List of Wedding Gifts, St. James's Palace, London, 1947.

R. Rhodes James 'The British Monarchy: Its Changing Constitutional Role', *RSA Journal*, Vol. 143, No. 5448, April 1994.

K. Rose and D. Kavanagh 'The Monarchy in Contemporary Political

Culture', *Comparative Politics*, Vol. 8, No. 4, July 1976, pp. 548–76.

S. Schama 'The Domestication of Majesty: Royal Family Portraiture 1500–1850', *Journal of Interdisciplinary History*, XVII: I, Summer 1986, pp. 155–83.

E. Shils and M. Young 'The Meaning of the Coronation', *Sociological Review*, Vol. I, No. 2, December 1953, pp. 63–70.

Their Majesties The King and Queen and Their Royal Highnesses the Princess Elizabeth and the Princess Margaret in the Union of South Africa, February–April 1947.

J. Thomas 'A Fairy Story? Popular Attitudes of Lesbians and Gays to the Death of Princess Diana', unpublished paper, 2001.

K.C. Wheare 'Walter Bagehot', *Proceedings of the British Academy*, Vol. LX (1974).

J. Weston 'Our Love of Elizabeth', Canadian Broadcasting Corporation transcript, 19.10.51.

INDEX

Grigg, John (Lord Altrincham): on
Coronation, 212; *National and English
Review* articles, 276–88, 289, 311, 412, 502,
566, 585; views on monarchy, 278–9, 293,
312; on Heir's education, 279, 359; BBC
ban, 286; political career, 292; on
Rhodesia issue, 353; on Queen's public
image, 411; on Silver Jubilee, 452; on
Queen's Commonwealth role, 506; on
royal household, 543; on *Elizabeth R* film,
547; on Australian republican movement,
563
Grimond, Jo, 404, 420
Grisewood, Harman, 286, 291
Guardian, 315, 339, 356, 447, 453, 507, 510, 537,
539, 548, 554, 561, 563, 568, 571, 579, 585, 589,
615, 620, 652, 677, 696
Guildhall, Queen's speech (1992), 558–9
Gulf War, 535, 536–8

Haakon, King of Norway, 169
Hague, William, 654, 702
Hahn, Kurt, 88–9
Haile Selassie, Emperor, 355
Hailsham, Douglas Hogg, Lord, 1
Hailsham, Quintin Hogg, Lord: Macmillan
succession question, 325, 327–8, 330,
333–4; general election (1974), 422; on
'elective dictatorship', 494
Haines, Joe, 344, 422, 435, 459
Haley, Sir William, 196, 236–8, 320
Halifax, Lord, 81, 170, 257
Hall, Philip, 405, 539
Hall, Radclyffe, 1
Hamilton, Alan, 547
Hamilton, William, 394, 400, 403, 424–5,
440, 529, 586
Hampton Court, 63–4, 107, 208, 263, 557
Handel, George Frederic, 213
Handley, Tommy, 70
Hanks, Tom, 628
Hannah, Sir Colin, 427
Hanover, Princess George of (Tiny), 88, 98
Hardinge, Sir Alexander, 71
Hare, David, 566
Harewood, George Lascelles, Earl of, 3, 14,
31, 217–18, 372–4, 435
Harpers and Queen, 533, 539
Harris, Robert, 515, 542
Harry, Prince: birth, 636; relationship with
mother, 562, 601; at Balmoral (summer

1997), 603, 605; mother's death, 609, 611;
Balmoral service, 623; appearance at
Kensington Palace, 626; mother's funeral,
627, 629; privacy issue, 656; South Africa
visit (1997), 658; relationship with father,
658, 684
Hartnell, Norman, 127, 134–5, 222–3, 248, 252
Harvey, Sir Oliver, 152
Haseler, Stephen, 568
Hastings-Bass, William (Earl of
Huntingdon), 360
Hattersley, Roy, 697
Hawke, Bob, 549
Hayden, Bill, 549
Healey, Denis, 425
Heath, Edward, 326, 395, 398–9, 418–22, 467
Heffer, Eric, 367
Heffer, Simon, 572
Helen, Queen (of Romania), 136
Henderson, Nicholas, 356–7
Hennessy, Peter, 575
Henry, Cardinal Duke of York, 642
Henry III, King, 584
Henry VIII, King, 72, 263
Herder, Johann Gottfried, 697
Heren, Louis, 411
Hern, Major Dick, 360
Heseltine, Michael, 535–6
Heseltine, Sir William: press secretary
appointment, 377–9, 409; background,
378; *Royal Family* film, 379–80; on
publication of family photographs, 387;
achievements, 396, 478; walkabout policy,
397; assistant private secretary, 410;
private secretary, 509; *Sunday Times* row,
510–11, 511; *Times* letter, 509–10; *Knockout*
doubts, 524; successor, 538
Heuss, Theodor, 355
Hewitt, James, 555, 577
Hicks, Lady Pamela (née Mountbatten): on
cousin Philip, 93; on royal wedding, 136,
139; on George VI's death, 176, 179; on
royal tour, 223, 225–6
Highgrove, 596–7
Hill House, 261
Hitchens, Christopher, 681, 697
Hitler, Adolf, 54, 57, 88
Hoare, *see* Templewood
Hocart, A.M., 211, 645
Hodcott House stables, 361
Hodge, Vickie, 485

Richard, Cliff, 575
Richards, Sir Gordon, 63, 81
Richards, Paul, 586, 587
Richardson, Sir John, 330
Richmond, 9th Duke of, 253
Riddell, Sir John, 513
Riddell, Peter, 587
Ring, Alice, 13
Robert II, King of the Franks, 640
Roberts, Alison, 698
Rook, Jean, 451
Roosevelt, Eleanor, 63, 68, 149
Roosevelt, Franklin D., 53–4
Rose, Kenneth, 164, 247, 388, 478, 588, 651
Rothschild, Baron Guy de, 359
Royal Collection, 264, 266, 336–7, 401, 534, 544
Royal College of Nursing, 83
Royal Family, The, film, 379–88, 392, 397, 402, 411, 452–3, 525, 546–7, 645
Royal Free Hospital School of Medicine for Women, 83
Royal Horse Guards, 84, 107
Royal Lodge, Windsor Great Park, 22, 34, 49–50, 57, 65
Royal Marriages Act (1772), 124, 202, 220, 299, 373, 475
Royal Maundy ceremony, 646, 694
Royal Mews, 27
Royal Naval College, Dartmouth, 86, 90, 359, 415
Royal Standard, 614–15, 663
Royal Titles Bill, 182
Royal Windsor Horse Show, 63
Runcie, Robert (Archbishop of Canterbury), 480, 496
Rusk, Dean, 317
Russell-Smith, Penny, 664–5
Rutherford, Malcolm, 505
Rwanda, Commonwealth membership 670

St Aldwyn, Lord, 327
St Andrew's University, 698
St James's Palace, 583–4, 595, 600, 616, 620, 702
St Mawr, Ruth, 12
St Paul's Walden Bury, 8, 10, 22, 54
Salisbury, Lord: opinion of Philip, 104, 124–5; Churchill retirement question, 186; Eden succession question, 256, 257–60, 327, 332
Salote, Queen of Tonga, 218

Salvation Army, 620
Sampson, Anthony, 256, 258, 296, 460, 484, 540, 550
Samuel, Raphael, 575, 691
Sandringham: Princess's childhood, 12, 22, 31, 57; stud, 108, 263, 451; royal lifestyle, 110, 451; childhood of Charles and Anne, 163, 255; King's illness, 174; Christmases, 255, 384, 397, 599; *Royal Family* film, 384; management, 402; press siege, 474
Sandys, Diana, 59
Sandys, Duncan, 306
Saturday Evening Post, 284
Saudi Arabia, 457–8
Schama, Simon, 60
Schmid, Carlo, 357
Scoon, Sir Paul, 496–7
Scotland: attitudes to monarchy, 538–9; devolution, 584, 668–9
scrofula, 640–5
Scruton, Roger, 694
Seaga, Edward, 466
Settlement, Act of (1701), 3
Shakespeare, William, 211, 640
Shand-Kydd, Frances, 474, 621, 653
Shaw, George Bernard, 374
Shea, Michael, 474, 482–3, 489, 492, 509–14
Sheldon, Robert, 557
Shelley, Percy Bysshe, 632–3
Sheridan, Lisa: memories of 145 Piccadilly, 7, 34; memories of young princesses, 20, 26, 34, 64–5, 69, 76; memoirs, 64–5; photographs, 65–6, 70; memories of Philip, 93
Sherrin, Ned, 320–1, 376
Shils, Edward, 216–17
Shinwell, Emmanuel, 394
Short, Edward, 366, 422
Shukburgh, Sir Evelyn, 231
Simon, Lord, 71
Simpson, Wallis, *see* Windsor, Duchess of
Singapore, royal visit (1974), 422
Sitwell, Edith, 187
Skinner, Dennis, 425
Smith, Adam, 502
Smith, Chris, 703
Smith, Doug, 265
Smith, Horace, 27–8, 63, 68, 76, 107
Smith, Ian, 346–54
Smith, John, 559
Smuts, Jan, 111, 115, 118, 119, 135